THE ULTIMATE
HIT
SINGLES
BOOK

THIS IS A CARLTON BOOK

This edition published 1998 for
Parragon Book Service Ltd
Unit 13–17 Avonbridge Trading Estate,
Atlantic Road, Avonmouth
Bristol BS11 9QD

Text and design
© copyright 1998 Carlton Books Limited

ISBN 0 75252 739 8

Printed and bound by Firmin-Didot (France)
Group Herissey
N° d'impression : 43662

THE ULTIMATE
HIT
Singles
BOOK

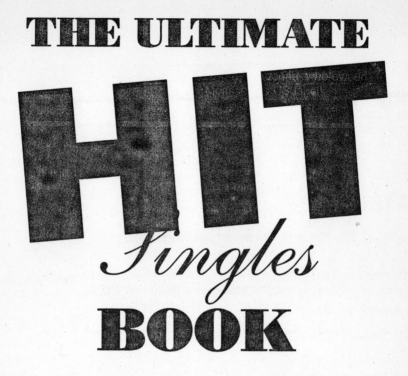

All the Top 20 Charts
for 45 years

COMPILED BY DAVE McALEER

SIENA

CONTENTS

CHART FILE   6

The complete Top 20 UK charts from 1954 to the present day. Each chart also details peak position, the number of weeks it spent in the Top 10, whether it was the artist's first or most recent hit and whether it sold over a million or two million copies.

LISTING BY TITLE   272

Alphabetical listing by song title showing the artist's name.

INTRODUCTION

The only way to get a real feel of the UK pop scene at any given moment is from the pop charts, as they instantly transport you back to the time concerned. There is also no better way to judge a record than in the context of its contemporaries and no other book makes these nostalgia trips easier or more interesting. The simple aim of this book is to put the 6,000 plus biggest UK hits of the last five decades into some kind of perspective, and to help you follow the careers of the 2,500 acts that put these singles into the Top 20.

Many musical changes have occurred in the last 45 years, and they are all chronicled in these pages. Indeed, it could be said that the only constants during the period were the fact most parents didn't appreciate their children's music, a good "novelty" record usually found a ready UK audience and there was always a handful of "wannabe" teen idols waiting to dethrone the current crop of pop stars.

The major happening was, of course, the arrival and rise of Rock music: the hybrid of US R&B, Pop and C&W that was first heard in Britain in 1954.Rock has, of course, changed its direction and sound many times over the years, but even as the millennium dawns it is still the nucleus of pop music.

From a British point of view, the most important change to the music scene during this period was the upsurge of interest in UK recording artists. In the 1950s, few British acts could equal their American peers' worldwide popularity, and most of them simply recorded cover versions of US hits for the British market. After the Beatles broke down the barriers, countless other UK artists became internationally successful and for the last 35 years the influence of British artists and the UK chart has been felt right around the globe.

CHARTS USED. The chart positions used for compiling the monthly Top 20s were those accepted at the time as the most accurate. The NME charts have been used for the first 10 years, and after that the information came from the UK record industry bible, Record Retailer, later known as Music Week.

CHART FILES. The Top 20 charts are compiled by means of a complex and comprehensive system, which considers not only a record's weekly chart placings and peak position, but also the number of weeks it spent in the Top 10 and Top 20, its weeks at No. 1 (if applicable) and its performance on other major charts.

Apart from normal chart features these Top 20s also show:
(a) The total number of weeks a record spent in the Top 20 during that chart run.
(b) Whether it was the artist's (or the first named artist in the case of duos) first (F) or most recent (L) Top 20 entry.
(c) Whether it sold a million (G) or over two million (P) copies.

LISTING BY SONG TITLE. An alphabetical listing of all song titles in this book with the artist's name.

1954

This Mnth	Prev Mnth	Title	Artist	Label	Wks	(US 20 Pos)	
1	12	Oh Mein Papa	Eddie Calvert	Columbia	21	(9)	F
2	1	Answer Me	Frankie Laine	Philips	17		
3	4	Let's Have A Party	Winifred Atwell	Philips	9		
4	3	Swedish Rhapsody	Mantovani	Decca	18		
5	15	Cloud Lucky Seven	Guy Mitchell	Philips	15		
6	-	Blowing Wild	Frankie Laine	Philips	12		
7	-	Rags To Riches	David Whitfield	Decca	11		
8	6	Chika Boom	Guy Mitchell	Philips	15		
9	2	Answer Me	David Whitfield	Decca	14		
10	18	Ricochet	Joan Regan	Decca	5		F
11	10	Poppa Piccolino	Diana Decker	Columbia	10		F L
12	-	Happy Wanderer	Obernkirchen Children's Choir	Parlophone	26		F L
13	-	That's Amore	Dean Martin	Capitol	11	(2)	
14	11	Crying In The Chapel	Lee Lawrence	Decca	6		F
15	-	The Creep	Ken Mackintosh	HMV	2		F
16	7	Swedish Rhapsody	Ray Martin	Columbia	4		L
17	8	I Saw Mommy Kissing Santa Claus	Beverley Sisters	Philips	5		F
18	5	I Saw Mommy Kissing Santa Claus	Jimmy Boyd	Columbia	6	(1)	F L
19	-	Oh! My Pa-Pa	Eddie Fisher	HMV	3	(1)	
20	16	Dragnet	Ray Anthony	Capitol	2	(3)	F L

This Mnth	Prev Mnth	Title	Artist	Label	Wks	(US 20 Pos)	
1	1	Oh Mein Papa	Eddie Calvert	Columbia	21	(9)	F
2	6	Blowing Wild	Frankie Laine	Philips	12		
3	5	Cloud Lucky Seven	Guy Mitchell	Philips	16		
4	13	That's Amore	Dean Martin	Capitol	11	(2)	
5	7	Rags To Riches	David Whitfield	Decca	11		
6	-	Tennessee Wig Walk	Bonnie Lou	Parlophone	10		F
7	12	Happy Wanderer	Obernkirchen Children's Choir	Parlophone	26		F
8	-	Woman (Uh-Huh)	Jose Ferrer	Philips	5	(18)	F
9	2	Answer Me	Frankie Laine	Philips	17		
10	4	Swedish Rhapsody	Mantovani	Decca	18		
11		Skin Deep	Ted Heath	Decca	3		
12	8	Chika Boom	Guy Mitchell	Philips	15		
13	-	Don't Laugh At Me	Norman Wisdom	Columbia	15		F
14	-	The Book	David Whitfield	Decca	15		
15	-	I See The Moon	Stargazers	Decca	15		
16	-	Ebb Tide	Frank Chacksfield	Decca	2	(2)	
17	19	Oh! My Pa-Pa	Eddie Fisher	HMV	4	(1)	
18	-	Cuff Of My Shirt	Guy Mitchell	Philips	3		
19	-	Sippin' Soda	Guy Mitchell	Philips	1		
20	-	Dragnet	Ted Heath	Decca	5		

◆ Swiss song 'Oh Mein Papa' (aka 'Oh! My Pa-Pa') was the top transatlantic hit. In the USA Eddie Fisher's vocal topped the chart with British-based trumpeter Eddie Calvert's version runner-up. In Britain the roles were reversed.

◆ American songwriter Joe Darion had a hot winter with his compositions 'Changing Partners' (Patti Page, Kay Starr, Bing Crosby) and 'Ricochet' (Teresa Brewer, Joan Regan) hitting on both sides of the Atlantic.

This Mnth	Prev Mnth	Title	Artist	Label	Wks	(US 20 Pos)	
1	15	I See The Moon	Stargazers	Decca	15		
2	1	Oh Mein Papa	Eddie Calvert	Columbia	21	(9)	F
3	7	Happy Wanderer	Obernkirchen Children's Choir	Parlophone	26		F
4	6	Tennessee Wig Walk	Bonnie Lou	Parlophone	10		F
5	13	Don't Laugh At Me	Norman Wisdom	Columbia	15		F
6	4	That's Amore	Dean Martin	Capitol	11	(2)	
7	14	The Book	David Whitfield	Decca	15		
8	2	Blowing Wild	Frankie Laine	Philips	12		
9	3	Cloud Lucky Seven	Guy Mitchell	Philips	16		
10	-	Skin Deep	Duke Ellington	Philips	3		F
11	-	Changing Partners	Kay Starr	Capitol	14	(13)	
12	-	Bell Bottom Blues	Alma Cogan	HMV	9		F
13	5	Rags To Riches	David Whitfield	Decca	11		
14	-	Changing Partners	Bing Crosby	Brunswick	3	(17)	
15	-	Granada	Frankie Laine	Philips	2		
16	8	Woman (Uh-Huh)	Jose Ferrer	Philips	5	(18)	F
17	17	Oh! My Pa-Pa	Eddie Fisher	HMV	4	(1)	
18	18	Cuff Of My Shirt	Guy Mitchell	Philips	3		
19	-	Moonlight Serenade	Glenn Miller	HMV	1		F
20	-	From Here To Eternity	Frank Sinatra	Capitol	9		

		Title	Artist	Label			
1	1	I See The Moon	Stargazers	Decca	15		
2	3	Happy Wanderer	Obernkirchen Children's Choir	Parlophone	26		F L
3	-	Secret Love	Doris Day	Philips	29	(1)	
4	10	Changing Partners	Kay Starr	Capitol	14	(13)	
5	5	Don't Laugh At Me	Norman Wisdom	Columbia	15		F
6	12	Bell Bottom Blues	Alma Cogan	HMV	9		F
7	2	Oh Mein Papa	Eddie Calvert	Columbia	21	(9)	F
8	-	Such A Night	Johnnie Ray	Philips	18		
9	7	The Book	David Whitfield	Decca	15		
10	-	The Kid's Last Fight	Frankie Laine	Philips	10		
11	-	Bimbo	Ruby Wright	Parlophone	5		F
12	4	Tennessee Wig Walk	Bonnie Lou	Parlophone	10		F L
13	15	Changing Partners	Bing Crosby	Brunswick	3	(17)	
14	6	That's Amore	Dean Martin	Capitol	11	(2)	
15	-	Dime And A Dollar	Guy Mitchell	Philips	5		
16	16	Granada	Frankie Laine	Philips	2		
17	-	Tenderly	Nat 'King' Cole	Capitol	1		
18	18	Cuff Of My Shirt	Guy Mitchell	Philips	3		
19	-	Friends And Neighbours	Billy Cotton & His Band	Decca	12		L
20	-	Happy Wanderer	Stargazers	Decca	1		

◆ Mixed quintet The Stargazers became the first British group to rack up two No. 1s; a feat that was not repeated until 1963 by The Beatles. The former group were produced by Dick Rowe, the Decca A&R man who turned down The Beatles.

◆ Al Martino was one of several American singers who covered US hits just for the British market. His own version of 'Wanted' sold just as well as original hitmaker Perry Como's recording in the UK.

1954

This Mnth	Prev Mnth	Title	Artist	Label	Wks	(US 20 Pos)	
1	3	Secret Love	Doris Day	Philips	29	(1)	
2	8	Such A Night	Johnnie Ray	Philips	18		
3	2	Happy Wanderer	Obernkirchen Children's Choir	Parlophone	26		F L
4	10	The Kid's Last Fight	Frankie Laine	Philips	10		
5	4	Changing Partners	Kay Starr	Capitol	14	(13)	
6	1	I See The Moon	Stargazers	Decca	15		
7	19	Friends And Neighbours	Billy Cotton & His Band	Decca	12		L
8	5	Don't Laugh At Me	Norman Wisdom	Columbia	15		F
9	-	Someone Else's Roses	Joan Regan	Decca	8		
10	-	Heart Of My Heart	Max Bygraves	HMV	8		
11	15	Dime And A Dollar	Guy Mitchell	Philips	5		
12	11	Bimbo	Ruby Wright	Parlophone	5		F
13	6	Bell Bottom Blues	Alma Cogan	HMV	9		F
14	9	The Book	David Whitfield	Decca	15		
15	-	Make Love To Me!	Jo Stafford	Philips	1	(1)	
16	7	Oh Mein Papa	Eddie Calvert	Columbia	21	(9)	F
17	-	Cross Over The Bridge	Patti Page	Oriole	8	(3)	L
18	-	Deadwood Stage	Doris Day	Columbia	7		
19	-	Shadow Waltz	Mantovani	Decca	5		
20	-	Heartless	Frankie Vaughan	HMV	5		

This Mnth	Prev Mnth	Title	Artist	Label	Wks	(US 20 Pos)	
1	1	Secret Love	Doris Day	Philips	29	(1)	
2	2	Such A Night	Johnnie Ray	Philips	18		
3	7	Friends And Neighbours	Billy Cotton & His Band	Decca	12		L
4	3	Happy Wanderer	Obernkirchen Children's Choir	Parlophone	26		F L
5	9	Someone Else's Roses	Joan Regan	Decca	8		
6	-	I Get So Lonely	Four Knights	Capitol	11	(3)	F L
7	-	Wanted	Perry Como	HMV	15	(1)	
8	10	Heart Of My Heart	Max Bygraves	HMV	8		
9	4	The Kid's Last Fight	Frankie Laine	Philips	10		
10	5	Changing Partners	Kay Starr	Capitol	14	(13)	
11	-	Cara Mia	David Whitfield	Decca	25	(10)	
12	-	Wanted	Al Martino	Capitol	15		
13	14	The Book	David Whitfield	Decca	15		
14	-	The Little Shoemaker	Petula Clark	Polygon	10		F
15	-	Idle Gossip	Perry Como	HMV	15		
16	11	Dime And A Dollar	Guy Mitchell	Philips	5		
17	17	Cross Over The Bridge	Patti Page	Oriole	8	(3)	L
18	-	The Happy Wanderer	Frank Weir	Decca	3	(4)	F
19	18	Deadwood Stage	Doris Day	Columbia	7		
20	-	Friends And Neighbours	Max Bygraves & The Tanner Sisters	HMV	3		

◆ British songstress Petula Clark made her UK chart debut with the French song, 'The Little Shoemaker'. This foot-tapping composition also gave The Gaylords their biggest American hit.

◆ American heart-throbs Frankie Laine, Guy Mitchell and Johnnie Ray had British hits with records that failed in their homeland. Among these was Ray's No. 1 'Such A Night', banned by the BBC for being too suggestive.

1954

This Mnth	Prev Mnth	Title	Artist	Label	Wks	(US 20 Pos)	
1	11	Cara Mia	David Whitfield	Decca	25	(10)	
2	1	Secret Love	Doris Day	Philips	29	(1)	
3	-	Little Things Mean A Lot	Kitty Kallen	Brunswick	23	(1)	F L
4	15	Idle Gossip	Perry Como	HMV	15		
5	12	Wanted	Al Martino	Capitol	15		
6	7	Wanted	Perry Como	HMV	15	(1)	
7	2	Such A Night	Johnnie Ray	Philips	18		
8	14	The Little Shoemaker	Petula Clark	Polygon	10		F
9	6	I Get So Lonely	Four Knights	Capitol	11	(3)	F L
10	3	Friends And Neighbours	Billy Cotton & His Band	Decca	12		L
11	-	Three Coins In The Fountain	Frank Sinatra	Capitol	19	(7)	
12	4	Happy Wanderer	Obernkirchen Children's Choir	Parlophone	26		F L
13	-	The Story Of Three Loves	Winifred Atwell	Decca	9		
14	-	Three Coins In The Fountain	Four Aces	Brunswick	6	(2)	F
15	5	Someone Else's Roses	Joan Regan	Decca	8		
16	8	Heart Of My Heart	Max Bygraves	HMV	8		
17	-	Young-At-Heart	Frank Sinatra	Capitol	1	(2)	F
18	-	Never Never Land	Frank Weir	Decca	13		
19	-	Charleston	Winifred Atwell	Decca	8		
20	-	The Little Shoemaker	Frank Weir	Decca	4		

1	1	Cara Mia	David Whitfield	Decca	25	(10)	
2	3	Little Things Mean A Lot	Kitty Kallen	Brunswick	23	(1)	F L
3	11	Three Coins In The Fountain	Frank Sinatra	Capitol	19	(7)	
4	4	Idle Gossip	Perry Como	HMV	15		
5	2	Secret Love	Doris Day	Philips	29	(1)	
6	5	Wanted	Al Martino	Capitol	15		
7	14	Three Coins In The Fountain	Four Aces	Brunswick	6	(2)	F
8	6	Wanted	Perry Como	HMV	15	(1)	
9	-	My Friend	Frankie Laine	Philips	15		
10	13	The Story Of Three Loves	Winifred Atwell	Decca	9		
11	8	The Little Shoemaker	Petula Clark	Polygon	10		F
12	9	I Get So Lonely	Four Knights	Capitol	11	(3)	F L
13	-	Black Hills Of Dakota	Doris Day	Philips	7		
14	-	Little Things Mean A Lot	Alma Cogan	HMV	5		
15	7	Such A Night	Johnnie Ray	Philips	18		
16	18	Never Never Land	Frank Weir	Decca	13		
17	-	Midnight	Eddie Calvert	Columbia	7		
18	-	Three Coins In The Fountain	Tony Brent	Columbia	6		
19	-	Destiny	Johnnie Ray	Columbia	4		
20	19	Charleston	Winifred Atwell	Decca	8		

◆ British balladeer David Whitfield had his biggest hit, 'Cara Mia'. It not only topped the UK chart but also reached the US Top 10, earning him a gold disc.

◆ Many US pop acts covered R&B hits: The McGuire Sisters scored with The Spaniels' 'Goodnight, Sweet-heart, Goodnight', June Valli's 'I Understand' joined the original by The Four Tunes on the American chart, and Canadian quartet The Crew-Cuts had a US No. 1 with The Chords' scat smash, 'Sh-Boom'. The latter becoming the first rock-related hit in Britain.

1954

September 1954

This Mnth	Prev Mnth	Title	Artist	Label	Wks (US 20 Pos)	
1	3	Three Coins In The Fountain	Frank Sinatra	Capitol	19 (7)	
2	1	Cara Mia	David Whitfield	Decca	25 (10)	
3	2	Little Things Mean A Lot	Kitty Kallen	Brunswick	23 (1)	F L
4	9	My Friend	Frankie Laine	Philips	15	
5	-	Hold My Hand	Don Cornell	Vogue	21 (5)	F
6	4	Idle Gossip	Perry Como	HMV	15	
7	5	Secret Love	Doris Day	Philips	29 (1)	
8	-	Smile	Nat 'King' Cole	Capitol	14 (14)	
9	13	Black Hills Of Dakota	Doris Day	Philips	7	
10	-	Gilly Gilly Ossenfeffer Katzenellen Bogen By The Sea	Max Bygraves	HMV	8	
11	-	West Of Zanzibar	Anthony Steel & The Radio Revellers	Polygon	6	F L
12	6	Wanted	Al Martino	Capitol	15	
13	10	The Story Of Three Loves	Winifred Atwell	Decca	9	
14	14	Little Things Mean A Lot	Alma Cogan	HMV	5	
15	8	Wanted	Perry Como	HMV	15 (1)	
16	-	Story Of Tina	Ronnie Harris	Columbia	2	F
17	-	Some Day	Frankie Laine	Columbia	3 (18)	
18	16	Never Never Land	Frank Weir	Decca	13	
19	-	Dixieland	Winifred Atwell	Decca	4	
20	-	Little Things Mean A Lot	Jimmy Young	Decca	2	

October 1954

This Mnth	Prev Mnth	Title	Artist	Label	Wks (US 20 Pos)	
1	5	Hold My Hand	Don Cornell	Vogue	21 (5)	F
2	8	Smile	Nat 'King' Cole	Capitol	14 (14)	
3	1	Three Coins In The Fountain	Frank Sinatra	Capitol	19 (7)	
4	4	My Friend	Frankie Laine	Philips	15	
5	3	Little Things Mean A Lot	Kitty Kallen	Brunswick	23 (1)	F
6	2	Cara Mia	David Whitfield	Decca	25 (10)	
7	-	If I Give My Heart To You	Doris Day	Philips	11 (4)	
8	-	Sway	Dean Martin	Capitol	7 (15)	
9	-	My Son My Son	Vera Lynn	Decca	14	
10	-	The Story Of Tina	Al Martino	Capitol	8	
11	-	This Ole House	Rosemary Clooney	Philips	18 (1)	
12	-	This Old House	Billie Anthony	Columbia	15	F
13	-	There Must Be A Reason	Frankie Laine	Philips	9	
14	-	Sh-Boom	Crew-Cuts	Mercury	9 (1)	F
15	10	Gilly Gilly Ossenfeffer Katzenellen Bogen By The Sea	MaxBygraves	HMV	8	
16	9	Black Hills Of Dakota	Doris Day	Philips	8	
17	7	Secret Love	Doris Day	Philips	29 (1)	
18	-	Rain Rain Rain	Frankie Laine	Philips	16 (30)	
19	16	The Story Of Tina	Ronnie Harris	Columbia	3	F
20	-	If I Give My Heart To You	Joan Regan	Decca	11	

◆ American vocalist Kitty Kallen failed to chart again after hitting the top.

◆ Both of West Indian pianist Winifred Atwell's Christmas hits, 'Let's Have A Party' and 'Let's Have Another Party', sold over a million copies worldwide.

November 1954

This Mnth	Prev Mnth	Title	Artist	Label	Wks (US 20 Pos)	
1	9	My Son My Son	Vera Lynn	Decca	14	
2	11	This Ole House	Rosemary Clooney	Philips	18 (1)	
3	1	Hold My Hand	Don Cornell	Vogue	21 (5)	F
4	20	If I Give My Heart To You	Joan Regan	Decca	11	
5	2	Smile	Nat 'King' Cole	Capitol	14 (14)	
6	7	If I Give My Heart To You	Doris Day	Philips	11 (4)	
7	12	This Old House	Billie Anthony	Columbia	15	F
8	18	Rain Rain Rain	Frankie Laine	Philips	16 (30)	
9	6	Cara Mia	David Whitfield	Decca	25 (10)	
10	5	Little Things Mean A Lot	Kitty Kallen	Brunswick	23 (1)	F
11	4	My Friend	Frankie Laine	Philips	15	
12	-	Santo Natale	David Whitfield	Decca	10	
13	-	No One But You	Billy Eckstine	MGM	17	F
14	13	There Must Be A Reason	Frankie Laine	Philips	9	
15	3	Three Coins In The Fountain	Frank Sinatra	Capitol	19 (7)	
16	14	Sh-Boom	Crew-Cuts	Mercury	9 (1)	F
17	-	I Need You Now	Eddie Fisher	HMV	10 (1)	
18	-	Let's Have Another Party	Winifred Atwell	Decca	8	
19	8	Sway	Dean Martin	Capitol	7 (15)	
20	-	Sh-Boom	Stan Freberg	Capitol	2	F

December 1954

This Mnth	Prev Mnth	Title	Artist	Label	Wks (US 20 Pos)	
1	18	Let's Have Another Party	Winifred Atwell	Decca	8	
2	12	Santo Natale	David Whitfield	Decca	10	
3	29	This Ole House	Rosemary Clooney	Philips	18 (1)	
4	13	No One But You	Billy Eckstine	MGM	17	F
5	-	I Still Believe	Ronnie Hilton	HMV	14	F
6	1	My Son My Son	Vera Lynn	Decca	14	
7	3	Hold My Hand	Don Cornell	Vogue	21 (5)	F
8	8	Rain Rain Rain	Frankie Laine	Philips	16	
9	7	This Ole House	Billie Anthony	Columbia	15	F
10	4	If I Give My Heart To You	Joan Regan	Decca	11	
11	-	Heartbeat	Ruby Murray	Columbia	16	F
12	-	Let's Get Together No. 1	Big Ben Banjo Band	Columbia	4	F
13	-	Finger Of Suspicion	Dickie Valentine	Decca	15	
14	17	I Need You Now	Eddie Fisher	HMV	10 (1)	
15	-	I Can't Tell A Waltz From A Tango	Alma Cogan	HMV	11	
16	5	Smile	Nat 'King' Cole	Capitol	14 (14)	
17	-	Shake, Rattle And Roll	Bill Haley & His Comets	Brunswick	14 (7)	
18	6	If I Give My Heart To You	Doris Day	Philips	10 (4)	
19	-	Veni Vidi Vici	Ronnie Hilton	HMV	8	
20	-	Let's Have A Party	Winifred Atwell	Philips	6	

◆ Elvis Presley, who had yet to have a UK release, was voted eighth Most Promising New C&W Singer in *Billboard's* US DJ poll – Tommy Collins took the crown.

◆ The flagging dance hall business on both sides of the Atlantic was revitalized firstly by the growth in interest in Latin American dances like the tango and mambo, and secondly by rock'n'roll. The latter was just starting to make an impression in the UK thanks to records like 'Sh-Boom' by The Crew-Cuts and 'Shake, Rattle And Roll' by Bill Haley & The Comets.

1955

This Mnth	Prev Mnth	Title	Artist	Label	Wks	(US 20 Pos)	
1	13	Finger Of Suspicion	Dickie Valentine	Decca	15		
2	-	Mambo Italiano	Rosemary Clooney	Philips	16	(10)	
3	4	No One But You	Billy Eckstine	MGM	17		F
4	5	I Still Believe	Ronnie Hilton	HMV	14		F
5	11	Heartbeat	Ruby Murray	Columbia	16		F
6	17	Shake, Rattle And Roll	Bill Haley & His Comets	Brunswick	14	(7)	
7	-	Mr. Sandman	Dickie Valentine	Decca	12		
8	15	I Can't Tell A Waltz From A Tango	Alma Cogan	HMV	11		
9	-	Mr. Sandman	Chordettes	Columbia	9	(1)	F
10	8	Rain Rain Rain	Frankie Laine	Philips	16		
11	-	Mr. Sandman	Four Aces	Brunswick	5	(10)	
12	3	This Ole House	Rosemary Clooney	Philips	18	(1)	
13	1	Let's Have Another Party	Winifred Atwell	Decca	8		
14	2	Santo Natale	David Whitfield	Decca	10		
15	7	Hold My Hand	Don Cornell	Vogue	21	(5)	F
16	-	Give Me Your Word	Tennessee Ernie Ford	Capitol	24		F
17	-	Count Your Blessings	Bing Crosby	Brunswick	3		
18	19	Veni Vidi Vici	Ronnie Hilton	HMV	8		
19	-	Softly Softly	Ruby Murray	Columbia	23		
20	9	This Ole House	Billie Anthony	Columbia	15		F

This Mnth	Prev Mnth	Title	Artist	Label	Wks	(US 20 Pos)	
1	19	Softly Softly	Ruby Murray	Columbia	23		
2	2	Mambo Italiano	Rosemary Clooney	Philips	16	(10)	
3	1	Finger Of Suspicion	Dickie Valentine	Decca	15		
4	16	Give Me Your Word	Tennessee Ernie Ford	Capitol	24		F
5	5	Heartbeat	Ruby Murray	Columbia	16		F
6	6	Shake, Rattle And Roll	Bill Haley & His Comets	Brunswick	14	(7)	
7	-	Naughty Lady Of Shady Lane	Dean Martin	Capitol	10		
8	-	The Naughty Lady Of Shady Lane	Ames Brothers	HMV	6	(3)	F L
9	3	No One But You	Billy Eckstine	MGM	17		F
10	7	Mr. Sandman	Dickie Valentine	Decca	12		
11	-	Happy Days And Lonely Nights	Ruby Murray	Columbia	8		
12	-	Let Me Go, Lover	Teresa Brewer	Vogue/Coral	10	(8)	F
13	-	Beyond The Stars	David Whitfield	Decca	9		
14	4	I Still Believe	Ronnie Hilton	HMV	14		F
15	-	Mobile	Ray Burns	Columbia	13		F
16	-	A Blossom Fell	Dickie Valentine	Decca	10		
17	-	Happy Days And Lonely Nights	Frankie Vaughan	HMV	3		
18	-	Majorca	Petula Clark	Polygon	5		
19	-	Mambo Italiano	Dean Martin	Capitol	2		
20	-	Drinking Song	Mario Lanza	HMV	1		

◆ Bill Haley's 'Rock Around The Clock' had a two-week chart run in Britain. In the US, it became the theme to the controversial film, *The Blackboard Jungle*.

◆ Not only were several versions of 'Let Me Go Lover' and 'Mr. Sandman' battling it out, but there were also two hit recordings of 'Mambo Italiano', 'This Ole House', 'Naughty Lady Of Shady Lane', and 'A Blossom Fell'.

1955

March 1955

This Mnth	Prev Mnth	Title	Artist	Label	Wks	(US 20 Pos)	
1	4	Give Me Your Word	Tennessee Ernie Ford	Capitol	24		F
2	1	Softly Softly	Ruby Murray	Columbia	23		
3	-	Let Me Go, Lover	Dean Martin	Capitol	9		
4	2	Mambo Italiano	Rosemary Clooney	Philips	16	(10)	
5	-	A Blossom Fell	Nat 'King' Cole	Capitol	10	(2)	
6	15	Mobile	Ray Burns	Columbia	13		F
7	7	Naughty Lady Of Shady Lane	Dean Martin	Capitol	10		
8	3	Finger Of Suspicion	Dickie Valentine	Decca	15		
9	5	Heartbeat	Ruby Murray	Columbia	16		F
10	-	Let Me Go, Lover	Ruby Murray	Columbia	7		
11	13	Beyond The Stars	David Whitfield	Decca	9		
12	12	Let Me Go, Lover	Teresa Brewer	Vogue/Coral	10	(8)	F
13	11	Happy Days And Lonely Nights	Ruby Murray	Columbia	8		
14	16	A Blossom Fell	Dickie Valentine	Decca	10		
15	-	Tomorrow	Johnny Brandon	Polygon	8		F
16	-	Wedding Bells	Eddie Fisher	HMV	11		
17	18	Majorca	Petula Clark	Polygon	5		
18	-	If Anyone Finds This I Love You	Ruby Murray	Columbia	11		
19	8	The Naughty Lady Of Shady Lane	Ames Brothers	HMV	6	(3)	F L
20	6	Shake, Rattle And Roll	Bill Haley & His Comets	Brunswick	14	(7)	

April 1955

This Mnth	Prev Mnth	Title	Artist	Label	Wks	(US 20 Pos)	
1	1	Give Me Your Word	Tennessee Ernie Ford	Capitol	24		F
2	-	Cherry Pink And Apple Blossom White	Perez Prado	HMV	17	(1)	F
3	2	Softly Softly	Ruby Murray	Columbia	23		
4	18	If Anyone Finds This I Love You	Ruby Murray	Columbia	11		
5	16	Wedding Bells	Eddie Fisher	HMV	11		
6	-	Under The Bridges Of Paris	Dean Martin	Capitol	8		
7	-	Cherry Pink And Apple Blossom White	Eddie Calvert	Columbia	21		
8	6	Mobile	Ray Burns	Columbia	13		F
9	-	Prize Of Gold	Joan Regan	Decca	8	(55)	
10	5	A Blossom Fell	Nat 'King' Cole	Capitol	10	(2)	
11	-	Under The Bridges Of Paris	Eartha Kitt	HMV	10		F L
12	-	Stranger In Paradise	Tony Bennett	Philips	16	(2)	F
13	-	Ready Willing And Able	Doris Day	Philips	9		
14	3	Let Me Go, Lover	Dean Martin	Capitol	9		
15	-	Earth Angel	Crew-Cuts	Mercury	20	(8)	L
16	-	Stranger In Paradise	Tony Martin	HMV	13	(10)	F
17	15	Tomorrow	Johnny Brandon	Polygon	8		F
18	14	A Blossom Fell	Dickie Valentine	Decca	10		
19	-	A Blossom Fell	Ronnie Hilton	HMV	5		
20	10	Let Me Go, Lover	Ruby Murray	Columbia	7		

◆ 'Give Me Your Word', which was the B-side of Tennessee Ernie Ford's minor US success, 'River Of No Return', surprised many people by topping the British chart.

◆ Less than four months after making her chart debut, distinctive Irish vocalist Ruby Murray had a record five singles simultaneously on the UK chart.

1955

This Mnth	Prev Mnth	Title	Artist	Label	Wks	(US 20 Pos)	
1	12	Stranger In Paradise	Tony Bennett	Philips	16	(2)	F
2	2	Cherry Pink And Apple Blossom White	Perez Prado	HMV	17	(1)	F
3	7	Cherry Pink And Apple Blossom White	Eddie Calvert	Columbia	21		
4	1	Give Me Your Word	Tennessee Ernie Ford	Capitol	24		F
5	15	Earth Angel	Crew-Cuts	Mercury	20	(8)	L
6	16	Stranger In Paradise	Tony Martin	HMV	13	(10)	F
7	3	Softly Softly	Ruby Murray	Columbia	23		
8	-	Unchained Melody	Al Hibbler	Brunswick	17	(5)	F L
9	5	Wedding Bells	Eddie Fisher	HMV	11		
10	-	Unchained Melody	Jimmy Young	Decca	19		
11	-	If You Believe	Johnnie Ray	Philips	11		
12	4	If Anyone Finds This I Love You	Ruby Murray	Columbia	11		
13	13	Ready Willing And Able	Doris Day	Philips	9		
14	11	Under The Bridges Of Paris	Eartha Kitt	HMV	10		F L
15	-	Unchained Melody	Les Baxter	Capitol	9	(2)	F L
16	-	Melody Of Love	Ink Spots	Parlophone	4		F L
17	-	Stranger In Paradise	Four Aces	Brunswick	6	(5)	
18	6	Under The Bridges Of Paris	Dean Martin	Capitol	8		
19	-	Stranger In Paradise	Eddie Calvert	Columbia	4		
20	-	Where Will The Baby's Dimple Be	Rosemary Clooney	Philips	13		

This Mnth	Prev Mnth	Title	Artist	Label	Wks	(US 20 Pos)	
1	3	Cherry Pink And Apple Blossom White	Eddie Calvert	Columbia	21		
2	8	Unchained Melody	Al Hibbler	Brunswick	17	(5)	F L
3	10	Unchained Melody	Jimmy Young	Decca	19		
4	1	Stranger In Paradise	Tony Bennett	Philips	16	(2)	F
5	5	Earth Angel	Crew-Cuts	Mercury	20	(8)	L
6	2	Cherry Pink And Apple Blossom White	Perez Prado	HMV	17	(1)	F
7	-	Dreamboat	Alma Cogan	HMV	16		
8	6	Stranger In Paradise	Tony Martin	HMV	13	(10)	F
9	20	Where Will The Baby's Dimple Be	Rosemary Clooney	Philips	13		
10	11	If You Believe	Johnnie Ray	Philips	11		
11	17	Stranger In Paradise	Four Aces	Brunswick	6	(5)	
12	4	Give Me Your Word	Tennessee Ernie Ford	Capitol	24		F
13	15	Unchained Melody	Les Baxter	Capitol	9	(2)	F L
14	-	I Wonder	Dickie Valentine	Decca	15		
15	-	Sing It With Joe	Joe 'Mr. Piano' Henderson	Polygon	4		F
16	-	You My Love	Frank Sinatra	Capitol	7		
17	7	Softly Softly	Ruby Murray	Columbia	23		
18	-	Cool Water	Frankie Laine	Philips	22		
19	-	Crazy Otto Rag	Stargazers	Decca	3		
20	-	Stowaway	Barbara Lyon	Columbia	8		F

◆ Latin American dance craze the mambo had its finest moment thanks to Perez Prado's transatlantic smash 'Cherry Pink And Apple Blossom White'.

◆ Sixteen months after they had simultaneously climbed the American Top 20, versions of 'Stranger In Paradise' by Tony Bennett, Tony Martin and The Four Aces also battled it out on the British chart. The song which was adapted from classical composer Borodin's 'Polovtsian Dances' came from the musical *Kismet*.

July 1955

This Mnth	Prev Mnth	Title	Artist	Label	Wks	(US 20 Pos)	
1	7	Dreamboat	Alma Cogan	HMV	16		
2	3	Unchained Melody	Jimmy Young	Decca	19		
3	2	Unchained Melody	Al Hibbler	Brunswick	17	(5)	F L
4	1	Cherry Pink And Apple Blossom White	Eddie Calvert	Columbia	21		
5	14	I Wonder	Dickie Valentine	Decca	15		
6	-	Evermore	Ruby Murray	Columbia	17		
7	18	Cool Water	Frankie Laine	Philips	22		
8	5	Earth Angel	Crew-Cuts	Mercury	20	(8)	L
9	9	Where Will The Baby's Dimple Be	Rosemary Clooney	Philips	13		
10	-	Rose Marie	Slim Whitman	London	19		F
11	4	Stranger In Paradise	Tony Bennett	Philips	16	(2)	F
12	-	Every Day Of My Life	Malcolm Vaughan	HMV	16		F
13	-	Ev'rywhere	David Whitfield	Decca	20		
14	20	Stowaway	Barbara Lyon	Columbia	8		F L
15	6	Cherry Pink And Apple Blossom White	Perez Prado	HMV	17	(1)	F
16	8	Stranger In Paradise	Tony Martin	HMV	13	(10)	F
17	-	Strange Lady In Town	Frankie Laine	Philips	13		
18	-	Sincerely	McGuire Sisters	Vogue Coral	4	(1)	
19	10	If You Believe	Johnnie Ray	Philips	11		
20	13	Unchained Melody	Les Baxter	Capitol	9	(2)	F L

August 1955

This Mnth	Prev Mnth	Title	Artist	Label	Wks	(US 20 Pos)	
1	10	Rose Marie	Slim Whitman	London	19		F
2	7	Cool Water	Frankie Laine	Philips	22		
3	6	Evermore	Ruby Murray	Columbia	17		
4	1	Dreamboat	Alma Cogan	HMV	16		
5	13	Ev'rywhere	David Whitfield	Decca	20		
6	12	Every Day Of My Life	Malcolm Vaughan	HMV	16		F
7	-	Learnin' The Blues	Frank Sinatra	Capitol	13	(2)	
8	17	Strange Lady In Town	Frankie Laine	Philips	13		
9	2	Unchained Melody	Jimmy Young	Decca	19		
10	5	I Wonder	Dickie Valentine	Decca	15		
11	4	Cherry Pink And Apple Blossom White	Eddie Calvert	Columbia	21		
12	3	Unchained Melody	Al Hibbler	Brunswick	17	(5)	F L
13	-	Mama	David Whitfield	Decca	11		
14	-	Indian Love Call	Slim Whitman	London American	12	(10)	
15	-	John And Julie	Eddie Calvert	Columbia	11		
16	-	The Breeze And I	Caterina Valente	Polydor	14	(13)	F L
17	8	Earth Angel	Crew-Cuts	Mercury	20	(8)	L
18	9	Where Will The Baby's Dimple Be	Rosemary Clooney	Philips	13		
19	14	Stowaway	Barbara Lyon	Columbia	8		F L
20	-	You My Love	Frank Sinatra	Capitol	7		

◆ Despite its failure in the US, 'Rose Marie' (from the 1925 musical of the same name) by Florida C&W artist Slim Whitman, held the top spot in Britain for 11 successive weeks – a record he held until 1991 when it was broken by Bryan Adams.

◆ Among the earliest R&B songs to chart in Britain were 'Earth Angel' and 'Sincerely', albeit the sanitized American pop versions by the Crew-Cuts and the McGuire Sisters respectively.

1955

This Mnth	Prev Mnth	Title	Artist	Label	Wks	(US 20 Pos)	
1	1	Rose Marie	Slim Whitman	London	19		F
2	7	Learnin' The Blues	Frank Sinatra	Capitol	13	(2)	
3	2	Cool Water	Frankie Laine	Philips	22		
4	5	Ev'rywhere	David Whitfield	Decca	20		
5	16	The Breeze And I	Caterina Valente	Polydor	14	(13)	F L
6	3	Evermore	Ruby Murray	Columbia	17		
7	8	Strange Lady In Town	Frankie Laine	Philips	13		
8	15	John And Julie	Eddie Calvert	Columbia	11		
9	6	Every Day Of My Life	Malcolm Vaughan	HMV	16		F
10	14	Indian Love Call	Slim Whitman	London American	12	(10)	
11	-	Close The Door	Stargazers	Decca	9		
12	-	The Man From Laramie	Jimmy Young	Decca	12		
13	-	Love Me Or Leave Me	Sammy Davis Jr.	Brunswick	6	(10)	
14	-	Stars Shine In Your Eyes	Ronnie Hilton	HMV	7		
15	-	Something's Gotta Give	Sammy Davis Jr.	Brunswick	7	(9)	F
16	-	That's How A Love Song Was Born	Ray Burns	Columbia	6		L
17	-	Blue Star	Cyril Stapleton	Decca	12		
18	13	Mama	David Whitfield	Decca	11		
19	4	Dreamboat	Alma Cogan	HMV	16		
20	-	China Doll	Slim Whitman	London American	2		

1	12	The Man From Laramie	Jimmy Young	Decca	12		
2	17	Blue Star	Cyril Stapleton	Decca	12		
3	1	Rose Marie	Slim Whitman	London	19		F
4	3	Cool Water	Frankie Laine	Philips	22		
5	-	Yellow Rose Of Texas	Mitch Miller	Philips	13	(1)	F L
6	4	Ev'rywhere	David Whitfield	Decca	20		
7	5	The Breeze And I	Caterina Valente	Polydor	14	(13)	F L
8	-	Hernando's Hideaway	Johnston Brothers	Decca	13		
9	2	Learnin' The Blues	Frank Sinatra	Capitol	13	(2)	
10	11	Close The Door	Stargazers	Decca	9		
11	-	Hey There	Rosemary Clooney	Philips	11	(1)	
12	-	Rock Around The Clock	Bill Haley & His Comets	Brunswick	17	(1)	G
13	-	Hernando's Hideaway	Johnnie Ray	Philips	5	(24)	
14	-	Hey There	Johnnie Ray	Philips	9		
15	10	Indian Love Call	Slim Whitman	London American	12	(10)	
16	-	I'll Come When You Call	Ruby Murray	Columbia	7		
17	9	Every Day Of My Life	Malcolm Vaughan	HMV	16		F
18	6	Evermore	Ruby Murray	Columbia	17		
19	13	Love Me Or Leave Me	Sammy Davis Jr.	Brunswick	6	(10)	
20	-	Go On By	Alma Cogan	HMV	4		

◆ Slim Whitman was not the only American artist hitting with a recording that had either failed in their homeland or had not merited release there. Other acts with Anglo-aimed singles included Rosemary Clooney, Johnnie Ray, Frank Sinatra and Frankie Laine. The latter was enjoying two UK-only successes 'Strange Lady In Town' and 'Cool Water'.

◆ American composer Jerry Ross died aged 29, as his compositions, 'Hernando's Hideaway' and 'Hey There', held three places in the UK Top 5.

November 1955

This Mnth	Prev Mnth	Title	Artist	Label	Wks 20	(US Pos)	
1	8	Hernando's Hideaway	Johnston Brothers	Decca	13		
2	12	Rock Around The Clock	Bill Haley & His Comets	Brunswick	17	(1)	G
3	1	The Man From Laramie	Jimmy Young	Decca	12		
4	14	Hey There	Johnnie Ray	Philips	9		
5	11	Hey There	Rosemary Clooney	Philips	11	(1)	
6	2	Blue Star	Cyril Stapleton	Decca	12		
7	5	Yellow Rose Of Texas	Mitch Miller	Philips	13	(1)	F L
8	16	I'll Come When You Call	Ruby Murray	Columbia	7		
9	-	Let's Have A Ding Dong	Winifred Atwell	Decca	10		
10	6	Ev'rywhere	David Whitfield	Decca	20		
11	-	Song Of The Dreamer	Johnnie Ray	Philips	5		
12	-	Love Is A Many Splendoured Thing	Four Aces	Brunswick	13	(1)	
13	4	Cool Water	Frankie Laine	Philips	22		
14	-	Twenty Tiny Fingers	Stargazers	Decca	11		L
15	3	Rose Marie	Slim Whitman	London	19		F
16	-	Yellow Rose Of Texas	Gary Miller	Nixa	5		F
17	7	The Breeze And I	Caterina Valente	Polydor	14	(13)	F L
18	-	Ain't That A Shame	Pat Boone	London American	9	(2)	F
19	-	Meet Me On The Corner	Max Bygraves	HMV	11		
20	-	Yellow Rose Of Texas	Ronnie Hilton	HMV	2		

December 1955

This Mnth	Prev Mnth	Title	Artist	Label	Wks 20	(US Pos)	
1	2	Rock Around The Clock	Bill Haley & His Comets	Brunswick	17	(1)	G
2	-	Christmas Alphabet	Dickie Valentine	Decca	7		
3	12	Love Is A Many Splendoured Thing	Four Aces	Brunswick	13	(1)	
4	9	Let's Have A Ding Dong	Winifred Atwell	Decca	10		
5	19	Meet Me On The Corner	Max Bygraves	HMV	11		
6	14	Twenty Tiny Fingers	Stargazers	Decca	11		L
7	7	Yellow Rose Of Texas	Mitch Miller	Philips	13	(1)	F L
8	1	Hernando's Hideaway	Johnston Brothers	Decca	13		
9	-	Suddenly There's A Valley	Petula Clark	Nixa	10		
10	18	Ain't That A Shame	Pat Boone	London American	9	(2)	F
11	-	Hawkeye	Frankie Laine	Philips	8		
12	-	When You Lose The One You Love	David Whitfield	Decca	11	(62)	
13	-	Suddenly There's A Valley	Jo Stafford	Philips	6	(21)	L
14	-	The Singing Dogs (Medley)	Singing Dogs	Nixa	4		F L
15	-	Never Do A Tango With An Eskimo	Alma Cogan	HMV	5		
16	4	Hey There	Johnnie Ray	Philips	9		
17	5	Hey There	Rosemary Clooney	Philips	11	(1)	
18	-	Suddenly There's A Valley	Lee Lawrence	Columbia	3		L
19	6	Blue Star	Cyril Stapleton	Decca	12		
20	-	On With The Motley	Harry Secombe	Philips	3		F

◆ Thanks to its exposure in the hit film *The Blackboard Jungle*, 'Rock Around The Clock' by Bill Haley & The Comets became the first rock'n'roll record to top the UK chart.

◆ Balladeer Jimmy Young became the first British artist to clock up two successive UK No. 1s. The record that completed the double was his version of the American film theme 'The Man From Laramie', a song which failed to chart Stateside.

1956

This Mnth	Prev Mnth	Title	Artist	Label	Wks	(US 20 Pos)	
1	1	Rock Around The Clock	Bill Haley & His Comets	Brunswick	17	(1)	G
2	3	Love Is A Many Splendoured Thing	Four Aces	Brunswick	13	(1)	
3	-	Rock-A-Beatin' Boogie	Bill Haley & His Comets	Brunswick	8	(23)	
4	-	Sixteen Tons	Tennessee Ernie Ford	Capitol	11	(1)	
5	-	The Ballad Of Davy Crockett	Bill Hayes	London American	9	(1)	F L
6	5	Meet Me On The Corner	Max Bygraves	HMV	11		
7	-	Love And Marriage	Frank Sinatra	Capitol	8	(6)	
8	-	The Ballad Of Davy Crockett	Tennessee Ernie Ford	Capitol	7	(6)	L
9	15	Never Do A Tango With An Eskimo	Alma Cogan	HMV	5		
10	12	When You Lose The One You Love	David Whitfield	Decca	11	(62)	
11	6	Twenty Tiny Fingers	Stargazers	Decca	11		L
12	9	Suddenly There's A Valley	Petula Clark	Nixa	10		
13	-	Rock Island Line	Lonnie Donegan	Decca	14	(8)	F
14	-	The Tender Trap	Frank Sinatra	Capitol	9	(24)	
15	-	Pickin' A Chicken	Eve Boswell	Parlophone	10		F L
16	-	Sixteen Tons	Frankie Laine	Philips	3		
17	11	Hawkeye	Frankie Laine	Philips	8		
18	-	Someone On Your Mind	Jimmy Young	Decca	5		
19	10	Ain't That A Shame	Pat Boone	London American	9	(2)	F
20	2	Christmas Alphabet	Dickie Valentine	Decca	7		

This Mnth	Prev Mnth	Title	Artist	Label	Wks	(US 20 Pos)	
1	4	Sixteen Tons	Tennessee Ernie Ford	Capitol	11	(1)	
2	14	The Tender Trap	Frank Sinatra	Capitol	9	(24)	
3	5	The Ballad Of Davy Crockett	Bill Hayes	London American	9	(1)	F L
4	-	Memories Are Made Of This	Dean Martin	Capitol	14	(1)	
5	-	Zambesi	Lou Busch	Capitol	15	(75)	F L
6	7	Love And Marriage	Frank Sinatra	Capitol	8	(6)	
7	-	Only You	Hilltoppers	London American	21	(15)	F
8	13	Rock Island Line	Lonnie Donegan	Decca	14	(8)	F
9	8	The Ballad Of Davy Crockett	Tennessee Ernie Ford	Capitol	7	(6)	L
10	-	Dreams Can Tell A Lie	Nat 'King' Cole	Capitol	9		
11	-	It's Almost Tomorrow	Dream Weavers	Brunswick	16	(8)	F L
12	3	Rock-A-Beatin' Boogie	Bill Haley & His Comets	Brunswick	8	(23)	
13	-	Rock And Roll Waltz	Kay Starr	HMV	18	(1)	L
14	-	Band Of Gold	Don Cherry	Philips	11	(5)	F L
15	-	Robin Hood	Gary Miller	Nixa	6		
16	2	Love Is A Many Splendoured Thing	Four Aces	Brunswick	13	(1)	
17	-	Robin Hood	Dick James	Parlophone	8		F
18	15	Pickin' A Chicken	Eve Boswell	Parlophone	10		F L
19	-	Memories Are Made Of This	Dave King	Decca	13		F
20	-	Young And Foolish	Edmund Hockridge	Nixa	7		F

◆ As Mercury Records had no UK outlet, the Platters' US smashes, 'Only You' and 'The Great Pretender', were not released in the UK until Autumn 1956. This left the way clear for The Hilltoppers and Jimmy Parkinson.

◆ Lonnie Donegan's 'Rock Island Line' introduced the transatlantic public to skiffle – a do-it-yourself folk/blues based music that launched a thousand British groups.

March 1956

This Mnth	Prev Mnth	Title	Artist	Label	Wks 20	(US Pos)	
1	11	It's Almost Tomorrow	Dream Weavers	Brunswick	16	(8)	F L
2	4	Memories Are Made Of This	Dean Martin	Capitol	14	(1)	
3	13	Rock And Roll Waltz	Kay Starr	HMV	18	(1)	L
4	5	Zambesi	Lou Busch	Capitol	15	(75)	F L
5	7	Only You	Hilltoppers	London American	21	(15)	F
6	19	Memories Are Made Of This	Dave King	Decca	13		F
7	14	Band Of Gold	Don Cherry	Philips	11	(5)	F L
8	-	See You Later Alligator	Bill Haley & His Comets	Brunswick	11	(6)	
9	20	Young And Foolish	Edmund Hockridge	Nixa	7		F
10	8	Rock Island Line	Lonnie Donegan	Decca	14	(8)	F
11	-	The Great Pretender	Jimmy Parkinson	Columbia	10		F
12	-	Poor People Of Paris	Winifred Atwell	Decca	15		
13	2	The Tender Trap	Frank Sinatra	Capitol	9	(24)	
14	1	Sixteen Tons	Tennessee Ernie Ford	Capitol	11	(1)	
15	-	Chain Gang	Jimmy Young	Decca	5		
16	-	Theme From 'The Three Penny Opera'	Dick Hyman Trio	MGM	9	(10)	F L
17	10	Dreams Can Tell A Lie	Nat 'King' Cole	Capitol	9		
18	-	Zambesi	Eddie Calvert	Columbia	5		
19	-	In Old Lisbon	Frank Chacksfield	Decca	4		L
20	18	Pickin' A Chicken	Eve Boswell	Parlophone	10		F L

April 1956

This Mnth	Prev Mnth	Title	Artist	Label	Wks 20	(US Pos)	
1	12	Poor People Of Paris	Winifred Atwell	Decca	15		
2	1	It's Almost Tomorrow	Dream Weavers	Brunswick	16	(8)	F L
3	3	Rock And Roll Waltz	Kay Starr	HMV	18	(1)	L
4	5	Only You	Hilltoppers	London American	21	(15)	F
5	6	Memories Are Made Of This	Dave King	Decca	13		F
6	4	Zambesi	Lou Busch	Capitol	15	(75)	F L
7	2	Memories Are Made Of This	Dean Martin	Capitol	14	(1)	
8	8	See You Later Alligator	Bill Haley & His Comets	Brunswick	11	(6)	
9	16	Theme From 'The Three Penny Opera'	Dick Hyman Trio	MGM	9	(10)	F L
10	-	My September Love	David Whitfield	Decca	21		
11	11	The Great Pretender	Jimmy Parkinson	Columbia	10		F
12	-	A Tear Fell	Teresa Brewer	Vogue/Coral	15	(9)	
13	-	Willie Can	Alma Cogan	HMV	7		
14	-	No Other Love	Ronnie Hilton	HMV	13		
15	-	Theme From 'The Threepenny Opera'	Billy Vaughn	London American	5	(37)	L
16	15	Chain Gang	Jimmy Young	Decca	5		
17	18	Zambesi	Eddie Calvert	Columbia	5		
18	-	Theme From The Threepenny Opera	Louis Armstrong	Philips	7		
19	7	Band Of Gold	Don Cherry	Philips	11	(5)	F L
20	-	You Can't Be True To Two	Dave King	Decca	7		

◆ George Martin had three productions simultaneously in the UK Top 20. The records being by TV personality Eamonn Andrews, Eve Boswell and (later Beatles' publisher) Dick James.

◆ For the first time in Britain an album sold enough copies to enter the best selling records chart. The LP **Songs For Swinging Lovers** contained such standards as 'Pennies From Heaven', 'Makin' Whoopee' and 'I've Got You Under My Skin'.

1956

This Mnth	Prev Mnth	Title	Artist	Label	Wks	(US 20 Pos)	
1	14	No Other Love	Ronnie Hilton	HMV	13		
2	1	Poor People Of Paris	Winifred Atwell	Decca	15		
3	12	A Tear Fell	Teresa Brewer	Vogue/Coral	15	(9)	
4	3	Rock And Roll Waltz	Kay Starr	HMV	18	(1)	L
5	10	My September Love	David Whitfield	Decca	21		
6	2	It's Almost Tomorrow	Dream Weavers	Brunswick	16	(8)	F L
7	4	Only You	Hilltoppers	London American	21	(15)	F
8	-	I'll Be Home	Pat Boone	London American	23	(6)	
9	-	Lost John/Stewball	Lonnie Donegan	Pye Nixa	14	(58)	
10	-	Main Title Theme From The Man With The Golden Arm	Billy May	Capitol	6	(49)	F L
11	18	Theme From The Threepenny Opera	Louis Armstrong	Philips	7		
12	20	You Can't Be True To Two	Dave King	Decca	7		
13	-	Heartbreak Hotel	Elvis Presley	HMV	19	(1)	F
14	-	The Happy Whistler	Don Robertson	Capitol	7	(9)	F L
15	8	See You Later Alligator	Bill Haley & His Comets	Brunswick	11	(6)	
16	5	Memories Are Made Of This	Dave King	Decca	13		F
17	7	Memories Are Made Of This	Dean Martin	Capitol	14	(1)	
18	-	Blue Suede Shoes	Carl Perkins	London American	7	(3)	F L
19	-	Mountain Greenery	Mel Torme	Vogue/Coral	17		F
20	9	Theme From 'The Three Penny Opera'	Dick Hyman Trio	MGM	9	(10)	F L

This Mnth	Prev Mnth	Title	Artist	Label	Wks	(US 20 Pos)	
1	8	I'll Be Home	Pat Boone	London American	23	(6)	
2	9	Lost John/Stewball	Lonnie Donegan	Pye Nixa	14	(58)	
3	1	No Other Love	Ronnie Hilton	HMV	13		
4	13	Heartbreak Hotel	Elvis Presley	HMV	19	(1)	F
5	3	A Tear Fell	Teresa Brewer	Vogue/Coral	15	(9)	
6	-	Hot Diggity	Perry Como	HMV	12	(2)	
7	-	The Saints Rock 'n Roll	Bill Haley & His Comets	Brunswick	22	(18)	
8	5	My September Love	David Whitfield	Decca	21		
9	-	Blue Suede Shoes	Elvis Presley	HMV	8	(20)	
10	-	Too Young To Go Steady	Nat 'King' Cole	Capitol	10		
11	14	The Happy Whistler	Don Robertson	Capitol	7	(9)	F L
12	-	Moonglow/Theme From 'Picnic'	Morris Stoloff	Brunswick	8	(2)	F L
13	2	Poor People Of Paris	Winifred Atwell	Decca	15		
14	4	Rock And Roll Waltz	Kay Starr	HMV	18	(1)	L
15	18	Blue Suede Shoes	Carl Perkins	London American	7	(3)	F L
16	7	Only You	Hilltoppers	London American	21	(15)	F
17	10	Main Title Theme From The Man With The Golden Arm	Billy May	Capitol	6	(49)	F L
18	-	Songs For Swinging Lovers (L.P.)	Frank Sinatra	Capitol	5		
19	-	Hot Diggity	Michael Holliday	Columbia	4		
20	-	Gal With The Yaller Shoes	Michael Holliday	Columbia	3		

◆ In the month that Elvis and Carl Perkins debuted on the British chart and Alan Freed was first heard in Europe, the first Eurovision Song Contest was held: it was won by Lys Assia from Switzerland with a song called 'Refrains'.

◆ The British singles chart was extended to a Top 30.
◆ As Elvis Presley was first seen on the front cover of *NME*, Britain's Lonnie Donegan appeared on the cover of the noted US music magazine *Cash Box*.

1956

This Mnth	Prev Mnth	Title	Artist	Label	Wks	(US 20 Pos)	
1	1	I'll Be Home	Pat Boone	London American	23	(6)	
2	4	Heartbreak Hotel	Elvis Presley	HMV	19	(1)	F
3	-	All Star Hit Parade	Various Artists	Decca	8		F L
4	-	Why Do Fools Fall In Love	Frankie Lymon/The Teenagers	Columbia	15	(6)	F
5	-	I'm Walking Backwards For Christmas/Bluebottle Blues	Goons	Decca	8		F
6	6	Hot Diggity	Perry Como	HMV	12	(2)	
7	2	Lost John/Stewball	Lonnie Donegan	Pye Nixa	14	(58)	
8	-	Experiments With Mice	Johnny Dankworth	Parlophone	8	(61)	F
9	-	The Wayward Wind	Gogi Grant	London American	9	(1)	F L
10	7	The Saints Rock 'n Roll	Bill Haley & His Comets	Brunswick	22	(18)	
11	-	Wayward Wind	Tex Ritter	Capitol	11	(28)	F L
12	8	My September Love	David Whitfield	Decca	21		
13	-	Who Are We	Ronnie Hilton	HMV	8		
14	-	Walk Hand In Hand	Tony Martin	HMV	13	(21)	L
15	-	Whatever Will Be Will Be	Doris Day	Philips	20	(3)	
16	12	Moonglow/Theme From 'Picnic'	Morris Stoloff	Brunswick	8	(2)	F L
17	3	No Other Love	Ronnie Hilton	HMV	13		
18	18	Songs For Swinging Lovers (L.P.)	Frank Sinatra	Capitol	5		
19	5	A Tear Fell	Teresa Brewer	Vogue/Coral	15	(9)	
20	10	Too Young To Go Steady	Nat 'King' Cole	Capitol	10		

This Mnth	Prev Mnth	Title	Artist	Label	Wks	(US 20 Pos)	
1	15	Whatever Will Be Will Be	Doris Day	Philips	20	(3)	
2	4	Why Do Fools Fall In Love	Frankie Lymon/The Teenagers	Columbia	15	(6)	F
3	14	Walk Hand In Hand	Tony Martin	HMV	13	(21)	L
4	-	Sweet Old-Fashioned Girl	Teresa Brewer	Vogue/Coral	13	(12)	L
5	-	Mountain Greenery	Mel Torme	Vogue/Coral	17		F
6	2	Heartbreak Hotel	Elvis Presley	HMV	19	(1)	F
7	1	I'll Be Home	Pat Boone	London American	23	(6)	
8	11	Wayward Wind	Tex Ritter	Capitol	11	(28)	F L
9	10	The Saints Rock 'n Roll	Bill Haley & His Comets	Brunswick	22	(18)	
10	13	Who Are We	Ronnie Hilton	HMV	8		
11	-	Rockin' Through The Rye	Bill Haley & His Comets	Brunswick	19	(78)	
12	3	All Star Hit Parade	Various Artists	Decca	8		F L
13	-	Serenade	Slim Whitman	London American	8		
14	5	I'm Walking Backwards For Christmas/Bluebottle Blues	Goons	Decca	8		F
15	-	Walk Hand In Hand	Ronnie Carroll	Philips	7		F
16	9	The Wayward Wind	Gogi Grant	London American	9	(1)	F L
17	8	Experiments With Mice	Johnny Dankworth	Parlophone	8	(61)	F
18	6	Hot Diggity	Perry Como	HMV	12	(2)	
19	-	I Almost Lost My Mind	Pat Boone	London American	6	(2)	
20	-	Left Bank	Winifred Atwell	Decca	5		

◆ Britain's first rock'n' roll riots were reported, as the film *Rock Around The Clock* went on general release. The film had teenagers jiving in the aisles and, sometimes, slashing cinema seats.

◆ At a time when American artists ruled the UK charts, Frankie Lymon & The Teenagers became the first black American act to top the British hit parade.

1956

This Mnth	Prev Mnth	Title	Artist	Label	Wks (US 20 Pos)	
1	1	Whatever Will Be Will Be	Doris Day	Philips	20 (3)	
2	-	Lay Down Your Arms	Anne Shelton	Philips	13 (59)	
3	11	Rockin' Through The Rye	Bill Haley & His Comets	Brunswick	19 (78)	
4	2	Why Do Fools Fall In Love	Frankie Lymon/The Teenagers	Columbia	15 (6)	F
5	4	Sweet Old-Fashioned Girl	Teresa Brewer	Vogue/Coral	13 (12)	L
6	3	Walk Hand In Hand	Tony Martin	HMV	13 (21)	L
7	-	The Great Pretender/Only You	Platters	Mercury	10 (2)	F
8	-	Bloodnok's Rock 'n' Roll Call/ Ying Tong Song	Goons	Decca	8	
9	5	Mountain Greenery	Mel Torme	Vogue/Coral	17	F
10	9	The Saints Rock 'n Roll	Bill Haley & His Comets	Brunswick	22 (18)	
11	-	Bring A Little Water Sylvie/ Dead Or Alive	Lonnie Donegan	Pye Nixa	8	
12	-	A Woman In Love	Frankie Laine	Philips	19 (19)	
13	-	Born To Be With You	Chordettes	London American	8 (8)	
14	13	Serenade	Slim Whitman	London American	8	
15	-	Hound Dog	Elvis Presley	HMV	22 (1)	
16	-	I Want You I Need You I Love You	Elvis Presley	HMV	6 (1)	
17	6	Heartbreak Hotel	Elvis Presley	HMV	19 (1)	F
18	19	I Almost Lost My Mind	Pat Boone	London American	6 (2)	
19	-	Rock Around The Clock	Bill Haley & His Comets	Brunswick	11	
20	-	I'm In Love Again	Fats Domino	London American	5 (4)	F

This Mnth	Prev Mnth	Title	Artist	Label	Wks (US 20 Pos)	
1	12	A Woman In Love	Frankie Laine	Philips	19 (19)	
2	2	Lay Down Your Arms	Anne Shelton	Philips	13 (59)	
3	15	Hound Dog	Elvis Presley	HMV	22 (1)	
4	1	Whatever Will Be Will Be	Doris Day	Philips	20 (3)	
5	-	Giddy-Up-A-Ding-Dong	Freddie Bell & The Bellboys	Mercury	8	F L
6	3	Rockin' Through The Rye	Bill Haley & His Comets	Brunswick	19 (78)	
7	7	The Great Pretender/Only You	Platters	Mercury	10 (2)	F
8	8	Bloodnok's Rock 'n' Roll Call/ Ying Tong Song	Goons	Decca	8	
9	11	Bring A Little Water Sylvie/ Dead Or Alive	Lonnie Donegan	Pye Nixa	8	
10	19	Rock Around The Clock	Bill Haley & His Comets	Brunswick	11	
11	-	Just Walkin' In The Rain	Johnnie Ray	Philips	18 (3)	
12	-	When Mexico Gave Up The Rumba	Mitchell Torok	Brunswick	15	F L
13	10	The Saints Rock 'n Roll	Bill Haley & His Comets	Brunswick	22 (18)	
14	-	More	Perry Como	HMV	8 (4)	
15	13	Born To Be With You	Chordettes	London American	8 (8)	
16	-	Razzle Dazzle	Bill Haley & His Comets	Brunswick	4 (15)	
17	-	See You Later Alligator	Bill Haley & His Comets	Brunswick	6 (6)	
18	4	Why Do Fools Fall In Love	Frankie Lymon/The Teenagers	Columbia	15 (6)	F
19	-	More	Jimmy Young	Decca	14	
20	5	Sweet Old-Fashioned Girl	Teresa Brewer	Vogue/Coral	13 (12)	L

◆ The first British hit with "rock" in the title came from the very popular radio comedy team The Goons (Peter Sellers, Harry Secombe and Spike Milligan). The B-side, 'Ying Tong Song', returned to the Top 10 in 1973.

◆ In the *NME* poll, Elvis was runner-up to Bill Haley as World's Most Outstanding Vocal Personality, and to Frank Sinatra as World's Outstanding Singer. In the *Billboard* DJ poll he was voted Most Played Male Pop and C&W Artist.

November 1956

This Mnth	Prev Mnth	Title	Artist	Label	Wks	(US 20 Pos)	
1	11	Just Walkin' In The Rain	Johnnie Ray	Philips	18	(3)	
2	1	A Woman In Love	Frankie Laine	Philips	19	(19)	
3	3	Hound Dog	Elvis Presley	HMV	22	(1)	
4	-	My Prayer	Platters	Mercury	10	(1)	
5	19	More	Jimmy Young	Decca	14		
6	6	Rockin' Through The Rye	Bill Haley & His Comets	Brunswick	19	(78)	
7	10	Rock Around The Clock	Bill Haley & His Comets	Brunswick	11		
8	12	When Mexico Gave Up The Rumba	Mitchell Torok	Brunswick	15		F L
9	-	Green Door	Frankie Vaughan	Philips	15		
10	2	Lay Down Your Arms	Anne Shelton	Philips	13	(59)	
11	-	Rip It Up	Bill Haley & His Comets	Brunswick	14	(25)	
12	-	Make It A Party	Winifred Atwell	Decca	10		
13	4	Whatever Will Be Will Be	Doris Day	Philips	20	(3)	
14	5	Giddy-Up-A-Ding-Dong	Freddie Bell & The Bellboys	Mercury	8		F L
15	-	St. Therese Of The Roses	Malcolm Vaughan	HMV	18		
16	-	The Green Door	Jim Lowe	London American	5	(2)	F L
17	-	Love Me As If There Were No Tomorrow	Nat 'King' Cole	Capitol	7		
18	-	Blue Moon	Elvis Presley	HMV	8	(55)	
19	14	More	Perry Como	HMV	8	(4)	
20	-	Cindy, Oh Cindy	Eddie Fisher	HMV	13	(10)	L

December 1956

This Mnth	Prev Mnth	Title	Artist	Label	Wks	(US 20 Pos)	
1	1	Just Walkin' In The Rain	Johnnie Ray	Philips	18	(3)	
2	9	Green Door	Frankie Vaughan	Philips	15		
3	15	St. Therese Of The Roses	Malcolm Vaughan	HMV	18		
4	11	Rip It Up	Bill Haley & His Comets	Brunswick	14	(25)	
5	20	Cindy, Oh Cindy	Eddie Fisher	HMV	13	(10)	L
6	4	My Prayer	Platters	Mercury	10	(1)	
7	-	True Love	Bing Crosby & Grace Kelly	Capitol	23	(5)	
8	2	A Woman In Love	Frankie Laine	Philips	19	(19)	
9	12	Make It A Party	Winifred Atwell	Decca	10		
10	3	Hound Dog	Elvis Presley	HMV	22	(1)	
11	5	More	Jimmy Young	Decca	14		
12	18	Blue Moon	Elvis Presley	HMV	8	(55)	
13	8	When Mexico Gave Up The Rumba	Mitchell Torok	Brunswick	15		F L
14	-	Christmas Island	Dickie Valentine	Decca	3		
15	-	Love Me Tender	Elvis Presley	HMV	9	(1)	
16	-	Two Different Worlds	Ronnie Hilton	HMV	7		
17	-	A House With Love In It	Vera Lynn	Decca	6		
18	-	Cindy Oh Cindy	Tony Brent	Columbia	3		
19	-	Moonlight Gambler	Frankie Laine	Philips	9	(5)	
20	-	Singing The Blues	Guy Mitchell	Philips	20	(1)	

◆ Although they failed to enter the Top 100 in their homeland, American rock'n'roll records by Freddie Bell and The Bellboys ('Giddy-Up-A-Ding-Dong') and Mitchell Torok ('When Mexico Gave Up The Rhumba') were big British hits.

◆ For several weeks Bill Haley & The Comets had five singles in the Top 20.

1957

This Mnth	Prev Mnth	Title	Artist	Label	Wks	(US 20 Pos)	
1	20	Singing The Blues	Guy Mitchell	Philips	20	(1)	
2	-	Singing The Blues	Tommy Steele	Decca	10		
3	3	St. Therese Of The Roses	Malcolm Vaughan	HMV	18		
4	1	Just Walkin' In The Rain	Johnnie Ray	Philips	18	(3)	
5	2	Green Door	Frankie Vaughan	Philips	15		
6	7	True Love	Bing Crosby & Grace Kelly	Capitol	23	(5)	
7	5	Cindy, Oh Cindy	Eddie Fisher	HMV	13	(10)	L
8	-	Friendly Persuasion	Pat Boone	London American	17	(9)	
9	-	Garden Of Eden	Frankie Vaughan	Philips	12		
10	10	Hound Dog	Elvis Presley	HMV	22	(1)	
11	4	Rip It Up	Bill Haley & His Comets	Brunswick	14	(25)	
12	15	Love Me Tender	Elvis Presley	HMV	9	(1)	
13	-	Blueberry Hill	Fats Domino	London American	10	(3)	
14	19	Moonlight Gambler	Frankie Laine	Philips	9	(5)	
15	8	A Woman In Love	Frankie Laine	Philips	19	(19)	
16	-	Don't You Rock Me Daddy-O	Lonnie Donegan	Pye Nixa	16		
17	-	Garden Of Eden	Gary Miller	Pye Nixa	2		
18	13	When Mexico Gave Up The Rumba	Mitchell Torok	Brunswick	15		F L
19	11	More	Jimmy Young	Decca	14		
20	9	Make It A Party	Winifred Atwell	Decca	10		

This Mnth	Prev Mnth	Title	Artist	Label	Wks	(US 20 Pos)	
1	9	Garden Of Eden	Frankie Vaughan	Philips	12		
2	1	Singing The Blues	Guy Mitchell	Philips	20	(1)	
3	8	Friendly Persuasion	Pat Boone	London American	17	(9)	
4	6	True Love	Bing Crosby & Grace Kelly	Capitol	23	(5)	
5	16	Don't You Rock Me Daddy-O	Lonnie Donegan	Pye Nixa	16		
6	3	St. Therese Of The Roses	Malcolm Vaughan	HMV	18		
7	13	Blueberry Hill	Fats Domino	London American	10	(3)	
8	-	Young Love	Tab Hunter	London American	17	(1)	F
9	2	Singing The Blues	Tommy Steele	Decca	10		
10	-	Don't Forbid Me	Pat Boone	London American	14	(3)	
11	7	Cindy, Oh Cindy	Eddie Fisher	HMV	13	(10)	L
12	-	Don't Knock The Rock	Bill Haley & His Comets	Brunswick	7	(45)	
13	-	Don't You Rock Me Daddy-O	Vipers Skiffle Group	Parlophone	6		F
14	10	Hound Dog	Elvis Presley	HMV	22	(1)	
15	5	Green Door	Frankie Vaughan	Philips	15		
16	-	Rock-A-Bye Your Baby (With A Dixie Melody)	Jerry Lewis	Brunswick	5	(10)	F L
17	4	Just Walkin' In The Rain	Johnnie Ray	Philips	18	(3)	
18	11	Rip It Up	Bill Haley & His Comets	Brunswick	14	(25)	
19	-	Adoration Waltz	David Whitfield	Decca	8		
20	-	You Don't Owe Me A Thing	Johnnie Ray	Philips	10	(10)	

◆ Less than three months after his chart debut, Tommy Steele (who was already filming his life story!) became the first British rock'n'roll artist to top the charts. His version of 'Singing The Blues' replaced Guy Mitchell's at No. 1.

◆ Britain launched its first pop TV shows: *Cool For Cats*, where professional dancers performed choreographed routines to current records, and the very influential *6-5 Special* which featured live artists.

1957

This Mnth	Prev Mnth	Title	Artist	Label	Wks	(US 20 Pos)	
1	8	Young Love	Tab Hunter	London American	17	(1)	F
2	10	Don't Forbid Me	Pat Boone	London American	14	(3)	
3	-	Knee Deep In The Blues	Guy Mitchell	Philips	11	(21)	
4	5	Don't You Rock Me Daddy-O	Lonnie Donegan	Pye Nixa	16		
5	2	Singing The Blues	Guy Mitchell	Philips	20	(1)	
6	-	Long Tall Sally	Little Richard	London American	14	(6)	F
7	1	Garden Of Eden	Frankie Vaughan	Philips	12		
8	4	True Love	Bing Crosby & Grace Kelly	Capitol	23	(5)	
9	-	Banana Boat Song	Harry Belafonte	HMV	14	(5)	F
10	3	Friendly Persuasion	Pat Boone	London American	17	(9)	
11	-	Banana Boat Song	Shirley Bassey	Philips	6		.F
12	19	Adoration Waltz	David Whitfield	Decca	8		
13	-	Young Love	Sonny James	Capitol	7	(2)	F L
14	12	Don't Knock The Rock	Bill Haley & His Comets	Brunswick	7	(45)	
15	7	Blueberry Hill	Fats Domino	London American	10	(3)	
16	-	The Girl Can't Help It	Little Richard	London American	10	(49)	
17	-	Wisdom Of A Fool	Norman Wisdom	Columbia	4		L
18	6	St. Therese Of The Roses	Malcolm Vaughan	HMV	18		
19	20	You Don't Owe Me A Thing	Johnnie Ray	Philips	10	(10)	
20	16	Rock-A-Bye Your Baby (With A Dixie Melody)	Jerry Lewis	Brunswick	5	(10)	F L

This Mnth	Prev Mnth	Title	Artist	Label	Wks	(US 20 Pos)	
1	1	Young Love	Tab Hunter	London American	17	(1)	F
2	-	Cumberland Gap	Lonnie Donegan	Pye Nixa	11		
3	9	Banana Boat Song	Harry Belafonte	HMV	14	(5)	F
4	2	Don't Forbid Me	Pat Boone	London American	14	(3)	
5	6	Long Tall Sally	Little Richard	London American	14	(6)	F
6	3	Knee Deep In The Blues	Guy Mitchell	Philips	11	(21)	
7	-	Look Homeward Angel	Johnnie Ray	Philips	10	(36)	
8	4	Don't You Rock Me Daddy-O	Lonnie Donegan	Pye Nixa	16		
9	8	True Love	Bing Crosby & Grace Kelly	Capitol	23	(5)	
10	16	The Girl Can't Help It	Little Richard	London American	10	(49)	
11	-	Baby Baby	Frankie Lymon/The Teenagers	Columbia	8		L
12	-	Ninety-Nine Ways	Tab Hunter	London American	10	(12)	L
13	-	Heart	Max Bygraves	Decca	7		
14	5	Singing The Blues	Guy Mitchell	Philips	20	(1)	
15	-	Cumberland Gap	Vipers Skiffle Group	Parlophone	4		L
16	-	I'm Not A Juvenile Delinquent	Frankie Lymon/The Teenagers	Columbia	4		
17	19	You Don't Owe Me A Thing	Johnnie Ray	Philips	10	(10)	
18	-	I'll Take You Home Again Kathleen	Slim Whitman	London American	11	(93)	
19	-	When I Fall In Love	Nat 'King' Cole	Capitol	19		
20	-	Freight Train	Chas McDevitt Skiffle Group	Oriole	14	(40)	F L

◆ Bill Haley & The Comets received an amazing media welcome to Britain, where *Rock Around The Clock* had became the first million seller. However, UK interest in them quickly faded and they left with minimal press coverage, and no future recordings made it into the Top 20.

◆ In April, Little Richard had three singles in the UK Top 20 and 14-year-old Frankie Lymon & The Teenagers had two. The youthful group, who successfully toured Britain and topped the bill at the London Palladium, were not to chart again.

1957

This Mnth	Prev Mnth	Title	Artist	Label	Wks	(US 20 Pos)	
1	-	Rock-A-Billy	Guy Mitchell	Philips	11	(10)	
2	-	Butterfly	Andy Williams	London American	12	(4)	F
3	2	Cumberland Gap	Lonnie Donegan	Pye Nixa	11		
4	19	When I Fall In Love	Nat 'King' Cole	Capitol	19		
5	12	Ninety-Nine Ways	Tab Hunter	London American	10	(12)	L
6	11	Baby Baby	Frankie Lymon/The Teenagers	Columbia	8		L
7	-	Yes Tonight Josephine	Johnnie Ray	Philips	15		
8	3	Banana Boat Song	Harry Belafonte	HMV	14	(5)	F
9	20	Freight Train	Chas McDevitt Skiffle Group	Oriole	14	(40)	F L
10	18	I'll Take You Home Again Kathleen	Slim Whitman	London American	11	(93)	
11	-	Too Much	Elvis Presley	HMV	8	(1)	
12	1	Young Love	Tab Hunter	London American	17	(1)	F
13	7	Look Homeward Angel	Johnnie Ray	Philips	10	(36)	
14	5	Long Tall Sally	Little Richard	London American	14	(6)	F
15	-	Chapel Of The Roses	Malcolm Vaughan	HMV	7		
16	10	The Girl Can't Help It	Little Richard	London American	10	(49)	
17	-	Mr. Wonderful	Peggy Lee	Brunswick	13	(25)	F
18	-	Butterfly	Charlie Gracie	Parlophone	3	(3)	F
19	-	Butterfingers	Tommy Steele	Decca	15		
20	4	Don't Forbid Me	Pat Boone	London American	14	(3)	

This Mnth	Prev Mnth	Title	Artist	Label	Wks	(US 20 Pos)	
1	7	Yes Tonight Josephine	Johnnie Ray	Philips	15		
2	4	When I Fall In Love	Nat 'King' Cole	Capitol	19		
3	2	Butterfly	Andy Williams	London American	12	(4)	F
4	-	Gamblin' Man/Putting On The Style	Lonnie Donegan	Pye Nixa	18		
5	-	Around The World	Ronnie Hilton	HMV	15		
6	-	Around The World	Bing Crosby	Brunswick	14	(25)	
7	1	Rock-A-Billy	Guy Mitchell	Philips	11	(10)	
8	-	Little Darlin'	Diamonds	Mercury	15	(2)	F L
9	9	Freight Train	Chas McDevitt Skiffle Group	Oriole	14	(40)	F L
10	17	Mr. Wonderful	Peggy Lee	Brunswick	13	(25)	F
11	-	Around The World	Gracie Fields	Columbia	7		F L
12	-	A White Sport Coat	King Brothers	Parlophone	11		F
13	-	We Will Make Love	Russ Hamilton	Oriole	16		F
14	11	Too Much	Elvis Presley	HMV	8	(1)	
15	10	I'll Take You Home Again Kathleen	Slim Whitman	London American	11	(93)	
16	15	Chapel Of The Roses	Malcolm Vaughan	HMV	7		
17	-	All Shook Up	Elvis Presley	HMV	18	(1)	
18	-	Fabulous	Charlie Gracie	Parlophone	13	(16)	
19	-	Island In The Sun	Harry Belafonte	RCA	22	(30)	
20	3	Cumberland Gap	Lonnie Donegan	Pye Nixa	11		

◆ Skiffle, now reaching its peak of popularity, had its first chart topper with Lonnie Donegan's adaptation of the traditional American folk song 'Cumberland Gap'.

◆ Amazingly, Nat 'King' Cole's version of the 1952 film theme 'When I Fall In Love' (which did not chart in America) returned to the UK Top 5 in 1987.

1957

This Mnth	Prev Mnth	Title	Artist	Label	Wks	(US 20 Pos)	
1	17	All Shook Up	Elvis Presley	HMV	18	(1)	
2	4	Gamblin' Man/Putting On The Style	Lonnie Donegan	Pye Nixa	18		
3	8	Little Darlin'	Diamonds	Mercury	15	(2)	F L
4	13	We Will Make Love	Russ Hamilton	Oriole	16		F
5	5	Around The World	Ronnie Hilton	HMV	15		
6	1	Yes Tonight Josephine	Johnnie Ray	Philips	15		
7	12	A White Sport Coat	King Brothers	Parlophone	11		F
8	2	When I Fall In Love	Nat 'King' Cole	Capitol	19		
9	6	Around The World	Bing Crosby	Brunswick	14	(25)	
10	-	Butterfingers	Tommy Steele	Decca	15		
11	10	Mr. Wonderful	Peggy Lee	Brunswick	13	(25)	F
12	-	Teddy Bear	Elvis Presley	HMV	18	(1)	
13	-	Love Letters In The Sand	Pat Boone	London American	21	(1)	
14	18	Fabulous	Charlie Gracie	Parlophone	13	(16)	
15	9	Freight Train	Chas McDevitt Skiffle Group	Oriole	14	(40)	F L
16	-	Lucille	Little Richard	London American	7	(21)	
17	19	Island In The Sun	Harry Belafonte	RCA	22	(30)	
18	-	Bye Bye Love	Everly Brothers	London American	13	(2)	F
19	3	Butterfly	Andy Williams	London American	12	(4)	F
20	-	I Like Your Kind Of Love	Andy Williams	London American	2	(10)	

This Mnth	Prev Mnth	Title	Artist	Label	Wks	(US 20 Pos)	
1	13	Love Letters In The Sand	Pat Boone	London American	21	(1)	
2	1	All Shook Up	Elvis Presley	HMV	18	(1)	
3	12	Teddy Bear	Elvis Presley	HMV	18	(1)	
4	17	Island In The Sun	Harry Belafonte	RCA	22	(30)	
5	2	Gamblin' Man/Putting On The Style	Lonnie Donegan	Pye Nixa	18		
6	4	We Will Make Love	Russ Hamilton	Oriole	16		F
7	3	Little Darlin'	Diamonds	Mercury	15	(2)	F L
8	18	Bye Bye Love	Everly Brothers	London American	13	(2)	F
9	-	Last Train To San Fernando	Johnny Duncan & The Blue Grass Boys	Columbia	16		F L
10	-	Diana	Paul Anka	Columbia	23	(1)	F G
11	5	Around The World	Ronnie Hilton	HMV	15		
12	-	With All My Heart	Petula Clark	Pye Nixa	16		
13	10	Butterfingers	Tommy Steele	Decca	15		
14	9	Around The World	Bing Crosby	Brunswick	14	(25)	
15	16	Lucille	Little Richard	London American	7	(21)	
16	14	Fabulous	Charlie Gracie	Parlophone	13	(16)	
17	6	Yes Tonight Josephine	Johnnie Ray	Philips	15		
18	8	When I Fall In Love	Nat 'King' Cole	Capitol	19		
19	7	A White Sport Coat	King Brothers	Parlophone	11		F
20	-	Start Movin'	Sal Mineo	Philips	6	(9)	F L

◆ The first successful British rock-related group were The King Brothers. This youthful trio scored the first of their hits with a cover of Marty Robbins' 'A White Sport Coat'.

◆ John Lennon and Paul McCartney met for the first time at a Church Garden Fete as fellow Merseyside singer/songwriter Russ Hamilton earned a pot of gold for his double sided transatlantic smash, 'We Will Make Love'/'Rainbow'.

1957

This Mnth	Prev Mnth	Title	Artist	Label	Wks	(US 20 Pos)	
1	10	Diana	Paul Anka	Columbia	23	(1)	F G
2	1	Love Letters In The Sand	Pat Boone	London American	21	(1)	
3	9	Last Train To San Fernando	Johnny Duncan & The Blue Grass Boys	Columbia	16		F L
4	4	Island In The Sun	Harry Belafonte	RCA	22	(30)	
5	12	With All My Heart	Petula Clark	Pye Nixa	16		
6	-	Water Water/Handful Of Songs	Tommy Steele	Decca	13		
7	2	All Shook Up	Elvis Presley	HMV	18	(1)	
8	-	Wanderin' Eyes/I Love You So Much It Hurts	Charlie Gracie	London American	12	(71)	L
9	-	Paralysed	Elvis Presley	HMV	9	(59)	
10	8	Bye Bye Love	Everly Brothers	London American	13	(2)	F
11	-	Tammy	Debbie Reynolds	Vogue Coral	15	(1)	F L
12	3	Teddy Bear	Elvis Presley	HMV	18	(1)	
13	5	Gamblin' Man/Putting On The Style	Lonnie Donegan	Pye Nixa	18		
14	16	Fabulous	Charlie Gracie	Parlophone	13	(16)	
15	-	Jenny Jenny	Little Richard	London American	5	(10)	
16	6	We Will Make Love	Russ Hamilton	Oriole	16		F
17	-	Stardust	Billy Ward & His Dominoes	London American	6	(14)	F L
18	-	Shiralee	Tommy Steele	Decca	3		
19	7	Little Darlin'	Diamonds	Mercury	15	(2)	F L
20	-	Build Your Love	Johnnie Ray	Philips	3	(58)	L

This Mnth	Prev Mnth	Title	Artist	Label	Wks	(US 20 Pos)	
1	1	Diana	Paul Anka	Columbia	23	(1)	F G
2	2	Love Letters In The Sand	Pat Boone	London American	21	(1)	
3	11	Tammy	Debbie Reynolds	Vogue Coral	15	(1)	F L
4	4	Island In The Sun	Harry Belafonte	RCA	22	(30)	
5	-	That'll Be The Day	Crickets	Vogue Coral	12	(1)	F
6	3	Last Train To San Fernando	Johnny Duncan & The Blue Grass Boys	Columbia	16		F L
7	8	Wanderin' Eyes/I Love You So Much It Hurts	Charlie Gracie	London American	12	(71)	L
8	5	With All My Heart	Petula Clark	Pye Nixa	16		
9	-	Party	Elvis Presley	RCA	14		
10	6	Water Water/Handful Of Songs	Tommy Steele	Decca	13		
11	12	Teddy Bear	Elvis Presley	HMV	18	(1)	
12	-	Remember You're Mine/There's A Goldmine In The Sky	Pat Boone	London American	13	(10)	
13	7	All Shook Up	Elvis Presley	HMV	18	(1)	
14	-	Man On Fire/Wanderin' Eyes	Frankie Vaughan	Philips	11		
15	-	Whole Lotta Shakin' Goin' On	Jerry Lee Lewis	London American	7	(3)	F
16	9	Paralysed	Elvis Presley	HMV	9	(59)	
17	-	My Dixie Darling	Lonnie Donegan	Pye Nixa	8		
18	17	Stardust	Billy Ward & His Dominoes	London American	6	(14)	F L
19	15	Jenny Jenny	Little Richard	London American	5	(10)	
20	-	Call Rosie On The Phone	Guy Mitchell	Philips	3		

◆ Fifteen-year-old Paul Anka topped the transatlantic chart with his composition 'Diana' (written about his childhood babysitter), which went on to sell over a million in Britain.

◆ *NME* readers voted Pat Boone World's Outstanding Male Singer, Elvis World's Outstanding Musical Personality, Doris Day World's Top Female Singer and The Platters World's Top Group.

1957

This Mnth	Prev Mnth	Title	Artist	Label	Wks (US 20 Pos)
1	5	That'll Be The Day	Crickets	Vogue Coral	12 (1) F
2	9	Party	Elvis Presley	RCA	14
3	3	Tammy	Debbie Reynolds	Vogue Coral	15 (1) F L
4	12	Remember You're Mine/There's A Goldmine In The Sky	Pat Boone	London American	13 (10)
5	-	Be My Girl	Jim Dale	Parlophone	12 F L
6	1	Diana	Paul Anka	Columbia	23 (1) F G
7	14	Man On Fire/Wanderin' Eyes	Frankie Vaughan	Philips	11
8	-	Mary's Boy Child	Harry Belafonte	RCA	9 (12) G
9	-	I Love You Baby	Paul Anka	Columbia	13 (97)
10	-	Gotta Have Something In The Bank Frank	Frankie Vaughan & The Kaye Sisters	Philips	7
11	-	Wake Up Little Susie	Everly Brothers	London American	11 (1)
12	17	My Dixie Darling	Lonnie Donegan	Pye Nixa	8
13	15	Whole Lotta Shakin' Goin' On	Jerry Lee Lewis	London American	7 (3) F
14	10	Water Water/Handful Of Songs	Tommy Steele	Decca	13
15	2	Love Letters In The Sand	Pat Boone	London American	21 (1)
16	7	Wanderin' Eyes/I Love You So Much It Hurts	Charlie Gracie	London American	12 (71) L
17	-	Santa Bring My Baby Back To Me	Elvis Presley	RCA	7
18	8	With All My Heart	Petula Clark	Pye Nixa	16
19	-	Alone	Petula Clark	Pye Nixa	9
20	-	Ma He's Making Eyes At Me	Johnny Otis Show	Capitol	15 F

This Mnth	Prev Mnth	Title	Artist	Label	Wks (US 20 Pos)
1	8	Mary's Boy Child	Harry Belafonte	RCA	9 (12) G
2	20	Ma He's Making Eyes At Me	Johnny Otis Show	Capitol	15 F
3	11	Wake Up Little Susie	Everly Brothers	London American	11 (1)
4	9	I Love You Baby	Paul Anka	Columbia	13 (97)
5	-	My Special Angel	Malcolm Vaughan	HMV	14
6	5	Be My Girl	Jim Dale	Parlophone	12 F L
7	-	Let's Have A Ball	Winifred Atwell	Decca	5
8	19	Alone	Petula Clark	Pye Nixa	9
9	-	Reet Petite	Jackie Wilson	Coral	11 (62) F
10	2	Party	Elvis Presley	RCA	14
11	-	All The Way	Frank Sinatra	Capitol	16 (15)
12	4	Remember You're Mine/There's A Goldmine In The Sky	Pat Boone	London American	13 (10)
13	17	Santa Bring My Baby Back To Me	Elvis Presley	RCA	7
14	6	Diana	Paul Anka	Columbia	23 (1) F G
15	-	Great Balls Of Fire	Jerry Lee Lewis	London American	11 (2)
16	-	He's Got The Whole World In His Hands	Laurie London	Parlophone	7 (2) F L
17	1	That'll Be The Day	Crickets	Vogue Coral	12 (1) F
18	10	Gotta Have Something In The Bank Frank	Frankie Vaughan/Kaye Sisters	Philips	7
19	-	April Love	Pat Boone	London American	17 (1)
20	7	Man On Fire/Wanderin' Eyes	Frankie Vaughan	Philips	11

◆ Elvis Presley had a record seven singles in the UK Top 30. In America Elvis' **Christmas Album**, with unprecedented American advance orders, replaced his **Lovin' You** at the top.

◆ Johnny Otis, who had been America's top R&B act of 1950, had a surprise British hit with a revival of 'Ma He's Making Eyes At Me', a flop in the USA.

1958

This Mnth	Prev Mnth	Title	Artist	Label	Wks	(US 20 Pos)	
1	2	Ma He's Making Eyes At Me	Johnny Otis Show	Capitol	15		F
2	15	Great Balls Of Fire	Jerry Lee Lewis	London American	11	(2)	
3	11	All The Way	Frank Sinatra	Capitol	16	(15)	
4	5	My Special Angel	Malcolm Vaughan	HMV	14		
5	9	Reet Petite	Jackie Wilson	Coral	11	(62)	F
6	-	Peggy Sue	Buddy Holly	Coral	12	(3)	F
7	-	Oh, Boy!	Crickets	Coral	12	(11)	
8	3	Wake Up Little Susie	Everly Brothers	London American	11	(1)	
9	4	I Love You Baby	Paul Anka	Columbia	13	(97)	
10	-	Kisses Sweeter Than Wine	Jimmie Rodgers	Columbia	10	(8)	F
11	-	Kisses Sweeter Than Wine	Frankie Vaughan	Philips	8		
12	19	April Love	Pat Boone	London American	17	(1)	
13	-	Jailhouse Rock	Elvis Presley	RCA	13	(1)	
14	-	The Story Of My Life	Michael Holliday	Columbia	14		
15	1	Mary's Boy Child	Harry Belafonte	RCA	9	(12)	G
16	8	Alone	Petula Clark	Pye Nixa	9		
17	-	Jack O' Diamonds	Lonnie Donegan	Pye Nixa	6		
18	14	Diana	Paul Anka	Columbia	23	(1)	F G
19	-	At The Hop	Danny & The Juniors	HMV	13	(1)	F L
20	-	Story Of My Life	Gary Miller	Pye Nixa	5		L

1	14	The Story Of My Life	Michael Holliday	Columbia	14		
2	13	Jailhouse Rock	Elvis Presley	RCA	13	(1)	
3	19	At The Hop	Danny & The Juniors	HMV	13	(1)	F L
4	7	Oh, Boy!	Crickets	Coral	12	(11)	
5	-	Magic Moments	Perry Como	RCA	15	(3)	
6	3	All The Way	Frank Sinatra	Capitol	16	(15)	
7	-	Love Me Forever	Marion Ryan	Pye Nixa	10		F L
8	6	Peggy Sue	Buddy Holly	Coral	12	(3)	F
9	12	April Love	Pat Boone	London American	17	(1)	
10	-	You Are My Destiny	Paul Anka	Columbia	10	(9)	
11	2	Great Balls Of Fire	Jerry Lee Lewis	London American	11	(2)	
12	-	Bony Moronie	Larry Williams	London American	7	(14)	F L
13	1	Ma He's Making Eyes At Me	Johnny Otis Show	Capitol	15		F
14	4	My Special Angel	Malcolm Vaughan	HMV	14		
15	-	Raunchy	Bill Justis	London American	4	(2)	F L
16	10	Kisses Sweeter Than Wine	Jimmie Rodgers	Columbia	10	(8)	F
17	-	Witchcraft	Frank Sinatra	Capitol	6	(20)	
18	11	Kisses Sweeter Than Wine	Frankie Vaughan	Philips	8		
19	-	Sugartime	McGuire Sisters	Coral	3	(7)	
20	-	Mandy	Eddie Calvert	Columbia	11		L

◆ Petula Clark had a hat-trick of hits with covers of US pop songs, 'With All My Heart', 'Alone' and 'Baby Lover'. When she recorded original material in the mid-1960s she became one of the top acts in America.

◆ Elvis Presley's 'Jailhouse Rock', with record advance orders of 250,000, became the first record to enter the chart at No. 1. Meanwhile, in America, 'Don't', became Presley's tenth chart topper in less than two years.

March 1958

This Mnth	Prev Mnth	Title	Artist	Label	Wks	(US 20 Pos)	
1	5	Magic Moments	Perry Como	RCA	15	(3)	
2	1	The Story Of My Life	Michael Holliday	Columbia	14		
3	2	Jailhouse Rock	Elvis Presley	RCA	13	(1)	
4	-	Don't	Elvis Presley	RCA	10	(1)	
5	3	At The Hop	Danny & The Juniors	HMV	13	(1)	F L
6	10	You Are My Destiny	Paul Anka	Columbia	10	(9)	
7	-	Nairobi	Tommy Steele	Decca	10		
8	7	Love Me Forever	Marion Ryan	Pye Nixa	10		F L
9	-	Good Golly Miss Molly	Little Richard	London American	7	(13)	
10	9	April Love	Pat Boone	London American	17	(1)	
11	4	Oh, Boy!	Crickets	Coral	12	(11)	
12	6	All The Way	Frank Sinatra	Capitol	16	(15)	
13	-	Whole Lotta Woman	Marvin Rainwater	MGM	14	(60)	F
14	-	Catch A Falling Star	Perry Como	RCA	7	(3)	
15	-	Can't Get Along Without You/ We're Not Alone	Frankie Vaughan	Philips	3		
16	-	Baby Lover	Petula Clark	Pye Nixa	4		
17	20	Mandy	Eddie Calvert	Columbia	11		L
18	-	Maybe Baby	Crickets	Coral	8	(18)	
19	-	La Dee Dah	Jackie Dennis	Decca	7		F L
20	8	Peggy Sue	Buddy Holly	Coral	12	(3)	F

April 1958

This Mnth	Prev Mnth	Title	Artist	Label	Wks	(US 20 Pos)	
1	1	Magic Moments	Perry Como	RCA	15	(3)	
2	13	Whole Lotta Woman	Marvin Rainwater	MGM	14	(60)	F
3	7	Nairobi	Tommy Steele	Decca	10		
4	-	Swingin' Shepherd Blues	Ted Heath	Decca	10		L
5	18	Maybe Baby	Crickets	Coral	8	(18)	
6	19	La Dee Dah	Jackie Dennis	Decca	7		F L
7	-	Tequila	Champs	London American	7	(1)	F L
8	4	Don't	Elvis Presley	RCA	10	(1)	
9	-	A Wonderful Time Up There	Pat Boone	London American	14	(4)	
10	-	Who's Sorry Now	Connie Francis	MGM	20	(5)	F
11	2	The Story Of My Life	Michael Holliday	Columbia	14		
12	-	It's Too Soon To Know	Pat Boone	London American	8	(4)	
13	17	Mandy	Eddie Calvert	Columbia	11		L
14	14	Catch A Falling Star	Perry Como	RCA	7	(3)	
15	-	Breathless	Jerry Lee Lewis	London American	6	(9)	
16	9	Good Golly Miss Molly	Little Richard	London American	7	(13)	
17	-	To Be Loved	Malcolm Vaughan	HMV	8		
18	5	At The Hop	Danny & The Juniors	HMV	13	(1)	F L
19	3	Jailhouse Rock	Elvis Presley	RCA	13	(1)	
20	-	Lollipop	Chordettes	London American	5	(2)	L

◆ Successful songwriter Hal David's collaboration with newcomer Burt Bacharach produced two successive UK No. 1s: 'The Story Of My Life' and 'Magic Moments'.

◆ Buddy Holly & The Crickets had a very successful tour of Britain, at a time when they were charting with four hits: 'Oh, Boy!', 'Peggy Sue', 'Maybe Baby' and 'Listen To Me'.

◆ Jerry Lee Lewis's British tour was cut short when the media discovered that his bigamously married third wife was his 14-year-old second cousin.

1958

This Mnth	Prev Mnth	Title	Artist	Label	Wks	(US 20 Pos)	
1	10	Who's Sorry Now	Connie Francis	MGM	20	(5)	F
2	2	Whole Lotta Woman	Marvin Rainwater	MGM	14	(60)	F
3	9	A Wonderful Time Up There	Pat Boone	London American	14	(4)	
4	-	Tom Hark	Elias & His Zigzag Jive Flutes	Columbia	12		F L
5	-	Wear My Ring Around Your Neck	Elvis Presley	RCA	7	(2)	
6	-	Lollipop	Mudlarks	Columbia	9		F
7	-	Grand Coolie Dam	Lonnie Donegan	Pye Nixa	9		
8	4	Swingin' Shepherd Blues	Ted Heath	Decca	10		L
9	20	Lollipop	Chordettes	London American	5	(2)	L
10	15	Breathless	Jerry Lee Lewis	London American	6	(9)	
11	7	Tequila	Champs	London American	7	(1)	F L
12	1	Magic Moments	Perry Como	RCA	15	(3)	
13	12	It's Too Soon To Know	Pat Boone	London American	8	(4)	
14	-	You Need Hands/ Tulips From Amsterdam	Max Bygraves	Decca	21		
15	-	On The Street Where You Live	Vic Damone	Philips	15	(8)	F L
16	-	I May Never Pass This Way Again	Robert Earl	Philips	9		F
17	-	Kewpie Doll	Perry Como	RCA	5	(12)	
18	17	To Be Loved	Malcolm Vaughan	HMV	8		
19	-	Kewpie Doll	Frankie Vaughan	Philips	9		
20	5	Maybe Baby	Crickets	Coral	8	(18)	

This Mnth	Prev Mnth	Title	Artist	Label	Wks	(US 20 Pos)	
1	1	Who's Sorry Now	Connie Francis	MGM	20	(5)	F
2	15	On The Street Where You Live	Vic Damone	Philips	15	(8)	F L
3	4	Tom Hark	Elias & His Zigzag Jive Flutes	Columbia	12		F L
4	-	Stairway Of Love	Michael Holliday	Columbia	11		
5	14	You Need Hands/ Tulips From Amsterdam	Max Bygraves	Decca	21		
6	-	All I Have To Do Is Dream/ Claudette	Everly Brothers	London American	19	(1)	
7	-	Witch Doctor	Don Lang	HMV	10		L
8	3	A Wonderful Time Up There	Pat Boone	London American	14	(4)	
9	-	Army Game	TV Cast	HMV	6		F L
10	6	Lollipop	Mudlarks	Columbia	9		F
11	19	Kewpie Doll	Frankie Vaughan	Philips	9		
12	7	Grand Coolie Dam	Lonnie Donegan	Pye Nixa	9		
13	-	Twilight Time	Platters	Mercury	12	(1)	
14	-	Book Of Love	Mudlarks	Columbia	7		L
15	5	Wear My Ring Around Your Neck	Elvis Presley	RCA	7	(2)	
16	-	I May Never Pass This Way Again	Perry Como	RCA	4		
17	-	Big Man	Four Preps	Capitol	12	(6)	F L
18	17	Kewpie Doll	Perry Como	RCA	5	(12)	
19	-	Witch Doctor	David Seville	London	5	(1)	F
20	16	I May Never Pass This Way Again	Robert Earl	Philips	9		F

◆ Jack Good, producer of *6-5 Special,* launched *Oh Boy!,* a TV show which first introduced the public to such acts as Cliff Richard and Billy Fury.

◆ A track recorded on the streets of South Africa by a tin-whistle band in 1956, 'Tom Hark' by Elias & His Zigzag Jive Flutes, was the year's most unexpected UK hit.

July 1958

This Mnth	Prev Mnth	Title	Artist	Label	Wks	(US 20 Pos)	
1	6	All I Have To Do Is Dream/ Claudette	Everly Brothers	London American	19	(1)	
2	2	On The Street Where You Live	Vic Damone	Philips	15	(8)	F L
3	5	You Need Hands/ Tulips From Amsterdam	Max Bygraves	Decca	21		
4	17	Big Man	Four Preps	Capitol	12	(6)	F L
5	13	Twilight Time	Platters	Mercury	12	(1)	
6	1	Who's Sorry Now	Connie Francis	MGM	20	(5)	F
7	-	Sugar Moon	Pat Boone	London American	10	(10)	
8	14	Book Of Love	Mudlarks	Columbia	7		L
9	-	Rave On	Buddy Holly	Coral	12	(41)	
10	7	Witch Doctor	Don Lang	HMV	10		L
11	4	Stairway Of Love	Michael Holliday	Columbia	11		
12	-	Sally Don't You Grieve/ Betty, Betty, Betty	Lonnie Donegan	Pye Nixa	6		
13	-	The Purple People Eater	Sheb Wooley	MGM	6	(1)	F L
14	3	Tom Hark	Elias & His Zigzag Jive Flutes	Columbia	12		F L
15	-	Endless Sleep	Marty Wilde	Philips	12		F
16	-	I'm Sorry I Made You Cry	Connie Francis	MGM	7	(36)	
17	9	Army Game	TV Cast	HMV	6		F L
18	9	On The Street Where You Live	David Whitfield	Decca	8		L
19	-	Hard Headed Woman	Elvis Presley	RCA	8	(1)	
20	11	Kewpie Doll	Frankie Vaughan	Philips	9		

August 1958

This Mnth	Prev Mnth	Title	Artist	Label	Wks	(US 20 Pos)	
1	1	All I Have To Do Is Dream/ Claudette	Everly Brothers	London American	19	(1)	
2	-	When	Kalin Twins	Brunswick	16	(5)	F L
3	19	Hard Headed Woman	Elvis Presley	RCA	8	(1)	
4	-	Return To Me	Dean Martin	Capitol	16	(4)	
5	3	You Need Hands/ Tulips From Amsterdam	Max Bygraves	Decca	21		
6	15	Endless Sleep	Marty Wilde	Philips	12		F
7	4	Big Man	Four Preps	Capitol	12	(6)	F L
8	9	Rave On	Buddy Holly	Coral	12	(41)	
9	5	Twilight Time	Platters	Mercury	12	(1)	
10	-	Patricia	Perez Prado	RCA	11	(2)	L
11	7	Sugar Moon	Pat Boone	London American	10	(10)	
12	6	Who's Sorry Now	Connie Francis	MGM	20	(5)	F
13	-	Think It Over	Crickets	Coral	5	(27)	
14	2	On The Street Where You Live	Vic Damone	Philips	15	(8)	F L
15	16	I'm Sorry I Made You Cry	Connie Francis	MGM	7	(36)	
16	-	Splish Splash	Charlie Drake	Parlophone	9		F
17	12	Sally Don't You Grieve/ Betty, Betty, Betty	Lonnie Donegan	Pye Nixa	6		
18	-	Fever	Peggy Lee	Capitol	8	(8)	L
19	-	Carolina Moon/Stupid Cupid	Connie Francis	MGM	17	(14)	
20	-	Poor Little Fool	Ricky Nelson	London American	13	(1)	F

◆ One of the most recorded songs of the year, 'On The Street Where You Live', took noted US balladeer Vic Damone to the top. His version had also outpaced all the competition in the USA two years earlier.

◆ Cliff Richard's debut single, 'Move It' (composed by Ian Samwell from his backing group, The Drifters), only narrowly missed topping the chart.

1958

1	2	When	Kalin Twins	Brunswick	16	(5)	F L
2	19	Carolina Moon/Stupid Cupid	Connie Francis	MGM	17	(14)	
3	4	Return To Me	Dean Martin	Capitol	16	(4)	
4	-	Volare	Dean Martin	Capitol	12	(15)	
5	1	All I Have To Do Is Dream/ Claudette	Everly Brothers	London American	19	(1)	
6	18	Fever	Peggy Lee	Capitol	8	(8)	L
7	20	Poor Little Fool	Ricky Nelson	London American	13	(1)	F
8	6	Endless Sleep	Marty Wilde	Philips	12		F
9	16	Splish Splash	Charlie Drake	Parlophone	9		F
10	10	Patricia	Perez Prado	RCA	11	(2)	L
11	-	Volare	Domenico Modugno	Oriole	8	(1)	F L
12	-	Mad Passionate Love	Bernard Bresslaw	HMV	9		F L
13	-	Yakety Yak	Coasters	London American	7	(2)	F
14	5	You Need Hands/Tulips From Amsterdam	Max Bygraves	Decca	21		
15	-	Bird Dog	Everly Brothers	London American	16	(2)	
16	3	Hard Headed Woman	Elvis Presley	RCA	8	(1)	
17	8	Rave On	Buddy Holly	Coral	12	(41)	
18	-	Trudie	Joe 'Mr. Piano' Henderson	Pye Nixa	6		L
19	-	Girl Of My Dreams	Tony Brent	Columbia	5		L
20	-	Born Too Late	Poni-Tails	HMV	10	(7)	F L

1	2	Carolina Moon/Stupid Cupid	Connie Francis	MGM	17	(14)	
2	15	Bird Dog	Everly Brothers	London American	16	(2)	
3	4	Volare	Dean Martin	Capitol	12	(15)	
4	-	King Creole	Elvis Presley	RCA	9		
5	-	Move It	Cliff Richard	Columbia	11		F
6	20	Born Too Late	Poni-Tails	HMV	10	(7)	F L
7	-	A Certain Smile	Johnny Mathis	Fontana	14	(21)	F
8	1	When	Kalin Twins	Brunswick	16	(5)	F L
9	7	Poor Little Fool	Ricky Nelson	London American	13	(1)	F
10	12	Mad Passionate Love	Bernard Bresslaw	HMV	9		F L
11	-	Come Prima	Marino Marini	Durium	13		L
12	-	It's All In The Game	Tommy Edwards	MGM	15	(1)	F L
13	3	Return To Me	Dean Martin	Capitol	16	(4)	
14	-	More Than Ever (Come Prima)	Malcolm Vaughan	HMV	13		
15	11	Volare	Domenico Modugno	Oriole	8	(1)	F L
16	-	Volare	Marino Marini	Durium	5		F
17	-	Western Movies	Olympics	HMV	7	(8)	F L
18	-	Hoots Mon	Lord Rockingham's XI	Decca	16		F
19	9	Splish Splash	Charlie Drake	Parlophone	9		F
20	6	Fever	Peggy Lee	Capitol	8	(8)	L

◆ Johnny Otis's biggest American hit, 'Willie & The Hand Jive', was inspired by a digital dance started in British coffee bars and popularized on6-5 *Special*.

◆ In August, the month that both Michael Jackson and Madonna were born, George Harrison joined John Lennon and Paul McCartney's group, The Quarry Men.

November 1958

This Mnth	Prev Mnth	Title	Artist	Label	Wks	(US 20 Pos)	
1	12	It's All In The Game	Tommy Edwards	MGM	15	(1)	F L
2	18	Hoots Mon	Lord Rockingham's XI	Decca	16		F
3	2	Bird Dog	Everly Brothers	London American	16	(2)	
4	11	Come Prima	Marino Marini	Durium	13		L
5	7	A Certain Smile	Johnny Mathis	Fontana	14	(21)	F
6	14	More Than Ever (Come Prima)	Malcolm Vaughan	HMV	13		
7	1	Carolina Moon/Stupid Cupid	Connie Francis	MGM	17	(14)	
8	5	Move It	Cliff Richard	Columbia	11		F
9	-	Tea For Two Cha Cha	Tommy Dorsey Orchestra	Brunswick	16	(7)	F L
10	-	It's Only Make Believe	Conway Twitty	MGM	14	(1)	F
11	4	King Creole	Elvis Presley	RCA	9		
12	-	My True Love	Jack Scott	London American	8	(3)	F
13	-	Love Makes The World Go Round	Perry Como	RCA	13	(33)	
14	-	Tom Dooley	Lonnie Donegan	Pye Nixa	12		
15	6	Born Too Late	Poni-Tails	HMV	10	(7)	F L
16	-	Someday	Jodie Sands	HMV	8	(95)	F L
17	-	Someday	Ricky Nelson	London American	8		
18	3	Volare	Dean Martin	Capitol	12	(15)	
19	17	Western Movies	Olympics	HMV	7	(8)	F L
20	-	Come On Let's Go	Tommy Steele	Decca	11		

December 1958

This Mnth	Prev Mnth	Title	Artist	Label	Wks	(US 20 Pos)	
1	10	It's Only Make Believe	Conway Twitty	MGM	14	(1)	F
2	2	Hoots Mon	Lord Rockingham's XI	Decca	16		F
3	14	Tom Dooley	Lonnie Donegan	Pye Nixa	12		
4	1	It's All In The Game	Tommy Edwards	MGM	15	(1)	F L
5	9	Tea For Two Cha Cha	Tommy Dorsey Orchestra	Brunswick	16	(7)	F L
6	-	Tom Dooley	Kingston Trio	Capitol	12	(1)	F L
7	13	Love Makes The World Go Round	Perry Como	RCA	13	(33)	
8	-	High Class Baby	Cliff Richard	Columbia	9		
9	6	More Than Ever (Come Prima)	Malcolm Vaughan	HMV	13		
10	5	A Certain Smile	Johnny Mathis	Fontana	14	(21)	F
11	17	Someday	Ricky Nelson	London American	8		
12	20	Come On Let's Go	Tommy Steele	Decca	11		
13	4	Come Prima	Marino Marini	Durium	13		L
14	-	The Day The Rains Came	Jane Morgan	London American	13	(21)	F L
15	-	Mary's Boy Child	Harry Belafonte	RCA	5		G
16	3	Bird Dog	Everly Brothers	London American	16	(2)	
17	-	Mandolins In The Moonlight	Perry Como	RCA	8	(47)	
18	-	More Party Pops	Russ Conway	Columbia	3		F
19	-	Real Love	Ruby Murray	Columbia	3		
20	8	Move It	Cliff Richard	Columbia	11		F

◆ *NME* poll winners included Elvis (World's Outstanding Male), Connie Francis (World's Outstanding Female), the Everly Brothers (World's Outstanding Group) and Cliff Richard, whose act had been labelled "crude" and "vulgar" was Favourite New Singer.

◆ Italian songs were enjoying an unprecedented amount of success in the UK. Three versions of Domenico Modugno's US chart topper, 'Volare', charted alongside two recordings of 'Come Prima' and Dean Martin's multi-lingual 'Return To Me'.

1959

This Mnth	Prev Mnth	Title	Artist	Label	Wks	(US 20 Pos)	
1	1	It's Only Make Believe	Conway Twitty	MGM	14	(1)	F
2	14	The Day The Rains Came	Jane Morgan	London American	13	(21)	F L
3	2	Hoots Mon	Lord Rockingham's XI	Decca	16		F
4	5	Tea For Two Cha Cha	Tommy Dorsey Orchestra	Brunswick	16	(7)	F L
5	3	Tom Dooley	Lonnie Donegan	Pye Nixa	12		
6	-	Baby Face	Little Richard	London American	10	(41)	
7	-	To Know Him, Is To Love Him	Teddy Bears	London American	11	(1)	F L
8	6	Tom Dooley	Kingston Trio	Capitol	12	(1)	F L
9	-	Kiss Me Honey Honey Kiss Me	Shirley Bassey	Philips	13		
10	7	Love Makes The World Go Round	Perry Como	RCA	13	(33)	
11	12	Come On Let's Go	Tommy Steele	Decca	11		
12	8	High Class Baby	Cliff Richard	Columbia	9		
13	-	One Night/I Got Stung	Elvis Presley	RCA	10	(4)	
14	-	As I Love You	Shirley Bassey	Philips	16		
15	17	Mandolins In The Moonlight	Perry Como	RCA	8	(47)	
16	4	It's All In The Game	Tommy Edwards	MGM	15	(1)	F L
17	-	You Always Hurt The One You Love	Connie Francis	MGM	5		
18	-	Smoke Gets In Your Eyes	Platters	Mercury	19	(1)	
19	-	Chantilly Lace	Big Bopper	Mercury	4	(6)	F L
20	-	Problems	Everly Brothers	London American	9	(2)	

This Mnth	Prev Mnth	Title	Artist	Label	Wks	(US 20 Pos)	
1	14	As I Love You	Shirley Bassey	Philips	16		
2	13	One Night/I Got Stung	Elvis Presley	RCA	10	(4)	
3	9	Kiss Me Honey Honey Kiss Me	Shirley Bassey	Philips	13		
4	18	Smoke Gets In Your Eyes	Platters	Mercury	19	(1)	
5	7	To Know Him is To Love Him	Teddy Bears	London American	11	(1)	F L
6	-	Does Your Chewing Gum Lose It's Flavour	Lonnie Donegan	Pye Nixa	11	(5)	
7	6	Baby Face	Little Richard	London American	10	(41)	
8	20	Problems	Everly Brothers	London American	9	(2)	
9	2	The Day The Rains Came	Jane Morgan	London American	13	(21)	F L
10	-	(All Of A Sudden) My Heart Sings	Paul Anka	Columbia	12	(15)	
11	-	A Pub With No Beer	Slim Dusty	Columbia	13		F L
12	-	Petite Fleur	Chris Barber's Jazz Band	Pye Nixa	18	(5)	F L
13	-	The Little Drummer Boy	Beverley Sisters	Decca	11		
14	-	High School Confidential	Jerry Lee Lewis	London American	4	(22)	
15	1	It's Only Make Believe	Conway Twitty	MGM	14	(1)	F
16	4	Tea For Two Cha Cha	Tommy Dorsey Orchestra	Brunswick	16	(7)	F L
17	-	My Happiness	Connie Francis	MGM	13	(2)	
18	-	Little Drummer Boy	Harry Simeone Chorale	Top Rank	4	(13)	F L
19	-	Apple Blossom Time	Rosemary June	Pye-Int	3		F L
20	-	Gigi	Billy Eckstine	Mercury	12		

◆ Among the acts charting with revivals of standard songs were US acts Little Richard, Paul Anka, the late Tommy Dorsey's Orchestra, Tommy Edwards, The Platters, Connie Francis and chart debutante Rosemary June.

◆ Lonnie Donegan, whose UK hit 'Does Your Chewing Gum Lose Its Flavour' reached the American Top 3 in 1961, signed a record £10,000 recording deal.

1959

This Mnth	Prev Mnth	Title	Artist	Label	Wks	(US 20 Pos)	
1	4	Smoke Gets In Your Eyes	Platters	Mercury	19	(1)	
2	1	As I Love You	Shirley Bassey	Philips	16		
3	-	Side Saddle	Russ Conway	Columbia	25		
4	11	A Pub With No Beer	Slim Dusty	Columbia	13		F L
5	12	Petite Fleur	Chris Barber's Jazz Band	Pye Nixa	18	(5)	F L
6	17	My Happiness	Connie Francis	MGM	13	(2)	
7	13	The Little Drummer Boy	Beverley Sisters	Decca	11		
8	6	Does Your Chewing Gum Lose It's Flavour	Lonnie Donegan	Pye Nixa	11	(5)	
9	-	Stagger Lee	Lloyd Price	HMV	11	(1)	F
10	10	(All Of A Sudden) My Heart Sings	Paul Anka	Columbia	12	(15)	
11	-	It Doesn't Matter Anymore	Buddy Holly	Coral	21	(13)	
12	2	One Night/I Got Stung	Elvis Presley	RCA	10	(4)	
13	20	Gigi	Billy Eckstine	Mercury	12		
14	3	Kiss Me Honey Honey Kiss Me	Shirley Bassey	Philips	13		
15	-	Tomboy	Perry Como	RCA	10	(29)	
16	8	Problems	Everly Brothers	London American	9	(2)	
17	-	C'mon Everybody	Eddie Cochran	London American	10	(35)	
18	5	To Know Him is To Love Him	Teddy Bears	London American	11	(1)	F L
19	-	Wonderful Secret Of Love	Robert Earl	Philips	4		L
20	18	Little Drummer Boy	Harry Simeone Chorale	Top Rank	4	(13)	F L

This Mnth	Prev Mnth	Title	Artist	Label	Wks	(US 20 Pos)	
1	3	Side Saddle	Russ Conway	Columbia	25		
2	11	It Doesn't Matter Anymore	Buddy Holly	Coral	21	(13)	
3	1	Smoke Gets In Your Eyes	Platters	Mercury	19	(1)	
4	5	Petite Fleur	Chris Barber's Jazz Band	Pye Nixa	18	(5)	F L
5	6	My Happiness	Connie Francis	MGM	13	(2)	
6	9	Stagger Lee	Lloyd Price	HMV	11	(1)	F
7	-	Donna	Marty Wilde	Philips	11		
8	2	As I Love You	Shirley Bassey	Philips	16		
9	13	Gigi	Billy Eckstine	Mercury	12		
10	-	Charlie Brown	Coasters	London American	11	(2)	
11	4	A Pub With No Beer	Slim Dusty	Columbia	13		F L
12	17	C'mon Everybody	Eddie Cochran	London American	10	(35)	
13	15	Tomboy	Perry Como	RCA	10	(29)	
14	7	The Little Drummer Boy	Beverley Sisters	Decca	11		
15	-	Wait For Me	Malcolm Vaughan	HMV	8		L
16	-	Sing Little Birdie	Pearl Carr & Teddy Johnson	Columbia	5		F
17	-	A Fool Such As I/ I Need Your Love Tonight	Elvis Presley	RCA	14	(2)	
18	8	Does Your Chewing Gum Lose It's Flavour	Lonnie Donegan	Pye Nixa	11	(5)	
19	-	By The Light Of The Silvery Moon	Little Richard	London American	3		
20	10	(All Of A Sudden) My Heart Sings	Paul Anka	Columbia	12	(15)	

◆ For the first time three British records simultaneously made the US Top 20: 'Petite Fleur' by Chris Barber, 'The Children's Marching Song' by Cyril Stapleton and 'Manhattan Spiritual' by Reg Owen - all instrumentals.

◆ Both the Beverly Sisters and The Harry Simone Chorale clicked with the Christmas song 'The Little Drummer Boy'.

1959

This Mnth	Prev Mnth	Title	Artist	Label	Wks 20	(US Pos)	
1	17	A Fool Such As I/ I Need Your Love Tonight	Elvis Presley	RCA	14	(2)	
2	2	It Doesn't Matter Anymore	Buddy Holly	Coral	21	(13)	
3	1	Side Saddle	Russ Conway	Columbia	25		
4	7	Donna	Marty Wilde	Philips	11		
5	-	It's Late	Ricky Nelson	London American	18	(9)	
6	4	Petite Fleur	Chris Barber's Jazz Band	Pye Nixa	18	(5)	F L
7	-	I've Waited So Long	Anthony Newley	Decca	13		
8	-	Come Softly To Me	Fleetwoods	London American	8	(1)	F L
9	10	Charlie Brown	Coasters	London American	11	(2)	
10	-	Come Softly To Me	Frankie Vaughan/Kaye Sisters	Philips	8		
11	-	I Go Ape	Neil Sedaka	RCA	10	(42)	F
12	-	Mean Streak	Cliff Richard	Columbia	8		
13	3	Smoke Gets In Your Eyes	Platters	Mercury	19	(1)	
14	12	C'mon Everybody	Eddie Cochran	London American	10	(35)	
15	-	Fort Worth Jail	Lonnie Donegan	Pye Nixa	4		
16	-	Roulette	Russ Conway	Columbia	18		
17	-	Guitar Boogie Shuffle	Bert Weedon	Top Rank	8		F L
18	-	May You Always	McGuire Sisters	Coral	5	(11)	L
19	-	Idle On Parade (EP)	Anthony Newley	Decca	2		F
20	6	Stagger Lee	Lloyd Price	HMV	11	(1)	F

This Mnth	Prev Mnth	Title	Artist	Label	Wks 20	(US Pos)	
1	1	A Fool Such As I/ I Need Your Love Tonight	Elvis Presley	RCA	14	(2)	
2	16	Roulette	Russ Conway	Columbia	18		
3	2	It Doesn't Matter Anymore	Buddy Holly	Coral	21	(13)	
4	7	I've Waited So Long	Anthony Newley	Decca	13		
5	5	It's Late	Ricky Nelson	London American	18	(9)	
6	-	Dream Lover	Bobby Darin	London American	17	(2)	
7	3	Side Saddle	Russ Conway	Columbia	25		
8	-	A Teenager In Love	Marty Wilde	Philips	13		
9	17	Guitar Boogie Shuffle	Bert Weedon	Top Rank	8		F L
10	12	Mean Streak	Cliff Richard	Columbia	8		
11	11	I Go Ape	Neil Sedaka	RCA	10	(42)	F
12	-	May You Always	Joan Regan	HMV	10		L
13	6	Petite Fleur	Chris Barber's Jazz Band	Pye Nixa	18	(5)	F L
14	4	Donna	Marty Wilde	Philips	11		
15	10	Come Softly To Me	Frankie Vaughan/Kaye Sisters	Philips	8		
16	-	Peter Gunn Theme	Duane Eddy	London American	10	(27)	
17	8	Come Softly To Me	Fleetwoods	London American	8	(1)	F L
18	-	Battle Of New Orleans	Lonnie Donegan	Pye	14		
19	9	Charlie Brown	Coasters	London American	11	(2)	
20	-	A Teenager In Love	Craig Douglas	Top Rank	8		F

◆ American rockers faring better in Britain included Little Richard, Eddie Cochran (whose 'C'mon Everybody' revisited the UK Top 20 in 1988) and the late Buddy Holly, whose 'It Doesn't Matter Anymore' topped the chart.

◆ The year's most successful singles artist in the UK was not a rock performer but easy-on-the-ear honky tonk pianist Russ Conway, whose self composed singles 'Side Saddle' and 'Roulette' both headed the chart.

July 1959

This Mnth	Prev Mnth	Title	Artist	Label	Wks	(US 20 Pos)	
1	6	Dream Lover	Bobby Darin	London American	17	(2)	
2	18	Battle Of New Orleans	Lonnie Donegan	Pye	14		
3	8	A Teenager In Love	Marty Wilde	Philips	13		
4	2	Roulette	Russ Conway	Columbia	18		
5	16	Peter Gunn Theme	Duane Eddy	London American	10	(27)	
6	-	Personality	Anthony Newley	Decca	9		
7	-	Living Doll	Cliff Richard	Columbia	19	(30)	
8	1	A Fool Such As I/ I Need Your Love Tonight	Elvis Presley	RCA	14	(2)	
9	-	Goodbye Jimmy, Goodbye	Ruby Murray	Columbia	11		L
10	5	It's Late	Ricky Nelson	London American	18	(9)	
11	-	Lipstick On Your Collar	Connie Francis	MGM	15	(5)	
12	4	I've Waited So Long	Anthony Newley	Decca	13		
13	7	Side Saddle	Russ Conway	Columbia	25		
14	-	Personality	Lloyd Price	HMV	7	(2)	L
15	12	May You Always	Joan Regan	HMV	10		L
16	-	Big Hunk O' Love	Elvis Presley	RCA	8	(1)	
17	3	It Doesn't Matter Anymore	Buddy Holly	Coral	21	(13)	
18	20	A Teenager In Love	Craig Douglas	Top Rank	8		F
19	-	Poor Jenny	Everly Brothers	London American	7	(22)	
20	-	I Know	Perry Como	RCA	12	(47)	

August 1959

1	7	Living Doll	Cliff Richard	Columbia	19	(30)	
2	1	Dream Lover	Bobby Darin	London American	17	(2)	
3	2	Battle Of New Orleans	Lonnie Donegan	Pye	14		
4	11	Lipstick On Your Collar	Connie Francis	MGM	15	(5)	
5	-	Lonely Boy	Paul Anka	Columbia	13	(1)	
6	16	Big Hunk O' Love	Elvis Presley	RCA	8	(1)	
7	3	A Teenager In Love	Marty Wilde	Philips	13		
8	4	Roulette	Russ Conway	Columbia	18		
9	-	The Heart Of A Man	Frankie Vaughan	Philips	12		
10	-	Only Sixteen	Craig Douglas	Top Rank	14		
11	-	Someone	Johnny Mathis	Fontana	13	(35)	
12	6	Personality	Anthony Newley	Decca	9		
13	-	Ragtime Cowboy Joe	Chipmunks	London American	5	(16)	L
14	20	I Know	Perry Como	RCA	12	(47)	
15	5	Peter Gunn Theme	Duane Eddy	London American	10	(27)	
16	10	It's Late	Ricky Nelson	London American	18	(9)	
17	9	Goodbye Jimmy, Goodbye	Ruby Murray	Columbia	11		L
18	-	China Tea	Russ Conway	Columbia	10		
19	-	Tallahassee Lassie	Tommy Steele	Decca	3		
20	-	Mona Lisa	Conway Twitty	MGM	12	(29)	L

◆ As Cliff Richard scored his first No. 1 with 'Living Doll', Duane Eddy hit with his version of 'Peter Gunn Theme' – in 1986 both artists returned to the Top 10 with re-recordings of the compositions.
◆ Mantovani, who had five albums on the US Top 30 stereo album chart, became the first British-based act to top the American LP chart when **Film Encores** moved into the top slot.
◆ Marty Wilde, Frankie Vaughan, Craig Douglas and Tommy Steele were just some of the artists in the 1950s whose UK hit tally was bolstered by cover versions of songs from the US chart.

1959

This Mnth	Prev Mnth	Title	Artist	Label	Wks (US 20 Pos)
1	10	Only Sixteen	Craig Douglas	Top Rank	14
2	1	Living Doll	Cliff Richard	Columbia	19 (30)
3	5	Lonely Boy	Paul Anka	Columbia	13 (1)
4	-	Here Comes Summer	Jerry Keller	London American	12 (14) F L
5	18	China Tea	Russ Conway	Columbia	10
6	4	Lipstick On Your Collar	Connie Francis	MGM	15 (5)
7	11	Someone	Johnny Mathis	Fontana	13 (35)
8	20	Mona Lisa	Conway Twitty	MGM	12 (29) L
9	9	The Heart Of A Man	Frankie Vaughan	Philips	12
10	3	Battle Of New Orleans	Lonnie Donegan	Pye	14
11	2	Dream Lover	Bobby Darin	London American	17 (2)
12	-	40 Miles Of Bad Road	Duane Eddy	London American	9 (9)
13	-	('Til) I Kissed You	Everly Brothers	London American	14 (4)
14	-	Just A Little Too Much	Ricky Nelson	London American	8 (9)
15	-	Sal's Got A Sugar Lip	Lonnie Donegan	Pye	3
16	14	I Know	Perry Como	RCA	12 (47)
17	6	Big Hunk O' Love	Elvis Presley	RCA	8 (1)
18	-	The Three Bells	Browns	RCA	11 (1) F L
19	-	High Hopes	Frank Sinatra	Capitol	12 (30)
20	8	Roulette	Russ Conway	Columbia	18

1	-	Mack The Knife	Bobby Darin	London American	14 (1)
2	4	Here Comes Summer	Jerry Keller	London American	12 (14) F L
3	13	('Til) I Kissed You	Everly Brothers	London American	14 (4)
4	1	Only Sixteen	Craig Douglas	Top Rank	14
5	2	Living Doll	Cliff Richard	Columbia	19 (30)
6	18	The Three Bells	Browns	RCA	11 (1) F L
7	-	Sea Of Love	Marty Wilde	Philips	11
8	-	Travellin' Light	Cliff Richard	Columbia	16
9	19	High Hopes	Frank Sinatra	Capitol	12 (30)
10	-	Broken Hearted Melody	Sarah Vaughan	Mercury	12 (7) F
11	8	Mona Lisa	Conway Twitty	MGM	12 (29) L
12	7	Someone	Johnny Mathis	Fontana	13 (35)
13	3	Lonely Boy	Paul Anka	Columbia	13 (1)
14	5	China Tea	Russ Conway	Columbia	10
15	14	Just A Little Too Much	Ricky Nelson	London American	8 (9)
16	-	Red River Rock	Johnny & The Hurricanes	London American	13 (5) F
17	12	40 Miles Of Bad Road	Duane Eddy	London American	9 (9)
18	-	Peggy Sue Got Married	Buddy Holly	Coral	5
19	-	Makin' Love	Floyd Robinson	RCA	7 (20) F L
20	9	The Heart Of A Man	Frankie Vaughan	Philips	12

◆ To avoid confusion with US hit makers The Drifters, Cliff Richard's group changed their name to The Shadows.

◆ Emile Ford became the first British-based black male performer to top the charts. His Johnny Otis-styled revival of 'What Do You Want To Make Those Eyes At Me For' sold over a million in the UK alone.

November 1959

This Mnth	Prev Mnth	Title	Artist	Label	Wks (US 20 Pos)	
1	8	Travellin' Light	Cliff Richard	Columbia	16	
2	1	Mack The Knife	Bobby Darin	London American	14 (1)	
3	16	Red River Rock	Johnny & The Hurricanes	London American	13 (5)	F
4	-	What Do You Want To Make Those Eyes At Me For	Emile Ford & The Checkmates	Pye	18	F
5	3	('Til) I Kissed You	Everly Brothers	London American	14 (4)	
6	7	Sea Of Love	Marty Wilde	Philips	11	
7	-	Put Your Head On My Shoulder	Paul Anka	Columbia	10 (2)	
8	10	Broken Hearted Melody	Sarah Vaughan	Mercury	12 (7)	F
9	9	High Hopes	Frank Sinatra	Capitol	12 (30)	
10	6	The Three Bells	Browns	RCA	11 (1)	F L
11	19	Makin' Love	Floyd Robinson	RCA	7 (20)	F L
12	-	Oh! Carol	Neil Sedaka	RCA	14 (9)	
13	-	One More Sunrise (Morgen)	Dickie Valentine	Pye	7	L
14	-	Teen Beat	Sandy Nelson	Top Rank	8 (4)	F
15	-	What Do You Want	Adam Faith	Parlophone	15	F
16	2	Here Comes Summer	Jerry Keller	London American	12 (14)	F L
17	-	Mr. Blue	Mike Preston	Decca	5	F
18	-	Snow Coach	Russ Conway	Columbia	8	
19	11	Mona Lisa	Conway Twitty	MGM	12 (29)	L
20	4	Only Sixteen	Craig Douglas	Top Rank	14	

December 1959

This Mnth	Prev Mnth	Title	Artist	Label	Wks (US 20 Pos)	
1	15	What Do You Want	Adam Faith	Parlophone	15	F
2	4	What Do You Want To Make Those Eyes At Me For	Emile Ford & The Checkmates	Pye	18	F
3	12	Oh! Carol	Neil Sedaka	RCA	14 (9)	
4	1	Travellin' Light	Cliff Richard	Columbia	16	
5	-	Seven Little Girls Sitting In The Back Seat	Avons	Columbia	10	F L
6	3	Red River Rock	Johnny & The Hurricanes	London American	13 (5)	F
7	7	Put Your Head On My Shoulder	Paul Anka	Columbia	10 (2)	
8	18	Snow Coach	Russ Conway	Columbia	8	
9	-	Rawhide	Frankie Laine	Philips	13	L
10	-	More And More Party Pops	Russ Conway	Columbia	5	
11	2	Mack The Knife	Bobby Darin	London American	14 (1)	
12	-	Little White Bull	Tommy Steele	Decca	12	
13	-	Piano Party	Winifred Atwell	Decca	5	L
14	14	Teen Beat	Sandy Nelson	Top Rank	8 (4)	F
15	-	Among My Souvenirs	Connie Francis	MGM	6 (7)	
16	-	Staccato's Theme	Elmer Bernstein	Capitol	10	F L
17	-	Jingle Bell Rock	Max Bygraves	Decca	3	
18	5	('Til) I Kissed You	Everly Brothers	London American	14 (4)	
19	-	Little Donkey	Beverley Sisters	Decca	4	L
20	6	Sea Of Love	Marty Wilde	Philips	11	

◆ Among the many other new groups in Britain were Johnny & The Moondogs (members included three Beatles) who reached the final in a TV *Star Search*.

◆ Transatlantic star Guy Mitchell, who had made his chart debut in 1950, ended the decade with the No. 1 single in America, 'Heartaches By The Number'.

1960

This Mnth	Prev Mnth	Title	Artist	Label	Wks	(US 20 Pos)	
1	2	What Do You Want To Make Those Eyes At Me For	Emile Ford & The Checkmates	Pye	18		F
2	1	What Do You Want	Adam Faith	Parlophone	15		F
3	3	Oh! Carol	Neil Sedaka	RCA	14	(9)	
4	16	Staccato's Theme	Elmer Bernstein	Capitol	10		F L
5	5	Seven Little Girls Sitting In The Back Seat	Avons	Columbia	10		F L
6	12	Little White Bull	Tommy Steele	Decca	12		
7	-	Starry Eyed	Michael Holliday	Columbia	9		L
8	9	Rawhide	Frankie Laine	Philips	13		L
9	-	Why	Anthony Newley	Decca	12		
10	-	Way Down Yonder In New Orleans	Freddy Cannon	Top Rank	11	(3)	
11	-	Heartaches By The Number	Guy Mitchell	Philips	9	(1)	L
12	-	Bad Boy	Marty Wilde	Philips	7	(45)	
13	6	Travellin' Light	Cliff Richard	Columbia	16		
14	-	Be My Guest	Fats Domino	London American	7	(8)	
15	-	Voice In The Wilderness	Cliff Richard	Columbia	10		
16	-	In The Mood	Ernie Fields	London American	5	(4)	F L
17	-	Some Kind-A Earthquake	Duane Eddy	London American	5	(37)	
18	15	Among My Souvenirs	Connie Francis	MGM	6	(7)	
19	-	Reveille Rock	Johnny & The Hurricanes	London American	4	(25)	
20	10	More And More Party Pops	Russ Conway	Columbia	5		

1	9	Why	Anthony Newley	Decca	12		
2	15	Voice In The Wilderness	Cliff Richard	Columbia	10		
3	10	Way Down Yonder In New Orleans	Freddy Cannon	Top Rank	11	(3)	
4	-	Poor Me	Adam Faith	Parlophone	11		
5	7	Starry Eyed	Michael Holliday	Columbia	9		L
6	-	Pretty Blue Eyes	Craig Douglas	Top Rank	8		
7	-	On A Slow Boat To China	Emile Ford	Pye	9		
8	1	What Do You Want To Make Those Eyes At Me For	Emile Ford & The Checkmates	Pye	18		F
9	-	Beyond The Sea (La Mer)	Bobby Darin	London American	6	(6)	
10	11	Heartaches By The Number	Guy Mitchell	Philips	9	(1)	L
11	-	Running Bear	Johnny Preston	Mercury	12	(1)	F
12	-	Summer Set	Acker Bilk	Columbia	10		F
13	-	Misty	Johnny Mathis	Fontana	6	(12)	
14	2	What Do You Want	Adam Faith	Parlophone	15		F
15	-	Harbour Lights	Platters	Mercury	7	(8)	L
16	4	Staccato's Theme	Elmer Bernstein	Capitol	10		F L
17	6	Little White Bull	Tommy Steele	Decca	12		
18	-	You Got What It Takes	Marv Johnson	London American	10	(10)	F
19	8	Rawhide	Frankie Laine	Philips	13		L
20	3	Oh! Carol	Neil Sedaka	RCA	14	(9)	

◆ Cliff Richard & The Shadows set a new record when 19.5 million people watched them on *Sunday Night At The London Palladium*. The following day they flew to the USA to tour with American chart stars Frankie Avalon, Freddy Cannon and Bobby Rydell.

◆ Elvis Presley set foot in Britain for the only time when changing planes in Scotland on his way back to the US from Germany to be demobbed.

March 1960

This Mnth	Prev Mnth	Title	Artist	Label	Wks	(US 20 Pos)	
1	4	Poor Me	Adam Faith	Parlophone	11		
2	11	Running Bear	Johnny Preston	Mercury	12	(1)	F
3	-	Delaware	Perry Como	RCA	8	(22)	
4	1	Why	Anthony Newley	Decca	12		
5	7	On A Slow Boat To China	Emile Ford & The Checkmates	Pye	9		
6	18	You Got What It Takes	Marv Johnson	London American	10	(10)	F
7	-	Theme From 'A Summer Place'	Percy Faith	Philips	12	(1)	F L
8	12	Summer Set	Acker Bilk	Columbia	10		F
9	2	Voice In The Wilderness	Cliff Richard	Columbia	10		
10	-	What In The World's Come Over You	Jack Scott	Top Rank	7	(5)	L
11	3	Way Down Yonder In New Orleans	Freddy Cannon	Top Rank	11	(3)	
12	6	Pretty Blue Eyes	Craig Douglas	Top Rank	8		
13	-	Be Mine	Lance Fortune	Pye	7		F L
14	-	Fings Ain't What They Used T'be	Max Bygraves	Decca	10		
15	-	My Old Man's A Dustman	Lonnie Donegan	Pye	9		
16	-	Who Could Be Bluer	Jerry Lordan	Parlophone	5		F L
17	9	Beyond The Sea (La Mer)	Bobby Darin	London American	6	(6)	
18	-	Beatnik Fly	Johnny & The Hurricanes	London American	9	(15)	
19	-	Bonnie Came Back	Duane Eddy	London American	4	(26)	
20	-	Royal Event	Russ Conway	Columbia	3		

April 1960

1	15	My Old Man's A Dustman	Lonnie Donegan	Pye	9		
2	-	Fall In Love With You	Cliff Richard	Columbia	11		
3	-	Handy Man	Jimmy Jones	MGM	17	(2)	F
4	-	Do You Mind	Anthony Newley	Decca	12	(91)	
5	14	Fings Ain't What They Used T'Be	Max Bygraves	Decca	10		
6	-	Stuck On You	Elvis Presley	RCA	8	(1)	
7	7	Theme From 'A Summer Place'	Percy Faith	Philips	12	(1)	F L
8	2	Running Bear	Johnny Preston	Mercury	12	(1)	F
9	18	Beatnik Fly	Johnny & The Hurricanes	London American	9	(15)	
10	-	Someone Else's Baby	Adam Faith	Parlophone	10		
11	-	Cathy's Clown	Everly Brothers	Warner	14	(1)	
12	3	Delaware	Perry Como	RCA	8	(22)	
13	-	Wild One	Bobby Rydell	Columbia	8	(2)	F
14	6	You Got What It Takes	Marv Johnson	London American	10	(10)	F
15	-	Sweet Nothin's	Brenda Lee	Brunswick	13	(4)	F
16	10	What In The World's Come Over You	Jack Scott	Top Rank	7	(5)	L
17	-	Clementine	Bobby Darin	London American	6	(21)	
18	-	Standing On The Corner	King Brothers	Parlophone	6		
19	1	Poor Me	Adam Faith	Parlophone	11		
20	-	Footsteps	Steve Lawrence	HMV	10	(7)	F

◆ British teen idol Adam Faith scored his second successive No. 1 single.

◆ *Record Retailer* introduced Britain's first Top 50 single and Top 20 album charts.

◆ The Everly Brothers' initial release on Warner Brothers, their own composition 'Cathy's Clown', topped the chart on both sides of the Atlantic.

1960

This Mnth	Prev Mnth	Title	Artist	Label	Wks	(US 20 Pos)	
1	11	Cathy's Clown	Everly Brothers	Warner	14	(1)	
2	10	Someone Else's Baby	Adam Faith	Parlophone	10		
3	3	Handy Man	Jimmy Jones	MGM	17	(2)	F
4	4	Do You Mind	Anthony Newley	Decca	12	(91)	
5	15	Sweet Nothin's	Brenda Lee	Brunswick	13	(4)	F
6	-	Cradle Of Love	Johnny Preston	Mercury	11	(7)	
7	-	Shazam	Duane Eddy	London American	9	(45)	
8	2	Fall In Love With You	Cliff Richard	Columbia	11		
9	18	Standing On The Corner	King Brothers	Parlophone	6		
10	20	Footsteps	Steve Lawrence	HMV	10	(7)	F
11	6	Stuck On You	Elvis Presley	RCA	8	(1)	
12	-	Three Steps To Heaven	Eddie Cochran	London American	12		
13	-	Heart Of A Teenage Girl	Craig Douglas	Top Rank	5		
14	7	Theme From 'A Summer Place'	Percy Faith	Philips	12	(1)	F L
15	1	My Old Man's A Dustman	Lonnie Donegan	Pye	9		
16	-	Stairway To Heaven	Neil Sedaka	RCA	7	(9)	
17	5	Fings Ain't What They Used T'be	Max Bygraves	Decca	10		
18	-	Mama	Connie Francis	MGM	11	(8)	
19	9	Beatnik Fly	Johnny & The Hurricanes	London American	9	(15)	
20	-	Let The Little Girl Dance	Billy Bland	London American	3	(7)	F L

This Mnth	Prev Mnth	Title	Artist	Label	Wks	(US 20 Pos)	
1	1	Cathy's Clown	Everly Brothers	Warner	14	(1)	
2	6	Cradle Of Love	Johnny Preston	Mercury	11	(7)	
3	3	Handy Man	Jimmy Jones	MGM	17	(2)	F
4	12	Three Steps To Heaven	Eddie Cochran	London American	12		
5	5	Sweet Nothin's	Brenda Lee	Brunswick	13	(4)	F
6	-	Robot Man	Connie Francis	MGM	11		
7	-	I Wanna Go Home	Lonnie Donegan	Pye	9		
8	7	Shazam	Duane Eddy	London American	9	(45)	
9	18	Mama	Connie Francis	MGM	11	(8)	
10	2	Someone Else's Baby	Adam Faith	Parlophone	10		
11	-	Ain't Misbehavin'	Tommy Bruce & The Bruisers	Columbia	11		F L
12	-	Sixteen Reasons	Connie Stevens	Warner	7	(3)	F L
13	-	He'll Have To Go	Jim Reeves	RCA	6	(2)	F
14	16	Stairway To Heaven	Neil Sedaka	RCA	7	(9)	
15	10	Footsteps	Steve Lawrence	HMV	10	(7)	F
16	-	Good Timin'	Jimmy Jones	MGM	13	(3)	L
17	-	Down Yonder	Johnny & The Hurricanes	London American	5	(48)	
18	-	Lucky Five	Russ Conway	Columbia	4		
19	4	Do You Mind	Anthony Newley	Decca	12	(91)	
20	20	Let The Little Girl Dance	Billy Bland	London American	3	(7)	F L

◆ Gene Vincent was injured and Eddie Cochran killed in a car crash in England. Cochran's first posthumous release, 'Three Steps To Heaven' topped the UK chart.

◆ The Silver Beetles (Beatles) toured Scotland as backing band to little heralded rocker Johnny Gentle, and appeared alongside Gerry & The Pacemakers at a gig on Merseyside.

July 1960

This Mnth	Prev Mnth	Title	Artist	Label	Wks	(US 20 Pos)	
1	16	Good Timin'	Jimmy Jones	MGM	13	(3)	L
2	-	Please Don't Tease	Cliff Richard	Columbia	13		
3	11	Ain't Misbehavin'	Tommy Bruce & The Bruisers	Columbia	11		F L
4	-	Shakin' All Over	Johnny Kidd & The Pirates	HMV	12		F
5	-	What A Mouth	Tommy Steele	Decca	7		L
6	6	Robot Man	Connie Francis	MGM	11		
7	-	Made You	Adam Faith	Parlophone	7		
8	4	Three Steps To Heaven	Eddie Cochran	London American	12		
9	-	Angela Jones	Michael Cox	Triumph	7		F L
10	-	Look For A Star	Garry Mills	Top Rank	7	(26)	F L
11	1	Cathy's Clown	Everly Brothers	Warner	14	(1)	
12	-	When Will I Be Loved	Everly Brothers	London American	12	(8)	
13	9	Mama	Connie Francis	MGM	11	(8)	
14	-	When Johnny Comes Marching Home	Adam Faith	Parlophone	7		
15	7	I Wanna Go Home	Lonnie Donegan	Pye	9		
16	17	Down Yonder	Johnny & The Hurricanes	London American	5	(48)	
17	-	If She Should Come To You	Anthony Newley	Decca	9	(67)	
18	-	Itsy Bitsy Teenie Weenie Yellow Polka Dot Bikini	Brian Hyland	London American	9	(1)	F
19	2	Cradle Of Love	Johnny Preston	Mercury	11	(7)	
20	3	Handy Man	Jimmy Jones	MGM	17	(2)	F

August 1960

This Mnth	Prev Mnth	Title	Artist	Label	Wks	(US 20 Pos)	
1	2	Please Don't Tease	Cliff Richard	Columbia	13		
2	-	Apache	Shadows	Columbia	15		F
3	-	A Mess Of Blues	Elvis Presley	RCA	14	(32)	
4	4	Shakin' All Over	Johnny Kidd & The Pirates	HMV	12		F
5	-	Because They're Young	Duane Eddy	London American	14	(4)	
6	12	When Will I Be Loved	Everly Brothers	London American	12	(8)	
7	1	Good Timin'	Jimmy Jones	MGM	13	(3)	L
8	17	If She Should Come To You	Anthony Newley	Decca	9	(67)	
9	-	Tie Me Kangaroo Down Sport	Rolf Harris	Columbia	8	(3)	F
10	18	Itsy Bitsy Teenie Weenie Yellow Polka Dot Bikini	Brian Hyland	London American	9	(1)	F
11	10	Look For A Star	Garry Mills	Top Rank	7	(26)	F L
12	-	I'm Sorry	Brenda Lee	Brunswick	8	(1)	
13	-	Paper Roses	Kaye Sisters	Philips	10		L
14	-	Girl Of My Best Friend	Elvis Presley	RCA	12		
15	3	Ain't Misbehavin'	Tommy Bruce & The Bruisers	Columbia	11		F L
16	-	As Long As He Needs Me	Shirley Bassey	Columbia	22		
17	-	Everybody's Somebody's Fool	Connie Francis	MGM	10	(1)	
18	6	Robot Man	Connie Francis	MGM	11		
19	-	Mais Oui	King Brothers	Parlophone	3		
20	14	When Johnny Comes Marching Home	Adam Faith	Parlophone	7		

◆ After several unsuccessful singles, Cliff Richard's backing group, The Shadows, had a No. 1 hit with 'Apache'. They also recorded one of the earliest video discs, which was seen on European video juke boxes.

◆ The Beatles, with Pete Best on drums, played outside of Liverpool for the first time when they started a three month stand at the Indra club in Hamburg, Germany.

1960

This Mnth	Prev Mnth	Title	Artist	Label	Wks	(US 20 Pos)	
1	2	Apache	Shadows	Columbia	15		F
2	5	Because They're Young	Duane Eddy	London American	14	(4)	
3	-	Tell Laura I Love Her	Ricky Valance	Columbia	12		F L
4	3	A Mess Of Blues	Elvis Presley	RCA	14	(32)	
5	14	Girl Of My Best Friend	Elvis Presley	RCA	12		
6	-	Only The Lonely	Roy Orbison	London American	15	(2)	F
7	16	As Long As He Needs Me	Shirley Bassey	Columbia	22		
8	1	Please Don't Tease	Cliff Richard	Columbia	13		
9	17	Everybody's Somebody's Fool	Connie Francis	MGM	10	(1)	
10	6	When Will I Be Loved	Everly Brothers	London American	12	(8)	
11	-	How About That	Adam Faith	Parlophone	10		
12	13	Paper Roses	Kaye Sisters	Philips	10		L
13	-	Nine Times Out Of Ten	Cliff Richard	Columbia	8		
14	-	Love Is Like A Violin	Ken Dodd	Decca	7		F
15	8	If She Should Come To You	Anthony Newley	Decca	9	(67)	
16	-	Walk-Don't Run	Ventures	Top Rank	8	(2)	F
17	4	Shakin' All Over	Johnny Kidd & The Pirates	HMV	12		F
18	-	Walk Don't Run	John Barry Seven	Columbia	9		
19	12	I'm Sorry	Brenda Lee	Brunswick	8	(1)	
20	9	Tie Me Kangaroo Down Sport	Rolf Harris	Columbia	8	(3)	F

This Mnth	Prev Mnth	Title	Artist	Label	Wks	(US 20 Pos)	
1	6	Only The Lonely	Roy Orbison	London American	15	(2)	F
2	3	Tell Laura I Love Her	Ricky Valance	Columbia	12		F L
3	7	As Long As He Needs Me	Shirley Bassey	Columbia	22		
4	11	How About That	Adam Faith	Parlophone	10		
5	13	Nine Times Out Of Ten	Cliff Richard	Columbia	8		
6	-	So Sad (To Watch Good Love Go Bad)	Everly Brothers	Warner	8	(7)	
7	18	Walk Don't Run	John Barry Seven	Columbia	9		
8	1	Apache	Shadows	Columbia	15		F
9	-	Chain Gang	Sam Cooke	RCA	8	(2)	F
10	-	Let's Think About Living	Bob Luman	Warner	9	(7)	F L
11	16	Walk-Don't Run	Ventures	Top Rank	8	(2)	F
12	5	Girl Of My Best Friend	Elvis Presley	RCA	12		
13	-	Dreamin'	Johnny Burnette	London American	12	(11)	F
14	-	Please Help Me, I'm Falling	Hank Locklin	RCA	7	(8)	F L
15	-	Rocking Goose	Johnny & The Hurricanes	London American	15	(60)	
16	4	A Mess Of Blues	Elvis Presley	RCA	14	(32)	
17	2	Because They're Young	Duane Eddy	London American	14	(4)	
18	-	MacDonald's Cave	Piltdown Men	Capitol	6		F
19	9	Everybody's Somebody's Fool	Connie Francis	MGM	10	(1)	
20	-	My Love For You	Johnny Mathis	Fontana	11	(47)	

◆ Sam Cooke's current US hit, 'Wonderful World' (which he had written with Herb Alpert), was a transatlantic Top 10 hit for Herman's Hermits in 1965, and became a major British hit by Cooke in 1986 (21 years after his death!)

◆ Elvis Presley's 'It's Now Or Never', which had record UK advance orders, sold over 750,000 copies in its first week and passed the million mark 40 days later. Meanwhile, in America, his revival of 'Are You Lonesome Tonight' became his 15th chart topping single.

November 1960

This Mnth	Prev Mnth	Title	Artist	Label	Wks	(US 20 Pos)	
1	-	It's Now Or Never	Elvis Presley	RCA	14	(1)	G
2	3	As Long As He Needs Me	Shirley Bassey	Columbia	22		
3	13	Dreamin'	Johnny Burnette	London American	12	(11)	F
4	1	Only The Lonely	Roy Orbison	London American	15	(2)	F
5	15	Rocking Goose	Johnny & The Hurricanes	London American	15	(60)	
6	-	My Heart Has A Mind Of Its Own	Connie Francis	MGM	8	(1)	
7	-	Save The Last Dance For Me	Drifters	London American	14	(1)	
8	10	Let's Think About Living	Bob Luman	Warner	9	(7)	F L
9	-	Goodness Gracious Me	Peter Sellers & Sophia Loren	Parlophone	12		
10	20	My Love For You	Johnny Mathis	Fontana	11	(47)	
11	18	MacDonald's Cave	Piltdown Men	Capitol	6		F
12	-	Man Of Mystery	Shadows	Columbia	10		
13	9	Chain Gang	Sam Cooke	RCA	8	(2)	F
14	4	How About That	Adam Faith	Parlophone	10		
15	-	Mr. Custer	Charlie Drake	Parlophone	4		
16	7	Walk Don't Run	John Barry Seven	Columbia	9		
17	-	The Stranger	Shadows	Columbia	4		
18	-	Kommotion	Duane Eddy	London American	3	(78)	
19	6	So Sad (To Watch Good Love Go Bad)	Everly Brothers	Warner	8	(7)	
20	5	Nine Times Out Of Ten	Cliff Richard	Columbia	8		

December 1960

This Mnth	Prev Mnth	Title	Artist	Label	Wks	(US 20 Pos)	
1	1	It's Now Or Never	Elvis Presley	RCA	14	(1)	G
2	7	Save The Last Dance For Me	Drifters	London American	14	(1)	
3	-	I Love You	Cliff Richard	Columbia	12		
4	-	Strawberry Fair	Anthony Newley	Decca	8		
5	9	Goodness Gracious Me	Peter Sellers & Sophia Loren	Parlophone	12		
6	-	Little Donkey	Nina & Frederick	Columbia	7		F
7	5	Rocking Goose	Johnny & The Hurricanes	London American	15	(60)	
8	12	Man Of Mystery	Shadows	Columbia	10		
9	-	Poetry In Motion	Johnny Tillotson	London American	13	(2)	F L
10	-	Lonely Pup (In A Christmas Shop)	Adam Faith	Parlophone	7		
11	-	Gurney Slade	Max Harris	Fontana	6		F L
12	6	My Heart Has A Mind Of Its Own	Connie Francis	MGM	8	(1)	
13	2	As Long As He Needs Me	Shirley Bassey	Columbia	22		
14	-	Perfidia	Ventures	London American	9	(15)	L
15	3	Dreamin'	Johnny Burnette	London American	12	(11)	F
16	10	My Love For You	Johnny Mathis	Fontana	11	(47)	
17	-	Blue Angel	Roy Orbison	London American	8	(9)	
18	-	Lively	Lonnie Donegan	Pye	6		
19	-	Ol' Macdonald	Frank Sinatra	Capitol	4	(25)	
20	-	Counting Teardrops	Emile Ford & The Checkmates	Pye	9		L

◆ Instrumentals were big business in Britain – at times accounting for 30% of the chart. The hottest instrumental acts were The Shadows, Johnny & The Hurricanes, Duane Eddy and American session-group The Piltdown Men.

◆ Frankie Vaughan, one of the top UK singers of the 1950s, became the first UK pop performer to be the subject of the US TV show *This Is Your Life* – an estimated 40 million viewers saw the show.

1961

This Mnth	Prev Mnth	Title	Artist	Label	Wks	(US 20 Pos)	
1	9	Poetry In Motion	Johnny Tillotson	London American	13	(2)	F L
2	3	I Love You	Cliff Richard	Columbia	12		
3	2	Save The Last Dance For Me	Drifters	London American	14	(1)	
4	-	Portrait Of My Love	Matt Monro	Parlophone	10		F
5	1	It's Now Or Never	Elvis Presley	RCA	14	(1)	G
6	14	Perfidia	Ventures	London American	9	(15)	L
7	20	Counting Teardrops	Emile Ford & The Checkmates	Pye	9		L
8	-	Are You Lonesome Tonight?	Elvis Presley	RCA	10	(1)	
9	5	Goodness Gracious Me	Peter Sellers & Sophia Loren	Parlophone	12		
10	-	Buona Sera	Acker Bilk	Columbia	8		
11	-	Pepe	Duane Eddy	London American	8	(18)	
12	10	Lonely Pup (In A Christmas Shop)	Adam Faith	Parlophone	7		
13	-	Stay	Maurice Williams & The Zodiacs	Top Rank	6	(1)	F L
14	7	Rocking Goose	Johnny & The Hurricanes	London American	15	(60)	
15	-	Sway	Bobby Rydell	Columbia	5	(14)	
16	17	Blue Angel	Roy Orbison	London American	8	(9)	
17	4	Strawberry Fair	Anthony Newley	Decca	8		
18	8	Man Of Mystery	Shadows	Columbia	10		
19	-	You're Sixteen	Johnny Burnette	London American	8	(8)	
20	-	Sailor	Petula Clark	Pye	9		

This Mnth	Prev Mnth	Title	Artist	Label	Wks	(US 20 Pos)	
1	8	Are You Lonesome Tonight?	Elvis Presley	RCA	10	(1)	
2	20	Sailor	Petula Clark	Pye	9		
3	-	Rubber Ball	Bobby Vee	London American	7	(6)	F
4	19	You're Sixteen	Johnny Burnette	London American	8	(8)	
5	11	Pepe	Duane Eddy	London American	8	(18)	
6	4	Portrait Of My Love	Matt Monro	Parlophone	10		F
7	-	F.B.I.	Shadows	Columbia	11		
8	1	Poetry In Motion	Johnny Tillotson	London American	13	(2)	F L
9	-	Walk Right Back	Everly Brothers	Warner	11	(7)	
10	-	Sailor	Anne Shelton	Philips	5		L
11	-	Rubber Ball	Marty Wilde	Philips	4		L
12	-	Who Am I/This Is It	Adam Faith	Parlophone	9		
13	10	Buona Sera	Acker Bilk	Columbia	8		
14	-	Will You Love Me Tomorrow	Shirelles	Top Rank	9	(1)	F L
15	-	Calendar Girl	Neil Sedaka	RCA	8	(4)	
16	2	I Love You	Cliff Richard	Columbia	12		
17	-	Many Tears Ago	Connie Francis	MGM	5	(7)	
18	7	Counting Teardrops	Emile Ford & The Checkmates	Pye	9		L
19	13	Stay	Maurice Williams & The Zodiacs	Top Rank	6	(1)	F L
20	-	Riders In The Sky	Ramrods	London American	7	(30)	F L

◆ Trad (based on old-time New Orleans- styled traditional jazz) was the latest UK music craze, with Acker Bilk, Kenny Ball and Chris Barber at the forefront of it.

◆ New transatlantic stars included the Buddy Holly-influenced 17-year-old Bobby Vee and singer/songwriter Johnny Tillotson whose 'Poetry In Motion' topped the chart on both sides of the Atlantic

March 1961

This Mnth	Prev Mnth	Title	Artist	Label	Wks 20	(US Pos)
1	9	Walk Right Back	Everly Brothers	Warner	11	(7)
2	-	Are You Sure	Allisons	Fontana	12	F L
3	-	Theme For A Dream	Cliff Richard	Columbia	9	
4	14	Will You Love Me Tomorrow	Shirelles	Top Rank	9	(1) F L
5	-	Wooden Heart	Elvis Presley	RCA	14	
6	7	F.B.I.	Shadows	Columbia	11	
7	20	Riders In The Sky	Ramrods	London American	7	(30) F L
8	-	My Kind Of Girl	Matt Monro	Parlophone	7	(18)
9	2	Sailor	Petula Clark	Pye	9	
10	15	Calendar Girl	Neil Sedaka	RCA	8	(4)
11	-	Exodus	Ferrante & Teicher	London American	10	(2) F L
12	12	Who Am I/This Is It	Adam Faith	Parlophone	9	
13	1	Are You Lonesome Tonight?	Elvis Presley	RCA	10	(1)
14	-	Wheels	String-A-Longs	London American	6	(3) F L
15	-	Samantha	Kenny Ball	Pye Jazz	10	F
16	-	And The Heavens Cried	Anthony Newley	Decca	7	
17	-	Lazy River	Bobby Darin	London American	8	(14)
18	-	Let's Jump The Broomstick	Brenda Lee	Brunswick	4	
19	-	Ja-Da	Johnny & The Hurricanes	London American	3	(86) L
20	3	Rubber Ball	Bobby Vee	London American	7	(6) F

April 1961

This Mnth	Prev Mnth	Title	Artist	Label	Wks 20	(US Pos)
1	5	Wooden Heart	Elvis Presley	RCA	14	
2	2	Are You Sure	Allisons	Fontana	12	F L
3	17	Lazy River	Bobby Darin	London American	8	(14)
4	-	You're Driving Me Crazy	Temperance Seven	Parlophone	12	F
5	11	Exodus	Ferrante & Teicher	London American	10	(2) F L
6	3	Theme For A Dream	Cliff Richard	Columbia	9	
7	-	Where The Boys Are	Connie Francis	MGM	6	(4)
8	-	Blue Moon	Marcels	Pye International	9	(1) F L
9	1	Walk Right Back	Everly Brothers	Warner	11	(7)
10	16	And The Heavens Cried	Anthony Newley	Decca	7	
11	-	Gee Whiz It's You	Cliff Richard	Columbia	8	
12	8	My Kind Of Girl	Matt Monro	Parlophone	7	(18)
13	6	F.B.I.	Shadows	Columbia	11	
14	15	Samantha	Kenny Ball	Pye Jazz	10	F
15	-	Warpaint	Brook Brothers	Pye	9	F
16	-	African Waltz	Johnny Dankworth	Columbia	8	L
17	4	Will You Love Me Tomorrow	Shirelles	Top Rank	9	(1) F L
18	-	A Hundred Pounds Of Clay	Craig Douglas	Top Rank	6	
19	-	Don't Treat Me Like A Child	Helen Shapiro	Columbia	11	F
20	-	Baby Sittin' Boogie	Buzz Clifford	Fontana	3	(6) F L

◆ The Allisons were the most talked about new act. The duo's self-composed 'Are You Sure' dethroned Elvis at the top and came runner-up in the most publicized Eurovision Song Contest to date.

◆ Ex-Drifter Ben E. King released 'Stand By Me' a song he had originally written for the group. It was a US Top 10 hit in both 1961 and 1986, and even topped the UK chart in 1987!

1961

May 1961

This Mnth	Prev Mnth	Title	Artist	Label	Wks	(US 20 Pos)
1	8	Blue Moon	Marcels	Pye International	9	(1) F L
2	4	You're Driving Me Crazy	Temperance Seven	Parlophone	12	F
3	-	On The Rebound	Floyd Cramer	RCA	9	(4) F L
4	-	Runaway	Del Shannon	London American	16	(1) F
5	-	More Than I Can Say	Bobby Vee	London American	9	(61)
6	19	Don't Treat Me Like A Child	Helen Shapiro	Columbia	11	F
7	1	Wooden Heart	Elvis Presley	RCA	14	
8	-	Theme From Dixie	Duane Eddy	London American	6	(39)
9	-	Frightened City	Shadows	Columbia	11	
10	-	Easy Going Me	Adam Faith	Parlophone	5	
11	18	A Hundred Pounds Of Clay	Craig Douglas	Top Rank	6	
12	-	What'd I Say	Jerry Lee Lewis	London American	6	(30) L
13	16	African Waltz	Johnny Dankworth	Columbia	8	L
14	-	You'll Never Know	Shirley Bassey	Columbia	8	
15	11	Gee Whiz It's You	Cliff Richard	Columbia	8	
16	15	Warpaint	Brook Brothers	Pye	9	F
17	3	Lazy River	Bobby Darin	London American	8	(14)
18	-	Surrender	Elvis Presley	RCA	10	(1)
19	-	But I Do	Clarence 'Frogman' Henry	Pye International	13	(4) F
20	5	Exodus	Ferrante & Teicher	London American	10	(2) F L

June 1961

1	4	Runaway	Del Shannon	London American	16	(1) F
2	18	Surrender	Elvis Presley	RCA	10	(1)
3	19	But I Do	Clarence 'Frogman' Henry	Pye International	13	(4) F
4	9	Frightened City	Shadows	Columbia	11	
5	14	You'll Never Know	Shirley Bassey	Columbia	8	
6	-	Hello Mary Lou/Travellin' Man	Ricky Nelson	London American	15	(9)
7	-	Halfway To Paradise	Billy Fury	Decca	18	
8	-	Have A Drink On Me	Lonnie Donegan	Pye	8	
9	-	Pasadena	Temperance Seven	Parlophone	12	
10	5	More Than I Can Say	Bobby Vee	London American	9	(61)
11	-	Temptation	Everly Brothers	Warner	12	(27)
12	-	Little Devil	Neil Sedaka	RCA	6	(11)
13	3	On The Rebound	Floyd Cramer	RCA	9	(4) F L
14	-	I've Told Every Little Star	Linda Scott	Columbia	6	(3) F L
15	-	Running Scared	Roy Orbison	London American	9	(1)
16	12	What'd I Say	Jerry Lee Lewis	London American	6	(30) L
17	-	A Girl Like You	Cliff Richard	Columbia	12	
18	-	Pop Goes The Weasel	Anthony Newley	Decca	6	(85)
19	-	Well I Ask You	Eden Kane	Decca	16	F
20	1	Blue Moon	Marcels	Pye International	9	(1) F L

◆ Elvis Presley's 'Surrender', which like its predecessor, 'It's Now Or Never', was based on an old Italian ballad, had a record 460,000 advance orders.

◆ The first American artist to appear on new pop TV show *Thank Your Lucky Stars* was Gene Vincent. This show, more than any other, would spread the Merseybeat sound.

◆ British teen idol Billy Fury clocked up his biggest hit to date with a cover of Tony Orlando's 'Halfway To Paradise'.

July 1961

This Mnth	Prev Mnth	Title	Artist	Label	Wks (US 20 Pos)	
1	11	Temptation	Everly Brothers	Warner	12 (27)	
2	1	Runaway	Del Shannon	London American	16 (1)	F
3	19	Well I Ask You	Eden Kane	Decca	16	F
4	6	Hello Mary Lou/Travellin' Man	Ricky Nelson	London American	15 (9)	
5	17	A Girl Like You	Cliff Richard	Columbia	12	
6	9	Pasadena	Temperance Seven	Parlophone	12	
7	7	Halfway To Paradise	Billy Fury	Decca	18	
8	3	But I Do	Clarence 'Frogman' Henry	Pye International	13 (4)	F
9	15	Running Scared	Roy Orbison	London American	9 (1)	
10	-	You Don't Know	Helen Shapiro	Columbia	14	
11	-	You Always Hurt The One You Love	Clarence 'Frogman' Henry	Pye International	9 (12)	L
12	2	Surrender	Elvis Presley	RCA	10 (1)	
13	-	Time	Craig Douglas	Top Rank	10	
14	18	Pop Goes The Weasel	Anthony Newley	Decca	6 (85)	
15	-	Romeo	Petula Clark	Pye	11	
16	-	Moody River	Pat Boone	London American	6 (1)	
17	4	Frightened City	Shadows	Columbia	11	
18	-	Weekend	Eddie Cochran	London American	3	L
19	-	Don't You Know It	Adam Faith	Parlophone	6	
20	-	Breakin' In A Brand New Broken Heart	Connie Francis	MGM	2 (7)	

August 1961

This Mnth	Prev Mnth	Title	Artist	Label	Wks (US 20 Pos)	
1	10	You Don't Know	Helen Shapiro	Columbia	14	
2	3	Well I Ask You	Eden Kane	Decca	16	F
3	-	Johnny Remember Me	John Leyton	Top Rank	11	F
4	7	Halfway To Paradise	Billy Fury	Decca	18	
5	15	Romeo	Petula Clark	Pye	11	
6	11	You Always Hurt The One You Love	Clarence 'Frogman' Henry	Pye International	9 (12)	L
7	6	Pasadena	Temperance Seven	Parlophone	12	
8	1	Temptation	Everly Brothers	Warner	12 (27)	
9	19	Don't You Know It	Adam Faith	Parlophone	6	
10	13	Time	Craig Douglas	Top Rank	10	
11	5	A Girl Like You	Cliff Richard	Columbia	12	
12	4	Hello Mary Lou/Travellin' Man	Ricky Nelson	London American	15 (9)	
13	-	Quarter To Three	Gary U.S. Bonds	Top Rank	9 (1)	L
14	-	Reach For The Stars/Climb Ev'ry Mountain	Shirley Bassey	Columbia	11	
15	2	Runaway	Del Shannon	London American	16 (1)	F
16	-	Climb Ev'ry Mountain	Shirley Bassey	Columbia	6	
17	-	Baby I Don't Care	Buddy Holly	Coral	6	
18	-	Marcheta	Karl Denver	Decca	7	F
19	-	That's My Home	Acker Bilk	Columbia	9	
20	-	Cupid	Sam Cooke	RCA	7 (17)	

◆ 'Michael', a 19th century slave song, gave American folk quintet The Highwaymen an unexpected transatlantic No. 1, despite heavy British competition from Lonnie Donegan. Incidentally, Donegan's 1959 UK hit 'Chewing Gum' was now huge in the USA.

◆ The Shadows became the first British rock act to top the UK album chart. Their boss, Cliff Richard, would be the second with his **21 Today** LP.

1961

This Mnth	Prev Mnth	Title	Artist	Label	Wks	20 (US Pos)	
1	3	Johnny Remember Me	John Leyton	Top Rank	11		F
2	1	You Don't Know	Helen Shapiro	Columbia	14		
3	14	Reach For The Stars/ Climb Ev'ry Mountain	Shirley Bassey	Columbia	11		
4	-	Wild In The Country	Elvis Presley	RCA	8	(26)	
5	-	Kon-Tiki	Shadows	Columbia	8		
6	20	Cupid	Sam Cooke	RCA	7	(17)	
7	2	Well I Ask You	Eden Kane	Decca	16		F
8	-	Michael	Highwaymen	HMV	10	(1)	F L
9	19	That's My Home	Acker Bilk	Columbia	9		
10	5	Romeo	Petula Clark	Pye	11		
11	-	Michael Row The Boat	Lonnie Donegan	Pye	6		
12	-	Jealousy	Billy Fury	Decca	8		
13	4	Halfway To Paradise	Billy Fury	Decca	18		
14	-	Get Lost	Eden Kane	Decca	8		
15	13	Quarter To Three	Gary U.S. Bonds	Top Rank	9	(1)	L
16	-	How Many Tears	Bobby Vee	London American	5	(63)	
17	-	Together	Connie Francis	MGM	6	(6)	
18	-	Hats Off To Larry	Del Shannon	London American	8	(5)	
19	11	A Girl Like You	Cliff Richard	Columbia	12		
20	-	You'll Answer To Me	Cleo Laine	Fontana	9		F L

This Mnth	Prev Mnth	Title	Artist	Label	Wks	20 (US Pos)	
1	-	Walkin' Back To Happiness	Helen Shapiro	Columbia	15(100)		
2	8	Michael	Highwaymen	HMV	10	(1)	F L
3	-	Wild Wind	John Leyton	Top Rank	6		
4	20	You'll Answer To Me	Cleo Laine	Fontana	9		F L
5	12	Jealousy	Billy Fury	Decca	8		
6	-	Sucu-Sucu	Laurie Johnson	Pye	10		F L
7	5	Kon-Tiki	Shadows	Columbia	8		
8	18	Hats Off To Larry	Del Shannon	London American	8	(5)	
9	4	Wild In The Country	Elvis Presley	RCA	8	(26)	
10	-	When The Girl In Your Arms Is The Girl In Your Heart	Cliff Richard	Columbia	7		
11	-	Bless You	Tony Orlando	Fontana	7	(15)	F L
12	14	Get Lost	Eden Kane	Decca	8		
13	-	Mexicali Rose	Karl Denver	Decca	9		
14	1	Johnny Remember Me	John Leyton	Top Rank	11		F
15	-	You Must Have Been A Beautiful Baby	Bobby Darin	London American	8	(5)	
16	-	Granada	Frank Sinatra	Reprise	4	(64)	
17	-	Hit The Road Jack	Ray Charles	HMV	8	(1)	
18	17	Together	Connie Francis	MGM	6	(6)	
19	-	My Boomerang Won't Come Back	Charlie Drake	Parlophone	6	(21)	L
20	2	You Don't Know	Helen Shapiro	Columbia	14		

◆ 15-year-old London schoolgirl Helen Shapiro had two successive chart toppers with the British songs 'You Don't Know' and 'Walkin' Back To Happiness'. Both records sold over a million copies worldwide.

◆ Unusually. three hitsby British acts also reached the US Top 10: 'Midnight In Moscow' by Kenny Ball, 'Stranger On The Shore' by Acker Bilk and 'Let's Get Together' by 14-year-old Hayley Mills.

1961

November 1961

This Mnth	Prev Mnth	Title	Artist	Label	Wks (US 20 Pos)
1	-	His Latest Flame	Elvis Presley	RCA	8 (4)
2	1	Walkin' Back To Happiness	Helen Shapiro	Columbia	15(100)
3	-	Take Good Care Of My Baby	Bobby Vee	London American	11 (1)
4	-	Big Bad John	Jimmy Dean	Philips	11 (1) F L
5	10	When The Girl In Your Arms Is The Girl In Your Heart	Cliff Richard	Columbia	7
6	-	Take Five	Dave Brubeck Quartet	Fontana	10 (25) F
7	17	Hit The Road Jack	Ray Charles	HMV	8 (1)
8	-	The Time Has Come	Adam Faith	Parlophone	8
9	6	Sucu-Sucu	Laurie Johnson	Pye	10 F L
10	13	Mexicali Rose	Karl Denver	Decca	9
11	-	Tower Of Strength	Frankie Vaughan	Philips	10
12	-	Moon River	Danny Williams	HMV	12 F
13	11	Bless You	Tony Orlando	Fontana	7 (15) F L
14	15	You Must Have Been A Beautiful Baby	Bobby Darin	London American	8 (5)
15	3	Wild Wind	John Leyton	Top Rank	6
16	-	Runaround Sue	Dion	Top Rank	5 (1) F
17	-	The Savage	Shadows	Columbia	5
18	-	Let's Get Together	Hayley Mills	Decca	5 (8) F L
19	-	Midnight In Moscow	Kenny Ball	Pye Jazz	11 (2)
20	4	You'll Answer To Me	Cleo Laine	Fontana	9 F L

December 1961

This Mnth	Prev Mnth	Title	Artist	Label	Wks (US 20 Pos)
1	11	Tower Of Strength	Frankie Vaughan	Philips	10
2	12	Moon River	Danny Williams	HMV	12 F
3	3	Take Good Care Of My Baby	Bobby Vee	London American	11 (1)
4	19	Midnight In Moscow	Kenny Ball	Pye Jazz	11 (2)
5	-	Stranger On The Shore	Mr. Acker Bilk	Columbia	33 (1) G
6	-	I'll Get By	Shirley Bassey	Columbia	6
7	2	Walkin' Back To Happiness	Helen Shapiro	Columbia	15(100)
8	1	His Latest Flame	Elvis Presley	RCA	8 (4)
9	-	Johnny Will	Pat Boone	London American	8 (35)
10	6	Take Five	Dave Brubeck Quartet	Fontana	10 (25) F
11	-	Let There Be Drums	Sandy Nelson	London American	9 (7) L
12	4	Big Bad John	Jimmy Dean	Philips	11 (1) F L
13	8	The Time Has Come	Adam Faith	Parlophone	8
14	-	My Friend The Sea	Petula Clark	Pye	4
15	-	So Long Baby	Del Shannon	London American	6 (28)
16	-	Don't Bring Lulu	Dorothy Provine	Warner	6 F L
17	-	Happy Birthday, Sweet Sixteen	Neil Sedaka	RCA	11 (6)
18	-	I Cried For You	Ricky Stevens	Columbia	4 F L
19	17	The Savage	Shadows	Columbia	5
20	-	I'd Never Find Another You	Billy Fury	Decca	11

◆ Mantovani received five American gold albums while fellow Briton Matt Monro was voted Most Promising Artist in the *Billboard* DJ Poll.

◆ American hits from C&W stars Leroy Van Dyke, Jimmy Dean and Patsy Cline also scored in Britain, although, in the case of Cline's 'Crazy' it was 30 years later!

◆ EMI Records proudly announced that **The Black And White Minstrel Show** by The George Mitchell Minstrels (which was based on the act's very popular TV series) was the company's first album to sell over 100,000 copies in the UK.

1962

This Mnth	Prev Mnth	Title	Artist	Label	Wks	(US 20 Pos)	
1	5	Stranger On The Shore	Mr. Acker Bilk	Columbia	33	(1)	G
2	20	I'd Never Find Another You	Billy Fury	Decca	11		
3	11	Let There Be Drums	Sandy Nelson	London American	9	(7)	L
4	-	The Young Ones	Cliff Richard	Columbia	13		G
5	17	Happy Birthday, Sweet Sixteen	Neil Sedaka	RCA	11	(6)	
6	-	Multiplication	Bobby Darin	London American	8	(30)	
7	-	Let's Twist Again	Chubby Checker	Columbia	18	(8)	
8	2	Moon River	Danny Williams	HMV	12		F
9	4	Midnight In Moscow	Kenny Ball	Pye Jazz	11	(2)	
10	9	Johnny Will	Pat Boone	London American	8	(35)	
11	-	Run To Him	Bobby Vee	Liberty	9	(2)	
12	-	The Twist	Chubby Checker	Columbia	5	(1)	F
13	1	Tower Of Strength	Frankie Vaughan	Philips	10		
14	-	The Lion Sleeps Tonight	Tokens	RCA	4	(1)	F L
15	-	Walk On By	Leroy Van Dyke	Mercury	9	(5)	F L
16	15	So Long Baby	Del Shannon	London American	6	(28)	
17	-	Forget Me Not	Eden Kane	Decca	9		
18	-	Language Of Love	John D. Loudermilk	RCA	4	(32)	F L
19	-	Toy Balloons	Russ Conway	Columbia	5		L
20	-	Cryin' In The Rain	Everly Brothers	Warner	9	(6)	

This Mnth	Prev Mnth	Title	Artist	Label	Wks	(US 20 Pos)	
1	4	The Young Ones	Cliff Richard	Columbia	13		G
2	7	Let's Twist Again	Chubby Checker	Columbia	18	(8)	
3	-	Rock-A-Hula-Baby	Elvis Presley	RCA	9	(23)	
4	17	Forget Me Not	Eden Kane	Decca	9		
5	15	Walk On By	Leroy Van Dyke	Mercury	9	(5)	F L
6	5	Happy Birthday, Sweet Sixteen	Neil Sedaka	RCA	11	(6)	
7	20	Cryin' In The Rain	Everly Brothers	Warner	9	(6)	
8	2	I'd Never Find Another You	Billy Fury	Decca	11		
9	1	Stranger On The Shore	Mr. Acker Bilk	Columbia	33	(1)	G
10	11	Run To Him	Bobby Vee	Liberty	9	(2)	
11	6	Multiplication	Bobby Darin	London American	8	(30)	
12	-	A Little Bitty Tear	Burl Ives	Brunswick	6	(9)	F L
13	-	Peppermint Twist	Joey Dee & The Starliters	Columbia	5	(1)	F L
14	-	Wimoweh	Karl Denver	Decca	10		
15	-	Lonesome	Adam Faith	Parlophone	4		
16	-	Can't Help Falling In Love	Elvis Presley	RCA	13	(2)	
17	-	The Comancheros	Lonnie Donegan	Pye	4		
18	-	March Of The Siamese Children	Kenny Ball	Pye Jazz	8	(88)	
19	3	Let There Be Drums	Sandy Nelson	London American	9	(7)	L
20	12	The Twist	Chubby Checker	Columbia	5	(1)	F

◆ The theme from Cliff Richard's film *The Young Ones* racked up 500,000 advance orders and entered the UK chart at No. 1. It went on to sell over a million in Britain. The soundtrack album also topped the chart.

◆ Elvis Presley earned his 29th gold single with the double-sided 'Rock-A-Hula Baby' and 'Can't Help Falling In Love'. The single came from the soundtrack album to the film *Blue Hawaii*, which topped the chart for four months on both sides of the Atlantic. 'Can't Help Falling In Love' charted again later for Andy Williams, The Stylistics and UB40.

March 1962

This Mnth	Prev Mnth	Title	Artist	Label	Wks	(US 20 Pos)	
1	18	March Of The Siamese Children	Kenny Ball	Pye Jazz	8	(88)	
2	-	Tell Me What He Said	Helen Shapiro	Columbia	10		
3	2	Let's Twist Again	Chubby Checker	Columbia	18	(8)	
4	-	Wonderful Land	Shadows	Columbia	16		
5	16	Can't Help Falling In Love	Elvis Presley	RCA	13	(2)	
6	14	Wimoweh	Karl Denver	Decca	10		
7	1	The Young Ones	Cliff Richard	Columbia	13		G
8	3	Rock-A-Hula-Baby	Elvis Presley	RCA	9	(23)	
9	9	Stranger On The Shore	Mr. Acker Bilk	Columbia	33	(1)	G
10	-	Hole In The Ground	Bernard Cribbins	Parlophone	7		F
11	-	Twistin' The Night Away	Sam Cooke	RCA	12	(9)	
12	-	Dream Baby	Roy Orbison	London American	11	(4)	
13	-	Softly As I Leave You	Matt Monro	Parlophone	8		
14	-	Hey! Baby	Bruce Channel	Mercury	9	(1)	F
15	7	Cryin' In The Rain	Everly Brothers	Warner	9	(6)	
16	-	The Wanderer	Dion	HMV	6	(2)	
17	4	Forget Me Not	Eden Kane	Decca	9		
18	12	A Little Bitty Tear	Burl Ives	Brunswick	6	(9)	F L
19	5	Walk On By	Leroy Van Dyke	Mercury	9	(5)	F L
20	-	Hey Little Girl	Del Shannon	London American	12	(38)	

April 1962

This Mnth	Prev Mnth	Title	Artist	Label	Wks	(US 20 Pos)	
1	4	Wonderful Land	Shadows	Columbia	16		
2	14	Hey! Baby	Bruce Channel	Mercury	9	(1)	F
3	12	Dream Baby	Roy Orbison	London American	11	(4)	
4	-	When My Little Girl Is Smiling	Jimmy Justice	Pye	9		F
5	11	Twistin' The Night Away	Sam Cooke	RCA	12	(9)	
6	2	Tell Me What He Said	Helen Shapiro	Columbia	10		
7	20	Hey Little Girl	Del Shannon	London American	12	(38)	
8	5	Can't Help Falling In Love	Elvis Presley	RCA	13	(2)	
9	-	Never Goodbye	Karl Denver	Decca	7		
10	-	Speak To Me Pretty	Brenda Lee	Brunswick	9		
11	3	Let's Twist Again	Chubby Checker	Columbia	18	(8)	
12	6	Wimoweh	Karl Denver	Decca	10		
13	-	When My Little Girl Is Smiling	Craig Douglas	Top Rank	6		
14	-	Dr. Kildare Theme	Johnny Spence	Parlophone	5		F L
15	9	Stranger On The Shore	Mr. Acker Bilk	Columbia	33	(1)	G
16	1	March Of The Siamese Children	Kenny Ball	Pye Jazz	8	(88)	
17	-	Love Letters	Ketty Lester	London American	9	(5)	F L
18	-	Nut Rocker	B. Bumble & The Stingers	Top Rank	11	(23)	F L
19	-	Wonderful World Of The Young	Danny Williams	HMV	7		L
20	-	Ev'rybody's Twistin'	Frank Sinatra	Reprise	5	(75)	

◆ Alexis Korner's group, Blues Incorporated (which at times included Charlie Watts, Jack Bruce, Ginger Baker, Mick Jagger and Brian Jones), played their debut gig at a club in Ealing.

◆ British trad star Acker Bilk topped the US chart with 'Stranger On The Shore'. In the 1962 *Billboard* DJ poll he won awards for Top Instrumentalist and Top Instrumental Single.

1962

This Mnth	Prev Mnth	Title	Artist	Label	Wks	(US 20 Pos)	
1	18	Nut Rocker	B. Bumble & The Stingers	Top Rank	11	(23)	F L
2	1	Wonderful Land	Shadows	Columbia	16		
3	17	Love Letters	Ketty Lester	London American	9	(5)	F L
4	-	Good Luck Charm	Elvis Presley	RCA	14	(1)	
5	10	Speak To Me Pretty	Brenda Lee	Brunswick	9		
6	-	I'm Looking Out The Window	Cliff Richard	Columbia	11		
7	7	Hey Little Girl	Del Shannon	London American	12	(38)	
8	4	When My Little Girl Is Smiling	Jimmy Justice	Pye	9		F
9	-	As You Like It	Adam Faith	Parlophone	10		
10	2	Hey! Baby	Bruce Channel	Mercury	9	(1)	F
11	19	Wonderful World Of The Young	Danny Williams	HMV	7		L
12	3	Dream Baby	Roy Orbison	London American	11	(4)	
13	5	Twistin' The Night Away	Sam Cooke	RCA	12	(9)	
14	-	Come Outside	Mike Sarne & Wendy Richard	Parlophone	14		F
15	-	Last Night Was Made For Love	Billy Fury	Decca	11		
16	-	The Party's Over	Lonnie Donegan	Pye	5		
17	15	Stranger On The Shore	Mr. Acker Bilk	Columbia	33	(1)	G
18	20	Ev'rybody's Twistin'	Frank Sinatra	Reprise	5	(75)	
19	-	Let's Talk About Love	Helen Shapiro	Columbia	3		
20	-	I Don't Know Why	Eden Kane	Decca	7		

This	Prev	Title	Artist	Label	Wks	(US 20 Pos)	
1	4	Good Luck Charm	Elvis Presley	RCA	14	(1)	
2	14	Come Outside	Mike Sarne & Wendy Richard	Parlophone	14		F
3	6	I'm Looking Out The Window	Cliff Richard	Columbia	11		
4	-	A Picture Of You	Joe Brown & The Bruvvers	Piccadilly	14		F
5	-	Ginny Come Lately	Brian Hyland	HMV	10	(21)	
6	15	Last Night Was Made For Love	Billy Fury	Decca	11		
7	20	I Don't Know Why	Eden Kane	Decca	7		
8	9	As You Like It	Adam Faith	Parlophone	10		
9	1	Nut Rocker	B. Bumble & The Stingers	Top Rank	11	(23)	F L
10	-	The Green Leaves Of Summer	Kenny Ball	Pye Jazz	9	(87)	
11	-	Do You Wanna Dance	Cliff Richard	Columbia	6		
12	17	Stranger On The Shore	Mr. Acker Bilk	Columbia	33	(1)	G
13	-	I Can't Stop Loving You	Ray Charles	HMV	12	(1)	
14	3	Love Letters	Ketty Lester	London American	9	(5)	F L
15	-	Theme From Dr. Kildare (Three Stars Will Shine Tonight)	Richard Chamberlain	MGM	4	(10)	F
16	-	Ain't That Funny	Jimmy Justice	Pye	8		L
17	-	A Little Love, A Little Kiss	Karl Denver	Decca	3		
18	2	Wonderful Land	Shadows	Columbia	16		
19	-	Here Comes That Feeling	Brenda Lee	Brunswick	8	(89)	
20	-	Follow That Dream E.P.	Elvis Presley	RCA	6	(15)	

◆ Three years after his first tour was scrapped (following the discovery that he had married his 14-year-old second cousin), Jerry Lee Lewis made a triumphant return to the UK. The piano-pounding performer helped re-awaken interest in wild rock'n'roll and breathed more life into the burgeoning British beat boom.

◆ The Beatles, attrac-ted a record 900 crowd to the Cavern Club after their successful EMI audition. Meanwhile, the Dave Clark Five released their debut single 'That's What I Said'.

◆ Mick Jagger met Brian Jones for the first time at the Ealing Jazz Club and decided to form a group.

July 1962

This Mnth	Prev Mnth	Title	Artist	Label	Wks 20	(US Pos)	
1	12	I Can't Stop Loving You	Ray Charles	HMV	12	(1)	
2	4	A Picture Of You	Joe Brown & The Bruvvers	Piccadilly	14		F
3	2	Come Outside	Mike Sarne & Wendy Richard	Parlophone	14		F
4	-	I Remember You	Frank Ifield	Columbia	19	(5)	F G
5	1	Good Luck Charm	Elvis Presley	RCA	14	(1)	
6	18	Here Comes That Feeling	Brenda Lee	Brunswick	8	(89)	
7	-	English Country Garden	Jimmie Rodgers	Columbia	9		L
8	5	Ginny Come Lately	Brian Hyland	HMV	10	(21)	
9	-	Don't Ever Change	Crickets	Liberty	9		L
10	-	Speedy Gonzales	Pat Boone	London American	12	(6)	
11	-	Our Favourite Melodies	Craig Douglas	Columbia	6		
12	10	The Green Leaves Of Summer	Kenny Ball	Pye Jazz	9	(87)	
13	3	I'm Looking Out The Window	Cliff Richard	Columbia	11		
14	15	Ain't That Funny	Jimmy Justice	Pye	8		L
15	6	Last Night Was Made For Love	Billy Fury	Decca	11		
16	-	Yes My Darling Daughter	Eydie Gorme	CBS	5		F
17	12	Stranger On The Shore	Mr. Acker Bilk	Columbia	33	(1)	G
18	-	Right Said Fred	Bernard Cribbins	Parlophone	6		L
19	19	Follow That Dream E.P.	Elvis Presley	RCA	6	(15)	
20	-	Ya Ya Twist	Petula Clark	Pye	5		

August 1962

This Mnth	Prev Mnth	Title	Artist	Label	Wks 20	(US Pos)	
1	4	I Remember You	Frank Ifield	Columbia	19	(5)	F G
2	10	Speedy Gonzales	Pat Boone	London American	12	(6)	
3	-	Guitar Tango	Shadows	Columbia	10		
4	-	Things	Bobby Darin	London American	12	(3)	
5	1	I Can't Stop Loving You	Ray Charles	HMV	12	(1)	
6	-	Roses Are Red	Ronnie Carroll	Philips	11		
7	2	A Picture Of You	Joe Brown & The Bruvvers	Piccadilly	14		F
8	9	Don't Ever Change	Crickets	Liberty	9		L
9	-	Once Upon A Dream	Billy Fury	Decca	8		
10	-	Little Miss Lonely	Helen Shapiro	Columbia	7		L
11	-	Let There Be Love	Nat 'King' Cole	Capitol	7		
12	-	Breaking Up Is Hard To Do	Neil Sedaka	RCA	11	(1)	
13	-	Sealed With A Kiss	Brian Hyland	HMV	8	(3)	
14	6	Here Comes That Feeling	Brenda Lee	Brunswick	8	(89)	
15	3	Come Outside	Mike Sarne & Wendy Richard	Parlophone	14		F
16	17	Right Said Fred	Bernard Cribbins	Parlophone	6		L
17	-	Roses Are Red (My Love)	Bobby Vinton	Columbia	4	(1)	F
18	-	Vacation	Connie Francis	MGM	4	(9)	L
19	7	English Country Garden	Jimmie Rodgers	Columbia	9		L
20	-	So Do I	Kenny Ball	Pye Jazz	3		

◆ Ringo Starr replaced drummer Pete Best in The Beatles, who recorded their Parlophone debut, 'Love Me Do'. The record, which took 17 takes, was a US No. 1 in 1964 and finally made the UK Top 10 twenty years later! Another group who were to change 1960s music, The Rolling Stones, made their live debut at the Marquee club in London.

◆ Frank Ifield scored the first of three successive No. 1s with 'I Remember You', which spent seven weeks at No. 1 in Britain and sold over a million copies.

1962

This Mnth	Prev Mnth	Title	Artist	Label	Wks	(US 20 Pos)	
1	-	She's Not You	Elvis Presley	RCA	11	(5)	
2	1	I Remember You	Frank Ifield	Columbia	19	(5)	F G
3	6	Roses Are Red	Ronnie Carroll	Philips	11		
4	-	It'll Be Me	Cliff Richard	Columbia	8		
5	4	Things	Bobby Darin	London American	12	(3)	
6	13	Sealed With A Kiss	Brian Hyland	HMV	10	(3)	
7	12	Breaking Up Is Hard To Do	Neil Sedaka	RCA	11	(1)	
8	-	Telstar	Tornados	Decca	19	(1)	F
9	2	Speedy Gonzales	Pat Boone	London American	12	(6)	
10	3	Guitar Tango	Shadows	Columbia	10		
11	-	Don't That Beat All	Adam Faith	Parlophone	8		
12	-	Sheila	Tommy Roe	HMV	11	(1)	F
13	-	The Loco-Motion	Little Eva	London American	12	(1)	F
14	-	Ballad Of Paladin	Duane Eddy	RCA	7	(33)	
15	9	Once Upon A Dream	Billy Fury	Decca	8		
16	-	Pick A Bale Of Cotton	Lonnie Donegan	Pye	5		L
17	-	You Don't Know Me	Ray Charles	HMV	8	(2)	
18	-	Will I What	Mike Sarne	Parlophone	5		L
19	-	Main Title Theme From 'Man With The Golden Arm'	Jet Harris	Decca	6		F
20	5	I Can't Stop Loving You	Ray Charles	HMV	13	(1)	

This Mnth	Prev Mnth	Title	Artist	Label	Wks	(US 20 Pos)	
1	8	Telstar	Tornados	Decca	19	(1)	F
2	12	Sheila	Tommy Roe	HMV	11	(1)	F
3	13	The Loco-Motion	Little Eva	London American	12	(1)	F
4	-	It Might As Well Rain Until September	Carole King	London American	9	(22)	F
5	1	She's Not You	Elvis Presley	RCA	11	(5)	
6	-	Ramblin' Rose	Nat 'King' Cole	Capitol	10	(2)	
7	17	You Don't Know Me	Ray Charles	HMV	8	(2)	
8	4	It'll Be Me	Cliff Richard	Columbia	8		
9	-	What Now My Love	Shirley Bassey	Columbia	8		
10	-	Venus In Blue Jeans	Mark Wynter	Pye	9		F
11	2	I Remember You	Frank Ifield	Columbia	19	(5)	F G
12	11	Don't That Beat All	Adam Faith	Parlophone	8		
13	-	Let's Dance	Chris Montez	London American	13	(4)	F
14	6	Sealed With A Kiss	Brian Hyland	HMV	10	(3)	
15	-	Sherry	Four Seasons	Stateside	10	(1)	F
16	-	Lonely	Acker Bilk	Columbia	5		
17	3	Roses Are Red	Ronnie Carroll	Philips	11		
18	-	Swiss Maid	Del Shannon	London American	12	(64)	
19	-	Lovesick Blues	Frank Ifield	Columbia	14	(44)	
20	5	Things	Bobby Darin	London American	12	(3)	

◆ Despite the fact that their current UK singles failed to enter the US Top 100, American performers Jimmie Rodgers, The Crickets (with a vocal from Glen Campbell), Eydie Gormé and Nat 'King' Cole had major British hits. Also faring far better in Britain were new releases from Brenda Lee, Duane Eddy and Carole King.

◆ Rock'n'roll great Little Richard played his first shows on British shores. He was supported by The Beatles, whom he thought "sounded like a black American act".

November 1962

This Mnth	Prev Mnth	Title	Artist	Label	Wks	(US 20 Pos)	
1	19	Lovesick Blues	Frank Ifield	Columbia	14	(44)	
2	13	Let's Dance	Chris Montez	London American	13	(4)	F
3	1	Telstar	Tornados	Decca	19	(1)	F
4	18	Swiss Maid	Del Shannon	London American	12	(64)	
5	10	Venus In Blue Jeans	Mark Wynter	Pye	9		F
6	3	The Loco-Motion	Little Eva	London American	12	(1)	F
7	-	Bobby's Girl	Susan Maughan	Philips	12		FL
8	15	Sherry	Four Seasons	Stateside	10	(1)	F
9	-	Devil Woman	Marty Robbins	CBS	10	(16)	L
10	6	Ramblin' Rose	Nat 'King' Cole	Capitol	10	(2)	
11	-	No One Can Make My Sunshine Smile	Everly Brothers	Warner	7		
12	4	It Might As Well Rain Until September	Carole King	London American	9	(22)	F
13	2	Sheila	Tommy Roe	HMV	11	(1)	F
14	-	Dance With The Guitar Man	Duane Eddy	RCA	11	(12)	
15	-	Sun Arise	Rolf Harris	Columbia	11	(61)	
16	-	Oh Lonesome Me	Craig Douglas	Decca	4		L
17	9	What Now My Love	Shirley Bassey	Columbia	8		
18	-	Return To Sender	Elvis Presley	RCA	11	(2)	
19	-	A Forever Kind Of Love	Bobby Vee	Liberty	5		
20	-	Kid Galahad E.P.	Elvis Presley	RCA	3		

December 1962

This Mnth	Prev Mnth	Title	Artist	Label	Wks	(US 20 Pos)	
1	18	Return To Sender	Elvis Presley	RCA	11	(2)	
2	1	Lovesick Blues	Frank Ifield	Columbia	14	(44)	
3	15	Sun Arise	Rolf Harris	Columbia	11	(61)	
4	-	The Next Time	Cliff Richard	Columbia	12		
5	14	Dance With The Guitar Man	Duane Eddy	RCA	11	(12)	
6	2	Let's Dance	Chris Montez	London American	13	(4)	F
7	7	Bobby's Girl	Susan Maughan	Philips	12		FL
8	4	Swiss Maid	Del Shannon	London American	12	(64)	
9	-	Rockin' Around The Christmas Tree	Brenda Lee	Brunswick	4	(14)	
10	3	Telstar	Tornados	Decca	19	(1)	F
11	-	Dance On	Shadows	Columbia	10		
12	-	Bachelor Boy	Cliff Richard	Columbia	12	(99)	
13	-	It Only Took A Minute	Joe Brown & The Bruvvers	Piccadilly	8		
14	9	Devil Woman	Marty Robbins	CBS	10	(16)	L
15	-	The Main Attraction	Pat Boone	London American	5		L
16	8	Sherry	Four Seasons	Stateside	10	(1)	F
17	-	Your Cheatin' Heart	Ray Charles	HMV	4	(29)	
18	-	Up On The Roof	Kenny Lynch	HMV	7		F
19	5	Venus In Blue Jeans	Mark Wynter	Pye	9		F
20	19	A Forever Kind Of Love	Bobby Vee	Liberty	5		

◆ Big winners at the *NME* poll were Elvis, Brenda Lee and The Everly Brothers, with The Beatles being voted 8th most popular British group.

◆ The first British group to top the American charts were instrumental combo The Tornados with 'Telstar'. The record's producer/composer, Joe Meek, earlier turned down a chance to work with The Beatles.

1963

This Mnth	Prev Mnth	Title	Artist	Label	Wks	(US 20 Pos)	
1	11	Dance On	Shadows	Columbia	10		
2	1	Return To Sender	Elvis Presley	RCA	11	(2)	
3	4	The Next Time	Cliff Richard	Columbia	12		
4	12	Bachelor Boy	Cliff Richard	Columbia	12	(99)	
5	5	Dance With The Guitar Man	Duane Eddy	RCA	11	(12)	
6	-	Like I Do	Maureen Evans	Oriole	9		F L
7	3	Sun Arise	Rolf Harris	Columbia	11	(61)	
8	2	Lovesick Blues	Frank Ifield	Columbia	14	(44)	
9	-	Globetrotter	Tornados	Decca	8		
10	-	Diamonds	Jet Harris & Tony Meehan	Decca	10		F
11	-	Go Away Little Girl	Mark Wynter	Pye	7		
12	18	Up On The Roof	Kenny Lynch	HMV	7		F
13	10	Telstar	Tornados	Decca	19	(1)	F
14	-	Coming Home Baby	Mel Tormé	London American	4	(36)	L
15	13	It Only Took A Minute	Joe Brown & The Bruvvers	Piccadilly	8		
16	7	Bobby's Girl	Susan Maughan	Philips	12		F L
17	-	Don't You Think It's Time	Mike Berry	HMV	7		F
18	6	Let's Dance	Chris Montez	London American	13	(4)	F
19	-	Little Town Flirt	Del Shannon	London American	8	(12)	
20	-	Desafinado	Stan Getz & Charlie Byrd	HMV	5	(15)	F L

This Mnth	Prev Mnth	Title	Artist	Label	Wks	(US 20 Pos)	
1	10	Diamonds	Jet Harris & Tony Meehan	Decca	10		F
2	-	Wayward Wind	Frank Ifield	Columbia	10		
3	19	Little Town Flirt	Del Shannon	London American	8	(12)	
4	-	Please Please Me	Beatles	Parlophone	10	(3)	F
5	9	Globetrotter	Tornados	Decca	8		
6	4	Bachelor Boy	Cliff Richard	Columbia	12	(99)	
7	-	Loop De Loop	Frankie Vaughan	Philips	8		
8	17	Don't You Think It's Time	Mike Berry	HMV	7		F
9	-	The Night Has A Thousand Eyes	Bobby Vee	Liberty	8	(3)	L
10	-	All Alone Am I	Brenda Lee	Brunswick	7	(3)	
11	-	Island Of Dreams	Springfields	Philips	12		F
12	6	Like I Do	Maureen Evans	Oriole	9		F L
13	1	Dance On	Shadows	Columbia	10		
14	3	The Next Time	Cliff Richard	Columbia	12		
15	-	Sukiyaki	Kenny Ball	Pye Jazz	5		
16	-	Walk Right In	Rooftop Singers	Fontana	5	(1)	F L
17	-	That's What Love Will Do	Joe Brown & The Bruvvers	Piccadilly	9		L
18	-	Big Girls Don't Cry	Four Seasons	Stateside	5	(1)	
19	2	Return To Sender	Elvis Presley	RCA	11	(2)	
20	-	Summer Holiday	Cliff Richard	Columbia	11		

◆ The Beatles' second single 'Please Please Me' topped the chart. It put Merseybeat on the musical map and launched the Beat Boom. In America it was rush released but failed to click.

◆ Rock instrumentals reached new heights in February when records by (ex-Shadows) Jet Harris & Tony Meehan, The Tornados and The Shadows took the top three spots.

March 1963

This Mnth	Prev Mnth	Title	Artist	Label	Wks	(US 20 Pos)	
1	20	Summer Holiday	Cliff Richard	Columbia	11		
2	4	Please Please Me	Beatles	Parlophone	10	(3)	F
3	-	Like I've Never Been Gone	Billy Fury	Decca	10		
4	17	That's What Love Will Do	Joe Brown & The Bruvvers	Piccadilly	9		L
5	9	The Night Has A Thousand Eyes	Bobby Vee	Liberty	8	(3)	L
6	-	Foot Tapper	Shadows	Columbia	9		
7	11	Island Of Dreams	Springfields	Philips	12		F
8	2	Wayward Wind	Frank Ifield	Columbia	10		
9	-	Charmaine	Bachelors	Decca	9		F
10	-	One Broken Heart For Sale	Elvis Presley	RCA	5	(11)	
11	7	Loop De Loop	Frankie Vaughan	Philips	8		
12	-	Hey Paula	Paul & Paula	Philips	7	(1)	F
13	-	From A Jack To A King	Ned Miller	London American	12	(6)	F L
14	-	Tell Him	Billie Davis	Decca	5		F L
15	1	Diamonds	Jet Harris & Tony Meehan	Decca	10		F
16	-	Say Wonderful Things	Ronnie Carroll	Philips	8	(91)	L
17	-	Rhythm Of The Rain	Cascades	Warner	10	(3)	F L
18	-	How Do You Do It?	Gerry & The Pacemakers	Columbia	11	(9)	F
19	-	Brown Eyed Handsome Man	Buddy Holly	Coral	10		
20	16	Walk Right In	Rooftop Singers	Fontana	5	(1)	F L

April 1963

This Mnth	Prev Mnth	Title	Artist	Label	Wks	(US 20 Pos)	
1	18	How Do You Do It?	Gerry & The Pacemakers	Columbia	11	(9)	F
2	13	From A Jack To A King	Ned Miller	London American	12	(6)	F L
3	6	Foot Tapper	Shadows	Columbia	9		
4	19	Brown Eyed Handsome Man	Buddy Holly	Coral	10		
5	17	Rhythm Of The Rain	Cascades	Warner	10	(3)	F L
6	-	Say I Won't Be There	Springfields	Philips	8		L
7	16	Say Wonderful Things	Ronnie Carroll	Philips	8	(91)	L
8	1	Summer Holiday	Cliff Richard	Columbia	11		
9	-	The Folk Singer	Tommy Roe	HMV	7	(84)	
10	-	Nobody's Darlin' But Mine	Frank Ifield	Columbia	8		
11	-	From Me To You	Beatles	Parlophone	15	(41)	
12	3	Like I've Never Been Gone	Billy Fury	Decca	10		
13	-	In Dreams	Roy Orbison	London American	13	(7)	
14	9	Charmaine	Bachelors	Decca	9		F
15	-	Walk Like A Man	Four Seasons	Stateside	6	(1)	
16	-	Can't Get Used To Losing You	Andy Williams	CBS	10	(2)	
17	7	Island Of Dreams	Springfields	Philips	12		F
18	-	Robot	Tornados	Decca	5		
19	4	That's What Love Will Do	Joe Brown & The Bruvvers	Piccadilly	9		L
20	-	Let's Turkey Trot	Little Eva	London American	6	(20)	

◆ The Scopitone video juke box was launched – it cost 5p a play to see acts like Craig Douglas and The Mudlarks – it proved to be a five minute wonder.
◆ Word came from Australia that The Bee Gees, an Everly Brothers influenced act, who originally hailed from Manchester, had signed with Festival Records. After making a name for themselves down under they became superstars later in the decade.
◆ The Beatles' manager Brian Epstein also looked after Billy J. Kramer & The Dakotas who had two successive No. 1s and Gerry & The Pacemakers who achieved three.

1963

May 1963

This Mnth	Prev Mnth	Title	Artist	Label	Wks	(US 20 Pos)	
1	11	From Me To You	Beatles	Parlophone	15	(41)	
2	-	Scarlett O'Hara	Jet Harris & Tony Meehan	Decca	11		
3	16	Can't Get Used To Losing You	Andy Williams	CBS	10	(2)	
4	1	How Do You Do It?	Gerry & The Pacemakers	Columbia	11	(9)	F
5	13	In Dreams	Roy Orbison	London American	13	(7)	
6	10	Nobody's Darlin' But Mine	Frank Ifield	Columbia	8		
7	-	Do You Want To Know A Secret	Billy J. Kramer & The Dakotas	Parlophone	10		F
8	-	Two Kinds Of Teardrops	Del Shannon	London American	8	(50)	
9	-	Lucky Lips	Cliff Richard	Columbia	9	(62)	
10	2	From A Jack To A King	Ned Miller	London American	12	(6)	F L
11	-	Losing You	Brenda Lee	Brunswick	9	(6)	
12	6	Say I Won't Be There	Springfields	Philips	8		L
13	-	He's So Fine	Chiffons	Stateside	5	(1)	F
14	-	Deck Of Cards	Wink Martindale	London American	15		L
15	-	When Will You Say I Love You	Billy Fury	Decca	7		
16	-	Young Lovers	Paul & Paula	Philips	6	(6)	L
17	5	Rhythm Of The Rain	Cascades	Warner	10	(3)	F L
18	-	Take These Chains From My Heart	Ray Charles	HMV	13	(8)	
19	4	Brown Eyed Handsome Man	Buddy Holly	Coral	10		
20	9	The Folk Singer	Tommy Roe	HMV	7	(84)	

June 1963

This Mnth	Prev Mnth	Title	Artist	Label	Wks	(US 20 Pos)	
1	-	I Like It	Gerry & The Pacemakers	Columbia	12	(17)	
2	7	Do You Want To Know A Secret	Billy J. Kramer & The Dakotas	Parlophone	10		F
3	1	From Me To You	Beatles	Parlophone	15	(41)	
4	18	Take These Chains From My Heart	Ray Charles	HMV	13	(8)	
5	-	If You Gotta Make A Fool Of Somebody	Freddie & The Dreamers	Columbia	9		F
6	-	Atlantis	Shadows	Columbia	11		
7	15	When Will You Say I Love You	Billy Fury	Decca	7		
8	14	Deck Of Cards	Wink Martindale	London American	15		L
9	2	Scarlett O'Hara	Jet Harris & Tony Meehan	Decca	11		
10	9	Lucky Lips	Cliff Richard	Columbia	9	(62)	
11	-	Falling	Roy Orbison	London American	8	(22)	
12	5	In Dreams	Roy Orbison	London American	13	(7)	
13	-	Bo Diddley	Buddy Holly	Coral	8		
14	8	Two Kinds Of Teardrops	Del Shannon	London American	8	(50)	
15	16	Young Lovers	Paul & Paula	Philips	6	(6)	L
16	-	Da Doo Ron Ron	Crystals	London American	10	(3)	
17	-	The Ice Cream Man	Tornados	Decca	4		L
18	-	It's My Party	Lesley Gore	Mercury	8	(1)	F
19	-	Forget Him	Bobby Rydell	Cameo Parkway	9	(4)	L
20	-	Confessin'	Frank Ifield	Columbia	11	(58)	

◆ Early examples of R&B covers in the "Beat Boom" included Freddie & The Dreamers' 'If You Gotta Make a Fool Of Somebody' and The Rolling Stones' version of Chuck Berry's 'Come On'. The late Buddy Holly hit the Top 5 with revivals of Chuck's 'Brown Eyed Handsome Man' and Bo Diddley's eponymous song, while in America The Beach Boys turned Berry's 'Sweet Little 16' into 'Surfin' USA' and Lonnie Mack charted with Chuck's 'Memphis'.

July 1963

This Mnth	Prev Mnth	Title	Artist	Label	Wks	(US 20 Pos)	
1	20	Confessin'	Frank Ifield	Columbia	11	(58)	
2	1	I Like It	Gerry & The Pacemakers	Columbia	12	(17)	
3	6	Atlantis	Shadows	Columbia	11		
4	-	Devil In Disguise	Elvis Presley	RCA	8	(3)	
5	16	Da Doo Ron Ron	Crystals	London American	10	(3)	
6	4	Take These Chains From My Heart	Ray Charles	HMV	13	(8)	
7	-	Sweets For My Sweet	Searchers	Pye	10		F
8	8	Deck Of Cards	Wink Martindale	London American	15		L
9	-	Welcome To My World	Jim Reeves	RCA	9		
10	18	It's My Party	Lesley Gore	Mercury	8	(1)	F
11	-	Twist And Shout	Brian Poole & The Tremeloes	Decca	9		F
12	13	Bo Diddley	Buddy Holly	Coral	8		
13	5	If You Gotta Make A Fool Of Somebody	Freddie & The Dreamers	Columbia	9		F
14	3	From Me To You	Beatles	Parlophone	15	(41)	
15	11	Falling	Roy Orbison	London American	8	(22)	
16	-	Twist And Shout E.P.	Beatles	Parlophone	15	(2)	
17	-	Sukiyaki	Kyu Sakamoto	HMV	9	(1)	F L
18	2	Do You Want To Know A Secret	Billy J. Kramer & The Dakotas	Parlophone	10		F
19	19	Forget Him	Bobby Rydell	Cameo Parkway	9	(4)	L
20	-	You Can Never Stop Me Loving You	Kenny Lynch	HMV	6		L

August 1963

This Mnth	Prev Mnth	Title	Artist	Label	Wks	(US 20 Pos)	
1	7	Sweets For My Sweet	Searchers	Pye	10		F
2	1	Confessin'	Frank Ifield	Columbia	11	(58)	
3	16	Twist And Shout E.P.	Beatles	Parlophone	15	(2)	
4	-	Bad To Me	Billy J. Kramer & The Dakotas	Parlophone	10	(9)	
5	11	Twist And Shout	Brian Poole & The Tremeloes	Decca	9		F
6	-	In Summer	Billy Fury	Decca	8		
7	4	Devil In Disguise	Elvis Presley	RCA	8	(3)	
8	-	Wipe Out	Surfaris	London American	8	(2)	F L
9	-	I'm Telling You Now	Freddie & The Dreamers	Columbia	7	(1)	
10	-	Theme From 'The Legion's Last Patrol'	Ken Thorne & His Orchestra	HMV	10		F L
11	5	Da Doo Ron Ron	Crystals	London American	10	(3)	
12	17	Sukiyaki	Kyu Sakamoto	HMV	9	(1)	F L
13	-	I'll Never Get Over You	Johnny Kidd & The Pirates	HMV	10		L
14	-	It's All In The Game	Cliff Richard	Columbia	9	(25)	
15	3	Atlantis	Shadows	Columbia	11		
16	-	You Don't Have To Be A Baby To Cry	Caravelles	Decca	7	(3)	F L
17	2	I Like It	Gerry & The Pacemakers	Columbia	12	(17)	
18	-	She Loves You	Beatles	Parlophone	24	(1)	G
19	6	Take These Chains From My Heart	Ray Charles	HMV	13	(8)	
20	20	You Can Never Stop Me Loving You	Kenny Lynch	HMV	6		L

◆ The Beatles' debut LP **Please Please Me** topped the chart for 30 weeks and the single 'She Loves You', which had record advance orders and sold over a million in the UK, cemented their position as Britain's top group.

◆ *Ready Steady Go* was launched – it was the British pop TV show which best reflected the times. Early guests included the Rolling Stones.

September 1963

This Mnth	Prev Mnth	Title	Artist	Label	Wks 20	(US Pos)	
1	18	She Loves You	Beatles	Parlophone	24	(1)	G
2	14	It's All In The Game	Cliff Richard	Columbia	9	(25)	
3	4	Bad To Me	Billy J. Kramer & The Dakotas	Parlophone	10	(9)	
4	-	I Want To Stay Here	Steve Lawrence & Eydie Gormé	CBS	8	(28)	L
5	13	I'll Never Get Over You	Johnny Kidd & The Pirates	HMV	10		L
6	9	I'm Telling You Now	Freddie & The Dreamers	Columbia	7	(1)	
7	-	Just Like Eddie	Heinz	Decca	10		F
8	16	You Don't Have To Be A Baby To Cry	Caravelles	Decca	7	(3)	F L
9	-	Applejack	Jet Harris & Tony Meehan	Decca	8		L
10	-	Do You Love Me	Brian Poole & The Tremeloes	Decca	11		
11	10	Theme From 'The Legion's Last Patrol'	Ken Thorne & His Orchestra	HMV	10		F L
12	8	Wipe Out	Surfaris	London American	8	(2)	F L
13	-	Then He Kissed Me	Crystals	London American	10	(6)	
14	-	If I Had A Hammer	Trini Lopez	Reprise	10	(3)	F L
15	1	Sweets For My Sweet	Searchers	Pye	10		F
16	-	Still	Karl Denver	Decca	6		L
17	3	Twist And Shout E.P.	Beatles	Parlophone	15	(2)	
18	-	Dance On	Kathy Kirby	Decca	5		F
19	-	Shindig	Shadows	Columbia	7		
20	-	Wishing	Buddy Holly	Coral	5		L

October 1963

This Mnth	Prev Mnth	Title	Artist	Label	Wks 20	(US Pos)	
1	10	Do You Love Me	Brian Poole & The Tremeloes	Decca	11		
2	13	Then He Kissed Me	Crystals	London American	10	(6)	
3	1	She Loves You	Beatles	Parlophone	24	(1)	G
4	14	If I Had A Hammer	Trini Lopez	Reprise	10	(3)	F L
5	-	Blue Bayou	Roy Orbison	London American	10	(29)	
6	-	The First Time	Adam Faith	Parlophone	8		
7	-	You'll Never Walk Alone	Gerry & The Pacemakers	Columbia	15	(48)	
8	19	Shindig	Shadows	Columbia	7		
9	-	I (Who Have Nothing)	Shirley Bassey	Columbia	9		
10	9	Applejack	Jet Harris & Tony Meehan	Decca	8		L
11	17	Twist And Shout E.P.	Beatles	Parlophone	15	(2)	
12	2	It's All In The Game	Cliff Richard	Columbia	9	(25)	
13	7	Just Like Eddie	Heinz	Decca	10		F
14	-	Hello Little Girl	Fourmost	Parlophone	6		F
15	4	I Want To Stay Here	Steve Lawrence & Eydie Gormé	CBS	8	(28)	L
16	-	Ain't Gonna Kiss Ya (E.P.)	Searchers	Pye	4		
17	-	Searchin'	Hollies	Parlophone	4		F
18	-	Everybody	Tommy Roe	HMV	4	(3)	
19	-	Memphis Tennessee	Chuck Berry	Pye International	7		
20	-	Be My Baby	Ronettes	London American	7	(2)	F

◆ Eric Clapton and Tom McGuinness (later of Manfred Mann) joined Casey Jones & The Engineers, and John Mayall launched The Bluesbreakers which included John McVie (later a founder of Fleetwood Mac.)

◆ As the year ended, The Beatles had five records in the Top 20 singles (including 2 EPs and an album) and the top two albums. The LP **With The Beatles** entered at No. 1 as did 'I Want To Hold Your Hand', which smashed all UK sales records, selling a million copies in three days. A big US launch was planned for early 1964.

November 1963

This Mnth	Prev Mnth	Title	Artist	Label	Wks (US 20 Pos)	
1	3	She Loves You	Beatles	Parlophone	24 (1)	G
2	7	You'll Never Walk Alone	Gerry & The Pacemakers	Columbia	15 (48)	
3	-	Sugar And Spice	Searchers	Pye	7 (44)	
4	20	Be My Baby	Ronettes	London American	7 (2)	F
5	9	I (Who Have Nothing)	Shirley Bassey	Columbia	9	
6	5	Blue Bayou	Roy Orbison	London American	10 (29)	
7	-	Don't Talk To Him	Cliff Richard	Columbia	10	
8	-	Secret Love	Kathy Kirby	Decca	12	
9	19	Memphis Tennessee	Chuck Berry	Pye International	7	
10	1	Do You Love Me	Brian Poole & The Tremeloes	Decca	11	
11	-	I'll Keep You Satisfied	Billy J. Kramer & The Dakotas	Parlophone	6 (30)	
12	-	You Were Made For Me	Freddie & The Dreamers	Columbia	11 (21)	
13	2	Then He Kissed Me	Crystals	London American	10 (6)	
14	-	Maria Elena	Los Indios Tabajaras	RCA	12 (6)	F L
15	-	Fools Rush In	Rick Nelson	London American	5 (12)	
16	6	The First Time	Adam Faith	Parlophone	8	
17	4	If I Had A Hammer	Trini Lopez	Reprise	10 (3)	F L
18	-	Blowin' In The Wind	Peter, Paul & Mary	Warner	5 (2)	F
19	-	It's Almost Tomorrow	Mark Wynter	Pye	6	L
20	-	I Only Want To Be With You	Dusty Springfield	Philips	14 (12)	F

December 1963

This Mnth	Prev Mnth	Title	Artist	Label	Wks (US 20 Pos)	
1	-	I Want To Hold Your Hand	Beatles	Parlophone	13 (1)	G
2	1	She Loves You	Beatles	Parlophone	24 (1)	G
3	8	Secret Love	Kathy Kirby	Decca	12	
4	-	Glad All Over	Dave Clark Five	Columbia	14 (6)	F
5	12	You Were Made For Me	Freddie & The Dreamers	Columbia	11 (21)	
6	7	Don't Talk To Him	Cliff Richard	Columbia	10	
7	20	I Only Want To Be With You	Dusty Springfield	Philips	14 (12)	F
8	-	Dominique	Singing Nun	Philips	8 (1)	FL
9	14	Maria Elena	Los Indios Tabajaras	RCA	12 (6)	FL
10	-	Twenty Four Hours From Tulsa	Gene Pitney	UA	13 (17F
11	11	I'll Keep You Satisfied	Billy J. Kramer & The Dakotas	Parlophone	6 (30)	
12	-	Twist And Shout (E.P.)	Beatles	Parlophone	15 (2)	
13	2	You'll Never Walk Alone	Gerry & The Pacemakers	Columbia	15 (48)	
14	-	Geronimo	Shadows	Columbia	6	
15	-	With The Beatles L.P.	Beatles	Parlophone	5	
16	-	Swinging On A Star	Big Dee Irwin	Colpix	10 (38)	FL
17	-	I Wanna Be Your Man	Rolling Stones	Decca	8	
18	19	It's Almost Tomorrow	Mark Wynter	Pye	6	L
19	-	All I Want For Christmas Is A Beatle	Dora Bryan	Fontana	3	FL
20	4	Be My Baby	Ronettes	London American	7 (2)	F

◆ For the first time, British acts, The Beatles and Cliff Richard (who had been voted Most Promising Male Singer in the top US teen magazine, 16), won awards in the World section of the NME readers poll.

◆ UK acts scoring with US songs included Brian Poole & The Tremeloes, Gerry & The Pacemakers, Cliff Richard, Shirley Bassey, Kathy Kirby, Mark Wynter, The Hollies, The Searchers ('Ain't Gonna Kiss Ya') and The Beatles ('Twist And Shout').

1964

This Mnth	Prev Mnth	Title	Artist	Label	Wks (US 20 Pos)	
1	4	Glad All Over	Dave Clark Five	Columbia	14 (6)	F
2	1	I Want To Hold Your Hand	Beatles	Parlophone	13 (1)	G
3	7	I Only Want To Be With You	Dusty Springfield	Philips	14 (12)	F
4	-	Hippy Hippy Shake	Swinging Blue Jeans	HMV	10 (24)	F
5	2	She Loves You	Beatles	Parlophone	24 (1)	G
6	10	Twenty Four Hours From Tulsa	Gene Pitney	UA	13 (17)	F
7	16	Swinging On A Star	Big Dee Irwin	Colpix	10 (38)	F
8	5	You Were Made For Me	Freddie & The Dreamers	Columbia	11 (21)	
9	8	Dominique	Singing Nun	Philips	8 (1)	F
10	-	Stay	Hollies	Parlophone	7	
11	3	Secret Love	Kathy Kirby	Decca	12	
12	9	Maria Elena	Los Indios Tabajaras	RCA	12 (6)	F
13	17	I Wanna Be Your Man	Rolling Stones	Decca	8	
14	-	Kiss Me Quick	Elvis Presley	RCA	6 (34)	
15	-	We Are In Love	Adam Faith	Parlophone	6	
16	6	Don't Talk To Him	Cliff Richard	Columbia	10	
17	-	As Usual	Brenda Lee	Brunswick	10 (12)	
18	-	Needles And Pins	Searchers	Pye	9 (13)	
19	14	Geronimo	Shadows	Columbia	6	
20	-	I'm The One	Gerry & The Pacemakers	Columbia	9 (82)	

1	18	Needles And Pins	Searchers	Pye	9 (13)	
2	20	I'm The One	Gerry & The Pacemakers	Columbia	9 (82)	
3	4	Hippy Hippy Shake	Swinging Blue Jeans	HMV	10 (24)	F
4	-	Diane	Bachelors	Decca	11 (10)	
5	1	Glad All Over	Dave Clark Five	Columbia	14 (6)	F
6	17	As Usual	Brenda Lee	Brunswick	10 (12)	
7	-	5-4-3-2-1	Manfred Mann	HMV	7	F
8	-	Don't Blame Me	Frank Ifield	Columbia	7	L
9	-	Anyone Who Had A Heart	Cilla Black	Parlophone	11	F
10	-	I Think Of You	Merseybeats	Fontana	11	F
11	6	Twenty Four Hours From Tulsa	Gene Pitney	UA	13 (17)	F
12	2	I Want To Hold Your Hand	Beatles	Parlophone	13 (1)	G
13	-	Baby I Love You	Ronettes	London American	7 (24)	L
14	3	I Only Want To Be With You	Dusty Springfield	Philips	14 (12)	F
15	-	I'm The Lonely One	Cliff Richard	Columbia	4 (92)	
16	10	Stay	Hollies	Parlophone	7	
17	-	Bits And Pieces	Dave Clark Five	Columbia	9 (4)	
18	-	Candy Man	Brian Poole & The Tremeloes	Decca	6	
19	-	For You	Rick Nelson	Brunswick	4 (6)	L
20	7	Swinging On A Star	Big Dee Irwin	Colpix	10 (38)	F L

◆ *Top Of The Pops* was launched. The TV show based on the Top 20 chart is still running thirty years later. Soon afterwards the first pirate radio station Radio Caroline started broadcasting from a ship in the North Sea.

◆ The Dave Clark Five's 'Bits And Pieces' had 250,000 advance orders and The Beatles 'Can't Buy Me Love' piled up record UK advance orders of over a million.

1964

March 1964

This Mnth	Prev Mnth	Title	Artist	Label	Wks	(US 20 Pos)	
1	9	Anyone Who Had A Heart	Cilla Black	Parlophone	11		F
2	17	Bits And Pieces	Dave Clark Five	Columbia	9	(4)	
3	-	Little Children	Billy J. Kramer & The Dakotas	Parlophone	9	(7)	
4	-	Not Fade Away	Rolling Stones	Decca	9	(48)	
5	4	Diane	Bachelors	Decca	11	(10)	
6	-	Just One Look	Hollies	Parlophone	9	(44)	
7	10	I Think Of You	Merseybeats	Fontana	11		F
8	-	Boys Cry	Eden Kane	Fontana	7		L
9	1	Needles And Pins	Searchers	Pye	9	(13)	
10	-	I Love You Because	Jim Reeves	RCA	26		
11	18	Candy Man	Brian Poole & The Tremeloes	Decca	6		
12	-	Let Me Go, Lover	Kathy Kirby	Decca	6		
13	-	That Girl Belongs To Yesterday	Gene Pitney	UA	7	(49)	
14	2	I'm The One	Gerry & The Pacemakers	Columbia	9	(82)	
15	-	Stay Awhile	Dusty Springfield	Philips	6	(38)	
16	-	Over You	Freddie & The Dreamers	Columbia	5		
17	6	As Usual	Brenda Lee	Brunswick	10	(12)	
18	-	Can't Buy Me Love	Beatles	Parlophone	9	(1)	G
19	7	5-4-3-2-1	Manfred Mann	HMV	7		F
20	-	Theme For Young Lovers	Shadows	Columbia	6		

April 1964

This Mnth	Prev Mnth	Title	Artist	Label	Wks	(US 20 Pos)	
1	18	Can't Buy Me Love	Beatles	Parlophone	9	(1)	G
2	-	I Believe	Bachelors	Decca	11	(33)	
3	3	Little Children	Billy J. Kramer & The Dakotas	Parlophone	9	(7)	
4	-	A World Without Love	Peter & Gordon	Columbia	9	(1)	F
5	10	I Love You Because	Jim Reeves	RCA	26		
6	6	Just One Look	Hollies	Parlophone	9	(44)	
7	4	Not Fade Away	Rolling Stones	Decca	9	(48)	
8	-	Tell Me When	Applejacks	Decca	8		F
9	13	That Girl Belongs To Yesterday	Gene Pitney	UA	7	(49)	
10	-	My Boy Lollipop	Millie	Fontana	10	(2)	F L
11	2	Bits And Pieces	Dave Clark Five	Columbia	9	(4)	
12	1	Anyone Who Had A Heart	Cilla Black	Parlophone	11		F
13	5	Diane	Bachelors	Decca	11	(10)	
14	-	Good Golly Miss Molly	Swinging Blue Jeans	HMV	5	(43)	
15	-	Move Over Darling	Doris Day	CBS	8		L
16	-	Everything's Alright	Mojos	Decca	6		F L
17	20	Theme For Young Lovers	Shadows	Columbia	6		
18	-	Don't Throw Your Love Away	Searchers	Pye	8	(16)	
19	-	Mockingbird Hill	Migil Five	Pye	6		F L
20	-	Viva Las Vegas	Elvis Presley	RCA	4	(29)	

◆ Blue beat was in with 'Madness' (Prince Buster) and 'Oh Carolina' (Folkes Brothers) selling well. A top 1980s band named themselves after the first track and the latter was a No. 1 in 1993 for Shaggy.

◆ Mods and Rockers clashed on British beaches, teenagers and drugs were linked for the first time in the press and the first drug-related British records, Mickey Finn's 'Pills' and 'Purple Pill Eater' by The Wild Ones, were released.

1964

This Mnth	Prev Mnth	Title	Artist	Label	Wks	(US 20 Pos)	
1	18	Don't Throw Your Love Away	Searchers	Pye	8	(16)	
2	10	My Boy Lollipop	Millie	Fontana	10	(2)	F L
3	-	Juliet	Four Pennies	Philips	10		F
4	2	I Believe	Bachelors	Decca	11	(33)	
5	4	A World Without Love	Peter & Gordon	Columbia	9	(1)	F
6	-	Don't Let The Sun Catch You Crying	Gerry & The Pacemakers	Columbia	6	(4)	
7	5	I Love You Because	Jim Reeves	RCA	26		
8	-	It's Over	Roy Orbison	London American	14	(9)	
9	-	A Little Loving	Fourmost	Parlophone	8		L
10	-	Walk On By	Dionne Warwick	Pye International	9	(6)	F
11	-	Constantly	Cliff Richard	Columbia	8		
12	-	You're My World	Cilla Black	Parlophone	10	(26)	
13	1	Can't Buy Me Love	Beatles	Parlophone	9	(1)	G
14	15	Move Over Darling	Doris Day	CBS	8		L
15	19	Mockingbird Hill	Migil Five	Pye	6		F L
16	-	Don't Turn Around	Merseybeats	Fontana	5		
17	-	The Rise & Fall Of Flingel Bunt	Shadows	Columbia	8		
18	16	Everything's Alright	Mojos	Decca	6		F L
19	-	I Will	Billy Fury	Decca	6		
20	-	Hubble Bubble Toil And Trouble	Manfred Mann	HMV	4		

This	Prev	Title	Artist	Label	Wks	(Pos)	
1	12	You're My World	Cilla Black	Parlophone	10	(26)	
2	8	It's Over	Roy Orbison	London American	14	(9)	
3	-	Someone Someone	Brian Poole & The Tremeloes	Decca	11	(97)	
4	-	No Particular Place To Go	Chuck Berry	Pye International	7	(10)	
5	-	Here I Go Again	Hollies	Parlophone	7		
6	-	My Guy	Mary Wells	Stateside	8	(1)	F
7	17	The Rise & Fall Of Flingel Bunt	Shadows	Columbia	8		
8	11	Constantly	Cliff Richard	Columbia	8		
9	3	Juliet	Four Pennies	Philips	10		F
10	-	Shout	Lulu	Decca	7	(94)	F
11	-	Hello, Dolly!	Louis Armstrong	London American	8	(1)	
12	-	Can't You See That She's Mine	Dave Clark Five	Columbia	6	(4)	
13	7	I Love You Because	Jim Reeves	RCA	26		
14	-	Ramona	Bachelors	Decca	8		
15	10	Walk On By	Dionne Warwick	Pye International	9	(6)	F
16	9	A Little Loving	Fourmost	Parlophone	8		L
17	2	My Boy Lollipop	Millie	Fontana	10	(2)	F L
18	-	You're No Good	Swinging Blue Jeans	HMV	8	(97)	L
19	-	Nobody I Know	Peter & Gordon	Columbia	5	(12)	
20	-	Non Ho L'Eta Per Amarti	Gigliola Cinquetti	Decca	4		F

◆ The Rolling Stones' eponymous debut album knocked The Beatles off the top after 51 consecutive weeks at the top.

◆ Peter & Gordon's 'World Without Love' was the eighth Lennon & McCartney song to top the UK chart in 14 months, and their fifth in the USA in less than five months.

◆ Mary Wells's last recording for Motown, 'My Guy', gave the label their first major transatlantic hit.

◆ Irish trio The Bachelors had two singles in the UK Top 10 while The Beatles had nine in the equivalent Canadian chart!

July 1964

This Mnth	Prev Mnth	Title	Artist	Label	Wks	(US 20 Pos)	
1	-	House Of The Rising Sun	Animals	Columbia	7	(1)	F
2	-	Hold Me	P.J. Proby	Decca	8	(70)	F
3	2	It's Over	Roy Orbison	London American	14	(9)	
4	-	It's All Over Now	Rolling Stones	Decca	11	(26)	
5	-	I Won't Forget You	Jim Reeves	RCA	19	(93)	
6	3	Someone Someone	Brian Poole & The Tremeloes	Decca	11	(97)	
7	18	You're No Good	Swinging Blue Jeans	HMV	8	(97)	L
8	14	Ramona	Bachelors	Decca	8		
9	-	A Hard Day's Night	Beatles	Parlophone	11	(1)	
10	11	Hello, Dolly!	Louis Armstrong	London American	8	(1)	
11	-	I Just Don't Know What To Do With Myself	Dusty Springfield	Philips	9		
12	-	On The Beach	Cliff Richard	Columbia	8		
13	-	Kissin' Cousins	Elvis Presley	RCA	6	(12)	
14	6	My Guy	Mary Wells	Stateside	8	(1)	F
15	19	Nobody I Know	Peter & Gordon	Columbia	5	(12)	
16	12	Can't You See That She's Mine	Dave Clark Five	Columbia	6	(4)	
17	1	You're My World	Cilla Black	Parlophone	10	(26)	
18	-	Call Up The Groups	Barron Knights	Columbia	9		F
19	10	Shout	Lulu	Decca	7	(94)	F
20	-	Do Wah Diddy Diddy	Manfred Mann	HMV	10	(1)	

August 1964

This Mnth	Prev Mnth	Title	Artist	Label	Wks	(US 20 Pos)	
1	9	A Hard Day's Night	Beatles	Parlophone	11	(1)	
2	20	Do Wah Diddy Diddy	Manfred Mann	HMV	10	(1)	
3	18	Call Up The Groups	Barron Knights	Columbia	9		F
4	4	It's All Over Now	Rolling Stones	Decca	11	(26)	
5	5	I Won't Forget You	Jim Reeves	RCA	19	(93)	
6	-	Tobacco Road	Nashville Teens	Decca	8	(14)	F
7	11	I Just Don't Know What To Do With Myself	Dusty Springfield	Philips	9		
8	-	I Get Around	Beach Boys	Capitol	8	(1)	F
9	12	On The Beach	Cliff Richard	Columbia	8		
10	-	Have I The Right?	Honeycombs	Pye	11	(5)	F
11	-	It's Only Make Believe	Billy Fury	Decca	5		
12	1	House Of The Rising Sun	Animals	Columbia	7	(1)	F
13	-	From A Window	Billy J. Kramer & The Dakotas	Parlophone	4	(23)	
14	-	Someday We're Gonna Love Again	Searchers	Pye	5	(34)	
15	2	Hold Me	P.J. Proby	Decca	8	(70)	F
16	-	It's For You	Cilla Black	Parlophone	6	(79)	
17	-	Wishin' And Hopin'	Merseybeats	Fontana	6		
18	-	You Really Got Me	Kinks	Pye	9	(7)	F
19	-	I Found Out The Hard Way	Four Pennies	Philips	3		
20	3	It's Over	Roy Orbison	London American	14	(9)	

◆ The Rolling Stones caused their first fan riots on tour in Britain. The quintet also clocked up their first UK chart topper, 'It's All Over Now', which was recorded in Chicago during their relatively disappointing debut US tour.

◆ The death of US country singer Jim Reeves (the top selling solo artist in Britain in 1964) resulted in a record eight of his albums simultaneously making the Top 20.

1964

This Mnth	Prev Mnth	Title	Artist	Label	Wks 20	(US Pos)	
1	10	Have I The Right?	Honeycombs	Pye	11	(5)	F
2	18	You Really Got Me	Kinks	Pye	9	(7)	F
3	5	I Won't Forget You	Jim Reeves	RCA	19	(93)	
4	-	I Wouldn't Trade You For The World	Bachelors	Decca	11	(69)	
5	-	The Crying Game	Dave Berry	Decca	7		
6	-	I'm Into Something Good	Herman's Hermits	Columbia	10	(13)	F
7	-	Rag Doll	Four Seasons	Philips	9	(1)	
8	2	Do Wah Diddy Diddy	Manfred Mann	HMV	10	(1)	
9	-	As Tears Go By	Marianne Faithfull	Decca	10	(22)	F
10	1	A Hard Day's Night	Beatles	Parlophone	11	(1)	
12	-	Where Did Our Love Go	Supremes	Stateside	10	(1)	F
13	-	She's Not There	Zombies	Decca	6	(2)	F L
14	16	It's For You	Cilla Black	Parlophone	6	(79)	
15	-	Such A Night	Elvis Presley	RCA	5	(16)	
16	-	The Wedding	Julie Rogers	Mercury	13	(10)	F L
17	8	I Get Around	Beach Boys	Capitol	8	(1)	F
18	-	Oh Pretty Woman	Roy Orbison	London American	12	(1)	
19	4	It's All Over Now	Rolling Stones	Decca	11	(26)	
20	-	Everybody Loves Somebody	Dean Martin	Reprise	7	(1)	

This Mnth	Prev Mnth	Title	Artist	Label	Wks 20	(US Pos)	
1	17	Oh Pretty Woman	Roy Orbison	London American	12	(1)	
2	11	Where Did Our Love Go	Supremes	Stateside	10	(1)	F
3	6	I'm Into Something Good	Herman's Hermits	Columbia	10	(13)	F
4	15	The Wedding	Julie Rogers	Mercury	13	(10)	F L
5	7	Rag Doll	Four Seasons	Philips	9	(1)	
6	-	When You Walk In The Room	Searchers	Pye	8	(35)	
7	4	I Wouldn't Trade You For The World	Bachelors	Decca	11	(69)	
8	3	I Won't Forget You	Jim Reeves	RCA	19	(93)	
9	-	(There's) Always Something There To Remind Me	Sandie Shaw	Pye	5	(52)	F
10	-	I'm Crying	Animals	Columbia	6	(19)	
11	-	We're Through	Hollies	Parlophone	7		
12	-	Walk Away	Matt Monro	Parlophone	11	(23)	
13	-	Together	P.J. Proby	Decca	6		
14	19	Everybody Loves Somebody	Dean Martin	Reprise	7	(1)	
15	9	As Tears Go By	Marianne Faithfull	Decca	10	(22)	F
16	-	The Twelfth Of Never	Cliff Richard	Columbia	6		
17	1	Have I The Right?	Honeycombs	Pye	11	(5)	F
18	-	How Soon	Henry Mancini & His Orchestra	RCA	4		L
19	-	One Way Love	Cliff Bennett & The Rebel Rousers	Parlophone	4		F
20	2	You Really Got Me	Kinks	Pye	9	(7)	F

◆ 60s superstars The Kinks and Herman's Hermits debuted on the UK chart, while the High Numbers (Who), Joe Cocker and Rod Stewart released unsuccessful singles.

◆ There was an upsurge of interest in "death discs" with Twinkle's self-penned 'Terry' and the US hit 'Leader Of The Pack' by the Shangri-La's (a hit in 1965, 1972 and 1976) both motoring up the chart. However, J. Frank Wilson's ghoulish American smash 'Last Kiss' was a stiff on this side of the Atlantic.

November 1964

This Mnth	Prev Mnth	Title	Artist	Label	Wks (US 20 Pos)	
1	-	Baby Love	Supremes	Stateside	10 (1)	
2	1	Oh Pretty Woman	Roy Orbison	London American	12 (1)	
3	-	Sha La La	Manfred Mann	HMV	7 (12)	
4	-	He's In Town	Rockin' Berries	Piccadilly	7	F
5	-	All Day And All Of The Night	Kinks	Pye	9 (7)	
6	12	Walk Away	Matt Monro	Parlophone	11 (23)	
7	-	Um Um Um Um Um Um	Wayne Fontana & The Mindbenders	Fontana	7	F
8	4	The Wedding	Julie Rogers	Mercury	13 (10)	F L
9	6	When You Walk In The Room	Searchers	Pye	8 (35)	
10	-	Tokyo Melody	Helmut Zacharias Orchestra	Polydor	6	F L
11	-	There's A Heartache Following Me	Jim Reeves	RCA	10	
12	16	The Twelfth Of Never	Cliff Richard	Columbia	6	
13	-	Google Eye	Nashville Teens	Decca	3	L
14	-	Don't Bring Me Down	Pretty Things	Fontana	5	F
15	-	I'm Gonna Be Strong	Gene Pitney	Stateside	10 (9)	
16	9	(There's) Always Something There To Remind Me	Sandie Shaw	Pye	5 (52)	F
17	-	Little Red Rooster	Rolling Stones	Decca	8	
18	2	Where Did Our Love Go	Supremes	Stateside	10 (1)	F
19	19	One Way Love	Cliff Bennettt/Rebel Rousers	Parlophone	4	F
20	-	Remember (Walkin' In The Sand)	Shangri-Las	Red Bird	3 (5)	F

December 1964

This Mnth	Prev Mnth	Title	Artist	Label	Wks (US 20 Pos)	
1	-	I Feel Fine	Beatles	Parlophone	10 (1)	G
2	15	I'm Gonna Be Strong	Gene Pitney	Stateside	10 (9)	
3	-	Downtown	Petula Clark	Pye	12 (1)	
4	17	Little Red Rooster	Rolling Stones	Decca	8	
5	-	Walk Tall	Val Doonican	Decca	10	F
6	-	Pretty Paper	Roy Orbison	London American	6 (15)	
7	1	Baby Love	Supremes	Stateside	10 (1)	
8	-	I Understand	Freddie & The Dreamers	Columbia	8 (36)	L
9	11	There's A Heartache Following Me	Jim Reeves	RCA	10	
10	5	All Day And All Of The Night	Kinks	Pye	9 (7)	
11	-	No Arms Could Ever Hold You	Bachelors	Decca	7 (27)	
12	10	Tokyo Melody	Helmut Zacharias Orchestra	Polydor	6	F L
13	-	Losing You	Dusty Springfield	Philips	5 (91)	
14	7	Um Um Um Um Um Um	Wayne Fontana/Mindbenders	Fontana	7	F
15	-	I Could Easily Fall	Cliff Richard	Columbia	8	
16	-	Message To Martha (Kentucky Bluebird)	Adam Faith	Parlophone	6	L
17	4	He's In Town	Rockin' Berries	Piccadilly	7	F
18	-	Somewhere	P.J. Proby	Liberty	8 (91)	
19	-	Blue Christmas	Elvis Presley	RCA	3	
20	-	Terry	Twinkle	Decca	9	F L

◆ The Beach Boys, who had a successful UK visit, ended the year topping the US album listings with Beach Boys Concert.

◆ 'Oh Pretty Woman' by Roy Orbison, was the only American record to top the transatlantic charts since 'I Can't Stop Loving You' by Ray Charles in 1962.

1965

This Mnth	Prev Mnth	Title	Artist	Label	Wks	(US 20 Pos)	
1	-	Yeh Yeh	Georgie Fame	Columbia	8	(21)	F
2	1	I Feel Fine	Beatles	Parlophone	10	(1)	G
3	20	Terry	Twinkle	Decca	9		F L
4	-	Girl Don't Come	Sandie Shaw	Pye	9	(42)	
5	-	Go Now!	Moody Blues	Decca	9	(10)	F
6	3	Downtown	Petula Clark	Pye	12	(1)	
7	5	Walk Tall	Val Doonican	Decca	10		F
8	18	Somewhere	P.J. Proby	Liberty	8	(91)	
9	15	I Could Easily Fall	Cliff Richard	Columbia	8		
10	2	I'm Gonna Be Strong	Gene Pitney	Stateside	10	(9)	
11	-	Cast Your Fate To The Wind	Sounds Orchestral	Piccadilly	10	(10)	F L
12	-	Ferry Across The Mersey	Gerry & The Pacemakers	Columbia	7	(6)	
13	11	No Arms Could Ever Hold You	Bachelors	Decca	7	(27)	
14	8	I Understand	Freddie & The Dreamers	Columbia	8	(36)	L
15	-	You've Lost That Lovin' Feelin'	Cilla Black	Parlophone	5		
16	-	Come Tomorrow	Manfred Mann	HMV	7	(50)	
17	-	What Have They Done To The Rain	Searchers	Pye	6	(29)	
18	-	Baby Please Don't Go	Them	Decca	6		F
19	16	Message To Martha (Kentucky Bluebird)	Adam Faith	Parlophone	6		L
20	-	You've Lost That Lovin' Feelin'	Righteous Brothers	London American	7	(1)	F

This Mnth	Prev Mnth	Title	Artist	Label	Wks	(US 20 Pos)	
1	20	You've Lost That Lovin' Feelin'	Righteous Brothers	London American	7	(1)	F
2	-	Tired Of Waiting For You	Kinks	Pye	7	(6)	
3	-	Keep Searchin' (We'll Follow The Sun)	Del Shannon	Stateside	8	(9)	L
4	-	I'll Never Find Another You	Seekers	Columbia	11	(4)	F
5	16	Come Tomorrow	Manfred Mann	HMV	7	(50)	
6	-	The Special Years	Val Doonican	Decca	8		
7	5	Go Now!	Moody Blues	Decca	9	(10)	F
8	-	Game Of Love	Wayne Fontana & The Mindbenders	Fontana	7	(1)	
9	-	Don't Let Me Be Misunderstood	Animals	Columbia	7	(15)	
10	11	Cast Your Fate To The Wind	Sounds Orchestral	Piccadilly	10	(10)	F L
11	15	You've Lost That Lovin' Feelin'	Cilla Black	Parlophone	5		
12	-	Funny How Love Can Be	Ivy League	Piccadilly	6		F
13	18	Baby Please Don't Go	Them	Decca	6		F
14	-	It Hurts So Much	Jim Reeves	RCA	6		
15	12	Ferry Across The Mersey	Gerry & The Pacemakers	Columbia	7	(6)	
16	-	Leader Of The Pack	Shangri-Las	Red Bird	4	(1)	
17	1	Yeh Yeh	Georgie Fame	Columbia	8	(21)	F
18	4	Girl Don't Come	Sandie Shaw	Pye	9	(42)	
19	3	Terry	Twinkle	Decca	9		F L
20	-	Yes I Will	Hollies	Parlophone	7		

◆ Folk rivals Bob Dylan and Donovan debuted on the UK singles chart in the same week.

◆ An all-star Motown package tour played to half empty houses. The Temptations' US chart topper, 'My Girl', finally hit in the UK in 1992. Fellow American, P.J. Proby, who was faring far better, was banned by the BBC, a major theatre chain and American show *Shindig*, after splitting his trousers on stage.

March 1965

This Mnth	Prev Mnth	Title	Artist	Label	Wks	(US 20 Pos)	
1	-	It's Not Unusual	Tom Jones	Decca	9	(10)	F
2	4	I'll Never Find Another You	Seekers	Columbia	11	(4)	F
3	-	Silhouettes	Herman's Hermits	Columbia	9	(5)	
4	-	Come And Stay With Me	Marianne Faithfull	Decca	7	(26)	
5	-	The Last Time	Rolling Stones	Decca	9	(9)	
6	-	I'll Stop At Nothing	Sandie Shaw	Pye	7	(97)	
7	-	I Must Be Seeing Things	Gene Pitney	Stateside	6	(31)	
8	8	Game Of Love	Wayne Fontana & The Mindbenders	Fontana	7	(1)	
9	9	Don't Let Me Be Misunderstood	Animals	Columbia	7	(15)	
10	20	Yes I Will	Hollies	Parlophone	7		
11	-	Goodbye My Love	Searchers	Pye	5	(52)	
12	6	The Special Years	Val Doonican	Decca	8		
13	12	Funny How Love Can Be	Ivy League	Piccadilly	6		F
14	-	I Apologise	P.J. Proby	Liberty	5		
15	-	Goodnight	Roy Orbison	London American	5	(21)	
16	14	It Hurts So Much	Jim Reeves	RCA	6		
17	2	Tired Of Waiting For You	Kinks	Pye	7	(6)	
18	-	Concrete And Clay	Unit 4 Plus 2	Decca	9	(28)	F
19	-	Honey I Need	Pretty Things	Fontana	3		L
20	-	The Minute You're Gone	Cliff Richard	Columbia	9		

April 1965

This Mnth	Prev Mnth	Title	Artist	Label	Wks	(US 20 Pos)	
1	20	The Minute You're Gone	Cliff Richard	Columbia	9		
2	-	For Your Love	Yardbirds	Columbia	7	(6)	F
3	18	Concrete And Clay	Unit 4 Plus 2	Decca	9	(28)	F
4	-	Catch The Wind	Donovan	Pye	8	(23)	F
5	5	The Last Time	Rolling Stones	Decca	9	(9)	
6	-	Here Comes The Night	Them	Decca	8	(24)	L
7	-	Times They Are A-Changin'	Bob Dylan	CBS	7		F
8	-	I Can't Explain	Who	Brunswick	7	(93)	F
9	-	Stop! In The Name Of Love	Supremes	Tamla Motown	6	(1)	
10	1	It's Not Unusual	Tom Jones	Decca	9	(10)	F
11	3	Silhouettes	Herman's Hermits	Columbia	9	(5)	
12	-	Ticket To Ride	Beatles	Parlophone	9	(1)	
13	11	Goodbye My Love	Searchers	Pye	5	(52)	
14	-	Little Things	Dave Berry	Decca	6		
15	4	Come And Stay With Me	Marianne Faithfull	Decca	7	(26)	
16	-	I'll Be There	Gerry & The Pacemakers	Columbia	4	(14)	L
17	-	You're Breakin' My Heart	Keely Smith	Reprise	5		F L
18	-	Everybody's Gonna Be Happy	Kinks	Pye	3		
19	2	I'll Never Find Another You	Seekers	Columbia	11	(4)	F
20	-	Pop Go The Workers	Barron Knights	Columbia	8		

◆ David Bowie's group, The Mannish Boys (named, as were the Rolling Stones, after a Muddy Waters' song), signed to Parlophone and released their debut single, 'I Pity The Fool' (a cover of Bobby Bland's R&B success).

◆ Bob Dylan concluded a very successful tour of Britain (the subject of the film *Don't Look Back*) where his album Bringing It All Back Home followed Freewheelin' at No. 1.

1965

This Mnth	Prev Mnth	Title	Artist	Label	Wks	(US 20 Pos)	
1	12	Ticket To Ride	Beatles	Parlophone	9	(1)	
2	-	King Of The Road	Roger Miller	Philips	9	(4)	F
3	-	True Love Ways	Peter & Gordon	Columbia	10	(14)	
4	-	A World Of Our Own	Seekers	Columbia	11	(19)	
5	-	Where Are You Now (My Love)	Jackie Trent	Pye	7		F L
6	20	Pop Go The Workers	Barron Knights	Columbia	8		
7	-	Bring It On Home To Me	Animals	Columbia	8	(32)	
8	6	Here Comes The Night	Them	Decca	8	(24)	L
9	1	The Minute You're Gone	Cliff Richard	Columbia	9		
10	-	Wonderful World	Herman's Hermits	Columbia	7	(4)	
11	-	Oh No Not My Baby	Manfred Mann	HMV	5		
12	-	Subterranean Homesick Blues	Bob Dylan	CBS	6	(39)	
13	-	This Little Bird	Marianne Faithfull	Decca	7	(32)	
14	4	Catch The Wind	Donovan	Pye	8	(23)	F
15	-	Long Live Love	Sandie Shaw	Pye	9		
16	14	Little Things	Dave Berry	Decca	6		
17	9	Stop! In The Name Of Love	Supremes	Tamla Motown	6	(1)	
18	3	Concrete And Clay	Unit 4 Plus 2	Decca	9	(28)	F
19	-	Poor Man's Son	Rockin' Berries	Piccadilly	7		L
20	-	The Clapping Song	Shirley Ellis	London American	8	(8)	F L

This Mnth	Prev Mnth	Title	Artist	Label	Wks	(US 20 Pos)	
1	15	Long Live Love	Sandie Shaw	Pye	9		
2	-	Crying In The Chapel	Elvis Presley	RCA	11	(3)	
3	-	The Price Of Love	Everly Brothers	Warner	10		
4	-	Trains And Boats And Planes	Burt Bacharach	London American	7		F L
5	19	Poor Man's Son	Rockin' Berries	Piccadilly	7		L
6	4	A World Of Our Own	Seekers	Columbia	11	(19)	
7	20	The Clapping Song	Shirley Ellis	London American	8	(8)	F L
8	-	I'm Alive	Hollies	Parlophone	10		
9	13	This Little Bird	Marianne Faithfull	Decca	7	(32)	
10	-	Marie	Bachelors	Decca	6	(15)	
11	5	Where Are You Now (My Love)	Jackie Trent	Pye	7		F L
12	3	True Love Ways	Peter & Gordon	Columbia	10	(14)	
13	-	Colours	Donovan	Pye	6	(61)	
14	-	Set Me Free	Kinks	Pye	6	(23)	
15	-	You've Never Been In Love Like This Before	Unit 4 Plus 2	Decca	5	(95)	L
16	1	Ticket To Ride	Beatles	Parlophone	9	(1)	
17	-	Anyway Anyhow Anywhere	Who	Brunswick	6		
18	-	Trains And Boats And Planes	Billy J. Kramer & The Dakotas	Parlophone	4	(47)	L
19	2	King Of The Road	Roger Miller	Philips	9	(4)	F
20	-	Looking Through The Eyes Of Love	Gene Pitney	Stateside	8	(28)	

◆ Cliff Richard clocked up his first No. 1 since the start of the beat boom with his Nashville-recorded version of Sonny James's country hit 'The Minute You're Gone'.

◆ Merseybeat pioneers Gerry & The Pacemakers and Billy J. Kramer & The Dakotas enjoyed their last Top 20 entries. From now on The Beatles were Epstein's only hitmaking group.

July 1965

This Mnth	Prev Mnth	Title	Artist	Label	Wks	(US 20 Pos)	
1	8	I'm Alive	Hollies	Parlophone	10		
2	-	Heart Full Of Soul	Yardbirds	Columbia	9	(9)	
3	2	Crying In The Chapel	Elvis Presley	RCA	11	(3)	
4	-	Mr. Tambourine Man	Byrds	CBS	9	(1)	F
5	20	Looking Through The Eyes Of Love	Gene Pitney	Stateside	8	(28)	
6	-	To Know You Is To Love You	Peter & Gordon	Columbia	6	(24)	
7	-	Tossing And Turning	Ivy League	Piccadilly	8		L
8	3	The Price Of Love	Everly Brothers	Warner	10		
9	-	Leave A Little Love	Lulu	Decca	5		
10	13	Colours	Donovan	Pye	6	(61)	
11	-	In The Middle Of Nowhere	Dusty Springfield	Philips	6		
12	17	Anyway Anyhow Anywhere	Who	Brunswick	6		
13	-	You've Got Your Troubles	Fortunes	Decca	9	(7)	F
14	-	There But For Fortune	Joan Baez	Fontana	7	(50)	F
15	4	Trains And Boats And Planes	Burt Bacharach	London American	7		F L
16	1	Long Live Love	Sandie Shaw	Pye	9		
17	-	Wooly Bully	Sam The Sham & The Pharaohs	MGM	6	(2)	F L
18	-	On My Word	Cliff Richard	Columbia	5		
19	14	Set Me Free	Kinks	Pye	6	(23)	
20	-	We Gotta Get Out Of This Place	Animals	Columbia	8	(13)	

August 1965

This Mnth	Prev Mnth	Title	Artist	Label	Wks	(US 20 Pos)	
1	-	Help!	Beatles	Parlophone	10	(1)	
2	20	We Gotta Get Out Of This Place	Animals	Columbia	8	(13)	
3	13	You've Got Your Troubles	Fortunes	Decca	9	(7)	F
4	4	Mr. Tambourine Man	Byrds	CBS	9	(1)	F
5	-	Catch Us If You Can	Dave Clark Five	Columbia	6	(4)	
6	-	Everyone's Gone To The Moon	Jonathan King	Decca	7	(17)	F
7	-	A Walk In The Black Forest	Horst Jankowski	Mercury	12	(12)	F L
8	7	Tossing And Turning	Ivy League	Piccadilly	8		L
9	14	There But For Fortune	Joan Baez	Fontana	7	(50)	F
10	-	I Got You Babe	Sonny & Cher	Atlantic	9	(1)	F
11	-	Zorba's Dance	Marcello Minerbi	Durium	10		F L
12	-	Summer Nights	Marianne Faithfull	Decca	5	(24)	L
13	-	In Thoughts Of You	Billy Fury	Decca	5		L
14	2	Heart Full Of Soul	Yardbirds	Columbia	9	(9)	
15	-	All I Really Want To Do	Byrds	CBS	5	(40)	
16	-	With These Hands	Tom Jones	Decca	4	(27)	
17	17	Wooly Bully	Sam The Sham & The Pharaohs	MGM	6	(2)	F L
18	11	In The Middle Of Nowhere	Dusty Springfield	Philips	6		
19	-	Don't Make My Baby Blue	Shadows	Columbia	5		
20	-	He's Got No Love	Searchers	Pye	5	(79)	

◆ The Rolling Stones played the prestigious London Palladium. Supporting them were Steam Packet featuring Rod Stewart.

◆ The Righteous Brothers' revival of 'Unchained Melody' became a transatlantic success. It would repeat that feat in 1990.

◆ Appearing at the National Jazz & Blues Festival at Richmond were such artists as The Spencer Davis Group, Manfred Mann, Rod Stewart, The Who and The Yardbirds.

1965

This Mnth	Prev Mnth	Title	Artist	Label	Wks (US 20 Pos)	
1	-	(I Can't Get No) Satisfaction	Rolling Stones	Decca	10 (1)	
2	-	Make It Easy On Yourself	Walker Brothers	Philips	10 (16)	
3	10	I Got You Babe	Sonny & Cher	Atlantic	9 (1)	F
4	7	A Walk In The Black Forest	Horst Jankowski	Mercury	12 (12)	F L
5	-	Like A Rolling Stone	Bob Dylan	CBS	8 (2)	
6	1	Help!	Beatles	Parlophone	10 (1)	
7	11	Zorba's Dance	Marcello Minerbi	Durium	10	F L
8	-	Look Through Any Window	Hollies	Parlophone	8 (32)	
9	15	All I Really Want To Do	Byrds	CBS	5 (40)	
10	-	Tears	Ken Dodd	Columbia	21	G
11	-	Laugh At Me	Sonny	Atlantic	6 (10)	F L
12	-	All I Really Want To Do	Cher	Liberty	5 (15)	F
13	-	That's The Way	Honeycombs	Pye	7	L
14	-	What's New Pussycat?	Tom Jones	Decca	5 (3)	
15	6	Everyone's Gone To The Moon	Jonathan King	Decca	7 (17)	F
16	-	Eve Of Destruction	Barry McGuire	RCA	10 (1)	F L
17	-	Unchained Melody	Righteous Brothers	London American	3 (4)	
18	-	See My Friend	Kinks	Pye	4	
19	-	Il Silenzio	Nini Rosso	Durium	7	F L
20	-	Just A Little Bit Better	Herman's Hermits	Columbia	5 (7)	

1	10	Tears	Ken Dodd	Columbia	21	G
2	-	If You Gotta Go, Go Now	Manfred Mann	HMV	8	
3	16	Eve Of Destruction	Barry McGuire	RCA	10 (1)	F
4	-	Almost There	Andy Williams	CBS	10 (67)	
5	2	Make It Easy On Yourself	Walker Brothers	Philips	10 (16)	
6	-	Hang On Sloopy	McCoys	Immediate	9 (1)	F
7	8	Look Through Any Window	Hollies	Parlophone	8 (32)	
8	19	Il Silenzio	Nini Rosso	Durium	7	F L
9	1	(I Can't Get No) Satisfaction	Rolling Stones	Decca	10 (1)	
10	-	Message Understood	Sandie Shaw	Pye	5	
11	-	Baby Don't Go	Sonny & Cher	Reprise	5 (8)	
12	4	A Walk In The Black Forest	Horst Jankowski	Mercury	12 (12)	F L
13	-	Some Of Your Lovin'	Dusty Springfield	Philips	6	
14	-	Evil Hearted You/Still I'm Sad	Yardbirds	Columbia	6	
15	5	Like A Rolling Stone	Bob Dylan	CBS	8 (2)	
16	3	I Got You Babe	Sonny & Cher	Atlantic	10 (1)	F
17	-	It's Good News Week	Hedgehoppers Anonymous	Decca	6 (48)	F L
18	-	In The Midnight Hour	Wilson Pickett	Atlantic	4 (21)	F
19	-	What Cha Gonna Do About It	Small Faces	Decca	5	F
20	-	Yesterday Man	Chris Andrews	Decca	11 (94)	F

◆ After a long absence, US groups started to chart again in Britain, with newcomers The Byrds, Sam The Sham & The Pharaohs and The Walker Brothers leading the way.

◆ Two British records which sold over a million in the UK but failed to even chart Stateside were: 'Tears' by Ken Dodd and 'The Carnival Is Over' by The Seekers.

◆ In a year when rock giants The Beatles, The Rolling Stones and Bob Dylan were the only acts to top the UK album chart, the longest running No. 1 was the MOR soundtrack album **The Sound Of Music**.

November 1965

This Mnth	Prev Mnth	Title	Artist	Label	Wks	(US 20 Pos)		
1	-	Get Off Of My Cloud	Rolling Stones	Decca	8	(1)		
2	1	Tears	Ken Dodd	Columbia	21		G	
3	20	Yesterday Man	Chris Andrews	Decca	11	(94)	F	
4	-	The Carnival Is Over	Seekers	Columbia	14		G	
5	-	Here It Comes Again	Fortunes	Decca	7	(27)		
6	14	Evil Hearted You/Still I'm Sad	Yardbirds	Columbia	6			
7	-	It's My Life	Animals	Columbia	6	(23)		
8	17	It's Good News Week	Hedgehoppers Anonymous	Decca	6	(48)	F	L
9	-	Yesterday	Matt Monro	Parlophone	7			L
10	-	My Generation	Who	Brunswick	10	(74)		
11	4	Almost There	Andy Williams	CBS	10	(67)		
12	-	1-2-3	Len Barry	Brunswick	11	(2)	F	
13	-	Positively 4th Street	Bob Dylan	CBS	9	(7)		
14	-	Love Is Strange	Everly Brothers	Warner	4			L
15	3	Eve Of Destruction	Barry McGuire	RCA	10	(1)	F	L
16	-	Wind Me Up (Let Me Go)	Cliff Richard	Columbia	12			
17	-	A Lover's Concerto	Toys	Stateside	9	(2)	F	L
18	6	Hang On Sloopy	McCoys	Immediate	9	(1)	F	L
19	2	If You Gotta Go, Go Now	Manfred Mann	HMV	8			
20	-	Princess In Rags	Gene Pitney	Stateside	8	(37)		

December 1965

This Mnth	Prev Mnth	Title	Artist	Label	Wks	(US 20 Pos)		
1	4	The Carnival Is Over	Seekers	Columbia	14		G	
2	16	Wind Me Up (Let Me Go)	Cliff Richard	Columbia	12			
3	10	My Generation	Who	Brunswick	10	(74)		
4	12	1-2-3	Len Barry	Brunswick	11	(2)	F	
5	-	Day Tripper/We Can Work it Out	Beatles	Parlophone	10	(5)	G	
6	2	Tears	Ken Dodd	Columbia	21		G	
7	-	The River	Ken Dodd	Columbia	11			
8	17	A Lovers Concerto	Toys	Stateside	9	(2)	F	L
9	-	Maria	P.J. Proby	Liberty	6			L
10	20	Princess In Rags	Gene Pitney	Stateside	8	(37)		
11	1	Get Off Of My Cloud	Rolling Stones	Decca	8	(1)		
12	-	My Ship Is Coming In	Walker Brothers	Philips	10	(63)		
13	13	Positively 4th Street	Bob Dylan	CBS	9	(7)		
14	-	Let's Hang On!	Four Seasons	Philips	11	(3)		
15	-	Rescue Me	Fontella Bass	Chess	7	(4)	F	L
16	3	Yesterday Man	Chris Andrews	Decca	11	(94)	F	
17	-	Don't Bring Me Your Heartaches	Paul & Barry Ryan	Decca	4		F	
18	7	It's My Life	Animals	Columbia	6	(23)		
19	-	To Whom It Concerns	Chris Andrews	Decca	5			L
20	-	Tell Me Why	Elvis Presley	RCA	4	(33)		

◆ As The Stones scored their fifth successive UK No. 1 with 'Get Off Of My Cloud', Motown (America's top label in 1965) act The Supremes notched up their sixth American topper, 'I Hear A Symphony'.

◆ Decca Records released Marc Bolan's debut disc, 'The Wizard'. The label also recorded the first solo tracks by Van Morrison, whose group, Them, had temporarily disbanded.

1966

January 1966

This Mnth	Prev Mnth	Title	Artist	Label	Wks	(US 20 Pos)	
1	5	Day Tripper/We Can Work it Out	Beatles	Parlophone	10	(1)	G
2	-	Keep On Runnin'	Spencer Davis Group	Fontana	10	(76)	F
3	12	My Ship Is Coming In	Walker Brothers	Philips	10	(63)	
4	2	Wind Me Up (Let Me Go)	Cliff Richard	Columbia	12		
5	7	The River	Ken Dodd	Columbia	11		
6	1	The Carnival Is Over	Seekers	Columbia	14		G
7	14	Let's Hang On!	Four Seasons	Philips	11	(3)	
8	-	Till The End Of The Day	Kinks	Pye	8	(50)	
9	6	Tears	Ken Dodd	Columbia	21		G
10	-	Spanish Flea	Herb Alpert	Pye International	12	(27)	F
11	-	A Must To Avoid	Herman's Hermits	Columbia	7	(8)	
12	4	1-2-3	Len Barry	Brunswick	11	(2)	F
13	-	Merrie Gentle Pops	Barron Knights	Columbia	5		
14	-	Michelle	Overlanders	Pye	6		F L
15	3	My Generation	Who	Brunswick	10	(74)	
16	15	Rescue Me	Fontella Bass	Chess	7	(4)	F L
17	-	My Girl	Otis Redding	Atlantic	7		F
18	-	A Hard Day's Night	Peter Sellers	Parlophone	4		L
19	8	A Lovers Concerto	Toys	Stateside	9	(2)	F L
20	19	To Whom It Concerns	Chris Andrews	Decca	5		L

February 1966

This Mnth	Prev Mnth	Title	Artist	Label	Wks	(US 20 Pos)	
1	-	You Were On My Mind	Crispian St. Peters	Decca	8	(36)	F
2	10	Spanish Flea	Herb Alpert	Pye International	12	(27)	F
3	-	These Boots Are Made For Walkin'	Nancy Sinatra	Reprise	10	(1)	F
4	-	Love's Just A Broken Heart	Cilla Black	Parlophone	6		
5	-	A Groovy Kind Of Love	Mindbenders	Fontana	10	(2)	F
6	14	Michelle	Overlanders	Pye	6		F L
7	2	Keep On Runnin'	Spencer Davis Group	Fontana	10	(76)	F
8	-	19th Nervous Breakdown	Rolling Stones	Decca	7	(2)	
9	11	A Must To Avoid	Herman's Hermits	Columbia	7	(8)	
10	-	Mirror Mirror	Pinkerton's Assorted Colours	Decca	4		F L
11	-	Tomorrow	Sandie Shaw	Pye	5		
12	-	Like A Baby	Len Barry	Brunswick	4	(27)	L
13	-	Girl	St. Louis Union	Decca	5		F L
14	-	My Love	Petula Clark	Pye	6	(1)	
15	1	Day Tripper/We Can Work it Out	Beatles	Parlophone	10	(1)	G
16	17	My Girl	Otis Redding	Atlantic	7		F
17	7	Let's Hang On!	Four Seasons	Philips	11	(3)	
18	-	Sha La La La Lee	Small Faces	Decca	8		
19	3	My Ship Is Coming In	Walker Brothers	Philips	10	(63)	
20	-	Michelle	David & Jonathan	Columbia	4	(18)	F

◆ Cover versions were still rife with re-treads of recent songs from The Walker Brothers, Cliff Richard, Otis Redding, Crispian St. Peters, The Mindbend-ers and The Hollies.

◆ A casual remark by John Lennon, which compared the popularity of The Beatles to Jesus, went virtually unnoticed in the UK. However, it caused problems in some American states.

March 1966

This Mnth	Prev Mnth	Title	Artist	Label	Wks	(US 20 Pos)	
1	5	A Groovy Kind Of Love	Mindbenders	Fontana	10	(2)	F
2	18	Sha La La La Lee	Small Faces	Decca	8		
3	-	Barbara Ann	Beach Boys	Capitol	8	(2)	
4	3	These Boots Are Made For Walkin'	Nancy Sinatra	Reprise	10	(1)	F
5	-	Backstage	Gene Pitney	Stateside	6	(25)	
6	-	I Can't Let Go	Hollies	Parlophone	6	(42)	
7	-	The Sun Ain't Gonna Shine Anymore	Walker Brothers	Philips	7	(13)	
8	8	19th Nervous Breakdown	Rolling Stones	Decca	7	(2)	
9	14	My Love	Petula Clark	Pye	6	(1)	
10	2	Spanish Flea	Herb Alpert	Pye International	12	(27)	F
11	-	Make The World Go Away	Eddy Arnold	RCA	10	(6)	F L
12	-	Shapes Of Things	Yardbirds	Columbia	7	(11)	
13	-	Lightnin' Strikes	Lou Christie	MGM	5	(1)	F
14	-	Dedicated Follower Of Fashion	Kinks	Pye	8	(36)	
15	-	Inside-Looking Out	Animals	Decca	4	(34)	
16	1	You Were On My Mind	Crispian St. Peters	Decca	8	(36)	F
17	11	Tomorrow	Sandie Shaw	Pye	5		
18	-	What Now My Love	Sonny & Cher	Atlantic	5	(14)	
19	-	Elusive Butterfly	Bob Lind	Fontana	5	(5)	F L
20	-	This Golden Ring	Fortunes	Decca	2	(82)	

April 1966

This Mnth	Prev Mnth	Title	Artist	Label	Wks	(US 20 Pos)	
1	-	Somebody Help Me	Spencer Davis Group	Fontana	7	(47)	
2	-	Hold Tight	Dave Dee, Dozy, Beaky, Mick & Tich	Fontana	10		F
3	-	The Sound Of Silence	Bachelors	Decca	9		
4	-	Elusive Butterfly	Val Doonican	Decca	8		
5	7	The Sun Ain't Gonna Shine Anymore	Walker Brothers	Philips	7	(13)	
6	-	Substitute	Who	Reaction	9		
7	19	Elusive Butterfly	Bob Lind	Fontana	5	(5)	F L
8	-	You Don't Have To Say You Love Me	Dusty Springfield	Philips	10	(4)	
9	14	Dedicated Follower Of Fashion	Kinks	Pye	8	(36)	
10	11	Make The World Go Away	Eddy Arnold	RCA	10	(6)	F L
11	-	Bang Bang (My Baby Shot Me Down)	Cher	Liberty	8	(2)	
12	12	Shapes Of Things	Yardbirds	Columbia	7	(11)	
13	6	I Can't Let Go	Hollies	Parlophone	6	(42)	
14	-	I Put A Spell On You	Alan Price Set	Decca	5	(80)	F
15	-	Alfie	Cilla Black	Parlophone	7	(95)	
16	-	Pied Piper	Crispian St. Peters	Decca	8	(4)	L
17	-	Someday One Day	Seekers	Columbia	6		
18	2	Sha La La La Lee	Small Faces	Decca	8		
19	3	Barbara Ann	Beach Boys	Capitol	8	(2)	
20	-	Pretty Flamingo	Manfred Mann	HMV	7	(29)	

◆ US soul music continued to thrive. Stevie Wonder had his first UK hit, 'Uptight'. James Brown had the whole of *Ready Steady Go* devoted to him, and Wilson Pickett and Mary Wells also had successful appearances on the show.

◆ The Beatles played their last UK date, alongside the Stones and The Who, at the *NME* poll winners' concert. They started their final World tour by returning to Hamburg.

1966

This Mnth	Prev Mnth	Title	Artist	Label	Wks	(US 20 Pos)	
1	20	Pretty Flamingo	Manfred Mann	HMV	7	(29)	
2	-	Sloop John B	Beach Boys	Capitol	9	(3)	
3	-	Daydream	Lovin' Spoonful	Pye International	8	(2)	F
4	8	You Don't Have To Say You Love Me	Dusty Springfield	Philips	10	(4)	
5	16	Pied Piper	Crispian St. Peters	Decca	8	(4)	L
6	11	Bang Bang (My Baby Shot Me Down)	Cher	Liberty	8	(2)	
7	-	Wild Thing	Troggs	Fontana	8	(1)	F
8	-	Shotgun Wedding	Roy 'C'	Island	6		F
9	2	Hold Tight	Dave Dee, Dozy, Beaky, Mick & Tich	Fontana	10		F
10	-	Sorrow	Merseys	Fontana	8		L
11	-	Paint It, Black	Rolling Stones	Decca	7	(1)	
12	-	Homeward Bound	Simon & Garfunkel	CBS	7	(5)	F
13	3	The Sound Of Silence	Bachelors	Decca	9		
14	-	Strangers In The Night	Frank Sinatra	Reprise	13	(1)	
15	15	Alfie	Cilla Black	Parlophone	7	(95)	
16	-	Rainy Day Women Nos. 12 & 35	Bob Dylan	CBS	5	(2)	
17	-	Monday Monday	Mamas & The Papas	RCA	10	(1)	F
18	-	Hey Girl	Small Faces	Decca	5		
19	-	Promises	Ken Dodd	Columbia	8		
20	1	Somebody Help Me	Spencer Davis Group	Fontana	7	(47)	

This Mnth	Prev Mnth	Title	Artist	Label	Wks	(US 20 Pos)	
1	14	Strangers In The Night	Frank Sinatra	Reprise	13	(1)	
2	17	Monday Monday	Mamas & The Papas	RCA	10	(1)	F
3	10	Sorrow	Merseys	Fontana	8		L
4	11	Paint It, Black	Rolling Stones	Decca	7	(1)	
5	-	When A Man Loves A Woman	Percy Sledge	Atlantic	9	(1)	F
6	7	Wild Thing	Troggs	Fontana	8	(1)	F
7	-	Don't Bring Me Down	Animals	Decca	6	(12)	
8	19	Promises	Ken Dodd	Columbia	8		
9	2	Sloop John B	Beach Boys	Capitol	9	(3)	
10	-	Paperback Writer	Beatles	Parlophone	7	(1)	
11	16	Rainy Day Women Nos. 12 & 35	Bob Dylan	CBS	5	(2)	
12	-	Over Under Sideways Down	Yardbirds	Columbia	5	(13)	L
13	18	Hey Girl	Small Faces	Decca	5		
14	-	Don't Answer Me	Cilla Black	Parlophone	6		
15	-	Sunny Afternoon	Kinks	Pye	9	(14)	
16	-	Nothing Comes Easy	Sandie Shaw	Pye	4		
17	-	River Deep Mountain High	Ike & Tina Turner	London American	9	(88)	F
18	8	Shotgun Wedding	Roy 'C'	Island	6		F
19	1	Pretty Flamingo	Manfred Mann	HMV	7	(29)	
20	-	Nobody Needs Your Love	Gene Pitney	Stateside	9		

◆ Like their earlier US No. 1s, 'Mrs. Brown You've Got A Lovely Daughter' and 'I'm Henry VIII I Am', Herman's Hermits latest American hit, a revival of George Formby's music hall favourite 'Leaning On The Lamp Post', was not deemed suitable for release in the group's homeland.

◆ American trio The Walker Brothers applied to become British Citizens, soon after British duo Chad & Jeremy had requested US citizenship.
◆ Frank Sinatra scored the only solo transatlantic chart topper of his career with Bert Kaempfert's composition 'Strangers In The Night'.

July 1966

This Mnth	Prev Mnth	Title	Artist	Label	Wks	(US 20 Pos)	
1	15	Sunny Afternoon	Kinks	Pye	9	(14)	
2	17	River Deep Mountain High	Ike & Tina Turner	London American	9	(88)	F
3	20	Nobody Needs Your Love	Gene Pitney	Stateside	9		
4	-	Get Away	Georgie Fame	Columbia	7	(70)	
5	1	Strangers In The Night	Frank Sinatra	Reprise	13	(1)	
6	-	Bus Stop	Hollies	Parlophone	7	(5)	
7	10	Paperback Writer	Beatles	Parlophone	7	(1)	
8	-	Out Of Time	Chris Farlowe	Immediate	8		F L
9	-	Black Is Black	Los Bravos	Decca	9	(4)	F
10	-	Hideaway	Dave Dee, Dozy, Beaky, Mick & Tich	Fontana	6		
11	-	I Couldn't Live Without Your Love	Petula Clark	Pye	7	(9)	
12	14	Don't Answer Me	Cilla Black	Parlophone	6		
13	5	When A Man Loves A Woman	Percy Sledge	Atlantic	9	(1)	F
14	-	Love Letters	Elvis Presley	RCA	7	(19)	
15	2	Monday Monday	Mamas & The Papas	RCA	10	(1)	F
16	-	With A Girl Like You	Troggs	Fontana	8	(29)	
17	-	The More I See You	Chris Montez	Pye International	9	(16)	
18	-	Goin' Back	Dusty Springfield	Philips	6		
19	-	Lana	Roy Orbison	London American	5		
20	7	Don't Bring Me Down	Animals	Decca	6	(12)	

August 1966

This Mnth	Prev Mnth	Title	Artist	Label	Wks	(US 20 Pos)	
1	16	With A Girl Like You	Troggs	Fontana	8	(29)	
2	9	Black Is Black	Los Bravos	Decca	9	(4)	F
3	17	The More I See You	Chris Montez	Pye International	9	(16)	
4	-	Mama	Dave Berry	Decca	10		L
5	-	God Only Knows	Beach Boys	Capitol	9	(39)	
6	8	Out Of Time	Chris Farlowe	Immediate	8		F L
7	-	Yellow Submarine/Eleanor Rigby	Beatles	Parlophone	9	(2)	
8	-	Visions	Cliff Richard	Columbia	8		
9	-	Summer In The City	Lovin' Spoonful	Kama Sutra	7	(1)	L
10	14	Love Letters	Elvis Presley	RCA	7	(19)	
11	11	I Couldn't Live Without Your Love	Petula Clark	Pye	7	(9)	
12	-	Hi-Lili-Hi-Lo	Alan Price Set	Decca	7		
13	-	They're Coming To Take Me Away Ha-Haaa!	Napoleon XIV	Warner	6	(3)	F L
14	4	Get Away	Georgie Fame	Columbia	7	(70)	
15	1	Sunny Afternoon	Kinks	Pye	9	(14)	
16	18	Goin' Back	Dusty Springfield	Philips	6		
17	-	Lovers Of The World Unite	David & Jonathan	Columbia	7		L
18	-	I Saw Her Again	Mamas & The Papas	RCA	6	(5)	
19	-	I Want You	Bob Dylan	CBS	5	(20)	
20	-	All Or Nothing	Small Faces	Decca	8		

◆ 'They're Coming To Take Me Away Ha-Haaa!' was one of the strangest transatlantic hits of all time. This "madman's monologue" was released by recording engineer-cum-successful MOR songsmith Jerry Samuels under the apt name Napoleon XIV. It cost him $15 to record and sold half a million copies in its first week.

1966

This Mnth	Prev Mnth	Title	Artist	Label	Wks	(US 20 Pos)	
1	20	All Or Nothing	Small Faces	Decca	8		
2	7	Yellow Submarine/Eleanor Rigby	Beatles	Parlophone	9	(2)	
3	5	God Only Knows	Beach Boys	Capitol	9	(39)	
4	-	Too Soon To Know	Roy Orbison	London American	10	(68)	
5	-	Distant Drums	Jim Reeves	RCA	19	(45)	
6	13	They're Coming To Take Me Away Ha-Haaa!	Napoleon XIV	Warner	6	(3)	F L
7	17	Lovers Of The World Unite	David & Jonathan	Columbia	7		L
8	4	Mama	Dave Berry	Decca	10		L
9	-	Working In The Coal Mine	Lee Dorsey	Stateside	6	(8)	F
10	-	Got To Get You Into My Life	Cliff Bennett & The Rebel Rousers	Parlophone	5		L
11	-	Just Like A Woman	Manfred Mann	Fontana	6		
12	1	With A Girl Like You	Troggs	Fontana	8	(29)	
13	-	I'm A Boy	Who	Reaction	10		
14	8	Visions	Cliff Richard	Columbia	8		
15	-	Little Man	Sonny & Cher	Atlantic	6	(21)	
16	-	You Can't Hurry Love	Supremes	Tamla Motown	8	(1)	
17	18	I Saw Her Again	Mamas & The Papas	RCA	6	(5)	
18	12	Hi-Lili-Hi-Lo	Alan Price Set	Decca	7		
19	9	Summer In The City	Lovin' Spoonful	Kama Sutra	7	(1)	L
20	-	When I Come Home	Spencer Davis Group	Fontana	4		

This Mnth	Prev Mnth	Title	Artist	Label	Wks	(US 20 Pos)	
1	5	Distant Drums	Jim Reeves	RCA	19	(45)	
2	-	Bend It	Dave Dee, Dozy, Beaky, Mick & Tich	Fontana	9		
3	13	I'm A Boy	Who	Reaction	10		
4	-	Winchester Cathedral	New Vaudeville Band	Fontana	9	(1)	F
5	16	You Can't Hurry Love	Supremes	Tamla Motown	8	(1)	
6	-	Have You Seen Your Mother, Baby, Standing In The Shadow	Rolling Stones	Decca	6	(9)	
7	-	Guantanamera	Sandpipers	Pye International	9	(9)	F L
8	15	Little Man	Sonny & Cher	Atlantic	6	(21)	
9	-	All I See Is You	Dusty Springfield	Philips	7	(20)	
10	-	I Can't Control Myself	Troggs	Page One	9	(43)	
11	-	Walk With Me	Seekers	Columbia	6		
12	4	Too Soon To Know	Roy Orbison	London American	10	(68)	
13	-	Reach Out I'll Be There	Four Tops	Tamla Motown	10	(1)	F
14	-	Stop Stop Stop	Hollies	Parlophone	8	(7)	
15	-	Sunny	Georgie Fame	Columbia	4		
16	-	Sunny	Bobby Hebb	Philips	3	(2)	F L
17	1	All Or Nothing	Small Faces	Decca	8		
18	-	Another Tear Falls	Walker Brothers	Philips	3		
19	-	No Milk Today	Herman's Hermits	Columbia	7	(35)	
20	2	Yellow Submarine/Eleanor Rigby	Beatles	Parlophone	9	(2)	

◆ The *NME* announced "The British Beat Boom is over". They pointed out there were now more American records on the US chart than British, and that sales of UK records in America were dropping. *NME* concluded, "Whatever happens, Britain has made her mark upon the world of pop, America now accepts us as a force to be reckoned with – the dark days when British hits in America were regarded as flukes are over."

November 1966

This Mnth	Prev Mnth	Title	Artist	Label	Wks 20	(US Pos)	
1	13	Reach Out I'll Be There	Four Tops	Tamla Motown	10	(1)	F
2	14	Stop Stop Stop	Hollies	Parlophone	8	(7)	
3	-	Semi-Detached Surburban Mr.James	Manfred Mann	Fontana	8		
4	-	High Time	Paul Jones	HMV	8		F
5	-	Good Vibrations	Beach Boys	Capitol	11	(1)	
6	10	I Can't Control Myself	Troggs	Page One	9	(43)	
7	1	Distant Drums	Jim Reeves	RCA	19	(45)	
8	-	Gimme Some Loving	Spencer Davis Group	Fontana	7	(7)	
9	-	If I Were A Carpenter	Bobby Darin	Atlantic	7	(8)	L
10	19	No Milk Today	Herman's Hermits	Columbia	7	(35)	
11	4	Winchester Cathedral	New Vaudeville Band	Fontana	9	(1)	F
12	-	Holy Cow	Lee Dorsey	Stateside	8	(23)	L
13	7	Guantanamera	Sandpipers	Pye International	9	(9)	F L
14	-	Green Green Grass Of Home	Tom Jones	Decca	15	(11)	G
15	-	Time Drags By	Cliff Richard	Columbia	4		
16	-	A Fool Am I	Cilla Black	Parlophone	4		
17	2	Bend It	Dave Dee, Dozy, Beaky etc.	Fontana	9		
18	-	What Would I Be	Val Doonican	Decca	11		
19	-	I've Got You Under My Skin	Four Seasons	Philips	5	(9)	
20	-	Help Me Girl	Eric Burdon & The Animals	Decca	4	(29)	

December 1966

This Mnth	Prev Mnth	Title	Artist	Label	Wks 20	(US Pos)	
1	14	Green Green Grass Of Home	Tom Jones	Decca	15	(11)	G
2	18	What Would I Be	Val Doonican	Decca	11		
3	5	Good Vibrations	Beach Boys	Capitol	11	(1)	
4	-	Morningtown Ride	Seekers	Columbia	10	(44)	
5	-	Friday On My Mind	Easybeats	UA	9	(16)	F
6	-	My Mind's Eye	Small Faces	Decca	6		
7	-	Dead End Street	Kinks	Pye	9	(73)	
8	8	Gimme Some Loving	Spencer Davis Group	Fontana	7	(7)	
9	-	What Becomes Of The Brokenhearted	Jimmy Ruffin	Tamla Motown	7	(7)	F
10	3	Semi-Detached Surburban Mr.James	Manfred Mann	Fontana	8		
11	-	Sunshine Superman	Donovan	Pye	7	(1)	
12	12	Holy Cow	Lee Dorsey	Stateside	8	(23)	L
13	-	Just One Smile	Gene Pitney	Stateside	6	(64)	
14	-	You Keep Me Hangin' On	Supremes	Tamla Motown	7	(1)	
15	-	Save Me	Dave Dee, Dozy, Beaky, Mick & Tich	Fontana	7		
16	7	Distant Drums	Jim Reeves	RCA	19	(45)	
17	-	If Every Day Was Like Christmas	Elvis Presley	RCA	4		
18	1	Reach Out I'll Be There	Four Tops	Tamla Motown	10	(1)	F
19	4	High Time	Paul Jones	HMV	8		F
20	-	There Won't Be Many Coming Home	Roy Orbison	London American	3		L

◆ The Beach Boys were mobbed when they arrived for a British tour. They ousted The Beatles as World's Top Group in the *NME* poll, and their transatlantic No. 1, 'Good Vibrations', showed how good pop records could be.

◆ A chart survey showed that the oddly named Dave Dee, Dozy, Beaky, Mick & Tich were the most successful singles act in the UK during 1966. The group went almost unnoticed across the Atlantic.

1967

January 1967

This Mnth	Prev Mnth	Title	Artist	Label	Wks	(US 20 Pos)	
1	1	Green Green Grass Of Home	Tom Jones	Decca	15	(11)	G
2	4	Morningtown Ride	Seekers	Columbia	10	(44)	
3	-	Happy Jack	Who	Reaction	7	(24)	
4	11	Sunshine Superman	Donovan	Pye	7	(1)	
5	-	I'm A Believer	Monkees	RCA	10	(1)	F
6	-	In The Country	Cliff Richard	Columbia	6		
7	15	Save Me	Dave Dee, Dozy, Beaky, Mick & Tich	Fontana	7		
8	-	Matthew And Son	Cat Stevens	Deram	7		F
9	-	Any Way That You Want Me	Troggs	Page One	5		
10	-	Night Of Fear	Move	Deram	7		F
11	7	Dead End Street	Kinks	Pye	9	(73)	
12	2	What Would I Be	Val Doonican	Decca	11		
13	-	Sittin' In The Park	Georgie Fame	Columbia	7		
14	14	You Keep Me Hangin' On	Supremes	Tamla Motown	7	(1)	
15	-	Pamela Pamela	Wayne Fontana	Fontana	6		L
16	-	Standing In The Shadows Of Love	Four Tops	Tamla Motown	4	(6)	
17	-	I Feel Free	Cream	Reaction	4		F
18	-	Hey Joe	Jimi Hendrix Experience	Polydor	5		F
19	3	Good Vibrations	Beach Boys	Capitol	11	(1)	
20	5	Friday On My Mind	Easybeats	UA	9	(16)	F

February 1967

This Mnth	Prev Mnth	Title	Artist	Label	Wks	(US 20 Pos)	
1	5	I'm A Believer	Monkees	RCA	10	(1)	F
2	-	Let's Spend The Night Together/Ruby Tuesday	Rolling Stones	Decca	7	(1)	
3	-	I've Been A Bad Bad Boy	Paul Jones	HMV	6		L
4	-	This Is My Song	Petula Clark	Pye	10	(3)	
5	8	Matthew And Son	Cat Stevens	Deram	7		F
6	10	Night Of Fear	Move	Deram	7		F
7	-	Release Me	Engelbert Humperdinck	Decca	15	(4)	F G
8	1	Green Green Grass Of Home	Tom Jones	Decca	15	(11)	G
9	-	Sugar Town	Nancy Sinatra	Reprise	5	(5)	
10	18	Hey Joe	Jimi Hendrix Experience	Polydor	5		F
11	-	Snoopy Vs The Red Baron	Royal Guardsmen	Stateside	8	(2)	F L
12	-	Peek-A-Boo	New Vaudeville Band	Fontana	7	(72)	
13	-	I Won't Come In While He's There	Jim Reeves	RCA	5		
14	-	Here Comes My Baby	Tremeloes	CBS	7	(13)	F
15	16	Standing In The Shadows Of Love	Four Tops	Tamla Motown	4	(6)	
16	-	I'm A Man	Spencer Davis Group	Fontana	3	(10)	L
17	-	Let Me Cry On Your Shoulder	Ken Dodd	Columbia	3		
18	-	Penny Lane/Strawberry Fields Forever	Beatles	Parlophone	8	(1)	
19	-	Mellow Yellow	Donovan	Pye	5	(2)	
20	17	I Feel Free	Cream	Reaction	4		F

◆ Tom Jones had his biggest UK hit with 'Green Green Grass Of Home'. Engelbert Humperdinck – who shared Jones's manager – also struck UK gold with a revi-val of another US country hit, 'Release Me'.

◆ Pink Floyd, The Jimi Hendrix Experience, Cream and The Monkees debuted on the UK chart. The Monkees' TV show was successful in Britain, catapulting them to the top of the charts.

March 1967

This Mnth	Prev Mnth	Title	Artist	Label	Wks	(US 20 Pos)	
1	7	Release Me	Engelbert Humperdinck	Decca	15	(4)	F G
2	18	Penny Lane/Strawberry Fields..	Beatles	Parlophone	8	(1)	
3	4	This Is My Song	Petula Clark	Pye	10	(3)	
4	-	Edelweiss	Vince Hill	Columbia	11		
5	14	Here Comes My Baby	Tremeloes	CBS	7	(13)	F
6	-	On A Carousel	Hollies	Parlophone	7	(11)	
7	-	There's A Kind Of Hush	Herman's Hermits	Columbia	7	(4)	
8	-	Georgy Girl	Seekers	Columbia	7	(2)	
9	-	Detroit City	Tom Jones	Decca	6	(27)	
10	11	Snoopy Vs The Red Baron	Royal Guardsmen	Stateside	8	(2)	F L
11	19	Mellow Yellow	Donovan	Pye	5	(2)	
12	12	Peek-A-Boo	New Vaudeville Band	Fontana	7	(72)	
13	-	This Is My Song	Harry Secombe	Philips	9		L
14	1	I'm A Believer	Monkees	RCA	10	(1)	F
15	-	Give It To Me	Troggs	Page One	4		
16	-	Simon Smith & His Amazing Dancing Bear	Alan Price Set	Decca	7		
17	-	I Was Kaiser Bill's Batman	Whistling Jack Smith	Deram	7	(20)	F L
18	-	Memories Are Made Of This	Val Doonican	Decca	5		
19	13	I Won't Come In While He's There	Jim Reeves	RCA	5		
20	2	Let's Spend The Night Together/Ruby Tuesday	Rolling Stones	Decca	7	(1)	

April 1967

This Mnth	Prev Mnth	Title	Artist	Label	Wks	(US 20 Pos)	
1	-	Somethin' Stupid	Nancy & Frank Sinatra	Reprise	11	(1)	
2	-	Puppet On A String	Sandie Shaw	Pye	13		
3	1	Release Me	Engelbert Humperdinck	Decca	15	(4)	F G
4	13	This Is My Song	Harry Secombe	Philips	9		L
5	-	A Little Bit Me, A Little Bit You	Monkees	RCA	8	(2)	
6	16	Simon Smith & His Amazing Dancing Bear	Alan Price Set	Decca	7		
7	17	I Was Kaiser Bill's Batman	Whistling Jack Smith	Deram	7	(20)	F L
8	-	Ha Ha Said The Clown	Manfred Mann	Fontana	7		
9	4	Edelweiss	Vince Hill	Columbia	11		
10	-	It's All Over	Cliff Richard	Columbia	6		
11	-	Purple Haze	Jimi Hendrix Experience	Track	8	(65)	
12	2	Penny Lane/Strawberry Fields Forever	Beatles	Parlophone	8	(1)	
13	8	Georgy Girl	Seekers	Columbia	7	(2)	
14	-	Bernadette	Four Tops	Tamla Motown	5	(4)	
15	3	This Is My Song	Petula Clark	Pye	10	(3)	
16	-	I'm Gonna Get Me A Gun	Cat Stevens	Deram	5		
17	18	Memories Are Made Of This	Val Doonican	Decca	5		
18	-	Happy Together	Turtles	London American	6	(1)	F
19	-	I Can Hear The Grass Grow	Move	Deram	6		
20	-	Touch Me Touch Me	Dave Dee, Dozy, Beaky, Mick & Tich	Fontana	3		

◆ Acts making their UK stage debuts included Otis Redding and Sam & Dave (on a Stax Records package show) and The Jeff Beck Group with vocalist Rod Stewart.

◆ The Beatles' album **Sergeant Pepper's Lonely Hearts Club Band** was released to much critical acclaim – it helped shape the future of pop and rock music.

1967

This Mnth	Prev Mnth	Title	Artist	Label	Wks	(US 20 Pos)	
1	2	Puppet On A String	Sandie Shaw	Pye	13		
2	-	Dedicated To The One I Love	Mamas & The Papas	RCA	10	(2)	
3	1	Somethin' Stupid	Nancy & Frank Sinatra	Reprise	11	(1)	
4	-	Silence Is Golden	Tremeloes	CBS	10	(11)	
5	-	The Boat That I Row	Lulu	Columbia	6		
6	-	Pictures Of Lily	Who	Track	6	(51)	
7	-	Funny Familiar Forgotten Feeling	Tom Jones	Decca	7	(49)	
8	11	Purple Haze	Jimi Hendrix Experience	Track	8	(65)	
9	-	Seven Drunken Nights	Dubliners	Major Minor	9		F
10	5	A Little Bit Me, A Little Bit You	Monkees	RCA	8	(2)	
11	19	I Can Hear The Grass Grow	Move	Deram	6		
12	-	Waterloo Sunset	Kinks	Pye	7		
13	-	Then I Kissed Her	Beach Boys	Capitol	8		
14	8	Ha Ha Said The Clown	Manfred Mann	Fontana	7		
15	-	Hi-Ho Silver Lining	Jeff Beck	Columbia	5		F
16	16	I'm Gonna Get Me A Gun	Cat Stevens	Deram	5		
17	-	The Wind Cries Mary	Jimi Hendrix Experience	Track	5		
18	3	Release Me	Engelbert Humperdinck	Decca	15	(4)	F G
19	-	New York Mining Disaster 1941	Bee Gees	Polydor	5	(14)	F
20	18	Happy Together	Turtles	London American	6	(1)	F

This	Prev	Title	Artist	Label	Wks	(US 20 Pos)	
1	-	A Whiter Shade Of Pale	Procol Harum	Deram	11	(5)	F
2	4	Silence Is Golden	Tremeloes	CBS	10	(11)	
3	12	Waterloo Sunset	Kinks	Pye	7		
4	-	There Goes My Everything	Engelbert Humperdinck	Decca	13	(20)	
5	-	The Happening	Supremes	Tamla Motown	8	(1)	
6	13	Then I Kissed Her	Beach Boys	Capitol	8		
7	2	Dedicated To The One I Love	Mamas & The Papas	RCA	10	(2)	
8	-	Sweet Soul Music	Arthur Conley	Atlantic	9	(2)	F L
9	-	Carrie-Anne	Hollies	Parlophone	8	(9)	
10	17	The Wind Cries Mary	Jimi Hendrix Experience	Track	5		
11	-	Okay!	Dave Dee, Dozy, Beaky, Mick & Tich	Fontana	6		
12	-	Finchley Central	New Vaudeville Band	Fontana	6		L
13	9	Seven Drunken Nights	Dubliners	Major Minor	9		F
14	6	Pictures Of Lily	Who	Track	6	(51)	
15	-	Paper Sun	Traffic	Island	5	(94)	F
16	1	Puppet On A String	Sandie Shaw	Pye	13		
17	-	Roses Of Picardy	Vince Hill	Columbia	4		
18	-	Groovin'	Young Rascals	Atlantic	7	(1)	F L
19	3	Somethin' Stupid	Nancy & Frank Sinatra	Reprise	11	(1)	
20	19	New York Mining Disaster 1941	Bee Gees	Polydor	5	(14)	F

◆ After coming second on five occasions the UK finally won the Eurovision Song Contest thanks to barefoot Sandie Shaw's bouncy 'Puppet On A String'.

◆ The Monkees, who continued adding to their transatlantic toppers, had a very successful British live debut at Wembley.

July 1967

This Mnth	Prev Mnth	Title	Artist	Label	Wks (US 20 Pos)	
1	1	A Whiter Shade Of Pale	Procol Harum	Deram	11 (5)	F
2	-	Alternate Title	Monkees	RCA	8	
3	4	There Goes My Everything	Engelbert Humperdinck	Decca	13 (20)	
4	-	She'd Rather Be With Me	Turtles	London American	10 (3)	
5	-	It Must Be Him (Seul Sur Son Etoile)	Vikki Carr	Liberty	10 (3)	F L
6	-	All You Need Is Love	Beatles	Parlophone	10 (1)	
7	9	Carrie-Anne	Hollies	Parlophone	8 (9)	
8	-	See Emily Play	Pink Floyd	Columbia	7	
9	-	If I Were A Rich Man	Topol	CBS	6	F L
10	-	San Francisco (Be Sure To Wear Some Flowers In Your Hair)	Scott McKenzie	CBS	14 (4)	F L
11	18	Groovin'	Young Rascals	Atlantic	7 (1)	F L
12	15	Paper Sun	Traffic	Island	5 (94)	F
13	-	Respect	Aretha Franklin	Atlantic	5 (1)	F
14	11	Okay!	Dave Dee, Dozy, Beaky, Mick & Tich	Fontana	6	
15	-	Here Come The Nice	Small Faces	Immediate	6	
16	8	Sweet Soul Music	Arthur Conley	Atlantic	9 (2)	F L
17	-	Seven Rooms Of Gloom	Four Tops	Tamla Motown	5 (14)	
18	5	The Happening	Supremes	Tamla Motown	8 (1)	
19	-	Don't Sleep In The Subway	Petula Clark	Pye	4 (5)	
20	-	You Only Live Twice/Jackson	Nancy Sinatra	Reprise	5 (44)	

August 1967

This Mnth	Prev Mnth	Title	Artist	Label	Wks (US 20 Pos)	
1	10	San Francisco (Be Sure To Wear Some Flowers In Your Hair)	Scott McKenzie	CBS	14 (4)	F L
2	6	All You Need Is Love	Beatles	Parlophone	10 (1)	
3	-	I'll Never Fall In Love Again	Tom Jones	Decca	10 (6)	
4	-	Death Of A Clown	Dave Davies	Pye	7	F
5	-	I Was Made To Love Her	Stevie Wonder	Tamla Motown	9 (2)	
6	5	It Must Be Him (Seul Sur Son Etoile)	Vikki Carr	Liberty	10 (3)	F L
7	-	Up Up And Away	Johnny Mann Singers	Liberty	7	F L
8	-	Just Loving You	Anita Harris	CBS	15	F L
9	4	She'd Rather Be With Me	Turtles	London American	10 (3)	
10	-	Even The Bad Times Are Good	Tremeloes	CBS	9 (36)	
11	2	Alternate Title	Monkees	RCA	8	
12	-	Creeque Alley	Mamas & The Papas	RCA	6 (5)	L
13	8	See Emily Play	Pink Floyd	Columbia	7	
14	-	The House That Jack Built	Alan Price Set	Decca	7	
15	3	There Goes My Everything	Engelbert Humperdinck	Decca	13 (20)	
16	-	Let's Pretend	Lulu	Columbia	4	
17	-	Gin House Blues	Amen Corner	Deram	5	F
18	1	A Whiter Shade Of Pale	Procol Harum	Deram	11 (5)	F
19	20	You Only Live Twice/Jackson	Nancy Sinatra	Reprise	5 (44)	
20	-	Pleasant Valley Sunday	Monkees	RCA	4 (3)	

◆ The UK government banned pirate radio stations and then launched Radio 1 – their own Top 40 station.
◆ Engelbert Humperdinck, one of the few acts not experimenting with psychedelic sounds, earned his second UK million seller of 1967 with 'The Last Waltz'.
◆ Beatles manager Brian Epstein and Bob Dylan's inspiration, folk singer/songwriter Woody Guthrie, died.

1967

This Mnth	Prev Mnth	Title	Artist	Label	Wks	(US 20 Pos)	
1	-	The Last Waltz	Engelbert Humperdinck	Decca	20	(25)	G
2	3	I'll Never Fall In Love Again	Tom Jones	Decca	10	(6)	
3	1	San Francisco (Be Sure To Wear Some Flowers In Your Hair)	Scott McKenzie	CBS	14	(4)	F L
4	-	Excerpt From A Teenage Opera	Keith West	Parlophone	11		F L
5	-	Itchycoo Park	Small Faces	Immediate	11	(16)	
6	10	Even The Bad Times Are Good	Tremeloes	CBS	9	(36)	
7	-	Let's Go To San Francisco	Flowerpot Men	Deram	7		F L
8	-	We Love You/Dandelion	Rolling Stones	Decca	6	(14)	
9	8	Just Loving You	Anita Harris	CBS	15		F L
10	-	Heroes And Villains	Beach Boys	Capitol	5	(12)	
11	14	The House That Jack Built	Alan Price Set	Decca	7		
12	5	I Was Made To Love Her	Stevie Wonder	Tamla Motown	9	(2)	
13	-	Reflections	Diana Ross & The Supremes	Tamla Motown	8	(2)	
14	-	Flowers In The Rain	Move	Regal Zonophone	10		
15	-	The Day I Met Marie	Cliff Richard	Columbia	8		
16	2	All You Need Is Love	Beatles	Parlophone	10	(1)	
17	-	Hole In My Shoe	Traffic	Island	10		
18	20	Pleasant Valley Sunday	Monkees	RCA	4	(3)	
19	-	There Must Be A Way	Frankie Vaughan	Columbia	14		L
20	4	Death Of A Clown	Dave Davies	Pye	7		F

This Mnth	Prev Mnth	Title	Artist	Label	Wks	(US 20 Pos)	
1	-	Massachusetts	Bee Gees	Polydor	10	(11)	
2	1	The Last Waltz	Engelbert Humperdinck	Decca	20	(25)	G
3	17	Hole In My Shoe	Traffic	Island	10		
4	14	Flowers In The Rain	Move	Regal Zonophone	10		
5	-	The Letter	Box Tops	Stateside	8	(1)	F
6	4	Excerpt From A Teenage Opera	Keith West	Parlophone	11		F L
7	13	Reflections	Diana Ross & The Supremes	Tamla Motown	8	(2)	
8	19	There Must Be A Way	Frankie Vaughan	Columbia	14		L
9	-	Homburg	Procol Harum	Regal Zonophone	7	(34)	
10	5	Itchycoo Park	Small Faces	Immediate	11	(16)	
11	-	From The Underworld	Herd	Fontana	8		F
12	-	When Will The Good Apples Fall	Seekers	Columbia	6		L
13	15	The Day I Met Marie	Cliff Richard	Columbia	8		
14	7	Let's Go To San Francisco	Flowerpot Men	Deram	7		F L
15	-	Baby, Now That I Found You	Foundations	Pye	9	(11)	F
16	-	Zabadak	Dave Dee, Dozy, Beaky, Mick & Tich	Fontana	8	(52)	
17	-	Ode To Billie Joe	Bobbie Gentry	Capitol	6	(1)	F
18	9	Just Loving You	Anita Harris	CBS	15		F L
19	-	Black Velvet Band	Dubliners	Major Minor	5		
20	2	I'll Never Fall In Love Again	Tom Jones	Decca	10	(6)	

◆ Innovative US act The Mothers Of Invention, whose **Freak Out** album was a milestone in rock, made a successful UK debut.

◆ The Beatles closed the year with 'Hello Goodbye' topping the transatlantic charts. However, in 1967, they were replaced as the world's most successful act by The Monkees, who, among other achievements, chalked up a (still unbeaten) record of four American chart topping albums in one calendar year.

November 1967

This Mnth	Prev Mnth	Title	Artist	Label	Wks	(US 20 Pos)	
1	15	Baby, Now That I Found You	Foundations	Pye	9	(11)	F
2	1	Massachusetts	Bee Gees	Polydor	10	(11)	
3	16	Zabadak	Dave Dee, Dozy, Beaky, Mick & Tich	Fontana	8	(52)	
4	-	Autumn Almanac	Kinks	Pye	7		
5	2	The Last Waltz	Engelbert Humperdinck	Decca	20	(25)	G
6	-	Love Is All Around	Troggs	Page One	7	(7)	L
7	11	From The Underworld	Herd	Fontana	8		F
8	-	San Franciscan Nights	Eric Burdon & The Animals	MGM	5	(9)	
9	9	Homburg	Procol Harum	Regal Zonophone	7	(34)	
10	-	There Is A Mountain	Donovan	Pye	5	(11)	
11	8	There Must Be A Way	Frankie Vaughan	Columbia	14		L
12	-	Let The Heartaches Begin	Long John Baldry	Pye	9	(88)	F
13	3	Hole In My Shoe	Traffic	Island	10		
14	-	If The Whole World Stopped Loving	Val Doonican	Pye	13		
15	-	I Can See For Miles	Who	Track	4	(9)	
16	-	Everybody Knows	Dave Clark Five	Columbia	8	(43)	
17	4	Flowers In The Rain	Move	Regal Zonophone	10		
18	5	The Letter	Box Tops	Stateside	8	(1)	F
19	-	I Feel Love Comin' On	Felice Taylor	President	6		F L
20	12	When Will The Good Apples Fall	Seekers	Columbia	6		L

December 1967

This Mnth	Prev Mnth	Title	Artist	Label	Wks	(US 20 Pos)	
1	-	Hello Goodbye	Beatles	Parlophone	10	(1)	
2	14	If The Whole World Stopped Loving	Val Doonican	Pye	13		
3	12	Let The Heartaches Begin	Long John Baldry	Pye	9	(88)	F
4	-	Something's Gotten Hold Of My Heart	Gene Pitney	Stateside	9		
5	-	I'm Comin' Home	Tom Jones	Decca	12	(57)	
6	16	Everybody Knows	Dave Clark Five	Columbia	8	(43)	
7	-	All My Love	Cliff Richard	Columbia	8		
8	-	Careless Hands	Des O'Connor	Columbia	9		F
9	-	Daydream Believer	Monkees	RCA	12	(1)	
10	-	World	Bee Gees	Polydor	10		
11	-	Thank U Very Much	Scaffold	Parlophone	8	(69)	F
12	-	Magical Mystery Tour (Double E.P.)	Beatles	Parlophone	9		
13	6	Love Is All Around	Troggs	Page One	7	(7)	L
14	-	Here We Go Round The Mulberry Bush	Traffic	Island	7		L
15	5	The Last Waltz	Engelbert Humperdinck	Decca	20	(25)	G
16	1	Baby, Now That I Found You	Foundations	Pye	9	(11)	F
17	19	I Feel Love Comin' On	Felice Taylor	President	6		F L
18	-	Kites	Simon Dupree & The Big Sound	Parlophone	8		F L
19	-	Walk Away Renee	Four Tops	Tamla Motown	8	(14)	
20	3	Zabadak	Dave Dee, Dozy, Beaky etc.	Fontana	8	(52)	

◆ In the year that US record sales first topped the $1 billion mark and, for the first time, albums outsold singles, the gap between the American and British markets widened, with only 25% of Top 20 hits scoring in both countries.

◆ 'To Sir With Love' by Lulu topped the US chart but was only a B-side in the UK.
◆ Critically acclaimed UK underground band Pink Floyd joined burgeoning teen idols Amen Corner and The Move to support headliner Jimi Hendrix on tour.

1968

This Mnth	Prev Mnth	Title	Artist	Label	Wks	(US 20 Pos)	
1	1	Hello Goodbye	Beatles	Parlophone	10	(1)	
2	12	Magical Mystery Tour (Double E.P.)	Beatles	Parlophone	9		
3	-	Ballad Of Bonnie & Clyde	Georgie Fame	CBS	8	(7)	
4	19	Walk Away Renee	Four Tops	Tamla Motown	8	(14)	
5	9	Daydream Believer	Monkees	RCA	12	(1)	
6	5	I'm Comin' Home	Tom Jones	Decca	12	(57)	
7	11	Thank U Very Much	Scaffold	Parlophone	8	(69)	F
8	-	Everlasting Love	Love Affair	CBS	10		F
9	2	If The Whole World Stopped Loving	Val Doonican	Pye	13		
10	10	World	Bee Gees	Polydor	10		
11	18	Kites	Simon Dupree & The Big Sound	Parlophone	8		F L
12	-	Am I That Easy To Forget	Engelbert Humperdinck	Decca	9	(18)	
13	4	Something's Gotten Hold Of My Heart	Gene Pitney	Stateside	9		
14	-	Tin Soldier	Small Faces	Immediate	8	(73)	
15	14	Here We Go Round The Mulberry Bush	Traffic	Island	7		L
16	-	Judy In Disguise (With Glasses)	John Fred & His Playboy Band	Pye International	7	(1)	F L
17	8	Careless Hands	Des O'Connor	Columbia	9		F
18	-	In And Out Of Love	Diana Ross & The Supremes	Tamla Motown	7	(9)	
19	-	Everything I Am	Plastic Penny	Page One	5		F L
20	-	She Wears My Ring	Solomon King	Columbia	11		F L

1	8	Everlasting Love	Love Affair	CBS	10		F
2	-	Mighty Quinn	Manfred Mann	Fontana	8	(10)	
3	12	Am I That Easy To Forget	Engelbert Humperdinck	Decca	9	(18)	
4	-	Bend Me Shape Me	Amen Corner	Deram	9		
5	16	Judy In Disguise (With Glasses)	John Fred & His Playboy Band	Pye International	7	(1)	F L
6	20	She Wears My Ring	Solomon King	Columbia	11		F L
7	-	Suddenly You Love Me	Tremeloes	CBS	8	(44)	
8	-	Gimme Little Sign	Brenton Wood	Liberty	7	(9)	F L
9	3	Ballad Of Bonnie & Clyde	Georgie Fame	CBS	8	(7)	
10	-	Pictures Of Matchstick Men	Status Quo	Pye	7	(12)	F
11	19	Everything I Am	Plastic Penny	Page One	5		F L
12	-	I Can Take Or Leave Your Lovin'	Herman's Hermits	Columbia	6	(22)	
13	-	Darlin'	Beach Boys	Capitol	9	(19)	
14	-	Fire Brigade	Move	Regal Zonophone	8		
15	-	Words	Bee Gees	Polydor	7	(15)	
16	-	Cinderella Rockafella	Esther & Abi Ofarim	Philips	9	(68)	F
17	5	Daydream Believer	Monkees	RCA	12	(1)	
18	-	Don't Stop The Carnival	Alan Price Set	Decca	4		
19	14	Tin Soldier	Small Faces	Immediate	8	(73)	
20	2	Magical Mystery Tour (Double E.P.)	Beatles	Parlophone	9		

◆ Music from *Magical Mystery Tour* kept the Beatles at the top, although the film itself was their first commercial and critical flop. Meanwhile, their previous project, **Sergeant Pepper**, grabbed four Grammies.

◆ Newcomers Love Affair were splashed over the front pages of the tabloids when they admitted that only lead singer Steve Ellis was actually on their chart topping cover of 'Everlasting Love'. This revelation did not stop them being elevated to teen idol status.

March 1968

This Mnth	Prev Mnth	Title	Artist	Label	Wks	(US 20 Pos)	
1	16	Cinderella Rockafella	Esther & Abi Ofarim	Philips	9	(68)	F
2	-	Legend Of Xanadu	Dave Dee, Dozy, Beaky, Mick & Tich	Fontana	8		
3	14	Fire Brigade	Move	Regal Zonophone	8		
4	-	Rosie	Don Partridge	Columbia	9		F
5	-	Jennifer Juniper	Donovan	Pye	6	(26)	
6	-	Delilah	Tom Jones	Decca	11	(15)	
7	2	Mighty Quinn	Manfred Mann	Fontana	8	(10)	
8	-	(Sittin' On) The Dock Of The Bay	Otis Redding	Stax	8	(1)	
9	-	Green Tambourine	Lemon Pipers	Pye International	6	(1)	F L
10	6	She Wears My Ring	Solomon King	Columbia	11		F L
11	4	Bend Me Shape Me	Amen Corner	Deram	9		
12	10	Pictures Of Matchstick Men	Status Quo	Pye	7	(12)	F
13	15	Words	Bee Gees	Polydor	7	(15)	
14	-	Me The Peaceful Heart	Lulu	Columbia	5	(53)	
15	13	Darlin'	Beach Boys	Capitol	9	(19)	
16	-	Lady Madonna	Beatles	Parlophone	6	(4)	
17	-	What A Wonderful World	Louis Armstrong	HMV	16	(32)	L
18	7	Suddenly You Love Me	Tremeloes	CBS	8	(44)	
19	-	If I Were A Carpenter	Four Tops	Tamla Motown	6	(20)	
20	8	Gimme Little Sign	Brenton Wood	Liberty	7	(9)	F L

April 1968

This Mnth	Prev Mnth	Title	Artist	Label	Wks	(US 20 Pos)	
1	-	Congratulations	Cliff Richard	Columbia	9	(99)	
2	17	What A Wonderful World	Louis Armstrong	HMV	16	(32)	L
3	6	Delilah	Tom Jones	Decca	11	(15)	
4	-	If I Only Had Time	John Rowles	MCA	11		F
5	8	(Sittin' On) The Dock Of The Bay	Otis Redding	Stax	8	(1)	
6	16	Lady Madonna	Beatles	Parlophone	6	(4)	
7	-	Simon Says	1910 Fruitgum Co.	Pye International	12	(4)	F L
8	-	Step Inside Love	Cilla Black	Parlophone	5		
9	19	If I Were A Carpenter	Four Tops	Tamla Motown	6	(20)	
10	-	Jennifer Eccles	Hollies	Parlophone	6	(40)	
11	-	Can't Take My Eyes Off You	Andy Williams	CBS	9		
12	1	Cinderella Rockafella	Esther & Abi Ofarim	Philips	9	(68)	F
13	-	I Can't Let Maggie Go	Honeybus	Deram	6		F L
14	-	Captain Of Your Ship	Reperata & The Delrons	Bell	5		F L
15	-	Ain't Nothin' But A Housparty	Showstoppers	Beacon	9		F L
16	-	Valleri	Monkees	RCA	5	(3)	
17	4	Rosie	Don Partridge	Columbia	9		F
18	2	Legend Of Xanadu	Dave Dee, Dozy, Beaky, Mick & Tich	Fontana	8		
19	-	Love Is Blue (L'Amour Est Bleu)	Paul Mauriat	Philips	5	(1)	F L
20	-	Something Here In My Heart (Keeps A-Tellin' Me No)	Paper Dolls	Pye	5		F L

◆ Status Quo (who subsequently had more UK chart singles than The Beatles or Stones) debuted on the Top 20. Fellow superstars Genesis released their first single, as did Elton John, described by his label as "1968's greatest new talent".

◆ Pink Floyd, Jethro Tull and Tyrannosaurus Rex appeared at the first free concert in London's Hyde Park.

1968

This Mnth	Prev Mnth	Title	Artist	Label	Wks	(US 20 Pos)	
1	2	What A Wonderful World	Louis Armstrong	HMV	16	(32)	L
2	-	Lazy Sunday	Small Faces	Immediate	7		
3	-	A Man Without Love	Engelbert Humperdinck	Decca	9	(19)	
4	7	Simon Says	1910 Fruitgum Co.	Pye International	12	(4)	F L
5	-	Young Girl	Gary Puckett & The Union Gap	CBS	12	(2)	F
6	11	Can't Take My Eyes Off You	Andy Williams	CBS	9		
7	-	I Don't Want Our Loving To Die	Herd	Fontana	8		L
8	4	If I Only Had Time	John Rowles	MCA	11		F
9	-	Honey	Bobby Goldsboro	UA	11	(1)	F
10	1	Congratulations	Cliff Richard	Columbia	9	(99)	
11	-	White Horses	Jacky	Philips	9		F L
12	10	Jennifer Eccles	Hollies	Parlophone	6	(40)	
13	-	Rainbow Valley	Love Affair	CBS	8		
14	15	Ain't Nothin' But A Housparty	Showstoppers	Beacon	9		F L
15	13	I Can't Let Maggie Go	Honeybus	Deram	6		F L
16	20	Something Here In My Heart (Keeps A-Tellin' Me No)	Paper Dolls	Pye	5		F L
17	3	Delilah	Tom Jones	Decca	11	(15)	
18	-	Sleepy Joe	Herman's Hermits	Columbia	6	(61)	
19	-	Joanna	Scott Walker	Philips	7		F
20	-	Cry Like A Baby	Box Tops	Bell	5	(2)	L

This Mnth	Prev Mnth	Title	Artist	Label	Wks	(US 20 Pos)	
1	5	Young Girl	Gary Puckett & The Union Gap	CBS	12	(2)	F
2	9	Honey	Bobby Goldsboro	UA	11	(1)	F
3	-	Jumping Jack Flash	Rolling Stones	Decca	9	(3)	
4	3	A Man Without Love	Engelbert Humperdinck	Decca	9	(19)	
5	-	This Wheel's On Fire	Julie Driscoll, Brian Auger & The Trinity	Marmalade	8		F L
6	13	Rainbow Valley	Love Affair	CBS	8		
7	-	Do You Know The Way To San José	Dionne Warwick	Pye International	8	(10)	
8	-	Blue Eyes	Don Partridge	Columbia	8		L
9	-	Hurdy Gurdy Man	Donovan	Pye	7	(5)	
10	7	I Don't Want Our Loving To Die	Herd	Fontana	8		L
11	19	Joanna	Scott Walker	Philips	7		F
12	-	Baby Come Back	Equals	President	12	(32)	F
13	1	What A Wonderful World	Louis Armstrong	HMV	16	(32)	L
14	-	I Pretend	Des O'Connor	Columbia	15		
15	2	Lazy Sunday	Small Faces	Immediate	7		
16	4	Simon Says	1910 Fruitgum Co.	Pye International	12	(4)	F L
17	18	Sleepy Joe	Herman's Hermits	Columbia	6	(61)	
18	-	Lovin' Things	Marmalade	CBS	6		F
19	-	Son Of Hickory Hollers Tramp	O.C. Smith	CBS	9	(40)	F L
20	-	Helule Helule	Tremeloes	CBS	5		

◆ American hits in Britain included: transatlantic No. 1 'Young Girl' by Gary Puckett & The Union Gap, 'Honey ' by Bobby Goldsboro, 'What A Wonderful World' by 66-year-old Louis Armstrong and rock's biggest seller, 'Rock Around The Clock' by Bill Haley.
◆ For a while street busker Don Partridge stopped playing outside theatres and headlined inside, thanks to two successive Top 5 singles, 'Rosie' and 'Blue Eyes'.

1968

July 1968

This Mnth	Prev Mnth	Title	Artist	Label	Wks	(US 20 Pos)	
1	12	Baby Come Back	Equals	President	12	(32)	F
2	14	I Pretend	Des O'Connor	Columbia	15		
3	19	Son Of Hickory Hollers Tramp	O.C. Smith	CBS	9	(40)	F L
4	-	Yesterday Has Gone	Cupid's Inspiration	Nems	7		F L
5	-	Yummy Yummy Yummy	Ohio Express	Pye International	9	(4)	F L
6	-	Mony Mony	Tommy James & The Shondells	Major Minor	11	(3)	F L
7	3	Jumping Jack Flash	Rolling Stones	Decca	9	(3)	
8	-	My Name Is Jack	Manfred Mann	Fontana	5		
9	-	MacArthur Park	Richard Harris	RCA	7	(2)	F L
10	8	Blue Eyes	Don Partridge	Columbia	8		L
11	18	Lovin' Things	Marmalade	CBS	6		F
12	9	Hurdy Gurdy Man	Donovan	Pye	7	(5)	
13	-	Hush Not A Word To Mary	John Rowles	MCA	5		L
14	-	Fire	Crazy World Of Arthur Brown	Track	10	(2)	F L
15	-	One More Dance	Esther & Abi Ofarim	Philips	4		L
16	1	Young Girl	Gary Puckett & The Union Gap	CBS	12	(2)	F
17	-	This Guy's In Love With You	Herb Alpert	A&M	11	(1)	
18	-	Mrs. Robinson	Simon & Garfunkel	CBS	7	(1)	
19	5	This Wheel's On Fire	Julie Driscoll, Brian Auger & The Trinity	Marmalade	8		F L
20	-	I Close My Eyes And Count To Ten	Dusty Springfield	Philips	6		

August 1968

This Mnth	Prev Mnth	Title	Artist	Label	Wks	(US 20 Pos)	
1	6	Mony Mony	Tommy James & The Shondells	Major Minor	11	(3)	F L
2	14	Fire	Crazy World Of Arthur Brown	Track	10	(2)	F L
3	17	This Guy's In Love With You	Herb Alpert	A&M	11	(1)	
4	2	I Pretend	Des O'Connor	Columbia	15		
5	20	I Close My Eyes And Count To Ten	Dusty Springfield	Philips	6		
6	-	Help Yourself	Tom Jones	Decca	10	(35)	
7	18	Mrs. Robinson	Simon & Garfunkel	CBS	7	(1)	
8	-	Sunshine Girl	Herman's Hermits	Columbia	8		
9	-	Dance To The Music	Sly & The Family Stone	Direction	7	(8)	F
10	-	Do It Again	Beach Boys	Capitol	10	(20)	
11	-	Last Night In Soho	Dave Dee, Dozy, Beaky, Mick & Tich	Fontana	6		
12	-	I've Gotta Get A Message To You	Bee Gees	Polydor	11	(8)	
13	9	MacArthur Park	Richard Harris	RCA	7	(2)	F L
14	-	Keep On	Bruce Channel	Bell	6		L
15	1	Baby Come Back	Equals	President	12	(32)	F
16	-	High In The Sky	Amen Corner	Deram	9		
17	-	Days	Kinks	Pye	6		
18	5	Yummy Yummy Yummy	Ohio Express	Pye International	9	(4)	F L
19	-	I Say A Little Prayer	Aretha Franklin	Atlantic	8	(10)	
20	3	Son Of Hickory Hollers Tramp	O.C. Smith	CBS	9	(40)	F L

◆ The Beatles launched their own label, Apple, and released their animated film *Yellow Submarine*. Incidentally, the group's No. 1 rivals of 1967, the Monkees, had their last US Top 20 entry with a Leiber & Stoller song, 'D.W. Washburn'.

◆ Cream announced they were splitting up, as did The Yardbirds. The Hollies started to make solo records, Janis Joplin quit Big Brother & The Holding Company, and Dennis Edwards replaced singer David Ruffin in The Temptations.

1968

September 1968

This Mnth	Prev Mnth	Title	Artist	Label	Wks	(US 20 Pos)	
1	12	I've Gotta Get A Message To You	Bee Gees	Polydor	11	(8)	
2	10	Do It Again	Beach Boys	Capitol	10	(20)	
3	19	I Say A Little Prayer	Aretha Franklin	Atlantic	8	(10)	
4	-	Hold Me Tight	Johnny Nash	Regal Zonophone	10	(5)	F
5	-	Hey Jude	Beatles	Apple	10	(1)	
6	-	Those Were The Days	Mary Hopkin	Apple	14	(2)	F
7	3	This Guy's In Love With You	Herb Alpert	A&M	11	(1)	
8	16	High In The Sky	Amen Corner	Deram	9		
9	6	Help Yourself	Tom Jones	Decca	10	(35)	
10	-	Jesamine	Casuals	Decca	11		F L
11	-	On The Road Again	Canned Heat	Liberty	7	(16)	F
12	-	Lady Willpower	Gary Puckett & The Union Gap	CBS	10	(2)	
13	-	Dream A Little Dream Of Me	Mama Cass	RCA	7	(12)	F
14	-	Little Arrows	Leapy Lee	MCA	13	(16)	F L
15	1	Mony Mony	Tommy James & The Shondells	Major Minor	11	(3)	F L
16	2	Fire	Crazy World Of Arthur Brown	Track	10	(2)	F L
17	-	Hard To Handle	Otis Redding	Atlantic	6	(51)	L
18	9	Dance To The Music	Sly & The Family Stone	Direction	7	(8)	F
19	-	Classical Gas	Mason Williams	Warner	8	(2)	F L
20	8	Sunshine Girl	Herman's Hermits	Columbia	8		

October 1968

This Mnth	Prev Mnth	Title	Artist	Label	Wks	(US 20 Pos)	
1	6	Those Were The Days	Mary Hopkin	Apple	14	(2)	F
2	5	Hey Jude	Beatles	Apple	10	(1)	
3	10	Jesamine	Casuals	Decca	11		F L
4	14	Little Arrows	Leapy Lee	MCA	13	(16)	F L
5	12	Lady Willpower	Gary Puckett & The Union Gap	CBS	10	(2)	
6	-	My Little Lady	Tremeloes	CBS	7		
7	-	Red Balloon	Dave Clark Five	Columbia	6		
8	-	A Day Without Love	Love Affair	CBS	7		
9	4	Hold Me Tight	Johnny Nash	Regal Zonophone	10	(5)	F
10	-	Les Bicyclettes De Belsize	Engelbert Humperdinck	Decca	7	(31)	
11	19	Classical Gas	Mason Williams	Warner	8	(2)	F L
12	-	Ice In The Sun	Status Quo	Pye	6	(70)	
13	1	I've Gotta Get A Message To You	Bee Gees	Polydor	11	(8)	
14		Light My Fire	José Feliciano	RCA	8	(3)	F L
15	-	The Good, The Bad And The Ugly	Hugo Montenegro & Orchestra	RCA	15	(2)	F L
16	3	I Say A Little Prayer	Aretha Franklin	Atlantic	8	(10)	
17	-	Listen To Me	Hollies	Parlophone	6		
18	-	Hello, I Love You	Doors	Elektra	6	(1)	F
19	8	High In The Sky	Amen Corner	Deram	9		
20	-	Only One Woman	Marbles	Polydor	8		F L

◆ The Album **Beat of the Brass** ended a fantastic run of eight consecutive Top 10 LPs for Herb Alpert & The Tijuana Brass

◆ John Sebastian left The Lovin' Spoonful, Eric Burdon disbanded The Animals and Graham Nash left The Hollies (to form Crosby, Stills & Nash). Also Mama Cass left The Mamas & The Papas, Peter Tork quit The Monkees and Cream's farewell American tour grossed over $700,000.

November 1968

This Mnth	Prev Mnth	Title	Artist	Label	Wks (US 20 Pos)
1	15	The Good, The Bad And The Ugly	Hugo Montenegro & Orchestra	RCA	15 (2) F L
2	-	With A Little Help From My Friends	Joe Cocker	Regal Zonophone	8 (68) F
3	-	Eloise	Barry Ryan	MGM	9 (86) F L
4	1	Those Were The Days	Mary Hopkin	Apple	14 (2) F
5	-	This Old Heart Of Mine	Isley Brothers	Tamla Motown	10 (12) F
6	20	Only One Woman	Marbles	Polydor	8 F L
7	-	All Along The Watchtower	Jimi Hendrix Experience	Track	6 (20)
8	14	Light My Fire	Jose Feliciano	RCA	8 (3) F L
9	-	Breakin' Down The Walls Of Heartache	Johnny Johnson & The Bandwagon	Direction	11 F
10	4	Little Arrows	Leapy Lee	MCA	13 (16) F L
11	3	Jesamine	Casuals	Decca	11 F L
12	2	Hey Jude	Beatles	Apple	10 (1)
13	-	Elenore	Turtles	London American	5 (6) L
14	10	Les Bicyclettes De Belsize	Engelbert Humperdinck	Decca	7 (31)
15	-	Ain't Got No - I Got Life/ Do What You Gotta Do	Nina Simone	RCA	12 (94) F
16	-	Lily The Pink	Scaffold	Parlophone	12
17	17	Listen To Me	Hollies	Parlophone	6
18	6	My Little Lady	Tremeloes	CBS	7
19	8	A Day Without Love	Love Affair	CBS	7
20	-	Mexico	Long John Baldry	Pye	4 L

December 1968

This Mnth	Prev Mnth	Title	Artist	Label	Wks (US 20 Pos)
1	16	Lily The Pink	Scaffold	Parlophone	12
2	15	Ain't Got No - I Got Life/ Do What You Gotta Do	Nina Simone	RCA	12 (94) F
3	1	The Good, The Bad And The Ugly	Hugo Montenegro & Orchestra	RCA	15 (2) F L
4	-	One Two Three O'Leary	Des O'Connor	Columbia	9
5	-	Build Me Up Buttercup	Foundations	Pye	9 (3)
6	-	I'm The Urban Spaceman	Bonzo Dog Doo-Dah Band	Liberty	10 F L
7	5	This Old Heart Of Mine	Isley Brothers	Tamla Motown	10 (12) F
8	9	Breakin' Down The Walls Of Heartache	Johnny Johnson & The Bandwagon	Direction	11 F
9	-	Race With The Devil	Gun	CBS	7 F L
10	-	I'm A Tiger	Lulu	Columbia	10
11	-	Sabre Dance	Love Sculpture	Parlophone	8 F L
12	3	Eloise	Barry Ryan	MGM	9 (86) F L
13	-	May I Have The Next Dream With You	Malcolm Roberts	Major Minor	8 F
14	-	Ob-La-Di Ob-La-Da	Marmalade	CBS	10
15	-	Harper Valley P.T.A.	Jeannie C. Riley	Polydor	5 (1) F L
16	13	Elenore	Turtles	London American	5 (6) L
17	-	Albatross	Fleetwood Mac	Blue Horizon	13 F
18	-	Private Number	Judy Clay & William Bell	Stax	9 (75) F L
19	-	A Minute Of Your Time	Tom Jones	Decca	7 (48)
20	7	All Along The Watchtower	Jimi Hendrix Experience	Track	6 (20)

◆ Double album, **The Beatles**, topped the charts, and the group's seven minute single, 'Hey Jude', amassed world sales of five million. The first solo Beatle LPs were released by George and John, and a single on their Apple imprint, 'Those Were The Days' by Mary Hopkin, became an international hit.

1969

This Mnth	Prev Mnth	Title	Artist	Label	Wks	(US 20 Pos)
1	14	Ob-La-Di Ob-La-Da	Marmalade	CBS	10	
2	1	Lily The Pink	Scaffold	Parlophone	12	
3	17	Albatross	Fleetwood Mac	Blue Horizon	13	F
4	5	Build Me Up Buttercup	Foundations	Pye	9 (3)	
5	6	I'm The Urban Spaceman	Bonzo Dog Doo-Dah Band	Liberty	10	F L
6	-	For Once In My Life	Stevie Wonder	Tamla Motown	10 (2)	
7	11	Sabre Dance	Love Sculpture	Parlophone	8	F L
8	-	Something's Happening	Herman's Hermits	Columbia	8	
9	2	Ain't Got No - I Got Life/ Do What You Gotta Do	Nina Simone	RCA	12 (94)	F
10	-	Son-Of-A Preacher Man	Dusty Springfield	Philips	6 (10)	
11	18	Private Number	Judy Clay & William Bell	Stax	9 (75)	F L
12	4	One Two Three O'Leary	Des O'Connor	Columbia	9	
13	-	Blackberry Way	Move	Regal Zonophone	8	
14	10	I'm A Tiger	Lulu	Columbia	10	
15	-	Fox On The Run	Manfred Mann	Fontana	6 (97)	
16	9	Race With The Devil	Gun	CBS	7	F L
17	3	The Good, The Bad And The Ugly	Hugo Montenegro & Orchestra	RCA	15 (2)	F L
18	-	Love Child	Diana Ross & The Supremes	Tamla Motown	9 (1)	
19	-	Stop Her On Sight (SOS)/ Headline News	Edwin Starr	Polydor	5 (48)	F
20	19	A Minute Of Your Time	Tom Jones	Decca	7 (48)	

1	3	Albatross	Fleetwood Mac	Blue Horizon	13	F
2	13	Blackberry Way	Move	Regal Zonophone	8	
3	6	For Once In My Life	Stevie Wonder	Tamla Motown	10 (2)	
4	-	Dancing In The Street	Martha & The Vandellas	Tamla Motown	7	F
5	-	You Got Soul	Johnny Nash	Major Minor	6 (58)	
6	-	Please Don't Go	Donald Peers	Columbia	9	F L
7	1	Ob-La-Di Ob-La-Da	Marmalade	CBS	10	
8	-	I'm Gonna Make You Love Me	Diana Ross & The Supremes & The Temptations	Tamla Motown	7 (2)	
9	-	To Love Somebody	Nina Simone	RCA	5	
10	-	(If Paradise Is) Half As Nice	Amen Corner	Immediate	7	
11	15	Fox On The Run	Manfred Mann	Fontana	6 (97)	
12	-	Where Do You Go To My Lovely	Peter Sarstedt	UA	10 (70)	F
13	8	Something's Happening	Herman's Hermits	Columbia	8	
14	-	I Guess I'll Always Love You	Isley Brothers	Tamla Motown	5 (61)	
15	11	Private Number	Judy Clay & William Bell	Stax	9 (75)	F L
16	19	Stop Her On Sight (SOS)/ Headline News	Edwin Starr	Polydor	5 (48)	F
17	-	The Way It Used To Be	Engelbert Humperdinck	Decca	8 (42)	
18	-	I'll Pick A Rose For My Rose	Marv Johnson	Tamla Motown	6	L
19	2	Lily The Pink	Scaffold	Parlophone	12	
20	-	Mrs. Robinson (E.P.)	Simon & Garfunkel	CBS	1	

◆ Martha & The Vandellas' 1964 American hit 'Dancing In The Streets' finally reached the UK Top 20 as did label-mates The Isley Brothers' 1966 recording of 'I Guess I'll Always Love You'.

◆ Led Zeppelin debuted in the US (supported by fellow newcomers Jethro Tull). They would become one of the biggest selling and most influential acts of all time.

1969

This Mnth	Prev Mnth	Title	Artist	Label	Wks	(US 20 Pos)	
1	12	Where Do You Go To My Lovely	Peter Sarstedt	UA	10	(70)	F
2	-	Surround Yourself With Sorrow	Cilla Black	Parlophone	9		
3	-	I Heard It Through The Grapevine	Marvin Gaye	Tamla Motown	10	(1)	
4	17	The Way It Used To Be	Engelbert Humperdinck	Decca	8	(42)	
5	6	Please Don't Go	Donald Peers	Columbia	9		F L
6	-	Gentle On My Mind	Dean Martin	Reprise	12		L
7	-	Wichita Lineman	Glen Campbell	Ember	6	(3)	F
8	-	Monsieur Dupont	Sandie Shaw	Pye	8		L
9	10	(If Paradise Is) Half As Nice	Amen Corner	Immediate	7		
10	-	First Of May	Bee Gees	Polydor	6	(37)	
11	8	I'm Gonna Make You Love Me	Diana Ross & The Supremes & The Temptations	Tamla Motown	7	(2)	
12	-	You've Lost That Lovin' Feelin'	Righteous Brothers	London American	6		
13	-	Sorry Suzanne	Hollies	Parlophone	7	(56)	
14	-	If I Can Dream	Elvis Presley	RCA	6	(12)	
15	-	Good Times (Better Times)	Cliff Richard	Columbia	7		
16	4	Dancing In The Street	Martha & The Vandellas	Tamla Motown	7		F
17	18	I'll Pick A Rose For My Rose	Marv Johnson	Tamla Motown	6		L
18	-	Games People Play	Joe South	Capitol	8	(12)	F L
19	2	Blackberry Way	Move	Regal Zonophone	8		
20	1	Albatross	Fleetwood Mac	Blue Horizon	13		F

This Mnth	Prev Mnth	Title	Artist	Label	Wks	(US 20 Pos)	
1	3	I Heard It Through The Grapevine	Marvin Gaye	Tamla Motown	10	(1)	
2	-	Israelites	Desmond Dekker & The Aces	Pyramid	8	(9)	
3	6	Gentle On My Mind	Dean Martin	Reprise	12		L
4	-	Boom Bang-A-Bang	Lulu	Columbia	7		
5	-	Goodbye	Mary Hopkin	Apple	9	(13)	
6	13	Sorry Suzanne	Hollies	Parlophone	7	(56)	
7	-	In The Bad Bad Old Days	Foundations	Pye	7	(51)	L
8	-	Pinball Wizard	Who	Track	8	(19)	
9	18	Games People Play	Joe South	Capitol	8	(12)	F L
10	-	Windmills Of Your Mind	Noel Harrison	Reprise	9		F L
11	8	Monsieur Dupont	Sandie Shaw	Pye	8		L
12	-	I Can Hear Music	Beach Boys	Capitol	7	(24)	
13	2	Surround Yourself With Sorrow	Cilla Black	Parlophone	9		
14	1	Where Do You Go To My Lovely	Peter Sarstedt	UA	10	(70)	F
15	-	Get Back	Beatles with Billy Preston	Apple	10	(1)	
16	-	Come Back And Shake Me	Clodagh Rodgers	RCA	8		F
17	-	Harlem Shuffle	Bob & Earl	Island	7	(44)	F L
18	-	Cupid	Johnny Nash	Major Minor	6	(39)	
19	-	Get Ready	Temptations	Tamla Motown	5	(29)	
20	10	First Of May	Bee Gees	Polydor	6	(37)	

◆ Cream's **Goodbye Cream** album was a Top 3 entry - although the film of the same name was panned. Ex-Cream members Eric Clapton and Ginger Baker were planning a new group (Blind Faith) with Stevie Winwood.

◆ Headliners at the first Country Music Festival in Britain included George Jones, Tammy Wynette, Conway Twitty and Loretta Lynn. Fellow Nashville superstar Johnny Cash appeared on a TV special with Bob Dylan.

1969

This Mnth	Prev Mnth	Title	Artist	Label	Wks	(US 20 Pos)	
1	15	Get Back	Beatles with Billy Preston	Apple	10	(1)	
2	-	Man Of The World	Fleetwood Mac	Immediate	9		
3	-	My Sentimental Friend	Herman's Hermits	Columbia	7		
4	5	Goodbye	Mary Hopkin	Apple	9	(13)	
5	16	Come Back And Shake Me	Clodagh Rodgers	RCA	8		F
6	-	My Way	Frank Sinatra	Reprise	9	(27)	
7	-	Behind A Painted Smile	Isley Brothers	Tamla Motown	7		
8	8	Pinball Wizard	Who	Track	8	(19)	
9	2	Israelites	Desmond Dekker & The Aces	Pyramid	8	(9)	
10	-	Dizzy	Tommy Roe	Stateside	10	(1)	L
11	-	The Boxer	Simon & Garfunkel	CBS	7	(7)	
12	-	(I'm A) Road Runner	Jr. Walker & The All Stars	Tamla Motown	6	(20)	F
13	17	Harlem Shuffle	Bob & Earl	Island	7	(44)	F L
14	18	Cupid	Johnny Nash	Major Minor	6	(39)	
15	-	Ragamuffin Man	Manfred Mann	Fontana	6		
16	3	Gentle On My Mind	Dean Martin	Reprise	12		L
17	-	Love Me Tonight	Tom Jones	Decca	6	(13)	
18	10	Windmills Of Your Mind	Noel Harrison	Reprise	9		F L
19	-	Aquarius/Let The Sunshine In (Medley)	Fifth Dimension	Liberty	4	(1)	F
20	-	I'm Living In Shame	Diana Ross & The Supremes	Tamla Motown	3	(10)	

This Mnth	Prev Mnth	Title	Artist	Label	Wks	(US 20 Pos)	
1	-	Ballad Of John And Yoko	Beatles	Apple	8	(8)	
2	10	Dizzy	Tommy Roe	Stateside	10	(1)	L
3	-	Oh Happy Day	Edwin Hawkins Singers	Buddah	8	(4)	F L
4	-	Time Is Tight	Booker T. & The M.G.'s	Stax	10	(6)	F
5	1	Get Back	Beatles with Nilly Preston	Apple	10	(1)	
6	6	My Way	Frank Sinatra	Reprise	9	(27)	
7	-	Living In The Past	Jethro Tull	Island	6	(11)	F
8	-	The Tracks Of My Tears	Smokey Robinson & The Miracles	Tamla Motown	6		F
9	2	Man Of The World	Fleetwood Mac	Immediate	9		
10	11	The Boxer	Simon & Garfunkel	CBS	7	(7)	
11	-	(Your Love Keeps Lifting Me) Higher And Higher	Jackie Wilson	MCA	6	(6)	
12	-	Big Ship	Cliff Richard	Columbia	5		
13	-	In The Ghetto	Elvis Presley	RCA	11	(3)	
14	15	Ragamuffin Man	Manfred Mann	Fontana	6		
15	17	Love Me Tonight	Tom Jones	Decca	6	(13)	
16	-	Something In The Air	Thunderclap Newman	Track	8	(37)	F L
17	3	My Sentimental Friend	Herman's Hermits	Columbia	7		
18	-	I'd Rather Go Blind	Chicken Shack	Blue Horizon	5		F L
19	-	Galveston	Glen Campbell	Ember	5	(4)	
20	7	Behind A Painted Smile	Isley Brothers	Tamla Motown	7		

◆ Shortly after marrying Bee Gee Maurice Gibb, Lulu won the Eurovision Song Contest (in an unprecedented four-way tie!) with 'Boom Bang-A-Bang'. The victory did not help her career, as this archetypal entry was her last major UK hit for five years.

◆ Blind Faith's debut show in London's Hyde Park was watched by a crowd of 150,000.

◆ Meanwhile, the first successful rock opera *Tommy* by The Who simultaneously entered the UK and US album charts.

July 1969

This Mnth	Prev Mnth	Title	Artist	Label	Wks	(US 20 Pos)	
1	16	Something In The Air	Thunderclap Newman	Track	8	(37)	F L
2	13	In The Ghetto	Elvis Presley	RCA	11	(3)	
3	-	Hello Susie	Amen Corner	Immediate	6		L
4	-	Way Of Life	Family Dogg	Bell	8		F L
5	1	Ballad Of John And Yoko	Beatles	Apple	8	(8)	
6	-	Break Away	Beach Boys	Capitol	6	(63)	
7	-	Honky Tonk Women	Rolling Stones	Decca	12	(1)	
8	-	Proud Mary	Creedence Clearwater Revival	Liberty	6	(2)	F
9	7	Living In The Past	Jethro Tull	Island	6	(11)	F
10	-	Give Peace A Chance	Plastic Ono Band	Apple	7	(14)	F
11	-	It Mek	Desmond Dekker & The Aces	Pyramid	5		
12	4	Time Is Tight	Booker T. & The M.G.'s	Stax	10	(6)	F
13	-	Lights Of Cincinatti	Scott Walker	Philips	5		L
14	-	Baby Make It Soon	Marmalade	CBS	7		
15	3	Oh Happy Day	Edwin Hawkins Singers	Buddah	8	(4)	F L
16	-	Frozen Orange Juice	Peter Sarstedt	UA	4		L
17	-	Gimme Gimme Good Lovin'	Crazy Elephant	Major Minor	5	(12)	F L
18	-	Saved By The Bell	Robin Gibb	Polydor	10		F L
19	12	Big Ship	Cliff Richard	Columbia	5		
20	-	That's The Way God Planned It	Billy Preston	Apple	6	(62)	F

August 1969

This Mnth	Prev Mnth	Title	Artist	Label	Wks	(US 20 Pos)	
1	7	Honky Tonk Women	Rolling Stones	Decca	12	(1)	
2	18	Saved By The Bell	Robin Gibb	Polydor	10		F L
3	-	Make Me An Island	Joe Dolan	Pye	10		F
4	10	Give Peace A Chance	Plastic Ono Band	Apple	7	(14)	F
5	-	My Cherie Amour	Stevie Wonder	Tamla Motown	9	(4)	
6	-	Goodnight Midnight	Clodagh Rodgers	RCA	8		
7	-	Conversations	Cilla Black	Parlophone	7		
8	2	In The Ghetto	Elvis Presley	RCA	11	(3)	
9	-	In The Year 2525 (Exordium & Terminus)	Zager & Evans	RCA	9	(1)	F L
10	-	Bringing On Back The Good Times	Love Affair	CBS	6		L
11	-	Early In The Morning	Vanity Fare	Page One	6	(12)	
12	-	Too Busy Thinking About My Baby	Marvin Gaye	Tamla Motown	8	(4)	
13	-	Wet Dream	Max Romeo	Unity	6		F L
14	14	Baby Make It Soon	Marmalade	CBS	7		
15	1	Something In The Air	Thunderclap Newman	Track	8	(37)	F L
16	20	That's The Way God Planned It	Billy Preston	Apple	6	(62)	F
17	11	It Mek	Desmond Dekker & The Aces	Pyramid	5		
18	-	Viva Bobbie Joe	Equals	President	8		
19	-	Goo Goo Barabajagal (Love Is Hot)	Donovan & Jeff Beck Group	Pye	4	(36)	L
20	-	Curly	Move	Regal Zonophone	7		

◆ The Rolling Stones attracted 250,000 fans to Hyde Park – during the show they paid tribute to ex-member Brian Jones who had drowned just days before. Other British shows included the Isle of Wight Festival headlined by Bob Dylan, and The National Jazz & Blues Festival featuring The Who, Yes and King Crimson.

1969

This Mnth	Prev Mnth	Title	Artist	Label	Wks 20	(US Pos)	
1	-	Bad Moon Rising	Creedence Clearwater Revival	Liberty	11	(2)	
2	9	In The Year 2525 (Exordium & Terminus)	Zager & Evans	RCA	9	(1)	F L
3	-	Don't Forget To Remember	Bee Gees	Polydor	11	(73)	
4	-	Je T'Aime...Moi Non Plus	Jane Birkin & Serge Gainsbourg	Fontana/ Major Minor	13	(58)	F L
5	-	Natural Born Bugie	Humble Pie	Immediate	7		F L
6	12	Too Busy Thinking About My Baby	Marvin Gaye	Tamla Motown	8	(4)	
7	18	Viva Bobbie Joe	Equals	President	8		
8	5	My Cherie Amour	Stevie Wonder	Tamla Motown	9	(4)	
9	1	Honky Tonk Women	Rolling Stones	Decca	12	(1)	
10	-	Good Morning Starshine	Oliver	CBS	10	(3)	F L
11	-	I'll Never Fall In Love Again	Bobbie Gentry	Capitol	9		
12	2	Saved By The Bell	Robin Gibb	Polydor	10		F L
13	3	Make Me An Island	Joe Dolan	Pye	10		F
14	-	A Boy Named Sue	Johnny Cash	CBS	9	(2)	F
15	20	Curly	Move	Regal Zonophone	7		
16	11	Early In The Morning	Vanity Fare	Page One	6	(12)	
17	-	It's Getting Better	Mama Cass	Stateside	6	(30)	L
18	-	Throw Down A Line	Cliff Richard	Columbia	6		
19	-	I'm A Better Man	Engelbert Humperdinck	Decca	4	(38)	
20	-	Cloud Nine	Temptations	Tamla Motown	3	(6)	

This Mnth	Prev Mnth	Title	Artist	Label	Wks 20	(US Pos)	
1	4	Je T'Aime...Moi Non Plus	Jane Birkin & Serge Gainsbourg	Fontana/ Major Minor	13	(58)	F L
2	11	I'll Never Fall In Love Again	Bobbie Gentry	Capitol	9		
3	14	A Boy Named Sue	Johnny Cash	CBS	9	(2)	F
4	-	Lay Lady Lay	Bob Dylan	CBS	7	(7)	
5	1	Bad Moon Rising	Creedence Clearwater Revival	Liberty	11	(2)	
6	-	I'm Gonna Make You Mine	Lou Christie	Buddah	8	(10)	L
7	10	Good Morning Starshine	Oliver	CBS	10	(3)	F L
8	-	Nobody's Child	Karen Young	Major Minor	12		F L
9	3	Don't Forget To Remember	Bee Gees	Polydor	11	(73)	
10	18	Throw Down A Line	Cliff Richard	Columbia	6		
11	17	It's Getting Better	Mama Cass	Stateside	6	(30)	L
12	-	He Ain't Heavy, He's My Brother	Hollies	Parlophone	8	(7)	
13	-	Space Oddity	David Bowie	Philips	8	(15)	F
14	-	Oh Well	Fleetwood Mac	Reprise	10	(55)	
15	-	Sugar Sugar	Archies	RCA	17	(1)	F L
16	-	Hare Krishna	Radha Krishna Temple	Apple	5		F L
17	2	In The Year 2525 (Exordium & Terminus)	Zager & Evans	RCA	9	(1)	F L
18	5	Natural Born Bugie	Humble Pie	Immediate	7		F L
19	-	Do What You Gotta Do	Four Tops	Tamla Motown	1		
20	7	Viva Bobbie Joe	Equals	President	8		

◆ nitially Zager & Evans only pressed 1000 copies of their pessimistic peek into the future, 'In The Year 2525'. As in the best fairy tales it sold five million copies and topped the charts.

◆ As the year closed, Elton John first collaborated with songwriter Bernie Taupin, Rod Stewart joined The Faces and Jimi Hendrix unveiled his Band Of Gypsies.

November 1969

This Mnth	Prev Mnth	Title	Artist	Label	Wks	(US 20 Pos)	
1	15	Sugar Sugar	Archies	RCA	17	(1)	F L
2	14	Oh Well	Fleetwood Mac	Reprise	10	(55)	
3	-	The Return Of Django	Upsetters	Upsetter	8		F L
4	-	(Call Me) Number One	Tremeloes	CBS	11		
5	12	He Ain't Heavy, He's My Brother	Hollies	Parlophone	8	(7)	
6	8	Nobody's Child	Karen Young	Major Minor	13		F L
7	-	Wonderful World Beautiful People	Jimmy Cliff	Trojan	9	(25)	F
8	6	I'm Gonna Make You Mine	Lou Christie	Buddah	8	(10)	L
9	-	Something/Come Together	Beatles	Apple	9	(1)	
10	-	Love's Been Good To Me	Frank Sinatra	Reprise	7	(75)	
11	13	Space Oddity	David Bowie	Philips	8	(15)	F
12	-	Delta Lady	Joe Cocker	Regal Zonophone	5	(69)	
13	-	Sweet Dream	Jethro Tull	Chrysalis	6		
14	2	I'll Never Fall In Love Again	Bobbie Gentry	Capitol	10		
15	-	Ruby, Don't Take Your Love To Town	Kenny Rogers & The First Edition	Reprise	16	(6)	F
16	-	Yester-Me, Yester-You, Yesterday	Stevie Wonder	Tamla Motown	9	(7)	
17	-	What Does It Take To Win Your Love	Jr. Walker & The All Stars	Tamla Motown	5	(4)	
18	3	A Boy Named Sue	Johnny Cash	CBS	9	(2)	F
19	-	Cold Turkey	Plastic Ono Band	Apple	5	(30)	
20	1	Je T'Aime...Moi Non Plus	Jane Birkin & Serge Gainsbourg	Fontana/MajorMinor	13	(58)	F L

December 1969

This Mnth	Prev Mnth	Title	Artist	Label	Wks	(US 20 Pos)	
1	1	Sugar Sugar	Archies	RCA	17	(1)	F L
2	15	Ruby, Don't Take Your Love To Town	Kenny Rogers & The First Edition	Reprise	16	(6)	F
3	-	Two Little Boys	Rolf Harris	Columbia	16		
4	16	Yester-Me, Yester-You, Yesterday	Stevie Wonder	Tamla Motown	9	(7)	
5	-	Melting Pot	Blue Mink	Philips	10		F
6	4	(Call Me) Number One	Tremeloes	CBS	11		
7	-	Suspicious Minds	Elvis Presley	RCA	11	(1)	
8	-	Winter World Of Love	Engelbert Humperdinck	Decca	9	(16)	
9	-	Liquidator	Harry J. & The All Stars	Trojan	13		F L
10	-	All I Have To Do Is Dream	Bobbie Gentry & GlenCampbell	Capitol	10	(27)	L
11	-	Onion Song	Marvin Gaye & Tammi Terrell	Tamla Motown	8	(50)	L
12	9	Something/Come Together	Beatles	Apple	9	(1)	
13	7	Wonderful World Beautiful People	Jimmy Cliff	Trojan	9	(25)	F
14	-	Tracy	Cuff Links	MCA	9	(9)	F
15	-	Love Is All	Malcolm Roberts	Major Minor	6		L
16	-	Durham Town (The Leavin')	Roger Whittaker	Columbia	9		F
17	2	Oh Well	Fleetwood Mac	Reprise	10	(55)	
18	-	Without Love	Tom Jones	Decca	6	(5)	
19	13	Sweet Dream	Jethro Tull	Chrysalis	6		
20	6	Nobody's Child	Karen Young	Major Minor	13		F L

◆ The Rolling Stones toured the US for the first time in three years. Their record breaking tour was marred by the death of a fan during their set at Altamont. The festival attracted 300,000 people.

◆ Jane Birkin and Serge Gainsbourg, survived both a BBC ban and being dropped by its original label. Their orgasmic ode became the first foreign language record to top the UK chart.

1970

This Mnth	Prev Mnth	Title	Artist	Label	Wks	(US 20 Pos)	
1	3	Two Little Boys	Rolf Harris	Columbia	16		
2	2	Ruby, Don't Take Your Love To Town	Kenny Rogers & First Edition	Reprise	16	(6)	F
3	10	All I Have To Do Is Dream	Bobbie Gentry & Glen Campbell	Capitol	10	(27)	L
4	7	Suspicious Minds	Elvis Presley	RCA	11	(1)	
5	14	Tracy	Cuff Links	MCA	9	(9)	F
6	1	Sugar Sugar	Archies	RCA	17	(1)	F L
7	5	Melting Pot	Blue Mink	Philips	10		F
8	-	Good Old Rock 'n' Roll	Dave Clark Five	Columbia	8		
9	-	Reflections Of My Life	Marmalade	Decca	7	(10)	
10	-	Come And Get It	Badfinger	Apple	7	(7)	F
11	4	Yester-Me, Yester-You, Yesterday	Stevie Wonder	Tamla Motown	9	(7)	
12	18	Without Love	Tom Jones	Decca	6	(5)	
13	16	Durham Town (The Leavin')	Roger Whittaker	Columbia	9		F
14	9	Liquidator	Harry J. & The All Stars	Trojan	13		F L
15	-	Love Grows (Where My Rosemary Goes)	Edison Lighthouse	Bell	10	(5)	F L
16	-	Friends	Arrival	Decca	5		F
17	8	Winter World Of Love	Engelbert Humperdinck	Decca	9	(16)	
18	11	Onion Song	Marvin Gaye & Tammi Terrell	Tamla Motown	8	(50)	
19	-	Someday We'll Be Together	Diana Ross & The Supremes	Tamla Motown	5	(1)	
20	-	Leavin' On A Jet Plane	Peter, Paul & Mary	Warner	9	(1)	L

This Mnth	Prev Mnth	Title	Artist	Label	Wks	(US 20 Pos)	
1	15	Love Grows (Where My Rosemary Goes)	Edison Lighthouse	Bell	10	(5)	F L
2	20	Leavin' On A Jet Plane	Peter, Paul & Mary	Warner	9	(1)	L
3	-	Let's Work Together	Canned Heat	Liberty	9	(26)	L
4	-	The Witch's Promise/Teacher	Jethro Tull	Chrysalis	5		
5	-	Temma Harbour	Mary Hopkin	Apple	6	(39)	
6	1	Two Little Boys	Rolf Harris	Columbia	16		
7	-	I Want You Back	Jackson Five	Tamla Motown	9	(1)	F
8	10	Come And Get It	Badfinger	Apple	7	(7)	F
9	9	Reflections Of My Life	Marmalade	Decca	7	(10)	
10	-	Wand'rin' Star	Lee Marvin	Paramount	11		F L
11	-	Venus	Shocking Blue	Penny Farthing	5	(1)	F L
12	-	I'm A Man	Chicago	CBS	6	(49)	F
13	-	Instant Karma	Lennon, Ono & The Plastic Ono Band	Apple	6	(3)	
14	2	Ruby, Don't Take Your Love To Town	Kenny Rogers & First Edition	Reprise	16	(6)	F
15	-	I Can't Get Next To You	Temptations	Tamla Motown	5	(1)	
16	16	Friends	Arrival	Decca	5		F
17	-	My Baby Loves Lovin'	White Plains	Deram	5	(13)	F
18	-	Years May Come, Years May Go	Herman's Hermits	Columbia	7		
19	3	All I Have To Do Is Dream	Bobbie Gentry & Glen Campbell	Capitol	10	(27)	L
20	-	United We Stand	Brotherhood Of Man	Deram	6	(13)	F

◆ American Ron Dante was the lead vocalist of transatlantic hit makers The Archies and The Cuff Links, while Englishman Tony Burrows sang in three transatlantic hit acts, Edison Lighthouse, White Plains and Brotherhood Of Man.

◆ Davy Jones quit The Monkees, British teen idol Steve Ellis left Love Affair and Joe Cocker split from the Grease Band before joining the *Mad Dogs And Englishmen* tour.

March 1970

This Mnth	Prev Mnth	Title	Artist	Label	Wks	(US 20 Pos)	
1	10	Wand'rin' Star	Lee Marvin	Paramount	11		F L
2	-	Bridge Over Troubled Water	Simon & Garfunkel	CBS	13	(1)	L
3	7	I Want You Back	Jackson Five	Tamla Motown	9	(1)	F
4	-	Let It Be	Beatles	Apple	6	(1)	
5	3	Let's Work Together	Canned Heat	Liberty	9	(26)	L
6	13	Instant Karma	Lennon/Ono/Plastic Ono Band	Apple	6	(3)	
7	-	That Same Old Feeling	Pickettywitch	Pye	8	(67)	F
8	18	Years May Come, Years May Go	Herman's Hermits	Columbia	7		
9	1	Love Grows (Where My Rosemary Goes)	Edison Lighthouse	Bell	10	(5)	F L
10	-	Na Na Hey Hey Kiss Him Goodbye	Steam	Fontana	6	(1)	F L
11	-	Don't Cry Daddy	Elvis Presley	RCA	7	(6)	
12	-	Can't Help Falling In Love	Andy Williams	CBS	11	(88)	
13	-	Raindrops Keep Fallin' On My Head	Sacha Distel	Warner	5		F L
14	20	United We Stand	Brotherhood Of Man	Deram	6	(13)	F
15	-	Something's Burning	Kenny Rogers & First Edition	Reprise	8	(11)	
16	-	Everybody Get Together	Dave Clark Five	Columbia	5		L
17	2	Leavin' On A Jet Plane	Peter, Paul & Mary	Warner	9	(1)	L
18	17	My Baby Loves Lovin'	White Plains	Deram	5	(13)	F
19	-	Young Gifted And Black	Bob & Marcia	Harry J.	8		F
20	-	Knock Knock Who's There	Mary Hopkin	Apple	7	(92)	

April 1970

This Mnth	Prev Mnth	Title	Artist	Label	Wks	(US 20 Pos)	
1	2	Bridge Over Troubled Water	Simon & Garfunkel	CBS	13	(1)	L
2	12	Can't Help Falling In Love	Andy Williams	CBS	11	(88)	
3	20	Knock Knock Who's There	Mary Hopkin	Apple	7	(92)	
4	-	All Kinds Of Everything	Dana	Rex	8		F
5	19	Young Gifted And Black	Bob & Marcia	Harry J.	8		F
6	-	Spirit In The Sky	Norman Greenbaum	Reprise	11	(3)	F L
7	1	Wand'rin' Star	Lee Marvin	Paramount	11		F L
8	7	That Same Old Feeling	Pickettywitch	Pye	8	(67)	F
9	-	Gimme Dat Ding	Pipkins	Columbia	6	(9)	F L
10	-	Farewell Is A Lonely Sound	Jimmy Ruffin	Tamla Motown	7		
11	15	Something's Burning	Kenny Rogers & The First Edition	Reprise	8	(11)	
12	-	I Can't Help Myself	Four Tops	Tamla Motown	5	(1)	
13	4	Let It Be	Beatles	Apple	6	(1)	
14	-	Never Had A Dream Come True	Stevie Wonder	Tamla Motown	7	(26)	
15	-	When Julie Comes Around	Cuff Links	MCA	6	(41)	L
16	11	Don't Cry Daddy	Elvis Presley	RCA	7	(6)	
17	16	Everybody Get Together	Dave Clark Five	Columbia	5		L
18	-	Good Morning Freedom	Blue Mink	Philips	4		
19	10	Na Na Hey Hey Kiss Him Goodbye	Steam	Fontana	6	(1)	F L
20	-	You're Such A Good Looking Woman	Joe Dolan	Pye	4		L

◆ Simon & Garfunkel topped the single and album charts with the multi Grammy winning Bridge Over Troubled Water. The album headed the UK charts for a record 41 weeks and remained in the Top 10 for 126 weeks!

◆ The new year heralded the introduction of the Minimoog. This instrument, an early synthesizer, was to greatly influence the recording scene over the next decades.

1970

May 1970

This Mnth	Prev Mnth	Title	Artist	Label	Wks	(US 20 Pos)	
1	-	Back Home	England World Cup Squad	Pye	9		F
2	6	Spirit In The Sky	Norman Greenbaum	Reprise	11	(3)	F L
3	-	House Of The Rising Sun	Frijid Pink	Deram	8	(7)	F L
4	4	All Kinds Of Everything	Dana	Rex	8		F
5	-	Daughter Of Darkness	Tom Jones	Decca	9	(13)	
6	-	Question	Moody Blues	Threshold	9	(21)	
7	-	Yellow River	Christie	CBS	11	(23)	F
8	1	Bridge Over Troubled Water	Simon & Garfunkel	CBS	13	(1)	L
9	-	Travellin' Band	Creedence Clearwater Revival	Liberty	7	(2)	
10	2	Can't Help Falling In Love	Andy Williams	CBS	11	(88)	
11	-	I Can't Tell The Bottom From The Top	Hollies	Parlophone	5	(82)	
12	-	Brontosaurus	Move	Regal Zonophone	6		
13	14	Never Had A Dream Come True	Stevie Wonder	Tamla Motown	7	(26)	
14	-	I Don't Believe In If Anymore	Roger Whittaker	Columbia	8		
15	15	When Julie Comes Around	Cuff Links	MCA	6	(41)	L
16	9	Gimme Dat Ding	Pipkins	Columbia	6	(9)	F L
17	10	Farewell Is A Lonely Sound	Jimmy Ruffin	Tamla Motown	7		
18	-	Honey Come Back	Glen Campbell	Capitol	10	(19)	
19	18	Good Morning Freedom	Blue Mink	Philips	4		
20	-	Up The Ladder To The Roof	Supremes	Tamla Motown	6	(10)	

June 1970

This Mnth	Prev Mnth	Title	Artist	Label	Wks	(US 20 Pos)	
1	7	Yellow River	Christie	CBS	11	(23)	F
2	-	In The Summertime	Mungo Jerry	Dawn	13	(3)	F
3	-	Groovin' With Mr. Bloe	Mr. Bloe	DJM	10		F L
4	18	Honey Come Back	Glen Campbell	Capitol	10	(19)	
5	1	Back Home	England World Cup Squad	Pye	9		F
6	-	Cottonfields	Beach Boys	Capitol	12		
7	-	Everything Is Beautiful	Ray Stevens	CBS	8	(1)	F
8	6	Question	Moody Blues	Threshold	9	(21)	
9	20	Up The Ladder To The Roof	Supremes	Tamla Motown	6	(10)	
10	-	Sally	Gerry Monroe	Chapter One	9		F
11	-	Abraham Martin & John	Marvin Gaye	Tamla Motown	7		
12	-	All Right Now	Free	Island	11	(4)	F
13	-	The Green Manalishi (With The Two Prong Crown)	Fleetwood Mac	Reprise	9		
14	-	ABC	Jackson Five	Tamla Motown	5	(1)	
15	14	I Don't Believe In If Anymore	Roger Whittaker	Columbia	8		
16	5	Daughter Of Darkness	Tom Jones	Decca	9	(13)	
17	-	Goodbye Sam Hello Samantha	Cliff Richard	Columbia	10		
18	2	Spirit In The Sky	Norman Greenbaum	Reprise	11	(3)	F L
19	-	It's All In The Game	Four Tops	Tamla Motown	9	(24)	
20	-	Down The Dustpipe	Status Quo	Pye	6		

◆ Grateful Dead made their UK debut at the Hollywood Rock Music Festival, where newcomers Mungo Jerry (whose 'In The Summertime' would sell seven million worldwide) were the surprise hit. One of several other UK festivals was the Bath Festival Of Blues And Progressive Music, whose headliners included Led Zeppelin, The Byrds, Donovan, Santana, Steppenwolf, Pink Floyd, John Mayall and Frank Zappa.

July 1970

This Mnth	Prev Mnth	Title	Artist	Label	Wks	(US 20 Pos)	
1	2	In The Summertime	Mungo Jerry	Dawn	13	(3)	F
2	12	All Right Now	Free	Island	11	(4)	F
3	-	Up Around The Bend	Creedence Clearwater Revival	Liberty	8	(4)	
4	19	It's All In The Game	Four Tops	Tamla Motown	9	(24)	
5	3	Groovin' With Mr. Bloe	Mr. Bloe	DJM	10		F L
6	6	Cottonfields	Beach Boys	Capitol	12		
7	10	Sally	Gerry Monroe	Chapter One	9		F
8	17	Goodbye Sam Hello Samantha	Cliff Richard	Columbia	10		
9	-	Love Of The Common People	Nicky Thomas	Trojan	7		F L
10	-	Lola	Kinks	Pye	10	(9)	
11	-	Something	Shirley Bassey	UA	12	(55)	
12	13	The Green Manalishi (With The Two Prong Crown)	Fleetwood Mac	Reprise	9		
13	20	Down The Dustpipe	Status Quo	Pye	6		
14	-	The Wonder Of You	Elvis Presley	RCA	16	(9)	
15	1	Yellow River	Christie	CBS	11	(23)	F
16	4	Honey Come Back	Glen Campbell	Capitol	10	(19)	
17	-	Lady D'Arbanville	Cat Stevens	Island	8		
18	11	Abraham Martin & John	Marvin Gaye	Tamla Motown	7		
19	-	Neanderthal Man	Hotlegs	Fontana	9	(22)	F L
20	-	Love Like A Man	Ten Years After	Deram	6	(98)	F L

August 1970

This Mnth	Prev Mnth	Title	Artist	Label	Wks	(US 20 Pos)	
1	14	The Wonder Of You	Elvis Presley	RCA	16	(9)	
2	19	Neanderthal Man	Hotlegs	Fontana	9	(22)	F L
3	10	Lola	Kinks	Pye	10	(9)	
4	11	Something	Shirley Bassey	UA	12	(55)	
5	2	All Right Now	Free	Island	11	(4)	F
6	1	In The Summertime	Mungo Jerry	Dawn	13	(3)	F
7	-	Rainbow	Marmalade	Decca	8	(51)	
8	-	I'll Say Forever My Love	Jimmy Ruffin	Tamla Motown	8	(77)	
9	-	Natural Sinner	Fair Weather	RCA	6		F L
10	-	The Tears Of A Clown	Smokey Robinson & The Miracles	Tamla Motown	10	(1)	
11	3	Up Around The Bend	Creedence Clearwater Revival	Liberty	8	(4)	
12	17	Lady D'Arbanville	Cat Stevens	Island	8		
13	4	It's All In The Game	Four Tops	Tamla Motown	9	(24)	
14	20	Love Like A Man	Ten Years After	Deram	6	(98)	F L
15	-	Big Yellow Taxi	Joni Mitchell	Reprise	5	(67)	F L
16	-	The Love You Save	Jackson Five	Tamla Motown	4	(1)	
17	-	25 Or 6 To 4	Chicago	CBS	7	(4)	
18	-	Signed, Sealed, Delivered I'm Yours	Stevie Wonder	Tamla Motown	5	(3)	
19	9	Love Of The Common People	Nicky Thomas	Trojan	7		F L
20	-	Sweet Inspiration	Johnny Johnson & The Bandwagon	Bell	5		

◆ The first of numerous hits by British football teams quickly shot to the top; it was by England's World Cup Squad (the winners of the previous World Cup) with the stirring 'Back Home'.

◆ Just weeks before his untimely death, Jimi Hendrix appeared at the Isle Of Wight Festival which also showcased The Who, The Doors, Chicago, Emerson, Lake & Palmer, The Moody Blues and Free, whose debut hit, 'All Right Now', returned to the UK Top 20 in 1973 and again in 1991.

1970

This Mnth	Prev Mnth	Title	Artist	Label	Wks	(US 20 Pos)	
1	10	The Tears Of A Clown	Smokey Robinson/The Miracles	Tamla Motown	10	(1)	
2	1	The Wonder Of You	Elvis Presley	RCA	16	(9)	
3	-	Give Me Just A Little More Time	Chairmen Of The Board	Invictus	8	(3)	F
4	-	Mama Told Me Not To Come	Three Dog Night	Stateside	8	(1)	F L
5	-	Band Of Gold	Freda Payne	Invictus	11	(3)	F L
6	-	Make It With You	Bread	Elektra	7	(1)	F
7	-	Love Is Life	Hot Chocolate	RAK	8		F
8	-	Wild World	Jimmy Cliff	Island	5		L
9	17	25 Or 6 To 4	Chicago	CBS	7	(4)	
10	7	Rainbow	Marmalade	Decca	8	(51)	
11	-	You Can Get It If You Really Want	Desmond Dekker	Trojan	10		
12	-	Which Way You Goin' Billy	Poppy Family	Decca	7	(2)	F L
13	2	Neanderthal Man	Hotlegs	Fontana	9	(22)	F L
14	4	Something	Shirley Bassey	UA	12	(55)	
15	20	Sweet Inspiration	Johnny Johnson & The Bandwagon	Bell	5		
16	-	Montego Bay	Bobby Bloom	Polydor	8	(8)	F L
17	-	It's So Easy	Andy Williams	CBS	4		
18	9	Natural Sinner	Fair Weather	RCA	6		F L
19	-	Don't Play That Song	Aretha Franklin	Atlantic	5	(11)	
20	-	Black Night	Deep Purple	Harvest	10	(66)	F

This Mnth	Prev Mnth	Title	Artist	Label	Wks	(US 20 Pos)	
1	5	Band Of Gold	Freda Payne	Invictus	11	(3)	F L
2	20	Black Night	Deep Purple	Harvest	10	(66)	F
3	11	You Can Get It If You Really Want	Desmond Dekker	Trojan	10		
4	-	Paranoid	Black Sabbath	Vertigo	8	(61)	F
5	16	Montego Bay	Bobby Bloom	Polydor	8	(8)	F L
6	-	Me And My Life	Tremeloes	CBS	9		L
7	-	Ain't No Mountain High Enough	Diana Ross	Tamla Motown	7	(1)	F
8	-	(They Long To Be) Close To You	Carpenters	A&M	8	(1)	F
9	12	Which Way You Goin' Billy	Poppy Family	Decca	7	(2)	F L
10	-	Patches	Clarence Carter	Atlantic	8	(4)	F L
11	-	Ball Of Confusion	Temptations	Tamla Motown	7	(3)	
12	-	Woodstock	Matthews Southern Comfort	Uni	8	(23)	F L
13	1	The Tears Of A Clown	Smokey Robinson & The Miracles	Tamla Motown	10	(1)	
14	3	Give Me Just A Little More Time	Chairmen Of The Board	Invictus	8	(3)	F
15	2	The Wonder Of You	Elvis Presley	RCA	16	(9)	
16	-	Strange Band	Family	Reprise	5		F
17	-	Black Pearl	Horace Faith	Trojan	4		F L
18	-	Still Water (Love)	Four Tops	Tamla Motown	6	(11)	
19	7	Love Is Life	Hot Chocolate	RAK	8		F
20	-	Gasoline Alley Bred	Hollies	Parlophone	4		

◆ The *Melody Maker* poll showed Janis Joplin as Top Female Singer and, after eight years, The Beatles were replaced as Top Group by Led Zeppelin. Incidentally, Zeppelin billed their sixth US tour as "The Greatest Live Event Since The Beatles".

◆ Matthews' Southern Comfort's version of 'Woodstock' topped the chart despite the "Summer of Love" being no more than a distant memory.

November 1970

This Mnth	Prev Mnth	Title	Artist	Label	Wks	(US 20 Pos)	
1	12	Woodstock	Matthews Southern Comfort	Uni	8	(23)	F L
2	10	Patches	Clarence Carter	Atlantic	8	(4)	F L
3	-	War	Edwin Starr	Tamla Motown	8	(1)	
4	-	Indian Reservation	Don Fardon	Young Blood	11	(20)	F L
5	-	Voodoo Chile	Jimi Hendrix Experience	Track	10		L
6	-	The Witch	Rattles	Decca	5	(79)	F L
7	-	Ruby Tuesday	Melanie	Buddah	7	(52)	F
8	-	San Bernadino	Christie	CBS	6	(100)	L
9	6	Me And My Life	Tremeloes	CBS	9		L
10	2	Black Night	Deep Purple	Harvest	10	(66)	F
11	-	It's Wonderful	Jimmy Ruffin	Tamla Motown	8		
12	1	Band Of Gold	Freda Payne	Invictus	11	(3)	F L
13	11	Ball Of Confusion	Temptations	Tamla Motown	7	(3)	
14	-	Cracklin' Rosie	Neil Diamond	Uni	13	(1)	F
15	-	I Hear You Knocking	Dave Edmunds	MAM	12	(4)	F
16	-	Julie, Do Ya Love Me	White Plains	Deram	9		
17	-	Ride A White Swan	T. Rex	Fly	14	(76)	F
18	4	Paranoid	Black Sabbath	Vertigo	8	(61)	F
19	18	Still Water (Love)	Four Tops	Tamla Motown	6	(11)	
20	-	I've Lost You	Elvis Presley	RCA	8	(32)	

December 1970

This Mnth	Prev Mnth	Title	Artist	Label	Wks	(US 20 Pos)	
1	15	I Hear You Knocking	Dave Edmunds	MAM	12	(4)	F
2	-	When I'm Dead And Gone	McGuinness Flint	Capitol	10	(47)	F
3	14	Cracklin' Rosie	Neil Diamond	Uni	13	(1)	F
4	-	It's Only Make Believe	Glen Campbell	Capitol	10	(10)	
5	-	You've Got Me Dangling On A String	Chairmen Of The Board	Invictus	10	(38)	
6	17	Ride A White Swan	T. Rex	Fly	14	(76)	F
7	5	Voodoo Chile	Jimi Hendrix Experience	Track	10		L
8	-	I'll Be There	Jackson Five	Tamla Motown	11	(1)	
9	-	Home Lovin' Man	Andy Williams	CBS	9		
10	4	Indian Reservation	Don Fardon	Young Blood	11	(20)	F L
11	-	My Prayer	Gerry Monroe	Chapter One	7		
12	-	Grandad	Clive Dunn	Columbia	14		F L
13	-	Nothing Rhymed	Gilbert O'Sullivan	MAM	7		F
14	20	I've Lost You	Elvis Presley	RCA	8	(32)	
15	16	Julie, Do Ya Love Me	White Plains	Deram	9		
16	-	Lady Barbara	Herman's Hermits	RAK	6		L
17	-	Blame It On The Pony Express	Johnny Johnson & The Bandwagon	Bell	8		L
18	11	It's Wonderful	Jimmy Ruffin	Tamla Motown	8		
19	8	San Bernadino	Christie	CBS	6	(100)	L
20	1	Woodstock	Matthews Southern Comfort	Uni	8	(23)	F L

◆ Double Grammy winners, The Carpenters, had their first transatlantic hit , '(They Long To Be) Close To You'. Also debuting on the UK chart were Neil Diamond, Gilbert O' Sullivan and T-Rex, while the US chart welcomed Dawn, James Taylor, and the stars of the latest pop-oriented TV series, The Partridge Family, featuring teen idol David Cassidy.

◆ The price of all record papers in Britain rose to 5p (12c).

1971

This Mnth	Prev Mnth	Title	Artist	Label	Wks	(US 20 Pos)	
1	12	Grandad	Clive Dunn	Columbia	14		F L
2	1	I Hear You Knocking	Dave Edmunds	MAM	12	(4)	F
3	6	Ride A White Swan	T. Rex	Fly	14	(76)	F
4	8	I'll Be There	Jackson Five	Tamla Motown	11	(1)	
5	2	When I'm Dead And Gone	McGuinness Flint	Capitol	10	(47)	F
6	3	Cracklin' Rosie	Neil Diamond	Uni	13	(1)	F
7	17	Blame It On The Pony Express	Johnny Johnson & The Bandwagon	Bell	8		L
8	4	It's Only Make Believe	Glen Campbell	Capitol	10	(10)	
9	-	Ape Man	Kinks	Pye	9	(45)	
10	9	Home Lovin' Man	Andy Williams	CBS	9		
11	13	Nothing Rhymed	Gilbert O'Sullivan	MAM	7		F
12	-	My Sweet Lord	George Harrison	Apple	12	(1)	F
13	-	Black Skin Blue Eyed Boys	Equals	President	6		L
14	5	You've Got Me Dangling On A String	Chairmen Of The Board	Invictus	10	(38)	
15	-	Amazing Grace	Judy Collins	Elektra	13	(15)	
16	-	The Pushbike Song	Mixtures	Polydor	13	(44)	F L
17	-	You Don't Have To Say You Love Me	Elvis Presley	RCA	6	(11)	
18	16	Lady Barbara	Herman's Hermits	RAK	6		L
19	11	My Prayer	Gerry Monroe	Chapter One	7		
20	-	You're Ready Now	Frankie Valli	Philips	6		F

This Mnth	Prev Mnth	Title	Artist	Label	Wks	(US 20 Pos)	
1	12	My Sweet Lord	George Harrison	Apple	12	(1)	F
2	16	The Pushbike Song	Mixtures	Polydor	13	(44)	F L
3	-	Stoned Love	Supremes	Tamla Motown	8	(7)	
4	-	Resurrection Shuffle	Ashton Gardner & Dyke	Capitol	9	(40)	F L
5	15	Amazing Grace	Judy Collins	Elektra	13	(15)	
6	-	No Matter What	Badfinger	Apple	8	(8)	
7	1	Grandad	Clive Dunn	Columbia	14		F L
8	-	Your Song	Elton John	DJM	6	(8)	F
9	-	Candida	Dawn	Bell	6	(3)	F
10	9	Ape Man	Kinks	Pye	9	(45)	
11	-	It's Impossible	Perry Como	RCA	11	(10)	
12	3	Ride A White Swan	T. Rex	Fly	14	(76)	F
13	20	You're Ready Now	Frankie Valli	Philips	6		F
14	-	She's A Lady	Tom Jones	Decca	5	(2)	
15	-	Baby Jump	Mungo Jerry	Dawn	9		
16	4	I'll Be There	Jackson Five	Tamla Motown	11	(1)	
17	-	Rupert	Jackie Lee	Pye	5		F L
18	17	You Don't Have To Say You Love Me	Elvis Presley	RCA	6	(11)	
19	-	(Come 'Round Here) I'm The One You Need	Smokey Robinson & The Miracles	Tamla Motown	4		
20	-	Sweet Caroline	Neil Diamond	Uni	7	(4)	

◆ George Harrison's triple LP, **All Things Must Pass,** topped the American charts, and his single 'My Sweet Lord' was a transatlantic No. 1. Soon afterwards, a court ruled that he had "unconsciously plagiarised" The Chiffons' (with whom The Beatles had toured in 1964) 'He's So Fine' when writing this hit.

March 1971

This Mnth	Prev Mnth	Title	Artist	Label	Wks (US 20 Pos)	
1	15	Baby Jump	Mungo Jerry	Dawn	9	
2	-	Another Day	Paul McCartney	Apple	9 (5)	F
3	1	My Sweet Lord	George Harrison	Apple	12 (1)	F
4	11	It's Impossible	Perry Como	RCA	11 (10)	
5	-	Rose Garden	Lynn Anderson	CBS	10 (3)	F L
6	-	Hot Love	T. Rex	Fly	12 (72)	
7	2	The Pushbike Song	Mixtures	Polydor	13 (44)	F L
8	20	Sweet Caroline	Neil Diamond	Uni	7 (4)	
9	5	Amazing Grace	Judy Collins	Elektra	13 (15)	
10	4	Resurrection Shuffle	Ashton Gardner & Dyke	Capitol	9 (40)	F L
11	-	Tomorrow Night	Atomic Rooster	B&C	5	F
12	3	Stoned Love	Supremes	Tamla Motown	8 (7)	
13	-	Everything's Tuesday	Chairmen Of The Board	Invictus	5 (38)	
14	-	Bridget The Midget (The Queen Of The Blues)	Ray Stevens	CBS	9 (50)	
15	-	Power To The People	John Lennon & The Plastic Ono Band	Apple	6 (11)	
16	-	Strange Kind Of Woman	Deep Purple	Harvest	5	
17	-	Forget Me Not	Martha & The Vandellas	Tamla Motown	3 (93)	L
18	-	Who Put The Lights Out	Dana	Rex	3	
19	-	Rose Garden	New World	RAK	5	F
20	-	Jack In The Box	Clodagh Rodgers	RCA	6	L

April 1971

This Mnth	Prev Mnth	Title	Artist	Label	Wks (US 20 Pos)	
1	6	Hot Love	T. Rex	Fly	12 (72)	
2	14	Bridget The Midget (The Queen Of The Blues)	Ray Stevens	CBS	9 (50)	
3	5	Rose Garden	Lynn Anderson	CBS	10 (3)	F L
4	20	Jack In The Box	Clodagh Rodgers	RCA	6	L
5	-	There Goes My Everything	Elvis Presley	RCA	6 (21)	
6	-	Walkin'	C.C.S.	RAK	7	
7	2	Another Day	Paul McCartney	Apple	9 (5)	F
8	-	If Not For You	Olivia Newton-John	Pye International	6 (25)	F
9	15	Power To The People	John Lennon	Apple	6 (11)	
10	-	(Where Do I Begin) Love Story	Andy Williams	CBS	8 (9)	
11	-	Double Barrel	Dave & Ansil Collins	Technique	9 (22)	F
12	1	Baby Jump	Mungo Jerry	Dawn	9	
13	4	It's Impossible	Perry Como	RCA	11 (10)	
14	-	Mozart Symphony No. 40 In G Minor	Waldo De Los Rios	A&M	10 (67)	F L
15	16	Strange Kind Of Woman	Deep Purple	Harvest	5	
16	8	Sweet Caroline	Neil Diamond	Uni	7 (4)	
17	-	Funny Funny	Sweet	RCA	6	F
18	3	My Sweet Lord	George Harrison	Apple	12 (1)	F
19	7	The Pushbike Song	Mixtures	Polydor	13 (44)	F L
20	-	Something Old, Something New	Fantastics	Bell	3	F L

◆ Judy Collins's live recording of the ancient hymn 'Amazing Grace' spent an amazing 67 weeks on the chart. Only Frank Sinatra's 'My Way' can claim a longer residence.

◆ Swedish quartet, The Engaged Couples, made their debut at a Gothenburg nightclub. They later changed their name to Abba.

May 1971

This Mnth	Prev Mnth	Title	Artist	Label	Wks	(US 20 Pos)	
1	-	Knock Three Times	Dawn	Bell	13	(1)	
2	-	Brown Sugar/Bitch/Let It Rock	Rolling Stones	Rolling Stone	9	(1)	
3	11	Double Barrel	Dave & Ansil Collins	Technique	9	(22)	F
4	-	It Don't Come Easy	Ringo Starr	Apple	8	(4)	F
5	14	Mozart Symphony No. 40 In G Minor	Waldo De Los Rios	A&M	10	(67)	F L
6	-	Indiana Wants Me	R. Dean Taylor	Tamla Motown	9	(5)	
7	-	Remember Me	Diana Ross	Tamla Motown	7	(16)	
8	1	Hot Love	T. Rex	Fly	12	(72)	
9	-	Jig A Jig	East Of Eden	Deram	6		F L
10	10	(Where Do I Begin) Love Story	Andy Williams	CBS	8	(9)	
11	-	Heaven Must Have Sent You	Elgins	Tamla Motown	9	(50)	F L
12	-	Malt And Barley Blues	McGuinness Flint	Capitol	7		L
13	-	Un Banc, Un Arbre, Une Rue	Severine	Philips	4		F L
14	2	Bridget The Midget (The Queen Of The Blues)	Ray Stevens	CBS	9	(50)	
15	-	My Brother Jake	Free	Island	7		
16	-	Sugar Sugar	Sakkarin	RCA	5		F L
17	17	Funny Funny	Sweet	RCA	6		F
18	-	It's A Sin To Tell A Lie	Gerry Monroe	Chapter One	5		L
19	-	Rosetta	Fame And Price Together	CBS	5		L
20	20	Something Old, Something New	Fantastics	Bell	3		F L

June 1971

This Mnth	Prev Mnth	Title	Artist	Label	Wks	(US 20 Pos)	
1	1	Knock Three Times	Dawn	Bell	13	(1)	
2	-	I Did What I Did For Maria	Tony Christie	MCA	9		F
3	11	Heaven Must Have Sent You	Elgins	Tamla Motown	9	(50)	F L
4	-	I'm Gonna Run Away From You	Tami Lynn	Mojo	8		F L
5	-	I Am ...I Said	Neil Diamond	Uni	8	(4)	
6	6	Indiana Wants Me	R. Dean Taylor	Tamla Motown	9	(5)	
7	-	Lady Rose	Mungo Jerry	Dawn	7		
8	-	Banner Man	Blue Mink	Regal Zonophone	9		
9	15	My Brother Jake	Free	Island	7		
10	-	Chirpy Chirpy Cheep Cheep	Middle Of The Road	RCA	12		F
11	-	Rags To Riches	Elvis Presley	RCA	6	(33)	
12	2	Brown Sugar/Bitch/Let It Rock	Rolling Stones	Rolling Stone	9	(1)	
13	-	He's Gonna Step On You Again	John Kongos	Fly	8	(70)	F
14	12	Malt And Barley Blues	McGuinness Flint	Capitol	7		L
15	-	Oh You Pretty Thing	Peter Noone	Rak	6		F L
16	9	Jig A Jig	East Of Eden	Deram	6		F L
17	-	I Think Of You	Perry Como	RCA	5	(53)	
18	-	Don't Let It Die	Hurricane Smith	Columbia	8		F
19	-	Co-Co	Sweet	RCA	10	(99)	
20	5	Mozart Symphony No. 40 In G Minor	Waldo De Los Rios	A&M	10	(67)	F L

◆ Photogenic Irish vocalist Clodagh Rodgers had her last hit with the UK's entry to the Eurovision Song Contest, 'Jack In A Box'. The winner 'Un Banc, Un Arbre, Une Rue' by Severine from Monaco also charted.

◆ Eric Clapton won a poll in *NME* for Greatest All-Time Guitarist, with Jimi Hendrix and B.B. King in runner-up positions.

1971

July 1971

This Mnth	Prev Mnth	Title	Artist	Label	Wks	(US 20 Pos)	
1	10	Chirpy Chirpy Cheep Cheep	Middle Of The Road	RCA	12		F
2	19	Co-Co	Sweet	RCA	10	(99)	
3	18	Don't Let It Die	Hurricane Smith	Columbia	8		F
4	8	Banner Man	Blue Mink	Regal Zonophone	9		
5	-	Me And You And A Dog Named Boo	Lobo	Philips	9	(5)	F
6	-	Get It On	T. Rex	Fly	9	(10)	
7	-	Black And White	Greyhound	Trojan	8		F
8	13	He's Gonna Step On You Again	John Kongos	Fly	8	(70)	F
9	-	Just My Imagination (Runnin' Away With Me)	Temptations	Tamla Motown	8	(1)	
10	-	Monkey Spanner	Dave & Ansil Collins	Technique	8		L
11	4	I'm Gonna Run Away From You	Tami Lynn	Mojo	8		F L
12	-	Tom-Tom Turnaround	New World	RAK	10		
13	2	I Did What I Did For Maria	Tony Christie	MCA	9		F
14	-	Pied Piper	Bob & Marcia	Trojan	5		L
15	7	Lady Rose	Mungo Jerry	Dawn	7		
16	-	River Deep-Mountain High	Supremes & Four Tops	Tamla	6	(14)	
17	-	I Don't Blame You At All	Smokey Robinson & The Miracles	Tamla Motown	5	(18)	
18	-	When You Are A King	White Plains	Deram	5		L
19	-	Never Ending Song Of Love	New Seekers	Philips	12		F
20	-	Tonight	Move	Harvest	5		

August 1971

This Mnth	Prev Mnth	Title	Artist	Label	Wks	(US 20 Pos)	
1	19	Never Ending Song Of Love	New Seekers	Philips	12		F
2	6	Get It On	T. Rex	Fly	9	(10)	
3	-	I'm Still Waiting	Diana Ross	Tamla Motown	11	(63)	
4	-	Devil's Answer	Atomic Rooster	B&C	7		L
5	-	In My Own Time	Family	Reprise	8		
6	1	Chirpy Chirpy Cheep Cheep	Middle Of The Road	RCA	12		F
7	12	Tom-Tom Turnaround	New World	RAK	10		
8	-	Won't Get Fooled Again	Who	Track	6	(15)	
9	-	What Are You Doing Sunday	Dawn	Bell	7	(39)	
10	5	Me And You And A Dog Named Boo	Lobo	Philips	9	(5)	F
11	2	Co-Co	Sweet	RCA	10	(99)	
12	-	Heartbreak Hotel/Hound Dog	Elvis Presley	RCA	5		
13	-	Leap Up And Down (Wave Your Knickers In The Air)	St. Cecilia	Polydor	7		F L
14	-	Soldier Blue	Buffy Sainte-Marie	RCA	8		F L
15	10	Monkey Spanner	Dave & Ansil Collins	Technique	8		L
16	-	Let Your Yeah Be Yeah	Pioneers	Trojan	6		F L
17	-	Bangla Desh	George Harrison	Apple	4	(23)	
18	7	Black And White	Greyhound	Trojan	8		F
19	-	Get Down And Get With It	Slade	Polydor	4		F
20	-	Hey Girl Don't Bother Me	Tams	Probe	11	(41)	F L

◆ Glitter-Rock (aka Glam Rock) was off and running in Britain, thanks to hits from Sweet, T-Rex and chart newcomers Slade.

◆ The Tams' seven-year-old 'Hey Girl Don't Bother Me' was one of several re-issues on the British chart – others came from Tami Lynn, The Elgins and even Elvis, with a coupling of 'Heartbreak Hotel' and 'Hound Dog'.

111

1971

This Mnth	Prev Mnth	Title	Artist	Label	Wks	(US 20 Pos)	
1	20	Hey Girl Don't Bother Me	Tams	Probe	11	(41)	F L
2	3	I'm Still Waiting	Diana Ross	Tamla Motown	11	(63)	
3	1	Never Ending Song Of Love	New Seekers	Philips	12		F
4	-	Did You Ever	Nancy Sinatra & Lee Hazlewood	Reprise	9		L
5	9	What Are You Doing Sunday	Dawn	Bell	7	(39)	
6	14	Soldier Blue	Buffy Sainte-Marie	RCA	8		F L
7	-	Back Street Luv	Curved Air	Warner	6		F L
8	-	Nathan Jones	Supremes	Tamla Motown	7	(16)	
9	-	It's Too Late	Carole King	A&M	6	(1)	L
10	16	Let Your Yeah Be Yeah	Pioneers	Trojan	6		F L
11	5	In My Own Time	Family	Reprise	8		
12	-	I Believe (In Love)	Hot Chocolate	RAK	6		
13	-	Maggie May	Rod Stewart	Mercury	14	(1)	F
14	-	You've Got A Friend	James Taylor	Warner	9	(1)	F L
15	-	Tweedle Dee Tweedle Dum	Middle Of The Road	RCA	9		
16	-	Cousin Norman	Marmalade	Decca	7		
17	2	Get It On	T. Rex	Fly	9	(10)	
18	17	Bangla Desh	George Harrison	Apple	4	(23)	
19	-	Tap Turns On The Water	C.C.S.	RAK	7		L
20	-	For All We Know	Shirley Bassey	UA	10		

This Mnth	Prev Mnth	Title	Artist	Label	Wks	(US 20 Pos)	
1	13	Maggie May	Rod Stewart	Mercury	14	(1)	F
2	15	Tweedle Dee Tweedle Dum	Middle Of The Road	RCA	9		
3	14	You've Got A Friend	James Taylor	Warner	9	(1)	F L
4	1	Hey Girl Don't Bother Me	Tams	Probe	11	(41)	F L
5	4	Did You Ever	Nancy Sinatra & Lee Hazlewood	Reprise	9		L
6	20	For All We Know	Shirley Bassey	UA	10		
7	19	Tap Turns On The Water	C.C.S.	RAK	7		L
8	-	Witch Queen Of New Orleans	Redbone	Epic	8	(21)	F L
9	-	Freedom Come Freedom Go	Fortunes	Capitol	7	(72)	
10	16	Cousin Norman	Marmalade	Decca	7		
11	-	Simple Game	Four Tops	Tamla Motown	8	(90)	
12	-	Sultana	Titanic	CBS	7		F L
13	-	Life Is A Long Song/Up The Pool	Jethro Tull	Chrysalis	5		L
14	8	Nathan Jones	Supremes	Tamla Motown	7	(16)	
15	-	Butterfly	Danyel Gerard	CBS	5	(78)	F L
16	12	I Believe (In Love)	Hot Chocolate	RAK	6		
17	-	Another Time Another Place	Engelbert Humperdinck	Decca	4	(43)	
18	-	You Don't Have To Be In The Army To Fight In The War	Mungo Jerry	Dawn	3		
19	7	Back Street Luv	Curved Air	Warner	6		F L
20	-	Keep On Dancing	Bay City Rollers	Bell	5		F

◆ Cliff Richard, who received an Ivor Novello award for his outstanding services to British music, was heavily promoting newcomer Olivia Newton-John on his weekly TV series.

◆ English comedian Benny Hill topped the chart with the novelty 'Ernie (The Fastest Milkman In The West)', which was loosely based on an earlier record by American humorist Frank Gallup.

1971

This Mnth	Prev Mnth	Title	Artist	Label	Wks 20	(US Pos)	
1	-	Coz I Luv You	Slade	Polydor	10		
2	1	Maggie May	Rod Stewart	Mercury	14	(1)	F
3	-	Till	Tom Jones	Decca	10	(41)	
4	-	Tired Of Being Alone	Al Green	London American	6	(11)	F
5	8	Witch Queen Of New Orleans	Redbone	Epic	8	(21)	F L
6	-	Johnny Reggae	Piglets	Bell	7		F L
7	-	I Will Return	Springwater	Polydor	6		F L
8	11	Simple Game	Four Tops	Tamla Motown	8	(90)	
9	-	The Night They Drove Old Dixie Down	Joan Baez	Vanguard	7	(3)	L
10	-	Banks Of The Ohio	Olivia Newton-John	Pye International	8	(94)	
11	-	Gypsys Tramps & Thieves	Cher	MCA	9	(1)	
12	-	Look Around	Vince Hill	Columbia	6		L
13	-	Jeepster	T. Rex	Fly	10		
14	12	Sultana	Titanic	CBS	7		F L
15	-	Brandy	Scott English	Horse	5	(91)	F L
16	-	Ernie (The Fastest Milkman In The West)	Benny Hill	Columbia	10		L
17	6	For All We Know	Shirley Bassey	UA	10		
18	2	Tweedle Dee Tweedle Dum	Middle Of The Road	RCA	9		
19	-	Run, Baby Run (Back Into My Arms)	Newbeats	London American	6		L
20	-	Surrender	Diana Ross	Tamla Motown	5	(38)	

This Mnth	Prev Mnth	Title	Artist	Label	Wks 20	(US Pos)	
1	16	Ernie (The Fastest Milkman In The.West)	Benny Hill	Columbia	10		L
2	13	Jeepster	T. Rex	Fly	10		
3	1	Coz I Luv You	Slade	Polydor	10		
4	-	Tokoloshe Man	John Kongos	Fly	7		L
5	11	Gypsys Tramps & Thieves	Cher	MCA	9	(1)	
6	-	Theme From 'Shaft'	Isaac Hayes	Stax	8	(1)	F
7	-	Something Tells Me (Something Is Gonna Happen Tonight)	Cilla Black	Parlophone	8		L
8	10	Banks Of The Ohio	Olivia Newton-John	Pye International	8	(94)	
9	-	No Matter How I Try	Gilbert O'Sullivan	MAM	9		
10	3	Till	Tom Jones	Decca	10	(41)	
11	6	Johnny Reggae	Piglets	Bell	7		F L
12	19	Run, Baby Run (Back Into My Arms)	Newbeats	London American	6		L
13	-	Softly Whispering I Love You	Congregation	Columbia	8	(29)	F L
14	-	Sing A Song Of Freedom	Cliff Richard	Columbia	4		
15	7	I Will Return	Springwater	Polydor	6		F L
16	20	Surrender	Diana Ross	Tamla Motown	5	(38)	
17	-	I'd Like To Teach The World To Sing	New Seekers	Polydor	12	(7)	
18	-	Soley Soley	Middle Of The Road	RCA	8		L
19	-	It Must Be Love	Labi Siffre	Pye International	6		F
20	-	Fireball	Deep Purple	Harvest	6		L

◆ Led Zeppelin's un-titled fourth album, which contained the FM classic 'Stairway To Heaven', was released. It spent five years on the American chart and sold eleven million in the US alone.

◆ Slade followed their first No. 1, 'Coz I Luv You', with another four phonetically spelled chart toppers. They were the first act to regularly misspell titles.

1972

This Mnth	Prev Mnth	Title	Artist	Label	Wks	(US 20 Pos)	
1	17	I'd Like To Teach The World To Sing	New Seekers	Polydor	12	(7)	
2	13	Softly Whispering I Love You	Congregation	Columbia	8	(29)	F L
3	-	Mother Of Mine	Neil Reid	Decca	14		F L
4	18	Soley Soley	Middle Of The Road	RCA	8		L
5	1	Ernie (The Fastest Milkman In The West)	Benny Hill	Columbia	10		L
6	-	I Just Can't Help Believing	Elvis Presley	RCA	8		
7	7	Something Tells Me (Something Is Gonna Happen Tonight)	Cilla Black	Parlophone	8		L
8	-	Sleepy Shores	Johnny Pearson Orchestra	Penny Farthing	7		F L
9	2	Jeepster	T. Rex	Fly	10		
10	9	No Matter How I Try	Gilbert O'Sullivan	MAM	9		
11	-	Brand New Key	Melanie	Buddah	7	(1)	L
12	-	Horse With No Name	America	Warner	7	(1)	F L
13	6	Theme From 'Shaft'	Isaac Hayes	Stax	8	(1)	F
14	-	Stay With Me	Faces	Warner	5	(17)	F
15	-	Morning Has Broken	Cat Stevens	Island	4	(6)	
16	-	Morning	Val Doonican	Philips	6		L
17	4	Tokoloshe Man	John Kongos	Fly	7		L
18	-	Telegram Sam	T. Rex	T. Rex	7	(67)	
19	-	Where Did Our Love Go	Donnie Elbert	London American	5	(15)	F
20	-	Let's Stay Together	Al Green	London American	7	(1)	

This Mnth	Prev Mnth	Title	Artist	Label	Wks	(US 20 Pos)	
1	18	Telegram Sam	T. Rex	T. Rex	7	(67)	
2	-	Son Of My Father	Chicory Tip	CBS	9		F
3	3	Mother Of Mine	Neil Reid	Decca	14		F L
4	-	Have You Seen Her	Chi-Lites	MCA	7	(3)	F
5	1	I'd Like To Teach The World To Sing	New Seekers	Polydor	12	(7)	
6	12	Horse With No Name	America	Warner	7	(1)	F L
7	-	Look Wot You Dun	Slade	Polydor	7		
8	20	Let's Stay Together	Al Green	London American	7	(1)	
9	-	American Pie	Don McLean	UA	11	(1)	F
10	11	Brand New Key	Melanie	Buddah	7	(1)	L
11	-	All I Ever Need Is You	Sonny & Cher	MCA	6	(7)	L
12	-	Storm In A Teacup	Fortunes	Capitol	6		L
13	14	Stay With Me	Faces	Warner	5	(17)	F
14	-	Moon River	Greyhound	Trojan	4		
15	19	Where Did Our Love Go	Donnie Elbert	London American	5	(15)	F
16	-	Day After Day	Badfinger	Apple	6	(4)	L
17	-	Without You	Nilsson	RCA	13	(1)	F L
18	6	I Just Can't Help Believing	Elvis Presley	RCA	8		
19	-	Baby I'm A Want You	Bread	Elektra	4	(3)	
20	-	Got To Be There	Michael Jackson	Tamla Motown	6	(4)	F

◆ Pink Floyd pre-viewed their **Dark Side Of The Moon** album at London's new home of rock music, The Rainbow Theatre. The LP, which was released a year later, smashed all longevity records.
◆ As Paul McCartney (& Wings) played his first dates since leaving The Beatles, John Lennon was having problems renewing his US visa. Ringo Starr, meanwhile, was making a film about Britain's latest pop sensations, T-Rex, whose live shows were "creating hysteria not seen since the early days of The Beatles".

March 1972

This Mnth	Prev Mnth	Title	Artist	Label	Wks	(US 20 Pos)	
1	17	Without You	Nilsson	RCA	13	(1)	F L
2	9	American Pie	Don McLean	UA	11	(1)	F
3	2	Son Of My Father	Chicory Tip	CBS	9		F
4	-	Beg Steal Or Borrow	New Seekers	Polydor	9	(81)	
5	-	Mother & Child Reunion	Paul Simon	CBS	7	(4)	F
6	20	Got To Be There	Michael Jackson	Tamla Motown	6	(4)	F
7	-	Blue Is The Colour	Chelsea F.C.	Penny Farthing	7		F L
8	-	Alone Again (Naturally)	Gilbert O'Sullivan	MAM	7	(1)	
9	7	Look Wot You Dun	Slade	Polydor	7		
10	-	Meet Me On The Corner	Lindisfarne	Charisma	6		F
11	-	Poppa Joe	Sweet	RCA	5		
12	3	Mother Of Mine	Neil Reid	Decca	14		F L
13	12	Storm In A Teacup	Fortunes	Capitol	6		L
14	-	I Can't Help Myself	Donnie Elbert	Avco	5	(22)	L
15	16	Day After Day	Badfinger	Apple	6	(4)	L
16	4	Have You Seen Her	Chi-Lites	MCA	7	(3)	F
17	-	Hold Your Head Up	Argent	Epic	7	(5)	F
18	-	Floy Joy	Supremes	Tamla Motown	6	(16)	
19	-	Say You Don't Mind	Colin Blunstone	Epic	3		F L
20	-	Desiderata	Les Crane	Warner	7	(8)	F L

April 1972

This Mnth	Prev Mnth	Title	Artist	Label	Wks	(US 20 Pos)	
1	1	Without You	Nilsson	RCA	13	(1)	F L
2	4	Beg Steal Or Borrow	New Seekers	Polydor	9	(81)	
3	-	Amazing Grace	Royal Scots Dragoon Guards	RCA	11	(11)	F
4	-	Sweet Talkin' Guy	Chiffons	London American	8		L
5	17	Hold Your Head Up	Argent	Epic	7	(5)	F
6	-	Back Off Boogaloo	Ringo Starr	Apple	8	(9)	
7	8	Alone Again (Naturally)	Gilbert O'Sullivan	MAM	7	(1)	
8	-	The Young New Mexican Puppeteer	Tom Jones	Decca	7	(80)	
9	20	Desiderata	Les Crane	Warner	7	(8)	F L
10	-	Heart Of Gold	Neil Young	Reprise	5	(1)	F L
11	10	Meet Me On The Corner	Lindisfarne	Charisma	6		F
12	2	American Pie	Don McLean	UA	11	(1)	F
13	18	Floy Joy	Supremes	Tamla Motown	6	(16)	
14	-	Until It's Time For You To Go	Elvis Presley	RCA	6	(40)	
15	-	Debora/One Inch Rock	Tyrannosaurus Rex	Magni Fly	6		
16	-	Run Run Run	Jo Jo Gunne	Asylum	7	(27)	F L
17	-	Crying Laughing Loving Lying	Labi Siffre	Pye International	5		
18	-	It's One Of Those Nights (Yes Love)	Partridge Family	Bell	5	(20)	
19	-	Come What May	Vicky Leandros	Philips	8		F L
20	5	Mother & Child Reunion	Paul Simon	CBS	7	(4)	F

◆ 'I'd Like To Teach The World To Sing' by The New Seekers was not the first recording from a TV advertisement, but this Coca Cola commercial was the one which proved that major UK hits can come via this route. Since then many more have charted in Britain.

◆ Among the record nine re-issued singles in the UK Top 50 were Procol Harum's 'A Whiter Shade of Pale' and tracks by The Chiffons and The Drifters.

1972

This Mnth	Prev Mnth	Title	Artist	Label	Wks (US 20 Pos)	
1	3	Amazing Grace	Royal Scots Dragoon Guards	RCA	11 (11)	F
2	-	Could It Be Forever/Cherish	David Cassidy	Bell	9 (37)	F
3	19	Come What May	Vicky Leandros	Philips	8	F L
4	-	A Thing Called Love	Johnny Cash	CBS	7	L
5	-	Rocket Man	Elton John	DJM	8 (6)	
6	-	Metal Guru	T. Rex	EMI	8	
7	-	Tumbling Dice	Rolling Stones	Rolling Stone	6 (7)	
8	-	Radancer	Marmalade	Decca	6	
9	16	Run Run Run	Jo Jo Gunne	Asylum	7 (27)	F L
10	6	Back Off Boogaloo	Ringo Starr	Apple	8 (9)	
11	4	Sweet Talkin' Guy	Chiffons	London American	8	L
12	-	At The Club/Saturday Night At The Movies	Drifters	Atlantic	9 (43)	
13	15	Debora/One Inch Rock	Tyrannosaurus Rex	Magni Fly	6	
14	-	Oh Babe What Would You Say?	Hurricane Smith	Columbia	7 (3)	L
15	-	Take A Look Around	Temptations	Tamla Motown	5 (30)	
16	-	Leeds United	Leeds United F.C.	Chapter One	5	F L
17	8	The Young New Mexican Puppeteer	Tom Jones	Decca	7 (80)	
18	1	Without You	Nilsson	RCA	13 (1)	F L
19	-	Stir It Up	Johnny Nash	CBS	5 (12)	
20	14	Until It's Time For You To Go	Elvis Presley	RCA	6 (40)	

This Mnth	Prev Mnth	Title	Artist	Label	Wks (US 20 Pos)	
1	6	Metal Guru	T. Rex	EMI	8	
2	-	Vincent	Don McLean	UA	9 (12)	
3	12	At The Club/Saturday Night At The Movies	Drifters	Atlantic	9 (43)	
4	-	Lady Eleanor	Lindisfarne	Charisma	6 (82)	
5	14	Oh Babe What Would You Say?	Hurricane Smith	Columbia	7 (3)	L
6	-	California Man	Move	Harvest	8	L
7	5	Rocket Man	Elton John	DJM	8 (6)	
8	-	Rockin' Robin	Michael Jackson	Tamla Motown	7 (2)	
9	-	Take Me Bak 'Ome	Slade	Polydor	9 (97)	
10	-	Sister Jane	New World	RAK	6	L
11	2	Could It Be Forever/Cherish	David Cassidy	Bell	9 (37)	F
12	-	Mary Had A Little Lamb	Wings	Apple	7 (28)	
13	1	Amazing Grace	Royal Scots Dragoon Guards	RCA	11 (11)	F
14	-	Isn't Life Strange	Moody Blues	Threshold	4 (29)	
15	-	Rock & Roll Part 2	Gary Glitter	Bell	10 (7)	F
16	3	Come What May	Vicky Leandros	Philips	8	F L
17	-	Doobedood'ndoobe Doobedood'ndoobe	Diana Ross	Tamla Motown	3	
18	-	A Whiter Shade Of Pale	Procol Harum	Magnifly	4	
19	4	A Thing Called Love	Johnny Cash	CBS	7	L
20	16	Leeds United	Leeds United F.C.	Chapter One	5	F L

◆ Clyde McPhatter, founder of The Drifters and one of the most imitated R&B singers in the 1950s, died of drink related causes.

◆ The Electric Light Orchestra and Roxy Music made their UK debuts, as Slade embarked on their first UK tour (supported by Status Quo). Other firsts included David Bowie's chart album, **The Rise And Fall Of Ziggy Stardust And The Spiders From Mars**, and Bob Marley's first hit as composer of American reggae star Johnny Nash's 'Stir It Up'.

July 1972

This Mnth	Prev Mnth	Title	Artist	Label	Wks	(US 20 Pos)	
1	-	Puppy Love	Donny Osmond	MGM	12	(3)	F
2	15	Rock & Roll Part 2	Gary Glitter	Bell	10	(7)	F
3	9	Take Me Bak 'Ome	Slade	Polydor	9	(97)	
4	-	Little Willie	Sweet	RCA	8	(3)	
5	-	Circles	New Seekers	Polydor	8	(87)	
6	-	Sylvia's Mother	Dr. Hook	CBS	8	(5)	F
7	-	I Can See Clearly Now	Johnny Nash	CBS	9	(1)	
8	-	An American Trilogy	Elvis Presley	RCA	5	(66)	
9	2	Vincent	Don McLean	UA	9	(12)	
10	8	Rockin' Robin	Michael Jackson	Tamla Motown	7	(2)	
11	-	Ooh-Wakka-Doo-Wakka-Day	Gilbert O'Sullivan	MAM	6		
12	-	Breaking Up Is Hard To Do	Partridge Family	Bell	9	(28)	
13	-	Join Together	Who	Track	6	(17)	
14	6	California Man	Move	Harvest	8		L
15	12	Mary Had A Little Lamb	Paul McCartney	Apple	7	(28)	
16	-	Seaside Shuffle	Terry Dactyl & The Dinosaurs	UK	8		F L
17	-	School's Out	Alice Cooper	Warner	9	(7)	F
18	-	Mad About You	Bruce Ruffin	Rhino	5		L
19	-	Walkin' In The Rain With The One I Love	Love Unlimited	Uni	4	(14)	F
20	-	Little Bit Of Love	Free	Island	5		

August 1972

This Mnth	Prev Mnth	Title	Artist	Label	Wks	(US 20 Pos)	
1	17	School's Out	Alice Cooper	Warner	9	(7)	F
2	16	Seaside Shuffle	Terry Dactyl & The Dinosaurs	UK	8		F L
3	1	Puppy Love	Donny Osmond	MGM	12	(3)	F
4	-	Silver Machine	Hawkwind	UA	10		F L
5	12	Breaking Up Is Hard To Do	Partridge Family	Bell	9	(28)	
6	-	Popcorn	Hot Butter	Pye International	8	(9)	F L
7	6	Sylvia's Mother	Dr. Hook	CBS	8	(5)	F
8	2	Rock & Roll Part 2	Gary Glitter	Bell	10	(7)	F
9	7	I Can See Clearly Now	Johnny Nash	CBS	9	(1)	
10	-	You Wear It Well	Rod Stewart	Mercury	7	(13)	
11	-	All The Young Dudes	Mott The Hoople	CBS	6	(37)	F
12	5	Circles	New Seekers	Polydor	8	(87)	
13	-	It's Four In The Morning	Faron Young	Mercury	10	(92)	F L
14	-	10538 Overture	Electric Light Orchestra	Harvest	6		F
15	-	Run To Me	Bee Gees	Polydor	5	(16)	
16	-	Automatically Sunshine	Supremes	Tamla Motown	4	(37)	L
17	-	Layla	Derek & The Dominoes	Polydor	5	(10)	F L
18	-	Starman	David Bowie	RCA	6	(65)	
19	18	Mad About You	Bruce Ruffin	Rhino	5		L
20	-	The Loco-Motion	Little Eva	London American	5		L

◆ Wembley Stadium hosted its first pop concert and 45,000 50s fans turned out to watch Bill Haley, Chuck Berry, Little Richard, Jerry Lee Lewis and Bo Diddley (filmed as *The London Rock And Roll Show*).

◆ The successful album-oriented TV show, *The Old Grey Whistle Test*, kicked off - it helped launch many less commercial acts in the 1970s.

1972

This Mnth	Prev Mnth	Title	Artist	Label	Wks (US 20 Pos)	
1	-	Mama Weer All Crazee Now	Slade	Polydor	7 (76)	
2	10	You Wear It Well	Rod Stewart	Mercury	7 (13)	
3	13	It's Four In The Morning	Faron Young	Mercury	10 (92)	F L
4	-	Sugar Me	Lynsey De Paul	MAM	6	F
5	-	Virginia Plain	Roxy Music	Island	6	F
6	-	Standing In The Road	Blackfoot Sue	Jam	6	F L
7	11	All The Young Dudes	Mott The Hoople	CBS	6 (37)	F
8	-	How Can I Be Sure	David Cassidy	Bell	8 (25)	
9	-	I Get The Sweetest Feeling	Jackie Wilson	MCA	6 (34)	
10	-	Children Of The Revolution	T. Rex	EMI	7	
11	-	Ain't No Sunshine	Michael Jackson	Tamla Motown	6	
12	4	Silver Machine	Hawkwind	UA	10	F L
13	17	Layla	Derek & The Dominoes	Polydor	5 (10)	F L
14	1	School's Out	Alice Cooper	Warner	9 (7)	F
15	-	Too Young	Donny Osmond	MGM	5 (13)	
16	-	Living In Harmony	Cliff Richard	Columbia	4	
17	20	The Loco-Motion	Little Eva	London American	5	L
18	6	Popcorn	Hot Butter	Pye International	8 (9)	F L
19	-	Come On Over To My Place	Drifters	Atlantic	6 (60)	
20	-	Wig Wam Bam	Sweet	RCA	7	

This Mnth	Prev Mnth	Title	Artist	Label	Wks (US 20 Pos)	
1	-	Mouldy Old Dough	Lieutenant Pigeon	Decca	11	F
2	8	How Can I Be Sure	David Cassidy	Bell	8 (25)	
3	-	You're A Lady	Peter Skellern	Decca	7 (50)	F
4	-	I Didn't Know I Loved You (Till I Saw You Rock 'n' Roll)	Gary Glitter	Bell	7 (35)	
5	20	Wig Wam Bam	Sweet	RCA	7	
6	-	Donna	10cc	UK	9	F
7	10	Children Of The Revolution	T. Rex	EMI	7	
8	-	Burning Love	Elvis Presley	RCA	6 (2)	
9	-	In A Broken Dream	Python Lee Jackson	Youngblood	7 (56)	F L
10	15	Too Young	Donny Osmond	MGM	5 (13)	
11	-	Big Six	Judge Dread	Big Shot	8	F
12	-	Elected	Alice Cooper	Warner	7 (26)	
13	-	John I'm Only Dancing	David Bowie	RCA	5	
14	-	There Are More Questions Than Answers	Johnny Nash	CBS	6	
15	-	Clair	Gilbert O'Sullivan	MAM	8 (2)	
16	19	Come On Over To My Place	Drifters	Atlantic	6 (60)	
17	3	It's Four In The Morning	Faron Young	Mercury	10 (92)	F L
18	1	Mama Weer All Crazee Now	Slade	Polydor	7 (76)	
19	-	Suzanne Beware Of The Devil	Dandy Livingstone	Horse	5	F L
20	-	Goodbye To Love/I Won't Last A Day Without You	Carpenters	A&M	6 (7)	

◆ Making their debuts were Wizzard, formed by ex-Move and Electric Light Orchestra front man Roy Wood, and 10cc, a collection of Manchester's finest, who had evolved from The Mindbenders and Hot Legs.

◆ Compilation albums of 1950s hits held the top spot for 14 consecutive weeks, and re-issues of earlier hits continued to clog the charts, the latest coming from Americans Neil Sedaka, The Shangri-Las, Chris Montez and Roy C.

1972

This Mnth	Prev Mnth	Title	Artist	Label	Wks	(US 20 Pos)	
1	15	Clair	Gilbert O'Sullivan	MAM	8	(2)	
2	1	Mouldy Old Dough	Lieutenant Pigeon	Decca	11		F
3	-	Leader Of The Pack	Shangri-Las	Kama Sutra	6		
4	-	Loop Di Love	Shag	UK	7		F L
5	-	My Ding-A-Ling	Chuck Berry	Chess	10	(1)	
6	6	Donna	10cc	UK	9		F
7	12	Elected	Alice Cooper	Warner	7	(26)	
8	9	In A Broken Dream	Python Lee Jackson	Youngblood	7	(56)	F L
9	20	Goodbye To Love/I Won't Last A Day Without You	Carpenters	A&M	6	(7)	
10	-	Crazy Horses	Osmonds	MGM	12	(14)	F
11	-	Why	Donny Osmond	MGM	9	(13)	
12	-	Crocodile Rock	Elton John	DJM	10	(1)	
13	-	Let's Dance	Chris Montez	London American	5		L
14	-	Hallelujah Freedom	Junior Campbell	Deram	5		F
15	-	I'm Stone In Love With You	Stylistics	Avco	5	(10)	
16	-	Here I Go Again	Archie Bell & The Drells	Atlantic	3		F
17	14	There Are More Questions Than Answers	Johnny Nash	CBS	6		
18	-	Burlesque	Family	Reprise	5		L
19	8	Burning Love	Elvis Presley	RCA	6	(2)	
20	3	You're A Lady	Peter Skellern	Decca	7	(50)	F

This Mnth	Prev Mnth	Title	Artist	Label	Wks	(US 20 Pos)	
1	5	My Ding-A-Ling	Chuck Berry	Chess	10	(1)	
2	10	Crazy Horses	Osmonds	MGM	12	(14)	F
3	-	Gudbuy T'Jane	Slade	Polydor	9	(68)	
4	11	Why	Donny Osmond	MGM	9	(13)	
5	-	Long Haired Lover From Liverpool	Little Jimmy Osmond	MGM	14	(38)	F
6	-	Solid Gold Easy Action	T. Rex	EMI	8		
7	12	Crocodile Rock	Elton John	DJM	10	(1)	
8	-	Ben	Michael Jackson	Tamla Motown	8	(1)	
9	-	Angel/What Made Milwaukee Famous	Rod Stewart	Mercury	5	(40)	
10	-	Happy Xmas (War Is Over)	John & Yoko/Plastic Ono Band	Apple	5		
11	-	Stay With Me	Blue Mink	Regal Zonophone	5		
12	-	Shotgun Wedding	Roy 'C'	UK	7		L
13	-	Lookin' Through The Windows	Jackson Five	Tamla Motown	6	(16)	
14	-	Rock Me Baby	David Cassidy	Bell	5	(38)	
15	-	Nights In White Satin	Moody Blues	Deram	6	(2)	
16	-	Lay Down	Strawbs	A&M	4		F
17	1	Clair	Gilbert O'Sullivan	MAM	8	(2)	
18	-	Help Me Make It Through The Night	Gladys Knight & The Pips	Tamla Motown	7	(33)	
19	15	I'm Stone In Love With You	Stylistics	Avco	5	(10)	
20	-	Little Drummer Boy	Royal Scots Dragoon Guards	RCA	4		L

◆ With Osmond-mania at its height in the UK, nine-year-old Little Jimmy's minor US hit, 'Long Haired Lover From Liverpool', became the biggest British seller by any of the family.

◆ The Moody Blues' US tour was a resounding success. The group, who had a transatlantic hit with the five-year-old, 'Nights in White Satin', topped the album chart with Seventh Sojourn.

◆ American band The New York Dolls made an impressive if not highly publicized UK debut.

1973

This Mnth	Prev Mnth	Title	Artist	Label	Wks	(US 20 Pos)	
1	5	Long Haired Lover From Liverpool	Little Jimmy Osmond	MGM	14	(38)	F
2	-	The Jean Genie	David Bowie	RCA	8	(71)	
3	-	Hi Hi Hi/C Moon	Wings	Apple	6	(10)	
4	6	Solid Gold Easy Action	T. Rex	EMI	8		
5	2	Crazy Horses	Osmonds	MGM	12	(14)	F
6	-	Ball Park Incident	Wizzard	Harvest	6		F
7	-	You're So Vain	Carly Simon	Elektra	8	(1)	F
8	-	Blockbuster	Sweet	RCA	10	(73)	
9	-	Big Seven	Judge Dread	Big Shot	7		
10	-	Always On My Mind	Elvis Presley	RCA	5		
11	3	Gudbuy T'Jane	Slade	Polydor	9	(68)	
12	12	Shotgun Wedding	Roy 'C'	UK	7		L
13	15	Nights In White Satin	Moody Blues	Deram	6	(2)	
14	10	Happy Xmas (War Is Over)	John & Yoko & The Plastic Ono Band	Apple	5		
15	1	My Ding-A-Ling	Chuck Berry	Chess	10	(1)	
16	18	Help Me Make It Through The Night	Gladys Knight & The Pips	Tamla Motown	7	(33)	
17	8	Ben	Michael Jackson	Tamla Motown	8	(1)	
18	-	Do You Wanna Touch Me (Oh Yeah)	Gary Glitter	Bell	7		
19	-	Wishing Well	Free	Island	5		
20	-	Can't Keep It In	Cat Stevens	Island	4		

This Mnth	Prev Mnth	Title	Artist	Label	Wks	(US 20 Pos)	
1	8	Blockbuster	Sweet	RCA	10	(73)	
2	18	Do You Wanna Touch Me (Oh Yeah)	Gary Glitter	Bell	7		
3	-	Part Of The Union	Strawbs	A&M	9		L
4	-	Daniel	Elton John	DJM	6	(2)	
5	7	You're So Vain	Carly Simon	Elektra	8	(1)	F
6	1	Long Haired Lover From Liverpool	Little Jimmy Osmond	MGM	14	(38)	F
7	-	Sylvia	Focus	Polydor	6	(89)	L
8	-	Roll Over Beethoven	Electric Light Orchestra	Harvest	5	(42)	
9	-	Paper Plane	Status Quo	Vertigo	5		
10	19	Wishing Well	Free	Island	5		
11	-	Whiskey In The Jar	Thin Lizzy	Decca	6		F
12	-	If You Don't Know Me By Now	Harold Melvin & The Blue Notes	CBS	4	(3)	F
13	2	The Jean Genie	David Bowie	RCA	8	(71)	
14	-	Superstition	Stevie Wonder	Tamla Motown	5	(1)	
15	-	Me And Mrs. Jones	Billy Paul	Epic	4	(1)	F L
16	-	Cindy Incidentally	Faces	Warner	7	(48)	
17	-	Baby I Love You	Dave Edmunds	Rockfield	6		
18	-	Lookin' Through The Eyes Of Love	Partridge Family	Bell	5	(39)	
19	6	Ball Park Incident	Wizzard	Harvest	6		F
20	20	Can't Keep It In	Cat Stevens	Island	4		

◆ Local glam rock greats, Sweet, Gary Glitter, T-Rex, David Bowie and Slade vied for the affection of British teeny boppers with American superstars The Osmonds and David Cassidy.

◆ Pink Floyd's album **Dark Side Of The Moon** entered the US chart, where it has remained for a record smashing 17 years (selling over 12 million copies)!

March 1973

This Mnth	Prev Mnth	Title	Artist	Label	Wks	(US 20 Pos)	
1	-	Cum On Feel The Noize	Slade	Polydor	7	(98)	
2	-	Feel The Need In Me	Detroit Emeralds	Janus	7	(90)	F
3	-	20th Century Boy	T. Rex	EMI	6		
4	16	Cindy Incidentally	Faces	Warner	7	(48)	
5	-	The Twelfth Of Never	Donny Osmond	MGM	9	(8)	
6	-	Killing Me Softly With His Song	Roberta Flack	Atlantic	8	(1)	
7	-	Hello Hurray	Alice Cooper	Warner	8	(35)	
8	3	Part Of The Union	Strawbs	A&M	9		L
9	-	Power To All Our Friends	Cliff Richard	EMI	7		
10	1	Blockbuster	Sweet	RCA	10	(73)	
11	-	Gonna Make You An Offer You Can't Refuse	Jimmy Helms	Cube	5		F L
12	7	Sylvia	Focus	Polydor	6	(89)	L
13	-	Doctor My Eyes	Jackson Five	Tamla Motown	5		
14	17	Baby I Love You	Dave Edmunds	Rockfield	6		
15	-	Get Down	Gilbert O'Sullivan	MAM	8	(7)	
16	11	Whiskey In The Jar	Thin Lizzy	Decca	6		F
17	2	Do You Wanna Touch Me (Oh Yeah)	Gary Glitter	Bell	7		
18	18	Lookin' Through The Eyes Of Love	Partridge Family	Bell	5	(39)	
19	-	Never Never Never	Shirley Bassey	UA	8	(48)	L
20	-	Heart Of Stone	Kenny	RAK	6		F L

April 1973

This Mnth	Prev Mnth	Title	Artist	Label	Wks	(US 20 Pos)	
1	-	Tie A Yellow Ribbon Round The Old Oak Tree	Dawn	Bell	17	(1)	
2	15	Get Down	Gilbert O'Sullivan	MAM	8	(7)	
3	-	I'm A Clown/Some Kind Of A Summer	David Cassidy	Bell	8		
4	5	The Twelfth Of Never	Donny Osmond	MGM	9	(8)	
5	-	Tweedle Dee	Little Jimmy Osmond	MGM	7	(59)	
6	-	Hello Hello I'm Back Again	Gary Glitter	Bell	10		
7	9	Power To All Our Friends	Cliff Richard	EMI	7		
8	19	Never Never Never	Shirley Bassey	UA	8	(48)	L
9	-	Love Train	O'Jays	CBS	6	(1)	
10	-	Pyjamarama	Roxy Music	Island	6		
11	-	All Because Of You	Geordie	EMI	6		F
12	-	Drive-In Saturday	David Bowie	RCA	7		
13	-	Crazy	Mud	RAK	5		F
14	20	Heart Of Stone	Kenny	RAK	6		F L
15	-	My Love	Paul McCartney & Wings	Apple	6	(1)	
16	-	Amanda	Stuart Gillies	Philips	5		F L
17	6	Killing Me Softly With His Song	Roberta Flack	Atlantic	8	(1)	
18	2	Feel The Need In Me	Detroit Emeralds	Janus	7	(90)	F
19	-	Why Can't We Live Together	Timmy Thomas	Mojo	4	(3)	F L
20	1	Cum On Feel The Noize	Slade	Polydor	7	(98)	

◆ Reluctant guitar hero Eric Clapton made his live comeback after two years with a performance at London's Rainbow Theatre. Pete Townshend organized the show which also featured Steve Winwood, Ron Wood and Jim Capaldi.

◆ As John Lennon denied that The Beatles would re-unite, the group's compilation album 1967-1970 was replaced at the top of the US chart by Red Rose Speedway from Paul McCartney & Wings.

1973

This Mnth	Prev Mnth	Title	Artist	Label	Wks	(US 20 Pos)	
1	1	Tie A Yellow Ribbon Round The Old Oak Tree	Dawn	Bell	17	(1)	
2	-	Hell Raiser	Sweet	RCA	6		
3	-	See My Baby Jive	Wizzard	Harvest	10		
4	6	Hello Hello I'm Back Again	Gary Glitter	Bell	10		
5	12	Drive-In Saturday	David Bowie	RCA	7		
6	-	Giving It All Away	Roger Daltrey	Track	6	(83)	F
7	-	Brother Louie	Hot Chocolate	RAK	6		
8	-	And I Love You So	Perry Como	RCA	12	(29)	
9	15	My Love	Paul McCartney & Wings	Apple	6	(1)	
10	-	No More Mr. Nice Guy	Alice Cooper	Warner	4	(25)	
11	11	All Because Of You	Geordie	EMI	6		F
12	-	Also Sprach Zarathustra (2001)	Deodata	CTI	5	(2)	F L
13	-	Wonderful Dream	Ann-Marie David	Epic	4		F L
14	5	Tweedle Dee	Little Jimmy Osmond	MGM	7	(59)	
15	-	One And One Is One	Medicine Head	Polydor	7		F
16	2	Get Down	Gilbert O'Sullivan	MAM	8	(7)	
17	3	I'm A Clown/Some Kind Of A Summer	David Cassidy	Bell	8		
18	-	Big Eight	Judge Dread	Big Shot	5		
19	-	Can The Can	Suzi Quatro	RAK	7	(56)	F
20	-	Broken Down Angel	Nazareth	Mooncrest	5		F

This Mnth	Prev Mnth	Title	Artist	Label	Wks	(US 20 Pos)	
1	19	Can The Can	Suzi Quatro	RAK	7	(56)	F
2	-	Rubber Bullets	10cc	UK	9	(73)	
3	3	See My Baby Jive	Wizzard	Harvest	10		
4	15	One And One Is One	Medicine Head	Polydor	7		F
5	-	Albatross	Fleetwood Mac	CBS	8		
6	8	And I Love You So	Perry Como	RCA	12	(29)	
7	-	The Groover	T. Rex	EMI	5		
8	-	Stuck In The Middle With You	Stealer's Wheel	A&M	6	(6)	F L
9	1	Tie A Yellow Ribbon Round The Old Oak Tree	Dawn	Bell	17	(1)	
10	-	Walking In The Rain	Partridge Family	Bell	5		L
11	-	You Are The Sunshine Of My Life	Stevie Wonder	Tamla Motown	5	(1)	
12	-	Welcome Home	Peters & Lee	Philips	15		F
13	-	Snoopy Vs. The Red Baron	Hotshots	Mooncrest	8		F L
14	-	Give Me Love (Give Me Peace On Earth)	George Harrison	Apple	6	(1)	
15	2	Hell Raiser	Sweet	RCA	6		
16	-	Walk On The Wild Side	Lou Reed	RCA	4	(16)	F L
17	-	Live And Let Die	Wings	Apple	7	(2)	
18	20	Broken Down Angel	Nazareth	Mooncrest	5		F
19	-	Skweeze Me Pleeze Me	Slade	Polydor	6		
20	12	Also Sprach Zarathustra (2001)	Deodata	CTI	5	(2)	F L

◆ Fleetwood Mac's re-issued instrumental 'Albatross' peaked at No. 2, narrowly failing to become the first record to top the UK chart on two separate occasions.

◆ 'Monster Mash' by Bobby 'Boris' Pickett & The Crypt Kickers, which had topped the US chart in 1962, not only returned to the Top 10 but also hit in re-issue-mad Britain for the first time.

July 1973

This Mnth	Prev Mnth	Title	Artist	Label	Wks	(US 20 Pos)	
1	12	Welcome Home	Peters & Lee	Philips	15		F
2	19	Skweeze Me Pleeze Me	Slade	Polydor	6		
3	-	Life On Mars	David Bowie	RCA	8		
4	-	Born To Be With You	Dave Edmunds	Rockfield	7		
5	13	Snoopy Vs. The Red Baron	Hotshots	Mooncrest	8		F L
6	-	Take Me To The Mardi Gras	Paul Simon	CBS	5		
7	2	Rubber Bullets	10cc	UK	9	(73)	
8	-	Saturday Night's Alright For Fighting	Elton John	DJM	5	(12)	
9	-	I'm The Leader Of The Gang (I Am)	Gary Glitter	Bell	8		
10	5	Albatross	Fleetwood Mac	CBS	8		
11	-	Going Home	Osmonds	MGM	6	(36)	
12	-	Alright Alright Alright	Mungo Jerry	Dawn	6		
13	-	Randy	Blue Mink	EMI	5		L
14	17	Live And Let Die	Wings	Apple	7	(2)	
15	-	Gaye	Clifford T. Ward	Charisma	5		F L
16	14	Give Me Love (Give Me Peace On Earth)	George Harrison	Apple	6	(1)	
17	-	Honaloochie Boogie	Mott The Hoople	CBS	3		
18	7	The Groover	T. Rex	EMI	5		
19	-	Can You Do It	Geordie	EMI	4		L
20	-	Step By Step	Joe Simon	Mojo	3	(37)	F L

August 1973

This Mnth	Prev Mnth	Title	Artist	Label	Wks	(US 20 Pos)	
1	9	I'm The Leader Of The Gang (I Am)	Gary Glitter	Bell	8		
2	1	Welcome Home	Peters & Lee	Philips	15		F
3	-	Yesterday Once More	Carpenters	A&M	8	(2)	
4	-	48 Crash	Suzi Quatro	RAK	5		
5	12	Alright Alright Alright	Mungo Jerry	Dawn	6		
6	-	Spanish Eyes	Al Martino	Capitol	13		L
7	11	Going Home	Osmonds	MGM	6	(36)	
8	-	You Can Do Magic	Limmie & The Family Cookin'	Avco	7	(84)	F
9	3	Life On Mars	David Bowie	RCA	8		
10	-	Touch Me In The Morning	Diana Ross	Tamla Motown	6	(1)	
11	-	Ying Tong Song	Goons	Decca	4		L
12	-	Bad Bad Boy	Nazareth	Mooncrest	5		
13	-	(Dancing) On A Saturday Night	Barry Blue	Bell	9		F
14	-	Young Love	Donny Osmond	MGM	7	(25)	
15	-	Smarty Pants	First Choice	Bell	5	(56)	L
16	13	Randy	Blue Mink	EMI	5		L
17	15	Gaye	Clifford T. Ward	Charisma	5		F L
18	-	All Right Now	Free	Island	3		
19	-	Rising Sun	Medicine Head	Polydor	5		L
20	-	Summer (The First Time)	Bobby Goldsboro	UA	5	(21)	

◆ David Bowie and Jethro Tull (who topped the US LP chart with A Passion Play) announced that their touring days were over. The Everly Brothers split up and Ray Davis quit The Kinks. More permanent, however, were the dissolution of The Doors and Eno's departure from Roxy Music.

◆ Soon after Freddie Mercury's debut single 'I Can Hear Music' (as Larry Lurex) failed to click, his group Queen's first 45, 'Keep Yourself Alive' also fell by the wayside. Despite this disappointing chart start, they went on to become one of the biggest selling and most influential British acts of all time.

1973

This Mnth	Prev Mnth	Title	Artist	Label	Wks	(US 20 Pos)	
1	-	Angel Fingers	Wizzard	Harvest	8		
2	14	Young Love	Donny Osmond	MGM	7	(25)	
3	-	Rock On	David Essex	CBS	7	(5)	F
4	13	(Dancing) On A Saturday Night	Barry Blue	Bell	9		F
5	6	Spanish Eyes	Al Martino	Capitol	13		L
6	-	Angie	Rolling Stones	Rolling Stone	5	(1)	
7	8	You Can Do Magic	Limmie & The Family Cookin'	Avco	7	(84)	F
8	-	Oh No Not My Baby	Rod Stewart	Mercury	5	(59)	
9	-	Say, Has Anybody Seen My Sweet Gypsy Rose	Dawn	Bell	5	(3)	L
10	-	Like Sister And Brother	Drifters	Bell	6		
11	3	Yesterday Once More	Carpenters	A&M	8	(2)	
12	-	Ballroom Blitz	Sweet	RCA	6	(5)	
13	-	Pick Up The Pieces	Hudson-Ford	A&M	4		F
14	-	Monster Mash	Bobby 'Boris' Pickett & The Crypt Kickers	London American	6	(10)	F L
15	-	The Dean And I	10cc	UK	4		
16	20	Summer (The First Time)	Bobby Goldsboro	UA	5	(21)	
17	-	Eye Level	Simon Park Orchestra	Columbia	10		F G L
18	2	Welcome Home	Peters & Lee	Philips	15		F
19	-	For The Good Times	Perry Como	RCA	10		L
20	1	I'm The Leader Of The Gang (I Am)	Gary Glitter	Bell	8		

This Mnth	Prev Mnth	Title	Artist	Label	Wks	(US 20 Pos)	
1	17	Eye Level	Simon Park Orchestra	Columbia	10		F G L
2	-	My Friend Stan	Slade	Polydor	6		
3	-	Nutbush City Limits	Ike & Tina Turner	UA	7	(22)	L
4	12	Ballroom Blitz	Sweet	RCA	6	(5)	
5	14	Monster Mash	Bobby 'Boris' Pickett & The Crypt Kickers	London American	6	(10)	F L
6	-	The Laughing Gnome	David Bowie	Deram	6		
7	19	For The Good Times	Perry Como	RCA	10		L
8	-	Daydreamer/The Puppy Song	David Cassidy	Bell	8		
9	-	Caroline	Status Quo	Vertigo	8		
10	-	Goodbye Yellow Brick Road	Elton John	DJM	7	(2)	
11	1	Angel Fingers	Wizzard	Harvest	8		
12	-	Joybringer	Manfred Mann's Earth Band	Vertigo	5		L
13	-	A Hard Rain's Gonna Fall	Bryan Ferry	Island	5		F
14	-	Sorrow	David Bowie	RCA	8		
15	-	Ghetto Child	Detroit Spinners	Atlantic	6	(29)	
16	8	Oh No Not My Baby	Rod Stewart	Mercury	5	(59)	
17	5	Spanish Eyes	Al Martino	Capitol	13		L
18	-	All The Way From Memphis	Mott The Hoople	CBS	4		
19	-	Showdown	Electric Light Orchestra	Harvest	5	(53)	
20	-	That Lady (Pt. 1)	Isley Brothers	Epic	2	(6)	

◆ It was announced that David Bowie had sold over eight million units in Britain in two years, making him the biggest seller since The Beatles.

◆ Hottest producer/ songwriters in Britain in 1973 were Nicky Chinn & Mike Chapman, who were responsible for hits from Sweet, American rocker Suzi Quatro and new teen idols Mud.

1973

This Mnth	Prev Mnth	Title	Artist	Label	Wks	(US 20 Pos)	
1	-	Let Me In	Osmonds	MGM	9	(36)	
2	14	Sorrow	David Bowie	RCA	8		
3	8	Daydreamer/The Puppy Song	David Cassidy	Bell	8		
4	-	Top Of The World	Carpenters	A&M	8	(1)	
5	-	Dyna-Mite	Mud	RAK	7		
6	1	Eye Level	Simon Park Orchestra	Columbia	10		F G L
7	-	I Love You Love Me Love	Gary Glitter	Bell	12		G
8	15	Ghetto Child	Detroit Spinners	Atlantic	6	(29)	
9	7	For The Good Times	Perry Como	RCA	10		L
10	-	Photograph	Ringo Starr	Apple	5	(1)	
11	-	This Flight Tonight	Nazareth	Mooncrest	5		
12	9	Caroline	Status Quo	Vertigo	8		
13	-	When I Fall In Love	Donny Osmond	MGM	9	(14)	
14	10	Goodbye Yellow Brick Road	Elton John	DJM	7	(2)	
15	-	Do You Wanna Dance	Barry Blue	Bell	6		
16	19	Showdown	Electric Light Orchestra	Harvest	5	(53)	
17	-	Deck Of Cards	Max Bygraves	Pye	5		L
18	-	Paper Roses	Marie Osmond	MGM	11	(5)	F L
19	2	My Friend Stan	Slade	Polydor	6		
20	-	Won't Somebody Dance With Me	Lynsey De Paul	MAM	5		

This Mnth	Prev Mnth	Title	Artist	Label	Wks	(US 20 Pos)	
1	7	I Love You Love Me Love	Gary Glitter	Bell	12		G
2	-	My Coo-Ca-Choo	Alvin Stardust	Magnet	12		F
3	-	You Won't Find Another Fool Like Me	New Seekers	Polydor	12		
4	18	Paper Roses	Marie Osmond	MGM	11	(5)	F L
5	-	Lamplight	David Essex	CBS	11	(71)	
6	-	Merry Xmas Everybody	Slade	Polydor	7		G
7	-	Why Oh Why Oh Why	Gilbert O'Sullivan	MAM	10		
8	-	Roll Away The Stone	Mott The Hoople	CBS	9		
9	-	I Wish It Could Be Christmas Everyday	Wizzard	Harvest	7		
10	-	Street Life	Roxy Music	Island	8		
11	13	When I Fall In Love	Donny Osmond	MGM	9	(14)	
12	5	Dyna-Mite	Mud	RAK	7		
13	1	Let Me In	Osmonds	MGM	9	(36)	
14	-	Truck On (Tyke)	T. Rex	EMI	7		
15	-	The Show Must Go On	Leo Sayer	Chrysalis	9		F
16	15	Do You Wanna Dance	Barry Blue	Bell	6		
17	-	Helen Wheels	Paul McCartney & Wings	Apple	4	(10)	
18	-	Forever	Roy Wood	Harvest	9		
19	-	Loving And Free/Amoureuse	Kiki Dee	Rocket	5		F
20	10	Photograph	Ringo Starr	Apple	5	(1)	

◆ John Rostill of The Shadows was electrocuted in his studio. His death came days after his song 'Let Me Be There' gave Olivia Newton-John her first American pop hit and days before her record became the first UK recording to crack the US country Top 10.

1974

This Mnth	Prev Mnth	Title	Artist	Label	Wks	(US 20 Pos)	
1	3	You Won't Find Another Fool Like Me	New Seekers	Polydor	12		
2	15	The Show Must Go On	Leo Sayer	Chrysalis	9		F
3	6	Merry Xmas Everybody	Slade	Polydor	7		G
4	2	My Coo-Ca-Choo	Alvin Stardust	Magnet	12		F
5	-	Dance With The Devil	Cozy Powell	RAK	10	(49)	F
6	1	I Love You Love Me Love	Gary Glitter	Bell	12		G
7	18	Forever	Roy Wood	Harvest	9		
8	4	Paper Roses	Marie Osmond	MGM	11	(5)	F L
9	-	Radar Love	Golden Earring	Track	6	(13)	F L
10	9	I Wish It Could Be Christmas Everyday	Wizzard	Harvest	7		
11	-	Pool Hall Richard/I Wish It Would Rain	Faces	Warner	7		
12	-	Love On A Mountain Top	Robert Knight	Monument	10		F
13	5	Lamplight	David Essex	CBS	11	(71)	
14	-	Teenage Rampage	Sweet	RCA	6		
15	-	Tiger Feet	Mud	RAK	8		
16	8	Roll Away The Stone	Mott The Hoople	CBS	9		
17	-	Solitaire	Andy Williams	CBS	8		L
18	10	Street Life	Roxy Music	Island	8		
19	7	Why Oh Why Oh Why	Gilbert O'Sullivan	MAM	10		
20	14	Truck On (Tyke)	T. Rex	EMI	7		

1	15	Tiger Feet	Mud	RAK	8		
2	14	Teenage Rampage	Sweet	RCA	6		
3	17	Solitaire	Andy Williams	CBS	8		L
4	-	The Man Who Sold The World	Lulu	Polydor	6		
5	5	Dance With The Devil	Cozy Powell	RAK	10	(49)	F
6	-	Devil Gate Drive	Suzi Quatro	RAK	7		
7	-	Rockin' Roll Baby	Stylistics	Avco	6	(14)	
8	-	All Of My Life	Diana Ross	Tamla Motown	6		
9	2	The Show Must Go On	Leo Sayer	Chrysalis	9		F
10	-	The Wombling Song	Wombles	CBS	7		F
11	1	You Won't Find Another Fool Like Me	New Seekers	Polydor	12		
12	-	How Come	Ronnie Lane	GM	4		F L
13	9	Radar Love	Golden Earring	Track	6	(13)	F L
14	7	Forever	Roy Wood	Harvest	9		
15	12	Love On A Mountain Top	Robert Knight	Monument	10		F
16	-	Jealous Mind	Alvin Stardust	Magnet	6		
17	4	My Coo-Ca-Choo	Alvin Stardust	Magnet	12		F
18	-	Teenage Lament '74	Alice Cooper	Warner	3	(48)	L
19	-	Teenage Dream	Marc Bolan & T. Rex	EMI	3		
20	-	Rebel Rebel	David Bowie	RCA	5	(64)	

◆ Newcomers who were creating interest included: Queen, Leo Sayer, Alvin Stardust, Bad Company, The Wombles, and a new-look Bay City Rollers.

◆ The main winners in the *NME* poll were David Bowie (Top Male), Diana Ross (Top Female) and Yes (Top Group). Incidentally, Yes, who quickly sold out their Madison Square Garden shows, scored their first UK chart topper with the LP **Tales From Topographic Oceans**.

March 1974

This Mnth	Prev Mnth	Title	Artist	Label	Wks	(US 20 Pos)	
1	-	The Air That I Breathe	Hollies	Polydor	7	(6)	
2	-	Billy, Don't Be A Hero	Paper Lace	Bus Stop	9	(96)	F
3	16	Jealous Mind	Alvin Stardust	Magnet	6		
4	-	You're Sixteen	Ringo Starr	Apple	7	(1)	L
5	-	The Most Beautiful Girl	Charlie Rich	CBS	9	(1)	F
6	6	Devil Gate Drive	Suzi Quatro	RAK	7		
7	-	Remember (Sha-La-La)	Bay City Rollers	Bell	6		
8	-	Jet	Paul McCartney & Wings	Apple	6	(7)	
9	10	The Wombling Song	Wombles	CBS	7		F
10	-	It's You	Freddie Starr	Tiffany	6		F L
11	20	Rebel Rebel	David Bowie	RCA	5	(64)	
12	-	I Get A Little Sentimental Over You	New Seekers	Polydor	6		L
13	-	Candle In The Wind	Elton John	DJM	6		
14	-	Ma He's Making Eyes At Me	Lena Zavaroni	Philips	6	(91)	F L
15	-	Emma	Hot Chocolate	RAK	7	(8)	
16	-	School Love	Barry Blue	Bell	5		L
17	1	Tiger Feet	Mud	Rak	8		
18	-	Seasons In The Sun	Terry Jacks	Bell	9	(1)	F
19	-	Never, Never Gonna Give Ya Up	Barry White	Pye International	4	(7)	F
20	-	Love's Theme	Love Unlimited Orchestra	Pye	6	(1)	F L

April 1974

This Mnth	Prev Mnth	Title	Artist	Label	Wks	(US 20 Pos)	
1	18	Seasons In The Sun	Terry Jacks	Bell	9	(1)	F
2	-	Angel Face	Glitter Band	Bell	7		F
3	-	Everyday	Slade	Polydor	5		
4	-	Remember Me This Way	Gary Glitter	Bell	6		
5	-	You Are Everything	Diana Ross	Tamla Motown	7		
6	2	Billy, Don't Be A Hero	Paper Lace	Bus Stop	9	(96)	F
7	15	Emma	Hot Chocolate	RAK	7	(8)	
8	-	The Cat Crept In	Mud	RAK	6		
9	-	Doctor's Orders	Sunny	CBS	5		F L
10	-	Seven Seas Of Rhye	Queen	EMI	6		F
11	-	Remember You're A Womble	Wombles	CBS	9		
12	5	The Most Beautiful Girl	Charlie Rich	CBS	9	(1)	F
13	12	I Get A Little Sentimental Over You	New Seekers	Polydor	6		L
14	-	I'm Gonna Knock On Your Door	Little Jimmy Osmond	MGM	4		L
15	-	Waterloo	Abba	Epic	7	(6)	F
16	-	Homely Girl	Chi-Lites	Brunswick	6	(54)	
17	-	Rock Around The Clock	Bill Haley & His Comets	MCA	5		L
18	-	A Walkin' Miracle	Limmie & The Family Cookin'	Avco	5		L
19	-	Long Live Love	Olivia Newton-John	Pye International	4		
20	-	Jambalaya	Carpenters	A&M	5		

◆ Soon after Elvis and Priscilla ended their marriage, Cher filed for divorce from Sonny and John Lennon and Yoko Ono temporarily separated.

◆ Rick Wakeman quit Yes and his solo album **Journey To The Centre Of The Earth** reached the transatlantic Top 3. Also stretching their wings were Bill Wyman, who became the first Rolling Stone to release a solo album, and The Who's Roger Daltrey, who staged his first solo concert.

1974

This Mnth	Prev Mnth	Title	Artist	Label	Wks	(US 20 Pos)	
1	15	Waterloo	Abba	Epic	7	(6)	F
2	-	Don't Stay Away Too Long	Peters & Lee	Philips	8		
3	-	Shang-A-Lang	Bay City Rollers	Bell	6		
4	-	Sugar Baby Love	Rubettes	Polydor	7	(37)	F
5	11	Remember You're A Womble	Wombles	CBS	9		
6	-	Rock 'n' Roll Winter	Wizzard	Warner	4		
7	16	Homely Girl	Chi-Lites	Brunswick	6	(54)	
8	-	The Night Chicago Died	Paper Lace	Bus Stop	6	(1)	
9	18	A Walkin' Miracle	Limmie & The Family Cookin'	Avco	5		L
10	-	Red Dress	Alvin Stardust	Magnet	5		
11	8	The Cat Crept In	Mud	RAK	6		
12	1	Seasons In The Sun	Terry Jacks	Bell	9	(1)	F
13	-	This Town Ain't Big Enough For Both Of Us	Sparks	Island	6		F
14	-	He's Misstra Know It All	Stevie Wonder	Tamla Motown	5		
15	-	I Can't Stop	Osmonds	MCA	5	(96)	
16	5	You Are Everything	Diana Ross	Tamla Motown	7		
17	9	Doctor's Orders	Sunny	CBS	5		F L
18	-	Long Legged Woman Dressed In Black	Mungo Jerry	Dawn	5		L
19	-	Spiders & Snakes	Jim Stafford	MGM	4	(3)	F
20	-	Break The Rules	Status Quo	Vertigo	4		

This Mnth	Prev Mnth	Title	Artist	Label	Wks	(US 20 Pos)	
1	-	Hey Rock And Roll	Showaddywaddy	Bell	8		F
2	-	There's A Ghost In My House	R. Dean Taylor	Tamla Motown	7		L
3	-	The Streak	Ray Stevens	Janus	7	(1)	
4	13	This Town Ain't Big Enough For Both Of Us	Sparks	Island	6		F
5	4	Sugar Baby Love	Rubettes	Polydor	7	(37)	F
6	-	Judy Teen	Cockney Rebel	EMI	6		F
7	-	Always Yours	Gary Glitter	Bell	6		
8	-	Jarrow Song	Alan Price	Warner	5		L
9	8	The Night Chicago Died	Paper Lace	Bus Stop	6	(1)	
10	-	A Touch Too Much	Arrows	RAK	5		F L
11	-	I See A Star	Mouth & McNeal	Decca	5		F L
12	-	Go (Before You Break My Heart)	Gigliola Cinquetti	CBS	4		L
13	-	She	Charles Aznavour	Barclay	8		F L
14	-	If I Didn't Care	David Cassidy	Bell	4		
15	2	Don't Stay Away Too Long	Peters & Lee	Philips	8		
16	-	Liverpool Lou	Scaffold	Warner	4		L
17	-	I'd Love You To Want Me	Lobo	UK	6	(2)	L
18	-	One Man Band	Leo Sayer	Chrysalis	5	(96)	
19	-	The In Crowd	Bryan Ferry	Island	4		
20	3	Shang-A-Lang	Bay City Rollers	Bell	6		

◆ NME writers selected **Sergeant Pepper** (The Beatles), **Blonde On Blonde** (Bob Dylan) and **Pet Sounds** (Beach Boys) as the three greatest albums ever recorded.

◆ Bill Haley & The Comets' original 1954 recording of 'Rock Around The Clock' returned to the chart; it was the fifth separate visit to the UK Top 20 for the single.

◆ As Blue Swede put Sweden on the US musical map, Abba gave Scandinavia its biggest British hit, with their Eurovision winner, 'Waterloo'.

July 1974

This Mnth	Prev Mnth	Title	Artist	Label	Wks	(US 20 Pos)	
1	13	She	Charles Aznavour	Barclay	8		F L
2	-	Kissin' In The Back Row Of The Movies	Drifters	Bell	8		
3	-	Bangin' Man	Slade	Polydor	5		
4	-	Rock Your Baby	George McCrae	Jayboy	9	(1)	F
5	17	I'd Love You To Want Me	Lobo	UK	6	(2)	L
6	-	Young Girl	Gary Puckett & The Union Gap	CBS	6		L
7	-	Band On The Run	Paul McCartney & Wings	Apple	6	(1)	
8	7	Always Yours	Gary Glitter	Bell	6		
9	-	Banana Rock	Wombles	CBS	5		
10	-	Wall Street Shuffle	10cc	UK	5		
11	1	Hey Rock And Roll	Showaddywaddy	Bell	8		F
12	18	One Man Band	Leo Sayer	Chrysalis	5	(96)	
13	-	Born With A Smile On My Face	Stephanie De Sykes	Bradley's	6		F
14	-	The Six Teens	Sweet	RCA	5		
15	-	If You Go Away	Terry Jacks	Bell	4	(68)	L
16	3	The Streak	Ray Stevens	Janus	7	(1)	
17	-	When Will I See You Again	Three Degrees	Philly International	10	(2)	
18	-	Guilty	Pearls	Bell	4		F L
19	-	Beach Baby	First Class	UK	4	(4)	F L
20	-	Going Down The Road	Roy Wood	Harvest	3		

August 1974

This Mnth	Prev Mnth	Title	Artist	Label	Wks	(US 20 Pos)	
1	17	When Will I See You Again	Three Degrees	Philly International	10	(2)	
2	-	You Make Me Feel Brand New	Stylistics	Avco	9	(2)	
3	4	Rock Your Baby	George McCrae	Jayboy	9	(1)	F
4	-	Summerlove Sensation	Bay City Rollers	Bell	7		
5	13	Born With A Smile On My Face	Stephanie De Sykes	Bradley's	6		F
6	-	Rocket	Mud	RAK	5		
7	-	Rock The Boat	Hues Corporation	RCA	5	(1)	F L
8	-	What Becomes Of The Brokenhearted	Jimmy Ruffin	Tamla Motown	8		
9	-	Amateur Hour	Sparks	Island	5		
10	7	Band On The Run	Paul McCartney & Wings	Apple	6	(1)	
11	-	I'm Leaving It (All) Up To You	Donny & Marie Osmond	MGM	8	(4)	F
12	-	I Shot The Sheriff	Eric Clapton	RSO	4	(1)	F
13	-	It's Only Rock 'n Roll (But I Like It)	Rolling Stones	Rolling Stone	4	(16)	
14	-	Tonight	Rubettes	Polydor	5		
15	2	Kissin' In The Back Row Of The...	Drifters	Bell	8		
16	-	Love Me For A Reason	Osmonds	MGM	7	(10)	
17	-	Mr. Soft	Cockney Rebel	EMI	5		
18	6	Young Girl	Gary Puckett & The Union Gap	CBS	6		L
19	-	Honey Honey	Sweet Dreams	Bradley's	6	(68)	F L
20	-	Just For You	Glitter Band	Bell	4		

◆ American oldies on the UK chart included Gary Puckett's 'Young Girl', 'Baby Love' by The Supremes and Jimmy Ruffin's 'What Becomes Of The Broken Hearted'.

◆ The Moody Blues opened the world's first quadrophonic (a system with four separate soundtracks as compared to stereo's two) recording studio in West London. One of the first projects recorded there was Blue Jays, a transatlantic Top 20 album by Moody members Justin Hayward & John Lodge.

1974

This Mnth	Prev Mnth	Title	Artist	Label	Wks	(US 20 Pos)	
1	-	Kung Fu Fighting	Carl Douglas	Pye	8	(1)	F L
2	16	Love Me For A Reason	Osmonds	MGM	7	(10)	
3	-	Annie's Song	John Denver	RCA	9	(1)	F L
4	-	Y Viva Espana	Sylvia	Sonet	8		L
5	11	I'm Leaving It (All) Up To You	Donny & Marie Osmond	MGM	8	(4)	F
6	-	Hang On In There Baby	Johnny Bristol	MGM	7	(8)	F L
7	-	You You You	Alvin Stardust	Magnet	6		
8	1	When Will I See You Again	Three Degrees	Philly International	10	(2)	
9	8	What Becomes Of The Brokenhearted	Jimmy Ruffin	Tamla Motown	8		
10	-	Queen Of Clubs	KC & The Sunshine Band	Jayboy	6	(66)	F
11	-	Na Na Na	Cozy Powell	RAK	6		L
12	-	Can't Get Enough Of Your Love, Babe	Barry White	Pye International	6	(1)	
13	19	Honey Honey	Sweet Dreams	Bradley's	6	(68)	F L
14	2	You Make Me Feel Brand New	Stylistics	Avco	9	(2)	
15	17	Mr. Soft	Cockney Rebel	EMI	5		
16	-	The Black Eyed Boys	Paper Lace	Bus Stop	4	(41)	L
17	-	Baby Love	Diana Ross & The Supremes	Tamla Motown	3		L
18	-	Rock 'n' Roll Lady	Showaddywaddy	Bell	4		
19	-	Rock Me Gently	Andy Kim	Capitol	5	(1)	F L
20	-	Long Tall Glasses	Leo Sayer	Chrysalis	5	(9)	

This Mnth	Prev Mnth	Title	Artist	Label	Wks	(US 20 Pos)	
1	-	Sad Sweet Dreamer	Sweet Sensation	Pye	7	(14)	F
2	3	Annie's Song	John Denver	RCA	9	(1)	F L
3	-	Gee Baby	Peter Shelley	Magnet	6	(81)	F
4	19	Rock Me Gently	Andy Kim	Capitol	5	(1)	F L
5	-	Everything I Own	Ken Boothe	Trojan	9		F
6	20	Long Tall Glasses	Leo Sayer	Chrysalis	5	(9)	
7	1	Kung Fu Fighting	Carl Douglas	Pye	8	(1)	F L
8	6	Hang On In There Baby	Johnny Bristol	MGM	7	(8)	F L
9	-	Far Far Away	Slade	Polydor	5		
10	-	I Get A Kick Out Of You	Gary Shearston	Charisma	5		F L
11	-	Farewell/Bring It On Home To Me	Rod Stewart	Mercury	4		
12	-	Reggae Tune	Andy Fairweather-Low	A&M	4		F
13	-	(You're) Having My Baby	Paul Anka & Odia Coates	UA	6	(1)	L
14	-	All Of Me Loves All Of You	Bay City Rollers	Bell	6		
15	7	You You You	Alvin Stardust	Magnet	6		
16	12	Can't Get Enough Of Your Love Babe	Barry White	Pye International	6	(1)	
17	-	I Can't Leave You Alone	George McCrae	Jayboy	5	(50)	
18	-	Knock On Wood	David Bowie	RCA	4		
19	10	Queen Of Clubs	KC & The Sunshine Band	Jayboy	6	(66)	F
20	-	Gonna Make You A Star	David Essex	CBS	9		

◆ Mama Cass, of The Mamas & The Papas, was found dead in Nilsson's London apartment. Four years later, The Who's extrovert drummer Keith Moon was to die in the same Park Street flat.

◆ Elton John re-signed with MCA Records. The five album deal netted him a record $8 million.

November 1974

This Mnth	Prev Mnth	Title	Artist	Label	Wks	(US 20 Pos)	
1	20	Gonna Make You A Star	David Essex	CBS	9		
2	-	Killer Queen	Queen	EMI	6	(12)	
3	5	Everything I Own	Ken Boothe	Trojan	9		F
4	-	(Hey There) Lonely Girl	Eddie Holman	ABC	7		F L
5	14	All Of Me Loves All Of You	Bay City Rollers	Bell	6		
6	-	You're The First, The Last, My Everything	Barry White	20th Century	9	(2)	
7	9	Far Far Away	Slade	Polydor	5		
8	-	Down On The Beach Tonight	Drifters	Bell	5		
9	-	Let's Put It All Together	Stylistics	Avco	5	(18)	
10	-	Let's Get Together Again	Glitter Band	Bell	5		
11	-	Pepper Box	Peppers	Spark	5		F L
12	13	(You're) Having My Baby	Paul Anka & Odia Coates	UA	6	(1)	L
13	-	Juke Box Jive	Rubettes	Polydor	9		
14	17	I Can't Leave You Alone	George McCrae	Jayboy	5	(50)	
15	-	The Wild One	Suzi Quatro	RAK	5		
16	-	All I Want Is You	Roxy Music	Island	6		
17	-	Oh Yes! You're Beautiful	Gary Glitter	Bell	7		
18	-	No Honestly	Lynsey De Paul	Jet	4		
19	-	Never Turn Your Back On Mother Earth	Sparks	Island	4		
20	-	Magic	Pilot	EMI	5	(5)	F

December 1974

This Mnth	Prev Mnth	Title	Artist	Label	Wks	(US 20 Pos)	
1	6	You're The First, The Last, My Everything	Barry White	20th Century	9	(2)	
2	-	You Ain't Seen Nothin' Yet	Bachman-Turner Overdrive	Mercury	9	(1)	F L
3	13	Juke Box Jive	Rubettes	Polydor	9		
4	17	Oh Yes! You're Beautiful	Gary Glitter	Bell	7		
5	-	Lonely This Christmas	Mud	RAK	8		
6	-	My Boy	Elvis Presley	RCA	9	(20)	
7	-	Tell Him	Hello	Bell	6		F
8	-	Get Dancing	Disco Tex & The Sex-O-Lettes	Chelsea	8	(10)	F
9	-	Streets Of London	Ralph McTell	Reprise	9		F L
10	-	Ire Feelings (Skanga)	Rupie Edwards	Cactus	6		F L
11	-	Lucy In The Sky With Diamonds	Elton John	DJM	8	(1)	
12	1	Gonna Make You A Star	David Essex	CBS	9		
13	-	Wombling Merry Christmas	Wombles	CBS	5		
14	20	Magic	Pilot	EMI	5	(5)	F
15	-	You Can Make Me Dance Sing Or Anything	Rod Stewart & The Faces	Warner	4		L
16	-	The In Betweenies/Father Christmas Do Not Touch Me	Goodies	Bradley's	6		F
17	-	Too Good To Be Forgotten	Chi-Lites	Brunswick	4		
18	4	(Hey There) Lonely Girl	Eddie Holman	ABC	7		F L
19	-	Down Down	Status Quo	Vertigo	8		
20	2	Killer Queen	Queen	EMI	6	(12)	

◆ British soul singers were making their mark. In the UK teenage Manchester group Sweet Sensation topped the chart with their debut 'Sad Sweet Dreamer' and in the USA Carl Douglas repeated his UK success by reaching No. 1 with 'Kung Fu Fighting'.

◆ The Drifters, who started as a trend-setting R&B act in 1953, were now resident in Britain and scored their third successive UK-written Top 10 hit, 'Down On The Beach Tonight'. Another US R&B group who would soon follow in their footsteps were The Three Degrees.

1975

January 1975

This Mnth	Prev Mnth	Title	Artist	Label	Wks	(US 20 Pos)	
1	9	Streets Of London	Ralph McTell	Reprise	9		F L
2	19	Down Down	Status Quo	Vertigo	8		
3	5	Lonely This Christmas	Mud	RAK	8		
4	-	The Bump	Kenny	RAK	6		F
5	-	Never Can Say Goodbye	Gloria Gaynor	MGM	5	(9)	F
6	-	Ms Grace	Tymes	RCA	5	(91)	L
7	8	Get Dancing	Disco Tex & The Sex-O-Lettes	Chelsea	8	(10)	F
8	-	I Can Help	Billy Swan	Monument	7	(1)	F L
9	13	Wombling Merry Christmas	Wombles	CBS	5		
10	6	My Boy	Elvis Presley	RCA	9	(20)	
11	16	The In Betweenies/Father Christmas Do Not Touch Me	Goodies	Bradley's	6		F
12	3	Juke Box Jive	Rubettes	Polydor	9		
13	-	Stardust	David Essex	CBS	4		
14	-	Are You Ready To Rock	Wizzard	Warner	5		L
15	2	You Ain't Seen Nothin' Yet	Bachman-Turner Overdrive	Mercury	9	(1)	F L
16	-	Help Me Make It Through The Night	John Holt	Trojan	6		F L
17	-	Crying Over You	Ken Boothe	Trojan	4		L
18	-	Morning Side Of The Mountain	Donny & Marie Osmond	MGM	5	(8)	
19	1	You're The First, The Last, My...	Barry White	20th Century	9	(2)	
20	11	Lucy In The Sky With Diamonds	Elton John	DJM	8	(1)	

February 1975

This Mnth	Prev Mnth	Title	Artist	Label	Wks	(US 20 Pos)	
1	-	January	Pilot	EMI	6	(87)	L
2	-	Goodbye My Love	Glitter Band	Bell	6		
3	-	Sugar Candy Kisses	Mac & Katie Kissoon	Polydor	5		F
4	-	Please Mr. Postman	Carpenters	A&M	7	(1)	
5	4	The Bump	Kenny	RAK	6		F
6	18	Morning Side Of The Mountain	Donny & Marie Osmond	MGM	5	(8)	
7	-	Angie Baby	Helen Reddy	Capitol	6	(1)	F L
8	6	Ms Grace	Tymes	RCA	5	(91)	L
9	5	Never Can Say Goodbye	Gloria Gaynor	MGM	5	(9)	F
10	-	Make Me Smile (Come Up And See Me)	Steve Harley & Cockney Rebel	EMI	6	(96)	
11	-	Black Superman (Muhammad Ali)	Johnny Wakelin & The Kinshasa Band	Pye	4	(21)	F
12	-	Promised Land	Elvis Presley	RCA	5	(14)	
13	16	Help Me Make It Through The Night	John Holt	Trojan	6		F L
14	-	Footsee	Wigan's Chosen Few	Disco Demand	5		F L
15	-	Now I'm Here	Queen	EMI	5		
16	-	Shame, Shame, Shame	Shirley And Company	All Platinum	5	(12)	F L
17	-	Purely By Coincidence	Sweet Sensation	Pye	4		L
18	-	Star On A TV Show	Stylistics	Avco	4	(47)	
19	-	Boogie On Reggae Woman	Stevie Wonder	Tamla Motown	3	(3)	
20	-	The Secrets That You Keep	Mud	RAK	5		

◆ Status Quo, who have put more singles in the UK charts than any other group, went up to the top for the only time in their long career with 'Down Down'.

◆ American acts whose current records were faring far better in Britain included: *Kojak* actor Telly Savalas, The Tymes, The Moments & The Whatnauts, Johnny Mathis and Love Unlimited.

March 1975

This Mnth	Prev Mnth	Title	Artist	Label	Wks	(US 20 Pos)	
1	-	If	Telly Savalas	MCA	7		F L
2	-	Only You Can	Fox	GTO	7	(53)	F
3	-	Bye Bye Baby	Bay City Rollers	Bell	11		
4	10	Make Me Smile (Come Up And See Me)	Steve Harley & Cockney Rebel	EMI	6	(96)	
5	20	The Secrets That You Keep	Mud	RAK	5		
6	-	My Eyes Adored You	Frankie Valli	Private Stock	5	(1)	
7	-	Pick Up The Pieces	Average White Band	Atlantic	5	(1)	F
8	-	There's A Whole Lot Of Loving	Guys & Dolls	Magnet	7		F
9	4	Please Mr. Postman	Carpenters	A&M	7	(1)	
10	-	What Am I Gonna Do With You	Barry White	20th Century	6	(8)	
11	16	Shame, Shame, Shame	Shirley And Company	All Platinum	5	(12)	F L
12	-	Girls	Moments And Whatnauts	All Platinum	6		F
13	-	Please Tell Him I Said Hello	Dana	GTO	6		
14	-	Fancy Pants	Kenny	RAK	6		
15	-	Mandy	Barry Manilow	Arista	4	(1)	F
16	-	I'm Stone In Love With You	Johnny Mathis	CBS	6		
17	-	I Can Do It	Rubettes	State	6		
18	-	Dreamer	Supertramp	A&M	4	(15)	F
19	14	Footsee	Wigan's Chosen Few	Disco Demand	5		F L
20	-	It May Be Winter Outside (But In My Heart It's Spring)	Love Unlimited	20th Century	4	(83)	L

April 1975

This Mnth	Prev Mnth	Title	Artist	Label	Wks	(US 20 Pos)	
1	3	Bye Bye Baby	Bay City Rollers	Bell	11		
2	-	Fox On The Run	Sweet	RCA	6	(5)	
3	-	Swing Your Daddy	Jim Gilstrap	Chelsea	7	(55)	F L
4	-	Love Me Love My Dog	Peter Shelley	Magnet	6		L
5	-	Funky Gibbon/Sick Man Blues	Goodies	Bradley's	6	(79)	
6	8	There's A Whole Lot Of Loving	Guys & Dolls	Magnet	7		F
7	12	Girls	Moments And Whatnauts	All Platinum	6		F
8	14	Fancy Pants	Kenny	RAK	6		
9	17	I Can Do It	Rubettes	State	6		
10	-	Honey	Bobby Goldsboro	UA	6		L
11	-	Play Me Like You Play Your Guitar	Duane Eddy & Rebelettes	GTO	5		
12	-	The Ugly Duckling	Mike Reid	Pye	4		F L
13	10	What Am I Gonna Do With You	Barry White	20th Century	6	(8)	
14	-	Let Me Be The One	Shadows	EMI	3		
15	-	Philadelphia Freedom	Elton John	DJM	6	(1)	
16	-	Skiing In The Snow	Wigan's Ovation	Spark	4		F L
17	-	Life Is A Minestone	10cc	Mercury	5		
18	-	Oh Boy	Mud	RAK	6		
19	-	Reach Out I'll Be There	Gloria Gaynor	MGM	4	(60)	
20	-	Loving You	Minnie Riperton	Epic	6	(1)	F L

◆ Disco was taking over the chart, with hits by Gloria Gaynor, Disco Tex, Barry White, Shirley & Co., Labelle and B. T. Express. Another type of dance music selling well in the UK was northern soul – the biggest hit from obscure Canadian band Wigan's Chosen Few.

1975

This Mnth	Prev Mnth	Title	Artist	Label	Wks	(US 20 Pos)	
1	18	Oh Boy	Mud	RAK	6		
2	20	Loving You	Minnie Riperton	Epic	6	(1)	F L
3	-	Stand By Your Man	Tammy Wynette	Epic	8		F
4	-	Hurt So Good	Susan Cadogan	Magnet	6		F L
5	-	Let Me Try Again	Tammy Jones	Epic	6		F L
6	10	Honey	Bobby Goldsboro	UA	6		L
7	-	I Wanna Dance Wit Choo'	Disco Tex & The Sex-O-Lettes	Chelsea	5	(23)	L
8	-	The Way We Were/Try To Remember (Medley)	Gladys Knight & The Pips	Buddah	7	(11)	
9	-	Sing Baby Sing	Stylistics	Avco	7		
10	-	Only Yesterday	Carpenters	A&M	5	(4)	
11	-	The Night	Frankie Valli & Four Seasons	Mowest	5		
12	-	Whispering Grass	Windsor Davies & Don Estelle	EMI	9		F L
13	1	Bye Bye Baby	Bay City Rollers	Bell	11		
14	-	Thanks For The Memory (Wham Bam Thank You Mam)	Slade	Polydor	5		
15	-	Take Good Care Of Yourself	Three Degrees	Philly Int.	4		
16	-	A Little Love And Understanding	Gilbert Becaud	Decca	5		F L
17	-	The Tears I Cried	Glitter Band	Bell	5		
18	-	Don't Do It Baby	Mac & Katie Kissoon	State	4		
19	-	Three Steps To Heaven	Showaddywaddy	Bell	8		
20	-	Send In The Clowns	Judy Collins	Elektra	5	(19)	L

This Mnth	Prev Mnth	Title	Artist	Label	Wks	(US 20 Pos)	
1	12	Whispering Grass	Windsor Davies & Don Estelle	EMI	9		F L
2	19	Three Steps To Heaven	Showaddywaddy	Bell	8		
3	-	I'm Not In Love	10cc	Mercury	8	(2)	
4	-	The Proud One	Osmonds	MGM	6	(22)	L
5	3	Stand By Your Man	Tammy Wynette	Epic	8		F
6	9	Sing Baby Sing	Stylistics	Avco	7		
7	-	The Hustle	Van McCoy	Avco	8	(1)	F
8	8	The Way We Were/Try To Remember (Medley)	Gladys Knight & The Pips	Buddah	7	(11)	
9	-	Listen To What The Man Said	Wings	Capitol	5	(1)	
10	20	Send In The Clowns	Judy Collins	Elektra	5	(19)	L
11	-	Disco Stomp	Hamilton Bohannon	Brunswick	7		F L
12	-	Disco Queen	Hot Chocolate	RAK	4	(28)	
13	-	Autobahn	Kraftwerk	Vertigo	5	(25)	F
14	-	Tears On My Pillow	Johnny Nash	CBS	9		L
15	-	Roll Over Lay Down	Status Quo	Vertigo	5		
16	-	The Israelites	Desmond Dekker & The Aces	Cactus	5		
17	-	Oh What A Shame	Roy Wood	Jet	4		L
18	-	Doing Alright With The Boys	Gary Glitter	Bell	4		
19	-	Baby I Love You, OK	Kenny	RAK	4		
20	14	Thanks For The Memory (Wham Bam Thank You Mam)	Slade	Polydor	5		

◆ A 12 city American tour by The Beach Boys and Chicago (whose **Chicago VIII** was a chart topper) was seen by 700,000, who paid over $7 million. The Beach Boys then joined Elton John, Rufus and The Eagles, playing to 80,000 at London's Wembley Stadium.

◆ Groundbreaking German group Kraftwerk had a transatlantic Top 40 hit with 'Autobahn'. Their electro-pop sound was a blueprint for many later electronic-dance acts.

July 1975

This Mnth	Prev Mnth	Title	Artist	Label	Wks 20	(US Pos)	
1	14	Tears On My Pillow	Johnny Nash	CBS	9		L
2	-	Misty	Ray Stevens	Janus	7	(14)	L
3	7	The Hustle	Van McCoy	Avco	8	(1)	F
4	-	Have You Seen Her/Oh Girl	Chi-Lites	Brunswick	5		
5	3	I'm Not In Love	10cc	Mercury	8	(2)	
6	-	Give A Little Love	Bay City Rollers	Bell	7		
7	11	Disco Stomp	Hamilton Bohannon	Brunswick	7		F L
8	-	Eighteen With A Bullet	Pete Wingfield	Island	5	(15)	F L
9	-	Barbados	Typically Tropical	Gull	9		F L
10	1	Whispering Grass	Windsor Davies & Don Estelle	EMI	9		F L
11	18	Doing Alright With The Boys	Gary Glitter	Bell	4		
12	-	Moonshine Sally	Mud	RAK	4		
13	-	Rollin' Stone	David Essex	CBS	4		
14	-	Je T'Aime (Moi Non Plus)	Judge Dread	Cactus	6		
15	2	Three Steps To Heaven	Showaddywaddy	Bell	8		
16	-	Jive Talkin'	Bee Gees	RSO	7	(1)	
17	-	Sealed With A Kiss	Brian Hyland	ABC	8		L
18	-	D.I.V.O.R.C.E.	Tammy Wynette	Epic	4	(63)	
19	-	My White Bicycle	Nazareth	Mooncrest	4		
20	19	Baby I Love You, OK	Kenny	RAK	4		

August 1975

This Mnth	Prev Mnth	Title	Artist	Label	Wks 20	(US Pos)	
1	9	Barbados	Typically Tropical	Gull	9		F L
2	-	Can't Give You Anything (But My Love)	Stylistics	Avco	8	(51)	
3	-	If You Think You Know How To Love Me	Smokey	RAK	7	(96)	F
4	6	Give A Little Love	Bay City Rollers	Bell	7		
5	16	Jive Talkin'	Bee Gees	RSO	7	(1)	
6	-	The Last Farewell	Roger Whittaker	EMI	9	(19)	
7	-	It's Been So Long	George McCrae	Jayboy	7		
8	17	Sealed With A Kiss	Brian Hyland	ABC	8		L
9	-	It's In His Kiss	Linda Lewis	Arista	5		L
10	-	Blanket On The Ground	Billie Jo Spears	UA	6	(78)	F
11	-	Delilah	Sensational Alex Harvey Band	Vertigo	5		F
12	-	Sailing	Rod Stewart	Warner	9	(58)	
13	1	Tears On My Pillow	Johnny Nash	CBS	9		L
14	-	Sherry	Adrian Baker	Magnet	4		F L
15	-	Dolly My Love	Moments	All Platinum	5		L
16	-	That's The Way (I Like It)	KC & The Sunshine Band	Jayboy	6	(1)	
17	14	Je T'Aime (Moi Non Plus)	Judge Dread	Cactus	6		
18	-	The Best Thing That Ever Happened	Gladys Knight & The Pips	Buddah	6	(3)	
19	2	Misty	Ray Stevens	Janus	7	(14)	L
20	-	El Bimbo	Bimbo Jet	EMI	4	(43)	F L

◆ Paul McCartney, who had yet to score a solo No. 1 single in his homeland, notched up his fourth American chart topping single, 'Listen To What The Man Said', and another transatlantic album topper, **Venus And Mars.**

◆ Soon after David Bowie announced "rock'n'roll is dead", he had his biggest American hit with 'Fame', co-written with John Lennon.

1975

This Mnth	Prev Mnth	Title	Artist	Label	Wks 20	(US Pos)	
1	12	Sailing	Rod Stewart	Warner	9	(58)	
2	6	The Last Farewell	Roger Whittaker	EMI	9	(19)	
3	-	Moonlighting	Leo Sayer	Chrysalis	6		
4	-	Summertime City	Mike Batt	Epic	5		F L
5	-	Funky Moped/Magic Roundabout	Jasper Carrott	DJM	10		F L
6	-	A Child's Prayer	Hot Chocolate	RAK	5		
7	2	Can't Give You Anything (But My Love)	Stylistics	Avco	8	(51)	
8	16	That's The Way (I Like It)	KC & The Sunshine Band	Jayboy	6	(1)	
9	-	I'm On Fire	5000 Volts	Philips	6	(26)	F
10	-	Heartbeat	Showaddywaddy	Bell	5		
11	-	Julie Ann	Kenny	RAK	5		L
12	7	It's Been So Long	George McCrae	Jayboy	7		
13	-	Hold Me Close	David Essex	CBS	8		
14	18	The Best Thing That Ever Happened	Gladys Knight & The Pips	Buddah	6	(3)	
15	10	Blanket On The Ground	Billie Jo Spears	UA	6	(78)	F
16	-	There Goes My First Love	Drifters	Bell	8		
17	-	Motor Biking	Chris Spedding	RAK	4		F L
18	-	Fattie Bum-Bum	Carl Malcolm	UK	5		F L
19	-	Love In The Sun	Glitter Band	Bell	4		
20	-	I Only Have Eyes For You	Art Garfunkel	CBS	8	(18)	F

This Mnth	Prev Mnth	Title	Artist	Label	Wks 20	(US Pos)	
1	13	Hold Me Close	David Essex	CBS	8		
2	20	I Only Have Eyes For You	Art Garfunkel	CBS	8	(18)	F
3	16	There Goes My First Love	Drifters	Bell	8		
4	-	It's Time For Love	Chi-Lites	Brunswick	5	(94)	
5	-	Una Paloma Blanca	Jonathan King	UK	6		L
6	-	Who Loves You	Four Seasons	Warner	5	(3)	
7	-	S.O.S.	Abba	Epic	6	(15)	
8	-	Scotch On The Rocks	Band Of The Black Watch	Spark	7		F L
9	-	Feelings	Morris Albert	Decca	6	(6)	F L
10	5	Funky Moped/Magic Roundabout	Jasper Carrott	DJM	10		F L
11	-	Paloma Blanca	George Baker Selection	Warner	4	(26)	F L
12	18	Fattie Bum-Bum	Carl Malcolm	UK	5		F L
13	9	I'm On Fire	5000 Volts	Philips	6	(26)	F
14	1	Sailing	Rod Stewart	Warner	9	(58)	
15	-	Space Oddity	David Bowie	RCA	8	(15)	
16	-	L-L-Lucy	Mud	Private Stock	4		
17	-	Don't Play Your Rock 'n' Roll To Me	Smokey	RAK	4		
18	3	Moonlighting	Leo Sayer	Chrysalis	6		
19	10	Heartbeat	Showaddywaddy	Bell	5		
20	-	Big Ten	Judge Dread	Cactus	4		

◆ Shortly before his group The Faces finally called it a day, lead singer Rod Stewart had the biggest British hit of his long and successful career with 'Sailing'. The single, which failed to make the American Top 40, returned to the Top 3 the following year, after its use as the theme to the BBC TV documentary *Sailor*, and was also a minor hit in 1987, with royalties being donated to the Zeebrugge Ferry Disaster Fund.

November 1975

This Mnth	Prev Mnth	Title	Artist	Label	Wks	(US 20 Pos)	
1	15	Space Oddity	David Bowie	RCA	8	(15)	
2	-	Love Is The Drug	Roxy Music	Island	6	(30)	
3	-	D.I.V.O.R.C.E.	Billy Connolly	Polydor	6		F L
4	-	Rhinestone Cowboy	Glen Campbell	Capitol	6	(1)	L
5	-	Love Hurts	Jim Capaldi	Island	6	(97)	F L
6	-	You Sexy Thing	Hot Chocolate	RAK	9	(3)	
7	2	I Only Have Eyes For You	Art Garfunkel	CBS	8	(18)	F
8	-	Imagine	John Lennon	Apple	5		G
9	-	Hold Back The Night	Trammps	Buddah	5	(35)	F
10	-	Blue Guitar	Justin Hayward & John Lodge	Threshold	5	(94)	F
11	-	What A Diff'rence A Day Makes	Esther Phillips	Kudu	5	(20)	F L
12	-	Bohemian Rhapsody	Queen	EMI	14	(9)	G
13	9	Feelings	Morris Albert	Decca	6	(6)	F L
14	-	New York Groove	Hello	Bell	4		L
15	-	Sky High	Jigsaw	Splash	5	(3)	F L
16	7	S.O.S.	Abba	Epic	6	(15)	
17	3	There Goes My First Love	Drifters	Bell	8		
18	-	This Old Heart Of Mine	Rod Stewart	Riva	5		
19	-	Right Back Where We Started From	Maxine Nightingale	UA	5	(2)	F
20	-	Money Honey	Bay City Rollers	Bell	8	(9)	

December 1975

This Mnth	Prev Mnth	Title	Artist	Label	Wks	(US 20 Pos)	
1	12	Bohemian Rhapsody	Queen	EMI	14	(9)	G
2	6	You Sexy Thing	Hot Chocolate	RAK	9	(3)	
3	-	Trail Of The Lonesome Pine	Laurel & Hardy	UA	7		F L
4	-	Na Na Is The Saddest Word	Stylistics	Avco	7		
5	20	Money Honey	Bay City Rollers	Bell	8	(9)	
6	-	Let's Twist Again	Chubby Checker	London American	8		
7	-	All Around My Hat	Steeleye Span	Chrysalis	7		L
8	-	I Believe In Father Christmas	Greg Lake	Manticore	6	(95)	F L
9	-	Happy To Be On An Island In The Sun	Demis Roussos	Philips	7		F
10	-	Show Me You're A Woman	Mud	Private Stock	6		
11	18	This Old Heart Of Mine	Rod Stewart	Riva	5		
12	-	Golden Years	David Bowie	RCA	7	(10)	
13	5	Love Hurts	Jim Capaldi	Island	6	(97)	F L
14	8	Imagine	John Lennon	Apple	5		G
15	-	Renta Santa	Chris Hill	Philips	3		F
16	-	It's Gonna Be A Cold Cold Christmas	Dana	GTO	5		
17	15	Sky High	Jigsaw	Splash	5	(3)	F L
18	3	D.I.V.O.R.C.E.	Billy Connolly	Polydor	6		F L
19	-	Can I Take You Home Little Girl	Drifters	Bell	6		
20	-	In For A Penny	Slade	Polydor	3		

♦ Queen's 'Bohemian Rhapsody' topped the chart and sold more than a million. In 1991, after Freddie Mercury's death, it returned and repeated the feat.
♦ The latest oldies to chart included Chubby Checker's 'Let's Twist Again' from 1961, David Bowie's 'Space Oddity' from 1969 and Laurel & Hardy's 1937 recording 'The Trail Of The Lonesome Pine'.
♦ Elton John's US tour closed with a spectacular show at the Dodger Stadium in L.A.

January 1976

This Mnth	Prev Mnth	Title	Artist	Label	Wks	(US 20 Pos)	
1	1	Bohemian Rhapsody	Queen	EMI	14	(9)	G
2	-	Glass Of Champagne	Sailor	Epic	8		F
3	-	Mamma Mia	Abba	Epic	8	(32)	
4	-	Wide Eyed And Legless	Andy Fairweather-Low	A&M	7		L
5	6	Let's Twist Again	Chubby Checker	London American	8		
6	3	Trail Of The Lonesome Pine	Laurel & Hardy	UA	7		F L
7	-	In Dulce Jubilo/On Horseback	Mike Oldfield	Virgin	4		F
8	-	Art For Art's Sake	10cc	UK			
9	-	King Of The Cops	Billy Howard	Penny Farthing	6		F L
10	8	I Believe In Father Christmas	Greg Lake	Manticore	6	(95)	F L
11	-	Love Machine	Miracles	Tamla Motown	7	( )	L
12	16	It's Gonna Be A Cold Cold Christmas	Dana	GTO	5		
13	12	Golden Years	David Bowie	RCA	7	(10)	
14	9	Happy To Be On An Island In The Sun	Demis Roussos	Philips	7		F
15	-	We Do It	R & J Stone	RCA	7		F L
16	-	Forever & Ever	Slik	Bell	7		F L
17	-	Itchycoo Park	Small Faces	Immediate	5		L
18	-	Let The Music Play	Barry White	20th Century	4	(32)	
19	19	Can I Take You Home Little Girl	Drifters	Bell	6		
20	2	You Sexy Thing	Hot Chocolate	RAK	9	(3)	

February 1976

This Mnth	Prev Mnth	Title	Artist	Label	Wks	(US 20 Pos)	
1	16	Forever & Ever	Slik	Bell	7		L
2	-	December '63 (Oh What A Night)	Four Seasons	Warner	8	(1)	
3	3	Mamma Mia	Abba	Epic	8	(32)	
4	-	Love To Love You Baby	Donna Summer	GTO	6	(2)	F
5	11	Love Machine	Miracles	Tamla Motown	7	(1)	L
6	-	Rodrigo's Guitar Concerto De Aranjuez	Manuel & His Music Of TheMountains	EMI	6		L
7	15	We Do It	R & J Stone	RCA	7		F L
8	-	No Regrets	Walker Brothers	GTO	5		L
9	-	I Love To Love (But My Baby Loves To Dance)	Tina Charles	CBS	7		F
10	-	Convoy	C.W. McCall	MGM	7	(1)	F L
11	-	Dat	Pluto Shervington	Opal	5		F
12	-	Moonlight Serenade/Little Brown Jug/In The Mood	Glenn Miller	RCA	5		F L
13	-	It Should Have Been Me	Yvonne Fair	Tamla Motown	5	(85)	F L
14	-	Low Rider	War	UA	5	(7)	F
15	1	Bohemian Rhapsody	Queen	EMI	14	(9)	G
16	-	Evil Woman	Electric Light Orchestra	JET	4	(10)	
17	-	Squeeze Box	Who	Polydor	6	(16)	
18	-	Walk Away From Love	David Ruffin	Tamla	4	(9)	F L
19	-	Midnight Rider	Paul Davidson	Tropical	4		F L
20	-	Rain	Status Quo	Vertigo	5		

◆ Thirteen years after taking the US charts by storm, The Four Seasons had their only transatlantic No. 1, 'December '63 (Oh What A Night)'.

◆ In Britain, album chart toppers included 1950s star Slim Whitman and 1960s chart regular Roy Orbison, whilst 1940s favourite Glenn Miller returned to the singles chart!

1976

This Mnth	Prev Mnth	Title	Artist	Label	Wks	(US 20 Pos)	
1	9	I Love To Love (But My Baby...)	Tina Charles	CBS	7		F
2	10	Convoy	C.W. McCall	MGM	7	(1)	F L
3	-	Love Really Hurts Without You	Billy Ocean	GTO	8	(22)	F
4	2	December '63 (Oh What A Night)	Four Seasons	Warner	8	(1)	
5	-	You Don't Have To Say You Love Me	Guys & Dolls	Magnet	5		L
6	-	People Like You And People Like Me	Glitter Band	Bell	6		L
7	-	Save Your Kisses For Me	Brotherhood Of Man	Pye	13	(27)	G
8	13	It Should Have Been Me	Yvonne Fair	Tamla Motown	5	(85)	F L
9	6	Rodrigo's Guitar Concerto....	Manuel/Music Of The Moutains	EMI	6		F L
10	-	You See The Trouble With Me	Barry White	20th Century	7		
11	-	I Wanna Stay With You	Gallagher & Lyle	A&M	6	(49)	F
12	-	(Do The) Spanish Hustle	Fatback Band	Polydor	4		
13	20	Rain	Status Quo	Vertigo	5		
14	11	Dat	Pluto Shervington	Opal	5		F
15	-	Funky Weekend	Stylistics	Avco	4	(76)	
16	-	Falling Apart At The Seams	Marmalade	Target	6	(49)	L
17	-	Miss You Nights	Cliff Richard	EMI	4		
18	-	Yesterday	Beatles	Apple	6		
19	17	Squeeze Box	Who	Polydor	6	(16)	
20	-	I Love Music	O'Jays	Philly International	4	(5)	

This Mnth	Prev Mnth	Title	Artist	Label	Wks	(US 20 Pos)	
1	7	Save Your Kisses For Me	Brotherhood Of Man	Pye	13	(27)	G
2	-	Music	John Miles	Decca	7	(88)	
3	10	You See The Trouble With Me	Barry White	20th Century	7		
4	-	Fernando	Abba	Epic	12	(13)	
5	-	I'm Mandy Fly Me	10cc	Mercury	6	(60)	
6	-	Jungle Rock	Hank Mizell	Charly	9		F L
7	-	Pinball Wizard	Elton John	DJM	4		
8	-	Theme From Mahogany (Do You Know Where You're Going To)	Diana Ross	Tamla Motown	5	(1)	
9	3	Love Really Hurts Without You	Billy Ocean	GTO	8	(22)	F
10	18	Yesterday	Beatles	Apple	6		
11	-	Girls Girls Girls	Sailor	Epic	5		L
12	11	I Wanna Stay With You	Gallagher & Lyle	A&M	6	(49)	F
13	16	Falling Apart At The Seams	Marmalade	Target	6	(49)	L
14	-	Hello Happiness	Drifters	Bell	5		
15	-	Love Me Like I Love You	Bay City Rollers	Bell	5		
16	-	Don't Stop It Now	Hot Chocolate	RAK	5	(42)	
17	-	Hey Jude	Beatles	Apple	4		
18	6	People Like You And People Like Me	Glitter Band	Bell	6		L
19	1	I Love To Love (But My Baby Loves To Dance)	Tina Charles	CBS	7		F
20	-	S-S-S-Single Bed	Fox	GTO	7		L

◆ Despite minimal British success Fleetwood Mac (with new members Stevie Nicks and Lindsey Buckingham) headed up the US LP chart with their eponymous album – it took 58 weeks to reach No. 1!

◆ The chart topper 'Save Your Kisses For Me' from mixed quartet Brotherhood Of Man went on to win the Eurovision Song Contest and sold over a million copies. Unlike all the earlier British entries this catchy single reached the US Top 40.

1976

This Mnth	Prev Mnth	Title	Artist	Label	Wks	(US 20 Pos)	
1	4	Fernando	Abba	Epic	12	(13)	
2	1	Save Your Kisses For Me	Brotherhood Of Man	Pye	13	(27)	G
3	6	Jungle Rock	Hank Mizell	Charly	9		F L
4	20	S-S-S-Single Bed	Fox	GTO	7		L
5	-	Silver Star	Four Seasons	Warner	5	(38)	L
6	-	More, More, More	Andrea True Connection	Buddah	7	(4)	F L
7	-	Arms Of Mary	Sutherland Brothers And Quiver	CBS	5	(81)	F L
8	-	Get Up And Boogie (That's Right)	Silver Convention	Magnet	6	(2)	F L
9	-	No Charge	J.J. Barrie	Power Exchange	7		F L
10	-	Convoy GB	Laurie Lingo & The Dipsticks	State	5		F L
11	-	Can't Help Falling In Love	Stylistics	Avco	6		
12	-	Fool To Cry	Rolling Stones	Rolling Stone	6	(10)	
13	-	Life Is Too Short Girl	Sheer Elegance	Pye International	6		L
14	8	Theme From Mahogany (Do You Where You're Going To)	Diana Ross	Tamla Motown	5	(1)	
15	-	My Resistance Is Low	Robin Sarstedt	Decca	5		F L
16	-	Combine Harvester (Brand New Key)	Wurzels	EMI	7		F
17	-	Love Hangover	Diana Ross	Tamla Motown	6	(1)	
18	-	Disco Connection	Isaac Hayes	ABC	5		L
19	11	Girls Girls Girls	Sailor	Epic	5		L
20	15	Love Me Like I Love You	Bay City Rollers	Bell	5		

This Mnth	Prev Mnth	Title	Artist	Label	Wks	(US 20 Pos)	
1	16	Combine Harvester (Brand New Key)	Wurzels	EMI	7		F
2	-	Silly Love Songs	Paul McCartney	Parlophone	8	(1)	
3	9	No Charge	J.J. Barrie	Power Exchange	7		F L
4	-	You To Me Are Everything	Real Thing	Pye International	8	(64)	F
5	15	My Resistance Is Low	Robin Sarstedt	Decca	5		F L
6	-	You Just Might See Me Cry	Our Kid	Polydor	7		F L
7	-	Let Your Love Flow	Bellamy Brothers	Warner	8	(1)	F
8	12	Fool To Cry	Rolling Stones	Rolling Stone	6	(10)	
9	1	Fernando	Abba	Epic	12	(13)	
10	-	Tonight's The Night (Gonna Be Alright)	Rod Stewart	Riva	7	(1)	
11	-	Jolene	Dolly Parton	RCA	6	(60)	F
12	-	Heart On My Sleeve	Gallagher & Lyle	A&M	7	(67)	L
13	-	Show Me The Way	Peter Frampton	A&M	5	(6)	F L
14	-	Devil Woman	Cliff Richard	EMI	4	(6)	
15	-	Midnight Train To Georgia	Gladys Knight & The Pips	Buddah	4	(1)	
16	7	Arms Of Mary	Sutherland Brothers & Quiver	CBS	7	(81)	F L
17	-	This Is It	Melba Moore	Buddah	4	(91)	F
18	-	Young Hearts Run Free	Candi Staton	Warner	9	(20)	F
19	17	Love Hangover	Diana Ross	Tamla Motown	6	(1)	
20	-	Shake It Down	Mud	Private Stock	2		

◆ The Rolling Stones, whose **Black And Blue** headed the American LP listings, played six nights at Earl's Court in London as part of their European tour. Other major UK events included The Who at Charlton Athletic Football Club and David Bowie at Wembley.

◆ A harbinger of the forthcoming British rockabilly revival was the success of 'Jungle Rock' by Hank Mizell. The old time rock'n'roll hit sold few copies in the USA when first released in 1957 but gave the 52-year-old sales manager a surprise European hit in 1976.

July 1976

This Mnth	Prev Mnth	Title	Artist	Label	Wks	(US 20 Pos)	
1	18	Young Hearts Run Free	Candi Staton	Warner	9	(20)	F
2	-	Roussos Phenomenon E.P.	Demis Roussos	Philips	9		
3	-	A Little Bit More	Dr. Hook	Capitol	11	(11)	
4	-	Kiss And Say Goodbye	Manhattans	CBS	8	(1)	F
5	4	You To Me Are Everything	Real Thing	Pye International	8	(64)	F
6	-	Don't Go Breaking My Heart	Elton John & Kiki Dee	Rocket	11	(1)	
7	-	Let's Stick Together	Bryan Ferry	Island	7		
8	6	You Just Might See Me Cry	Our Kid	Polydor	7		F L
9	-	Misty Blue	Dorothy Moore	Contempo	9	(3)	F
10	-	You're My Best Friend	Queen	EMI	5	(16)	
11	10	Tonight's The Night (Gonna Be Alright)	Rod Stewart	Riva	7	(1)	
12	-	Leader Of The Pack	Shangri-Las	Charly/Contempo	5		L
13	-	It Only Takes A Minute	One Hundred Ton & A Feather	UK	5		F L
14	-	The Boys Are Back In Town	Thin Lizzy	Vertigo	5	(12)	
15	-	You Are My Love	Liverpool Express	Warner	6		F
16	-	Heaven Must Be Missing An Angel	Tavares	Capitol	7	(15)	F
17	12	Heart On My Sleeve	Gallagher & Lyle	A&M	7	(67)	L
18	2	Silly Love Songs	Paul McCartney	Parlophone	8	(1)	
19	-	I Love To Boogie	T. Rex	EMI	5		
20	-	Man To Man	Hot Chocolate	RAK	4		

August 1976

This Mnth	Prev Mnth	Title	Artist	Label	Wks	(US 20 Pos)	
1	6	Don't Go Breaking My Heart	Elton John & Kiki Dee	Rocket	11	(1)	
2	3	A Little Bit More	Dr. Hook	Capitol	11	(11)	
3	-	Jeans On	David Dundas	Air	6	(17)	F L
4	16	Heaven Must Be Missing An Angel	Tavares	Capitol	7	(15)	F
5	-	In Zaire	Johnny Wakelin	Pye	6		L
6	-	Now Is The Time	Jimmy James & The Vagabonds	Pye	6		F L
7	-	Dr Kiss Kiss	5000 Volts	Philips	6		L
8	-	Let 'Em In	Wings	Parlophone	8	(3)	
9	9	Misty Blue	Dorothy Moore	Contempo	9	(3)	F
10	-	You Should Be Dancing	Bee Gees	RSO	7	(1)	
11	2	Roussos Phenomenon E.P.	Demis Roussos	Philips	9		
12	-	Mystery Song	Status Quo	Vertigo	5		
13	-	Harvest For The World	Isley Brothers	Epic	4	(63)	
14	4	Kiss And Say Goodbye	Manhattans	CBS	8	(1)	F
15	-	Here Comes The Sun	Steve Harley	EMI	4		
16	-	You Don't Have To Go	Chi-Lites	Brunswick	7		L
17	-	Extended Play (E.P.)	Bryan Ferry	Island	6		
18	-	What I've Got In Mind	Billie Jo Spears	UA	5		L
19	1	Young Hearts Run Free	Candi Staton	Warner	9	(20)	F
20	-	You'll Never Find Another Love Like Mine	Lou Rawls	Philly International	4	(2)	F L

◆ A UK visit by The Ramones helped to heighten interest in punk. The Sex Pistols appeared on TV, and The Clash, The Buzzcocks and Siouxsie & The Banshees made their live debuts. Stiff Records was launched, and the first issue of fanzine *Sniffin' Glue* hit the streets.

◆ The Rolling Stones, Lynyrd Skynyrd, and 10cc attracted 200,000 to the Knebworth Festival, while 60,000 attended Queen's Hyde Park concert and Grateful Dead and Santana packed the crowds into Wembley.

1976

This Mnth	Prev Mnth	Title	Artist	Label	Wks	(US 20 Pos)
1	-	Dancing Queen	Abba	Epic	12	(1)
2	8	Let 'Em In	Wings	Parlophone	8	(3)
3	-	The Killing Of Georgie	Rod Stewart	Riva	7	(30)
4	16	You Don't Have To Go	Chi-Lites	Brunswick	7	L
5	-	(Light Of Experience) Doina De Jale	Georghe Zamfir	Epic	6	F L
6	-	Can't Get By Without You	Real Thing	Pye	8	
7	-	16 Bars	Stylistics	H & L	7	L
8	1	Don't Go Breaking My Heart	Elton John & Kiki Dee	Rocket	11	(1)
9	18	What I've Got In Mind	Billie Jo Spears	UA	5	L
10	-	Aria	Acker Bilk	Pye	6	L
11	-	Blinded By The Light	Manfred Mann's Earth Band	Bronze	6	(1) F
12	-	I Am A Cider Drinker (Paloma Blanca)	Wurzels	EMI	5	L
13	-	I Only Wanna Be With You	Bay City Rollers	Bell	6	(12)
14	17	Extended Play (E.P.)	Bryan Ferry	Island	6	
15	10	You Should Be Dancing	Bee Gees	RSO	7	(1)
16	-	Mississippi	Pussycat	Sonet	13	F L
17	2	A Little Bit More	Dr. Hook	Capitol	11	(11)
18	-	Dance Little Lady Dance	Tina Charles	CBS	6	
19	20	You'll Never Find Another Love Like Mine	Lou Rawls	Philly International	4	(2) F L
20	5	In Zaire	Johnny Wakelin	Pye	6	L

This Mnth	Prev Mnth	Title	Artist	Label	Wks	(US 20 Pos)
1	16	Mississippi	Pussycat	Sonet	13	F L
2	1	Dancing Queen	Abba	Epic	12	(1)
3	-	Sailing	Rod Stewart	Warner	8	(58)
4	6	Can't Get By Without You	Real Thing	Pye	8	
5	-	When Forever Has Gone	Demis Roussos	Philips	7	L
6	-	Disco Duck	Rick Dees & His Cast Of Idiots	RSO	6	(1) F L
7	-	Howzat	Sherbet	Epic	7	(61) F L
8	-	Girl Of My Best Friend	Elvis Presley	RCA	6	
9	18	Dance Little Lady Dance	Tina Charles	CBS	6	
10	13	I Only Wanna Be With You	Bay City Rollers	Bell	6	(12)
11	-	Hurt	Manhattans	CBS	8	(97) L
12	-	If You Leave Me Now	Chicago	CBS	12	(1)
13	-	The Best Disco In Town	Ritchie Family	Polydor	5	(17) F L
14	12	I Am A Cider Drinker (Paloma Blanca)	Wurzels	EMI	5	L
15	-	Summer Of My Life	Simon May	Pye	6	F L
16	-	Don't Take Away The Music	Tavares	Capitol	7	(34)
17	10	Aria	Acker Bilk	Pye	6	L
18	11	Blinded By The Light	Manfred Mann's Earth Band	Bronze	6	(1) F
19	-	I'll Meet You At Midnight	Smokie	RAK	5	
20	-	Loving And Free/Amoureuse	Kiki Dee	Rocket	5	

◆ Britain's top solo artist, Cliff Richard, finally cracked the US Top 10 with 'Devil Woman'. His 20 date Russian tour was also a great success.

◆ Sid Bernstein, who had promoted The Beatles' famous Shea Stadium gig, reportedly offered the group $200 million to reform and tour for him.

November 1976

This Mnth	Prev Mnth	Title	Artist	Label	Wks	(US 20 Pos)	
1	12	If You Leave Me Now	Chicago	CBS	12	(1)	
2	1	Mississippi	Pussycat	Sonet	13		F L
3	-	You Make Me Feel Like Dancing	Leo Sayer	Chrysalis	7	(1)	
4	16	Don't Take Away The Music	Tavares	Capitol	7	(34)	
5	-	Play That Funky Music	Wild Cherry	Epic	7	(1)	F L
6	11	Hurt	Manhattans	CBS	8	(97)	L
7	5	When Forever Has Gone	Demis Roussos	Philips	7		L
8	-	If Not You	Dr. Hook	Capitol	6	(55)	
9	-	Under The Moon Of Love	Showaddywaddy	Bell	12		
10	-	Couldn't Get It Right	Climax Blues Band	BTM	6	(3)	F L
11	7	Howzat	Sherbet	Epic	7	(61)	F L
12	15	Summer Of My Life	Simon May	Pye	6		F L
13	-	Dancing With The Captain	Paul Nicholas	RSO	5		
14	-	Substitute	Who	Polydor	5		
15	-	Love And Affection	Joan Armatrading	A&M	5		F
16	-	Beautiful Noise	Neil Diamond	CBS	4		
17	-	Lost In France	Bonnie Tyler	RCA	5		F
18	-	Somebody To Love	Queen	EMI	8	(13)	
19	-	Jaws	Lalo Schifrin	CTI	4		F L
20	3	Sailing	Rod Stewart	Warner	8	(58)	

December 1976

This Mnth	Prev Mnth	Title	Artist	Label	Wks	(US 20 Pos)	
1	9	Under The Moon Of Love	Showaddywaddy	Bell	12		
2	18	Somebody To Love	Queen	EMI	8	(13)	
3	-	Money Money Money	Abba	Epic	10	(56)	
4	-	Livin' Thing	Electric Light Orchestra	Jet	8	(13)	
5	-	When A Child Is Born (Soleado)	Johnny Mathis	CBS	8		
6	-	Love Me	Yvonne Elliman	RSO	8	(14)	F
7	1	If You Leave Me Now	Chicago	CBS	12	(1)	
8	3	You Make Me Feel Like Dancing	Leo Sayer	Chrysalis	7	(1)	
9	-	Lean On Me	Mud	Private Stock	7		L
10	-	Portsmouth	Mike Oldfield	Virgin	9		
11	-	Get Back	Rod Stewart	Riva	6		
12	17	Lost In France	Bonnie Tyler	RCA	5		F
13	8	If Not You	Dr. Hook	Capitol	6	(55)	
14	-	Sorry Seems To Be The Hardest Word	Elton John	Rocket	3	(6)	
15	-	Living Next Door To Alice	Smokie	RAK	7	(25)	
16	-	Bionic Santa	Chris Hill	Philips	5		L
17	-	Little Does She Know	Kursaal Flyers	CBS	6		F L
18	-	Dr. Love	Tina Charles	CBS	8		L
19	-	Stop Me (If You've Heard It All Before)	Billy Ocean	GTO	4		
20	-	Rock'n Me	Steve Miller Band	Mercury	4	(1)	F

◆ 'New Rose' by The Damned, widely accepted as the first British punk single, was released. The Sex Pistols' debut disc 'Anarchy In The UK' charted, but EMI, offended by their "disgraceful... aggressive behaviour", withdrew the record, paid them off with £40,000 ($100,000) and dropped them!

◆ One of the leading exponents of the current British craze Pub Rock, Dr. Feelgood (named after an earlier US R&B singer), took their R&B-styled live album **Stupidity** to the top without the benefit of a hit single.

1977

This Mnth	Prev Mnth	Title	Artist	Label	Wks 20	(US Pos)	
1	-	Don't Give Up On Us	David Soul	Private Stock	12	(1)	F G
2	1	Under The Moon Of Love	Showaddywaddy	Bell	12		
3	3	Money Money Money	Abba	Epic	10	(56)	
4	5	When A Child Is Born (Soleado)	Johnny Mathis	CBS	8		
5	18	Dr. Love	Tina Charles	CBS	8		L
6	10	Portsmouth	Mike Oldfield	Virgin	9		
7	15	Living Next Door To Alice	Smokie	RAK	7	(25)	
8	-	Things We Do For Love	10cc	Mercury	8	(5)	
9	-	Side Show	Barry Biggs	Dynamic	9		F L
10	-	Don't Cry For Me Argentina	Julie Covington	MCA	10		F
11	-	Wild Side Of Life	Status Quo	Vertigo	9		
12	-	I Wish	Stevie Wonder	Tamla Motown	6	(1)	
13	2	Somebody To Love	Queen	EMI	8	(13)	
14	-	Grandma's Party	Paul Nicholas	RSO	8		L
15	-	You're More Than A Number In My Little Red Book	Drifters	Arista	6		L
16	9	Lean On Me	Mud	Private Stock	7		L
17	-	Isn't She Lovely	David Parton	Pye	7		F L
18	4	Livin' Thing	Electric Light Orchestra	Jet	8	(13)	
19	-	Fairytale	Dana	GTO	6		L
20	16	Bionic Santa	Chris Hill	Philips	5		L

This Mnth	Prev Mnth	Title	Artist	Label	Wks 20	(US Pos)	
1	10	Don't Cry For Me Argentina	Julie Covington	MCA	10		F
2	1	Don't Give Up On Us	David Soul	Private Stock	12	(1)	F G
3	-	When I Need You	Leo Sayer	Chrysalis	9	(1)	
4	9	Side Show	Barry Biggs	Dynamic	9		F L
5	17	Isn't She Lovely	David Parton	Pye	7		F L
6	-	Don't Leave Me This Way	Harold Melvin & The Blue Notes	Philly Int.	7		L
7	-	Daddy Cool	Boney M	Atlantic	6	(65)	F
8	-	Jack In The Box	Moments	All Platinum	6		L
9	-	Boogie Nights	Heatwave	GTO	10	(2)	F
10	-	Car Wash	Rose Royce	MCA	6	(1)	F
11	-	Suspicion	Elvis Presley	RCA	6		
12	15	You're More Than A Number In My Little Red Book	Drifters	Arista	6		L
13	-	Chanson D'Amour	Manhattan Transfer	Atlantic	11		F
14	-	Sing Me	Brothers	Bus Stop	6		F L
15	-	Don't Believe A Word	Thin Lizzy	Vertigo	4		
16	8	Things We Do For Love	10cc	Mercury	8	(5)	
17	11	Wild Side Of Life	Status Quo	Vertigo	9		
18	-	This Is Tomorrow	Bryan Ferry	Polydor	6		
19	-	Romeo	Mr. Big	EMI	7	(87)	F L
20	12	I Wish	Stevie Wonder	Tamla Motown	6	(1)	

◆ American actor David Soul's version of the British-written 'Don't Give Up On Us', topped the transatlantic charts and sold a million copies in the UK alone.
Interestingly, teen-heartthrob Soul had previously recorded unsuccessfully in 1966 as The Covered Man (advertisements showed him with a bag on his head)!
◆ Punk was making the headlines, and most major labels quickly clambered onto the fast moving bandwagon. United Artists signed The Stranglers, Polydor nabbed The Jam and A&M briefly inked The Sex Pistols.

March 1977

This Mnth	Prev Mnth	Title	Artist	Label	Wks 20	(US Pos)	
1	13	Chanson D'Amour	Manhattan Transfer	Atlantic	11		F
2	9	Boogie Nights	Heatwave	GTO	10	(2)	F
3	3	When I Need You	Leo Sayer	Chrysalis	9	(1)	
4	19	Romeo	Mr. Big	EMI	7	(87)	F L
5	-	Knowing Me Knowing You	Abba	Epic	11	(14)	
6	-	Sound And Vision	David Bowie	RCA	9	(69)	
7	-	Torn Between Two Lovers	Mary MacGregor	Ariola America	8	(1)	F L
8	1	Don't Cry For Me Argentina	Julie Covington	MCA	10		F
9	-	When	Showaddywaddy	Arista	8		
10	18	This Is Tomorrow	Bryan Ferry	Polydor	6		
11	-	Baby I Know	Rubettes	State	7		L
12	-	Rockaria	Electric Light Orchestra	Jet	5		
13	-	What Can I Say	Boz Scaggs	CBS	5	(42)	F
14	6	Don't Leave Me This Way	Harold Melvin & The Blue Notes	Philly Int.	7		L
15	14	Sing Me	Brothers	Bus Stop	6		F L
16	2	Don't Give Up On Us	David Soul	Private Stock	12	(1)	F G
17	-	Moody Blue	Elvis Presley	RCA	5	(31)	
18	-	Don't Leave Me This Way	Thelma Houston	Motown	4	(1)	F L
19	8	Jack In The Box	Moments	All Platinum	6		L
20	-	Going In With My Eyes Open	David Soul	Private Stock	6	(54)	

April 1977

This Mnth	Prev Mnth	Title	Artist	Label	Wks 20	(US Pos)	
1	5	Knowing Me Knowing You	Abba	Epic	11	(14)	
2	20	Going In With My Eyes Open	David Soul	Private Stock	6	(54)	
3	-	I Don't Want To Put A Hold On You	Berni Flint	EMI	8		F L
4	-	Red Light Spells Danger	Billy Ocean	GTO	9		
5	9	When	Showaddywaddy	Arista	8		
6	-	Sunny	Boney M	Atlantic	6		
7	6	Sound And Vision	David Bowie	RCA	9	(69)	
8	-	Oh Boy	Brotherhood Of Man	Pye	7		
9	1	Chanson D'Amour	Manhattan Transfer	Atlantic	11		F
10	-	You Don't Have To Be A Star (To Be In My Show)	Marilyn McCoo & Billy Davis Jr	ABC	5	(1)	F L
11	17	Moody Blue	Elvis Presley	RCA	5	(31)	
12	-	Free	Deniece Williams	CBS	9	(25)	F
13	-	Have I The Right?	Dead End Kids	CBS	7		F L
14	-	Sir Duke	Stevie Wonder	Motown	7	(1)	
15	-	Lay Back In The Arms Of Someone	Smokie	RAK	6		
16	-	Love Hit Me	Maxine Nightingale	UA	3		L
17	-	Gimme Some	Brendon	Magnet	5		F L
18	7	Torn Between Two Lovers	Mary MacGregor	Ariola America	8	(1)	F L
19	-	Pearl's A Singer	Elkie Brooks	A&M	6		F
20	2	Boogie Nights	Heatwave	GTO	10	(2)	F

◆ Two American acts faring better in Britain were Manhattan Transfer with the chart-topping single 'Chanson D'Amour', and 53-year-old country singer Slim Whitman, who had a No. 1 album, **Red River Valley** – neither record charted Stateside.

◆ The Sex Pistols topped some charts with 'God Save The Queen'. The Clash and The Stranglers had hit albums and newcomers The Boomtown Rats and Adam & The Ants attracted media acclaim.

1977

This Mnth	Prev Mnth	Title	Artist	Label	Wks	(US 20 Pos)	
1	-	I Don't Want To Talk About It/ First Cut Is The Deepest	Rod Stewart	Riva	10	(46)	
2	12	Free	Deniece Williams	CBS	9	(25)	F
3	-	Ain't Gonna Bump No More (WithNo Big Fat Woman)	Joe Tex	Epic	8	(12)	F L
4	14	Sir Duke	Stevie Wonder	Motown	7	(1)	
5	-	The Shuffle	Van McCoy	H & L	8		L
6	-	Whodunit	Tavares	Capitol	7	(22)	
7	-	Evergreen ('A Star Is Born')	Barbra Streisand	CBS	12	(1)	
8	-	Hotel California	Eagles	Asylum	5	(1)	L
9	-	Good Morning Judge	10cc	Mercury	7	(69)	
10	-	Lucille	Kenny Rogers	UA	10	(5)	
11	13	Have I The Right?	Dead End Kids	CBS	7		F L
12	4	Red Light Spells Danger	Billy Ocean	GTO	9		
13	-	Mah Na Mah Na	Piero Umiliani	EMI International	5	(55)	F L
14	19	Pearl's A Singer	Elkie Brooks	A&M	6		F
15	-	Solsbury Hill	Peter Gabriel	Charisma	5	(68)	F
16	1	Knowing Me Knowing You	Abba	Epic	11	(14)	
17	-	Got To Give It Up	Marvin Gaye	Motown	6	(1)	
18	-	How Much Love	Leo Sayer	Chrysalis	5	(17)	
19	-	Lonely Boy	Andrew Gold	Asylum	5	(7)	F
20	3	I Don't Want To Put A Hold On You	Berni Flint	EMI	8		F L

This Mnth	Prev Mnth	Title	Artist	Label	Wks	(US 20 Pos)	
1	10	Lucille	Kenny Rogers	UA	10	(5)	
2	1	I Don't Want To Talk About It/ First Cut Is The Deepest	Rod Stewart	Riva	10	(46)	
3	7	Evergreen ('A Star Is Born')	Barbra Streisand	CBS	12	(1)	
4	-	God Save The Queen	Sex Pistols	Virgin	6		F
5	3	Ain't Gonna Bump No More (With No Big Fat Woman)	Joe Tex	Epic	8	(12)	F L
6	-	Show You The Way To Go	Jacksons	Epic	7	(28)	
7	-	You're Moving Out Today	Carole Bayer Sager	Elektra	7	(69)	F L
8	-	Halfway Down The Stairs	Muppets	Pye	6		F
9	5	The Shuffle	Van McCoy	H & L	8		L
10	17	Got To Give It Up	Marvin Gaye	Motown	6	(1)	
11	9	Good Morning Judge	10cc	Mercury	7	(69)	
12	-	Telephone Line	Electric Light Orchestra	Jet	7	(7)	
13	-	Lido Shuffle	Boz Scaggs	CBS	7	(11)	L
14	-	O.K.	Rock Follies	Polydor	4		F L
15	-	Baby Don't Change Your Mind	Gladys Knight & The Pips	Buddah	7	(52)	
16	-	So You Win Again	Hot Chocolate	RAK	10	(31)	
17	-	Too Hot To Handle/Slip Your Disc To This	Heatwave	GTO	7		
18	-	Fanfare For The Common Man	Emerson, Lake & Palmer	Atlantic	10		F L
19	13	Mah Na Mah Na	Piero Umiliani	EMI International	5	(55)	F L
20	-	Spot The Pigeon (E.P.)	Genesis	Charisma	2		F

◆ US cult heroes Blondie, Television, Talking Heads and The Ramones toured the UK, and The Damned became the first UK punk act to perform at CBGB's in New York.

◆ Debuting in the UK Top 20 were Genesis with 'Spot The Pigeon' and their former lead singer, Peter Gabriel, with 'Solsbury Hill'.

July 1977

This Mnth	Prev Mnth	Title	Artist	Label	Wks	(US 20 Pos)	
1	16	So You Win Again	Hot Chocolate	RAK	10	(31)	
2	18	Fanfare For The Common Man	Emerson, Lake & Palmer	Atlantic	10		F L
3	15	Baby Don't Change Your Mind	Gladys Knight & The Pips	Buddah	7	(52)	
4	-	Ma Baker	Boney M	Atlantic	10	(96)	
5	-	I Feel Love	Donna Summer	GTO	9	(6)	
6	6	Show You The Way To Go	Jacksons	Epic	7	(28)	
7	-	Sam	Olivia Newton-John	EMI	7	(20)	
8	-	Peaches/Go Buddy Go	Stranglers	UA	7		F
9	-	Angelo	Brotherhood Of Man	Pye	11		
10	-	Pretty Vacant	Sex Pistols	Virgin	5		
11	-	Oh Lori	Alessi	A&M	8		F L
12	7	You're Moving Out Today	Carole Bayer Sager	Elektra	7	(69)	F L
13	1	Lucille	Kenny Rogers	UA	10	(5)	
14	3	Evergreen (Love Theme From 'A Star Is Born')	Barbra Streisand	CBS	12	(1)	
15	-	Slow Down	John Miles	Decca	6	(34)	L
16	-	You're Gonna Get Next To Me	Bo Kirkland & Ruth Davis	EMI International	5		F L
17	-	Feel The Need In Me	Detroit Emeralds	Atlantic	8	(90)	L
18	-	Do What You Wanna Do	T-Connection	TK	3	(46)	F
19	12	Telephone Line	Electric Light Orchestra	Jet	7	(7)	
20	8	Halfway Down The Stairs	Muppets	Pye	6		F

August 1977

This Mnth	Prev Mnth	Title	Artist	Label	Wks	(US 20 Pos)	
1	9	Angelo	Brotherhood Of Man	Pye	11		
2	5	I Feel Love	Donna Summer	GTO	9	(6)	
3	-	You Got What It Takes	Showaddywaddy	Arista	8		
4	-	Float On	Floaters	ABC	9	(2)	F L
5	4	Ma Baker	Boney M	Atlantic	10	(96)	
6	-	We're All Alone	Rita Coolidge	A&M	8	(7)	F L
7	-	The Crunch	Rah Band	Good Earth	8		F
8	-	It's Your Life	Smokie	RAK	6		
9	-	Easy	Commodores	Motown	6	(4)	
10	-	Something Better Change/ Straighten Out	Stranglers	UA	5		
11	2	Fanfare For The Common Man	Emerson, Lake & Palmer	Atlantic	10		F L
12	1	So You Win Again	Hot Chocolate	RAK	10	(31)	
13	-	That's What Friends Are For	Deniece Williams	CBS	7		
14	-	Roadrunner	Jonathan Richman & The Modern Lovers	Berserkley	3		F
15	10	Pretty Vacant	Sex Pistols	Virgin	5		
16	-	Nights On Broadway	Candi Staton	Warner	8		
17	11	Oh Lori	Alessi	A&M	8		F L
18	-	Nobody Does It Better	Carly Simon	Elektra	8	(2)	
19	-	Way Down	Elvis Presley	RCA	10	(18)	
20	17	Feel The Need In Me	Detroit Emeralds	Atlantic	8	(90)	L

◆ As one of the era's top female singers Debbie Harry, and her group Blondie, signed with Chrysalis, an earlier teen queen, Connie Francis, was the first woman to top the UK LP chart.

◆ The Bay City Rollers, whose star had already waned in the UK, scored their last American Top 20 entry, as new teen idols Shaun Cassidy (David's brother) and Andy Gibb (Brother of the Bee Gees) debuted on the chart.

1977

September 1977

This Mnth	Prev Mnth	Title	Artist	Label	Wks (US 20 Pos)		
1	19	Way Down	Elvis Presley	RCA	10 (18)		
2	-	Magic Fly	Space	Pye International	8		F L
3	-	Silver Lady	David Soul	Private Stock	11 (52)		
4	-	Oxygene Part IV	Jean-Michel Jarre	Polydor	7		F L
5	4	Float On	Floaters	ABC	9	(2)	F L
6	-	Deep Down Inside	Donna Summer	Casablanca	7		
7	16	Nights On Broadway	Candi Staton	Warner	8		
8	18	Nobody Does It Better	Carly Simon	Elektra	8	(2)	
9	1	Angelo	Brotherhood Of Man	Pye	11		
10	13	That's What Friends Are For	Deniece Williams	CBS	7		
11	3	You Got What It Takes	Showaddywaddy	Arista	8		
12	-	Telephone Man	Meri Wilson	Pye International	7	(18)	F L
13	7	The Crunch	Rah Band	Good Earth	8		F
14	-	Do Anything You Wanna Do	Rods	Island	7		F L
15	-	Tulane	Steve Gibbons Band	Polydor	4		F L
16	-	Dancin' In The Moonlight (It's Caught Me In The Spotlight)	Thin Lizzy	Vertigo	4		
17	-	Looking After Number One	Boomtown Rats	Ensign	5		F
18	-	Best Of My Love	Emotions	CBS	7	(1)	F
19	2	I Feel Love	Donna Summer	GTO	9	(6)	
20	-	Wonderous Stories	Yes	Atlantic	7		F L

October 1977

This Mnth	Prev Mnth	Title	Artist	Label	Wks (US 20 Pos)		
1	3	Silver Lady	David Soul	Private Stock	11 (52)		
2	-	Black Is Black	La Belle Epoque	Harvest	9		F L
3	18	Best Of My Love	Emotions	CBS	7	(1)	F
4	-	I Remember Elvis Presley (The King Is Dead)	Danny Mirror	Sonet	6		F L
5	1	Way Down	Elvis Presley	RCA	10 (18)		
6	-	Yes Sir I Can Boogie	Baccara	RCA	9		F
7	-	You're In My Heart	Rod Stewart	Riva	8	(4)	
8	-	From New York To L.A.	Patsy Gallant	EMI	5		F L
9	2	Magic Fly	Space	Pye International	8		F L
10	-	Black Betty	Ram Jam	Epic	8	(18)	F
11	-	No More Heroes	Stranglers	UA	6		
12	12	Telephone Man	Meri Wilson	Pye International	7	(18)	F L
13	20	Wonderous Stories	Yes	Atlantic	7		F L
14	6	Deep Down Inside	Donna Summer	Casablanca	7		
15	-	Star Wars Theme - Cantina Band	Meco	RCA	5	(1)	F L
16	4	Oxygene Part IV	Jean-Michel Jarre	Polydor	7		F L
17	-	Rockin' All Over The World	Status Quo	Vertigo	10		
18	-	Sunshine After The Rain	Elkie Brooks	A&M	4		
19	-	I Remember Yesterday	Donna Summer	GTO	5		
20	-	Holidays In The Sun	Sex Pistols	Virgin	5		

◆ Marc Bolan, front man of the highly successful glam rock duo T-Rex, died in a car crash. He was a major figure in British rock music.

◆ Bing Crosby died. The well-loved singer, who had amassed 299 American Top 20 hits, found himself back in the British Top 10 with the evergreen 'White Christmas'.

148

November 1977

This Mnth	Prev Mnth	Title	Artist	Label	Wks	(US 20 Pos)	
1	-	The Name Of The Game	Abba	Epic	9	(12)	
2	17	Rockin' All Over The World	Status Quo	Vertigo	10		
3	-	We Are The Champions	Queen	EMI	8	(4)	
4	6	Yes Sir I Can Boogie	Baccara	RCA	9		F
5	7	You're In My Heart	Rod Stewart	Riva	8	(4)	
6	-	2-4-6-8 Motorway	Tom Robinson Band	EMI	6		F
7	2	Black Is Black	La Belle Epoque	Harvest	9		F L
8	-	Calling Occupants Of Interplanetary Craft	Carpenters	A&M	6	(32)	L
9	-	How Deep Is Your Love	Bee Gees	RSO	11	(1)	
10	-	Needles And Pins	Smokie	RAK	6	(68)	
11	-	Dancin' Party	Showaddywaddy	Arista	9		
12	-	Live In Trouble	Barron Knights	Epic	5		
13	-	Virginia Plain	Roxy Music	Polydor	5		
14	10	Black Betty	Ram Jam	Epic	8	(18)	F
15	20	Holidays In The Sun	Sex Pistols	Virgin	5		
16	-	Daddy Cool/The Girl Can't Help It	Darts	Magnet	10		F
17	1	Silver Lady	David Soul	Private Stock	11	(52)	
18	-	She's Not There	Santana	CBS	5	(27)	F L
19	-	Mull Of Kintyre/Girls' School	Wings	Capitol	13	(33)	P
20	-	Hot Track E.P.	Nazareth	Mountain	4		L

December 1977

This Mnth	Prev Mnth	Title	Artist	Label	Wks	(US 20 Pos)	
1	19	Mull Of Kintyre/Girls' School	Wings	Capitol	13	(33)	P
2	-	The Floral Dance	Brighouse & Rastrick Brass Band	Transatlantic	10		F L
3	9	How Deep Is Your Love	Bee Gees	RSO	11	(1)	
4	-	I Will	Ruby Winters	Creole	9		F
5	16	Daddy Cool/The Girl Can't Help It	Darts	Magnet	10		F
6	11	Dancin' Party	Showaddywaddy	Arista	9		
7	-	Egyptian Reggae	Jonathan Richman & The Modern Lovers	Berserkley	6		L
8	-	Belfast	Boney M	Atlantic	7		
9	3	We Are The Champions	Queen	EMI	8	(4)	
10	-	Love's Unkind	Donna Summer	GTO	10		
11	2	Rockin' All Over The World	Status Quo	Vertigo	10		
12	-	White Christmas	Bing Crosby	MCA	4		G
13	-	It's A Heartache	Bonnie Tyler	RCA	9	(3)	
14	-	Love Of My Life	Dooleys	GTO	5		
15	-	Put Your Love In Me	Hot Chocolate	RAK	6		
16	1	The Name Of The Game	Abba	Epic	9	(12)	
17	-	Mary Of The Fourth Form	Boomtown Rats	Ensign	5		
18	-	Watching The Detectives	Elvis Costello	Stiff	5		F
19	-	My Way	Elvis Presley	RCA	6	(22)	
20	12	Live In Trouble	Barron Knights	Epic	5		

◆ The Vortex opened. Among the early headliners were Adam & The Ants, controversial girl group The Slits and Siouxsie & The Banshees.

◆ Understandably, British punk had few initial takers Stateside. However the Sex Pistols' chart topping UK debut LP **Never Mind the Bollocks** and Elvis Costello's **My Aim Is True** (which included musical contributions from Huey Lewis) were minor US successes.

1978

January 1978

This Mnth	Prev Mnth	Title	Artist	Label	Wks	(US 20 Pos)	
1	1	Mull Of Kintyre/Girls' School	Wings	Capitol	13	(33)	P
2	10	Love's Unkind	Donna Summer	GTO	10		
3	13	It's A Heartache	Bonnie Tyler	RCA	9	(3)	
4	2	The Floral Dance	Brighouse/Rastrick Brass Band	Transatlantic	10		F L
5	-	Don't It Make My Brown Eyes Blue	Crystal Gayle	UA	8	(2)	F
6	-	Dance Dance Dance (Yowsah Yowsah Yowsah)	Chic	Atlantic	8	(6)	F
7	-	Uptown Top Ranking	Althia And Donna	Lightning	8		F L
8	3	How Deep Is Your Love	Bee Gees	RSO	11	(1)	
9	-	Let's Have A Quiet Night In	David Soul	Private Stock	7		
10	4	I Will	Ruby Winters	Creole	9		F
11	-	Native New Yorker	Odyssey	RCA	7	(21)	F
12	-	Who Pays The Ferryman	Yannis Markopoulos	BBC	4		F L
13	5	Daddy Cool/The Girl Can't Help It	Darts	Magnet	10		F
14	-	Figaro	Brotherhood Of Man	Pye	9		
15	-	Jamming/Punky Reggae Party	Bob Marley & The Wailers	Island	5		
16	-	Only Women Bleed	Julie Covington	Virgin	4		L
17	-	I Love You	Donna Summer	Casablanca	3	(37)	
18	19	My Way	Elvis Presley	RCA	6	(22)	
19	-	Lovely Day	Bill Withers	CBS	6	(30)	
20	-	If I Had Words	Scott Fitzgerald/Yvonne Keeley	Pepper	7		F L

February 1978

This Mnth	Prev Mnth	Title	Artist	Label	Wks	(US 20 Pos)	
1	14	Figaro	Brotherhood Of Man	Pye	9		
2	-	Take A Chance On Me	Abba	Epic	10	(3)	
3	20	If I Had Words	Scott Fitzgerald/Yvonne Keeley	Pepper	7		F L
4	7	Uptown Top Ranking	Althia And Donna	Lightning	8		F L
5	-	Come Back My Love	Darts	Magnet	10		
6	-	Sorry I'm A Lady	Baccara	RCA	5		L
7	1	Mull Of Kintyre/Girls' School	Wings	Capitol	13	(33)	P
8	11	Native New Yorker	Odyssey	RCA	7	(21)	F
9	19	Lovely Day	Bill Withers	CBS	6	(30)	
10	-	Wishing On A Star	Rose Royce	Warner	8		
11	-	Hotlegs/I Was Only Joking	Rod Stewart	Riva	6	(28)	
12	-	Mr. Blue Sky	Electric Light Orchestra	Jet	8	(35)	
13	2	Love's Unkind	Donna Summer	GTO	10		
14	-	Love Is Like Oxygen	Sweet	Polydor	5	(8)	L
15	-	The Groove Line	Heatwave	GTO	5	(7)	
16	15	Jamming/Punky Reggae Party	Bob Marley & The Wailers	Island	5		
17	-	Drummer Man	Tonight	Target	3		F L
18	-	Just One More Night	Yellow Dog	Virgin	5		F L
19	3	It's A Heartache	Bonnie Tyler	RCA	9	(3)	
20	6	Dance Dance Dance (Yowsah Yowsah Yaowsah)	Chic	Atlantic	8	(6)	F

◆ British acts working the USA included Genesis, David Bowie, The Stranglers, The Jam and The Sex Pistols, whose leader, Johnny Rotten, announced at the end of their short and controversial tour, that they were disbanding. .

◆ Pink Floyd's Dave Gilmour helped Kate Bush get a record deal with EMI. The multi-talented teenager's first single 'Wuthering Heights' shot her to instant stardom in Britain.

March 1978

This Mnth	Prev Mnth	Title	Artist	Label	Wks	(US 20 Pos)	
1	-	Wuthering Heights	Kate Bush	EMI	9		F
2	2	Take A Chance On Me	Abba	Epic	10	(3)	
3	5	Come Back My Love	Darts	Magnet	10		
4	10	Wishing On A Star	Rose Royce	Warner	8		
5	-	Denis	Blondie	Chrysalis	9		F
6	-	Stayin' Alive	Bee Gees	RSO	7	(1)	
7	-	Baker Street	Gerry Rafferty	UA	10	(2)	F
8	-	I Can't Stand The Rain	Eruption	Atlantic	8	(18)	F
9	12	Mr. Blue Sky	Electric Light Orchestra	Jet	8	(35)	
10	-	Matchstalk Men And Matchstalk Cats And Dogs	Brian & Michael	Pye	11		F L
11	-	Is This Love	Bob Marley & The Wailers	Island	6		
12	18	Just One More Night	Yellow Dog	Virgin	5		F L
13	-	Emotions	Samantha Sang	Private Stock	8	(3)	F L
14	1	Figaro	Brotherhood Of Man	Pye	9		
15	-	Free (E.P.)	Free	Island	4		L
16	-	Fantasy	Earth, Wind & Fire	CBS	4	(32)	
17	14	Love Is Like Oxygen	Sweet	Polydor	5	(8)	L
18	3	If I Had Words	Scott Fitzgerald/Yvonne Keeley	Pepper	7		F L
19	-	Ally's Tartan Army	Andy Cameron	Klub	5		F L
20	-	I Love The Sound Of Breaking Glass	Nick Lowe & His Cowboy Outfit	Radar	4		F

April 1978

This Mnth	Prev Mnth	Title	Artist	Label	Wks	(US 20 Pos)	
1	10	Matchstalk Men And Matchstalk Cats And Dogs	Brian & Michael	Pye	11		F L
2	-	I Wonder Why	Showaddywaddy	Arista	7		
3	7	Baker Street	Gerry Rafferty	UA	10	(2)	F
4	-	If You Can't Give Me Love	Suzi Quatro	RAK	8	(45)	
5	5	Denis	Blondie	Chrysalis	9		F
6	1	Wuthering Heights	Kate Bush	EMI	9		F
7	-	Follow You Follow Me	Genesis	Charisma	7	(23)	
8	-	Never Let Her Slip Away	Andrew Gold	Asylum	8	(67)	
9	-	With A Little Luck	Wings	Parlophone	5	(1)	
10	-	Night Fever	Bee Gees	RSO	12	(1)	
11	8	I Can't Stand The Rain	Eruption	Atlantic	8	(18)	F
12	-	Too Much, Too Little, Too Late	Johnny Mathis & Deniece Williams	CBS	9	(1)	
13	20	I Love The Sound Of Breaking Glass	Nick Lowe & His Cowboy Outfit	Radar	4		F
14	19	Ally's Tartan Army	Andy Cameron	Klub	5		F L
15	-	Walk In Love	Manhattan Transfer	Atlantic	5		
16	-	Every 1's A Winner	Hot Chocolate	RAK	6	(6)	
17	-	Singin' In The Rain (Pt. 1)	Sheila B. Devotion	Carrere	4		F
18	-	Sometimes When We Touch	Dan Hill	20th Century	5	(3)	F L
19	11	Is This Love	Bob Marley & The Wailers	Island	6		
20	-	More Like The Movies	Dr. Hook	Capitol	5		

◆ For the third time in the 1970s, Free's recording of 'All Right Now' reached the UK Top 20. This time around it was on the 'Free EP'.

◆ As The Bee Gees scored their only transatlantic topper of the 1970s with the Grammy winning 'Night Fever', its parent album, **Saturday Night Fever**, started an 18 week run (a record for the decade) at the top in Britain.

1978

This Mnth	Prev Mnth	Title	Artist	Label	Wks (US 20 Pos)	
1	-	Rivers Of Babylon/Brown Girl In The Ring	Boney M	Atlantic/Hansa	22 (30)	P
2	10	Night Fever	Bee Gees	RSO	12 (1)	
3	12	Too Much, Too Little, Too Late	Johnny Mathis/Deniece Williams	CBS	9 (1)	
4	-	Automatic Lover	Dee D. Jackson	Mercury	5	F L
5	8	Never Let Her Slip Away	Andrew Gold	Asylum	8 (67)	
6	-	Boy From New York City	Darts	Magnet	8	
7	-	Because The Night	Patti Smith Group	Arista	6 (13)	F L
8	-	Let's All Chant	Michael Zager Band	Private Stock	6 (36)	F L
9	1	Matchstalk Men And Matchstalk...	Brian & Michael	Pye	11	F L
10	-	Jack And Jill	Raydio	Arista	5 (8)	F
11	-	If I Can't Have You	Yvonne Elliman	RSO	7 (1)	L
12	-	Love Is In The Air	John Paul Young	Ariola	6 (7)	F L
13	-	She's So Modern	Boomtown Rats	Ensign	6	
14	-	Do It Again	Raffaella Carra	Epic	5	F L
15	4	If You Can't Give Me Love	Suzi Quatro	RAK	8 (45)	
16	-	More Than A Woman	Tavares	Capitol	6 (32)	
17	-	Everybody Dance	Chic	Atlantic	5 (38)	
18	2	I Wonder Why	Showaddywaddy	Arista	7	
19	-	Bad Old Days	Co-Co	Ariola/Hansa	3	F L
20	-	(I'm Always Touched By Your) Presence Dear	Blondie	Chrysalis	5	

This Mnth	Prev Mnth	Title	Artist	Label	Wks (US 20 Pos)	
1	1	Rivers Of Babylon/Brown Girl In...	Boney M	Atlantic/Hansa	22 (30)	P
2	-	You're The One That I Want	John Travolta/Olivia Newton-John	RSO	17 (1)	F P
3	6	Boy From New York City	Darts	Magnet	8	
4	11	If I Can't Have You	Yvonne Elliman	RSO	7 (1)	L
5	2	Night Fever	Bee Gees	RSO	12 (1)	
6	-	Ca Plane Pour Moi	Plastic Bertrand	Sire	7	F L
7	-	Oh Carol	Smokie	RAK	6	
8	12	Love Is In The Air	John Paul Young	Ariola	6 (7)	F L
9	-	Davy's On The Road Again	Manfred Mann's Earth Band	Bronze	5	L
10	-	Annie's Song	James Galway	RCA Red Seal	8	F L
11	16	More Than A Woman	Tavares	Capitol	6 (32)	
12	-	Miss You	Rolling Stones	Rolling Stone	6 (1)	
13	7	Because The Night	Patti Smith Group	Arista	6 (13)	F L
14	-	The Smurf Song	Father Abraham & The Smurfs	Decca	11	F
15	-	Ole Ola (Muhler Brasileira)	Rod Stewart	Riva	3	
16	-	What A Waste	Ian Dury & The Blockheads	Stiff	4	F
17	-	Making Up Again	Goldie	Bronze	5	F L
18	-	Hi Tension	Hi Tension	Island	3	F
19	-	It Sure Brings Out The Love In Your Eyes	David Soul	Private Stock	4	L
20	-	Come To Me	Ruby Winters	Creole	4	L

◆ Boney M's double-sided chart topper, 'Rivers Of Babylon'/ 'Brown Girl In The Ring', which sold over two million in Britain, was the only American Top 40 entry for these regular European hit makers.

◆ Dire Straits' debut single 'Sultans Of Swing' was released. It caused little interest until 1979 when it first charted in the USA.

1978

This Mnth	Prev Mnth	Title	Artist	Label	Wks	(US 20 Pos)
1	2	You're The One That I Want	John Travolta & Olivia Newton-John	RSO	17	(1) F P
2	14	The Smurf Song	Father Abraham & The Smurfs	Decca	11	F
3	-	Dancing In The City	Marshall Hain	Harvest	9	(43) F L
4	-	Airport	Motors	Virgin	7	F
5	10	Annie's Song	James Galway	RCA Red Seal	8	F L
6	-	Like Clockwork	Boomtown Rats	Ensign	7	
7	-	Man With The Child In His Eyes	Kate Bush	EMI	6	(85)
8	-	A Little Bit Of Soap	Showaddywaddy	Arista	6	
9	12	Miss You	Rolling Stones	Rolling Stone	6	(1)
10	-	Substitute	Clout	Carrere	9	(67) F L
11	-	Boogie Oogie Oogie	Taste Of Honey	Capitol	8	(1) F L
12	-	No One Is Innocent/My Way	Sex Pistols	Virgin	5	
13	1	Rivers Of Babylon/Brown Girl In The Ring	Boney M	Atlantic/Hansa	22	(30) P
14	-	Mind Blowing Decisions	Heatwave	GTO	4	
15	-	Used Ta Be My Girl	O'Jays	Philly International	5	(4) L
16	-	Wild West Hero	Electric Light Orchestra	Jet	6	
17	-	Run For Home	Lindisfarne	Mercury	5	(33)
18	17	Making Up Again	Goldie	Bronze	5	F L
19	9	Davy's On The Road Again	Manfred Mann's Earth Band	Bronze	5	L
20	-	Argentine Melody (Cancion De Argentina)	San Jose	MCA	3	F L

This Mnth	Prev Mnth	Title	Artist	Label	Wks	(US 20 Pos)
1	1	You're The One That I Want	John Travolta & Olivia Newton-John	RSO	17	(1) F P
2	10	Substitute	Clout	Carrere	9	(67) F L
3	11	Boogie Oogie Oogie	Taste Of Honey	Capitol	8	(1) F L
4	13	Rivers Of Babylon/Brown Girl	Boney M	Atlantic/Hansa	22	(30) P
5	-	Three Times A Lady	Commodores	Motown	10	(1)
6	-	Forever Autumn	Justin Hayward	CBS	6	(47) L
7	2	The Smurf Song	Father Abraham & The Smurfs	Decca	11	F
8	-	5-7-0-5	City Boy	Vertigo	5	(27) F L
9	-	If The Kids Are United	Sham 69	Polydor	5	
10	-	It's Raining	Darts	Magnet	8	
11	3	Dancing In The City	Marshall Hain	Harvest	9	(43) F L
12	-	Northern Lights	Renaissance	Warner	5	F L
13	16	Wild West Hero	Electric Light Orchestra	Jet	6	
14	-	Supernature	Cerrone	Atlantic	5	(70) F L
15	8	A Little Bit Of Soap	Showaddywaddy	Arista	6	
16	6	Like Clockwork	Boomtown Rats	Ensign	7	
17	-	Dreadlock Holiday	10cc	Mercury	9	(44) L
18	-	Come Back And Finish What You Started	Gladys Knight & The Pips	Buddah	5	
19	-	Stay	Jackson Browne	Asylum	4	(20) F L
20	-	Baby Stop Crying	Bob Dylan	CBS	5	L

◆ The soundtrack album to John Travolta's latest box office smash *Grease* topped the American album chart for three months and it repeated that feat in Britain. It contained the transatlantic smash duets, 'You're The One That I Want' and 'Summer Nights' by Travolta and Olivia Newton-John (both selling over a million in the UK alone), as well as the chart topping title song by Frankie Valli.

1978

This Mnth	Prev Mnth	Title	Artist	Label	Wks	(US 20 Pos)	
1	5	Three Times A Lady	Commodores	Motown	10	(1)	
2	17	Dreadlock Holiday	10cc	Mercury	9	(44)	L
3	4	Rivers Of Babylon/Brown Girl In The Ring	Boney M	Atlantic/Hansa	22	(30)	P
4	-	Oh What A Circus	David Essex	Mercury	8		
5	-	Jilted John	Jilted John	EMI International	7		F L
6	10	It's Raining	Darts	Magnet	8		
7	1	You're The One That I Want	John Travolta/O. Newton-John	RSO	17	(1)	F P
8	-	Kiss You All Over	Exile	RAK	6	(1)	F L
9	-	British Hustle/Peace On Earth	Hi Tension	Island	5		L
10	-	Hong Kong Garden	Siouxsie & The Banshees	Polydor	5		F
11	14	Supernature	Cerrone	Atlantic	5	(70)	F L
12	-	Grease	Frankie Valli	RSO	6	(1)	L
13	-	Picture This	Blondie	Chrysalis	6		
14	-	Summer Nights	John Travolta/O. Newton-John	RSO	11	(5)	G
15	-	An Everlasting Love	Andy Gibb	RSO	5	(5)	F L
16	-	Summer Night City	Abba	Epic	5		
17	-	It's Only Make Believe	Child	Ariola Hansa	5		F L
18	-	Forget About You	Motors	Virgin	4		L
19	-	Again And Again	Status Quo	Vertigo	4		
20	-	Love Don't Live Here Anymore	Rose Royce	Whitfield	7	(32)	

This Mnth	Prev Mnth	Title	Artist	Label	Wks	(US 20 Pos)	
1	14	Summer Nights	John Travolta & Olivia Newton-John	RSO	11	(5)	G
2	-	Rasputin	Boney M	Atlantic/Hansa	7		
3	20	Love Don't Live Here Anymore	Rose Royce	Whitfield	7	(32)	
4	-	Lucky Stars	Dean Friedman	Lifesong	6		F L
5	-	I Can't Stop Lovin' You (Though I Try)	Leo Sayer	Chrysalis	6		
6	-	Sandy	John Travolta	Polydor	7		
7	-	Sweet Talkin' Woman	Electric Light Orchestra	Jet	7	(17)	
8	12	Grease	Frankie Valli	RSO	6	(1)	L
9	-	You Make Me Feel (Mighty Real)	Sylvester	Fantasy	5	(36)	F L
10	-	Now That We've Found Love	Third World	Island	4	(47)	F
11	-	Talking In Your Sleep	Crystal Gayle	UA	5	(18)	L
12	-	Blame It On The Boogie	Jacksons	Epic	7	(54)	
13	16	Summer Night City	Abba	Epic	5		
14	-	Rat Trap	Boomtown Rats	Ensign	9		
15	-	Macarthur Park	Donna Summer	Casablanca	6	(1)	
16	2	Dreadlock Holiday	10cc	Mercury	9	(44)	L
17	-	A Rose Has To Die	Dooleys	GTO	4		
18	8	Kiss You All Over	Exile	RAK	6	(1)	F L
19	1	Three Times A Lady	Commodores	Motown	10	(1)	
20	4	Oh What A Circus	David Essex	Mercury	8		

◆ Soon after The Who's original manager Pete Meaden committed suicide, the group's colourful and extrovert drummer Keith Moon died from drug and drink-related causes.

◆ It was reported that The Rolling Stones' US tour had grossed a record-breaking $6 million.

November 1978

This Mnth	Prev Mnth	Title	Artist	Label	Wks	(US 20 Pos)	
1	14	Rat Trap	Boomtown Rats	Ensign	9		
2	1	Summer Nights	John Travolta & Olivia Newton-John	RSO	11	(5)	G
3	6	Sandy	John Travolta	Polydor	7		
4	-	Hopelessly Devoted To You	Olivia Newton-John	RSO	5	(3)	
5	-	Darlin'	Frankie Miller	Chrysalis	7		F L
6	15	Macarthur Park	Donna Summer	Casablanca	6	(1)	
7	-	My Best Friend's Girl	Cars	Elektra	5	(35)	F
8	12	Blame It On The Boogie	Jacksons	Epic	7	(54)	
9	2	Rasputin	Boney M	Atlantic/Hansa	7		
10	-	Pretty Little Angel Eyes	Showaddywaddy	Arista	6		
11	7	Sweet Talkin' Woman	Electric Light Orchestra	Jet	7	(17)	
12	-	Instant Replay	Dan Hartman	Sky	6	(29)	F
13	-	Givin' Up Givin' In	Three Degrees	Ariola	5		
14	-	Public Image	Public Image Ltd.	Virgin	4		F
15	-	Bicycle Race/Fat Bottomed Girls	Queen	EMI	4	(24)	
16	-	Da Ya Think I'm Sexy	Rod Stewart	Riva	9	(1)	
17	4	Lucky Stars	Dean Friedman	Lifesong	6		F L
18	-	Dippety Day	Father Abraham & The Smurfs	Decca	5		
19	-	Hurry Up Harry	Sham 69	Polydor	5		
20	-	Hanging On The Telephone	Blondie	Chrysalis	7		

December 1978

This Mnth	Prev Mnth	Title	Artist	Label	Wks	(US 20 Pos)	
1	-	Mary's Boy Child-Oh My Lord	Boney M	Atlantic/Hansa	7	(85)	G
2	16	Da Ya Think I'm Sexy	Rod Stewart	Riva	9	(1)	
3	-	Too Much Heaven	Bee Gees	RSO	9	(1)	
4	-	A Taste Of Aggro	Barron Knights	Epic	8		
5	-	I Lost My Heart To A Starship Trooper	Sarah Brightman & Hot Gossip	Ariola	8		F
6	-	Y.M.C.A.	Village People	Mercury	10	(2)	F G
7	-	Le Freak	Chic	Atlantic	10	(1)	
8	-	Always And Forever/Mind Blowing Decisions	Heatwave	GTO	9	(18)	
9	20	Hanging On The Telephone	Blondie	Chrysalis	7		
10	-	You Don't Bring Me Flowers	Barbra & Neil	Columbia	6	(1)	
11	1	Rat Trap	Boomtown Rats	Ensign	9		
12	-	Lay Your Love On Me	Racey	RAK	9		F
13	-	Don't Cry Out Loud	Elkie Brooks	A&M	5		
14	4	Hopelessly Devoted To You	Olivia Newton-John	RSO	5	(3)	
15	10	Pretty Little Angel Eyes	Showaddywaddy	Arista	6		
16	7	My Best Friend's Girl	Cars	Elektra	5	(35)	F
17	-	Greased Lightning	John Travolta	Polydor	5	(47)	
18	-	Song For Guy	Elton John	Rocket	6		
19	12	Instant Replay	Dan Hartman	Sky	6	(29)	F
20	-	In The Bush	Musique	CBS	5	(58)	F L

◆ The film *Grease* continued to spawn hits, with three songs, 'Summer Nights', 'Sandy' and 'Hopelessly Devoted To You', taking slots in the British Top 4 in November.

◆ The Cars , who were voted Best New Band in *Rolling Stone,* started a European tour. Their debut hit, 'My Best Friend's Girl', was the first picture disc to be successfully marketed in Britain.

◆ Sex Pistol Sid Vicious was charged in New York with the murder of his girlfriend Nancy Spungen.

January 1979

This Mnth	Prev Mnth	Title	Artist	Label	Wks 20	(US Pos)	
1	6	Y.M.C.A.	Village People	Mercury	10	(2)	F G
2	-	Hit Me With Your Rhythm Stick	Ian Dury & The Blockheads	Stiff	10		
3	12	Lay Your Love On Me	Racey	RAK	9		F
4	-	September	Earth, Wind & Fire	CBS	7	(8)	
5	18	Song For Guy	Elton John	Rocket	6		
6	7	Le Freak	Chic	Atlantic	10	(1)	
7	-	A Little More Love	Olivia Newton-John	EMI	6	(3)	
8	4	A Taste Of Aggro	Barron Knights	Epic	8		
9	-	Hello This Is Joannie (Telephone Answering Machine Song)	Paul Evans	Spring	5		F L
10	10	You Don't Bring Me Flowers	Barbra & Neil	Columbia	6	(1)	
11	1	Mary's Boy Child-Oh My Lord	Boney M	Atlantic/Hansa	7	(85)	G
12	3	Too Much Heaven	Bee Gees	RSO	9	(1)	
13	-	I'm Every Woman	Chaka Khan	Warner	7	(21)	F
14	5	I Lost My Heart To A Starship Trooper	Sarah Brightman & Hot Gossip	Ariola	8		F
15	-	One Nation Under A Groove (Pt. 1)	Funkadelic	Warner	4	(28)	F L
16	-	Car 67	Driver 67	Logo	5		F L
17	-	I'll Put You Together Again	Hot Chocolate	RAK	4		
18	-	Women In Love	Three Degrees	Ariola	8		
19	-	Heart Of Glass	Blondie	Chrysalis	8	(1)	G
20	8	Always And Forever/Mind Blowing Decisions	Heatwave	GTO	9	(18)	

February 1979

This Mnth	Prev Mnth	Title	Artist	Label	Wks 20	(US Pos)	
1	19	Heart Of Glass	Blondie	Chrysalis	8	(1)	G
2	18	Women In Love	Three Degrees	Ariola	8		
3	-	Chiquitita	Abba	Epic	7	(29)	
4	-	Don't Cry For Me Argentina	Shadows	EMI	6		
5	2	Hit Me With Your Rhythm Stick	Ian Dury & The Blockheads	Stiff	10		
6	-	I Was Made For Dancin'	Leif Garrett	Scotti Bros	5	(10)	F L
7	-	Contact	Edwin Starr	20th Century	6	(65)	
8	16	Car 67	Driver 67	Logo	5		F L
9	4	September	Earth, Wind & Fire	CBS	7	(8)	
10	-	Milk And Alcohol	Dr. Feelgood	UA	5		F L
11	-	Tragedy	Bee Gees	RSO	7	(1)	
12	1	Y.M.C.A.	Village People	Mercury	10	(2)	F G
13	7	A Little More Love	Olivia Newton-John	EMI	6	(3)	
14	-	My Life	Billy Joel	CBS	4	(3)	
15	-	Oliver's Army	Elvis Costello	Radar	9		
16	-	King Rocker	Generation X	Chrysalis	4		F L
17	-	Just The Way You Are	Barry White	20th Century	5		
18	9	Hello This Is Joannie (Telephone...)	Paul Evans	Spring	5		F L
19	-	I Will Survive	Gloria Gaynor	Polydor	9	(1)	
20	3	Lay Your Love On Me	Racey	RAK	9		F

◆ British single sales continued to amaze, with hits from the Village People ('Y.M.C.A.') and Blondie ('Heart Of Glass') selling more than a million and Ian Dury's 'Hit Me With Your Rhythm Stick', only narrowly missing.

◆ British success for local groups Dire Straits and Police only came after their respective singles 'Sultans Of Swing' and 'Roxanne' charted in America.

March 1979

This Mnth	Prev Mnth	Title	Artist	Label	Wks	(US 20 Pos)	
1	19	I Will Survive	Gloria Gaynor	Polydor	9	(1)	
2	15	Oliver's Army	Elvis Costello	Radar	9		
3	11	Tragedy	Bee Gees	RSO	7	(1)	
4	-	Lucky Number	Lene Lovich	Stiff	7		F
5	-	Can You Feel The Force	Real Thing	Pye	7		
6	-	Something Else/Friggin' In The Riggin'	Sex Pistols	Virgin	7		
7	-	I Want Your Love	Chic	Atlantic	7	(7)	
8	1	Heart Of Glass	Blondie	Chrysalis	8	(1)	G
9	-	Keep On Dancin'	Gary's Gang	CBS	5	(41)	F L
10	7	Contact	Edwin Starr	20th Century	6	(65)	
11	-	Get Down	Gene Chandler	20th Century	5	(53)	F L
12	-	Into The Valley	Skids	Virgin	6		F
13	3	Chiquitita	Abba	Epic	7	(29)	
14	-	Painter Man	Boney M	Atlantic/Hansa	3		
15	-	Get It	Darts	Magnet	4		
16	-	Waiting For An Alibi	Thin Lizzy	Vertigo	4		
17	-	In The Navy	Village People	Mercury	6	(3)	
18	-	Don't Stop Me Now	Queen	EMI	4	(86)	
19	-	Sound Of The Suburbs	Members	Virgin	4		F L
20	6	I Was Made For Dancin'	Leif Garrett	Scotti Bros	5	(10)	F L

April 1979

This Mnth	Prev Mnth	Title	Artist	Label	Wks	(US 20 Pos)	
1	-	Bright Eyes	Art Garfunkel	CBS	11		G L
2	-	Cool For Cats	Squeeze	A&M	7		
3	-	Some Girls	Racey	RAK	7		
4	17	In The Navy	Village People	Mercury	6	(3)	
5	1	I Will Survive	Gloria Gaynor	Polydor	9	(1)	
6	-	Shake Your Body (Down To The Ground)	Jacksons	Epic	6	(7)	
7	-	Sultans Of Swing	Dire Straits	Vertigo	5	(4)	F
8	-	He's The Greatest Dancer	Sister Sledge	Atlantic/Cotillion	5	(9)	
9	-	Silly Thing/Who Killed Bambi	Sex Pistols	Virgin	4		
10	-	The Runner	Three Degrees	Ariola	4		
11	7	I Want Your Love	Chic	Atlantic	7	(7)	
12	-	Hallelujah	Milk & Honey	Polydor	4		F L
13	6	Something Else/Friggin' In The Riggin'	Sex Pistols	Virgin	7		
14	-	Pop Muzik	M	MCA	9	(1)	F
15	-	Wow	Kate Bush	EMI	4		
16	-	Turn The Music Up	Players Association	Vanguard	4		F L
17	-	I Don't Wanna Lose You	Kandidate	RAK	5		F L
18	4	Lucky Number	Lene Lovich	Stiff	7		F
19	2	Oliver's Army	Elvis Costello	Radar	9		
20	-	The Logical Song	Supertramp	A&M	5	(6)	

◆ The biggest transatlantic hits of the period were Gloria Gaynor's smash 'I Will Survive' and Rod Stewart's disco-oriented 'Da Ya Think I'm Sexy'.

◆ The film *Quadrophenia*, based on The Who album, and featuring Sting and Toyah, premiered in London, on the night of The Who's first gig with new drummer Kenny Jones (Keith Moon having died in September 1978). Soon afterwards, The Who's movie *The Kids Are Alright* premiered in New York.

1979

May 1979

This Mnth	Prev Mnth	Title	Artist	Label	Wks (US 20 Pos)	
1	1	Bright Eyes	Art Garfunkel	CBS	11	G L
2	14	Pop Muzik	M	MCA	9 (1)	F
3	-	Hooray Hooray It's A Holi-Holiday	Boney M	Atlantic/Hansa	6	
4	-	Does Your Mother Know	Abba	Epic	6 (19)	
5	-	Knock On Wood	Amii Stewart	Atlantic/Hansa	6 (1)	F
6	-	Reunited	Peaches & Herb	CBS	7 (1)	F L
7	3	Some Girls	Racey	RAK	7	
8	-	Goodnight Tonight	Wings	Parlophone	5 (5)	
9	20	The Logical Song	Supertramp	A&M	5 (6)	
10	-	Dance Away	Roxy Music	Polydor	10 (44)	
11	-	One Way Ticket	Eruption	Atlantic/Hansa	6	L
12	-	Sunday Girl	Blondie	Chrysalis	8	
13	-	Banana Splits (Tra La La Song)	Dickies	A&M	3	F L
14	6	Shake Your Body (Down To The Ground)	Jacksons	Epic	6 (7)	
15	-	Parisienne Walkways	Gary Moore	MCA	5	F
16	12	Hallelujah	Milk & Honey	Polydor	4	F L
17	-	Love You Inside Out	Bee Gees	RSO	3 (1)	
18	-	Boys Keep Swingin'	David Bowie	RCA	6	
19	-	Roxanne	Police	A&M	5 (32)	F
20	2	Cool For Cats	Squeeze	A&M	7	

June 1979

This Mnth	Prev Mnth	Title	Artist	Label	Wks (US 20 Pos)	
1	10	Dance Away	Roxy Music	Polydor	10 (44)	
2	12	Sunday Girl	Blondie	Chrysalis	8	
3	-	Boogie Wonderland	Earth, Wind & Fire With The Emotions	CBS	7 (6)	
4	-	Ring My Bell	Anita Ward	TK	7 (1)	F L
5	-	Ain't No Stoppin' Us Now	McFadden & Whitehead	Philly Int.	6 (13)	F L
6	-	Theme From The Deer Hunter (Cavatina)	Shadows	EMI	6	
7	-	Are 'Friends' Electric	Tubeway Army	Beggars Banquet	10	F L
8	-	Shine A Little Love	Electric Light Orchestra	Jet	6 (8)	
9	6	Reunited	Peaches & Herb	CBS	7 (1)	F L
10	-	Up The Junction	Squeeze	A&M	6	
11	-	We Are Family	Sister Sledge	Atlantic	4 (2)	
12	2	Pop Muzik	M	MCA	9 (1)	F
13	-	The Lone Ranger	Quantum Jump	Electric	5	F L
14	-	Hot Stuff	Donna Summer	Casablanca	4 (1)	
15	18	Boys Keep Swingin'	David Bowie	RCA	6	
16	-	H.A.P.P.Y. Radio	Edwin Starr	RCA	5 (79)	L
17	4	Does Your Mother Know	Abba	Epic	6 (19)	
18	-	Masquerade	Skids	Virgin	4	
19	15	Parisienne Walkways	Gary Moore	MCA	5	F
20	-	Night Owl	Gerry Rafferty	UA	5	L

◆ As the Sex Pistols clicked with Eddie Cochran's 'Something Else', German-based Eruption charted with a revival of another lesser known late 1950s song, Neil Sedaka's 'One Way Ticket'.

◆ Art Garfunkel's 'Bright Eyes', from the animated film *Watership Down,* topped the UK chart, selling over a million copies. Surprisingly it failed to chart in his homeland.

◆ For the first time in 16 years The Shadows had two successive Top 10 hits, 'Don't Cry For Me Argentina' and 'Theme From The Deer Hunter'.

July 1979

This Mnth	Prev Mnth	Title	Artist	Label	Wks	(US 20 Pos)	
1	7	Are 'Friends' Electric		...quet	10		F L
2	-	Silly Games			6		F L
3	-	C'mon Everybody			5		L
4	-	Light My Fire-137 Disco Hea... (Medley)	A...	...ntic	5	(69)	
5	10	Up The Junction	Squee...	A&M	6		
6	20	Night Owl	Gerry Rafferty	UA	5		L
7	-	Lady Lynda	Beach Boys	Caribou	4		
8	-	Good Times	Chic	Atlantic	5	(1)	
9	-	Wanted	Dooleys	GTO	7		
10	-	Girls Talk	Dave Edmunds	Swansong	5	(65)	
11	4	Ring My Bell	Anita Ward	Tk	7	(1)	F L
12	-	Babylon's Burning	Ruts	Virgin	4		F L
13	-	I Don't Like Mondays	Boomtown Rats	Ensign	9	(73)	
14	13	The Lone Ranger	Quantum Jump	Electric	5		F L
15	-	Living On The Front Line	Eddy Grant	Ensign	4		F
16	-	Breakfast In America	Supertramp	A&M	4	(62)	L
17	-	Maybe	Thom Pace	RSO	4		F L
18	-	Born To Be Alive	Patrick Hernandez	GEM	5	(16)	F L
19	-	My Sharona	Knack	Capitol	3		F L
20	-	Do Anything You Want To	Thin Lizzy	Vertigo	3		

(Handwritten annotations overlaying part of this chart: "JONATHAN RICHMAN & THE MODERN LOVERS", "SAD", "CAFE", "TUBEWAY ARMY", "HUDSON FORD", "JONATHAN", "SMOKIE")

August 1979

This Mnth	Prev Mnth	Title	Artist	Label	Wks	(US 20 Pos)	
1	13	I Don't Like Mondays	Boomtown Rats	Ensign	9	(73)	
2	-	We Don't Talk Anymore	Cliff Richard	EMI	10	(7)	
3	-	Angel Eyes/Voulez Vous	Abba	Epic	6	(64)	
4	-	Can't Stand Losing You	Police	A&M	6		
5	9	Wanted	Dooleys	GTO	7		
6	-	Reasons To Be Cheerful (Part 3)	Ian Dury & The Blockheads	Stiff	5		L
7	-	Hersham Boys	Sham 69	Polydor	4		L
8	-	After The Love Has Gone	Earth, Wind & Fire	CBS	6	2)	
9	-	The Diary Of Horace Wimp	Electric Light Orchestra	Jet	5		
10	-	Beat The Clock	Sparks	Virgin	4		L
11	10	Girls Talk	Dave Edmunds	Swansong	5	(65)	
12	-	Duke Of Earl	Darts	Magnet	6		
13	-	Bang Bang	B.A. Robertson	Asylum	7		F
14	18	Born To Be Alive	Patrick Hernandez	GEM	5	(16)	F L
15	19	My Sharona	Knack	Capitol	3		F L
16	-	Gangsters	Specials	2 Tone	6		F
17	16	Breakfast In America	Supertramp	A&M	4	(62)	L
18	-	Angel Eyes	Roxy Music	Polydor	7		
19	2	Silly Games	Janet Kay	Scope	6		F L
20	1	Are 'Friends' Electric	Tubeway Army	Beggars Banquet	10		F L

◆ West Indian sounds continued to gain popularity thanks in part to ska-based 2-Tone music, whose foremost purveyors, The Specials and Madness, debuted on the British chart.

◆ *Rolling Stone* called videotapes "The newest selling tool in rock", citing David Bowie's 'Boys Keep Swinging' and Queen's 'Bohemian Rhapsody' as good examples.

1979

This Mnth	Prev Mnth	Title	Artist	Label	Wks	(US 20 Pos)	
1	2	We Don't Talk Anymore	Cliff Richard	EMI	10	(7)	
2	-	Cars	Gary Numan	Beggars Banquet	8	(9)	F
3	13	Bang Bang	B.A. Robertson	Asylum	7		F
4	-	Street Life	Crusaders	MCA	6	(36)	F L
5	-	Don't Bring Me Down	Electric Light Orchestra	Jet	6	(4)	
6	18	Angel Eyes	Roxy Music	Polydor	7		
7	-	If I Said You Had A Beautiful Body, Would You Hold It Against Me	Bellamy Brothers	Warner	7	(39)	L
8	-	Just When I Needed You Most	Randy Vanwarmer	Bearsville	5	(4)	F L
9	-	Love's Gotta Hold On Me	Dollar	Carrere	6		
10	-	Money	Flying Lizards	Virgin	5	(50)	F L
11	16	Gangsters	Specials	2 Tone	6		F
12	1	I Don't Like Mondays	Boomtown Rats	Ensign	9	(73)	
13	-	Message In A Bottle	Police	A&M	7	(74)	
14	8	After The Love Has Gone	Earth, Wind & Fire	CBS	6	(2)	
15	-	Gotta Go Home/El Lute	Boney M	Atlantic/Hansa	4		L
16	-	Ooh! What A Life	Gibson Brothers	Island	5		F
17	-	Strut Your Funky Stuff	Frantique	Philly Int.	4		F L
18	-	Sail On	Commodores	Motown	4	(4)	
19	12	Duke Of Earl	Darts	Magnet	6		
20	-	Reggae For It Now	Bill Lovelady	Charisma	4		F L

This Mnth	Prev Mnth	Title	Artist	Label	Wks	(US 20 Pos)	
1	-	Video Killed The Radio Star	Buggles	Island	6	(40)	F
2	13	Message In A Bottle	Police	A&M	7	(74)	
3	-	Don't Stop Till You Get Enough	Michael Jackson	Epic	7	(1)	
4	-	Dreaming	Blondie	Chrysalis	6	(27)	
5	-	Whatever You Want	Status Quo	Vertigo	6		
6	-	Since You've Been Gone	Rainbow	Polydor	6	(57)	F
7	-	One Day At A Time	Lena Martell	Pye	8		F L
8	-	Every Day Hurts	Sad Café	RCA	6		F
9	2	Cars	Gary Numan	Beggars Banquet	8	(9)	F
10	7	If I Said You Had A Beautiful Body, Would You Hold It Against Me	Bellamy Brothers	Warner	7	(39)	L
11	-	When You're In Love With A Beautiful Woman	Dr. Hook	Capitol	9	(6)	
12	-	The Chosen Few	Dooleys	GTO	5		L
13	-	Kate Bush On Stage E.P.	Kate Bush	EMI	3		
14	9	Love's Gotta Hold On Me	Dollar	Carrere	6		
15	-	Queen Of Hearts	Dave Edmunds	Swansong	5		L
16	-	O.K. Fred	Erroll Dunkley	Scope	5		F L
17	-	Cruel To Be Kind	Nick Lowe	Radar	5	(12)	L
18	18	Sail On	Commodores	Motown	4	(4)	
19	-	Gimme Gimme Gimme (A Man After Midnight)	Abba	Epic	6		
20	-	Tusk	Fleetwood Mac	Warner	5	(8)	

◆ Disco performer Patrick Hernandez had his sole Top 20 entry with 'Born To Be Alive'. Among the Frenchman's backing vocalists in the early 1980s was a certain Madonna Ciccone.

◆ Almost overnight The Police became teen idols. They had two consecutive chart toppers, 'Message in A Bottle' and 'Walking on The Moon', and the first of five No. 1 LPs, **Regatta De Blanc**.

1979

This Mnth	Prev Mnth	Title	Artist	Label	Wks	(US 20 Pos)
1	11	When You're In Love With A...	Dr. Hook	Capitol	9	(6)
2	7	One Day At A Time	Lena Martell	Pye	8	F L
3	-	Crazy Little Thing Called Love	Queen	EMI	7	(1)
4	19	Gimme Gimme Gimme (A Man After Midnight)	Abba	Epic	6	
5	-	The Eton Rifles	Jam	Polydor	5	
6	8	Every Day Hurts	Sad Café	RCA	6	F
7	-	Still	Commodores	Motown	6	(1)
8	20	Tusk	Fleetwood Mac	Warner	5	(8)
9	-	Gonna Get Along Without You Now	Viola Wills	Ariola/Hansa	5	F L
10	-	On My Radio	Selecter	2 Tone	3	F
11	-	She's In Love With You	Suzi Quatro	RAK	4	(41) L
12	1	Video Killed The Radio Star	Buggles	Island	6	(40) F
13	-	The Sparrow	Ramblers	Decca	5	F L
14	-	No More Tears (Enough Is Enough)	Barbra Streisand/Donna Summer	Casablanca/CBS	8	(1)
15	-	A Message To You Rudy/Nite Klub	Specials	2 Tone	4	
16	12	The Chosen Few	Dooleys	GTO	5	L
17	3	Don't Stop Till You Get Enough	Michael Jackson	Epic	7	(1)
18	16	O.K. Fred	Erroll Dunkley	Scope	5	F L
19	-	Knocked It Off	B.A. Robertson	Asylum	4	
20	-	Ladies Night	Kool & The Gang	Mercury	4	(8) F

This	Prev	Title	Artist	Label	Wks	(US 20 Pos)
1	-	Walking On The Moon	Police	A&M	7	
2	-	Another Brick In The Wall (Pt. 2)	Pink Floyd	Harvest	8	(1) G L
3	14	No More Tears (Enough Is Enough)	Barbra Streisand & D. Summer	Casablanca/CBS	8	(1)
4	-	Que Sera Mi Vida (If You Should Go)	Gibson Brothers	Island	8	
5	-	I Only Want To Be With You	Tourists	Logo	7	(83) F
6	-	Rapper's Delight	Sugarhill Gang	Sugarhill	7	(36) F L
7	1	When You're In Love With A...	Dr. Hook	Capitol	9	(6)
8	-	Confusion/Last Train To London	Electric Light Orchestra	Jet	6	(37)
9	3	Crazy Little Thing Called Love	Queen	EMI	7	(1)
10	-	One Step Beyond	Madness	Stiff	6	
11	-	I Have A Dream	Abba	Epic	6	
12	-	My Simple Heart	Three Degrees	Ariola	6	L
13	-	Day Trip To Bangor (Didn't We Have A Lovely Time)	Fiddler's Dram	Dingles	5	F L
14	-	Complex	Gary Numan	Beggars Banquet	4	
15	-	Off The Wall	Michael Jackson	Epic	4	(10)
16	7	Still	Commodores	Motown	6	(1)
17	-	Wonderful Christmastime	Paul McCartney	Parlophone	5	
18	-	Union City Blue	Blondie	Chrysalis	5	
19	-	Brass In Pocket	Pretenders	Real	9	(14) F
20	5	The Eton Rifles	Jam	Polydor	5	

◆ Among the year's top record deals were Paul McCartney signing to Columbia for $20 million, and Paul Simon's seven album deal with Warner, which was reportedly worth $14 million.

◆ Annie Lennox first charted with The Tourists, 16-year-olds George Michael and Andrew Ridgeley formed a group and The Buggles warned that 'Video Killed The Radio Star'.

1980

This Mnth	Prev Mnth	Title	Artist	Label	Wks 20	(US Pos)	
1	19	Brass In Pocket	Pretenders	Real	9	(14)	F
2	2	Another Brick In The Wall (Pt. 2)	Pink Floyd	Harvest	8	(1)	G L
3	11	I Have A Dream	Abba	Epic	6		
4	-	Please Don't Go	KC & The Sunshine Band	TK	6	(1)	
5	-	With You I'm Born Again	Billy Preston & Syreeta	Motown	5	(4)	L
6	13	Day Trip To Bangor (Didn't We Have A Lovely Time)	Fiddler's Dram	Dingles	5		F L
7	5	I Only Want To Be With You	Tourists	Logo	7	(83)	F
8	-	My Girl	Madness	Stiff	6		
9	-	Tears Of A Clown/Ranking Full Stop	Beat	2 Tone	7		F
10	-	I'm In The Mood For Dancing	Nolans	Epic	8		F
11	6	Rapper's Delight	Sugarhill Gang	Sugarhill	7	(36)	F L
12	12	My Simple Heart	Three Degrees	Ariola	6		L
13	1	Walking On The Moon	Police	A&M	7		
14	-	Is It Love You're After	Rose Royce	Whitfield	6		
15	-	Green Onions	Booker T. & The M.G.'s	Atlantic	4		L
16	-	London Calling	Clash	CBS	3		
17	-	John I'm Only Danncing (Again)	David Bowie	RCA	5		
18	-	Better Love Next Time	Dr. Hook	Capitol	4	(12)	
19	-	Babe	Styx	A&M	6	(1)	F L
20	17	Wonderful Christmastime	Paul McCartney	Parlophone	5		

This Mnth	Prev Mnth	Title	Artist	Label	Wks 20	(US Pos)	
1	-	Too Much Too Young E.P. (Special AKA Live!)	Specials	2 Tone	6		
2	-	Coward Of The County	Kenny Rogers	UA	8	(3)	
3	10	I'm In The Mood For Dancing	Nolans	Epic	8		F
4	-	Someone's Looking At You	Boomtown Rats	Ensign	5		
5	-	It's Different For Girls	Joe Jackson	A&M	5		
6	8	My Girl	Madness	Stiff	6		
7	19	Babe	Styx	A&M	6	(1)	F L
8	-	Captain Beaky/Wilfred The Weasel	Keith Michel	Polydor	5		F L
9	-	And The Beat Goes On	Whispers	Solar	7	(19)	F
10	-	I Hear You Now	Jon & Vangelis	Polydor	6	(58)	F
11	1	Brass In Pocket	Pretenders	Real	9	(14)	F
12	-	7 Teen	Regents	Rialto	4		F L
13	5	With You I'm Born Again	Billy Preston & Syreeta	Motown	5	(4)	L
14	-	Carrie	Cliff Richard	EMI	6	(34)	
15	15	Green Onions	Booker T. & The M.G.'s	Atlantic	4		L
16	4	Please Don't Go	KC & The Sunshine Band	TK	6	(1)	
17	-	Atomic	Blondie	Chrysalis	6	(39)	
18	-	Rock With You	Michael Jackson	Epic	5	(1)	
19	-	I Can't Stand Up For Falling Down	Elvis Costello	F. Beat	5		
20	-	Living By Numbers	New Muzik	GTO	3		F L

◆ In the week that he was awarded an OBE by the Queen, Cliff Richard had the second US Top 10 entry of his long career with 'We Don't Talk Anymore'.

◆ Among the past hit makers who died as the decade dawned were Mantovani, R&B legends Amos Milburn and Professor Longhair, early rocker Larry Williams and million selling 1950s British balladeer David Whitfield.

March 1980

This Mnth	Prev Mnth	Title	Artist	Label	Wks	(US 20 Pos)	
1	-	Together We Are Beautiful	Fern Kinney	WEA	7		F L
2	-	Take That Look Off Your Face	Marti Webb	Polydor	6		F
3	17	Atomic	Blondie	Chrysalis	6	(39)	
4	-	Games Without Frontiers	Peter Gabriel	Charisma	5	(48)	
5	-	All Night Long	Rainbow	Polydor	6		
6	-	Turning Japanese	Vapors	UA	7	(36)	F L
7	9	And The Beat Goes On	Whispers	Solar	7	(19)	F
8	2	Coward Of The County	Kenny Rogers	UA	8	(3)	
9	14	Carrie	Cliff Richard	EMI	6	(34)	
10	19	I Can't Stand Up For Falling Down	Elvis Costello	F. Beat	5		
11	-	So Lonely	Police	A&M	5		
12	-	Going Underground/Dreams Of Children	Jam	Polydor	6		
13	-	Dance Yourself Dizzy	Liquid Gold	Polo	8		F
14	-	Do That To Me One More Time	Captain & Tennille	Casablanca	4	(1)	F L
15	18	Rock With You	Michael Jackson	Epic	5	(1)	
16	-	Hands Off-She's Mine	Beat	Go Feet	4		
17	-	Working My Way Back To You-Forgive Me, Girl (Medley)	Detroit Spinners	Atlantic	9	(2)	
18	-	So Good To Be Back Home Again	Tourists	Logo	5		L
19	-	Riders In The Sky	Shadows	EMI	4		L
20	-	Cuba/Better Do It Salsa	Gibson Brothers	Island	3	(81)	

April 1980

This Mnth	Prev Mnth	Title	Artist	Label	Wks	(US 20 Pos)	
1	17	Working My Way Back To You	Detroit Spinners	Atlantic	9	(2)	
2	13	Dance Yourself Dizzy	Liquid Gold	Polo	8		F
3	-	King/Food For Thought	UB40	Graduate	7		F
4	-	Sexy Eyes	Dr. Hook	Capitol	6	(5)	L
5	12	Going Underground/Dreams Of Children	Jam	Polydor	6		
6	-	Work Rest & Play (E.P.)	Madness	Stiff	5		
7	-	Poison Ivy	Lambrettas	Rocket	5		F
8	-	Call Me	Blondie	Chrysalis	5	(1)	
9	-	Turn It On Again	Genesis	Charisma	4	(58)	
10	-	January February	Barbara Dickson	Epic	6		
11	6	Turning Japanese	Vapors	UA	7	(36)	F L
12	-	Stomp!	Brothers Johnson	A&M	5	(7)	F L
13	-	Talk Of The Town	Pretenders	Real	4		
14	-	Silver Dream Machine (Pt. 1)	David Essex	Mercury	7		
15	-	Geno	Dexy's Midnight Runners	Late Night Feelings	8		F
16	1	Together We Are Beautiful	Fern Kinney	WEA	7		F L
17	-	Living After Midnight	Judas Priest	CBS	4		
18	-	Don't Push It, Don't Force It	Leon Haywood	20th Century	6	(49)	F L
19	-	Echo Beach	Martha & The Muffins	Dindisc	4		F L
20	-	Coming Up	Paul McCartney	Parlophone	5	(1)	

◆ The first indie LP chart in the UK showed **Dirk Wears White Sox** by Adam & The Ants at No. 1.

◆ Mirror In The Bathroom' by 2-Tone act The Beat, was the UK's first digitally recorded hit. Another first was The Police's 'Six Pack' – six separate singles sold as a package – which reached the Top 20.

1980

This Mnth	Prev Mnth	Title	Artist	Label	Wks	(US 20 Pos)	
1	15	Geno	Dexy's Midnight Runners	Late Night...	8		F
2	-	What's Another Year	Johnny Logan	Epic	6		F
3	-	No Doubt About It	Hot Chocolate	RAK	8		
4	20	Coming Up	Paul McCartney	Parlophone	5	(1)	
5	-	Mirror In The Bathroom	Beat	Go Feet	5		
6	-	She's Out Of My Life	Michael Jackson	Epic	5	(10)	
7	14	Silver Dream Machine (Pt. 1)	David Essex	Mercury	7		
8	-	Hold On To My Love	Jimmy Ruffin	RSO	5	(10)	L
9	8	Call Me	Blondie	Chrysalis	5	(1)	
10	-	I Shoulda Loved Ya	Narada Michael Walden	Atlantic	5	(66)	F
11	-	The Groove	Rodney Franklin	CBS	4		F L
12	-	Toccata	Sky	Ariola	4		F L
13	-	Theme From M*A*S*H (Suicide Is Painless)	Mash	CBS	7		F L
14	-	My Perfect Cousin	Undertones	Sire	3		
15	-	Over You	Roxy Music	Polydor	7	(80)	
16	-	Don't Make Waves	Nolans	Epic	4		
17	-	We Are Glass	Gary Numan	Beggars Banquet	5		
18	-	Check Out The Groove	Bobby Thurston	Epic	3		F L
19	3	King/Food For Thought	UB40	Graduate	7		F
20	-	The Golden Years (E.P.)	Motorhead	Bronze	3		F

This Mnth	Prev Mnth	Title	Artist	Label	Wks	(US 20 Pos)	
1	-	Crying	Don McLean	EMI	9	(5)	
2	13	Theme From M*A*S*H (Suicide...)	Mash	CBS	7		F L
3	-	Funkytown	Lipps Inc.	Casablanca	8	(1)	F L
4	3	No Doubt About It	Hot Chocolate	Rak	8		
5	-	Back Together Again	Roberta Flack & Donny Hathaway	Atlantic	7	(56)	
6	-	Rat Race/Rude Buoys Outa Jail	Specials	2 Tone	6		
7	-	Let's Get Serious	Jermaine Jackson	Motown	5	(9)	F
8	15	Over You	Roxy Music	Polydor	7	(80)	
9	-	You Gave Me Love	Crown Heights Affair	De-Lite	6		F L
10	-	Everybody's Got To Learn Sometime	Korgis	Rialto	6	(18)	L
11	-	Behind The Groove	Teena Marie	Motown	5		F L
12	17	We Are Glass	Gary Numan	Beggars Banquet	5		
13	6	She's Out Of My Life	Michael Jackson	Epic	5	(10)	
14	-	Messages	Orchestral Manoeuvres In The Dark	Dindisc	4		F
15	-	Midnite Dynamos	Matchbox	Magnet	5		
16	-	Substitute	Liquid Gold	Polo	4		L
17	-	Let's Go Round Again Pt. 1	Average White Band	RCA	5	(53)	L
18	-	Breaking The Law	Judas Priest	CBS	3		L
19	-	D-a-a-ance	Lambrettas	Rocket	3		L
20	-	Simon Templar/Two Pints Of Lager And A Packet Of Crisps Please	Splodgenessabounds	Deram	4		F L

◆ American records creating interest in Britain included dance tracks from Crown Heights Affair and Teena Marie, a duet by Robert Flack & the late Donny Hathaway, and the chart topping ten-year-old TV series theme *M*A*S*H*.

◆ Two of the 1980s' most successful acts made their Top 20 debuts. UB40 scored with 'King' (a tribute to Martin Luther King) and Orchestral Manoeuvres In The Dark charted with 'Messages'.

July 1980

This Mnth	Prev Mnth	Title	Artist	Label	Wks	(US 20 Pos)	
1	-	Xanadu	Olivia Newton-John/ Electric Light Orchestra	Jet	8	(8)	
2	-	Jump To The Beat	Stacy Lattisaw	Atlantic	7		F L
3	-	Use It Up And Wear It Out	Odyssey	RCA	8		
4	1	Crying	Don McLean	EMI	9	(5)	
5	-	Cupid-I've Loved You For A Long Time (Medley)	Detroit Spinners	Atlantic	6	(4)	L
6	-	My Way Of Thinking/I Think It's Going To Rain	UB40	Graduate	6		
7	-	Could You Be Loved	Bob Marley & The Wailers	Island	6		
8	3	Funkytown	Lipps Inc.	Casablanca	8	(1)	F L
9	-	Waterfalls	Paul McCartney	Parlophone	5		
10	10	Everybody's Got To Learn Sometime	Korgis	Rialto	6	(18)	L
11	-	Babooshka	Kate Bush	EMI	6		
12	20	Simon Templar/Two Pints Of Lager...	Splodgenessabounds	Deram	4		F L
13	-	To Be Or Not To Be	B.A. Robertson	Asylum	3		
14	-	More Than I Can Say	Leo Sayer	Chrysalis	6	(2)	
15	5	Back Together Again	Roberta Flack/Donny Hathaway	Atlantic	7	(56)	
16	-	747 (Strangers In The Night)	Saxon	Carrere	4		
17	11	Behind The Groove	Teena Marie	Motown	5		F L
18	-	Emotional Rescue	Rolling Stones	Rolling Stone	5	(3)	
19	-	Let's Hang On	Darts	Magnet	4		L
20	-	Love Will Tear Us Apart	Joy Division	Factory	4		F

August 1980

This Mnth	Prev Mnth	Title	Artist	Label	Wks	(US 20 Pos)	
1	-	The Winner Takes It All	Abba	Epic	7	(8)	
2	-	Upside Down	Diana Ross	Motown	7	(1)	
3	-	9 to 5 (A.K.A. Morning Train)	Sheena Easton	EMI	9	(1)	F
4	-	Oops Upside Your Head	Gap Band	Mercury	8		F
5	-	Ashes To Ashes	David Bowie	RCA	7		
6	14	More Than I Can Say	Leo Sayer	Chrysalis	6	(2)	
7	3	Use It Up And Wear It Out	Odyssey	RCA	8		
8	-	Oh Yeah (On The Radio)	Roxy Music	Polydor	5		
9	-	Give Me The Night	George Benson	Warner	5	(4)	F
10	11	Babooshka	Kate Bush	EMI	6		
11	-	Start	Jam	Polydor	6		
12	7	Could You Be Loved	Bob Marley & The Wailers	Island	6		
13	-	Tom Hark	Piranhas	Sire	6		F
14	-	Feels Like I'm In Love	Kelly Marie	Calibre	9		F L
15	-	Funkin' For Jamaica (N.Y.)	Tom Browne	Arista	4		F L
16	1	Xanadu	Olivia Newton-John/E.L.O.	Jet	8	(8)	
17	-	There There My Dear	Dexy's Midnight Runners	Late Night Feelings	5		
18	-	Mariana	Gibson Brothers	Island	3		L
19	-	Lip Up Fatty	Bad Manners	Magnet	4		F
20	-	Sunshine Of Your Smile	Mike Berry	Polydor	6		L

◆ Critically acclaimed Manchester group Joy Division's 'Love Will Tear Us Apart' reached the Top 20 shortly after the group's leader Ian Curtis had committed suicide.

◆ Scottish singer Sheena Easton found herself with two singles in the Top 10 after being the subject of the TV series *The Big Time*. She went on to win the Grammy for Best New Artist of 1981.

1980

This Mnth	Prev Mnth	Title	Artist	Label	Wks	(US 20 Pos)
1	14	Feels Like I'm In Love	Kelly Marie	Calibre	9	F L
2	11	Start	Jam	Polydor	6	
3	-	Eighth Day	Hazel O'Connor	A&M	6	F
4	5	Ashes To Ashes	David Bowie	RCA	7	
5	-	One Day I'll Fly Away	Randy Crawford	Warner	6	F
6	-	It's Only Love/Beyond The Reef	Elvis Presley	RCA	6	(51) L
7	3	9 to 5	Sheena Easton	EMI	9	(1) F
8	-	Dreaming	Cliff Richard	EMI	6	(10)
9	-	Modern Girl	Sheena Easton	EMI	6	(18)
10	-	Master Blaster (Jammin')	Stevie Wonder	Motown	6	(5)
11	20	Sunshine Of Your Smile	Mike Berry	Polydor	6	L
12	13	Tom Hark	Piranhas	Sire	6	F
13	-	Another One Bites The Dust	Queen	EMI	5	(1)
14	-	I Die: You Die	Gary Numan	Beggars Banquet	4	
15	-	Can't Stop The Music	Village People	Mercury	4	L
16	-	Bank Robber	Clash	CBS	4	
17	-	Don't Stand So Close To Me	Police	A&M	7	(10)
18	-	It's Still Rock And Roll To Me	Billy Joel	CBS	6	(1)
19	1	The Winner Takes It All	Abba	Epic	7	(8)
20	-	Baggy Trousers	Madness	Stiff	7	

This Mnth	Prev Mnth	Title	Artist	Label	Wks	(US 20 Pos)
1	17	Don't Stand So Close To Me	Police	A&M	7	(10)
2	-	D.I.S.C.O.	Ottawan	Carrere	7	F
3	20	Baggy Trousers	Madness	Stiff	7	
4	10	Master Blaster (Jammin')	Stevie Wonder	Motown	6	(5)
5	-	My Old Piano	Diana Ross	Motown	5	
6	-	If You're Lookin' For A Way Out	Odyssey	RCA	8	
7	-	Et Les Oiseaux Chantaient (And The Birds Were Singing)	Sweet People	Polydor	4	F L
8	-	Amigo	Black Slate	Ensign	4	F L
9	-	What You're Proposing	Status Quo	Vertigo	4	
10	-	Woman In Love	Barbra Streisand	CBS	8	(1)
11	-	When You Ask About Love	Matchbox	Magnet	7	
12	5	One Day I'll Fly Away	Randy Crawford	Warner	6	F
13	-	Killer On The Loose	Thin Lizzy	Vertigo	4	
14	1	Feels Like I'm In Love	Kelly Marie	Calibre	9	F L
15	-	Searching	Change	WEA	3	
16	-	Gotta Pull Myself Together	Nolans	Epic	5	
17	13	Another One Bites The Dust	Queen	EMI	5	(1)
18	-	Casanova	Coffee	De-Lite	4	F L
19	-	Stereotype/International Jet Set	Specials	2 Tone	1	
20	6	It's Only Love/Beyond The Reef	Elvis Presley	RCA	6	(51) L

◆ On the album charts **Emotional Rescue** gave The Rolling Stones their only transatlantic No. 1 of the decade and singer/songwriter Kate Bush's **Never For Ever** became the first LP by a female British singer to head the UK charts. The Police had the year's top UK single and album with the Grammy winning 'Don't Stand So Close To Me' and **Zenyatta Mondatta**, both of which entered at No. 1.

◆ Abba's 'Super Trooper' gave them their ninth and last chart topper, as the album of the same name chalked up over a million British advance orders.

November 1980

This Mnth	Prev Mnth	Title	Artist	Label	Wks	(US 20 Pos)	
1	10	Woman In Love	Barbra Streisand	CBS	8	(1)	
2	-	The Tide Is High	Blondie	Chrysalis	9	(1)	
3	-	Special Brew	Bad Manners	Magnet	6		
4	-	Fashion	David Bowie	RCA	6	(70)	
5	-	Enola Gay	OMD	Dindisc	7		
6	-	I Could Be So Good For You	Dennis Waterman	EMI	6		F L
7	-	Dog Eat Dog	Adam & The Ants	CBS	6		F
8	-	Super Trouper	Abba	Epic	9	(45)	
9	-	Never Knew Love Like This Before	Stephanie Mills	20th Century	7	(6)	F L
10	11	When You Ask About Love	Matchbox	Magnet	7		
11	6	If You're Lookin' For A Way Out	Odyssey	RCA	8		
12	9	What You're Proposing	Status Quo	Vertigo	4		
13	2	D.I.S.C.O.	Ottawan	Carrere	7		F
14	-	The Earth Dies Screaming/ Dream A Lie	UB40	Graduate	5		
15	16	Gotta Pull Myself Together	Nolans	Epic	5		
16	-	Celebration	Kool & The Gang	De-Lite	5	(1)	
17	3	Baggy Trousers	Madness	Stiff	7		
18	-	(Just Like) Starting Over	John Lennon	Geffen	10	(1)	
19	-	All Out Of Love	Air Supply	Arista	4	(2)	F L
20	-	The Same Old Scene	Roxy Music	Polydor	3		

December 1980

This Mnth	Prev Mnth	Title	Artist	Label	Wks	(US 20 Pos)	
1	8	Super Trouper	Abba	Epic	9	(45)	
2	-	There's No One Quite Like Grandma	St. Winifred's School Choir	MFP	6		F L
3	-	Embarrassment	Madness	Stiff	8		
4	-	Stop The Cavalry	Jona Lewie	Stiff	8		L
5	-	Banana Republic	Boomtown Rats	Ensign	7		L
6	18	(Just Like) Starting Over	John Lennon	Geffen	10	(1)	
7	-	To Cut A Long Story Short	Spandau Ballet	Reformation	8		F
8	-	De Do Do Do, De Da Da Da	Police	A&M	6	(10)	
9	2	The Tide Is High	Blondie	Chrysalis	9	(1)	
10	-	Do You Feel My Love	Eddy Grant	Ensign	4		
11	-	Runaway Boys	Stray Cats	Arista	6		F
12	-	Antmusic	Adam & The Ants	CBS	12		
13	16	Celebration	Kool & The Gang	De-Lite	5	(1)	
14	-	Lady	Kenny Rogers	UA	5	(1)	
15	9	Never Knew Love Like This Before	Stephanie Mills	20th Century	7	(6)	F L
16	6	I Could Be So Good For You	Dennis Waterman	EMI	6		F L
17	-	Lies/Don't Drive My Car	Status Quo	Vertigo	6		
18	-	Happy Xmas (War Is Over)	John & Yoko & The Plastic Ono Band	Apple	5		
19	-	Flash	Queen	EMI	8	(42)	
20	-	Rock 'n' Roll Ain't Noise Pollution	AC/DC	Atlantic	3		F

◆ Fleetwood Mac followed the record breaking **Rumours** album with **Tusk,** which reportedly cost over $1 million to record

◆ Queen notched up their second US chart topper of the year when 'Another One Bites The Dust' followed in the footsteps of their retro-rockabilly track 'Crazy Little Thing Called Love'.

1981

This Mnth	Prev Mnth	Title	Artist	Label	Wks	20	(US Pos)	
1	-	Imagine	John Lennon	Apple	9			
2	12	Antmusic	Adam & The Ants	CBS	12			
3	18	Happy Xmas (War Is Over)	John & Yoko & The Plastic Ono Band	Apple	5			
4	6	(Just Like) Starting Over	John Lennon	Geffen	10		(1)	
5	4	Stop The Cavalry	Jona Lewie	Stiff	8			L
6	-	Do Nothing/Maggie's Farm	Specials	2 Tone	5			
7	19	Flash	Queen	EMI	8		(42)	
8	8	De Do Do Do, De Da Da Da	Police	A&M	6		(10)	
9	-	Woman	John Lennon	Geffen	7		(2)	
10	-	Too Nice To Talk To	Beat	Go Feet	4			
11	2	There's No One Quite Like Grandma	St. Winifred's School Choir	MFP	6			F L
12	-	In The Air Tonight	Phil Collins	Virgin	6		(19)	F
13	-	I Am The Beat	Look	MCA	5			F L
14	-	Rabbit	Chas & Dave	Rockney	6			
15	3	Embarrassment	Madness	Stiff	8			
16	1	Super Trouper	Abba	Epic	9		(45)	
17	-	Don't Stop The Music	Yarbrough & Peoples	Mercury	6		(19)	F L
18	17	Lies/Don't Drive My Car	Status Quo	Vertigo	6			
19	11	Runaway Boys	Stray Cats	Arista	6			F
20	-	I Ain't Gonna Stand For It	Stevie Wonder	Motown	4		(11)	

This Mnth	Prev Mnth	Title	Artist	Label	Wks	20	(US Pos)	
1	9	Woman	John Lennon	Geffen	7		(2)	
2	-	Vienna	Ultravox	Chrysalis	10			F
3	12	In The Air Tonight	Phil Collins	Virgin	6		(19)	F
4	-	I Surrender	Rainbow	Polydor	6			
5	-	Shaddup You Face	Joe Dolce Music Theatre	Epic	6		(53)	F L
6	-	Return Of The Los Palmas 7	Madness	Stiff	7			
7	-	Oldest Swinger In Town	Fred Wedlock	Rocket	5			F L
8	-	Romeo And Juliet	Dire Straits	Vertigo	6			
9	-	Rapture	Blondie	Chrysalis	5		(1)	
10	1	Imagine	John Lennon	Apple	9			
11	-	Fade To Grey	Visage	Polydor	5			F
12	2	Antmusic	Adam & The Ants	CBS	12			
13	-	Rock This Town	Stray Cats	Arista	5		(9)	
14	17	Don't Stop The Music	Yarbrough & Peoples	Mercury	6		(19)	F L
15	-	We'll Bring The House Down	Slade	Cheapskate	4			
16	-	St. Valentine's Day Massacre E.P.	Motorhead & Girlschool	Bronze	5			
17	-	(Do) The Hucklebuck	Coast To Coast	Polydor	8			F L
18	-	Young Parisians	Adam & The Ants	Decca	4			
19	-	Message Of Love	Pretenders	Real	3			
20	-	Jealous Guy	Roxy Music	EG	7			

◆ In January, the late John Lennon held three of the Top 4 places in the UK chart. His recordings of 'Woman' and the re-released 'Imagine' hit the top, as did Roxy Music's interpretation of his composition 'Jealous Guy'.

◆ The rockabilly revival continued with American trio The Stray Cats and Welsh rocker Shakin' Stevens leading the way. Interest was also growing in Brit-funk, thanks to Freeez and Beggar & Co.

March 1981

This Mnth	Prev Mnth	Title	Artist	Label	Wks	(US 20 Pos)	
1	20	Jealous Guy	Roxy Music	EG	7		
2	-	Kings Of The Wild Frontier	Adam & The Ants	CBS	6		
3	17	(Do) The Hucklebuck	Coast To Coast	Polydor	8		F L
4	2	Vienna	Ultravox	Chrysalis	10		F
5	-	Kids In America	Kim Wilde	RAK	8	(25)	F
6	-	This Ole House	Shakin' Stevens	Epic	9		
7	5	Shaddup You Face	Joe Dolce Music Theatre	Epic	6	(53)	F L
8	-	Four From Toyah E.P.	Toyah	Safari	7		F
9	-	Reward	Teardrop Explodes	Vertigo	4		F
10	-	Southern Freeez	Freeez	Beggars Banquet	4		F
11	16	St. Valentine's Day Massacre E.P.	Motorhead & Girlschool	Bronze	5		
12	-	Something 'Bout You Baby I Like	Status Quo	Vertigo	4		
13	-	You Better You Bet	Who	Polydor	4	(18)	L
14	4	I Surrender	Rainbow	Polydor	6		
15	-	Once In A Lifetime	Talking Heads	Sire	3	(91)	F
16	-	Lately	Stevie Wonder	Motown	7	(64)	
17	-	Star	Kiki Dee	Ariola	4		L
18	6	Return Of The Los Palmas 7	Madness	Stiff	7		
19	-	(Somebody) Help Me Out	Beggar & Co	Ensign	3		F L
20	-	I Missed Again	Phil Collins	Virgin	3	(19)	

April 1981

This Mnth	Prev Mnth	Title	Artist	Label	Wks	(US 20 Pos)	
1	6	This Ole House	Shakin' Stevens	Epic	9		
2	-	Making Your Mind Up	Bucks Fizz	RCA	8		F
3	16	Lately	Stevie Wonder	Motown	7	(64)	
4	-	Einstein A Go-Go	Landscape	RCA	7		F L
5	5	Kids In America	Kim Wilde	RAK	8	(25)	F
6	-	Intuition	Linx	Chrysalis	6		
7	-	It's A Love Thing	Whispers	Solar	7	(28)	L
8	-	Chi Mai Theme (From The TV Series The Life And Times Of David Lloyd George)	Ennio Morricone	BBC	8		F L
9	-	Good Thing Going (We've Got A Good Thing Going)	Sugar Minott	RCA	6		F L
10	-	Capstick Comes Home/ Sheffield Grinder	Tony Capstick	Dingles	4		F L
11	-	Night Games	Graham Bonnett	Vertigo	5		F L
12	-	Can You Feel It	Jacksons	Epic	6	(77)	
13	-	D-Days	Hazel O'Connor	Albion	5		
14	8	Four From Toyah E.P.	Toyah	Safari	7		F
15	-	Attention To Me	Nolans	Epic	7		
16	-	What Becomes Of The Broken Hearted	Dave Stewart & Colin Blunstone	Stiff	5		F
17	1	Jealous Guy	Roxy Music	Eg	7		
18	3	(Do) The Hucklebuck	Coast To Coast	Polydor	8		F L
19	-	Just A Feeling	Bad Manners	Magnet	5		
20	-	Mind Of A Toy	Visage	Polydor	3		

◆ Major new artists on the UK charts included Phil Collins (whose first solo album Face Value entered at No. 1), 'new romantics' Spandau Ballet and Duran Duran, Kim Wilde and influential bands New Order and Ultravox.

◆ The first demonstration of the CD took place in Europe. The revolutionary digital playback system for music, which utilised laser beam technology, was to vinyl as the most popular system of carrying recorded sound.

1981

This Mnth	Prev Mnth	Title	Artist	Label	Wks	(US 20 Pos)	
1	-	Stars On 45	Starsound	CBS	8	(1)	F
2	-	Stand And Deliver	Adam & The Ants	CBS	8		
3	-	You Drive Me Crazy	Shakin' Stevens	Epic	8		
4	-	Grey Day	Madness	Stiff	6		
5	8	Chi Mai Theme (From The TV Series The Life And Times Of David Lloyd George)	Ennio Morricone	BBC	8		F L
6	2	Making Your Mind Up	Bucks Fizz	RCA	8		F
7	-	Chequered Love	Kim Wilde	RAK	5		
8	-	Ossie's Dream (Spurs Are On Their Way To Wembley)	Tottenham Hotspur F.A. Cup Final Squad	Rockney	4		F
9	-	Swords Of A Thousand Men	Ten Pole Tudor	Stiff	6		F
10	-	Keep On Loving You	REO Speedwagon	Epic	5	(1)	F
11	9	Good Thing Going (We've Got A Good Thing Going)	Sugar Minott	RCA	6		F L
12	12	Can You Feel It	Jacksons	Epic	6	(77)	
13	15	Attention To Me	Nolans	Epic	7		
14	-	Musclebound/Glow	Spandau Ballet	Reformation	5		
15	-	Stray Cat Strut	Stray Cats	Arista	4	(3)	L
16	-	Only Crying	Keith Marshall	Arrival	4		F L
17	11	Night Games	Graham Bonnett	Vertigo	5		F L
18	-	Bette Davis Eyes	Kim Carnes	Emi America	5	(1)	F L
19	-	I Want To Be Free	Toyah	Safari	6		
20	7	It's A Love Thing	Whispers	Solar	7	(28)	L

1	-	Being With You	Smokey Robinson	Motown	7	(2)	F L
2	-	One Day In Your Life	Michael Jackson	Motown	8	(55)	
3	-	More Than In Love	Kate Robbins & Beyond	RCA	6		F L
4	-	How 'Bout Us	Champaign	CBS	7	(12)	F L
5	2	Stand And Deliver	Adam & The Ants	CBS	8		
6	3	You Drive Me Crazy	Shakin' Stevens	Epic	8		
7	-	Will You	Hazel O'Connor	A&M	5		L
8	-	Going Back To My Roots	Odyssey	RCA	7		
9	-	Funeral Pyre	Jam	Polydor	3		
10	19	I Want To Be Free	Toyah	Safari	6		
11	-	Teddy Bear	Red Sovine	Starday	4	(40)	F L
12	-	All Stood Still	Ultravox	Chrysalis	5		
13	-	Ain't No Stoppin'	Enigma	Creole	5		F
14	1	Stars On 45	Starsound	CBS	8	(1)	F
15	9	Swords Of A Thousand Men	Ten Pole Tudor	Stiff	6		F
16	7	Chequered Love	Kim Wilde	RAK	5		
17	-	Memory	Elaine Paige	Polydor	6		F
18	-	Chariots Of Fire - Titles	Vangelis	Polydor	3	(1)	F L
19	18	Bette Davis Eyes	Kim Carnes	EMI America	5	(1)	F L
20	-	Ghost Town	Specials	2 Tone	8		

◆ A re-issue of his 1975 recording 'One Day In Your Life', which had previously failed to take Michael Jackson into the US Top 40, gave him his first British chart topper.

◆ Toni Basil's Word of Mouth (which included the future No. 1 'Mickey') claimed to be the first album to be simultaneously released on record and video.

◆ The first US shows by Britain's hottest act Adam & The Ants were successful, but American sales were minimal. In the UK their seventh chart entry in nine months, 'Stand And Deliver', came in at No. 1.

1981

This Mnth	Prev Mnth	Title	Artist	Label	Wks	(US 20 Pos)	
1	20	Ghost Town	Specials	2 Tone	8		
2	-	Can Can	Bad Manners	Magnet	8		
3	2	One Day In Your Life	Michael Jackson	Motown	8	(55)	
4	-	Body Talk	Imagination	R&B	9		F
5	-	Stars On 45 (Vol 2)	Starsound	CBS	6		
6	8	Going Back To My Roots	Odyssey	RCA	7		
7	-	Wordy Rappinghood	Tom Tom Club	Island	5		F L
8	-	No Woman No Cry	Bob Marley & The Wailers	Island	6		
9	17	Memory	Elaine Paige	Polydor	6		F
10	-	Motorhead Live	Motorhead	Bronze	4		L
11	-	You Might Need Somebody	Randy Crawford	Warner	5		
12	1	Being With You	Smokey Robinson	Motown	7	(2)	F L
13	-	Dancing On The Floor (Hooked On Love)	Third World	CBS	6		L
14	-	Razzamatazz	Quincy Jones	A&M	3		L
15	-	Chant No. 1 (I Don't Need This Pressure On)	Spandau Ballet	Reformation	7		
16	-	Piece Of The Action	Bucks Fizz	RCA	5		
17	-	Lay All Your Love On Me	Abba	Epic	4		
18	3	More Than In Love	Kate Robbins & Beyond	RCA	6		F L
19	-	Sat In Your Lap	Kate Bush	EMI	4		
20	11	Teddy Bear	Red Sovine	Starday	4	(40)	F L

This Mnth	Prev Mnth	Title	Artist	Label	Wks	(US 20 Pos)	
1	-	Green Door	Shakin' Stevens	Epic	6		
2	-	Hooked On Classics	Royal Philharmonic Orchestra	RCA	7	(10)	F L
3	-	Happy Birthday	Stevie Wonder	Motown	7		
4	15	Chant No. 1 (I Don't Need This Pressure On)	Spandau Ballet	Reformation	7		
5	-	Back To The Sixties	Tight Fit	Jive	6	(89)	F
6	-	Girls On Film	Duran Duran	EMI	6		
7	-	Love Action (I Believe In Love)	Human League	Virgin	7		
8	-	Hold On Tight	Electric Light Orchestra	Jet	9	(10)	
9	1	Ghost Town	Specials	2 Tone	8		
10	-	For Your Eyes Only	Sheena Easton	EMI	5	(4)	
11	-	Japanese Boy	Aneka	Hansa	7		F L
12	-	Walk Right Now	Jacksons	Epic	5	(73)	
13	2	Can Can	Bad Manners	Magnet	8		
14	-	Tainted Love	Soft Cell	Some Bizzare	9	(8)	F
15	-	Caribbean Disco	Lobo	Polydor	5		F L
16	-	Water On Glass/Boys	Kim Wilde	RAK	4		
17	5	Stars On 45 (Vol 2)	Starsound	CBS	6		
18	-	New Life	Depeche Mode	Mute	6		F
19	-	Beach Boy Gold	Gidea Park	Sonet	4		F L
20	13	Dancing On The Floor (Hooked On Love)	Third World	CBS	6		L

◆ When Soft Cell's revival of the northern soul favourite 'Tainted Love' was re-issued it became Britain's Top Single of 1981. It also went on to spend a record 43 weeks in the US Hot 100.

◆ Meat Loaf's long-awaited album, **Dead Ringer**, was the first LP by an American artist to enter the British chart at No. 1.

◆ The most successful purveyors of 2-Tone music, The Specials, topped the chart with their last single, 'Ghost Town'. It was their seventh Top 10 entry in two years.

1981

This Mnth	Prev Mnth	Title	Artist	Label	Wks	(US 20 Pos)	
1	14	Tainted Love	Soft Cell	Some Bizzare	9	(8)	F
2	11	Japanese Boy	Aneka	Hansa	7		F L
3	-	Prince Charming	Adam & The Ants	CBS	7		
4	-	Wired For Sound	Cliff Richard	EMI	6	(71)	
5	8	Hold On Tight	Electric Light Orchestra	Jet	9	(10)	
6	7	Love Action (I Believe In Love)	Human League	Virgin	7		
7	-	Souvenir	Orchestral Manoeuvres In The Dark	Dindisc	6		
8	-	Hands Up (Give Me Your Heart)	Ottawan	Carrere	8		L
9	-	Start Me Up	Rolling Stones	Rolling Stone	4	(2)	
10	-	One In Ten	UB40	Dep International	5		
11	-	She's Got Claws	Gary Numan	Beggars Banquet	4		
12	-	Pretend	Alvin Stardust	Stiff	6		
13	-	Slow Hand	Pointer Sisters	Planet	5	(2)	F
14	-	Abacab	Genesis	Charisma	4	(26)	
15	2	Hooked On Classics	Royal Philharmonic Orchestra	RCA	7	(10)	F L
16	-	Endless Love	Diana Ross & Lionel Richie	Motown	6	(1)	
17	-	Everybody Salsa	Modern Romance	WEA	3		F
18	-	The Thin Wall	Ultravox	Chrysalis	4		
19	15	Caribbean Disco	Lobo	Polydor	5		F L
20	1	Green Door	Shakin' Stevens	Epic	6		

This Mnth	Prev Mnth	Title	Artist	Label	Wks	(US 20 Pos)	
1	-	The Birdie Song (Birdie Dance)	Tweets	PRT	8		F L
2	-	It's My Party	Dave Stewart & Barbara Gaskin	Broken	8	(72)	L
3	-	Under Your Thumb	Godley & Creme	Polydor	6		F
4	3	Prince Charming	Adam & The Ants	CBS	7		
5	8	Hands Up (Give Me Your Heart)	Ottawan	Carrere	8		L
6	-	Thunder In Mountains	Toyah	Safari	5		
7	-	Invisible Sun	Police	A&M	4		
8	-	Just Can't Get Enough	Depeche Mode	Mute	5		
9	-	Shut Up	Madness	Stiff	5		
10	-	Happy Birthday	Altered Images	Epic	7		F
11	-	O Superman	Laurie Anderson	Warner	4		F L
12	-	Open Your Heart	Human League	Virgin	5		
13	12	Pretend	Alvin Stardust	Stiff	6		
14	16	Endless Love	Diana Ross & Lionel Richie	Motown	6	(1)	
15	-	A Good Year For The Roses	Elvis Costello	F. Beat	6		L
16	-	It's Raining	Shakin' Stevens	Epic	5		
17	-	Absolute Beginners	Jam	Polydor	4		
18	7	Souvenir	Orchestral Manoeuvres In The Dark	Dindisc	6		
19	-	Walkin' In The Sunshine	Bad Manners	Magnet	5		
20	1	Tainted Love	Soft Cell	Some Bizzare	9	(8)	F

◆ The medley craze was at its height; artists scoring in this vein were Tight Fit, Gidea Park, Royal Philharmonic Orchestra and genre pioneers Starsound, who scored a second successive hit. Meanwhile in the USA, a segue single of past hits by The Beach Boys was riding high.

◆ The Rolling Stones' American tour grossed a record $35 million, with each Stone supposedly pocketing $4 million.

November 1981

This Mnth	Prev Mnth	Title	Artist	Label	Wks	(US 20 Pos)	
1	-	Every Little Thing She Does Is Magic	Police	A&M	6	(3)	
2	-	Joan Of Arc	OMD	Dindisc	5		
3	-	When She Was My Girl	Four Tops	Casablanca	5	(11)	
4	-	Under Pressure	Queen & David Bowie	EMI	6	(29)	
5	10	Happy Birthday	Altered Images	Epic	7		F
6	-	Begin The Beguine (Volver A Empezar)	Julio Iglesias	CBS	8		F
7	-	Labelled With Love	Squeeze	A&M	6		
8	-	Favourite Shirts (Boy Meets Girl)	Haircut 100	Arista	5		F
9	-	Tonight I'm Yours (Don't Hurt Me)	Rod Stewart	Riva	6	(20)	
10	2	It's My Party	Dave Stewart & Barbara Gaskin	Broken	8	(72)	L
11	-	Physical	Olivia Newton-John	EMI	6	(1)	
12	-	Let's Groove	Earth, Wind & Fire	CBS	6	(3)	L
13	15	A Good Year For The Roses	Elvis Costello	F. Beat	6		L
14	-	Bed Sitter	Soft Cell	Some Bizzare	7		
15	-	I Go To Sleep	Pretenders	Real	5		
16	-	Hold Me	B.A. Robertson & Maggie Bell	Swansong	5		L
17	-	When You Were Sweet Sixteen	Fureys & Davey Arthur	Ritz	4		F L
18	1	The Birdie Song (Birdie Dance)	Tweets	PRT	8		F L
19	12	Open Your Heart	Human League	Virgin	5		
20	-	Why Do Fools Fall In Love	Diana Ross	Capitol	8	(7)	

December 1981

This Mnth	Prev Mnth	Title	Artist	Label	Wks	(US 20 Pos)	
1	-	Don't You Want Me	Human League	Virgin	9	(1)	G
2	-	Daddy's Home	Cliff Richard	EMI	8	(23)	
3	6	Begin The Beguine (Volver A...)	Julio Iglesias	CBS	8		F
4	20	Why Do Fools Fall In Love	Diana Ross	Capitol	8	(7)	
5	14	Bed Sitter	Soft Cell	Some Bizzare	7		
6	-	One Of Us	Abba	Epic	7		L
7	-	Ant Rap	Adam & The Ants	CBS	7		
8	-	It Must Be Love	Madness	Stiff	7	(33)	
9	12	Let's Groove	Earth, Wind & Fire	CBS	6	(3)	L
10	-	Wedding Bells	Godley & Creme	Polydor	6		
11	4	Under Pressure	Queen & David Bowie	EMI	6	(29)	
12	-	Land Of Make Believe	Bucks Fizz	RCA	10		
13	15	I Go To Sleep	Pretenders	Real	5		
14	-	Rock 'n' Roll	Status Quo	Vertigo	6		
15	-	Cambodia	Kim Wilde	RAK	6		
16	-	Ay Ay Ay Ay Moosey	Modern Romance	WEA	4		
17	-	Spirits In The Material World	Police	A&M	5	(11)	
18	-	Mirror Mirror (Mon Amour)	Dollar	WEA	8		
19	-	Four More From Toyah E.P.	Toyah	Safari	2		L
20	8	Favourite Shirts (Boy Meets Girl)	Haircut 100	Arista	5		F

◆ The Human League's 'Don't You Want Me' sold almost 1.5 million in the UK alone. Six months later it topped the US chart and opened the doors to other British synth bands. The group's **Dare** album also reached No. 1 in Britain.

◆ Early rock songs enjoying a return to favour included 'Why Do Fools Fall In Love' by Diana Ross, 'It's My Party' by Dave Stewart & Barbara Gaskin and Cliff Richard's revival of 'Daddy's Home'.

1982

This Mnth	Prev Mnth	Title	Artist	Label	Wks	(US 20 Pos)	
1	12	Land Of Make Believe	Bucks Fizz	RCA	10		
2	1	Don't You Want Me	Human League	Virgin	9	(1)	G
3	-	Get Down On It	Kool & The Gang	De-Lite	7	(10)	
4	18	Mirror Mirror (Mon Amour)	Dollar	WEA	8		
5	-	I'll Find My Way Home	Jon & Vangelis	Polydor	8	(51)	L
6	7	Ant Rap	Adam & The Ants	CBS	7		
7	6	One Of Us	Abba	Epic	7		L
8	8	It Must Be Love	Madness	Stiff	7	(33)	
9	-	The Model/Computer Love	Kraftwerk	EMI	7		
10	-	Oh Julie	Shakin' Stevens	Epic	7		
11	-	I Could Be Happy	Altered Images	Epic	7		
12	-	Waiting For A Girl Like You	Foreigner	Atlantic	8	(2)	F
13	2	Daddy's Home	Cliff Richard	EMI	8	(23)	
14	-	Being Boiled	Human League	Virgin	5		
15	10	Wedding Bells	Godley & Creme	Polydor	6		
16	14	Rock 'n' Roll	Status Quo	Vertigo	6		
17	-	Dead Ringer For Love	Meat Loaf	Epic	6		
18	-	Young Turks	Rod Stewart	Riva	4	(5)	
19	-	Golden Brown	Stranglers	Liberty	7		
20	17	Spirits In The Material World	Police	A&M	5	(11)	

This	Prev	Title	Artist	Label	Wks	(US Pos)	
1	19	Golden Brown	Stranglers	Liberty	7		
2	9	The Model/Computer Love	Kraftwerk	EMI	7		
3	-	Maid Of Orleans (The Waltz Joan Of Arc)	Orchestral Manoeuvres In The Dark	Dindisc	7		
4	-	Town Called Malice/Precious	Jam	Polydor	6		
5	10	Oh Julie	Shakin' Stevens	Epic	7		
6	17	Dead Ringer For Love	Meat Loaf	Epic	6		
7	-	Arthur's Theme (Best That You Can Do)	Christopher Cross	Warner	6	(1)	F L
8	-	The Lion Sleeps Tonight	Tight Fit	Jive	9		
9	-	Say Hello Wave Goodbye	Soft Cell	Some Bizzare	6		
10	-	Love Plus One	Haircut 100	Arista	7	(37)	
11	-	I Can't Go For That (No Can Do)	Daryl Hall & John Oates	RCA	5	(1)	F
12	1	Land Of Make Believe	Bucks Fizz	RCA	10		
13	-	Drowning In Berlin	Mobiles	Rialto	5		F L
14	-	Senses Working Overtime	XTC	Virgin	5		L
15	-	Easier Said Than Done	Shakatak	Polydor	4		F
16	-	Centrefold	J. Geils Band	EMI America	6	(1)	F L
17	3	Get Down On It	Kool & The Gang	De-Lite	7	(10)	
18	14	Bein' Boiled	Human League	Virgin	5		
19	-	Let's Get It Up	AC/DC	Atlantic	2	(44)	
20	12	Waiting For A Girl Like You	Foreigner	Atlantic	8	(2)	F

◆ Retro rock'n'roller Shakin' Stevens scored his third No. 1 with 'Oh Julie' (covered in America by Barry Manilow). The Jam had their third chart topping single with 'Town Called Malice' and their only No. 1 LP, The Gift.

◆ UB40's new record deal with Dep International was described as "The best since Paul McCartney signed with Columbia".

March 1982

This Mnth	Prev Mnth	Title	Artist	Label	Wks	(US 20 Pos)	
1	8	The Lion Sleeps Tonight	Tight Fit	Jive	9		
2	-	Mickey	Toni Basil	Radialchoice	6	(1)	F L
3	10	Love Plus One	Haircut 100	Arista	7	(37)	
4	-	It Ain't What You Do It's The Way That You Do It	Fun Boy Three & Bananarama	Chrysalis	5		
5	-	Seven Tears	Goombay Dance Band	Epic	7		F L
6	16	Centrefold	J. Geils Band	EMI America	6	(1)	F L
7	-	Poison Arrow	ABC	Neutron	6	(25)	
8	-	See You	Depeche Mode	Mute	5		
9	-	Go Wild In The Country	Bow Wow Wow	RCA	5		F
10	-	Run To The Hills	Iron Maiden	EMI	5		F
11	-	Classic	Adrian Gurvitz	RAK	5		F L
12	-	Just An Illusion	Imagination	R&B	7		
13	4	Town Called Malice/Precious	Jam	Polydor	6		
14	-	Quiereme Mucho (Yours)	Julio Iglesias	CBS	4		
15	-	Cardiac Arrest	Madness	Stiff	4		
16	-	Layla	Derek & The Dominoes	RSO	5		F L
17	9	Say Hello Wave Goodbye	Soft Cell	Some Bizzare	6		
18	-	Party Fears Two	Associates	Associates	3		F
19	-	Deutscher Girls	Adam & The Ants	Ego	4		
20	3	Maid Of Orleans (The Waltz Joan Of Arc)	Orchestral Manoeuvres In The Dark	Dindisc	7		

April 1982

This Mnth	Prev Mnth	Title	Artist	Label	Wks	(US 20 Pos)	
1	-	My Camera Never Lies	Bucks Fizz	RCA	5		
2	-	Ain't No Pleasing You	Chas & Dave	Rockney	6		
3	5	Seven Tears	Goombay Dance Band	Epic	7		F L
4	12	Just An Illusion	Imagination	R&B	7		
5	-	Give Me Back My Heart	Dollar	WEA	6		
6	-	Ghosts	Japan	Virgin	5		
7	-	More Than This	Roxy Music	EG	5		
8	-	Ebony And Ivory	Paul McCartney & Stevie Wonder	Parlophone	7	(1)	
9	16	Layla	Derek & The Dominoes	RSO	5		F L
10	14	Quiereme Mucho (Yours)	Julio Iglesias	CBS	4		
11	-	Papa's Got A Brand New Pigbag	Pigbag	Y	5		F L
12	-	Have You Ever Been In Love	Leo Sayer	Chrysalis	3		
13	-	Dear John	Status Quo	Vertigo	4		
14	-	Is It A Dream	Classix Nouveaux	Liberty	3		F L
15	-	Night Birds	Shakatak	Polydor	4		
16	-	One Step Further	Bardo	Epic	4		F L
17	-	See Those Eyes	Altered Images	Epic	4		
18	7	Poison Arrow	ABC	Neutron	6	(25)	
19	-	Damned Don't Cry	Visage	Polydor	3		
20	-	Blue Eyes	Elton John	Rocket	4	(12)	

◆ Few pundits at the time would have prophesied that Bananarama, who made their chart debut alongside The Specials' off-shoot Fun Boy Three, would go on to amass more UK and US hits than any other female British group.

◆ In their homeland, British supergroup Asia's eponymous album, which headed the US chart for nine weeks, failed to make the Top 10.

1982

This Mnth	Prev Mnth	Title	Artist	Label	Wks	(US 20 Pos)	
1	-	I Won't Let You Down	PhD	WEA	7		F L
2	8	Ebony And Ivory	Paul McCartney/Stevie Wonder	Parlophone	7	(1)	
3	-	A Little Peace	Nicole	CBS	6		F L
4	-	I Love Rock 'n' Roll	Joan Jett & The Blackhearts	Epic	6	(1)	F L
5	-	Only You	Yazoo	Mute	7	(67)	F
6	-	Really Saying Something	Bananarama & Funboy Three	Deram	5		
7	-	This Time (We'll Get It Right)/ England We'll Fly The Flag	England World Cup Squad	England	5		
8	-	We Have A Dream	Scotland World Cup Squad	WEA	5		L
9	-	Girl Crazy	Hot Chocolate	RAK	6		
10	11	Papa's Got A Brand New Pigbag	Pigbag	Y	5		F L
11	-	Goody Two Shoes	Adam Ant	CBS	7	(12)	
12	16	One Step Further	Bardo	Epic	4		F L
13	-	Forget Me Nots	Patrice Rushen	Elektra	5	(23)	F L
14	-	House Of Fun	Madness	Stiff	6		
15	-	Fantasy Island	Tight Fit	Jive	7		L
16	-	I Can Make You Feel Good	Shalamar	Solar	5		
17	-	Fantastic Day	Haircut 100	Arista	5		
18	-	Shirley	Shakin' Stevens	Epic	2		
19	-	The Look Of Love (Part 1)	ABC	Neutron	7	(18)	
20	-	Instinction	Spandau Ballet	Chrysalis	4		

This Mnth	Prev Mnth	Title	Artist	Label	Wks	(US 20 Pos)	
1	11	Goody Two Shoes	Adam Ant	CBS	7	(12)	
2	-	Torch	Soft Cell	Some Bizzare	6		
3	19	The Look Of Love (Part 1)	ABC	Neutron	7	(18)	
4	14	House Of Fun	Madness	Stiff	6		
5	-	Hungry Like The Wolf	Duran Duran	EMI	8	(3)	
6	-	I've Never Been To Me	Charlene	Motown	6	(3)	F L
7	15	Fantasy Island	Tight Fit	Jive	7		L
8	-	Mama Used To Say	Junior	Mercury	7	(30)	F
9	5	Only You	Yazoo	Mute	7	(67)	F
10	-	I'm A Wonderful Thing (Baby)	Kid Creole & The Coconuts	Ze	5		F
11	-	I Want Candy	Bow Wow Wow	RCA	4	(62)	L
12	-	Work That Body	Diana Ross	Capitol	5	(44)	
13	-	3 X 3 (E.P.)	Genesis	Charisma	4	(32)	
14	-	We Take Mystery (To Bed)	Gary Numan	Beggars Banquet	2		
15	-	Island Of Lost Souls	Blondie	Chrysalis	4	(37)	
16	-	Club Country	Associates	Associates	4		L
17	13	Forget Me Nots	Patrice Rushen	Elektra	5	(23)	F L
18	1	I Won't Let You Down	PhD	WEA	7		F L
19	-	Inside Out	Odyssey	RCA	7		L
20	-	Do I Do	Stevie Wonder	Motown	3	(13)	

◆ Adam & The Ants split, and Adam's first solo effort, 'Goody Two Shoes', topped the UK listings and became his first US Top 20 entry.

◆ The Rolling Stones made their first UK appearance in six years. Their two Wembley shows attracted 140,000 fans.

◆ The UK's 500th chart topper was Eurovision Song Contest winner 'A Little Peace' by 17-year-old German Nicole (Hohloch). It entered at No. 8 – a record for a new artist.

1982

This Mnth	Prev Mnth	Title	Artist	Label	Wks	(US 20 Pos)	
1	-	Abracadabra	Steve Miller Band	Mercury	7	(1)	
2	-	Fame	Irene Cara	RSO	10	(4)	F
3	19	Inside Out	Odyssey	RCA	7		L
4	-	Happy Talk	Captain Sensible	A&M	4		F
5	-	A Night To Remember	Shalamar	Solar	6	(44)	
6	-	Music And Lights	Imagination	R&B	5		L
7	-	Da Da Da	Trio	Mobile Suit	5		F L
8	-	Shy Boy	Bananarama	London	7	(83)	
9	-	Now Those Days Are Gone	Bucks Fizz	RCA	5		
10	-	It Started With A Kiss	Hot Chocolate	RAK	8		
11	-	Don't Go	Yazoo	Mute	6		
12	-	No Regrets	Midge Ure	Chrysalis	5		F
13	6	I've Never Been To Me	Charlene	Motown	6	(3)	F L
14	-	Iko Iko	Natasha	Towerbell	5		F L
15	-	Driving In My Car	Madness	Stiff	6		
16	-	Come On Eileen	Dexy's Midnight Runners	Mercury	11	(1)	G
17	12	Work That Body	Diana Ross	Capitol	5	(44)	
18	-	Just Who Is The Five O'Clock Hero	Jam	Polydor	3		
19	-	Beatles Movie Medley	Beatles	Parlophone	4	(12)	
20	-	Night Train	Visage	Polydor	4		L

This Mnth	Prev Mnth	Title	Artist	Label	Wks	(US 20 Pos)	
1	16	Come On Eileen	Dexy's Midnight Runners	Mercury	11	(1)	G
2	2	Fame	Irene Cara	RSO	10	(4)	F
3	11	Don't Go	Yazoo	Mute	6		
4	10	It Started With A Kiss	Hot Chocolate	RAK	8		
5	-	Eye Of The Tiger	Survivor	Scotti Brothers	10	(1)	F
6	15	Driving My Car	Madness	Stiff	6		
7	-	Strange Little Girl	Stranglers	Liberty	5		
8	-	Stool Pigeon	Kid Creole & The Coconuts	Ze	5		
9	-	Can't Take My Eyes Off You	Boystown Gang	ERC	6		F L
10	-	My Girl Lollipop (My Boy Lollipop)	Bad Manners	Magnet	3		L
11	8	Shy Boy	Bananarama	London	7	(83)	
12	-	What	Soft Cell	Some Bizzare	5		
13	-	The Clapping Song	Belle Stars	Stiff	4		F
14	7	Da Da Da	Trio	Mobile Suit	5		F L
15	-	I Second That Emotion	Japan	Hansa	6		L
16	-	I Eat Cannibals Pt. 1	Toto Coelo	Radialchoice	5	(66)	F L
17	-	The Only Way Out	Cliff Richard	EMI	4	(64)	
18	-	Save A Prayer	Duran Duran	EMI	6	(16)	
19	-	Arthur Daley ('E's Alright)	Firm	Bark	3		F
20	-	John Wayne Is Big Leggy	Haysi Fantayzee	Regard	4		F

◆ Come On Eileen', by Dexy's Midnight Runners, which sold over a million in the UK, was Britain's top single of 1982 and went on to top the American charts too.

◆ Thanks to the TV series *Fame* (based on the 1980 film), Irene Cara's 'Fame' headed the British listings, two years after reaching the US Top 5. The film's soundtrack album also hit No. 1, being replaced by the million selling Kids From Fame from the TV series. This American series spawned five UK hit albums and four singles – none of which were successful in the act's homeland.

1982

This Mnth	Prev Mnth	Title	Artist	Label	Wks	(US 20 Pos)	
1	5	Eye Of The Tiger	Survivor	Scotti Brothers	10	(1)	F
2	18	Save A Prayer	Duran Duran	EMI	6	(16)	
3	-	Walking On Sunshine	Rocker's Revenge	London	8		F L
4	-	Private Investigations	Dire Straits	Vertigo	6		
5	1	Come On Eileen	Dexy's Midnight Runners	Mercury	11	(1)	G
6	-	Hi-Fidelity	Kids From 'Fame' (Featuring Valerie Landsberg)	RCA	6		F
7	-	All Of My Heart	ABC	Neutron	5		
8	-	Give Me Your Heart Tonight	Shakin' Stevens	Epic	4		
9	12	What	Soft Cell	Some Bizzare	5		
10	-	The Message	Grandmaster Flash, Melle Mel & The Furious Five	Sugar Hill	4	(62)	F
11	-	The Bitterest Pill (I Ever Had To Swallow)	Jam	Polydor	5		
12	16	I Eat Cannibals Pt. 1	Toto Coelo	Radialchoice	5	(66)	F L
13	-	There It Is	Shalamar	Solar	7		
14	9	Can't Take My Eyes Off You	Boystown Gang	ERC	6		F L
15	-	Nobody's Fool	Haircut 100	Arista	4		L
16	-	Today	Talk Talk	EMI	4		F
17	-	Saddle Up	David Christie	KR	5		F L
18	20	John Wayne Is Big Leggy	Haysi Fantayzee	Regard	4		F
19	-	Why	Carly Simon	WEA	5	(74)	
20	2	Fame	Irene Cara	RSO	10	(4)	F

1	-	Pass The Dutchie	Musical Youth	MCA	6	(10)	F
2	-	Zoom	Fat Larry's Band	Virgin	7		F L
3	-	Do You Really Want To Hurt Me	Culture Club	Virgin	9	(2)	F
4	-	Hard To Say I'm Sorry	Chicago	Full Moon	6	(1)	
5	-	Starmaker	Kids From 'Fame'	RCA	7		
6	-	Love Come Down	Evelyn King	EMI	7	(17)	F L
7	-	Jackie Wilson Said	Dexy's Midnight Runners	Mercury	4		
8	13	There It Is	Shalamar	Solar	7		
9	-	Love Me Do	Beatles	Parlophone	5		
10	-	Just What I Always Wanted	Mari Wilson	Compact	5		F L
11	-	Lifeline	Spandau Ballet	Chrysalis	5		
12	-	Annie I'm Not Your Daddy	Kid Creole & The Coconuts	Ze	5		L
13	11	The Bitterest Pill (I Ever Had To Swallow)	Jam	Polydor	5		
14	-	Friend Or Foe	Adam Ant	CBS	4		
15	1	Eye Of The Tiger	Survivor	Scotti Brothers	10	(1)	F
16	3	Walking On Sunshine	Rocker's Revenge	London	8		F L
17	19	Why	Carly Simon	WEA	5	(74)	
18	-	House Of The Rising Sun	Animals	RAK	4		L
19	-	Danger Games	Pinkees	Creole	2		F L
20	-	Mad World	Tears For Fears	Mercury	7		F

◆ Survivor become the first US rock group to top the British charts in six years with their American No. 1, 'Eye of The Tiger'. The Steve Miller Band had nearly accomplished this feat just weeks earlier with 'Abracadabra'.

◆ Big American hits from the first British invasion, 'Love Me Do' by The Beatles and 'House Of The Rising Sun' by The Animals returned to the UK chart. Debuting on that chart were Culture Club, Wham! and Tears for Fears – artists who would help lead the second UK invasion.

November 1982

This Mnth	Prev Mnth	Title	Artist	Label	Wks (US 20	Pos)	
1	-	I Don't Wanna Dance	Eddy Grant	Ice	7	(53)	
2	-	Heartbreaker	Dionne Warwick	Arista	6	(10)	
3	20	Mad World	Tears For Fears	Mercury	7		F
4	3	Do You Really Want To Hurt Me	Culture Club	Virgin	9	(2)	F
5	-	(Sexual) Healing	Marvin Gaye	CBS	6	(3)	
6	-	Theme From Harry's Game	Clannad	RCA	4		F
7	-	Maneater	Daryl Hall & John Oates	RCA	4	(1)	
8	-	Ooh La La La (Let's Go Dancing)	Kool & The Gang	De-Lite	4	(30)	
9	-	The Girl Is Mine	Michael Jackson & Paul McCartney	Epic	3	(2)	
10	5	Starmaker	Kids From 'Fame'	RCA	7		
11	-	Mirror Man	Human League	Virgin	8	(30)	
12	-	I Wanna Do It With You	Barry Manilow	Arista	5		
13	-	Young Guns (Go For It)	Wham!	Innervision	9		F
14	-	Living On The Ceiling	Blancmange	London	6		F
15	12	Annie I'm Not Your Daddy	Kid Creole & The Coconuts	Ze	5		L
16	9	Love Me Do	Beatles	Parlophone	5		
17	-	I'll Be Satisfied	Shakin' Stevens	Epic	4		
18	-	Caroline (Live At The N.E.C.)	Status Quo	Vertigo	3		
19	-	Rio	Duran Duran	EMI	5	(14)	
20	11	Lifeline	Spandau Ballet	Chrysalis	5		

December 1982

This Mnth	Prev Mnth	Title	Artist	Label	Wks (US 20	Pos)	
1	-	Save Your Love	Renee And Renato	Hollywood	10		F L
2	-	Beat Surrender	Jam	Polydor	6		L
3	-	Time (Clock Of The Heart)	Culture Club	Virgin	8	(2)	
4	11	Mirror Man	Human League	Virgin	8	(30)	
5	-	Truly	Lionel Richie	Motown	7	(1)	
6	13	Young Guns (Go For It)	Wham!	Innervision	9		F
7	-	Our House	Madness	Stiff	8	(7)	
8	14	Living On The Ceiling	Blancmange	London	6		F
9	-	Best Years Of Our Lives	Modern Romance	WEA	8		
10	-	The Shakin' Stevens E.P.	Shakin' Stevens	Epic	4		
11	1	I Don't Wanna Dance	Eddy Grant	Ice	7	(53)	
12	19	Rio	Duran Duran	EMI	5	(14)	
13	-	Peace On Earth/Little DrummerBoy	David Bowie & Bing Crosby	RCA	4		
14	-	Wishing (If I Had A Photograph Of You)	Flock Of Seagulls	Jive	4	(26)	F L
15	-	Hymn	Ultravox	Chrysalis	8		
16	-	The Other Side Of Love	Yazoo	Mute	4		
17	-	You Can't Hurry Love	Phil Collins	Virgin	10	(10)	
18	2	Heartbreaker	Dionne Warwick	Arista	6	(10)	
19	-	Friends	Shalamar	Solar	6		
20	-	A Winter's Tale	David Essex	Mercury	6		

◆ Shortly after Musical Youth (featuring 11-year-old Kelvin Grant) became the youngest group to top the chart, David Bowie & the late Bing Crosby became the oldest duo to reach the Top 5.

◆ The 1980s' most influential British pop TV show, The Tube, was launched.

1983

January 1983

This Mnth	Prev Mnth	Title	Artist	Label	Wks	(US 20 Pos)	
1	17	You Can't Hurry Love	Phil Collins	Virgin	10	(10)	
2	20	A Winter's Tale	David Essex	Mercury	6		
3	1	Save Your Love	Renee And Renato	Hollywood	10		F L
4	-	Orville's Song	Keith Harris & Orville	BBC	5		F L
5	-	Down Under	Men At Work	Epic	7	(1)	F L
6	9	Best Years Of Our Lives	Modern Romance	WEA	8		
7	7	Our House	Madness	Stiff	8	(7)	
8	-	The Story Of The Blues	Wah!	Eternal	6		F
9	3	Time (Clock Of The Heart)	Culture Club	Virgin	8	(2)	
10	-	Buffalo Gals	Malcolm McLaren & The World's Famous Supreme Team	Charisma	7		F
11	15	Hymn	Ultravox	Chrysalis	8		
12	-	Electric Avenue	Eddy Grant	Ice	5	(2)	
13	-	Heartache Avenue	Maisonettes	Ready Steady Go!	4		F L
14	10	The Shakin' Stevens E.P.	Shakin' Stevens	Epic	4		
15	-	All The Love In The World	Dionne Warwick	Arista	5		
16	13	Peace On Earth/Little Drummer Boy	David Bowie & Bing Crosby	RCA	4		
17	-	Steppin' Out	Joe Jackson	A&M	5	(6)	L
18	-	Cacharpaya (Andes Pumpsa Daesi)	Incantation	Beggars Banquet	4		F L
19	-	European Female	Stranglers	Epic	3		
20	-	If You Can't Stand The Heat	Bucks Fizz	RCA	6		

February 1983

This Mnth	Prev Mnth	Title	Artist	Label	Wks	(US 20 Pos)	
1	-	Too Shy	Kajagoogoo	EMI	8	(5)	F
2	5	Down Under	Men At Work	Epic	7	(1)	F L
3	-	Sign Of The Times	Belle Stars	Stiff	7	(75)	L
4	-	Change	Tears For Fears	Mercury	6	(73)	
5	-	Up Where We Belong	Joe Cocker & Jennifer Warnes	Island	6	(1)	
6	12	Electric Avenue	Eddy Grant	Ice	5	(2)	
7	-	Wham Rap	Wham!	Innervision	5		
8	-	Gloria	Laura Branigan	Atlantic	6	(2)	F
9	-	Billie Jean	Michael Jackson	Epic	10	(1)	
10	-	Oh Diane	Fleetwood Mac	Warner	5		
11	1	You Can't Hurry Love	Phil Collins	Virgin	10	(10)	
12	-	Africa	Toto	CBS	6	(1)	
13	-	The Cutter	Echo & The Bunnymen	Korova	4		
14	8	The Story Of The Blues	Wah!	Eternal	6		F
15	-	Last Night A D.J. Saved My Life	Indeep	Sound Of New York	4		F L
16	-	New Year's Day	U2	Island	3	(53)	F
17	-	Never Gonna Give You Up	Musical Youth	MCA	5		L
18	-	Christian	China Crisis	Virgin	3		F
19	17	Steppin' Out	Joe Jackson	A&M	5	(6)	L
20	-	The Tunnel Of Love	Fun Boy Three	Chrysalis	5		

◆ Noteworthy newcomers on the UK chart included future transatlantic stars U2 (whose album War entered at No. 1), The Eurythmics and the Thompson Twins.

◆ Shortly after disbanding, The Jam had a record 15 singles in the UK Top 100, and lead singer Paul Weller signed a £250,000 deal for his new act Style Council.

1983

March 1983

This Mnth	Prev Mnth	Title	Artist	Label	Wks	(US 20 Pos)	
1	-	Total Eclipse Of The Heart	Bonnie Tyler	CBS	8	(1)	
2	-	Sweet Dreams (Are Made Of This)	Eurythmics	RCA	7	(1)	F
3	9	Billie Jean	Michael Jackson	Epic	10	(1)	
4	-	Rock The Boat	Forrest	CBS	6		F
5	12	Africa	Toto	CBS	6	(1)	
6	-	Na Na Hey Hey Kiss Him Goodbye	Bananarama	London	5		
7	1	Too Shy	Kajagoogoo	EMI	8	(5)	F
8	-	Love On Your Side	Thompson Twins	Arista	5	(45)	F
9	-	Speak Like A Child	Style Council	Polydor	5		F
10	-	Tomorrow's (Just Another Day)/ Madness (Is All In The Mind)	Madness	Stiff	4		
11	17	Never Gonna Give You Up	Musical Youth	MCA	5		L
12	-	High Life	Modern Romance	WEA	3		
13	-	She Means Nothing To Me	Phil Everly & Cliff Richard	Capitol	4		F
14	-	Baby, Come To Me	Patti Austin & James Ingram	Qwest	5	(1)	F L
15	-	Communication	Spandau Ballet	Reformation	4	(59)	
16	-	Rip It Up	Orange Juice	Polydor	5		F L
17	20	The Tunnel Of Love	Fun Boy Three	Chrysalis	5		
18	-	Is There Something I Should Know	Duran Duran	EMI	5	(4)	
19	4	Change	Tears For Fears	Mercury	6	(73)	
20	-	Let's Dance	David Bowie	EMI America	8	(1)	

April 1983

This Mnth	Prev Mnth	Title	Artist	Label	Wks	(US 20 Pos)	
1	20	Let's Dance	David Bowie	EMI America	8	(1)	
2	18	Is There Something I Should Know	Duran Duran	EMI	5	(4)	
3	-	Church Of The Poison Mind	Culture Club	Virgin	6	(10)	
4	-	Boxer Beat	Joboxers	RCA	5		F
5	-	Breakaway	Tracey Ullman	Stiff	6	(70)	F
6	-	Beat It	Michael Jackson	Epic	6	(1)	
7	-	Words	F.R. David	Carrere	7	(62)	F L
8	-	Ooh To Be Ah	Kajagoogoo	EMI	5		
9	9	Speak Like A Child	Style Council	Polydor	5		F
10	2	Sweet Dreams (Are Made Of This)	Eurythmics	RCA	7	(1)	F
11	1	Total Eclipse Of The Heart	Bonnie Tyler	CBS	8	(1)	
12	-	Blue Monday	New Order	Factory	8		F
13	-	Fields Of Fire (400 Miles)	Big Country	Mercury	4	(52)	F
14	-	True	Spandau Ballet	Reformation	8	(4)	
15	-	Snot Rap	Kenny Everett	RCA	3		F L
16	-	Love Is A Stranger	Eurythmics	RCA	4	(23)	
17	-	Don't Talk To Me About Love	Altered Images	Epic	4		L
18	-	The House That Jack Built	Tracie	Respond	3		F L
19	16	Rip It Up	Orange Juice	Polydor	5		F L
20	-	Whistle Down The Wind	Nick Heyward	Arista	4		F

◆ CDs (which stored sounds digitally, thus eliminating most distortion) went on sale for the first time.
◆ Billy Fury, one of Britain's first home grown rock stars, died from heart problems, aged 41.

◆ Police scored the last of their five UK No. 1 singles and albums with 'Every Breath You Take' and **Synchronicity**. Both records also topped the US chart, with the latter holding sway for 17 weeks.

1983

May 1983

This Mnth	Prev Mnth	Title	Artist	Label	Wks	(US 20 Pos)	
1	14	True	Spandau Ballet	Reformation	8	(4)	
2	-	Temptation	Heaven 17	Virgin	7		F
3	-	Dancing Tight	Galaxy Featuring Phil Fearon	Ensign	6		F
4	-	(Keep Feeling) Fascination	Human League	Virgin	6	(8)	
5	-	Candy Girl	New Edition	London	6	(46)	F
6	7	Words	F.R. David	Carrere	7	(62)	F L
7	-	Pale Shelter	Tears For Fears	Mercury	4		
8	-	Can't Get Used To Losing You	Beat	Go Feet	5		L
9	-	Our Lips Are Sealed	Fun Boy Three	Chrysalis	5		L
10	-	We Are Detective	Thompson Twins	Arista	4		
11	6	Beat It	Michael Jackson	Epic	6	(1)	
12	-	Blind Vision	Blancmange	London	4		
13	-	Bad Boys	Wham!	Innervision	8	(60)	
14	1	Let's Dance	David Bowie	EMI America	8	(1)	
15	-	What Kinda Boy You Looking For (Girl)	Hot Chocolate	RAK	4		
16	-	True Love Ways	Cliff Richard	EMI	4		
17	-	Friday Night (Live Version)	Kids From 'Fame'	RCA	4		L
18	3	Church Of The Poison Mind	Culture Club	Virgin	6	(10)	
19	-	Every Breath You Take	Police	A&M	8	(1)	
20	-	Nobody's Diary	Yazoo	Mute	7		

June 1983

This Mnth	Prev Mnth	Title	Artist	Label	Wks	(US 20 Pos)	
1	19	Every Breath You Take	Police	A&M	8	(1)	
2	13	Bad Boys	Wham!	Innervision	8	(60)	
3	20	Nobody's Diary	Yazoo	Mute	7		
4	-	Buffalo Soldier	Bob Marley & The Wailers	Island	6		
5	-	China Girl	David Bowie	EMI America	5	(10)	
6	-	Love Town	Booker Newberry III	Polydor	5		F L
7	-	Flashdance....What A Feeling	Irene Cara	Casablanca	9	(1)	L
8	5	Candy Girl	New Edition	London	6	(46)	F
9	-	Just Got Lucky	Joboxers	RCA	4	(36)	L
10	-	Baby Jane	Rod Stewart	Warner	9	(14)	
11	-	Lady Love Me (One More Time)	George Benson	Warner	5	(30)	
12	-	Waiting For A Train	Flash And The Pan	Ensign	5		F L
13	-	I Guess That's Why They Call It The Blues	Elton John	Rocket	6	(4)	
14	8	Can't Get Used To Losing You	Beat	Go Feet	5		L
15	-	Wanna Be Startin' Something	Michael Jackson	Epic	3	(5)	
16	2	Temptation	Heaven 17	Virgin	7		F
17	-	Money Go Round (Pt.1)	Style Council	Polydor	3		
18	-	Hang On Now	Kajagoogoo	EMI	3	(78)	
19	1	True	Spandau Ballet	Reformation	8	(4)	
20	-	Dark Is The Night	Shakatak	Polydor	2		

◆ David Bowie signed a $10 million deal with EMI, and the first release 'Let's Dance' (co-produced with Nile Rodgers) became his biggest transatlantic hit. He also launched his *Serious Moonlight* tour, which would be seen by over 2.5 million people.

◆ Blue Monday', the 12-inch only release from New Order, was released. It became the UK's biggest selling single on that particular format and spent nearly a year on the chart.

July 1983

This Mnth	Prev Mnth	Title	Artist	Label	Wks	(US 20 Pos)	
1	10	Baby Jane	Rod Stewart	Warner	9	(14)	
2	-	Wherever I Lay My Hat (That's My Home)	Paul Young	CBS	9	(70)	F
3	-	I.O.U.	Freeez	Beggars Banquet	9		L
4	-	Moonlight Shadow	Mike Oldfield	Virgin	9		
5	7	Flashdance....What A Feeling	Irene Cara	Casablanca	9	(1)	L
6	-	Come Live With Me	Heaven 17	Virgin	7		
7	-	War Baby	Tom Robinson	Panic	5		L
8	-	Who's That Girl	Eurythmics	RCA	6	(21)	
9	-	Double Dutch	Malcolm McLaren	Charisma	9		
10	-	It's Over	Funk Masters	Master Funk	4		F L
11	-	Dead Giveaway	Shalamar	Solar	5	(22)	
12	13	I Guess That's Why They Call It The Blues	Elton John	Rocket	6	(4)	
13	1	Every Breath You Take	Police	A&M	8	(1)	
14	-	Rock 'n' Roll Is King	Electric Light Orchestra	Jet	4	(19)	L
15	-	Take That Situation	Nick Heyward	Arista	3		
16	-	Cruel Summer	Bananarama	London	5	(9)	
17	-	Wrapped Around Your Finger	Police	A&M	4	(8)	
18	-	The Trooper	Iron Maiden	EMI	3		
19	5	China Girl	David Bowie	EMI America	5	(10)	
20	-	When We Were Young	Bucks Fizz	RCA	3		

August 1983

This Mnth	Prev Mnth	Title	Artist	Label	Wks	(US 20 Pos)	
1	-	Give It Up	KC & The Sunshine Band	Epic	9	(18)	L
2	-	Club Tropicana	Wham!	Innervision	7		
3	9	Double Dutch	Malcolm McLaren	Charisma	9		
4	3	I.O.U.	Freeez	Beggars Banquet	9		L
5	2	Wherever I Lay My Hat (That's My Home)	Paul Young	CBS	9	(70)	F
6	-	Long Hot Summer	Style Council	Polydor	5		
7	-	Gold	Spandau Ballet	Reformation	6	(29)	
8	-	I'm Still Standing	Elton John	Rocket	6	(12)	
9	-	Everything Counts	Depeche Mode	Mute	5		
10	-	The Crown	Gary Byrd & The GB Experience	Motown	5		F L
11	8	Who's That Girl	Eurythmics	RCA	6	(21)	
12	-	Rockit	Herbie Hancock	CBS	5	(71)	L
13	-	Big Log	Robert Plant	WEA	4	(20)	F L
14	16	Cruel Summer	Bananarama	London	5	(9)	
15	-	Wings Of A Dove	Madness	Stiff	6		
16	17	Wrapped Around Your Finger	Police	A&M	4	(8)	
17	-	It's Late	Shakin' Stevens	Epic	3		
18	4	Moonlight Shadow	Mike Oldfield	Virgin	9		
19	-	Watching You Watching Me	David Grant	Chrysalis	5		
20	6	Come Live With Me	Heaven 17	Virgin	7		

◆ David Bowie had ten albums in the British Top 100 (a feat bettered only by Elvis Presley), including the transatlantic Top 5 hit, **Let's Dance**.

◆ Stars of the Castle Donnington Rock Festival included ZZ Top, Meat Loaf, Twisted Sister and Whitesnake. Other successful live shows included Barry Manilow at Blenheim Palace, and The Prince's Trust Gala which included Duran Duran and Dire Straits.

1983

This Mnth	Prev Mnth	Title	Artist	Label	Wks	(US 20 Pos)	
1	-	Red Red Wine	UB40	Dep International	10	(34)	
2	15	Wings Of A Dove	Madness	Stiff	6		
3	-	Tonight I Celebrate My Love	Peabo Bryson & Roberta Flack	Capitol	7	(16)	F
4	-	What Am I Gonna Do	Rod Stewart	Warner	5	(35)	
5	-	Mama	Genesis	Virgin/Charisma	7	(73)	
6	-	Walking In The Rain	Modern Romance	WEA	6		L
7	1	Give It Up	KC & The Sunshine Band	Epic	9	(18)	L
8	-	The Sun Goes Down (Living It Up)	Level 42	Polydor	5		F
9	-	Karma Chameleon	Culture Club	Virgin	11	(1)	G
10	7	Gold	Spandau Ballet	Reformation	6	(29)	
11	8	I'm Still Standing	Elton John	Rocket	6	(12)	
12	-	Come Back And Stay	Paul Young	CBS	5	(22)	
13	-	Dolce Vita	Ryan Paris	Carrere	5		F L
14	2	Club Tropicana	Wham!	Innervision	7		
15	-	Chance	Big Country	Mercury	5		
16	6	Long Hot Summer	Style Council	Polydor	5		
17	-	Ol' Rag Blues	Status Quo	Vertigo	4		
18	19	Watching You Watching Me	David Grant	Chrysalis	5		
19	-	Confusion	New Order	Factory	3		
20	-	Modern Love	David Bowie	EMI America	6	(14)	

This Mnth	Prev Mnth	Title	Artist	Label	Wks	(US 20 Pos)	
1	9	Karma Chameleon	Culture Club	Virgin	11	(1)	G
2	20	Modern Love	David Bowie	EMI America	6	(14)	
3	-	They Don't Know	Tracey Ullman	Stiff	6	(8)	
4	-	Dear Prudence	Siouxsie & The Banshees	Wonderland	6		
5	-	New Song	Howard Jones	WEA	6	(27)	F
6	1	Red Red Wine	UB40	Dep International	10	(34)	
7	-	This Is Not A Love Song	Public Image Ltd.	Virgin	5		
8	-	Blue Monday	New Order	Factory	7		
9	-	In Your Eyes	George Benson	Warner	6		
10	-	All Night Long (All Night)	Lionel Richie	Motown	8	(1)	
11	-	(Hey You) The Rocksteady Crew	Rocksteady Crew	Virgin	6		F L
12	12	Come Back And Stay	Paul Young	CBS	5	(22)	
13	3	Tonight I Celebrate My Love	Peabo Bryson & Roberta Flack	Capitol	7	(16)	F
14	-	Superman (Gioca Jouer)	Black Lace	Flair	5		F
15	-	Tahiti (From Mutiny On The Bounty)	David Essex	Mercury	5		L
16	5	Mama	Genesis	Virgin	7	(73)	
17	-	Big Apple	Kajagoogoo	EMI	4		L
18	-	The Safety Dance	Men Without Hats	Statik	6	(3)	F L
19	13	Dolce Vita	Ryan Paris	Carrere	5		F L
20	15	Chance	Big Country	Mercury	5		

◆ As 'Wings Of A Dove' gave Madness their 16th successive Top 20 hit, 'Our House' became their only US Top 20 entry.

◆ Culture Club's only transatlantic chart topper, 'Karma Chameleon', was Britain's top single in 1983, selling nearly 1.5 million.

November 1983

This Mnth	Prev Mnth	Title	Artist	Label	Wks	(US 20 Pos)	
1	-	Uptown Girl	Billy Joel	CBS	12	(3)	
2	10	All Night Long (All Night)	Lionel Richie	Motown	8	(1)	
3	-	Say Say Say	Paul McCartney & Michael Jackson	Parlophone	9	(1)	
4	-	Cry Just A Little Bit	Shakin' Stevens	Epic	7	(67)	
5	-	Puss 'n Boots	Adam Ant	CBS	4		
6	-	The Love Cats	Cure	Fiction	5		
7	1	Karma Chameleon	Culture Club	Virgin	11	(1)	G
8	18	The Safety Dance	Men Without Hats	Statik	6	(3)	F L
9	-	The Sun And The Rain	Madness	Stiff	4	(72)	
10	-	Union Of The Snake	Duran Duran	EMI	4	(3)	
11	-	Never Never	Assembly	Mute	4		F L
12	-	Please Don't Make Me Cry	UB40	Dep International	5		
13	11	(Hey You) The Rocksteady Crew	Rocksteady Crew	Virgin	6		F L
14	3	They Don't Know	Tracey Ullman	Stiff	6	(8)	
15	5	New Song	Howard Jones	WEA	6	(27)	F
16	-	Love Of The Common People	Paul Young	CBS	10	(45)	
17	-	Solid Bond In Your Heart	Style Council	Polydor	3		
18	-	Undercover Of The Night	Rolling Stones	Rolling Stone	3	(9)	
19	-	Calling Your Name	Marilyn	Mercury	4		F L
20	-	Unconditional Love	Donna Summer	Mercury	2	(43)	

December 1983

This Mnth	Prev Mnth	Title	Artist	Label	Wks	(US 20 Pos)	
1	-	Only You	Flying Pickets	10	7		F
2	16	Love Of The Common People	Paul Young	CBS	10	(45)	
3	-	Hold Me Now	Thompson Twins	Arista	9	(3)	
4	-	My Oh My	Slade	RCA	7	(37)	
5	-	Let's Stay Together	Tina Turner	Capitol	8	(26)	F
6	1	Uptown Girl	Billy Joel	CBS	12	(3)	
7	-	Victims	Culture Club	Virgin	6		
8	-	Please Don't Fall In Love	Cliff Richard	EMI	6		
9	-	Move Over Darling	Tracey Ullman	Stiff	5		
10	-	Islands In The Stream	Kenny Rogers & Dolly Parton	RCA	7	(1)	L
11	-	Tell Her About It	Billy Joel	CBS	7	(1)	
12	-	Thriller	Michael Jackson	Epic	9	(4)	
13	19	Calling Your Name	Marilyn	Mercury	4		F L
14	-	Marguerita Time	Status Quo	Vertigo	6		
15	3	Say Say Say	Paul McCartney & Michael Jackson	Parlophone	9	(1)	
16	-	What Is Love	Howard Jones	WEA	8	(33)	
17	11	Never Never	Assembly	Mute	4		F L
18	4	Cry Just A Little Bit	Shakin' Stevens	Epic	7	(67)	
19	-	Right By Your Side	Eurythmics	RCA	4	(29)	
20	-	That's All!	Genesis	Charisma/virgin	4	(6)	

◆ In 1983, Michael Jackson not only had the biggest album, **Thriller**, he also earned the first platinum music video for *The Making Of Thriller*, and amassed seven US Top 10 singles –. the best yearly performance since The Beatles in 1964!

◆ Britain's most successful chart year in the US since 1964 ended with legendary hitmakers The Who splitting and chart regulars ELO starting a long sabbatical.

1984

This Mnth	Prev Mnth	Title	Artist	Label	Wks	(US 20 Pos)	
1	-	Pipes Of Peace	Paul McCartney	Parlophone	6		
2	16	What Is Love	Howard Jones	WEA	8	(33)	
3	-	Relax	Frankie Goes To Hollywood	ZTT	25	(10)	F G
4	14	Marguerita Time	Status Quo	Vertigo	6		
5	11	Tell Her About It	Billy Joel	CBS	7	(1)	
6	2	Love Of The Common People	Paul Young	CBS	10	(45)	
7	-	A Rockin' Good Way	Shaky & Bonnie	CBS	5		
8	-	That's Living (Alright)	Joe Fagin	Towerbell	7		F L
9	10	Islands In The Stream	Kenny Rogers & Dolly Parton	RCA	7	(1)	L
10	3	Hold Me Now	Thompson Twins	Arista	9	(3)	
11	1	Only You	Flying Pickets	10	7		F
12	7	Victims	Culture Club	Virgin	6		
13	-	Bird Of Paradise	Snowy White	Towerbell	4		F L
14	4	My Oh My	Slade	RCA	7	(37)	
15	-	Nobody Told Me	John Lennon	Ono/Polydor	3	(5)	L
16	12	Thriller	Michael Jackson	Epic	9	(4)	
17	-	Wonderland	Big Country	Mercury	4	(86)	
18	-	Running With The Night	Lionel Richie	Motown	2	(7)	
19	-	Wishful Thinking	China Crisis	Virgin	4		
20	5	Let's Stay Together	Tina Turner	Capitol	8	(26)	F

This Mnth	Prev Mnth	Title	Artist	Label	Wks	(US 20 Pos)	
1	3	Relax	Frankie Goes To Hollywood	ZTT	25	(10)	F G
2	-	Radio Ga Ga	Queen	EMI	6	(16)	
3	-	Girls Just Want To Have Fun	Cyndi Lauper	Portrait	7	(2)	F
4	-	Break My Stride	Matthew Wilder	Epic	7	(5)	F L
5	-	Doctor Doctor	Thompson Twins	Arista	7	(11)	
6	8	That's Living (Alright)	Joe Fagin	Towerbell	7		F L
7	-	Holiday	Madonna	Sire	5	(16)	F
8	-	New Moon On Monday	Duran Duran	EMI	4	(10)	
9	-	(Feels Like) Heaven	Fiction Factory	CBS	4		F L
10	-	99 Red Balloons	Nena	Epic	8	(2)	F L
11	-	My Ever Changing Moods	Style Council	Polydor	4		
12	-	Here Comes The Rain Again	Eurythmics	RCA	5	(4)	
13	-	The Killing Moon	Echo & The Bunnymen	Korova	3		
14	-	What Difference Does It Make	Smiths	Rough Trade	4		F
15	-	Somebody's Watching Me	Rockwell	Motown	6	(2)	F L
16	-	Love Theme From 'The Thorn Birds'	Juan Martin	WEA	2		F L
17	-	Wouldn't It Be Good	Nik Kershaw	MCA	7	(46)	F
18	17	Wonderland	Big Country	Mercury	4	(86)	
19	-	Michael Caine	Madness	Stiff	3		
20	1	Pipes Of Peace	Paul McCartney	Parlophone	6		

◆ As 'Nobody Told Me' gave John Lennon his last transatlantic Top 20 hit, Paul McCartney scored his only British No. 1 of the 1980s, 'Pipes Of Peace', which, oddly, failed to chart Stateside.

◆ Despite being banned by the BBC, 'Relax' by Frankie Goes To Hollywood became one of Britain's biggest ever sellers.

March 1984

This Mnth	Prev Mnth	Title	Artist	Label	Wks (US 20 Pos)	
1	10	99 Red Balloons	Nena	Epic	8 (2)	F L
2	-	Joanna/Tonight	Kool & The Gang	De-Lite	7 (2)	
3	-	Street Dance	Break Machine	Record Shack	8	F
4	17	Wouldn't It Be Good	Nik Kershaw	MCA	7 (46)	F
5	1	Relax	Frankie Goes To Hollywood	ZTT	25 (10)	F G
6	-	Hello	Lionel Richie	Motown	10 (1)	
7	-	An Innocent Man	Billy Joel	CBS	7 (10)	
8	15	Somebody's Watching Me	Rockwell	Motown	6 (2)	F L
9	-	It's Raining Men	Weather Girls	CBS	6 (46)	F L
10	-	Jump	Van Halen	Warner	5 (1)	F
11	-	What Do I Do	Phil Fearon & Galaxy	Ensign	5	
12	-	The Music Of Torvill & Dean EP	Richard Hartley/ Michael Reed Orchestra	Safari	5	F L
13	-	Run Runaway	Slade	RCA	5 (20)	
14	-	Robert De Niro's Waiting	Bananarama	London	5 (95)	
15	5	Doctor Doctor	Thompson Twins	Arista	7 (11)	
16	-	Your Love Is King	Sade	Epic	5 (54)	F
17	-	Hide And Seek	Howard Jones	WEA	5	
18	-	It's A Miracle	Culture Club	Virgin	5 (13)	
19	2	Radio Ga Ga	Queen	EMI	6 (16)	
20	11	My Ever Changing Moods	Style Council	Polydor	4	

April 1984

This Mnth	Prev Mnth	Title	Artist	Label	Wks (US 20 Pos)	
1	6	Hello	Lionel Richie	Motown	10 (1)	
2	-	You Take Me Up	Thompson Twins	Arista	6 (44)	
3	-	A Love Worth Waiting For	Shakin' Stevens	Epic	6	
4	-	People Are People	Depeche Mode	Mute	6 (13)	
5	-	Glad It's All Over/Damned On 45	Captain Sensible	A&M	5	L
6	-	Against All Odds (Take A Look At Me Now)	Phil Collins	Virgin	8 (1)	
7	14	Robert De Niro's Waiting	Bananarama	London	5 (95)	
8	-	I Want To Break Free	Queen	EMI	9 (45)	
9	-	Nelson Mandela	Special AKA	2 Tone	4	L
10	18	It's A Miracle	Culture Club	Virgin	5 (13)	
11	-	Ain't Nobody	Rufus & Chaka Khan	Warner	6 (22)	F
12	9	It's Raining Men	Weather Girls	CBS	6 (46)	F L
13	-	(When You Say You Love Somebody) In The Heart	Kool & The Gang	De-Lite	4	
14	11	What Do I Do	Phil Fearon & Galaxy	Ensign	5	
15	-	Wood Beez (Pray Like Aretha Franklin)	Scritti Politti	Virgin	3 (91)	F
16	-	P.Y.T. (Pretty Young Thing)	Michael Jackson	Epic	3 (10)	
17	16	Your Love Is King	Sade	Epic	5 (54)	F
18	-	The Reflex	Duran Duran	EMI	8 (1)	
19	-	Don't Tell Me	Blancmange	London	6	L
20	-	Cherry Oh Baby	UB40	Dep International	3	

◆ The *NME* Poll showed New Order as Best Group, their 'Blue Monday' as Top Record, and fellow Mancunians The Smiths as Best New Group. In January, The Smiths' first three releases held the top three rungs on the Indie chart.

◆ The Beatles Exhibition Centre opened in Liverpool, Yoko Ono presented a cheque for £250,000 to Liverpool's Strawberry Fields old people's home (immortalized in The Beatles song 'Strawberry Fields Forever').

1984

This Mnth	Prev Mnth	Title	Artist	Label	Wks	(US 20 Pos)	
1	18	The Reflex	Duran Duran	EMI	8	(1)	
2	-	Automatic	Pointer Sisters	Planet	7	(5)	
3	6	Against All Odds (Take A Look At...)	Phil Collins	Virgin	8	(1)	
4	8	I Want To Break Free	Queen	EMI	9	(45)	
5	-	One Love/People Get Ready	Bob Marley & The Wailers	Island	5		L
6	-	Locomotion	O.M.D.	Virgin	7		
7	-	When You're Young And In Love	Flying Pickets	10	5		L
8	19	Don't Tell Me	Blancmange	London	6		L
9	-	Footloose	Kenny Loggins	CBS	4	(1)	F L
10	-	Let's Hear It For The Boy	Deniece Williams	CBS	7	(1)	L
11	1	Hello	Lionel Richie	Motown	10	(1)	
12	-	Dancing Girls	Nik Kershaw	MCA	3		
13	-	The Lebanon	Human League	Virgin	3	(64)	
14	-	I'm Falling	Bluebells	London	4		F
15	-	Love Games	Belle & The Devotions	CBS	2		F L
16	-	Wake Me Up Before You Go Go	Wham!	Epic	8	(1)	
17	-	Break Dance Party	Break Machine	Record Shack	4		L
18	13	(When You Say You...) In The Heart	Kool & The Gang	De-Lite	4		
19	-	Somebody Else's Guy	Jocelyn Brown	4th & Broadway	3	(75)	F
20	2	You Take Me Up	Thompson Twins	Arista	6	(44)	

This	Prev	Title	Artist	Label	Wks	(US Pos)	
1	16	Wake Me Up Before You Go Go	Wham!	Epic	8	(1)	
2	-	Two Tribes	Frankie Goes To Hollywood	ZTT	14	(43)	G
3	-	Smalltown Boy	Bronski Beat	Forbidden Fruit	7	(48)	F
4	-	High Energy	Evelyn Thomas	Record Shack	5	(85)	F L
5	10	Let's Hear It For The Boy	Deniece Williams	CBS	7	(1)	L
6	-	Dancing With Tears In My Eyes	Ultravox	Chrysalis	5		
7	-	Only When You Leave	Spandau Ballet	Reformation	4	(34)	
8	-	Relax	Frankie Goes To Hollywood	ZTT	25	(10)	F G
9	-	Sad Songs (Say So Much)	Elton John	Rocket	5	(5)	
10	-	Pearl In The Shell	Howard Jones	WEA	4		
11	-	Searchin' (I Gotta Find A Man)	Hazell Dean	Proto	5		F
12	-	Groovin' (You're The Best Thing)/ Big Boss Groove)	Style Council	Polydor	5		
13	-	I Won't Let The Sun Go Down On Me	Nik Kershaw	MCA	8		
14	1	The Reflex	Duran Duran	EMI	8	(1)	
15	-	Farewell My Summer Love	Michael Jackson	Motown	6	(38)	
16	-	Heaven Knows I'm Miserable Now	Smiths	Rough Trade	5		
17	-	I Feel Like Buddy Holly	Alvin Stardust	Stiff	5		
18	-	Thinking Of You	Sister Sledge	Cotillion/Atlantic	6		
19	2	Automatic	Pointer Sisters	Planet	7	(5)	
20	4	I Want To Break Free	Queen	EMI	9	(45)	

◆ The Beatles, who had recently had streets named after them in Liverpool, were made Freemen of that city – its highest honour.

◆ The late Bob Marley's **Legend** entered the LP chart at No. 1 and held that spot for three months.

◆ Frankie Goes To Hollywood's second single, 'Two Tribes', entered at No. 1 and spent nine weeks at the summit. Soon afterwards 'Relax' moved back up to No. 2. Both sold over a million.

1984

July 1984

This Mnth	Prev Mnth	Title	Artist	Label	Wks	(US 20 Pos)	
1	2	Two Tribes	Frankie Goes To Hollywood	ZTT	14	(43)	G
2	-	Relax	Frankie Goes To Hollywood	ZTT	25	(10)	F G
3	-	Time After Time	Cyndi Lauper	Portrait	7	(1)	
4	13	I Won't Let The Sun Go Down On Me	Nik Kershaw	MCA	8		
5	-	Hole In My Shoe	neil	WEA	6		F L
6	-	Jump (For My Love)	Pointer Sisters	Planet	5	(3)	
7	-	White Lines (Don't Don't Do It)	Grandmaster Flash, Melle Mel & The Furious Five	Sugar Hill	12		L
8	-	When Doves Cry	Prince	Warner	8	(1)	F
9	-	Breakin'...There's No Stopping Us	Ollie & Jerry	Polydor	5	(9)	F L
10	-	What's Love Got To Do With It	Tina Turner	Capitol	10	(1)	
11	-	Love Resurrection	Alison Moyet	CBS	5	(82)	F
12	-	Young At Heart	Bluebells	London	6		
13	-	Sister Of Mercy	Thompson Twins	Arista	3		
14	3	Smalltown Boy	Bronski Beat	Forbidden	7	(48)	F
15	-	Talking Loud And Clear	Orchestral Manoeuvres In The Dark	Virgin	4		
16	15	Farewell My Summer Love	Michael Jackson	Motown	6	(38)	
17	-	Stuck On You	Lionel Richie	Motown	4	(3)	
18	1	Wake Me Up Before You Go Go	Wham!	Epic	8	(1)	
19	-	Everybody's Laughing	Phil Fearon & Galaxy	Ensign	5		
20	18	Thinking Of You	Sister Sledge	Cotillion/Atlantic	6		

August 1984

This Mnth	Prev Mnth	Title	Artist	Label	Wks	(US 20 Pos)	
1	1	Two Tribes	Frankie Goes To Hollywood	ZTT	14	(43)	G
2	-	Careless Whisper	George Michael	Epic	12	(1)	F G
3	10	What's Love Got To Do With It	Tina Turner	Capitol	10	(1)	
4	-	Agadoo	Black Lace	Flair	10		
5	-	Relax	Frankie Goes To Hollywood	ZTT	25	(10)	F G
6	8	When Doves Cry	Prince	Warner	8	(1)	F
7	-	Whatever I Do (Wherever I Go)	Hazell Dean	Proto	7		
8	5	Hole In My Shoe	neil	WEA	6		F L
9	-	It's A Hard Life	Queen	EMI	4	(72)	
10	-	Self Control	Laura Branigan	Atlantic	7	(4)	L
11	7	White Lines (Don't Don't Do It)	Grandmaster Flash, Melle Mel & The Furious Five	Sugar Hill	12		L
12	-	Like To Get To Know You Well	Howard Jones	WEA	7	(49)	
13	19	Everybody's Laughing	Phil Fearon & Galaxy	Ensign	5		
14	-	On The Wings Of Love	Jeffrey Osborne	A&M	5	(29)	L
15	-	Down On The Street	Shakatak	Polydor	4		L
16	-	Closest Thing To Heaven	Kane Gang	Kitchenware	5		F L
17	-	I Just Called To Say I Love You	Stevie Wonder	Motown	13	(1)	G
18	3	Time After Time	Cyndi Lauper	Portrait	7	(1)	
19	-	Stuck On You	Trevor Walters	Sanity	4		F L
20	12	Young At Heart	Bluebells	London	6		

◆ Elton John, Kool & The Gang and Brits winner Paul Young (whose **No Parlez** album sold over a million) performed in front of 72,000 at Wembley Stadium.

◆ Stevie Wonder's 36th British hit 'I Just Called To Say I Love You' was not only his first solo No. 1, but also Motown's first UK million seller. It was the third British million seller in a row to head the chart (following 'Two Tribes' and 'Careless Whisper').

1984

This Mnth	Prev Mnth	Title	Artist	Label	Wks (US 20 Pos)	
1	16	I Just Called To Say I Love You	Stevie Wonder	Motown	13 (1)	G
2	2	Careless Whisper	George Michael	Epic	12 (1)	F G
3	4	Agadoo	Black Lace	Flair	10	
4	-	Ghostbusters	Ray Parker Jr.	Arista	17 (1)	
5	-	Dr. Beat	Miami Sound Machine	Epic	7	F
6	11	Like To Get To Know You Well	Howard Jones	WEA	7 (49)	
7	-	Passengers	Elton John	Rocket	5	
8	-	Pride (In The Name Of Love)	U2	Island	7 (33)	
9	9	Self Control	Laura Branigan	Atlantic	7 (4)	L
10	-	Big In Japan	Alphaville	WEA International	5 (66)	F L
11	-	Lost In Music	Sister Sledge	Cotillion/Atlantic	6	
12	-	Master And Servant	Depeche Mode	Mute	4 (87)	
13	-	I'll Fly For You	Spandau Ballet	Reformation	4	
14	6	Whatever I Do (Wherever I Go)	Hazell Dean	Proto	7	
15	-	Madame Butterfly	Malcolm McLaren	Charisma	4	L
16	1	Two Tribes	Frankie Goes To Hollywood	ZTT	14 (43)	G
17	10	White Lines (Don't Don't Do It)	Grandmaster Flash, Melle Mel & The Furious Five	Sugar Hill	12	L
18	-	A Letter To You	Shakin' Stevens	Epic	4	
19	-	Blue Jean	David Bowie	EMI America	4 (8)	
20	18	Stuck On You	Trevor Walters	Sanity	4	F L

This Mnth	Prev Mnth	Title	Artist	Label	Wks (US 20 Pos)	
1	1	I Just Called To Say I Love You	Stevie Wonder	Motown	13 (1)	G
2	-	The War Song	Culture Club	Virgin	5 (17)	
3	-	Freedom	Wham!	Epic	8 (3)	
4	4	Ghostbusters	Ray Parker Jr.	Arista	17 (1)	
5	-	No More Lonely Nights (Ballad)	Paul McCartney	Parlophone	6 (6)	
6	-	Drive	Cars	Elektra	6 (3)	
7	-	Together In Electric Dreams	Giorgio Moroder & Phil Oakey	Virgin	6	L
8	-	Why?	Bronski Beat	Forbidden Fruit	5	
9	8	Pride (In The Name Of Love)	U2	Island	7 (33)	
10	-	Shout To The Top	Style Council	Polydor	4	
11	-	Purple Rain	Prince & The Revolution	Warner	4 (2)	
12	11	Lost In Music	Sister Sledge	Cotillion/Atlantic	6	
13	-	Missing You	John Waite	EMI	6 (1)	F L
14	-	If It Happens Again	UB40	Dep International	4	
15	-	I'm Gonna Tear Your Playhouse Down	Paul Young	CBS	3 (13)	
16	-	All Cried Out	Alison Moyet	CBS	6	
17	-	Love Kills	Freddie Mercury	CBS	4 (69)	F
18	19	Blue Jean	David Bowie	Emi America	4 (8)	
19	-	I Feel For You	Chaka Khan	Warner	8 (3)	
20	2	Careless Whisper	George Michael	Epic	12 (1)	F G

◆ Soon after releasing a duet with Cliff Richard, 'Two To The Power', Michael Jackson's 18-year-old sister Janet eloped with El Debarge, from the group Debarge.

◆ Bob Geldof and Midge Ure organized an all-star group, Band Aid, whose 'Do They Know It's Christmas' not only raised a fortune for the starving in Ethiopia but also became Britain's biggest ever seller (over 3.5 million).

November 1984

This Mnth	Prev Mnth	Title	Artist	Label	Wks	(US 20 Pos)	
1	19	I Feel For You	Chaka Khan	Warner	8	(3)	
2	-	The Wild Boys	Duran Duran	Parlophone	6	(2)	
3	3	Freedom	Wham!	Epic	8	(3)	
4	-	The Wanderer	Status Quo	Vertigo	5		
5	-	Caribbean Queen (No More Love On The Run)	Billy Ocean	Jive	6	(1)	
6	16	All Cried Out	Alison Moyet	CBS	6		
7	-	I Should Have Known Better	Jim Diamond	A&M	8		F
8	-	Never Ending Story	Limahl	EMI	7	(17)	L
9	-	Too Late For Goodbyes	Julian Lennon	Charisma	5	(5)	F
10	5	No More Lonely Nights (Ballad)	Paul McCartney	Parlophone	6	(6)	
11	7	Together In Electric Dreams	Giorgio Moroder & Phil Oakey	Virgin	6		L
12	-	Gimme All Your Lovin'	ZZ Top	Warner	4	(37)	F
13	-	Love's Great Adventure	Ultravox	Chrysalis	5		
14	-	Hard Habit To Break	Chicago	Full Moon	4	(3)	
15	-	I'm So Excited	Pointer Sisters	Planet	4	(9)	
16	1	I Just Called To Say I Love You	Stevie Wonder	Motown	13	(1)	G
17	-	The Riddle	Nik Kershaw	MCA	9		
18	13	Missing You	John Waite	EMI	6	(1)	F L
19	-	Sexcrime (Nineteen Eighty Four)	Eurythmics	Virgin	7	(81)	
20	6	Drive	Cars	Elektra	6	(3)	

December 1984

This Mnth	Prev Mnth	Title	Artist	Label	Wks	(US 20 Pos)	
1	-	The Power Of Love	Frankie Goes To Hollywood	ZTT	8		
2	18	The Riddle	Nik Kershaw	MCA	9		
3	-	We All Stand Together	Paul McCartney	Parlophone	7		
4	-	Like A Virgin	Madonna	Sire	10	(1)	
5	-	Do They Know It's Christmas	Band Aid	Mercury	8	(13)	F P
6	-	Teardrops	Shakin' Stevens	Epic	6		
7	7	I Should Have Known Better	Jim Diamond	A&M	8		F
8	-	Last Christmas/Everything She Wants	Wham!	Epic	8	(1)	G
9	20	Sexcrime (Nineteen Eighty Four)	Eurythmics	Virgin	7	(81)	
10	-	I Won't Run Away	Alvin Stardust	Chrysalis	6		L
11	1	I Feel For You	Chaka Khan	Warner	8	(3)	
12	-	Fresh	Kool & The Gang	De-Lite	7	(9)	
13	-	Nellie The Elephant	Toy Dolls	Volume	6		F L
14	-	Do The Conga	Black Lace	Flair	6		L
15	-	One Night In Bangkok	Murray Head	RCA	7	(3)	F L
16	8	Never Ending Story	Limahl	EMI	7	(17)	L
17	-	Everything Must Change	Paul Young	CBS	7	(56)	
18	-	Another Rock And Roll Christmas	Gary Glitter	Arista	3		L
19	15	Hard Habit To Break	Chicago	Full Moon	4	(3)	
20	-	Shout	Tears For Fears	Mercury	9	(1)	

◆ 'The Power Of Love' gave the year's most successful UK act, Frankie Goes To Hollywood, their third consecutive No. 1 with their first three hits, equalling a record set by fellow Liverpudlians Gerry & The Pacemakers.

◆ U2's first Top 5 entry 'Pride (In The Name Of Love)' was dedicated to Martin Luther King.

1985

This Mnth	Prev Mnth	Title	Artist	Label	Wks 20	(US Pos)	
1	5	Do They Know It's Christmas	Band Aid	Mercury	8	(13)	F P
2	8	Last Christmas/Everything She Wants	Wham!	Epic	8	(1)	G
3	-	I Want To Know What Love Is	Foreigner	Atlantic	9	(1)	L
4	4	Like A Virgin	Madonna	Sire	10	(1)	
5	4	Ghostbusters	Ray Parker Jr.	Arista	17	(1)	
6	20	Shout	Tears For Fears	Mercury	9	(1)	
7	3	We All Stand Together	Paul McCartney	Parlophone	7		
8	18	Everything Must Change	Paul Young	CBS	7	(56)	
9	13	Nellie The Elephant	Toy Dolls	Volume	6		F L
10	-	I Know Him So Well	Elaine Paige & Barbara Dickson	RCA	10		L
11	-	Step Off (Pt. 1)	Grandmaster Melle Mel & The Furious Five	Sugar Hill	4		F L
12	-	1999/Little Red Corvette	Prince & The Revolution	Warner	7	(12)	
13	-	Since Yesterday	Strawberry Switchblade	Korova	5		F L
14	1	The Power Of Love	Frankie Goes To Hollywood	ZTT	8		
15	-	Police Officer	Smiley Culture	Fashion	3		F L
16	2	The Riddle	Nik Kershaw	MCA	9		
17	12	Fresh	Kool & The Gang	De-Lite	7	(9)	
18	-	Love & Pride	King	CBS	8	(55)	F
19	-	Atmosphere	Russ Abbot	Spirit	7		F
20	-	Friends	Amii Stewart	RCA	4		

This Mnth	Prev Mnth	Title	Artist	Label	Wks 20	(US Pos)	
1	9	I Know Him So Well	Elaine Paige & Barbara Dickson	RCA	10		L
2	17	Love & Pride	King	CBS	8	(55)	F
3	-	Solid	Ashford & Simpson	Capitol	8	(12)	F L
4	3	I Want To Know What Love Is	Foreigner	Atlantic	9	(1)	L
5	11	1999/Little Red Corvette	Prince & The Revolution	Warner	7	(12)	
6	-	Dancing In The Dark	Bruce Springsteen	CBS	9	(2)	F
7	18	Atmosphere	Russ Abbot	Spirit	7		F
8	-	Close (To The Edit)	Art Of Noise	ZTT	4		F
9	5	Shout	Tears For Fears	Mercury	9	(1)	
10	-	A New England	Kirsty MacColl	Stiff	5		
11	-	Run To You	Bryan Adams	A&M	6	(6)	F
12	-	Things Can Only Get Better	Howard Jones	WEA	6	(5)	
13	12	Since Yesterday	Strawberry Switchblade	Korova	5		F L
14	-	Sussudio	Phil Collins	Virgin	4	(1)	
15	-	Loverboy	Billy Ocean	Jive	5	(2)	
16	-	Thinking Of You	Colour Field	Chrysalis	4		F L
17	-	You Spin Me Round (Like A Record)	Dead Or Alive	Epic	8	(11)	F
18	-	Nightshift	Commodores	Motown	8	(3)	
19	4	Like A Virgin	Madonna	Sire	10	(1)	
20	-	Yah Mo B There	James Ingram & Michael McDonald	A&M	2	(19)	

◆ Bruce Springsteen's 12 million selling **Born In The USA** topped the transatlantic charts as 'Dancing In The Dark' gave him his first major British hit.
◆ Wham! were voted British Group of the Year at the Brits, and George Michael became the youngest person to win the Songwriter of the Year trophy at the Ivor Novello Awards, where the transatlantic chart topper 'Careless Whisper' was named Most Performed Song of the Year.

March 1985

This Mnth	Prev Mnth	Title	Artist	Label	Wks	(US 20 Pos)	
1	17	You Spin Me Round (Like A Record)	Dead Or Alive	Epic	8	(11)	F
2	-	Material Girl	Madonna	Sire	6	(2)	
3	1	I Know Him So Well	Elaine Paige & Barbara Dickson	RCA	10		L
4	18	Nightshift	Commodores	Motown	8	(3)	
5	-	Kiss Me	Stephen 'Tin Tin' Duffy	10	6		F
6	-	Easy Lover	Philip Bailey & Phil Collins	CBS	9	(2)	F L
7	-	That Ole Devil Called Love	Alison Moyet	CBS	6		
8	-	The Last Kiss	David Cassidy	Arista	5		L
9	-	Everytime You Go Away	Paul Young	CBS	6	(1)	
10	-	Do What You Do	Jermaine Jackson	Arista	6	(13)	L
11	6	Dancing In The Dark	Bruce Springsteen	CBS	9	(2)	F
12	-	Let's Go Crazy/Take Me With You	Prince & The Revolution	Warner	4	(1)	
13	3	Solid	Ashford & Simpson	Capitol	8	(12)	F L
14	2	Love & Pride	King	CBS	8	(55)	F
15	-	We Close Our Eyes	Go West	Chrysalis	8	(41)	F
16	12	Things Can Only Get Better	Howard Jones	WEA	6	(5)	
17	-	Wide Boy	Nik Kershaw	MCA	6		
18	-	Pie Jesu	Sarah Brightman & Paul Miles-Kingston	HMV	5		
19	10	A New England	Kirsty MacColl	Stiff	5		
20	-	The Boys Of Summer	Don Henley	Geffen	3	(5)	F L

April 1985

This Mnth	Prev Mnth	Title	Artist	Label	Wks	(US 20 Pos)	
1	-	Everybody Wants To Rule The World	Tears For Fears	Mercury	9	(1)	
2	6	Easy Lover	Philip Bailey & Phil Collins	CBS	9	(2)	F L
3	-	Welcome To The Pleasure Dome	Frankie Goes To Hollywood	ZTT	5	(48)	
4	15	We Close Our Eyes	Go West	Chrysalis	8	(41)	F
5	-	Move Closer	Phyllis Nelson	Carrere	11		F L
6	-	We Are The World	USA For Africa	CBS	6	(1)	F L
7	-	Could It Be I'm Falling In Love	David Grant & Jaki Graham	Chrysalis	6		
8	18	Pie Jesu	Sarah Brightman & Paul Miles-Kingston	HMV	5		
9	7	That Ole Devil Called Love	Alison Moyet	CBS	6		
10	9	Everytime You Go Away	Paul Young	CBS	6	(1)	
11	-	One More Night	Phil Collins	Virgin	5	(1)	
12	-	Clouds Across The Moon	Rah Band	RCA	5		L
13	-	Spend The Night	Coolnotes	Abstract Dance	4		F
14	17	Wide Boy	Nik Kershaw	MCA	6		
15	-	The Heat Is On	Glenn Frey	MCA	4	(2)	F L
16	10	Do What You Do	Jermaine Jackson	Arista	6	(13)	L
17	5	Kiss Me	Stephen 'Tin Tin' Duffy	10	6		F
18	2	Material Girl	Madonna	Sire	6	(2)	
19	-	I Feel Love	Bronski Beat & Marc Almond	Forbidden Fruit	7		
20	-	Don't You (Forget About Me)	Simple Minds	Virgin	5	(1)	

◆ Queen, Rod Stewart, Yes, Iron Maiden, AC/DC, Whitesnake, The Scorpions and Ozzy Osbourne were among the headliners at the massive *Rock In Rio* festival.

◆ Few Chinese noticed as Wham! became the first western pop group to play in China and to have records released there. In contrast, few Britons could have been unaware of Bruce Springsteen's UK tour.

1985

This Mnth	Prev Mnth	Title	Artist	Label	Wks	(US 20 Pos)	
1	-	19	Paul Hardcastle	Chrysalis	9	(15)	F
2	5	Move Closer	Phyllis Nelson	Carrere	11		F L
3	19	I Feel Love	Bronski Beat & Marc Almond	Forbidden Fruit	7		
4	1	Everybody Wants To Rule The World	Tears For Fears	Mercury	9	(1)	
5	-	Feel So Real	Steve Arrington	Atlantic	7		F L
6	-	Rhythm Of The Night	DeBarge	Gordy	6	(3)	F L
7	20	Don't You (Forget About Me)	Simple Minds	Virgin	5	(1)	
8	6	We Are The World	USA For Africa	CBS	6	(1)	F L
9	-	The Unforgettable Fire	U2	Island	3		
10	-	I Was Born To Love You	Freddie Mercury	CBS	5	(76)	
11	-	Walls Come Tumbling Down!	Style Council	Polydor	4		
12	-	A View To Kill	Duran Duran	Parlophone	7	(1)	
13	-	Love Don't Live Here Anymore	Jimmy Nail	Virgin	6		F
14	11	One More Night	Phil Collins	Virgin	5	(1)	
15	12	Clouds Across The Moon	Rah Band	RCA	5		L
16	-	Kayleigh	Marillion	EMI	9		
17	7	Could It Be I'm Falling In Love	David Grant & Jaki Graham	Chrysalis	6		
18	-	Slave To Love	Bryan Ferry	EG	4		
19	-	Lover Come Back To Me	Dead Or Alive	Epic	3	(75)	
20	-	I Want Your Lovin' (Just A Little Bit)	Curtis Hairston	London	2		F L

This Mnth	Prev Mnth	Title	Artist	Label	Wks	(US 20 Pos)	
1	16	Kayleigh	Marillion	EMI	9		
2	-	You'll Never Walk Alone	The Crowd	Spartan	6		F L
3	1	19	Paul Hardcastle	Chrysalis	9	(15)	F
4	12	A View To Kill	Duran Duran	Parlophone	7	(1)	
5	-	Suddenly	Billy Ocean	Jive	8	(4)	
6	-	Obsession	Animotion	Mercury	6	(6)	F L
7	-	The Word Girl	Scritti Politti Feat. Ranking Ann	Virgin	6		
8	-	Frankie	Sister Sledge	Atlantic	10	(75)	
9	-	Crazy For You	Madonna	Geffen	10	(1)	
10	-	Out In The Fields	Gary Moore & Phil Lynott	10	6		
11	-	History	Mai Tai	Virgin	7		F
12	-	Cherish	Kool & The Gang	De-Lite	12	(2)	L
13	-	Walking On Sunshine	Katrina & The Waves	Capitol	5	(9)	F
14	13	Love Don't Live Here Anymore	Jimmy Nail	Virgin	6		F
15	-	Axel F	Harold Faltermeyer	MCA	9	(3)	F L
16	6	Rhythm Of The Night	DeBarge	Gordy	6	(3)	F L
17	-	Ben	Marti Webb	Starblend	6		
18	-	Call Me	Go West	Chrysalis	3	(54)	
19	3	I Feel Love	Bronski Beat & Marc Almond	Forbidden Fruit	7		
20	-	Johnny Come Home	Fine Young Cannibals	London	7	(76)	F

◆ Paul Hardcastle, ex- keyboard player with Brit-funk band Direct Drive, took sampling to new heights with his groundbreaking transatlantic hit '19'. Its success helped make him the most in-demand remixer of the time.

◆ Dancing In The Street' by David Bowie & Mick Jagger, entered at No. 1. Proceeds from the hit helped the starving in Ethiopia.

July 1985

This Mnth	Prev Mnth	Title	Artist	Label	Wks	(US 20 Pos)	
1	8	Frankie	Sister Sledge	Atlantic	10	(75)	
2	15	Axel F	Harold Faltermeyer	MCA	9	(3)	F L
3	9	Crazy For You	Madonna	Geffen	10	(1)	
4	12	Cherish	Kool & The Gang	De-Lite	12	(2)	L
5	-	I'm On Fire/Born In The U.S.A.	Bruce Springsteen	CBS	7	(6)	
6	-	There Must Be An Angel (Playing With My Heart)	Eurythmics	RCA	8	(22)	
7	-	My Toot Toot	Denise La Salle	Epic	6		F L
8	17	Ben	Marti Webb	Starblend	6		
9	20	Johnny Come Home	Fine Young Cannibals	London	7	(76)	F
10	-	Live Is Life	Opus	Polydor	7	(32)	F L
11	11	History	Mai Tai	Virgin	7		F
12	5	Suddenly	Billy Ocean	Jive	8	(4)	
13	-	Head Over Heels	Tears For Fears	Mercury	4	(3)	
14	-	Round And Round	Jaki Graham	EMI	4		
15	1	Kayleigh	Marillion	EMI	9		
16	-	Into The Groove	Madonna	Sire	10		
17	2	You'll Never Walk Alone	The Crowd	Spartan	6		F L
18	-	Turn It Up	Conway Brothers	10	3		F L
19	-	Money's Too Tight (To Mention)	Simply Red	Elektra	3	(28)	F
20	-	Living On Video	Trans-X	Boiling Point	5	(61)	F L

August 1985

This Mnth	Prev Mnth	Title	Artist	Label	Wks	(US 20 Pos)	
1	16	Into The Groove	Madonna	Sire	10		
2	-	We Don't Need Another Hero (Thunderdome)	Tina Turner	Capitol	7	(2)	
3	-	Money For Nothing	Dire Straits	Vertigo	8	(1)	
4	6	There Must Be An Angel (Playing With My Heart)	Eurythmics	RCA	8	(22)	
5	-	I Got You Babe	UB40 Feat Chrissie Hynde	Dep International	8	(28)	
6	-	Holiday	Madonna	Sire	5		
7	-	White Wedding	Billy Idol	Chrysalis	8	(36)	
8	-	Running Up That Hill	Kate Bush	EMI	6	(30)	
9	-	Drive	Cars	Elektra	7		L
10	10	Live Is Life	Opus	Polydor	7	(32)	F L
11	4	Cherish	Kool & The Gang	De-Lite	12	(2)	L
12	-	Say I'm Your No. 1	Princess	Supreme	6		F
13	1	Frankie	Sister Sledge	Atlantic	10	(75)	
14	2	Axel F	Harold Faltermeyer	MCA	9	(3)	F L
15	-	Don Quixote	Nik Kershaw	MCA	3		L
16	-	Tarzan Boy	Baltimora	Columbia	7	(13)	F L
17	-	Excitable	Amazulu	Island	3		F
18	20	Living On Video	Trans-X	Boiling Point	5	(61)	F L
19	-	Alone Without You	King	CBS	5		
20	14	Round And Round	Jaki Graham	EMI	4		

◆ n September, a record nine re-issued singles were simultaneously in the UK Top 40, including re-mixes of Amii Stewart's 1979 'Knock On Wood' and 'Light My Fire' – the earliest of dozens of dance re-mixes to chart in Britain.

◆ Dire Straits scored simultaneous US chart-toppers with **Brothers In Arms** (which eventually sold six million in America, nearly four million in the UK and topped the chart in 22 countries!), and the Grammy winning 'Money For Nothing' on which co-writer Sting apeared.

1985

This Mnth	Prev Mnth	Title	Artist	Label	Wks	(US 20 Pos)	
1	-	Dancing In The Street	David Bowie & Mick Jagger	EMI America	7	(7)	
2	-	Holding Out For A Hero	Bonnie Tyler	CBS	8	(34)	L
3	16	Tarzan Boy	Baltimora	Columbia	7	(13)	F L
4	5	I Got You Babe	UB40 Feat. Chrissie Hynde	Dep International	8	(28)	
5	-	Part Time Lover	Stevie Wonder	Motown	5	(1)	
6	-	Body And Soul	Mai Tai	Virgin	6		L
7	1	Into The Groove	Madonna	Sire	10		
8	-	Knock On Wood/Light My Fire	Amii Stewart	Sedition	5		L
9	9	Drive	Cars	Elektra	7		L
10	-	Lavender	Marillion	EMI	5		
11	8	Running Up That Hill	Kate Bush	EMI	6	(30)	
12	12	Say I'm Your No. 1	Princess	Supreme	6		F
13	-	If I Was	Midge Ure	Chrysalis	7		
14	-	Angel	Madonna	Sire	5	(5)	
15	19	Alone Without You	King	CBS	5		
16	-	The Power Of Love	Huey Lewis & The News	Chrysalis	5	(1)	F
17	3	Money For Nothing	Dire Straits	Vertigo	8	(1)	
18	-	Lean On Me (Ah-Li-Ayo)	Red Box	Sire	8		F
19	-	Body Rock	Maria Vidal	EMI America	5	(48)	F L
20	-	I Can Dream About You	Dan Hartman	MCA	3	(6)	L

This Mnth	Prev Mnth	Title	Artist	Label	Wks	(US 20 Pos)	
1	-	The Power Of Love	Jennifer Rush	CBS	11	(57)	F G
2	13	If I Was	Midge Ure	Chrysalis	7		
3	-	Trapped	Colonel Abrams	MCA	10		F L
4	18	Lean On Me (Ah-Li-Ayo)	Red Box	Sire	7		
5	-	Rebel Yell	Billy Idol	Chrysalis	6	(46)	
6	5	Part Time Lover	Stevie Wonder	Motown	8	(1)	
7	-	Take On Me	A-Ha	Warner	9	(1)	F
8	-	St. Elmo's Fire (Man In Motion)	John Parr	London	6	(1)	F L
9	1	Dancing In The Street	David Bowie & Mick Jagger	EMI America	7	(7)	
10	2	Holding Out For A Hero	Bonnie Tyler	CBS	8	(34)	L
11	-	Alive And Kicking	Simple Minds	Virgin	6	(3)	
12	14	Angel	Madonna	Sire	5	(5)	
13	-	Gambler	Madonna	Geffen	6		
14	-	Miami Vice Theme	Jan Hammer	MCA	4	(1)	F
15	10	Lavender	Marillion	EMI	5		
16	19	Body Rock	Maria Vidal	EMI America	5	(48)	F L
17	16	The Power Of Love	Huey Lewis & The News	Chrysalis	5	(1)	F
18	-	Slave To The Rhythm	Grace Jones	ZTT	4		
19	-	Nikita	Elton John	Rocket	9	(7)	
20	-	Single Life	Cameo	Club	3		F

◆ Madonna became the first female to simultaneously hold the top 2 places, thanks to 'Into The Groove' (which only appeared on the 12" version of 'Angel' in the US) and a re-issue of 'Holiday'.

◆ It was claimed that Dire Straits' 'Brothers In Arms' was the first commercially succsseful CD single.

1985

November 1985

This Mnth	Prev Mnth	Title	Artist	Label	Wks	(US 20 Pos)	
1	1	The Power Of Love	Jennifer Rush	CBS	11	(57)	F G
2	-	A Good Heart	Feargal Sharkey	Virgin	10	(67)	F
3	7	Take On Me	A-Ha	Warner	9	(1)	F
4	19	Nikita	Elton John	Rocket	9	(7)	
5	-	Don't Break My Heart	UB40	Dep International	8		
6	-	Something About You	Level 42	Polydor	6	(7)	
7	3	Trapped	Colonel Abrams	MCA	10		F L
8	-	I'm Your Man	Wham!	Epic	8	(3)	
9	-	Road To Nowhere	Talking Heads	EMI	6		
10	-	One Vision	Queen	EMI	4	(61)	
11	13	Gambler	Madonna	Geffen	6		
12	-	Sisters Are Doin' It For Themselves	Eurythmics & Aretha Franklin	RCA	5	(18)	
13	-	Stairway To Heaven	Far Corporation	Arista	4	(89)	F L
14	8	St. Elmo's Fire (Man In Motion)	John Parr	London	6	(1)	F L
15	-	The Show	Doug E. Fresh & The Get Fresh Crew	Cooltempo	6		F L
16	-	The Taste Of Your Tears	King	CBS	5		L
17	-	Election Day	Arcadia	Odeon	4	(6)	F L
18	11	Alive And Kicking	Simple Minds	Virgin	6	(3)	
19	-	See The Day	Dee C. Lee	CBS	8		F L
20	14	Miami Vice Theme	Jan Hammer	MCA	4	(1)	F

December 1985

This Mnth	Prev Mnth	Title	Artist	Label	Wks	(US 20 Pos)	
1	-	Saving All My Love For You	Whitney Houston	Arista	9	(1)	F
2	8	I'm Your Man	Wham!	Epic	8	(3)	
3	19	See The Day	Dee C. Lee	CBS	8		F L
4	-	Separate Lives	Phil Collins & Marilyn Martin	Virgin	8	(1)	
5	-	Do They Know It's Christmas	Band Aid	Mercury	5		L
6	-	Merry Christmas Everyone	Shakin' Stevens	Epic	6		
7	-	Dress You Up	Madonna	Sire	6	(5)	
8	-	West End Girls	Pet Shop Boys	Parlophone	8	(1)	
9	2	A Good Heart	Feargal Sharkey	Virgin	10	(67)	F
10	-	Say You, Say Me	Lionel Richie	Motown	7	( )	
11	15	The Show	Doug E. Fresh & The Get Fresh Crew	Cooltempo	6		F L
12	-	We Built This City	Starship	RCA	6	(1)	F
13	-	Last Christmas	Wham!	Epic	4		G
14	-	Santa Claus Is Comin' To Town/My Hometown	Bruce Springsteen	Epic	4		
15	5	Don't Break My Heart	UB40	Dep International	8		
16	-	Don't Look Down-The Sequel	Go West	Chrysalis	6	(39)	
17	-	Walking In The Air	Aled Jones	HMV	5		F L
18	9	Road To Nowhere	Talking Heads	EMI	6		
19	-	Spies Like Us	Paul McCartney	Parlophone	6	(7)	
20	4	Nikita	Elton John	Rocket	9	(7)	

◆ American Jennifer Rush topped the chart with 'The Power Of Love'. It became the first UK million seller by a female artist. In her homeland it failed to reach the Top 40. The song, however, became an American No. 1 by French-Canadian Celine Dion in 1994.

◆ NME writers chose The Jesus & Mary Chain's 'Never Understood' and **Psychocandy** as the Top Single and Album of the Year respectively.

January 1986

This Mnth	Prev Mnth	Title	Artist	Label	Wks	(US 20 Pos)	
1	8	West End Girls	Pet Shop Boys	Parlophone	8	(1)	F
2	-	Hit That Perfect Beat	Bronski Beat	Forbidden	7		
3	-	The Sun Always Shines On T.V.	A-Ha	Warner	7	(20)	
4	1	Saving All My Love For You	Whitney Houston	Arista	9	(1)	F
5	-	Saturday Love	Cherrelle & Alexander O'Neal	Tabu	5	(26)	F L
6	-	Girlie Girlie	Sophia George	Winner	5		F L
7	6	Merry Christmas Everyone	Shakin' Stevens	Epic	6		
8	-	Walk Of Life	Dire Straits	Vertigo	6	(7)	L
9	17	Walking In The Air	Aled Jones	HMV	5		F L
10	-	You Little Thief	Feargal Sharkey	Virgin	4		
11	-	Broken Wings	Mr Mister	RCA	4	(1)	F
12	7	Dress You Up	Madonna	Sire	6	(5)	
13	5	Do They Know It's Christmas	Band Aid	Mercury	5		L
14	2	I'm Your Man	Wham!	Epic	8	(3)	
15	4	Separate Lives	Phil Collins & Marilyn Martin	Virgin	8	(1)	
16	-	Alice I Want You Just For Me	Full Force	CBS	3		F L
17	13	Last Christmas	Wham!	Epic	4		G
18	-	Who's Zoomin' Who	Aretha Franklin	Arista	3	(7)	
19	-	Russians	Sting	A&M	3	(16)	
20	-	It's Alright (Baby's Coming Back)	Eurythmics	RCA	4	(78)	

February 1986

This	Prev	Title	Artist	Label	Wks	(US Pos)	
1	-	When The Going Gets Tough, The Tough Get Going	Billy Ocean	Jive	8	(2)	
2	-	Borderline	Madonna	Sire	6	(10)	
3	3	The Sun Always Shines On T.V.	A-Ha	Warner	7	(20)	
4	-	Only Love	Nana Mouskouri	Philips	6		F L
5	-	System Addict	Five Star	Tent	6		
6	8	Walk Of Life	Dire Straits	Vertigo	6	(7)	L
7	-	Living In America	James Brown	Scotti Bros	6	(4)	
8	-	Eloise	Damned	MCA	6		L
9	-	The Phantom Of The Opera	Sarah Brightman/Steve Harley	Polydor	4		
10	-	Starting Together	Su Pollard	Rainbow	5		F L
11	-	The Captain Of Her Heart	Double	Polydor	4	(16)	F L
12	-	How Will I Know	Whitney Houston	Arista	6	(1)	
13	-	Suspicious Minds	Fine Young Cannibals	London	5		
14	11	Broken Wings	Mr Mister	RCA	4	(1)	F
15	-	Chain Reaction	Diana Ross	Capitol	10	(66)	
16	5	Saturday Love	Cherrelle & Alexander O'Neal	Tabu	5	(26)	F L
17	-	Rise	Public Image Ltd.	Virgin	5		L
18	-	Pull Up To The Bumper/La Vie En Rose	Grace Jones	Island	4		L
19	-	Burning Heart	Survivor	Scotti Brothers	5	(2)	L
20	-	Sanctify Yourself	Simple Minds	Virgin	3	(14)	

◆ An *NME* survey showed that Madonna was the UK's Top Singles Artist in 1985 and that Bruce Springsteen was Top Album Artist.

◆ Annie Lennox again collected the Best Female Artist trophy at the Brit Awards. Other winners included Phil Collins (Best Male), Dire Straits (Best Group), Go West (Best Newcomer), Bruce Springsteen (Best International Artist) and Huey Lewis & The News (Best International Group).

March 1986

This Mnth	Prev Mnth	Title	Artist	Label	Wks	(US 20 Pos)	
1	15	Chain Reaction	Diana Ross	Capitol	10	(66)	
2	-	Manic Monday	Bangles	CBS	6	(2)	F
3	1	When The Going Gets Tough, The Tough Get Going	Billy Ocean	Jive	8	(2)	
4	-	Love Missile F1-11	Sigue Sigue Sputnik	Parlophone	4		F
5	-	Absolute Beginners	David Bowie	Virgin	5	(53)	
6	-	Hi Ho Silver	Jim Diamond	A&M	7		L
7	10	Starting Together	Su Pollard	Rainbow	5		F L
8	19	Burning Heart	Survivor	Scotti Brothers	5	(2)	L
9	-	Theme From New York New York	Frank Sinatra	Reprise	3	(32)	L
10	-	(Nothin' Serious) Just Buggin'	Whistle	Champion	4		F L
11	12	How Will I Know	Whitney Houston	Arista	6	(1)	
12	-	Living Doll	Cliff Richard & The Young Ones	WEA	7		
13	-	Kiss	Prince & The Revolution	Paisley Park	4	(1)	
14	-	The Power Of Love/Do You Believe In Love	Huey Lewis & The News	Chrysalis	4		
15	8	Eloise	Damned	MCA	6		L
16	-	Don't Waste My Time	Paul Hardcastle	Chrysalis	4		
17	-	Move Away	Culture Club	Virgin	4	(12)	L
18	-	Kyrie	Mr. Mister	RCA	5	(1)	L
19	-	Digging Your Scene	Blow Monkeys	RCA	4	(14)	F
20	-	Touch Me (I Want Your Body)	Samantha Fox	Jive	6	(4)	F

April 1986

This Mnth	Prev Mnth	Title	Artist	Label	Wks	(US 20 Pos)	
1	12	Living Doll	Cliff Richard & The Young Ones	WEA	7		
2	-	A Different Corner	George Michael	Epic	7	(7)	
3	-	Rock Me Amadeus	Falco	A&M	9	(1)	F
4	20	Touch Me (I Want Your Body)	Samantha Fox	Jive	6	(4)	F
5	-	A Kind Of Magic	Queen	EMI	8	(42)	
6	-	Wonderful World	Sam Cooke	RCA	6		L
7	-	You To Me Are Everything	Real Thing	PRT	7		
8	-	Peter Gunn	Art Of Noise & Duane Eddy	China	4	(50)	
9	-	Secret Lovers	Atlantic Starr	A&M	6	(3)	F
10	-	Train Of Thought	A-Ha	Warner	3		
11	-	Look Away	Big Country	Mercury	5		
12	-	All The Things She Said	Simple Minds	Virgin	5	(28)	
13	1	Chain Reaction	Diana Ross	Capitol	10	(66)	
14	5	Absolute Beginners	David Bowie	Virgin	5	(53)	
15	-	E=MC^2	Big Audio Dynamite	CBS	4		F L
16	-	What Have You Done For Me Lately	Janet Jackson	A&M	6	(4)	F
17	-	Can't Wait Another Minute	Five Star	Tent	7	(41)	
18	-	Just Say No	Grange Hill Cast	BBC	3		F L
19	6	Hi Ho Silver	Jim Diamond	A&M	7		L
20	18	Kyrie	Mr. Mister	RCA	5	(1)	L

◆ Among the American re-releases hitting the heights were 'Borderline' by Madonna, 'The Power of Love' by Huey Lewis & The News and, perhaps most surprisingly, 'Theme From New York New York' by Frank Sinatra.

◆ Bob Geldof received an honorary knighthood for his charity work. Among the current charity hits were 'Everybody Wants To Run the World' (for Sports Aid) by Tears For Fears and an update of 'Living Doll' by Cliff Richard & The Young Ones (for Comic Relief).

1986

This Mnth	Prev Mnth	Title	Artist	Label	Wks 20	(US Pos)	
1	-	Lessons In Love	Level 42	Polydor	7	(12)	
2	3	Rock Me Amadeus	Falco	A&M	9	(1)	F
3	-	On My Own	Patti Labelle/Michael McDonald	MCA	8	(1)	F L
4	-	The Chicken Song	Spitting Image	Virgin	6		F L
5	-	Live To Tell	Madonna	Sire	6	(1)	
6	16	What Have You Done For Me Lately	Janet Jackson	A&M	6	(4)	F
7	-	Sledgehammer	Peter Gabriel	Virgin	8	(1)	
8	17	Can't Wait Another Minute	Five Star	Tent	7	(41)	
9	-	Greatest Love Of All	Whitney Houston	Arista	5	(1)	
10	2	A Different Corner	George Michael	Epic	7	(7)	
11	-	Snooker Loopy	Matchroom Mob With Chas & Dave	Rockney	4		F L
12	-	Spirit In The Sky	Doctor & The Medics	IRS	9	(69)	F L
13	-	I Heard It Through The Grapevine	Marvin Gaye	Tamla Motown	4		L
14	-	Why Can't This Be Love	Van Halen	Warner	4	(3)	L
15	5	A Kind Of Magic	Queen	EMI	8	(42)	
16	18	Just Say No	Grange Hill Cast	BBC	3		F L
17	-	There'll Be Sad Songs (To Make You Cry)	Billy Ocean	Jive	4	(1)	
18	-	Rolling Home	Status Quo	Vertigo	3		
19	11	Look Away	Big Country	Mercury	5		
20	-	You And Me Tonight	Aurra	10	4		F L

This Mnth	Prev Mnth	Title	Artist	Label	Wks 20	(US Pos)	
1	12	Spirit In The Sky	Doctor & The Medics	IRS	9	(69)	F L
2	-	Holding Back The Years	Simply Red	WEA	8	(1)	
3	-	I Can't Wait	Nu Shooz	Atlantic	7	(3)	F L
4	-	Addicted To Love	Robert Palmer	Island	7	(1)	
5	7	Sledgehammer	Peter Gabriel	Virgin	8	(1)	
6	-	Can't Get By Without You	Real Thing	PRT	6		L
7	-	The Edge Of Heaven/ Where Did Your Heart Go	Wham!	Epic	6	(10)	L
8	-	Hunting High And Low	A-Ha	Warner	5		
9	-	Set Me Free	Jaki Graham	EMI	5		
10	-	Everybody Wants To Run The World	Tears For Fears	Mercury	3		
11	-	Too Good To Be Forgotten	Amazulu	Island	6		
12	-	Vienna Calling	Falco	A&M	4	(18)	L
13	4	The Chicken Song	Spitting Image	Virgin	6		F L
14	-	Happy Hour	Housemartins	Go! Discs	7		F
15	3	On My Own	Patti Labelle/Michael McDonald	MCA	8	(1)	F L
16	-	New Beginning (Mamba Seyra)	Bucks Fizz	Polydor	5		L
17	1	Lessons In Love	Level 42	Polydor	7	(12)	
18	-	My Favourite Waste Of Time	Owen Paul	Epic	7		F L
19	-	Opportunities (Let's Make Lots Of Money)	Pet Shop Boys	Parlophone	4	(10)	
20	-	Amityville (The House On...)	Lovebug Starski	Epic	4		F L

◆ Sam Cooke's 'Wonderful World' (from 1960) and Marvin Gaye's 'I Heard it Through The Grapevine' (from 1968), were the first of many oldies that hit after being heard in Levis' jeans advertisements.

◆ Shortly before his last gig with Wham!, George Michael's 'A Different Corner' became the first British No. 1 sung, written, produced, arranged and played (all instruments!) by the same person.

1986

This Mnth	Prev Mnth	Title	Artist	Label	Wks	(US 20 Pos)
1	-	Papa Don't Preach	Madonna	Sire	9	(1)
2	18	My Favourite Waste Of Time	Owen Paul	Epic	7	F L
3	7	The Edge Of Heaven/Where Did Your Heart Go	Wham!	Epic	6	(10) L
4	14	Happy Hour	Housemartins	Go! Discs	7	F
5	-	Let's Go All The Way	Sly Fox	Capitol	6	(7) F L
6	-	Venus	Bananarama	London	5	(1)
7	11	Too Good To Be Forgotten	Amazulu	Island	6	
8	-	Every Beat Of My Heart	Rod Stewart	Warner	6	(83)
9	3	I Can't Wait	Nu Shooz	Atlantic	7	(3) F L
10	-	Sing Our Own Song	UB40	Dep International	4	
11	-	The Lady In Red	Chris De Burgh	A&M	9	(3) F
12	16	New Beginning (Mamba Seyra)	Bucks Fizz	Polydor	5	L
13	-	Bang Zoom (Let's Go Go)	Real Roxanne With Hitman Howie Tee	Cooltempo	4	F L
14	-	Do Ya Do Ya (Wanna Please Me)	Samantha Fox	Jive	3	(87)
15	8	Hunting High And Low	A-Ha	Warner	5	
16	-	Paranoimia	Art Of Noise	China	3	(34)
17	-	Camouflage	Stan Ridgway	IRS	6	F L
18	1	Spirit In The Sky	Doctor & The Medics	IRS	9	(69) F L
19	-	It's 'Orrible Being In Love (When You're 8½)	Claire & Friends	BBC	3	F L
20	-	Higher Love	Steve Winwood	Island	3	(1) F

August 1986

This Mnth	Prev Mnth	Title	Artist	Label	Wks	(US 20 Pos)
1	11	The Lady In Red	Chris De Burgh	A&M	9	(3) F
2	-	So Macho/Cruising	Sinitta	Fanfare	9	F
3	-	I Want To Wake Up With You	Boris Gardiner	Revue	9	
4	17	Camouflage	Stan Ridgway	IRS	6	F L
5	-	Ain't Nothing Goin' On But The Rent	Gwen Guthrie	Boiling Point	7	(42) F L
6	1	Papa Don't Preach	Madonna	Sire	9	(1)
7	-	Anyone Can Fall In Love	Anita Dobson	BBC	4	F L
8	5	Let's Go All The Way	Sly Fox	Capitol	6	(7) F L
9	-	Find The Time	Five Star	Tent	4	
10	-	Calling All The Heroes	It Bites	Virgin	5	F L
11	8	Every Beat Of My Heart	Rod Stewart	Warner	6	(83)
12	-	What's The Colour Of Money?	Hollywood Beyond	WEA	5	F L
13	-	Shout	Lulu	Jive/Decca	4	
14	-	Panic	Smiths	Rough Trade	4	
15	-	I Didn't Mean To Turn You On	Robert Palmer	Island	4	(2)
16	-	Dancing On The Ceiling	Lionel Richie	Motown	4	(2)
17	-	Brother Louie	Modern Talking	RCA	6	F L
18	-	I Can Prove It	Phil Fearon	Ensign	4	L
19	-	We Don't Have To ...	Jermaine Stewart	10	9	(5) F
20	10	Sing Our Own Song	UB40	Dep International	4	

◆ Madonna's self-penned and produced 'Papa Don't Preach' was a transatlantic topper, as was her album **True Blue,** the first LP by an American female to enter the UK chart at the summit.
◆ Chicago club DJ Farley 'Jackmaster' Funk's 'Love Can't Turn You Around' is generally regarded as the earliest "house music" hit.
◆ Frankie Goes To Hollywood announced they were to disband, septet Madness shrunk to a quartet and Stiff Records closed – it was the end of another era in British pop.

1986

September 1986

This Mnth	Prev Mnth	Title	Artist	Label	Wks	(US 20 Pos)	
1	-	Don't Leave Me This Way	Communards	London	9	(40)	F
2	19	We Don't Have To ...	Jermaine Stewart	10	9	(5)	F
3	3	I Want To Wake Up With You	Boris Gardiner	Revue	9		
4	-	Glory Of Love	Peter Cetera	Full Moon	7	(1)	F L
5	-	(I Just) Died In Your Arms	Cutting Crew	Siren	6	(1)	F L
6	-	Rage Hard	Frankie Goes To Hollywood	ZTT	4		
7	17	Brother Louie	Modern Talking	RCA	6		F L
8	-	Word Up	Cameo	Club	7	(6)	
9	-	Holiday Rap	M.C. Miker 'G' & Deejay Sven	Debut	3		F L
10	-	Love Can't Turn Around	Farley 'Jackmaster' Funk	D.J. International	6		F L
11	2	So Macho/Cruising	Sinitta	Fanfare	9		F
12	-	Walk This Way	Run D.M.C.	London	6	(4)	F
13	-	Thorn In My Side	Eurythmics	RCA	7	(68)	
14	-	Human	Human League	Virgin	5	(1)	
15	-	Rain Or Shine	Five Star	Tent	7		
16	-	When I Think Of You	Janet Jackson	A&M	4	(1)	
17	1	The Lady In Red	Chris De Burgh	A&M	9	(3)	F
18	-	You Give Love A Bad Name	Bon Jovi	Vertigo	3	(1)	F
19	-	Sweet Freedom	Michael McDonald	MCA	3	(7)	L
20	5	Ain't Nothing Goin' On But The Rent	Gwen Guthrie	Boiling Point	7	(42)	F L

October 1986

This Mnth	Prev Mnth	Title	Artist	Label	Wks	(US 20 Pos)	
1	-	True Blue	Madonna	Sire	7	(3)	
2	15	Rain Or Shine	Five Star	Tent	7		
3	1	Don't Leave Me This Way	Communards	London	9	(40)	F
4	-	You Can Call Me Al	Paul Simon	Warner	6	(23)	
5	-	Every Loser Wins	Nick Berry	BBC	6		F
6	-	In The Army Now	Status Quo	Vertigo	7		
7	8	Word Up	Cameo	Club	7	(6)	
8	13	Thorn In My Side	Eurythmics	RCA	7	(68)	
9	-	Suburbia	Pet Shop Boys	Parlophone	7	(70)	
10	-	I've Been Losing You	A-Ha	Warner	4		
11	-	All I Ask Of You	Cliff Richard & Sarah Brightman	Polydor	8		
12	-	Walk Like An Egyptian	Bangles	CBS	8	(1)	
13	2	We Don't Have To ...	Jermaine Stewart	10	9	(5)	F
14	-	(Forever) Live And Die	Orchestral Manoeuvres In The Dark	Virgin	5	(19)	
15	-	Always There	Marti Webb	BBC	5		L
16	12	Walk This Way	Run D.M.C.	London	6	(4)	F
17	5	(I Just) Died In Your Arms	Cutting Crew	Siren	6	(1)	F L
18	-	True Colors	Cyndi Lauper	Portrait	5	(1)	
19	-	Stuck With You	Huey Lewis & The News	Chrysalis	4	(1)	L
20	-	Montego Bay	Amazulu	Island	3	(90)	L

◆ Irish singer/songwriter Chris De Burgh, who had sold 10 million albums globally, gained his first UK Top 40 single with his 24th release, the chart topping 'The Lady In Red'. It was also his only US Top 20 entry.

◆ Status Quo scored their 20th Top 10 hit, 'In The Army Now'. The Beatles and The Rolling Stones were the only other groups to achieve this feat.

1986

This Mnth	Prev Mnth	Title	Artist	Label	Wks	(US 20 Pos)	
1	-	Take My Breath Away	Berlin	CBS	11	(1)	F
2	-	You Keep Me Hangin' On	Kim Wilde	MCA	7	(1)	
3	12	Walk Like An Egyptian	Bangles	CBS	8	(1)	
4	-	Showing Out (Get Fresh At The Weekend)	Mel & Kim	Supreme	6	(78)	F
5	6	In The Army Now	Status Quo	Vertigo	7		
6	5	Every Loser Wins	Nick Berry	BBC	6		F
7	-	Breakout	Swing Out Sister	Mercury	7	(6)	F
8	11	All I Ask Of You	Cliff Richard & Sarah Brightman	Polydor	8		
9	-	Livin' On A Prayer	Bon Jovi	Vertigo	10	(1)	
10	-	The Final Countdown	Europe	Epic	10	(8)	F
11	-	Through The Barricades	Spandau Ballet	Reformation	5		L
12	-	Don't Give Up	Peter Gabriel & Kate Bush	Virgin	4	(72)	
13	-	Notorious	Duran Duran	EMI	4	(2)	
14	-	For America	Red Box	Sire	5		L
15	-	Midas Touch	Midnight Star	Solar	4	(42)	L
16	1	True Blue	Madonna	Sire	7	(3)	
17	-	Don't Get Me Wrong	Pretenders	Real	4	(10)	
18	4	You Can Call Me Al	Paul Simon	Warner	6	(23)	
19	-	Each Time You Break My Heart	Nick Kamen	WEA	5		F
20	-	French Kissin' In The USA	Debbie Harry	Chrysalis	7	(57)	F

This Mnth	Prev Mnth	Title	Artist	Label	Wks	(US 20 Pos)	
1	10	The Final Countdown	Europe	Epic	10	(8)	F
2	-	Sometimes	Erasure	Mute	10		F
3	-	Caravan Of Love	Housemartins	Go! Discs	6		
4	-	The Rain	Oran 'Juice' Jones	Def Jam	8	(9)	F L
5	9	Livin' On A Prayer	Bon Jovi	Vertigo	10	(1)	
6	1	Take My Breath Away	Berlin	CBS	11	(1)	F
7	-	Open Your Heart	Madonna	Sire	6	(1)	
8	-	Shake You Down	Gregory Abbott	CBS	7	(1)	F L
9	-	Reet Petite	Jackie Wilson	SMP	9		
10	-	So Cold The Night	Communards	London	6		
11	19	Each Time You Break My Heart	Nick Kamen	WEA	5		F
12	20	French Kissin' In The USA	Debbie Harry	Chrysalis	7	(57)	F
13	-	Cry Wolf	A-Ha	Warner	6	(50)	
14	7	Breakout	Swing Out Sister	Mercury	7	(6)	F
15	-	The Skye Boat Song	Roger Whittaker & Des O'Connor	Tembo	5		L
16	-	Is This Love	Alison Moyet	CBS	9		
17	2	You Keep Me Hangin' On	Kim Wilde	MCA	7	(1)	
18	4	Showing Out (Get Fesh At The Weekend)	Mel & Kim	Supreme	6	(78)	F
19	-	Big Fun	Gap Band	Total Experience	8		
20	-	Land Of Confusion	Genesis	Virgin	7	(4)	

◆ Take My Breath Away' (from the five million selling **Top Gun** soundtrack) gave Berlin a transatlantic chart-topper. It also returned to the British Top 3 in 1990.

◆ In October, for the first time, the top three US singles were by different solo female singers, Janet Jackson, Tina Turner and Cyndi Lauper. A month later female vocalists held a record Top 5 slots on the UK chart.

1987

This Mnth	Prev Mnth	Title	Artist	Label	Wks	(US 20 Pos)	
1	9	Reet Petite	Jackie Wilson	SMP	9		
2	16	Is This Love	Alison Moyet	CBS	9		
3	19	Big Fun	Gap Band	Total Experience	8		
4	-	Jack Your Body	Steve 'Silk' Hurley	DJ International	7		F L
5	-	No More The Fool	Elkie Brooks	Legend	8		L
6	3	Caravan Of Love	Housemartins	Go! Discs	6		
7	-	C'est La Vie	Robbie Nevil	Manhattan	5	(2)	F L
8	2	Sometimes	Erasure	Mute	10		F
9	1	The Final Countdown	Europe	Epic	10	(8)	F
10	7	Open Your Heart	Madonna	Sire	6	(1)	
11	4	The Rain	Oran 'Juice' Jones	Def Jam	8	(9)	F L
12	13	Cry Wolf	A-Ha	Warner	6	(50)	
13	-	Surrender	Swing Out Sister	Mercury	4		L
14	-	Hymn To Her	Pretenders	Real	5		
15	8	Shake You Down	Gregory Abbott	CBS	7	(1)	F L
16	-	It Didn't Matter	Style Council	Polydor	3		
17	-	I Knew You Were Waiting (For Me)	Aretha Franklin/George Michael	Epic	6	(1)	
18	-	Down To Earth	Curiosity Killed The Cat	Mercury	8		F
19	5	Livin' On A Prayer	Bon Jovi	Vertigo	10	(1)	
20	10	So Cold The Night	Communards	London	6		

This Mnth	Prev Mnth	Title	Artist	Label	Wks	(US 20 Pos)	
1	17	I Knew You Were Waiting (For Me)	Aretha Franklin/George Michael	Epic	6	(1)	
2	-	Heartache	Pepsi & Shirlie	Polydor	6	(78)	F
3	18	Down To Earth	Curiosity Killed The Cat	Mercury	8		F
4	-	Almaz	Randy Crawford	Warner	5		L
5	-	It Doesn't Have To Be That Way	Blow Monkeys	RCA	4		L
6	-	Male Stripper	Man 2 Man Meet Man Parrish	Bolts	7		F L
7	-	Stand By Me	Ben E. King	Atlantic	7	(9)	F L
8	-	I Love My Radio	Taffy	Transglobal	4		F L
9	-	When A Man Loves A Woman	Percy Sledge	Atlantic	6		L
10	4	Jack Your Body	Steve 'Silk' Hurley	DJ International	7		F L
11	-	Stay Out Of My Life	Five Star	Tent	4		
12	-	The Music Of The Night/ Wishing You Were Somehow Here Again	Michael Crawford/Sarah Brightman	Polydor	4		F L
13	-	Running In The Family	Level 42	Polydor	6	(83)	
14	-	You Sexy Thing	Hot Chocolate	EMI	4		
15	5	No More The Fool	Elkie Brooks	Legend	8		L
16	7	C'est La Vie	Robbie Nevil	Manhattan	5	(2)	F L
17	-	Coming Around Again	Carly Simon	Arista	5	(18)	L
18	-	Shoplifters Of The World Unite	Smiths	Rough Trade	2		
19	2	Is This Love	Alison Moyet	CBS	9		
20	-	Once Bitten Twice Shy	Vesta Williams	A&M	3		F L

◆ Ben E. King's 25-year-old 'Stand By Me' was a transatlantic Top 10 hit, while in Britain Percy Sledge's 1966 smash, 'When A Man Loves A Woman', scored again. Jackie Wilson's 29-year-old 'Reet Petite' hit the top and half the Top 10 in March were re-issues.

◆ *Record Mirror's* readers poll showed Prince as Top Male, Madonna as Top Female and The Smiths as Top Group.

1987

March 1987

This Mnth	Prev Mnth	Title	Artist	Label	Wks	(US 20 Pos)	
1	-	Everything I Own	Boy George	Virgin	6		F
2	-	I Get The Sweetest Feeling	Jackie Wilson	SMP	6		
3	-	Live It Up	Mental As Anything	Epic	7		F L
4	-	The Great Pretender	Freddie Mercury	Parlophone	6		
5	7	Stand By Me	Ben E. King	Atlantic	7	(9)	F L
6	-	Respectable	Mel & Kim	Supreme	9		
7	9	When A Man Loves A Woman	Percy Sledge	Atlantic	6		L
8	-	Crush On You	Jets	MCA	6	(3)	F L
9	6	Male Stripper	Man 2 Man Meet Man Parrish	Bolts	7		F L
10	13	Running In The Family	Level 42	Polydor	6	(83)	
11	-	Weak In The Presence Of Beauty	Alison Moyet	CBS	6		
12	-	Moonlighting ('Theme')	Al Jarreau	WEA	4	(23)	F L
13	-	Respect Yourself	Bruce Willis	Motown	4	(5)	F
14	-	The Right Thing	Simply Red	WEA	4	(27)	
15	-	It Doesn't Have To Be	Erasure	Mute	5		
16	3	Down To Earth	Curiosity Killed The Cat	Mercury	8		F
17	17	Coming Around Again	Carly Simon	Arista	5	(18)	L
18	-	With Or Without You	U2	Island	6	(1)	
19	-	Sign 'O' The Times	Prince	Paisley Park	5	(3)	
20	-	(You Gotta) Fight For Your Right (To Party)	Beastie Boys	Def Jam	3	(7)	F

April 1987

This	Prev	Title	Artist	Label	Wks	(US 20 Pos)	
1	-	Let It Be	Ferry Aid	The Sun	5		F L
2	-	La Isla Bonita	Madonna	Sire	8	(4)	
3	6	Respectable	Mel & Kim	Supreme	9		
4	-	Lean On Me	Club Nouveau	King Jay	7	(1)	F L
5	-	Let's Wait Awhile	Janet Jackson	Breakout	6	(2)	
6	18	With Or Without You	U2	Island	6	(1)	
7	-	If You Let Me Stay	Terence Trent D'Arby	CBS	7	(68)	F
8	-	Can't Be With You Tonight	Judy Boucher	Orbitone	9		F
9	-	Ever Fallen In Love	Fine Young Cannibals	London	6		
10	11	Weak In The Presence Of Beauty	Alison Moyet	CBS	6		
11	-	Living In A Box	Living In A Box	Chrysalis	8	(17)	F
12	-	The Irish Rover	Pogues & The Dubliners	Stiff	3		
13	1	Everything I Own	Boy George	Virgin	6		F
14	2	I Get The Sweetest Feeling	Jackie Wilson	SMP	6		
15	-	Ordinary Day	Curiosity Killed The Cat	Mercury	3		
16	-	The Slightest Touch	Five Star	Tent	6		
17	-	Wanted Dead Or Alive	Bon Jovi	Vertigo	4	(7)	
18	19	Sign 'O' The Times	Prince	Paisley Park	5	(3)	
19	13	Respect Yourself	Bruce Willis	Motown	4	(5)	F
20	-	Big Time	Peter Gabriel	Charisma	3	(8)	

◆ Kate Bush, who was voted Best Female Artist at the Brit Awards, became the first British female to chalk up three No. 1 LPs when **The Whole Story** completed her hat-trick.
◆ This year's Prince's Trust Gala starred Eric Clapton, Bryan Adams, Ben E. King, Alison Moyet and new teeny bop idols Curiosity Killed The Cat. Acts enjoying sell out shows at Wembley included Americans Lionel Richie, Luther Vandross and Tina Turner and UK-based Duran Duran, David Bowie, U2 and The Pretenders.

1987

This Mnth	Prev Mnth	Title	Artist	Label	Wks	(US 20 Pos)	
1	-	Nothing's Gonna Stop Us Now	Starship	RCA	11	(1)	L
2	8	Can't Be With You Tonight	Judy Boucher	Orbitone	9		F
3	-	A Boy From Nowhere	Tom Jones	Epic	8		
4	11	Living In A Box	Living In A Box	Chrysalis	8	(17)	F
5	-	(Something Inside) So Strong	Labi Siffre	China	7		L
6	2	La Isla Bonita	Madonna	Sire	8	(4)	
7	-	Another Step (Closer To You)	Kim Wilde & Junior	MCA	7		
8	16	The Slightest Touch	Five Star	Tent	6		
9	-	Big Love	Fleetwood Mac	Warner	5	(5)	
10	-	Shattered Dreams	Johnny Hates Jazz	Virgin	6	(2)	F
11	-	Back And Forth	Cameo	Club	5	(50)	L
12	-	I Wanna Dance With Somebody (Who Loves Me)	Whitney Houston	Arista	10	(1)	
13	4	Lean On Me	Club Nouveau	King Jay	7	(1)	F L
14	-	Incommunicado	Marillion	EMI	3		
15	-	April Skies	Jesus And Mary Chain	Blanco	3		
16	-	To Be With You Again	Level 42	Polydor	3		
17	7	If You Let Me Stay	Terence Trent D'Arby	CBS	7	(68)	F
18	-	Lil' Devil	Cult	Beggars Banquet	4		
19	-	Boops (Here To Go)	Sly And Robbie	4th & Broadway	3		F L
20	-	Hold Me Now	Johnny Logan	Epic	7		L

This Mnth	Prev Mnth	Title	Artist	Label	Wks	(US 20 Pos)	
1	12	I Wanna Dance With Somebody (Who Loves Me)	Whitney Houston	Arista	10	(1)	
2	20	Hold Me Now	Johnny Logan	Epic	7		L
3	1	Nothing's Gonna Stop Us Now	Starship	RCA	11	(1)	L
4	-	I Want Your Sex	George Michael	Epic	5	(2)	
5	-	Star Trekkin'	Firm	Bark	7		L
6	-	I Still Haven't Found What I'm Looking For	U2	Island	4	(1)	
7	-	Jack Mix II	Mirage	Debut	5		F
8	-	Victim Of Love	Erasure	Mute	4		
9	-	Nothing's Gonna Stop Me Now	Samantha Fox	Jive	5	(80)	
10	-	Under The Boardwalk	Bruce Willis	Motown	10	(59)	L
11	-	Goodbye Stranger	Pepsi & Shirlie	Polydor	4		L
12	10	Shattered Dreams	Johnny Hates Jazz	Virgin	6	(2)	F
13	-	Wishing I Was Lucky	Wet Wet Wet	Precious	5	(58)	F
14	-	You're The Voice	John Farnham	Wheatley	6	(82)	F L
15	-	Serious	Donna Allen	Portrait	3	(21)	F
16	-	It's A Sin	Pet Shop Boys	Parlophone	8	(9)	
17	-	When Smokey Sings	ABC	Neutron	4	(5)	L
18	-	Looking For A New Love	Jody Watley	MCA	3	(2)	F L
19	-	Is This Love	Whitesnake	EMI	5	(2)	
20	-	No Sleep Till Brooklyn	Beastie Boys	Def Jam	3		

◆ Headliners at Switzerland's Montreux Rock Festival included Whitney Houston, Cameo, Duran Duran, Spandau Ballet, Run DMC and The Beastie Boys. The latter two then toured Britain where The Beasties received a hammering from the British press for their alleged anti-social behaviour.
◆ The influx of old songs onto the chart continued and even classic old recordings such as Tom Jones's debut hit single 'It's Not Unusual' and The Beatles' **Sergeant Pepper** album returned to the Top 20.

July 1987

This Mnth	Prev Mnth	Title	Artist	Label	Wks (US 20 Pos)	
1	16	It's A Sin	Pet Shop Boys	Parlophone	8 (9)	
2	10	Under The Boardwalk	Bruce Willis	Motown	10 (59)	L
3	-	Wishing Well	Terence Trent D'Arby	CBS	6 (1)	
4	5	Star Trekkin'	Firm	Bark	7	L
5	-	Always	Atlantic Starr	Warner	8 (1)	L
6	-	The Living Daylights	A-Ha	Warner	5	
7	1	I Wanna Dance With Somebody (Who Loves Me)	WhitneyHouston	Arista	10 (1)	
8	-	My Pretty One	Cliff Richard	EMI	4	
9	-	Who's That Girl	Madonna	Sire	7 (1)	
10	-	Sweetest Smile	Black	A&M	4	F
11	-	Alone	Heart	Capitol	7 (1)	F
12	-	F.L.M.	Mel & Kim	Supreme	5	
13	14	You're The Voice	John Farnham	Wheatley	6 (82)	F L
14	-	Misfit	Curiosity Killed The Cat	Mercury	4 (42)	
15	19	Is This Love	Whitesnake	EMI	5 (2)	
16	-	Jive Talkin'	Boogie Box High	Hardback	5	F L
17	-	Let's Dance	Chris Rea	Magnet	4 (81)	F
18	17	When Smokey Sings	ABC	Neutron	4 (5)	L
19	-	La Bamba	Los Lobos	Slash	6 (1)	F
20	-	A Little Boogie Woogie (In The Back Of My Mind)	Shakin' Stevens	Epic	4	

August 1987

1	19	La Bamba	Los Lobos	Slash	6 (1)	F
2	-	I Just Can't Stop Loving You	Michael Jackson (duet with Seidah Garrett)	Epic	6 (1)	
3	-	Call Me	Spagna	CBS	6	F L
4	-	True Faith	New Order	Factory	6	
5	9	Who's That Girl	Madonna	Sire	7 (1)	
6	11	Alone	Heart	Capitol	7 (1)	F
7	5	Always	Atlantic Starr	Warner	8 (1)	L
8	-	Labour Of Love	Hue & Cry	Circa	6	F
9	-	Never Gonna Give You Up	Rick Astley	RCA	10 (1)	F
10	-	Toy Boy	Sinitta	Fanfare	8	
11	-	Animal	Def Leppard	Bludgeon Riffola	5 (19)	F
12	-	Sweet Little Mystery	Wet Wet Wet	Precious	6	
13	-	Somewhere Out There	Linda Ronstadt	MCA	4 (2)	F
14	-	What Have I Done To Deserve This	Pet Shop Boys & Dusty Springfield	Parlophone	6 (2)	
15	16	Jive Talkin'	Boogie Box High	Hardback	5	F L
16	1	It's A Sin	Pet Shop Boys	Parlophone	8 (9)	
17	-	Just Don't Want To Be Lonely	Freddie McGregor	Germain	4	F L
18	-	She's On It	Beastie Boys	Def Jam	4	L
19	2	Under The Boardwalk	Bruce Willis	Motown	10 (59)	L
20	-	Funky Town	Pseudo Echo	RCA	4 (6)	F L

◆ The video for Peter Gabriel's 'Sledgehammer' won a record 10 MTV awards.

◆ Cliff Richard scored his 50th British Top 10 hit, 'My Pretty One', and

Bananarama collected their 13th chart entry – a record for a British female group.

◆ Rick Astley had Britain's biggest selling single of 1987, 'Never Gonna Give You Up'.

1987

This Mnth	Prev Mnth	Title	Artist	Label	Wks	(US 20 Pos)	
1	9	Never Gonna Give You Up	Rick Astley	RCA	10	(1)	F
2	-	Wipeout	Fat Boys & Beach Boys	Urban	7	(12)	F
3	-	Heart And Soul	T'Pau	Siren	6	(4)	F
4	14	What Have I Done To Deserve This	Pet Shop Boys/Dusty Springfield	Parlophone	6	(2)	
5	-	Some People	Cliff Richard	EMI	7		
6	10	Toy Boy	Sinitta	Fanfare	8		
7	-	Pump Up The Volume	M/A/R/R/S	4AD	8	(13)	F L
8	-	Where The Streets Have No Name	U2	Island	3	(13)	
9	-	Wonderful Life	Black	A&M	5		L
10	12	Sweet Little Mystery	Wet Wet Wet	Precious	6		
11	-	Casanova	Levert	Atlantic	5	(5)	F L
12	-	Causing A Commotion	Madonna	Sire	5	(2)	
13	-	Bridge To Your Heart	Wax	RCA	5		F L
14	3	Call Me	Spagna	CBS	6		F L
15	-	House Nation	House Master Boyz & The Rude Boy Of House	Magnetic Dance	4		F L
16	-	It's Over	Level 42	Polydor	4		
17	2	I Just Can't Stop Loving You	Michael Jackson	Epic	6	(1)	
18	-	I Don't Want To Be A Hero	Johnny Hates Jazz	Virgin	5	(31)	
19	-	U Got The Look	Prince	Paisley Park	4	(2)	
20	-	Bad	Michael Jackson	Epic	5	(1)	

This Mnth	Prev Mnth	Title	Artist	Label	Wks	(US 20 Pos)	
1	-	Crockett's Theme	Jan Hammer	MCA	8		L
2	-	Full Metal Jacket (I Wanna Be Your Drill Instructor)	Abigail Mead & Nigel Goulding	Warner Bros.	6		F L
3	7	Pump Up The Volume	M/A/R/R/S	4AD	8	(13)	F L
4	-	You Win Again	Bee Gees	Warner Bros.	8	(75)	
5	-	Crazy Crazy Nights	Kiss	Vertigo	5	(65)	F
6	20	Bad	Michael Jackson	Epic	5	(1)	
7	1	Never Gonna Give You Up	Rick Astley	RCA	10	(1)	F
8	-	I Need Love	L.L. Cool J	CBS	5	(14)	F L
9	-	The Circus	Erasure	Mute	5		
10	5	Some People	Cliff Richard	EMI	7		
11	-	I Found Lovin'	Fatback Band	Master Mix	4		L
12	-	Love In The First Degree/ Mr. Sleaze	Bananarama/S.A.W.	London	6	(48)	
13	12	Causing A Commotion	Madonna	Sire	5	(2)	
14	-	This Corrosion	Sisters Of Mercy	Merciful Release	3		F
15	-	Mony Mony	Billy Idol	Chrysalis	6	(1)	
16	-	Faith	George Michael	Epic	5	(1)	
17	-	Little Lies	Fleetwood Mac	Warner Bros.	5	(4)	
18	-	The Real Thing	Jellybean Feat.\ Steven Dante	Chrysalis	4	(82)	F
19	15	House Nation	House Master Boyz/Rude Boy...	Magnetic Dance	4		F L
20	-	Walk The Dinosaur	Was (Not Was)	Fontana	5	(7)	F

◆ **Introducing The Hardline According To Terence Trent D'Arby** was the first debut album by an American act to enter the UK chart at No. 1. In his homeland it spent 26 weeks on the chart before reaching the Top 10.

◆ Half the songs on December's UK chart were oldies. Among them were re-issues of 'When I Fall In Love' by Nat 'King' Cole (1957) and 'My Baby Just Cares For Me' by Nina Simone (1959).

This Mnth	Prev Mnth	Title	Artist	Label	Wks	(US 20 Pos)	
1	-	China In Your Hand	T'Pau	Siren	11		
2	-	Got My Mind Set On You	George Harrison	Dark Horse	9	(1)	L
3	-	Whenever You Need Somebody	Rick Astley	RCA	6		
4	4	You Win Again	Bee Gees	Warner	8	(75)	
5	-	Never Can Say Goodbye	Communards	London	7	(51)	
6	16	Faith	George Michael	Epic	5	(1)	
7	12	Love In The First Degree/ Mr. Sleaze	Bananarama/S.A.W.	London	6	(48)	
8	-	(I've Had) The Time Of My Life	Bill Medley & Jennifer Warnes	RCA	4	(1)	F
9	-	My Baby Just Cares For Me	Nina Simone	Charly	4		L
10	-	Barcelona	Freddie Mercury/M. Caballé	Polydor	4		
11	-	Here I Go Again	Whitesnake	EMI	5	(1)	
12	17	Little Lies	Fleetwood Mac	Warner	5	(4)	
13	-	Jack Mix IV	Mirage	Debut	4		L
14	-	So Emotional	Whitney Houston	Arista	6	(1)	
15	15	Mony Mony	Billy Idol	Chrysalis	6	(1)	
16	-	Criticize	Alexander O'Neal	Tabu	8	(70)	
17	1	Crockett's Theme	Jan Hammer	MCA	8		L
18	20	Walk The Dinosaur	Was (Not Was)	Fontana	5	(7)	F
19	-	I Don't Think That Man Should Sleep Alone	Ray Parker Jr.	Geffen	3	(68)	L
20	9	The Circus	Erasure	Mute	5		

This Mnth	Prev Mnth	Title	Artist	Label	Wks	(US 20 Pos)	
1	1	China In Your Hand	T'Pau	Siren	11		
2	-	Always On My Mind	Pet Shop Boys	Parlophone	8	(4)	
3	-	The Way You Make Me Feel	Michael Jackson	Epic	7	(1)	
4	-	When I Fall In Love/My Arms Keep Missing You	Rick Astley	RCA	6		
5	-	What Do You Want To Make Those Eyes At Me For	Shakin' Stevens	Epic	5		
6	-	Letter From America	Proclaimers	Chrysalis	6		F
7	-	Love Letters	Alison Moyet	CBS	6		
8	2	Got My Mind Set On You	George Harrison	Dark Horse	9	(1)	L
9	16	Criticize	Alexander O'Neal	Tabu	8	(70)	
10	-	Rockin' Around The Christmas Tree	Mel & Kim (Smith & Wilde)	10	5		
11	-	Fairytale Of New York	Pogues Feat. Kirsty MacColl	Pogue Mahone	6		F
12	-	Who Found Who	Jellybean Feat. Elisa Fiorillo	Chrysalis	6	(16)	
13	14	So Emotional	Whitney Houston	Arista	6	(1)	
14	5	Never Can Say Goodbye	Communards	London	7	(51)	
15	-	The Look Of Love	Madonna	Sire	5		
16	-	Once Upon A Long Ago	Paul McCartney	Parlophone	3		
17	-	When I Fall In Love	Nat 'King' Cole	Capitol	4		L
18	-	Heaven Is A Place On Earth	Belinda Carlisle	Virgin	10	(1)	F
19	-	Ev'ry Time We Say Goodbye	Simply Red	Elektra	3		
20	-	Some Guys Have All The Luck	Maxi Priest	10	4		F

◆ 1987 was the year when "sampling" surfaced, three inch CDs were unsuccessfully launched, Japanese company Sony bought CBS Records and MTV debuted in Europe.

◆ The boundary breaking single 'Pump Up The Volume' by M/A/R/R/S was the first record to top the indie, dance and pop charts.

1988

This Mnth	Prev Mnth	Title	Artist	Label	Wks	(US 20 Pos)	
1	18	Heaven Is A Place On Earth	Belinda Carlisle	Virgin	10	(1)	F
2	2	Always On My Mind	Pet Shop Boys	Parlophone	8	(4)	
3	-	House Arrest	Krush	Club	7		F L
4	-	Stutter Rap (No Sleep 'Til Bedtime)	Morris Minor & The Majors	10/Virgin	5		F L
5	-	Angel Eyes (Home And Away)	Wet Wet Wet	Precious	6		
6	-	I Found Someone	Cher	Geffen	4	(10)	
7	-	Sign Your Name	Terence Trent D'Arby	CBS	6	(4)	
8	-	I Think We're Alone Now	Tiffany	MCA	9	(1)	F
9	-	Come Into My Life	Joyce Sims	London	5		L
10	11	Fairytale Of New York	Pogues Feat. Kirsty MacColl	Pogue Mahone	6		F
11	-	All Day And All Of The Night	Stranglers	Epic	4		
12	3	The Way You Make Me Feel	Michael Jackson	Epic	7	(1)	
13	7	Love Letters	Alison Moyet	CBS	6		
14	-	Rise To The Occasion	Climie Fisher	EMI	4		F
15	4	When I Fall In Love/My Arms Keep Missing You	Rick Astley	RCA	6		
16	10	Rockin' Around The Christmas Tree	Mel & Kim (Smith & Wilde)	10	5		
17	17	When I Fall In Love	Nat 'King' Cole	Capitol	4		
18	-	Heatseeker	AC/DC	Atlantic	3		
19	-	When Will I Be Famous	Bros	CBS	6	(83)	F
20	-	Rok Da House	Beatmasters Feat. Cookie Crew	Rhythm King	5		F

This Mnth	Prev Mnth	Title	Artist	Label	Wks	(US 20 Pos)	
1	8	I Think We're Alone Now	Tiffany	MCA	9	(1)	F
2	-	Tell It To My Heart	Taylor Dayne	Arista	6	(7)	F
3	-	I Should Be So Lucky	Kylie Minogue	PWL	10	(28)	F
4	19	When Will I Be Famous	Bros	CBS	6	(83)	F
5	-	Get Outta My Dreams Get Into My Car	Billy Ocean	Jive	6	(1)	L
6	-	Candle In The Wind (Live)	Elton John	Rocket	5	(6)	
7	-	Shake Your Love	Debbie Gibson	Atlantic	5	(4)	F
8	-	Say It Again	Jermaine Stewart	10	5	(27)	
9	-	The Jack That House Built	Jack 'n' Chill	Oval	5		F L
10	-	Beat Dis	Bomb The Bass	Mister-Ron	5		F
11	20	Rok Da House	Beatmasters Feat. Cookie Crew	Rhythm King	5		F
12	7	Sign Your Name	Terence Trent D'Arby	CBS	6	(4)	
13	1	Heaven Is A Place On Earth	Belinda Carlisle	Virgin	10	(1)	F
14	-	O L'Amour	Dollar	London	5		L
15	-	Valentine	T'Pau	Siren	4		
16	-	Gimme Hope Jo'anna	Eddy Grant	Ice	5		L
17	3	House Arrest	Krush	Club	7		F L
18	-	Hot In The City	Billy Idol	Chrysalis	4	(23)	L
19	-	Tower Of Strength	Mission	Mercury	4		
20	-	Suedehead	Morrissey	HMV	3		F

◆ Female artists scored a record three successive No. 1s when Australian soap star Kylie Minogue followed transatlantic toppers Belinda Carlisle and Tiffany to the top spot.

◆ A survey showed that the richest people in the music business in Britain were Virgin Records' head Richard Branson followed by Paul McCartney and Elton John.

1988

March 1988

This Mnth	Prev Mnth	Title	Artist	Label	Wks	(US 20 Pos)	
1	3	I Should Be So Lucky	Kylie Minogue	PWL	10	(28)	F
2	-	Together Forever	Rick Astley	RCA	5	(1)	
3	-	Joe Le Taxi	Vanessa Paradis	FA Prods	6		F
4	10	Beat Dis	Bomb The Bass	Mister-Ron	5		F
5	-	Crash	Primitives	Lazy	5		F L
6	5	Get Outta My Dreams Get Into My Car	Billy Ocean	Jive	6	(1)	L
7	-	Doctorin' The House	Coldcut Featuring Yazz & The Plastic Population	Ahead Of Our Time	5		F
8	-	Don't Turn Around	Aswad	Mango	5		F
9	-	Ship Of Fools	Erasure	Mute	5		
10	16	Gimme Hope Jo'anna	Eddy Grant	Ice	5		L
11	-	I Get Weak	Belinda Carlisle	Virgin	5	(2)	
12	20	Suedehead	Morrissey	HMV	3		F
13	-	Love Is Contagious	Taja Sevelle	Paisley Park	3		F L
14	-	Drop The Boy	Bros	CBS	7		
15	-	Never/These Dreams	Heart	Capitol	5	(4)	
16	2	Tell It To My Heart	Taylor Dayne	Arista	6	(7)	F
17	-	That's The Way It Is	Mel & Kim	Supreme	3		L
18	-	Hazy Shade Of Winter	Bangles	Def Jam	3	(2)	
19	-	Can I Play With Madness	Iron Maiden	EMI	4		
20	-	Could've Been	Tiffany	MCA	5	(1)	

April 1988

This Mnth	Prev Mnth	Title	Artist	Label	Wks	(US 20 Pos)	
1	-	Heart	Pet Shop Boys	Parlophone	7		
2	-	Love Changes (Everything)	Climie Fisher	EMI	6	(23)	L
3	14	Drop The Boy	Bros	CBS	7		
4	20	Could've Been	Tiffany	MCA	5	(1)	
5	-	Everywhere	Fleetwood Mac	Warner Bros.	5	(14)	L
6	8	Don't Turn Around	Aswad	Mango	5		F
7	-	Cross My Broken Heart	Sinitta	Fanfare	5		
8	-	Who's Leaving Who	Hazell Dean	EMI	7		
9	-	Pink Cadillac	Natalie Cole	Manhattan	6	(5)	F
10	-	I'm Not Scared	Eighth Wonder	CBS	6		F
11	-	Theme From S'Express	S'Express	Rhythm King	7	(91)	F
12	19	Can I Play With Madness	Iron Maiden	EMI	4		
13	-	I Want You Back	Bananarama	London	6		
14	-	Stay On These Roads	A-Ha	Warner	4		
15	-	Prove Your Love	Taylor Dayne	Arista	4	(7)	L
16	-	Girlfriend	Pebbles	MCA	3	(5)	F L
17	-	Mary's Prayer	Danny Wilson	Virgin	6	(23)	F L
18	1	I Should Be So Lucky	Kylie Minogue	PWL	10	(28)	F
19	-	I Want You Back '88	Michael Jackson With The Jackson Five	Epic	5	(1)	
20	-	Only In My Dreams	Debbie Gibson	Atlantic	3	(4)	

◆ Expose became the first group to have four American Top 10 singles on their debut LP. Surprisingly, the female trio never had a major UK hit.

◆ Nelson Mandela's 70th birthday show was the most star-studded event since 'Live Aid'. Appearing were such notables as Bryan Adams, The Bee Gees, Natalie Cole, Phil Collins, Dire Straits, Eurythmics, Al Green, Whitney Houston, George Michael, Salt-N-Pepa, Sting and Stevie Wonder. The suprise hit of the show was Grammy winning American newcomer Tracy Chapman.

1988

May 1988

This Mnth	Prev Mnth	Title	Artist	Label	Wks	(US 20 Pos)	
1	-	Perfect	Fairground Attraction	RCA	8	(80)	F
2	11	Theme From S'express	S'express	Rhythm King	7	(91)	F
3	-	Blue Monday 1988	New Order	Factory	6	(68)	
4	-	With A Little Help From My Friends/She's Leaving Home	Wet Wet Wet/ Billy Bragg & Cara Tivey	Childline	7		
5	-	Loadsamoney (Doin' Up The House)	Harry Enfield	Mercury	4		F L
6	17	Mary's Prayer	Danny Wilson	Virgin	6	(23)	F L
7	-	Anfield Rap (Red Machine In Full Effect)	Liverpool F.C.	Virgin	4		L
8	13	I Want You Back	Bananarama	London	6		
9	-	Got To Be Certain	Kylie Minogue	PWL	8		
10	8	Who's Leaving Who	Hazell Dean	EMI	7		
11	9	Pink Cadillac	Natalie Cole	Manhattan	6	(5)	F
12	-	Divine Emotions	Narada	Reprise	4		L
13	19	I Want You Back '88	Michael Jackson/Jackson Five	Epic	5	(1)	
14	-	Alphabet Street	Prince	Paisley Park	3	(8)	
15	-	Circle In The Sand	Belinda Carlisle	Virgin	5	(7)	
16	-	The King Of Rock 'n' Roll	Prefab Sprout	Kitchenware	4		F L
17	1	Heart	Pet Shop Boys	Parlophone	7		
18	-	Somewhere In My Heart	Aztec Camera	WEA	6		
19	-	Let's All Chant	Mick And Pat	PWL	4		F L
20	-	Pump Up The Bitter	Star Turn On 45 Pints	Pacific	2		F L

June 1988

This Mnth	Prev Mnth	Title	Artist	Label	Wks	(US 20 Pos)	
1	4	With A Little Help From My Friends/She's Leaving...	Wet Wet Wet/ Billy Bragg & Cara Tivey	Childline	7		
2	9	Got To Be Certain	Kylie Minogue	PWL	8		
3	-	Doctorin' The Tardis	Timelords	KLF Comms.	5	(66)	F L
4	18	Somewhere In My Heart	Aztec Camera	WEA	6		
5	-	Voyage Voyage	Desireless	CBS	6		F L
6	15	Circle In The Sand	Belinda Carlisle	Virgin	5	(7)	
7	-	I Owe You Nothing	Bros	CBS	7		
8	-	My One Temptation	Mica Paris	4th & Broadway	5	(97)	F
9	-	Wild World	Maxi Priest	10	6	(25)	
10	-	Boys (Summertime Love)	Sabrina	CBS	6		F L
11	1	Perfect	Fairground Attraction	RCA	8	(80)	F
12	-	Check This Out	L.A. Mix	Breakout	4		F L
13	-	I Saw Him Standing There	Tiffany	MCA	3	(7)	
14	-	Everyday Is Like Sunday	Morrissey	HMV	3		
15	16	The King Of Rock 'n' Roll	Prefab Sprout	Kitchenware	4		F L
16	-	Chains Of Love	Erasure	Mute	4	(12)	
17	-	Tribute (Right On)	Pasadenas	CBS	7	(52)	F
18	-	Give A Little Love	Aswad	Mango	3		
19	-	The Twist (Yo, Twist)	Fat Boys/Chubby Checker	Urban	7	(16)	L
20	-	Love Will Save The Day	Whitney Houston	Arista	2	(9)	

◆ Bros, whose UK tour incited mass hysteria among Britain's teenyboppers, topped the chart with a re-issue of their first single 'I Owe You Nothing'.

◆ Indie-dance act The Justified Ancients Of Mu Mu were convinced they knew the formula to get a UK No. 1 single. Their made-to-measure track 'Doctorin' The Tardis', released under the name The Timelords, not only reached the top, it also spent three months on the US chart.

July 1988

This Mnth	Prev Mnth	Title	Artist	Label	Wks	(US 20 Pos)	
1	-	Nothing's Gonna Change My Love For You	Glenn Medeiros	London	8	(12)	F
2	-	Push It/Tramp	Salt 'n' Pepa	Champion/ffrr	8	(19)	F
3	19	The Twist (Yo, Twist)	Fat Boys/Chubby Checker	Urban	7	(16)	L
4	7	I Owe You Nothing	Bros	CBS	7		
5	-	Fast Car	Tracy Chapman	Elektra	6	(6)	F L
6	-	Breakfast In Bed	UB40 Featuring Chrissie Hynde	Dep International	6		
7	10	Boys (Summertime Love)	Sabrina	CBS	6		F L
8	-	I Don't Want To Talk About It	Everything But The Girl	Blanco Y Negro	6		F
9	-	In The Air Tonight	Phil Collins	Virgin	5		
10	-	Roses Are Red	Mac Band Featuring The McCampbell Brothers	MCA	7		F L
11	17	Tribute (Right On)	Pasadenas	CBS	7	(52)	F
12	-	Dirty Diana	Michael Jackson	Epic	5	(1)	
13	-	I Want Your Love	Transvision Vamp	MCA	6		F
14	-	Don't Blame It On That Girl/ Wap Bam Boogie	Matt Bianco	WEA	6		L
15	9	Wild World	Maxi Priest	10	6	(25)	
16	-	Foolish Beat	Debbie Gibson	Atlantic	5	(1)	
17	3	Doctorin' The Tardis	Timelords	KLF	5	(66)	F L
18	-	You Came	Kim Wilde	MCA	7	(41)	
19	-	Love Bites	Def Leppard	Bludgeon Riffola	4	(1)	
20	-	Tougher Than The Rest	Bruce Springsteen	CBS	3		

August 1988

This Mnth	Prev Mnth	Title	Artist	Label	Wks	(US 20 Pos)	
1	-	The Only Way Is Up	Yazz & The Plastic Population	Big Life	9	(96)	
2	-	The Loco-Motion	Kylie Minogue	PWL	7	(3)	
3	18	You Came	Kim Wilde	MCA	7	(41)	
4	-	I Need You	B.V.S.M.P.	Debut	6		F L
5	-	Superfly Guy	S'Express	Rhythm King	6		
6	-	Find My Love	Fairground Attraction	RCA	6		L
7	-	The Evil That Men Do	Iron Maiden	EMI	3		
8	1	Nothing's Gonna Change My Love...	Glenn Medeiros	London	8	(12)	F
9	-	Reach Out I'll Be There	Four Tops	Motown	5		
10	-	Hands To Heaven	Breathe	Siren	6	(2)	F L
11	2	Push It/Tramp	Salt 'n' Pepa	Champion/ffrr	8	(19)	F
12	-	The Harder I Try	Brother Beyond	Parlophone	6		F
13	13	I Want Your Love	Transvision Vamp	MCA	6		F
14	-	Martha's Harbour	All About Eve	Mercury	3		F L
15	8	I Don't Want To Talk About It	Everything But The Girl	Blanco Y Negro	6		F
16	-	Hustle! (To The Music...)	Funky Worm	Fon	4		F L
17	10	Roses Are Red	Mac Band/McCampbell Brothers	MCA	7		F L
18	-	My Love	Julio Iglesias (featuring Stevie Wonder)	CBS	5	(80)	L
19	-	Good Tradition	Tanita Tikaram	WEA	4		F L
20	12	Dirty Diana	Michael Jackson	Epic	5	(1)	

◆ Two fans died at the *Monsters Of Rock* festival at Castle Donnington. Headlining were Iron Maiden, Kiss, Guns N' Roses, Megadeth and David Lee Roth.

◆ The Hollies' 19-year-old 'He Ain't Heavy, He's My Brother' hit the top. Other oldies returning included 'Lovely Day' by Bill Withers, 'Easy' by The Commodores and 'Reach Out I'll Be There' by The Four Tops.

1988

This Mnth	Prev Mnth	Title	Artist	Label	Wks	(US 20 Pos)	
1	-	Groovy Kind Of Love	Phil Collins	Virgin	10	(1)	
2	-	Teardrops	Womack & Womack	4th & Broadway	11		
3	12	The Harder I Try	Brother Beyond	Parlophone	6		F
4	1	The Only Way Is Up	Yazz & The Plastic Population	Big Life	9	(96)	
5	-	He Ain't Heavy, He's My Brother	Hollies	EMI	7		L
6	-	Megablast/Don't Make Me Wait	Bomb The Bass	Mister-Ron	5		
7	-	The Race	Yello	Mercury	6		F L
8	18	My Love	Julio Iglesias/Stevie Wonder	CBS	5	(80)	L
9	2	The Loco-Motion	Kylie Minogue	PWL	7	(3)	
10	10	Hands To Heaven	Breathe	Siren	6	(2)	F L
11	-	Lovely Day	Bill Withers	CBS	5		L
12	-	I Quit	Bros	CBS	3		
13	-	Anything For You	Gloria Estefan/Miami Sound Machine	Epic	6	(1)	
14	-	Rush Hour	Jane Wiedlin	Manhattan	4	(9)	F L
15	-	Nothing Can Divide Us	Jason Donovan	PWL	7		F
16	-	Touchy!	A-Ha	Warner	3		
17	4	I Need You	B.V.S.M.P.	Debut	6		F L
18	-	I'm Gonna Be	Proclaimers	Chrysalis	5		
19	-	Big Fun	Inner City	10	7		F
20	6	Find My Love	Fairground Attraction	RCA	6		L

This Mnth	Prev Mnth	Title	Artist	Label	Wks	(US 20 Pos)	
1	-	One Moment In Time	Whitney Houston	Arista	8	(5)	
2	2	Teardrops	Womack & Womack	4th & Broadway	11		
3	5	He Ain't Heavy, He's My Brother	Hollies	EMI	7		L
4	-	Don't Worry Be Happy	Bobby McFerrin	Manhattan	5	(1)	F L
5	-	Desire	U2	Island	4	(3)	
6	-	She Wants To Dance With Me	Rick Astley	RCA	7	(6)	
7	1	Groovy Kind Of Love	Phil Collins	Virgin	10	(1)	
8	-	A Little Respect	Erasure	Mute	8	(14)	
9	15	Nothing Can Divide Us	Jason Donovan	PWL	7		F
10	-	Wee Rule	Wee Papa Girl Rappers	Jive	6		F L
11	19	Big Fun	Inner City	10	7		F
12	-	Orinoco Flow	Enya	WEA	6	(24)	F
13	-	We Call It Acieed	D. Mob Feat. Gary Haisman	ffrr	6		F
14	11	Lovely Day	Bill Withers	CBS	5		L
15	-	Domino Dancing	Pet Shop Boys	Parlophone	4	(18)	
16	-	Never Trust A Stranger	Kim Wilde	MCA	5		
17	-	Je Ne Sais Pas Pourquoi	Kylie Minogue	PWL	6		
18	-	Riding On A Train	Pasadenas	CBS	5		
19	-	Harvest For The World	Christians	Island	4		
20	-	Burn It Up	Beatmasters With P.P. Arnold	Rhythm King	4		

◆ Even though it sold few copies in their homeland, 'Jackie' by Blue Zone charted in America. It featured vocalist Lisa Stansfield.

◆ The Proclaimers' current hit 'I'm Gonna Be', reached the US Top 20 five years later.

◆ U2's film *Rattle And Hum* premiered: the double album soundtrack sold a record one million copies in its first week in America and 300,000 in Britain.

November 1988

This Mnth	Prev Mnth	Title	Artist	Label	Wks	(US 20 Pos)	
1	-	Stand Up For Your Love Rights	Yazz	Big Life	6		
2	17	Je Ne Sais Pas Pourquoi	Kylie Minogue	PWL	6		
3	12	Orinoco Flow	Enya	WEA	6	(24)	F
4	-	The First Time	Robin Beck	Mercury	9		F L
5	-	Girl You Know It's True	Milli Vanilli	Cooltempo	6	(2)	F
6	-	She Makes My Day	Robert Palmer	EMI	5		
7	-	Real Gone Kid	Deacon Blue	CBS	5		F
8	-	He Ain't No Competiition	Brother Beyond	Parlophone	4		
9	-	Need You Tonight	INXS	Mercury	5	(1)	F
10	-	Missing You	Chris De Burgh	A&M	6		L
11	-	Kiss	Art Of Noise & Tom Jones	China	4	(31)	L
12	-	1-2-3	Gloria Estefan & The Miami Sound Machine	Epic	3	(3)	
13	13	We Call It Acieed	D. Mob Feat. Gary Haisman	ffrr	6		F
14	-	Twist And Shout	Salt 'n' Pepa	ffrr	4		
15	1	One Moment In Time	Whitney Houston	Arista	8	(5)	
16	-	The Clairvoyant	Iron Maiden	EMI	3		
17	8	A Little Respect	Erasure	Mute	8	(14)	
18	-	Let's Stick Together	Bryan Ferry	EG	2		
19	19	Harvest For The World	Christians	Island	4		
20	-	Left To My Own Devices	Pet Shop Boys	Parlophone	4	(84)	

December 1988

This Mnth	Prev Mnth	Title	Artist	Label	Wks	(US 20 Pos)	
1	-	Mistletoe And Wine	Cliff Richard	EMI	7		
2	-	Cat Among The Pigeons/ Silent Night	Bros	CBS	6		
3	-	Especially For You	Kylie Minogue/Jason Donovan	PWL	10		
4	-	Suddenly	Angry Anderson	Food For Thought	8		F L
5	-	Two Hearts	Phil Collins	Virgin	8	(1)	
6	-	Crackers International (E.P.)	Erasure	Mute	10		
7	4	The First Time	Robin Beck	Mercury	9		F L
8	-	Smooth Criminal	Michael Jackson	Epic	8	(7)	
9	-	Take Me To Your Heart	Rick Astley	RCA	7		
10	-	Good Life	Inner City	10	8	(73)	
11	-	Burning Bridges (On And Off And On Again)	Status Quo	Vertigo	6		
12	10	Missing You	Chris De Burgh	A&M	6		L
13	-	Angel Of Harlem	U2	Island	4	(14)	
14	-	Say A Little Prayer	Bomb The Bass	Rhythm King	5		
15	20	Left To My Own Devices	Pet Shop Boys	Parlophone	4	(84)	
16	-	Downtown '88	Petula Clark	PRT	4		L
17	9	Need You Tonight	INXS	Mercury	5	(1)	F
18	-	Buffalo Stance	Neneh Cherry	Circa	7	(3)	F
19	-	Fine Time	New Order	Factory	4		
20	-	Loco In Acapulco	Four Tops	Arista	5		L

◆ Britain's fastest selling single of 1988 was 'Mistletoe And Wine', which gave Cliff Richard his 100th chart record and his 55th Top 10 hit (equalling Elvis Presley's record).

◆ Australian Kylie Minogue became the first female singer in the UK to have her first four singles sell over 250,000 copies each.

◆ Stock, Aitken & Waterman wrote and produced a record six singles in the Top 30 in October.

1989

This Mnth	Prev Mnth	Title	Artist	Label	Wks 20	(US Pos)	
1	3	Especially For You	Kylie Minogue/Jason Donovan	PWL	10		
2	6	Crackers International (E.P.)	Erasure	Mute	10		
3	18	Buffalo Stance	Neneh Cherry	Circa	7	(3)	F
4	10	Good Life	Inner City	10	8	(73)	
5	-	She Drives Me Crazy	Fine Young Cannibals	London	6	(1)	
6	-	The Living Years	Mike + The Mechanics	WEA	7	(1)	F
7	4	Suddenly	Angry Anderson	Food For Thought	8		F L
8	-	Four Letter Word	Kim Wilde	MCA	6		
9	-	Baby I Love Your Way/Freebird	Will To Power	Epic	5	(1)	F L
10	20	Loco In Acapulco	Four Tops	Arista	5		L
11	-	Something's Gotten Hold Of My Heart	Marc Almond Featuring Gene Pitney	Parlophone	9		
12	-	You Got It	Roy Orbison	Virgin	6	(9)	
13	-	Waiting For A Star To Fall	Boy Meets Girl	RCA	4	(5)	F L
14	-	Cuddly Toy	Roachford	CBS	5		F L
15	11	Burning Bridges (On And Off...)	Status Quo	Vertigo	6		
16	-	All She Wants Is	Duran Duran	EMI	2	(22)	
17	1	Mistletoe And Wine	Cliff Richard	EMI	7		
18	-	Keeping The Dream Alive	Freiheit	CBS	4		F L
19	5	Two Hearts	Phil Collins	Virgin	8	(1)	
20	-	You Are The One	A-Ha	Warner	5		

This Mnth	Prev Mnth	Title	Artist	Label	Wks 20	(US Pos)	
1	11	Something's Gotten Hold Of My Heart	Marc Almond Featuring Gene Pitney	Parlophone	9		
2	6	The Living Years	Mike + The Mechanics	WEA	7	(1)	F
3	-	Love Train	Holly Johnson	MCA	6	(65)	F
4	12	You Got It	Roy Orbison	Virgin	6	(9)	
5	-	Love Changes Everything	Michael Ball	Really Useful	8		F L
6	-	My Prerogative	Bobby Brown	MCA	6	(1)	F
7	14	Cuddly Toy	Roachford	CBS	5		F L
8	-	Wait	Robert Howard & Kym Mazelle	RCA	5		F L
9	-	Belfast Child	Simple Minds	Virgin	5		
10	-	That's The Way Love Is	Ten City	Atlantic	5		F L
11	-	Fine Time	Yazz	Big Life	4		
12	5	She Drives Me Crazy	Fine Young Cannibals	London	6	(1)	
13	-	Last Of The Famous International Playboys	Morrissey	HMV	2		
14	-	Hold Me In Your Arms	Rick Astley	RCA	4		
15	-	Stop	Sam Brown	A&M	7	(65)	F
16	1	Especially For You	Kylie Minogue/Jason Donovan	PWL	10		
17	-	Leave Me Alone	Michael Jackson	Epic	6		
18	2	Crackers International (E.P.)	Erasure	Mute	10		
19	-	It's Only Love	Simply Red	Elektra	2	(57)	
20	-	Big Area	Then Jerico	London	2		L

◆ A new album chart was introduced which contained only multi-artist albums, leaving the main chart for solo artist sets.

◆ American producers L.A. & Babyface had five singles simultaneously in the US Top 40. In Britain, Stock, Aitken & Waterman scored their 80th UK Top 75 hit in less than five years, and in March produced three of the Top 4 singles.

◆ The quasi-religious video for Madonna's transatlantic topper, 'Like A Prayer', caused a major controversy, resulting in Pepsi dropping an $8 million advertising campaign.

1989

March 1989

This Mnth	Prev Mnth	Title	Artist	Label	Wks	(US 20 Pos)	
1	-	Too Many Broken Hearts	Jason Donovan	PWL	9		
2	-	Help	Bananarama/La Na Nee Nee Noo Noo	London	6		
3	15	Stop	Sam Brown	A&M	7	(65)	F
4	5	Love Changes Everything	Michael Ball	Really Useful	8		F L
5	-	Can't Stay Away From You	Gloria Estefan & The Miami Sound Machine	Epic	6	(6)	
6	17	Leave Me Alone	Michael Jackson	Epic	6		
7	-	Hey Music Lover	S'Express	Rhythm King	5		L
8	-	This Time I Know It's For Real	Donna Summer	Warner	8	(7)	
9	9	Belfast Child	Simple Minds	Virgin	5		
10	-	Like A Prayer	Madonna	Sire	7	(1)	
11	-	Straight Up	Paula Abdul	Siren	9	(1)	F
12	-	I Don't Want A Lover	Texas	Mercury	5	(77)	F
13	-	Blow The House Down	Living In A Box	Chrysalis	4		
14	-	I'd Rather Jack	Reynolds Girls	PWL	6		F L
15	-	Keep On Movin'	Soul II Soul Feat. Caron Wheeler	10	6	(11)	F
16	6	My Prerogative	Bobby Brown	MCA	6	(1)	F
17	-	Turn Up The Bass	Tyree Feat. Kool Rock Steady	ffrr	3		F L
18	-	Every Rose Has Its Thorn	Poison	Enigma	4	(1)	F
19	-	Paradise City	Guns N' Roses	Geffen	5	(5)	F
20	14	Hold Me In Your Arms	Rick Astley	RCA	4		

April 1989

This Mnth	Prev Mnth	Title	Artist	Label	Wks	(US 20 Pos)	
1	-	Eternal Flame	Bangles	CBS	9	(1)	L
2	10	Like A Prayer	Madonna	Sire	7	(1)	
3	11	Straight Up	Paula Abdul	Siren	9	(1)	F
4	-	I Beg Your Pardon	Kon Kan	Atlantic	7	(15)	F L
5	1	Too Many Broken Hearts	Jason Donovan	PWL	9		
6	8	This Time I Know It's For Real	Donna Summer	Warner	8	(7)	
7	-	If You Don't Know Me By Now	Simply Red	Elektra	7	(1)	
8	-	Baby I Don't Care	Transvision Vamp	MCA	8		
9	-	Americanos	Holly Johnson	MCA	7		
10	15	Keep On Movin'	Soul II Soul Feat. Caron Wheeler	10	6	(11)	F
11	19	Paradise City	Guns N' Roses	Geffen	5	(5)	F
12	-	When Love Comes To Town	U2 With B.B. King	Island	3	(68)	
13	-	People Hold On	Coldcut Feat. Lisa Stansfield	Ahead Of Our Time	4		L
14	-	Good Thing	Fine Young Cannibals	London	5	(1)	
15	14	I'd Rather Jack	Reynolds Girls	PWL	6		F L
16	-	Lullaby	Cure	Fiction	3	(74)	
17	-	I Haven't Stopped Dancing Yet	Pat & Mick	PWL	3		F L
18	-	International Rescue	Fuzzbox	WEA	4		F
19	-	Don't Be Cruel	Bobby Brown	MCA	3	(8)	
20	5	Can't Stay Away From You	Gloria Estefa/Miami Sound...	Epic	6	(6)	

◆ 1960s superstar Gene Pitney had his only No. 1 with a revival of his last Top 10 entry (from 1967), 'Something's Gotten Hold Of My Heart'. He shared billing on this re-recording with Marc Almond.

◆ TV's *Top Of The Pops* celebrated its 25th birthday.

◆ Wembley crowd-pullers included The Bee Gees, Bobby Brown, Bob Dylan, Elton John, R.E.M., Diana Ross and Stevie Wonder.

1989

This Mnth	Prev Mnth	Title	Artist	Label	Wks	(US 20 Pos)	
1	-	Hand On Your Heart	Kylie Minogue	PWL	7		
2	-	Requiem	London Boys	WEA	7		F
3	-	Miss You Like Crazy	Natalie Cole	EMI	8	(7)	
4	1	Eternal Flame	Bangles	CBS	9	(1)	L
5	-	I Want It All	Queen	Parlophone	4	(50)	
6	-	Bring Me Edelweiss	Edelweiss	WEA	5		F L
7	-	Beds Are Burning	Midnight Oil	CBS	5	(17)	F L
8	-	Ferry 'Cross The Mersey	Christians/Holly Johnson/Paul McCartney/Gerry Marsden & Stock Aitken Waterman	PWL	5		F L
9	8	Baby I Don't Care	Transvision Vamp	MCA	8		
10	-	I'm Every Woman	Chaka Khan	Warner	4		L
11	9	Americanos	Holly Johnson	MCA	7		
12	7	If You Don't Know Me By Now	Simply Red	Elektra	7	(1)	
13	-	The Look	Roxette	EMI	4	(1)	F
14	-	Who's In The House	Beatmasters	Rhythm King	4		
15	-	Electric Youth	Debbie Gibson	Atlantic	3	(11)	
16	-	Every Little Step	Bobby Brown	MCA	4	(3)	
17	-	Your Mama Don't Dance	Poison	Capitol	3	(10)	
18	14	Good Thing	Fine Young Cannibals	London	5	(1)	
19	-	Manchild	Neneh Cherry	Circa	5		
20	-	Where Has All The Love Gone	Yazz	Big Life	3		

This	Prev	Title	Artist	Label	Wks	(US Pos)	
1	-	Sealed With A Kiss	Jason Donovan	PWL	5		
2	3	Miss You Like Crazy	Natalie Cole	EMI	8	(7)	
3	-	Express Yourself	Madonna	Sire	5	(2)	
4	-	The Best Of Me	Cliff Richard	EMI	4		
5	-	Right Back Where We Started From	Sinitta	Fanfare	7	(84)	
6	-	Back To Life (However Do You Want Me)	Soul II Soul Featuring Caron Wheeler	10	10	(4)	
7	-	Sweet Child O' Mine	Guns N' Roses	Geffen	6	(1)	
8	8	Ferry 'Cross The Mersey	Christians, Holly Johnson etc.	PWL	5		F L
9	19	Manchild	Neneh Cherry	Circa	5		
10	-	I Don't Wanna Get Hurt	Donna Summer	Warner	5		
11	-	On The Inside (Theme 'Prisoner- Cell Block H')	Lynne Hamilton	A1	4		F L
12	-	I Drove All Night	Cyndi Lauper	Epic	6	(6)	
13	1	Hand On Your Heart	Kylie Minogue	PWL	7		
14	2	Requiem	London Boys	WEA	7		F
15	-	Song For Whoever	Beautiful South	Go! Discs	7		F
16	-	It Is Time To Get Funky	D. Mob Featuring LRS	London	5		
17	6	Bring Me Edelweiss	Edelweiss	WEA	5		F L
18	16	Every Little Step	Bobby Brown	MCA	4	(3)	
19	-	Batdance	Prince	Warner	5	(1)	
20	-	Just Keep Rockin'	Double Trouble & Rebel M.C.	Desire	7		F

◆ Stock, Aitken & Waterman scored a record three successive No. 1s with singles by Kylie Minogue, Jason Donovan and an all star group featuring Gerry (& The Pacemakers) Marsden, whose re-recording of 'Ferry Cross The Mersey' was the eighth charity chart topper in five years.

◆ Cliff Richard released his 100th single, 'The Best Of Me'. It coincided with the 100th anniversary of the first commercially released record.

1989

This Mnth	Prev Mnth	Title	Artist	Label	Wks	(US 20 Pos)	
1	6	Back To Life (However Do You Want Me)	Soul II Soul Featuring Caron Wheeler	10	10	(4)	
2	-	London Nights	London Boys	Teldec/WEA	7		
3	15	Song For Whoever	Beautiful South	Go! Discs	7		F
4	-	You'll Never Stop Me From Loving You	Sonia	Chrysalis	8		F
5	-	Licence To Kill	Gladys Knight	MCA	7		L
6	-	It's Alright	Pet Shop Boys	Parlophone	4		
7	19	Batdance	Prince	Warner	5	(1)	
8	-	Ain't Nobody	Rufus & Chaka Khan	Warner	7	(22)	L
9	-	On Our Own	Bobby Brown	MCA	6	(2)	
10	-	Wind Beneath My Wings	Bette Midler	Atlantic	6	(1)	F L
11	12	I Drove All Night	Cyndi Lauper	Epic	6	(6)	
12	-	All I Want Is You	U2	Island	3	(83)	
13	-	Breakthru'	Queen	Parlophone	3		
14	-	Superwoman	Karyn White	Warner	4	(8)	F L
15	-	Don't Wanna Lose You	Gloria Estefan	Epic	6	(1)	
16	20	Just Keep Rockin'	Double Trouble & Rebel M.C.	Desire	7		F
17	5	Right Back Where We Started From	Sinitta	Fanfare	7	(84)	
18	-	Voodoo Ray (EP)	A Guy Called Gerald	Rham!	4		F L
19	1	Sealed With A Kiss	Jason Donovan	PWL	5		
20	-	Patience	Guns N' Roses	Geffen	3	(4)	

This Mnth	Prev Mnth	Title	Artist	Label	Wks	(US 20 Pos)	
1	-	Swing The Mood	Jive Bunny & The Mastermixers	Music Factory	10	(11)	F
2	-	Wouldn't Change A Thing	Kylie Minogue	PWL	6		
3	-	French Kiss	Lil Louis	ffrr	7	(50)	F
4	-	Poison	Alice Cooper	Epic	7	(7)	L
5	4	You'll Never Stop Me From Loving...	Sonia	Chrysalis	8		F
6	15	Don't Wanna Lose You	Gloria Estefan	Epic	6	(1)	
7	-	Toy Soldiers	Martika	CBS	6	(1)	F
8	-	Too Much	Bros	CBS	4		
9	9	On Our Own	Bobby Brown	MCA	6	(2)	
10	-	You're History	Shakespear's Sister	ffrr	4		F
11	-	Losing My Mind	Liza Minnelli	Epic	3		F L
12	-	Ride On Time	Black Box	De Construction	14		F
13	-	Blame It On The Boogie	Big Fun	Jive	6		F
14	8	Ain't Nobody	Rufus & Chaka Khan	Warner	7	(22)	L
15	10	Wind Beneath My Wings	Bette Midler	Atlantic	6	(1)	F L
16	2	London Nights	London Boys	Teldec/WEA	7		
17	-	Hey D.J. I Can't Dance To That Music You're Playing/Ska Train	Beatmasters Featuring Betty Boo	Rhythm King	6		L
18	-	Days	Kirsty MacColl	Virgin	4		L
19	-	Do The Right Thing	Redhead Kingpin & The FBI	10	3		F L
20	1	Back To Life (However Do You ...)	Soul II Soul/Caron Wheeler	10	10	(4)	

◆ Madonna scored a record 16th successive Top 5 single in the USA with 'Cherish'. In the UK Kylie Minogue's 'Wouldn't Change A Thing' was the fourth of her six singles to enter in runner-up position (surprisingly she never had a record enter at No. 1).
◆ Paul McCartney started his first world tour for 13 years in Sweden, and The Pet Shop Boys, who chalked up their 12th Top 20 hit with 'It's Alright', toured the UK for the first time.

1989

This Mnth	Prev Mnth	Title	Artist	Label	Wks	(US 20 Pos)	
1	12	Ride On Time	Black Box	De Construction	14		F
2	1	Swing The Mood	Jive Bunny & Mastermixers	Music Factory	10	(11)	F
3	-	Sowing The Seeds Of Love	Tears For Fears	Fontana	5	(2)	
4	-	Right Here Waiting	Richard Marx	EMI	7	(1)	F
5	13	Blame It On The Boogie	Big Fun	Jive	6		F
6	-	Every Day (I Love You More)	Jason Donovan	PWL	4		
7	-	I Need Your Lovin'	Alyson Williams	Def Jam	7		L
8	-	The Time Warp	Damian	Jive	5		F L
9	-	The Best	Tina Turner	Capitol	7	(15)	
10	-	I Just Don't Have The Heart	Cliff Richard	EMI	5		
11	-	Numero Uno	Starlight	City Beat	6		F L
12	17	Hey D.J. I Can't Dance To That Music You're Playing/Ska Train	Beatmasters Featuring Betty Boo	Rhythm King	6		L
13	-	Pump Up The Jam	Technotronic Featuring Felly	Swanyard	9	(2)	F
14	-	Cherish	Madonna	Sire	5	(2)	
15	4	Poison	Alice Cooper	Epic	7	(7)	L
16	-	If Only I Could	Sydney Youngblood	Circa	9		F
17	7	Toy Soldiers	Martika	CBS	6	(1)	F
18	3	French Kiss	Lil Louis	ffrr	7	(50)	F
19	2	Wouldn't Change A Thing	Kylie Minogue	PWL	6		
20	-	Personal Jesus	Depeche Mode	Mute	3	(28)	

1	1	Ride On Time	Black Box	De Construction	14		F
2	13	Pump Up The Jam	Technotronic Featuring Felly	Swanyard	9	(2)	F
3	16	If Only I Could	Sydney Youngblood	Circa	9		F
4	-	Street Tuff	Rebel MC/Double Trouble	Desire	8		L
5	-	That's What I Like	Jive Bunny & The Mastermixers	Music Factory	8	(69)	
6	-	We Didn't Start The Fire	Billy Joel	CBS	6	(1)	
7	-	Girl I'm Gonna Miss You	Milli Vanilli	Cooltempo	8	(1)	L
8	-	Sweet Surrender	Wet Wet Wet	Precious	5		
9	-	Drama!	Erasure	Mute	4		
10	-	If I Could Turn Back Time	Cher	Geffen	7	(3)	
11	-	Leave A Light On	Belinda Carlisle	Virgin	6	(11)	
12	-	You Keep It All In	Beautiful South	Go! Discs	5		
13	4	Right Here Waiting	Richard Marx	EMI	7	(1)	F
14	-	Room In Your Heart	Living In A Box	Chrysalis	7		L
15	9	The Best	Tina Turner	Capitol	7	(15)	
16	-	Wishing On A Star	Fresh 4 Featuring Lizz E	10	3		F L
17	-	Chocolate Box	Bros	CBS	2		
18	-	Name And Number	Curiosity Killed The Cat	Mercury	3		
19	-	The Road To Hell (Pt. 2)	Chris Rea	WEA	5		
20	14	Cherish	Madonna	Sire	5	(2)	

◆ In September, Italian records held the top three places in the UK dance chart with the chart topping 'Ride On Time' by Black Box outselling all other singles in 1989.

◆ Phonogram bought Island Records for $480 (£300) million with shareholders U2 making $48 (£30) million from the deal.

◆ Richard Marx's debut UK Top 20 entry, 'Right Here Waiting', had been his sixth successive US Top 3 entry.

November 1989

This Mnth	Prev Mnth	Title	Artist	Label	Wks	(US 20 Pos)	
1	-	All Around The World	Lisa Stansfield	Arista	7	(3)	
2	7	Girl I'm Gonna Miss You	Milli Vanilli	Cooltempo	8	(1)	L
3	5	That's What I Like	Jive Bunny & The Mastermixers	Music Factory	8	(69)	L
4	-	Never Too Late	Kylie Minogue	PWL	5		
5	-	Another Day In Paradise	Phil Collins	Virgin	5	(1)	
6	4	Street Tuff	Rebel MC/Double Trouble	Desire	8		L
7	-	I Feel The Earth Move	Martika	CBS	6	(25)	
8	14	Room In Your Heart	Living In A Box	Chrysalis	7		L
9	-	You Got It (The Right Stuff)	New Kids On The Block	CBS	8	(3)	F
10	11	Leave A Light On	Belinda Carlisle	Virgin	6	(11)	
11	-	Don't Know Much	Linda Ronstadt (featuring Aaron Neville)	Elektra	7	(2)	L
12	-	Grand Piano	Mixmaster	BCM	4		F L
13	10	If I Could Turn Back Time	Cher	Geffen	7	(3)	
14	19	The Road To Hell (Pt. 2)	Chris Rea	WEA	5		
15	-	Infinite Dreams	Iron Maiden	EMI	2		
16	1	Ride On Time	Black Box	De Construction	14		F
17	-	I Want That Man	Deborah Harry	Chrysalis	4		L
18	-	Never Too Much (89 Remix)	Luther Vandross	Epic	3	(33)	
19	-	C'mon And Get My Love	D. Mob Featuring Cathy Dennis	Ffrr	4	(10)	
20	3	If Only I Could	Sydney Youngblood	Circa	9		F

December 1989

This Mnth	Prev Mnth	Title	Artist	Label	Wks	(US 20 Pos)	
1	11	Don't Know Much	Linda Ronstadt (featuring Aaron Neville)	Elektra	7	(2)	L
2	9	You Got It (The Right Stuff)	New Kids On The Block	CBS	8	(3)	F
3	-	Lambada	Kaoma	CBS	9	(46)	F L
4	-	When You Come Back To Me	Jason Donovan	PWL	8		
5	-	Get A Life	Soul II Soul	10	8	(54)	
6	-	Eve Of The War	Jeff Wayne	CBS	6		F L
7	-	Let's Party	Jive Bunny & The Mastermixers	Music Factory	5		
8	-	I Don't Wanna Lose You	Tina Turner	Capitol	5	(9)	
9	-	Donald Where's Your Troosers	Andy Stewart	Stone	5	(77)	F L
10	-	Dear Jessie	Madonna	Sire	6		
11	-	Do They Know It's Christmas?	Band Aid II	PWL/Polydor	4		F L
12	-	Homely Girl	UB40	Dep International	4		
13	-	Can't Shake The Feeling	Big Fun	Jive	5		
14	-	Got To Get	Rob 'n' Raz Featuring Leila K	Arista	9		F L
15	1	All Around The World	Lisa Stansfield	Arista	7	(3)	
16	-	Fool's Gold/What The World Is Waiting For	Stone Roses	Silvertone	4		F
17	5	Another Day In Paradise	Phil Collins	Virgin	5	(1)	
18	-	In Private	Dusty Springfield	Parlophone	4		L
19	-	Sister	Bros	CBS	3		
20	-	Pacific	808 State	ZTT	4		F

◆ Jive Bunny & The Mastermixers scored a third successive No. 1 with their third release 'Let's Party', equalling the record set by Gerry & The Pacemakers and Frankie Goes To Hollywood.

◆ Stock, Aitken & Waterman produced a record breaking 11 of the year's Top 40 British singles.

◆ The decade ended with Band Aid II (a collection of current UK stars) topping the chart with an update of 'Do They Know It's Christmas'.

1990

This Mnth	Prev Mnth	Title	Artist	Label	Wks (US	20 Pos)	
1	-	Hangin' Tough	New Kids On The Block	CBS	6	(1)	
2	5	Get A Life	Soul II Soul	10	8	(54)	
3	4	When You Come Back To Me	Jason Donovan	PWL	8		
4	-	Touch Me	49ers	4th & Broadway	7		F
5	14	Got To Get	Rob 'n' Raz Featuring Leila K	Arista	9		F L
6	-	Got To Have Your Love	Mantronix Featuring Wondress	Capitol	7	(82)	F
7	-	Tears On My Pillow	Kylie Minogue	PWL	6		
8	-	The Magic Number/Buddy	De La Soul	Big Life	5		
9	11	Do They Know It's Christmas?	Band Aid II	PWL/Polydor	4		F L
10	10	Dear Jessie	Madonna	Sire	6		
11	3	Lambada	Kaoma	CBS	9	(46)	F L
12	-	Put Your Hands Together	D. Mob Featuring Nuff Juice	London	4		L
13	-	You Make Me Feel (Mighty Real)	Jimmy Somerville	London	4	(87)	
14	-	Going Back To My Roots/ Rich In Paradise	FPI Project	Rumour	4		F L
15	-	Deep Heat '89	Latino Rave	Deep Heat	6		F L
16	-	Could Have Told You So	Halo James	Epic	5		F L
17	7	Let's Party	Jive Bunny & The Mastermixers	Music Factory	5		
18	-	Listen To Your Heart	Sonia	Chrysalis	3		
19	-	Nothing Compares 2 U	Sinead O'Connor	Ensign	10	(1)	F L
20	9	Donald Where's Your Troosers	Andy Stewart	Stone	5	(77)	F L

This Mnth	Prev Mnth	Title	Artist	Label	Wks (US	20 Pos)	
1	19	Nothing Compares 2 U	Sinead O'Connor	Ensign	10	(1)	F L
2	-	Get Up (Before The Night Is Over)	Technotronic Feat. Ya Kid K	Swanyard	7	(7)	
3	-	Happenin' All Over Again	Lonnie Gordon	Supreme	6		F L
4	7	Tears On My Pillow	Kylie Minogue	PWL	6		
5	6	Got To Have Your Love	Mantronix Featuring Wondress	Capitol	7	(82)	F
6	-	I Wish It Would Rain Down	Phil Collins	Virgin	5	(3)	
7	-	Dub Be Good To Me	Beats International Featuring Lindy Layton	Go Beat	10	(76)	F
8	4	Touch Me	49ers	4th & Broadway	7		F
9	-	Walk On By	Sybil	PWL	5	(74)	
10	-	Instant Replay	Yell!	Fanfare	4		F L
11	-	I Don't Know Anybody Else	Black Box	Deconstruction	5	(23)	
12	16	Could Have Told You So	Halo James	Epic	5		F L
13	-	Live Together	Lisa Stansfield	Arista	3		
14	-	Nothing Ever Happens	Del Amitri	A&M	4		F
15	1	Hangin' Tough	New Kids On The Block	CBS	6	(1)	
16	-	Enjoy The Silence	Depeche Mode	Mute	6	(8)	
17	-	Just Like Jesse James	Cher	Geffen	4	(8)	
18	13	You Make Me Feel (Mighty Real)	Jimmy Somerville	London	4	(87)	
19	-	18 And Life	Skid Row	Atlantic	2	(4)	F
20	-	How Am I Supposed To Live Without You	Michael Bolton	CBS	6	(1)	F

◆ Ruby Turner became the first female British singer to top the US black music chart. A month later Lisa Stansfield followed in her footsteps.

◆ In February female-fronted singles held the top five places. Chart topper Sinead O'Connor also became the first Irish woman to top the LP chart.

March 1990

This Mnth	Prev Mnth	Title	Artist	Label	Wks	(US 20 Pos)	
1	7	Dub Be Good To Me	Beats International/Lindy Layton	Go Beat	10	(76)	F
2	20	How Am I Supposed To Live...	Michael Bolton	CBS	6	(1)	F
3	-	The Brits 1990	Various Artists	RCA	5		F L
4	-	Infinity	Guru Josh	Deconstruction	5		F L
5	-	Love Shack	B-52's	Reprise	8	(3)	
6	1	Nothing Compares 2 U	Sinead O'Connor	Ensign	10	(1)	F
7	-	Blue Savannah	Erasure	Mute	7		
8	-	That Sounds Good To Me	Jive Bunny & Mastermixers	Music Factory	3		
9	-	Moments In Soul	JT And The Big Family	Champion	4		F L
10	-	Lily Was Here	David A. Stewart Featuring Candy Dulfer	Anxious	7	(11)	F L
11	-	I'll Be Loving You (Forever)	New Kids On The Block	CBS	4	(1)	
12	16	Enjoy The Silence	Depeche Mode	Mute	6	(8)	
13	11	I Don't Know Anybody Else	Black Box	Deconstruction	5	(23)	
14	-	Strawberry Fields Forever	Candy Flip	Debut	7		F L
15	2	Get Up (Before The Night Is Over)	Technotronic Feat. Ya Kid K	Swanyard	7	(7)	
16	-	The Power	Snap	Arista	10	(2)	F
17	-	Elephant Stone	Stone Roses	Silvertone	2		
18	-	Downtown Train	Rod Stewart	Warner	4	(3)	
19	-	Black Betty	Ram Jam	Epic	3		L
20	-	Birdhouse In Your Soul	They Might Be Giants	Elektra	6		F L

April 1990

This Mnth	Prev Mnth	Title	Artist	Label	Wks	(US 20 Pos)	
1	-	Vogue	Madonna	Sire	10	(1)	
2	16	The Power	Snap	Arista	10	(2)	F
3	-	Black Velvet	Alannah Myles	Atlantic	8	(1)	F L
4	-	Kingston Town	UB40	Dep International	8		
5	-	Don't Miss The Partyline	Bizz Nizz	Cooltempo	5		F L
6	5	Love Shack	B-52's	Reprise	8	(3)	
7	-	Step On	Happy Mondays	Factory	7	(57)	
8	-	Hang On To Your Love	Jason Donovan	PWL	4		
9	-	All I Wanna Do Is Make Love To You	Heart	Capitol	8	(2)	
10	14	Strawberry Fields Forever	Candy Flip	Debut	7		F L
11	20	Birdhouse In Your Soul	They Might Be Giants	Elektra	6		F L
12	-	Opposites Attract	Paula Abdul (with The Wild Pair)	Siren	9	(1)	
13	-	Ghetto Heaven	Family Stand	Atlantic	8		F L
14	10	Lily Was Here	David A. Stewart/Candy Dulfer	Anxious	7	(11)	F L
15	7	Blue Savannah	Erasure	Mute	7		
16	-	This Beat Is Technotronic	Technotronic Feat. MC Eric	Swanyard	3		
17	-	Killer	Adamski	MCA	13		
18	-	Mamma Gave Birth To The Soul Children	Queen Latifah & De La Soul	Tommy Boy	4		F L
19	1	Dub Be Good To Me	Beats International/Lindy Layton	Go Beat	10	(76)	F
20	-	Everybody Needs Somebody To Love	Blues Brothers	Atlantic	3		F L

◆ Phil Collins' ...But Seriously sold a million in Britain in a record five weeks, topping the charts for 15 weeks. Oddly, for a week in February, Collins' 'I Wish It Would Rain Down' was the only male vocal record in the UK Top 10!

◆ The biggest recorded audience for a one act pop show was broken by Paul McCartney who attracted 184,000 to the Maracana Stadium in Brazil.

May 1990

This Mnth	Prev Mnth	Title	Artist	Label	Wks	(US 20 Pos)	
1	17	Killer	Adamski	MCA	13		
2	-	Dirty Cash	Adventures Of Stevie V	Mercury	9	(25)	F L
3	12	Opposites Attract	Paula Abdul (with The Wild Pair)	Siren	9	(1)	
4	1	Vogue	Madonna	Sire	10	(1)	
5	-	Better The Devil You Know	Kylie Minogue	PWL	6		
6	3	Black Velvet	Alannah Myles	Atlantic	8	(1)	F L
7	-	Cover Girl	New Kids On The Block	CBS	5	(2)	
8	-	A Dream's A Dream	Soul II Soul	Virgin	4	(85)	
9	4	Kingston Town	UB40	Dep International	8		
10	-	Hold On	En Vogue	Atlantic	6	(2)	F
11	2	The Power	Snap	Arista	10	(2)	F
12	9	All I Wanna Do Is Make Love To You	Heart	Capitol	8	(2)	
13	-	Won't Talk About It	Beats International	Go Beat	5	(76)	L
14	13	Ghetto Heaven	Family Stand	Atlantic	8		F L
15	-	Take Your Time	Mantronix Featuring Wondress	Capitol	4		L
16	7	Step On	Happy Mondays	Factory	7	(57)	
17	-	I Still Haven't Found What I'm Looking For	Chimes	CBS	5		F L
18	-	How Can We Be Lovers	Michael Bolton	CBS	4	(3)	
19	-	November Spawned A Monster	Morrissey	HMV	2		
20	-	Something Happened On The Way To Heaven	Phil Collins	Virgin	3	(4)	

June 1990

This Mnth	Prev Mnth	Title	Artist	Label	Wks	(US 20 Pos)	
1	-	World In Motion	Englandneworder	Factory	9		L
2	1	Killer	Adamski	MCA	13		
3	-	Hear The Drummer (Get Wicked)	Chad Jackson	Big Wave	6		F L
4	-	Doin' The Doo	Betty Boo	Rhythm King	7		F
5	-	Sacrifice/Healing Hands	Elton John	Rocket	10	(18)	
6	-	Venus	Don Pablo's Animals	Rumour	6		F L
7	-	It Must Have Been Love	Roxette	EMI	9	(1)	
8	2	Dirty Cash	Adventures Of Stevie V	Mercury	9	(25)	F L
9	-	Step By Step	New Kids On The Block	CBS	3	(1)	
10	-	The Only One I Know	Charlatans	Situation Two	5		F
11	5	Better The Devil You Know	Kylie Minogue	PWL	6		
12	-	Oops Up	Snap	Arista	8	(35)	
13	-	Hold On	Wilson Phillips	SBK	7	(1)	F
14	-	Nessun Dorma	Luciano Pavarotti	Decca	6		F
15	10	Hold On	En Vogue	Atlantic	6	(2)	F L
16	17	I Still Haven't Found What I'm...	Chimes	CBS	5		F L
17	-	Star	Erasure	Mute	4		
18	-	The Only Rhyme That Bites	MC Tunes Versus 808 State	ZTT	6		F
19	-	Papa Was A Rolling Stone	Was (Not Was)	Fontana	3		
20	7	Cover Girl	New Kids On The Block	CBS	5	(2)	

◆ Stars at a Wembley show, celebrating the release of Nelson Mandela from a South African prison, included Tracy Chapman, Peter Gabriel, Patti Labelle, Simple Minds and Neil Young. An all-star John Lennon tribute show in Liverpool featured Natalie Cole, Terence Trent D'Arby, Roberta Flack, Daryll Hall & John Oates, Cyndi Lauper, Kylie Minogue and Wet Wet Wet. Headliners at a huge charity show at Knebworth included Phil Collins, Paul McCartney, Pink Floyd and Status Quo.

July 1990

This Mnth	Prev Mnth	Title	Artist	Label	Wks (US 20 Pos)	
1	5	Sacrifice/Healing Hands	Elton John	Rocket	10 (18)	
2	-	Mona	Craig McLachlan & Check 1-2	Epic	8	F
3	7	It Must Have Been Love	Roxette	EMI	9 (1)	
4	14	Nessun Dorma	Luciano Pavarotti	Decca	6	F
5	-	U Can't Touch This	M.C. Hammer	Capitol	11 (8)	F
6	-	Thunderbirds Are Go	FAB Featuring MC Parker	Brothers Org.	5	F L
7	12	Oops Up	Snap	Arista	8 (35)	
8	1	World In Motion	Englandneworder	Factory	9	L
9	-	Close To You	Maxi Priest	10	6 (1)	
10	-	Turtle Power	Partners In Kryme	SBK	8 (13)	F L
11	-	One Love	Stone Roses	Silvertone	4	
12	13	Hold On	Wilson Phillips	SBK	7 (1)	F
13	-	She Ain't Worth It	Glenn Medeiros Featuring Bobby Brown	London	4 (1)	L
14	-	Hanky Panky	Madonna	Sire	6 (10)	
15	18	The Only Rhyme That Bites	MC Tunes Versus 808 State	ZTT	6	F
16	-	I'm Free	Soup Dragons	Big Life	8 (79)	F L
17	-	Rockin' Over The Beat	Technotronic Featuring Ya Kid K	Swanyard	5 (95)	
18	-	Naked In The Rain	Blue Pearl	W.A.U.!Mr.Modo	9	F
19	-	Thinking Of You	Maureen	Urban	4	F L
20	4	Doin' The Doo	Betty Boo	Rhythm King	7	F

August 1990

This Mnth	Prev Mnth	Title	Artist	Label	Wks (US 20 Pos)	
1	10	Turtle Power	Partners In Kryme	SBK	8 (13)	F L
2	-	Tom's Diner	DNA Featuring Suzanne Vega	A&M	7 (5)	F
3	18	Naked In The Rain	Blue Pearl	W.A.U.!Mr.Modo	9	F
4	5	U Can't Touch This	M.C. Hammer	Capitol	11 (8)	F
5	16	I'm Free	Soup Dragons	Big Life	8 (79)	F L
6	14	Hanky Panky	Madonna	Sire	6 (10)	
7	-	Tonight	New Kids On The Block	CBS	8 (7)	
8	-	Itsy Bitsy Teeny Weeny Yellow Polka Dot Bikini	Bombalurina	Carpet	8	F
9	1	Sacrifice/Healing Hands	Elton John	Rocket	10 (18)	
10	-	Thieves In The Temple	Prince	Paisley Park	3 (6)	
11	17	Rockin' Over The Beat	Technotronic Feat. Ya Kid K	Swanyard	5 (95)	
12	-	Listen To Your Heart/Dangerous	Roxette	EMI	5 (1)	
13	2	Mona	Craig McLachlan & Check 1-2	Epic	8	F
14	-	Hardcore Uproar	Together	Ffrr	4	F L
15	-	LFO	LFO	Warp	3	F L
16	-	Where Are You Baby?	Betty Boo	Rhythm King	6	
17	-	California Dreamin'/Carry The Blame	River City People	EMI	5	F L
18	-	Blaze Of Glory	Jon Bon Jovi	Vertigo	3 (1)	F L
19	3	It Must Have Been Love	Roxette	EMI	9 (1)	
20	-	Tricky Disco	Tricky Disco	Warp	3	F L

◆ Pink Floyd's *The Wall* show in Berlin drew 200,000 people and an estimated one billion saw it on TV. Among those appearing were Bryan Adams, The Band, Van Morrison, Sinead O'Connor and The Scorpions.

◆ Elton John's 'Sacrifice'/'Healing Hands' not only helped him equal Elvis Presley's American record of (at least) one Top 40 hit a year for 21 years, it also gave him his first British solo chart topper.

1990

September 1990

This Mnth	Prev Mnth	Title	Artist	Label	Wks	(US 20 Pos)	
1	-	The Joker	Steve Miller Band	Capitol	7		L
2	-	Groove Is In The Heart	Deee-Lite	Elektra	8	(4)	F L
3	-	Four Bacharach & David Songs (EP)	Deacon Blue	CBS	6		
4	8	Itsy Bitsy Teeny Weeny Yellow Polka Dot Bikini	Bombalurina	Carpet	8		F
5	-	What Time Is Love	KLF/Children Of The Revolution	KLF Comms.	7	(57)	F
6	16	Where Are You Baby?	Betty Boo	Rhythm King	6		
7	7	Tonight	New Kids On The Block	CBS	8	(7)	
8	-	Vision Of Love	Mariah Carey	CBS	5	(1)	F
9	-	The Space Jungle	Adamski	MCA	4		L
10	-	Show Me Heaven	Maria McKee	Epic	9		F L
11	-	Groovy Train	Farm	Produce	5	(41)	F
12	-	Praying For Time	George Michael	Epic	4	(1)	
13	-	Holy Smoke	Iron Maiden	EMI	2		
14	3	Naked In The Rain	Blue Pearl	W.A.U.!Mr.Modo	9		F
15	-	I've Been Thinking About You	Londonbeat	Anxious	7	(1)	L
16	12	Listen To Your Heart	Roxette	EMI	5	(1)	
17	-	Can Can You Party	Jive Bunny & The Mastermixers	Music Factory	3		
18	-	Rhythm Of The Rain	Jason Donovan	PWL	2		
19	2	Tom's Diner	DNA Featuring Suzanne Vega	A&M	7	(5)	F
20	-	Silhouettes	Cliff Richard	EMI	4		

October 1990

This Mnth	Prev Mnth	Title	Artist	Label	Wks	(US 20 Pos)	
1	10	Show Me Heaven	Maria McKee	Epic	9		F L
2	-	Blue Velvet	Bobby Vinton	Epic	8		L
3	-	The Anniversary Waltz - Part 1	Status Quo	Vertigo	6		
4	15	I've Been Thinking About You	Londonbeat	Anxious	7	(1)	L
5	-	I Can't Stand It	Twenty 4 Seven Featuring Captain Hollywood	BCM	6		F
6	-	Megamix	Technotronic	Swanyard	5		L
7	-	A Little Time	Beautiful South	Go! Discs	8		
8	-	So Hard	Pet Shop Boys	Parlophone	3	(62)	
9	-	Have You Seen Her	M.C. Hammer	Capitol	4	(4)	
10	-	Fascinating Rhythm	Bass-O-Matic	Virgin	5		F L
11	2	Groove Is In The Heart	Deee-Lite	Elektra	8	(4)	F L
12	1	The Joker	Steve Miller Band	Capitol	7		L
13	-	It's A Shame (My Sister)	Monie Love Feat. True Image	Cooltempo	4	(26)	
14	-	Let's Try Again/Didn't I Blow Your Mind	New Kids On The Block	CBS	3	(53)	
15	-	I'm Your Baby Tonight	Whitney Houston	Arista	6	(1)	
16	11	Groovy Train	Farm	Produce	5	(41)	F
17	-	Unchained Melody	Righteous Brothers	Verve	11	(13)	
18	-	Kinky Afro	Happy Mondays	Factory	4		
19	-	From A Distance	Cliff Richard	EMI	3		
20	-	Cult Of Snap	Snap	Arista	3		

◆ Steve Miller's 1974 US No. 1, 'The Joker', finally repeated that feat in the UK after it was heard in a TV advertisement for Levi jeans.

◆ Bobby Vinton's 1963 US chart topper, 'Blue Velvet', hit in Britain as Berlin's 'Take My Breath Away' returned. The Righteous Brothers' 'You've Lost That Lovin' Feeling' spent a record third time in the Top 10, and the duo's 25-year-old 'Unchained Melody' became the year's top seller.

November 1990

This Mnth	Prev Mnth	Title	Artist	Label	Wks	(US 20 Pos)		
1	17	Unchained Melody	Righteous Brothers	Verve	11	(13)		
2	7	A Little Time	Beautiful South	Go! Discs	8			
3	-	Don't Worry	Kim Appleby	Parlophone	8		F	
4	-	Take My Breath Away	Berlin	CBS	6		L	
5	-	Step Back In Time	Kylie Minogue	PWL	4			
6		(We Want) The Same Thing	Belinda Carlisle	MCA	5			
7	-	Fog On The Tyne (Revisited)	Gazza And Lindisfarne	Best	4		F L	
8	-	Fantasy	Black Box	De Construction	6			
9	15	I'm Your Baby Tonight	Whitney Houston	Arista	6	(1)		
10	-	I'll Be Your Baby Tonight	Robert Palmer And UB40	EMI	6			
11	1	Show Me Heaven	Maria McKee	Epic	9		F L	
12	-	Unbelievable	EMF	Parlophone	8	(1)	F	
13	-	To Love Somebody	Jimmy Somerville	London	4			
14	-	Working Man	Rita McNeil	Polydor	4		F L	
15	18	Kinky Afro	Happy Mondays	Factory	4			
16	-	Cubik/Olympic	808 State	ZTT	3			
17	-	Ice Ice Baby	Vanilla Ice	SBK	10	(1)	F	
18	3	The Anniversary Waltz - Part 1	Status Quo	Vertigo	6			
19	-	Close To Me	Cure	Elektra	3	(97)		
20	2	Blue Velvet	Bobby Vinton	Epic	8		L	

December 1990

This Mnth	Prev Mnth	Title	Artist	Label	Wks	(US 20 Pos)		
1	17	Ice Ice Baby	Vanilla Ice	SBK	10	(1)	F	
2	12	Unbelievable	EMF	Parlophone	8	(1)	F	
3	1	Unchained Melody	Righteous Brothers	Verve	11	(13)		
4	-	Saviour's Day	Cliff Richard	EMI	6			
5	-	Justify My Love	Madonna	Sire	6	(1)		
6	-	All Together Now	Farm	Produce	8			
7	3	Don't Worry	Kim Appleby	Parlophone	8		F	
8	-	You've Lost That Lovin' Feeling/Ebb Tide	Righteous Brothers	Verve	6		L	
9	-	Kinky Boots	Patrick MacNee & Honor Blackman	Deram	4		F L	
10	-	Wicked Game	Chris Isaak	London	5	(6)	F	
11	-	Mary Had A Little Boy	Snap	Arista	6			
12	-	Pray	M.C. Hammer	Capitol	7	(2)		
13	-	Sadness Part 1	Enigma	Virgin Int.	9	(5)		
14	-	It Takes Two	Rod Stewart & Tina Turner	Warner Bros.	4			
15	-	Falling	Julee Cruise	Warner Bros.	4		F L	
16	-	This One's For The Children	New Kids On The Block	CBS	4	(7)		
17	8	Fantasy	Black Box	Deconstruction	6			
18	-	The Grease Megamix	John Travolta/O. Newton-John	Polydor	6		L	
19	-	Just This Side Of Love	Malandra Burrows	YTV	4		F L	
20	-	King Of The Road (EP)	Proclaimers	Chrysalis	3		L	

◆ In October, for the first time since March 1986, there were no Stock Aitken & Waterman records in the Top 40. They had produced over 100 Top 75 entries.

◆ New Kids On The Block scored their seventh Top 10 single in 1990 equalling Bill Haley & The Comets' 1956 record. NKOTB reportedly earned $115 million in 1990.

◆ Queen, who had not graced the American Top 20 since 1984, signed a $10 million deal with the Walt Disney-owned Hollywood label.

1991

This Mnth	Prev Mnth	Title	Artist	Label	Wks	(US 20 Pos)	
1	13	Sadness Part 1	Enigma	Virgin Int.	9	(5)	
2	-	Crazy	Seal	ZTT	9	(8)	F
3	18	The Grease Megamix	John Travolta/O. Newton-John	Polydor	6		L
4	1	Ice Ice Baby	Vanilla Ice	SBK	10	(1)	F
5	-	Bring Your Daughter...To The Slaughter	Iron Maiden	EMI	3		
6	6	All Together Now	Farm	Produce	8		
7	-	Gonna Make You Sweat	C&C Music Factory/F. Williams	CBS	6	(1)	F
8	-	3 A.M. Eternal	KLF/Children Of The Revolution	KLF Comms.	8	(5)	
9	-	(I've Had) The Time Of My Life	Bill Medley & Jennifer Warnes	RCA	4		L
10	8	You've Lost That Lovin' Feeling	Righteous Brothers	Verve	6		L
11	12	Pray	M.C. Hammer	Capitol	7	(2)	
12	11	Mary Had A Little Boy	Snap	Arista	6		
13	-	International Bright Young Thing	Jesus Jones	Food	3		F L
14	-	I Can't Take The Power	Off-Shore	CBS	4		F L
15	5	Justify My Love	Madonna	Sire	6	(1)	
16	-	Mercy Mercy Me - I Want You	Robert Palmer	EMI	4	(16)	L
17	-	Innuendo	Queen	Parlophone	3		
18	4	Saviour's Day	Cliff Richard	EMI	6		
19	-	The Total Mix	Black Box	Deconstruction	4		
20	-	All The Man That I Need	Whitney Houston	Arista	3	(1)	

1	-	Do The Bartman	Simpsons	Geffen	10		F
2	8	3 A.M. Eternal	KLF/Children Of The Revolution	KLF Comms.	8	(5)	
3	-	Wiggle It	2 In A Room	Big Life	6	(15)	F L
4	-	(I Wanna Give You) Devotion	Nomad/MC Mikee Freedom	Rumour	8		F
5	-	What Do I Have To Do	Kylie Minogue	PWL	5		
6	-	Only You	Praise	Epic	5		F L
7	-	I Believe	EMF	Parlophone	4		
8	-	Hippychick	Soho	S&M	5	(14)	F L
9	-	Get Here	Oleta Adams	Fontana	7	(5)	F L
10	-	Cry For Help	Rick Astley	RCA	5	(7)	L
11	2	Crazy	Seal	ZTT	9	(8)	F
12	-	Play That Funky Music	Vanilla Ice	SBK	4	(4)	L
13	17	Innuendo	Queen	Parlophone	3		
14	1	Sadness Part 1	Enigma	Virgin Int.	9	(5)	
15	-	You Got The Love	Source Featuring Candi Staton	Truelove	7		F
16	-	G.L.A.D.	Kim Appleby	Parlophone	3		
17	7	Gonna Make You Sweat	C&C Music Factory/F. Williams	CBS	6	(1)	F
18	-	In Yer Face	808 State	ZTT	4		
19	-	All Right Now	Free	Island	5		L
20	16	Mercy Mercy Me - I Want You	Robert Palmer	EMI	4	(16)	L

◆ Another spate of re-entries hit the UK Top 20 including records by Bill Medley & Jennifer Warnes, The Clash, Madonna, John Travolta & Olivia Newton-John and Free, while Patsy Cline's 1961 American hit, 'Crazy' made its UK debut.

◆ Eric Clapton played a record 24 nights at London's prestigious Royal Albert Hall.

◆ Michael Jackson, whose Bad album had now passed the 25 million sales mark globally, signed the world's biggest record deal (reportedly worth somewhere between $50 million and a billion!) with Sony.

March 1991

This Mnth	Prev Mnth	Title	Artist	Label	Wks	(US 20 Pos)	
1	-	Should I Stay Or Should I Go	Clash	CBS	6		
2	15	You Got The Love	Source Featuring Candi Staton	Truelove	7		F
3	1	Do The Bartman	Simpsons	Geffen	10		F
4	-	The Stonk	Hale & Pace & The Stonkers	London	5		F L
5	-	Crazy For You	Madonna	Sire	4		
6	-	Because I Love You (Postman Song)	Stevie B	LMR	6	(1)	F L
7	-	Move Your Body (Elevation)	Xpansions	Optimism	5		F L
8	-	Joyride	Roxette	EMI	7	(1)	
9	4	(I Wanna Give You) Devotion	Nomad/MC Mikee Freedom	Rumour	8		F
10	-	The One And Only	Chesney Hawkes	Chrysalis	6	(10)	F L
11	-	It's Too Late	Quartz Introducing Dina Carroll	Mercury	6		F L
12	-	Rhythm Of My Heart	Rod Stewart	Warner Bros.	8		
13	19	All Right Now	Free	Island	5		L
14	9	Get Here	Oleta Adams	Fontana	7	(5)	F L
15	-	Where The Streets Have No Name-Can't Take My Eyes Off You/How Can You Expect To Be Taken Seriously	Pet Shop Boys	EMI	4	(72)	
16	-	Love Rears It's Ugly Head	Living Colour	Epic	5		F L
17	2	3 A.M. Eternal	KLF/Children Of The Revolution	KLF Comms.	8	(5)	
18	-	Let There Be Love	Simple Minds	Virgin	4		
19	18	In Yer Face	808 State	ZTT	4		
20	-	Secret Love	Bee Gees	Warner Bros.	5		

April 1991

This Mnth	Prev Mnth	Title	Artist	Label	Wks	(US 20 Pos)	
1	-	Sit Down	James	Fontana	8		F
2	-	The Whole Of The Moon	Waterboys	Ensign	6		F L
3	10	The One And Only	Chesney Hawkes	Chrysalis	6	(10)	F L
4	12	Rhythm Of My Heart	Rod Stewart	Warner	8		
5	-	Rescue Me	Madonna	Sire	5	(9)	
6	-	The Size Of A Cow	Wonder Stuff	Polydor	5		
7	8	Joyride	Roxette	EMI	7	(1)	
8	-	Deep, Deep Trouble	Simpsons Feat. Bart & Homer	Geffen	5	(69)	L
9	-	Love & Kisses	Dannii Minogue	MCA	5		F
10	-	Human Nature	Gary Clail On-U Sound System	Perfecto	5		F L
11	-	Anthem	N-Joi	Deconstruction	5		F
12	20	Secret Love	Bee Gees	Warner	5		
13	-	I've Got News For You	Feargal Sharkey	Virgin	4		L
14	11	It's Too Late	Quartz Introducing Dina Carroll	Mercury	6		F L
15	18	Let There Be Love	Simple Minds	Virgin	4		
16	-	The Shoop Shoop Song (It's In His Kiss)	Cher	Geffen	11	(33)	
17	15	Where The Streets Have No Name...	Pet Shop Boys	EMI	4	(72)	
18	-	Snap Mega Mix	Snap	Arista	3		
19	-	Sailing On The Seven Seas	OMD	Virgin	8		
20	4	The Stonk	Hale & Pace & The Stonkers	London	5		F L

◆ Despite the fact that The Simpsons cartoon TV series was only seen by a minority of the British public who had satellite or cable TV, the single, 'Do The Bartman', took the quirky quintet to the top.

◆ New Kids On The Block ended their European tour at Wembley. They had played 31 dates and grossed $8.8 million.

May 1991

This Mnth	Prev Mnth	Title	Artist	Label	Wks	(US 20 Pos)	
1	16	The Shoop Shoop Song (It's In His...)	Cher	Geffen	11	(33)	
2	-	Last Train To Trancentral	KLF	KLF Comms.	7		
3	19	Sailing On The Seven Seas	OMD	Virgin	8		
4	-	Senza Una Donna (Without A Woman)	Zucchero & Paul Young	London	6		F
5	-	Touch Me (All Night Long)	Cathy Dennis	Polydor	6	(2)	
6	-	Promise Me	Beverley Craven	Epic	8		F L
7	-	There's No Other Way	Blur	Food	5	(82)	F
8	-	Gypsy Woman (La Da Dee)	Crystal Waters	A&M	6	(8)	F
9	-	Get The Message	Electronic	Factory	4		
10	-	Born Free	Vic Reeves/The Roman Numerals	Sense	4		F
11	1	Sit Down	James	Fontana	8		F
12	-	Tainted Love	Soft Cell/Marc Almond	Mercury	5		L
13	-	Ring Ring Ring (Ha Ha Hey)	De La Soul	Big Life	4		L
14	2	The Whole Of The Moon	Waterboys	Ensign	6		F L
15	-	Future Love (EP)	Seal	ZTT	3		
16	-	Fading Like A Flower (Every Time You Leave)	Roxette	EMI	3	(2)	
17	-	I Wanna Sex You Up	Color Me Badd	Giant	9	(2)	F
18	-	Quadrophonia	Quadrophonia	ARS	2		F L
19	-	Anasthasia	T99	Citybeat	2		F L
20	-	Baby Baby	Amy Grant	A&M	7	(1)	F

June 1991

This Mnth	Prev Mnth	Title	Artist	Label	Wks	(US 20 Pos)	
1	17	I Wanna Sex You Up	Color Me Badd	Giant	9	(2)	F
2	1	The Shoop Shoop Song (It's In His Kiss)	Cher	Geffen	11	(33)	
3	20	Baby Baby	Amy Grant	A&M	7	(1)	F L
4	6	Promise Me	Beverley Craven	Epic	8		F L
5	-	Shiny Happy People	R.E.M.	Warner	6	(10)	
6	9	Gypsy Woman (La Da Dee)	Crystal Waters	A&M	6	(8)	F
7	-	Thinking About Your Love	Kenny Thomas	Cooltempo	8		
8	-	Shocked	Kylie Minogue	PWL	4		
9	-	Any Dream Will Do	Jason Donovan	Really Useful	9		
10	-	Do You Want Me	Salt-N-Pepa	ffrr	6	(21)	
11	12	Tainted Love	Soft Cell/Marc Almond	Mercury	5		L
12	-	Light My Fire	Doors	Elektra	3		L
13	-	Only Fools (Never Fall In Love)	Sonia	IQ	5		
14	-	Holiday	Madonna	Sire	3		
15	2	Last Train To Trancentral	KLF	KLF	7		
16	5	Touch Me (All Night Long)	Cathy Dennis	Polydor	6	(2)	
17	5	Touch Me (All Night Long)	Cathy Dennis	Polydor	6	(2)	
18	-	Move That Body	Technotronic Featuring Reggie	Ars	3		
19	-	The Motown Song	Rod Stewart	Warner Bros.	4	(10)	
20	-	Success	Dannii Minogue	MCA	3		

◆ As sister Dannii scored her second successive hit, Kylie Minogue became the first artist to see her first 13 hit singles all go into the Top 10.

◆ Small Faces' singer Steve Marriott died in a fire, and ex-Temptation David Ruffin died of drug-related causes.

◆ For the first time three consecutive No. 1s came from films. 'The One And Only' (*Buddy's Song*), 'The Shoop Shoop Song' (*Mermaids*) and 'I Wanna Sex You Up' (*New Jack City*).

July 1991

This Mnth	Prev Mnth	Title	Artist	Label	Wks	(US 20 Pos)	
1	-	(Everything I Do) I Do It For You	Bryan Adams	A&M	22	(1)	G
2	9	Any Dream Will Do	Jason Donovan	Really Useful	9		
3	-	Chorus	Erasure	Mute	6		
4	-	Rush Rush	Paula Abdul	Virgin	7	(1)	
5	7	Thinking About Your Love	Kenny Thomas	Cooltempo	8		
6	-	You Could Be Mine	Guns n' Roses	Geffen	7	(29)	
7	-	Now That We've Found Love	Heavy D. & The Boyz	MCA	8	(11)	F L
8	-	Always There	Incognito Featuring Jocelyn Brown	Talkin' Loud	5		F
9	1	I Wanna Sex You Up	Color Me Badd	Giant	9	(2)	F
10	10	Do You Want Me	Salt-N-Pepa	Ffrr	6	(21)	
11	-	Things That Make You Go Hmmmm....	C&C Music Factory	Columbia	7	(4)	L
12	-	7 Ways To Love	Cola Boy	Arista	4		F L
13	-	Pandora's Box	OMD	Virgin	5		L
14	-	Are You Mine?	Bros	Columbia	3		L
15	-	It Ain't Over 'Til It's Over	Lenny Kravitz	Virgin America	4	(2)	F
16		16			5		L
17	-	Love And Understanding	Cher	Geffen	5	(17)	L
18	-	I Touch Myself	Divinyls	Virgin America	5	(4)	F L
19	-	More Than Words	Extreme	A&M	8	(1)	
20	19	The Motown Song	Rod Stewart	Warner Bros	4	(10)	

August 1991

This Mnth	Prev Mnth	Title	Artist	Label	Wks	(US 20 Pos)	
1	1	(Everything I Do) I Do It For You	Bryan Adams	A&M	22	(1)	G
2	19	More Than Words	Extreme	A&M	8	(1)	
3	-	I'm Too Sexy	Right Said Fred	Tug	12	(1)	F
4	-	Move Any Mountain	Shamen	One Little Indian	7	(38)	F
5	7	Now That We've Found Love	Heavy D. & The Boyz	MCA	8	(11)	F L
6	-	All For Love	Color Me Badd	Giant	6	(1)	L
7	-	Winter In July	Bomb The Bass	Rhythm King	5		L
8	-	Set Adrift On Memory Bliss	P.M. Dawn	Gee Street	5	(1)	F
9	11	Things That Make You Go Hmmmm....	C&C Music Factory	Columbia	7	(4)	L
10	-	Summertime	D.J. Jazzy Jeff & The Fresh Prince	Jive	5	(4)	F
11	-	Twist & Shout	Deacon Blue	Columbia	4		
12	13	Pandora's Box	OMD	Virgin	5		L
13	2	Any Dream Will Do	Jason Donovan	Really Useful	9		
14	-	Charly	Prodigy	XL	7		F
15	-	Enter Sandman	Metallica	Vertigo	2	(16)	
16	6	You Could Be Mine	Guns n' Roses	Geffen	7	(29)	
17	-	Sunshine On A Rainy Day	Zoe	M&G	9		F L
18	-	Jump To The Beat	Dannii Minogue	MCA	3		
19	-	Happy Together	Jason Donovan	PWL	4		
20	17	Love And Understanding	Cher	Geffen	5	(17)	

◆ Bryan Adams's recording of '(Everything I Do) I Do It For You' was the world's top selling single in 1991. It sold over three million in America and became the first million seller for six years in Britain, where it spent a record 16 successive weeks at the top.

◆ Of the current wave of new UK chart makers only EMF, Jesus Jones, The KLF, Cathy Dennis and Seal were selling well in the USA.

1991

This Mnth	Prev Mnth	Title	Artist	Label	Wks	(US 20 Pos)	
1	1	(Everything I Do) I Do It For You	Bryan Adams	A&M	22	(1)	G
2	3	I'm Too Sexy	Right Said Fred	Tug	11	(1)	F
3	-	Insanity	Oceanic	Dead Dead Good	11		F
4	14	Charly	Prodigy	XL	7		F
5	17	Sunshine On A Rainy Day	Zoe	M&G	9		F L
6	-	Let's Talk About Sex	Salt-N-Pepa	ffrr	9	(13)	
7	-	Gett Off	Prince/New Power Generation	Paisley Park	5	(21)	
8	-	What Can You Do For Me	Utah Saints	ffrr	7		F
9	-	I'll Be Back	Arnee & The Terminaters	Epic	4		F L
10	-	Love...Thy Will Be Done	Martika	Columbia	5	(10)	
11	-	Love To Hate You	Erasure	Mute	6		
12	-	Peace	Sabrina Johnson	East West	6		F L
13	8	Set Adrift On Memory Bliss	P.M. Dawn	Gee Street	5	(1)	F
14	-	Everybody's Free (To Feel Good)	Rozalla	Pulse 8	6	(37)	F
15	6	All For Love	Color Me Badd	Giant	6	(1)	L
16	-	20th Century Boy	Marc Bolan & T. Rex	Marc On Wax	4		L
17	-	Don't Cry	Guns N' Roses	Geffen	2	(10)	
18	2	More Than Words	Extreme	A&M	8	(1)	
19	-	Good Vibrations	Marky Mark & The Funky Bunch Featuring Loleatta Holloway	Interscope	3	(1)	F L
20	-	Something Got Me Started	Simply Red	East West	4	(23)	

This Mnth	Prev Mnth	Title	Artist	Label	Wks	(US 20 Pos)	
1	1	(Everything I Do) I Do It For You	Bryan Adams	A&M	22	(1)	G
2	-	Wind Of Change	Scorpions	Mercury	7	(4)	F L
3	3	Insanity	Oceanic	Dead Dead Good	11		F
4	6	Let's Talk About Sex	Salt-N-Pepa	ffrr	9	(13)	
5	-	Saltwater	Julian Lennon	Virgin	6		L
6	11	Love To Hate You	Erasure	Mute	6		
7	14	Everybody's Free (To Feel Good)	Rozalla	Pulse 8	6	(37)	F
8	-	Always Look On The Bright Side Of Life	Monty Python	Virgin	5		F L
9	-	World In Union	Kiri Te Kanawa	Columbia	7		F L
10	-	Get Ready For This	2 Unlimited	PWL Continental	8	(76)	F
11	12	Peace	Sabrina Johnson	East West	6		F L
12	5	Sunshine On A Rainy Day	Zoe	M&G	9		F L
13	2	I'm Too Sexy	Right Said Fred	Tug	11	(1)	F
14	-	Best Of You	Kenny Thomas	Cooltempo	3		
15	-	Such A Feeling	Bizarre Inc	Vinyl Solution	5		F
16	-	Change	Lisa Stansfield	Arista	4	(30)	
17	-	Live Your Life Be Free	Belinda Carlisle	Virgin	3		
18	-	Dizzy	Vic Reeves & The Wonder Stuff	Sense	8		
19	20	Something Got Me Started	Simply Red	East West	4	(23)	
20	-	Baby Love	Dannii Minogue	MCA	2		

◆ Opera singer Luciano Pavarotti topped the LP chart with Essential Pavarotti II. In America his In Concert album completed a year at the helm of the classical chart.

◆ In 1991, more singles charted than ever. Records tended to enter higher and have shorter chart life spans.

November 1991

This Mnth	Prev Mnth	Title	Artist	Label	Wks	(US 20 Pos)	
1	18	Dizzy	Vic Reeves & The Wonder Stuff	Sense	8		
2	10	Get Ready For This	2 Unlimited	PWL Continental	8	(76)	F
3	1	(Everything I Do) I Do It For You	Bryan Adams	A&M	22	(1)	G
4	-	Rhythm Is A Mystery	K-Klass	De Construction	4		F
5	-	The Fly	U2	Island	3	(58)	
6	-	If You Were Here With Me Now	Kylie Minogue/K. Washington	PWL	5		
7	9	World In Union	Kiri Te Kanawa	Columbia	7		F L
8	-	Activ 8 (Come With Me)	Altern 8	Network	5		F
9	-	Is There Anybody Out There?	Bassheads	Deconstruction	4		F
10	-	Black Or White	Michael Jackson	Epic	9	(1)	
11	-	No Son Of Mine	Genesis	Virgin	3	(12)	
12	-	Playing With Knives	Bizarre Inc	Vinyl Solution	3		
13	2	Wind Of Change	Scorpions	Mercury	7	(4)	F L
14	8	Always Look On The Bright Side Of Life	Monty Python	Virgin	5		F L
15	-	American Pie	Don McLean	Liberty	4		L
16	-	Killer (EP)	Seal	ZTT	3	(100)	
17	-	When A Man Loves A Woman	Michael Bolton	Columbia	3	(1)	
18	-	Go	Moby	Outer-Rhythm	4		F
19	3	Insanity	Oceanic	Dead Dead Good	11		F
20	-	DJs Take Control/Way In My Brain	SL2	XL	2		F

December 1991

This Mnth	Prev Mnth	Title	Artist	Label	Wks	(US 20 Pos)	
1	-	Don't Let The Sun Go Down On Me	George Michael/Elton John	Epic	6	(1)	
2	-	When You Tell Me That You Love Me	Diana Ross	EMI	9		
3	-	Justified And Ancient	KLF/Tammy Wynette	KLF Communications	9	(11)	
4	10	Black Or White	Michael Jackson	Epic	9	(1)	
5	-	Driven By You	Brian May	Parlophone	6		F
6	-	Ride Like The Wind	East Side Beat	Ffrr	7		F L
7	-	Too Blind To See It	Kym Sims	Atco	8	(38)	F
8	-	Stars	Simply Red	East West	6	(44)	
9	-	Bohemian Rhapsody/These Are The Days Of Our Lives	Queen	Parlophone	10	(2)	G
10	-	Don't Talk Just Kiss	Right Said Fred/Jocelyn Brown	Tug	7	(76)	
11	-	Live And Let Die	Guns n' Roses	Geffen	4	(33)	
12	8	Activ 8 (Come With Me)	Altern 8	Network	5		F
13	-	Smells Like Teen Spirit	Nirvana	DGC	3	(6)	F
14	-	We Should Be Together	Cliff Richard	EMI	3		
15	-	Rocket Man (I Think It's Going To Be A Long Long Time)	Kate Bush	Mercury	4		
16	1	Dizzy	Vic Reeves & WonderStuff	Sense	8		L
17	-	If You Go Away	New Kids On The Block	Columbia	2		L
18	-	Addams Groove	Hammer	Capitol	7	(7)	
19	-	Sound	James	Fontana	3		
20	-	Bare Necessities Megamix	UK Mixmasters	Connect	4		F L

◆ The Top 6 all came from different countries: Ireland, England, Holland, Canada, New Zealand and Germany.
◆ The Rolling Stones signed to Virgin for a $40 million advance, while Madonna's new deal guaranteed her at least $5 million per album.
◆ Freddie Mercury died. His group Queen ended the year as Britain's top album act and top singles group, and their Greatest Hits album was certified as a three million seller.

1992

This Mnth	Prev Mnth	Title	Artist	Label	Wks	(US 20 Pos)	
1	9	Bohemian Rhapsody/These Are The Days Of OurLives	Queen	Parlophone	10	(2)	G
2	3	Justified And Ancient	KLF/Tammy Wynette	KLF Communications	9	(11)	
3	7	Too Blind To See It	Kym Sims	Atco	8	(38)	F
4	19	Addams Groove	Hammer	Capitol	7	(7)	
5	10	Don't Talk Just Kiss	Right Said Fred/Jocelyn Brown	Tug	7	(76)	
6	-	Goodnight Girl	Wet Wet Wet	Precious	9		
7	-	Everybody In The Place (EP)	Prodigy	XL	5		
8	2	When You Tell Me That You Love Me	Diana Ross	EMI	9		
9	-	We Got A Love Thang	Ce Ce Peniston	A&M	5	(20)	F
10	17				5		F L
11	1	Don't Let The Sun Go Down On Me	George Michael/Elton John	Epic	6	(1)	
12	-	God Gave Rock & Roll To You II	Kiss	Interscope	5		L
13	11	Live And Let Die	Guns n' Roses	Geffen	4	(33)	
14	-	I Can't Dance	Genesis	Virgin	5	(7)	
15	5	Driven By You	Brian May	Parlophone	6		F
16	4	Black Or White	Michael Jackson	Epic	9	(1)	
17	-	Give Me Just A Little More Time	Kylie Minogue	PWL	5		
18	-	Different Strokes	Isotonik	Ffrreedom	2		F L
19	-	Feel So High	Des'ree	Dusted Sound	4		F
20	-	(Can You) Feel The Passion	Blue Pearl	Big Life	3		L

This Mnth	Prev Mnth	Title	Artist	Label	Wks	(US 20 Pos)	
1	6	Goodnight Girl	Wet Wet Wet	Precious	9		
2	-	Stay	Shakespears Sister	London	14	(4)	
3	-	Twilight Zone	2 Unlimited	PWL Continental	7	(49)	
4	-	I'm Doing Fine Now	Pasadenas	Columbia	7		
5	-	I Wonder Why	Curtis Stigers	Arista	6	(9)	F
6	17	Give Me Just A Little More Time	Kylie Minogue	PWL	5		
7	-	Remember The Time	Michael Jackson	Epic	4	(3)	
8	-	My Girl	Temptations	Epic	8		L
9	1	Bohemian Rhapsody/These Are The Days Of Our Lives	Queen	Parlophone	10	(2)	G
10	-	The Bouncer	Kicks Like A Mule	Tribal Bass	4		F L
11	-	For Your Babies	Simply Red	East West	5		
12	12	God Gave Rock & Roll To You II	Kiss	Interscope	5		L
13	-	I Love Your Smile	Shanice	Motown	7	(2)	F L
14	14	I Can't Dance	Genesis	Virgin	5	(7)	
15	-	It's A Fine Day	Opus III	PWL Int	5		F L
16	7	Everybody In The Place (EP)	Prodigy	XL	5		
17	-	Thought I'd Died And Gone To Heaven	Bryan Adams	A&M	4	(13)	
18	-	Welcome To The Cheap Seats (EP)	Wonder StufF	Polydor	3		
19	-	Dixie-Narco (EP)	Primal Scream	Creation	2		
20	-	It Must Be Love	Madness	Virgin	5		L

◆ Following Freddie Mercury's death, Queen had the top 4 music videos and 'Bohemian Rhapsody' became the first record ever to top the charts twice (selling over a million on both occasions). Its double A-side, 'These Are The Days Of Our Lives', was voted Record of The Year at the Brit Awards.

◆ UK acts inducted into the *Rock And Roll Hall Of Fame* between 1989 and 1992 were Eric Clapton, The Kinks, Jimmy Page and The Who.

March 1992

This Mnth	Prev Mnth	Title	Artist	Label	Wks	(US 20 Pos)
1	2	Stay	Shakespears Sister	London	14	(4)
2	13	I Love Your Smile	Shanice	Motown	7	(2) F L
3	8	My Girl	Temptations	Epic	8	L
4	-	America: What Time Is Love?	KLF	KLF Communications	4	(57) L
5	-	Weather With You	Crowded House	Capitol	5	
6	15	It's A Fine Day	Opus III	PWL Int	5	F L
7	-	November Rain	Guns n' Roses	Geffen	3	(3)
8	-	Tears In Heaven	Eric Clapton	Reprise	5	(2) L
9	-	Finally	Ce Ce Peniston	A&M	6	(5)
10	-	To Be With You	Mr. Big	Atlantic	7	(1) F L
11	20	It Must Be Love	Madness	Virgin	5	L
12	-	One	U2	Island	2	
13	4	I'm Doing Fine Now	Pasadenas	Columbia	7	
14	-	Deeply Dippy	Right Said Fred	Tug	10	
15	-	Come As You Are	Nirvana	DGC	2	(32)
16	-	Human Touch	Bruce Springsteen	Columbia	2	(16) L
17	-	I Know	New Atlantic	3 Beat	4	F L
18	17	Thought I'd Died And Gone To Heaven	Bryan Adams	A&M	4	(13)
19	-	Let's Get Rocked	Def Leppard	Bludgeon Riffola	4	(15)
20	-	Dragging Me Down	Inspiral Carpets	Cow	3	

April 1992

This Mnth	Prev Mnth	Title	Artist	Label	Wks	(US 20 Pos)
1	14	Deeply Dippy	Right Said Fred	Tug	10	
2	1	Stay	Shakespears Sister	London	14	(4)
3	10	To Be With You	Mr. Big	Atlantic	7	(1) F L
4	-	Save The Best For Last	Vanessa Williams	Polydor	7	(1) F L
5	-	Joy	Soul II Soul	Ten	4	L
6	9	Finally	Ce Ce Peniston	A&M	6	(5)
7	-	Why	Annie Lennox	RCA	5	(34) F
8	19	Let's Get Rocked	Def Leppard	Bludgeon Riffola	4	(15)
9	-	Evapor 8	Altern 8	Network	3	
10	-	On A Ragga Tip	SL2	XL	9	L
11	-	You're All That Matters To Me	Curtis Stigers	Arista	7	(98) L
12	-	Breath Of Life	Erasure	Mute	4	
13	-	(I Want To Be) Elected	Mr. Bean & Smear Campaign	London	3	F L
14	-	Viva Las Vegas	ZZ Top	Warner	4	
15	8	Tears In Heaven	Eric Clapton	Reprise	5	(2) L
16	-	You	Ten Sharp	Columbia	7	F L
17	-	Be Quick Or Be Dead	Iron Maiden	EMI	2	
18	-	Take My Advice	Kym Sims	Atco	2	(86) L
19	-	Time To Make You Mine	Lisa Stansfield	Arista	4	
20	-	The Only Living Boy In New Cross	Carter-USM	Big Cat	3	

◆ The KLF announced they were quitting the music business, on stage at the Brit Awards where they were voted Best British Group. Their 'Justified And Ancient' gave guest vocalist Tammy Wynette the highest placed US pop hit of her career.

◆ Bruce Springsteen's latest albums Human Touch and Lucky Town entered the UK chart in positions 1 and 2 (Nos. 2 and 3 in the USA) - the feat is more remarkable considering only three days' sales were taken into account - the albums were released on a Thursday rather than Monday as is usual in Britain.

1992

This Mnth	Prev Mnth	Title	Artist	Label	Wks	(US 20 Pos)	
1	-	Please Don't Go	KWS	Network	12	(6)	F
2	10	On A Ragga Tip	SL2	XL	9		L
3	-	Hang On In There Baby	Curiosity	RCA	6		L
4	1	Deeply Dippy	Right Said Fred	Tug	10		
5	-	The Days Of Pearly Spencer	Marc Almond	Some Bizzare	4		L
6	-	Workaholic	2 Unlimited	PWL Continental	4		
7	-	My Lovin'	En Vogue	East West America	5	(2)	
8	11	You're All That Matters To Me	Curtis Stigers	Arista	7	(98)	L
9	-	Everything About You	Ugly Kid Joe	Mercury	7	(9)	F
10	-	Nothing Else Matters	Metallica	Vertigo	3	(35)	
11	-	Knockin' On Heaven's Door	Guns N' Roses	Geffen	6		
12	-	Temple Of Love (1992)	Sisters Of Mercy	Merciful Release	3		
13	15	You	Ten Sharp	Columbia	7		F L
14	-	I Don't Care	Shakespears Sister	London	4	(55)	
15	-	In The Closet	Michael Jackson	Epic	3	(6)	
16	4	Save The Best For Last	Vanessa Williams	Polydor	7	(1)	F L
17	-	Beauty And The Beast	Celine Dion & Peabo Bryson	Epic	3	(9)	F
18	-	Keep On Walkin'	Ce Ce Peniston	A&M	3	(15)	
19	-	Song For Love	Extreme	A&M	3		
20	20	The Only Living Boy In New Cross	Carter-Unstoppable Sex Machine	Big Cat	3		

This Mnth	Prev Mnth	Title	Artist	Label	Wks	(US 20 Pos)	
1	1	Please Don't Go	KWS	Network	12	(6)	F
2	-	Hazard	Richard Marx	Capitol	10	(9)	
3	-	Jump	Kris Kross	Ruffhouse	6	(1)	F
4	-	Abba-Esque (EP)	Erasure	Mute	8		
5	-	Something Good	Utah Saints	ffrr	7	(98)	
6	-	Heartbeat	Nick Berry	Columbia	5		L
7	-	Toofunky	George Michael	Epic	5	(10)	
8	9	Everything About You	Ugly Kid Joe	Mercury	7	(9)	F
9	-	It Only Takes A Minute	Take That	RCA	6		F
10	11	Knockin' On Heaven's Door	Guns N' Roses	Geffen	6		
11	-	The One	Elton John	Rocket	5	(9)	
12	-	Friday, I'm In Love	Cure	Fiction	4	(18)	L
13	-	Blue Room	Orb	Big Life	3		F
14	2	On A Ragga Tip	SL2	XL	9		L
15	7	My Lovin'	En Vogue	East West America	5	(2)	
16	-	Midlife Crisis	Faith No More	Slash	2		F
17	-	Even Better Than The Real Thing	U2	Island	6	(32)	
18	-	Ain't 2 Proud 2 Beg	TLC	Arista	3	(6)	F
19	-	I'll Be There	Mariah Carey	Columbia	6	(1)	
20	14	I Don't Care	Shakespears Sister	London	4	(55)	

◆ Stars appearing in a successful tribute show for Freddie Mercury at Wembley included David Bowie, Def Leppard, Guns N' Roses, Elton John, Metallica, George Michael, Liza Minnelli, Robert Plant, Queen, Lisa Stansfield and U2.

◆ U2, who at times had seven albums on the UK chart, signed a £10 ($15) million publishing deal with Phonogram.
◆ Erasure's 17th Top 20 entry, the Abba tribute 'Abba-Esque', was their first chart topper. It also headed the list in Abba's homeland, Sweden.

July 1992

This Mnth	Prev Mnth	Title	Artist	Label	Wks	(US 20 Pos)	
1	4	Abba-Esque (EP)	Erasure	Mute	8		
2	19	I'll Be There	Mariah Carey	Columbia	6	(1)	
3	-	Rhythm Is A Dancer	Snap	Arista	16	(5)	
4	-	Ain't No Doubt	Jimmy Nail	East West	9		
5	-	Sesame's Treet	Smart E's	Suburban Base	6	(60)	F L
6	2	Hazard	Richard Marx	Capitol	10	(9)	
7	-	A Trip To Trumpton	Urban Hype	Faze	5		F L
8	5	Something Good	Utah Saints	ffrr	7	(98)	
9	17	Even Better Than The Real Thing	U2	Island	6	(32)	
10	-	One Shining Moment	Diana Ross	EMI	6		
11	-	Sexy MF/Strollin'	Prince/New Power Generation	Paisley Park	4	(66)	
12	6	Heartbeat	Nick Berry	Columbia	5		L
13	-	I Drove All Night	Roy Orbison	MCA	6		
14	-	Disappointed	Electronic	Parlophone	2		L
15	-	L.S.I.	Shamen	One Little Indian	6		
16	1	Please Don't Go	KWS	Network	12	(6)	F L
17	7	Toofunky	George Michael	Epic	5	(10)	
18	-	Shake Your Head	Was (Not Was)	Fontana	8		L
19	-	This Used To Be My Playground	Madonna	Sire	6	(1)	
20	9	It Only Takes A Minute	Take That	RCA	6		F

August 1992

This Mnth	Prev Mnth	Title	Artist	Label	Wks	(US 20 Pos)	
1	3	Rhythm Is A Dancer	Snap	Arista	16	(5)	
2	4	Ain't No Doubt	Jimmy Nail	East West	9		
3	-	Achy Breaky Heart	Billy Ray Cyrus	Mercury	8	(4)	F L
4	-	Barcelona	Freddie Mercury & Montserrat Caballe	Polydor	5		
5	19	This Used To Be My Playground	Madonna	Sire	6	(1)	
6	18	Shake Your Head	Was (Not Was)	Fontana	8		L
7	-	Just Another Day	Jon Secada	SBK	10	(5)	F L
8	-	The Best Things In Life Are Free	Luther Vandross/Janet Jackson	Epic	10	(10)	L
9	-	Don't You Want Me	Felix	Deconstruction	8		F
10	15	L.S.I.	Shamen	One Little Indian	6		
11	5	Sesame's Treet	Smart E's	Suburban Base	6	(60)	F L
12	13	I Drove All Night	Roy Orbison	MCA	6		
13	-	Baker Street	Undercover	PWL International	11		F
14	-	This Charming Man	Smiths	WEA	2		
15	-	Book Of Days	Enya	WEA	3		
16	-	Who Is It	Michael Jackson	Epic	4	(14)	
17	-	Rock Your Baby	KWS	Network	4		L
18	-	How Do You Do!	Roxette	EMI	4	(58)	
19	-	Magic Friend	2 Unlimited	PWL Continental	4		
20	7	A Trip To Trumpton	Urban Hype	Faze	5		F L

◆ Elton John overtook The Beatles when he collected his 50th US Top 40 entry with 'The One'. Madonna's 'This Used To Be My Playground', not only gave her a (female) record 10th American No. 1, but also meant she had more UK Top 10 hits than The Beatles.

◆ Morrissey sold out the Hollywood Bowl in 23 minutes breaking another record set by The Beatles.

◆ Elvis Presley's estate received 110 gold and platinum records which went on display at Graceland.

1992

September 1992

This Mnth	Prev Mnth	Title	Artist	Label	Wks	(US 20 Pos)	
1	1	Rhythm Is A Dancer	Snap	Arista	16	(5)	
2	-	Ebeneezer Goode	Shamen	One Little Indian	8		
3	13	Baker Street	Undercover	PWL Int.	11		F
4	8	The Best Things In Life Are Free	Luther Vandross/Janet Jackson	Epic	10	(10)	
5	-	Too Much Love Will Kill You	Brian May	Parlophone	6		
6	7	Just Another Day	Jon Secada	SBK	10	(5)	F L
7	-	It's My Life	Dr. Alban	Arista	9	(88)	F
8	-	My Destiny	Lionel Richie	Motown	9		L
9	3	Achy Breaky Heart	Billy Ray Cyrus	Mercury	8	(4)	F L
10	-	Walking On Broken Glass	Annie Lennox	RCA	5	(14)	
11	9	Don't You Want Me	Felix	Deconstruction	8		F
12	-	House Of Love	East 17	London	4		F
13	-	Theme From M*A*S*H/ (...) I Do It For You	Manic Street Preachers/ Fatima Mansions	Columbia	4		
14	-	Iron Lion Zion	Bob Marley & The Wailers	Tuff Gong	5		
15	17	Rock Your Baby	KWS	Network	4		L
16	-	Jam	Michael Jackson	Epic	2	(26)	
17	-	Take This Heart	Richard Marx	Capitol	2	(20)	
18	4	Barcelona	Freddie Mercury & Montserrat Caballe	Polydor	5		
19	-	Fire/Jericho	Prodigy	XL	2		
20	-	Rest In Peace	Extreme	A&M	2	(96)	

October 1992

1	-	Sleeping Satellite	Tasmin Archer	EMI	9	(32)	F
2	-	End Of The Road	Boyz II Men	Motown	12	(1)	F
3	7	It's My Life	Dr. Alban	Arista	9	(88)	F
4	2	Ebeneezer Goode	Shamen	One Little Indian	8		
5	-	I'm Gonna Get You	Bizarre Inc	Vinyl Solution	8	(47)	
6	3	Baker Street	Undercover	PWL International	11		F
7	-	Erotica	Madonna	Maverick/sire	5	(3)	
8	-	Tetris	Doctor Spin	Carpet	5		F L
9	14	Iron Lion Zion	Bob Marley & The Wailers	Tuff Gong	5		L
10	-	A Million Love Songs (EP)	Take That	RCA	5		
11	8	My Destiny	Lionel Richie	Motown	9		L
12	-	Love Song/Alive And Kicking	Simple Minds	Virgin	3		L
13	-	Keep The Faith	Bon Jovi	Jambco	4	(29)	
14	-	My Name Is Prince	Prince & The New Power Generation	Paisley Park	3	(36)	
15	-	People Everyday	Arrested Development	Cooltempo	8	(8)	F
16	-	Sentinel	Mike Oldfield	WEA	3		L
17	1	Rhythm Is A Dancer	Snap	Arista	16	(5)	
18	4	The Best Things In Life Are Free	Luther Vandross & Janet Jackson	Epic	10	(10)	
19	5	Too Much Love Will Kill You	Brian May	Parlophone	6		
20	13	Theme From M*A*S*H/ (...) I Do It For You	Manic Street Preachers/ Fatima Mansions	Columbia	4		

◆ Motown hitmaker Mary Wells, reggae star Jackie Edwards and Tony Williams, the voice of The Platters, all died.

◆ American shows by Elton John, George Michael, Lionel Richie, Madonna and Billy Idol raised over $7 million for AIDS research. At the same time, Elton signed his publishing to Warner for a world record $26 million.

1992

November 1992

This Mnth	Prev Mnth	Title	Artist	Label	Wks	(US 20 Pos)	
1	2	End Of The Road	Boyz II Men	Motown	12	(1)	F L
2	15	People Everyday	Arrested Development	Cooltempo	8	(8)	F
3	-	Would I Lie To You?	Charles & Eddie	Capitol	12	(13)	L
4	-	Boss Drum	Shamen	One Little Indian	5		
5	-	Never Let Her Slip Away	Undercover	PWL International	5		L
5	-	Run To You	Rage	Pulse 8	5		F L
7	-	I Will Always Love You	Whitney Houston	Arista	17	(1)	G
8	-	Be My Baby	Vanessa Paradis	Remark	6		L
9	-	Supermarioland	Ambassadors Of Funk/MC Mario	Living Beat	5		F L
10	5	I'm Gonna Get You	Bizarre Inc	Vinyl Solution	8	(47)	
11	-	(Take A Little) Piece Of My Heart	Erma Franklin	Epic	5		F L
12	-	Temptation	Heaven 17	Virgin	8		L
13	1	Sleeping Satellite	Tasmin Archer	EMI	9	(32)	F
14	-	Invisible Touch (Live)	Genesis	Virgin	2		L
15	-	Who Needs Love (Like That)	Erasure	Mute	3		
16	-	Out Of Space/Ruff In The Jungle Bizness	Prodigy	XL	9		
17	-	Yesterdays/November Rain	Guns n' Roses	Geffen	3	(3)	
18	-	Montreux EP	Simply Red	East West	7		
19	8	A Million Love Songs (EP)	Take That	RCA	5		
20	7	Erotica	Madonna	Maverick	5	(3)	

December 1992

This Mnth	Prev Mnth	Title	Artist	Label	Wks	(US 20 Pos)	
1	7	I Will Always Love You	Whitney Houston	Arista	17	(1)	G
2	-	Heal The World	Michael Jackson	Epic	8	(27)	
3	3	Would I Lie To You?	Charles & Eddie	Capitol	12	(13)	F L
4	-	Tom Traubert's Blues (Waltzing Matilda)	Rod Stewart	Warner Bros.	5		
5	-	Slam Jam	WWF Superstars	Arista	5		F
6	16	Out Of Space/Ruff In The Jungle Bizness	Prodigy	XL	9		
7	-	Could It Be Magic	Take That	RCA	9		
8	12	Temptation	Heaven 17	Virgin	8		L
9	-	I Still Believe In You	Cliff Richard	EMI	4		
10	-	Deeper And Deeper	Madonna	Maverick	5	(7)	
11	-	Boney M Megamix	Boney M	Arista	5		L
12	-	In My Defence	Freddie Mercury	Parlophone	4		L
13	-	Phorever People	Shamen	One Little Indian	7		
14	18	Montreux EP	Simply Red	East West	7		
15	-	Step It Up	Stereo MCs	Fourth & Broadway	7		
16	-	If We Hold On Together	Diana Ross	EMI	6		
17	1	End Of The Road	Boyz II Men	Motown	12	(1)	F
18	5	Never Let Her Slip Away	Undercover	PWL International	5		L
19	-	Miami Hit Mix/Christmas Through Your Eyes	Gloria Estefan	Epic	5		
20	2	People Everyday	Arrested Development	Cooltempo	8	(8)	F

◆ U2 grossed $64 million from their 1992 US tour; Barbra Streisand's new record contract with Columbia was slated to earn her a similar figure.
◆ Soon after the launch of her book, *Sex*, Madonna's equally controversial 'Erotica' single rocketed to No. 3 on both sides of the Atlantic and her album of the same name reached runner-up spot in the UK and USA.

1993

This Mnth	Prev Mnth	Title	Artist	Label	Wks	(US 20 Pos)	
1	1	I Will Always Love You	Whitney Houston	Arista	17	(1)	G
2	7	Could It Be Magic	Take That	RCA	9		
3	-	Exterminate!	Snap Featuring Niki Haris	Arista	8		
4	2	Heal The World	Michael Jackson	Epic	8	(27)	
5	13	Phorever People	Shamen	One Little Indian	7		
6	-	Mr. Wendal/Revolution	Arrested Development	Cooltempo	5	(6)	
7	3	Would I Lie To You?	Charles & Eddie	Capitol	12	(13)	F L
8	-	I'm Easy/Be Aggressive	Faith No More	Slash	5	(58)	
9	-	The Love I Lost	West End Featuring Sybil	PWL Sanctuary	9		F L
10	5	Slam Jam	WWF Superstars	Arista	5		F
11	-	We Are Family	Sister Sledge	Atlantic	4		
12	-	Open Your Mind	Usura	Deconstruction	5		F L
13	18	Miami Hit Mix/Christmas Through Your Eyes	Gloria Estefan	Epic	5		
14	-	Sweet Harmony	Beloved	East West	5		L
15	-	After All	Frank And Walters	Setanta	3		F L
16	11	Boney M Megamix	Boney M	Arista	5		L
17	6	Out Of Space/Ruff In The Jungle Bizness	Prodigy	XL	9		
18	-	Someday (I'm Coming Back)	Lisa Stansfield	Arista	5		
19	-	Steam	Peter Gabriel	Realworld	3	(32)	L
20	-	No Limit	2 Unlimited	PWL Continental	13		

This Mnth	Prev Mnth	Title	Artist	Label	Wks	(US 20 Pos)	
1	20	No Limit	2 Unlimited	PWL Continental	13		
2	1	I Will Always Love You	Whitney Houston	Arista	17	(1)	G
3	-	Deep	East 17	London	8		
4	9	The Love I Lost	West End Featuring Sybil	PWL Sanctuary	9		F L
5	-	Little Bird/Love Song For A Vampire	Annie Lennox	RCA	8	(49)	
6	-	Ordinary World	Duran Duran	Parlophone	6	(3)	
7	3	Exterminate!	Snap Featuring Niki Haris	Arista	8		
8	-	How Can I Love You More?	M People	Deconstruction	4		F
9	-	Why Can't I Wake Up With You?	Take That	RCA	4		
10	-	I'm Every Woman	Whitney Houston	Arista	6	(4)	
11	-	Stairway To Heaven	Rolf Harris	Vertigo	3		L
12	14	Sweet Harmony	Beloved	East West	5		L
13	12	Open Your Mind	Usura	Deconstruction	5		F L
14	-	Are You Gonna Go My Way	Lenny Kravitz	Virgin America	7		
15	11	We Are Family	Sister Sledge	Atlantic	4		
16	-	Independence	Lulu	Dome	3		
17	-	Give In To Me	Michael Jackson	Epic	6		
18	-	You're In A Bad Way	Saint Etienne	Heavenly	2		F
19	-	Ruby Tuesday	Rod Stewart	Warner Bros.	3		
20	-	I Feel You	Depeche Mode	Mute	2	(37)	

♦ Revivals enjoyed a revival with updated hits from such diverse acts as Take That, Faith No More, West End, Whitney Houston, Shaggy and Ugly Kid Joe, plus veterans Rolf Harris and Rod Stewart.

♦ Thirty-four years after his death, Buddy Holly's album Words of Love topped the UK chart.

March 1993

This Mnth	Prev Mnth	Title	Artist	Label	Wks	(US 20 Pos)	
1	1	No Limit	2 Unlimited	PWL Continental	13		
2	-	Oh Carolina	Shaggy	Greensleeves	12	(59)	F
3	17	Give In To Me	Michael Jackson	Epic	6		
4	5	Little Bird/Love Song For A Vampire	Annie Lennox	RCA	8	(49)	
5	14	Are You Gonna Go My Way	Lenny Kravitz	Virgin America	7		
6	-	Mr. Loverman	Shabba Ranks	Epic	8	(40)	
7	-	Stick It Out	Right Said Fred & Friends	Tug	5		L
8	10	I'm Every Woman	Whitney Houston	Arista	6	(4)	
9	-	Animal Nitrate	Suede	Nude	3		
10	-	Informer	Snow	East West America	11	(1)	F L
11	3	Deep	East 17	London	8		
12	-	Too Young To Die	Jamiroquai	Sony S^2	3		F
13	-	Cat's In The Cradle	Ugly Kid Joe	Mercury	6	(6)	L
14	-	Shortsharpshock (EP)	Therapy?	A&M	2		F
15	-	Bad Girl	Madonna	Maverick	3	(36)	
16	9	Why Can't I Wake Up With You?	Take That	RCA	4		
17	-	Looking Through Patient Eyes	PM Dawn	Gee Street	4	(6)	L
18	-	Young At Heart	Bluebells	London	8		L
19	-	Fear Of The Dark (Live)	Iron Maiden	EMI	2		
20	-	Peace In Our Time	Cliff Richard	EMI	2		

April 1993

This Mnth	Prev Mnth	Title	Artist	Label	Wks	(US 20 Pos)	
1	18	Young At Heart	Bluebells	London	8		L
2	10	Informer	Snow	East West America	11	(1)	F L
3	2	Oh Carolina	Shaggy	Greensleeves	12	(59)	F
4	-	When I'm Good And Ready	Sybil	PWL International	8		L
5	6	Mr. Loverman	Shabba Ranks	Epic	8	(40)	
6	-	Show Me Love	Robin S.	Champion	6	(5)	F
7	-	Don't Walk Away	Jade	Giant	6	(4)	F
8	-	Ain't No Love (Ain't No Use)	Sub Sub Featuring Melanie Williams	Rob's	8		F L
9	1	No Limit	2 Unlimited	PWL Continental	13		
10	-	U Got 2 Know	Cappella	Internal	7		
11	13	Cat's In The Cradle	Ugly Kid Joe	Mercury	6	(6)	L
12	-	Fever	Madonna	Maverick	3		
13	-	Regret	New Order	London	3	(28)	
14	-	Go Away	Gloria Estefan	Epic	4		
15	-	Wind It Up (Rewound)	Prodigy	XL	3		
16	-	Come Undone	Duran Duran	Parlophone	4	(7)	
17	-	Wrestlemania	WWF Superstars	Arista	3		L
18	-	Slow It Down	East 17	London	3		
19	-	I Have Nothing	Whitney Houston	Arista	6	(4)	
20	-	Jump They Say	David Bowie	Arista	2		L

◆ At the end of March, for the first time reggae records held the top three places on the UK chart. They were 'Oh Carolina' by Shaggy, 'Informer' by white Canadian rapper Snow and 'Mr. Loverman' by Shabba Ranks.

◆ Depeche Mode, whose 'Walking in My Shoes' was their 21st Top 20 entry, entered the transatlantic charts at No. 1 with their album Songs Of Faith & Devotion.

1993

This Mnth	Prev Mnth	Title	Artist	Label	Wks	(US 20 Pos)	
1	-	Five Live (EP)	George Michael & Queen	Parlophone	7		
2	-	All That She Wants	Ace Of Base	London	12	(2)	F
3	-	Sweat (A La La La La Long)	Inner Circle	Magnet	8	(16)	F
4	-	That's The Way Love Goes	Janet Jackson	Virgin	6	(1)	
5	-	Tribal Dance	2 Unlimited	PWL Continental	7		
6	19	I Have Nothing	Whitney Houston	Arista	6	(4)	
7	-	Everybody Hurts	REM	Warner	8	(29)	
8	8	Ain't No Love (Ain't No Use)	Sub Sub Feat. Melanie Williams	Rob's	8		F L
9	2	Informer	Snow	East West	11	(1)	F L
10	1	Young At Heart	Bluebells	London	8		L
11	-	Housecall	Shabba Ranks Feat. Maxi Priest	Epic	5	(37)	
12	-	(I Can't Help) Falling In Love With You	UB40	Dep International	12	(1)	
13	10	U Got 2 Know	Cappella	Internal	7		
14	-	Believe In Me	Utah Saints	ffrr	3		L
15	4	When I'm Good And Ready	Sybil	PWL Int.	8		L
16	-	In These Arms	Bon Jovi	Jambco	3	(28)	
17	-	I Don't Wanna Fight	Tina Turner	Parlophone	5	(9)	
18	-	Jump Around	House Of Pain	Ruffness	4	(3)	F
19	6	Show Me Love	Robin S.	Champion	6	(5)	F
20	-	Express	Dina Carroll	A&M	3		

This Mnth	Prev Mnth	Title	Artist	Label	Wks	(US 20 Pos)	
1	12	(I Can't Help) Falling In Love With You	UB40	Dep International	12	(1)	
2	2	All That She Wants	Ace Of Base	London	12	(2)	F
3	-	Two Princes	Spin Doctors	Epic	10	(7)	F L
4	-	What Is Love	Haddaway	Arista	12	(11)	F
5	-	Three Little Pigs	Green Jelly	Zoo	5	(17)	F L
6	3	Sweat (A La La La La Long)	Inner Circle	Magnet	8	(16)	F
7	-	In All The Right Places	Lisa Stansfield	Arista	7		
8	-	Dreams	Gabrielle	Go.Beat	11	(32)	F
9	-	Shout	Louchie Lou & Michie One	ffrr	5		F L
10	-	Tease Me	Chaka Demus & Pliers	Mango	13		F
11	-	Can You Forgive Her?	Pet Shop Boys	Parlophone	3		
12	-	Do You See The Light (Looking For)	Snap Featuring Niki Haris	Arista	4		
13	5	Tribal Dance	2 Unlimited	PWL Continental	7		
14	-	Blow Your Mind	Jamiroquai	Sony S²	3		
15	17	I Don't Wanna Fight	Tina Turner	Parlophone	5	(9)	
16	1	Five Live (EP)	George Michael & Queen	Parlophone	7		
17	18	Jump Around	House Of Pain	Ruffness	4	(3)	F
18	4	That's The Way Love Goes	Janet Jackson	Virgin	6	(1)	
19	-	Have I Told You Lately	Rod Stewart	Warner Bros.	5	(5)	
20	-	One Night In Heaven	M People	Deconstruction	8		

◆ In April, nine of the British Top 10 were dance records, and at times only five of the Top 20 records were by British artists - two more firsts.

◆ Over 180,000 people saw France's top selling rock artist Johnny Halliday at the Parc Des Princes Stadium in Paris. To celebrate his 50th birthday a 40 CD box set was released – the biggest ever by a solo artist.

July 1993

This Mnth	Prev Mnth	Title	Artist	Label	Wks (US 20 Pos)	
1	8	Dreams	Gabrielle	Go.Beat	11 (32)	F
2	4	What Is Love	Haddaway	Arista	12 (11)	F
3	10	Tease Me	Chaka Demus & Pliers	Mango	13	F
4	20	One Night In Heaven	M People	Deconstruction	8	
5	-	What's Up	4 Non Blondes	Interscope	11 (16)	F L
6	1	(I Can't Help) Falling In Love With You	UB40	Dep International	12 (1)	
7	-	I Will Survive	Gloria Gaynor	Polydor	6	L
8	-	Pray	Take That	RCA	7	
9	19	Have I Told You Lately	Rod Stewart	Warner Bros.	5 (5)	
10	3	Two Princes	Spin Doctors	Epic	10 (7)	F L
11	-	Will You Be There	Michael Jackson	Epic	4 (7)	
12	2	All That She Wants	Ace Of Base	London	12 (2)	F
13	-	If I Can't Have You	Kim Wilde	MCA	4	L
14	-	Almost Unreal	Roxette	EMI	5 (94)	
15	-	This Is It	Dannii Minogue	MCA	5	
16	7	In All The Right Places	Lisa Stansfield	Arista	7	
17	-	Living On My Own	Freddie Mercury	Parlophone	9	L
18	-	Nothin' My Love Can't Fix	Joey Lawrence	EMI	3 (19)	F L
19	-	I Wanna Love You	Jade	Giant	3 (16)	
20	-	Can't Get Enough Of Your Love	Taylor Dayne	Arista	3 (20)	L

August 1993

1	17	Living On My Own	Freddie Mercury	Parlophone	9	L
2	-	The Key The Secret	Urban Cookie Collective	Pulse 8	10	F
3	5	What's Up	4 Non Blondes	Interscope	11 (16)	F L
4	-	The River Of Dreams	Billy Joel	Columbia	9 (3)	L
5	8	Pray	Take That	RCA	7	
6	-	It Keeps Rainin' (Tears From My Eyes)	Bitty McLean	Brilliant	9	F
7	3	Tease Me	Chaka Demus & Pliers	Mango	13	F
8	-	Mr. Vain	Culture Beat	Epic	11 (20)	F
9	-	Nuff Vibes (EP)	Apache Indian	Island	6	L
10	1	Dreams	Gabrielle	Go.Beat	11 (32)	F
11	-	Rain	Madonna	Maverick	4 (14)	
12	-	Looking Up	Michelle Gayle	RCA	4	F
13	14	Almost Unreal	Roxette	EMI	5 (94)	
14	-	Higher Ground	UB40	Dep International	5 (46)	
15	-	Luv 4 Luv	Robin S.	Champion	4	L
16	-	I Will Always Love You	Sarah Washington	Almighty	4	F L
17	2	What Is Love	Haddaway	Arista	12 (11)	F
18	-	Dreamlover	Mariah Carey	Columbia	6 (1)	
19	15	This Is It	Dannii Minogue	MCA	5	
20	-	Right Here	SWV	RCA	8 (2)	

◆ Several disco classics from the 1970s returned: 'If I Can't Have You' (Yvonne Elliman/Kim Wilde), 'This Is It' (Melba Moore/Dannii Minogue), 'Go West' (Village People/Pet Shop Boys), 'Disco Inferno' (Trammps/Tina Turner) and a remix of Gloria Gaynor's 'I Will Survive'.

◆ European music conglomerate Polygram bought Motown Records' 30,000 masters for $325 million, as the label re-signed Boyz II Men in a deal that could earn the act $30 million.

September 1993

This Mnth	Prev Mnth	Title	Artist	Label	Wks	(US 20 Pos)	
1	8	Mr. Vain	Culture Beat	Epic	11	(20)	F
2	6	It Keeps Rainin' (Tears From My Eyes)	Bitty McLean	Brilliant	9		F
3	20	Right Here	SWV	RCA	8	(2)	
4	4	The River Of Dreams	Billy Joel	Columbia	9	(3)	L
5	-	Boom! Shake The Room	Jazzy Jeff & Fresh Prince	Jive	10	(13)	F L
6	1	Living On My Own	Freddie Mercury	Parlophone	9		L
7	-	Faces	2 Unlimited	PWL Continental	4		
8	18	Dreamlover	Mariah Carey	Columbia	6	(1)	
9	-	Go West	Pet Shop Boys	Parlophone	6		
10	2	The Key The Secret	Urban Cookie Collective	Pulse 8	10		F
11	9	Nuff Vibes (EP)	Apache Indian	Island	6		L
12	14	Higher Ground	UB40	Dep International	5	(46)	
13	-	Heart-Shaped Box	Nirvana	Geffen	2		L
14	-	Creep	Radiohead	Parlophone	3	(34)	F
15	-	Slave To The Vibe	Aftershock	Virgin	5		F L
16	-	She Don't Let Nobody	Chaka Demus & Pliers	Mango	7		
17	-	Moving On Up	M People	Deconstruction	7		
18	-	Rubberband Girl	Kate Bush	EMI	2	(88)	L
19	-	Disco Inferno	Tina Turner	Parlophone	3		
20	-	It Must Have Been Love	Roxette	EMI	4		

October 1993

This Mnth	Prev Mnth	Title	Artist	Label	Wks	(US 20 Pos)	
1	5	Boom! Shake The Room	Jazzy Jeff & Fresh Prince	Jive	10	(13)	F L
2	17	Moving On Up	M People	Deconstruction	7		
3	16	She Don't Let Nobody	Chaka Demus & Pliers	Mango	7		
4	-	I'd Do Anything For Love (But I Won't Do That)	Meat Loaf	Virgin	12	(1)	
5	-	Relight My Fire	Take That Featuring Lulu	RCA	5		
6	-	Stay	Eternal	EMI	6		F
7	-	Relax	Frankie Goes To Hollywood	ZTT	5		
8	-	Life	Haddaway	Logic	5	(83)	
9	9	Go West	Pet Shop Boys	Parlophone	6		
10	1	Mr. Vain	Culture Beat	Epic	11	(20)	F
11	-	U Got 2 Let The Music	Cappella	Internal	6		
12	-	One Love	Prodigy	XL	4		
13	-	Going Nowhere	Gabrielle	Go.Beat	4		
14	-	Don't Be A Stranger	Dina Carroll	A&M	11		
15	3	Right Here	SWV	RCA	8	(2)	
16	-	Here We Go	Stakka Bo	Polydor	4		F L
17	-	Please Forgive Me	Bryan Adams	A&M	9	(7)	
18	-	Play Dead	Bjork & David Arnold	Island	4		F
19	20	It Must Have Been Love	Roxette	EMI	4		
20	-	Both Sides Of The Story	Phil Collins	Virgin	2	(25)	

◆ UK acts Cream, Elton John, The Animals, John Lennon, Van Morrison and Rod Stewart joined other 1993 *Rock And Roll Hall Of Fame* inductees The Band, Ruth Brownl, Doors, Duane Eddy, Grateful Dead, Etta James, Frankie Lymon & The Teenagers, Bob Marley and Sly & The Family Stone.

◆ In the US, only 10 different singles made No. 1 in 1993 (a new low), and records, in general, stayed on the charts longer. In contrast, in Britain more records charted and a hit's life-span was shorter than ever. 1993 was the year of the American rock act, and the worst year for British artists in the US.

November 1993

This Mnth	Prev Mnth	Title	Artist	Label	Wks	(US 20 Pos)	
1	4	I'll Do Anything For Love (But I Won't Do That)	Meat Loaf	Virgin	15	(1)	
2	17	Please Forgive Me	Bryan Adams	A&M	11	(7)	
3	14	Don't Be A Stranger	Dina Carroll	A&M	11		
4	-	Got To Get It	Culture Beat	Epic	5		
5	11	U Got 2 Let The Music	Cappella	Internal	6		
6	-	Give It Up	Goodmen	Fresh Fruit	5		F L
7	-	Hero	Mariah Carey	Columbia	10	(1)	
8	-	Feels Like Heaven	Urban Cookie Collective	Pulse 8	4		
9	-	Runaway Train	Soul Asylum	Columbia	5	(5)	F L
10	-	True Love	Elton John & Kiki Dee	Rocket	7	(56)	
11	-	Real Love '93	Time Frequency	Internal Affairs	3		L
12	-	Again	Janet Jackson	Virgin	8	(1)	
13	-	Feel Like Making Love	Pauline Henry	Sony	4		F L
14	-	Ain't It Fun	Guns N' Roses	Geffen	2		L
15	-	Little Fluffy Clouds	Orb	Big Life	2		
16	1	Boom! Shake That Room	Jazzy Jeff & Fresh Prince	Jive	10	(13)	F L
17	6	Stay	Eternal	EMI	6	(19)	F
18	-	Queen Of The Night	Whitney Houston	Arista	2		
19	-	Long Train Runnin'	Doobie Brothers	Warner Bros.	4		F L
20	20	Both Sides Of The Story	Phil Collins	Virgin	2	(25)	

December 1993

This Mnth	Prev Mnth	Title	Artist	Label	Wks	(US 20 Pos)	
1	-	Mr. Blobby	Mr. Blobby	Destiny Music	7		F L
2	1	I'll Do Anything For Love (But I Won't Do That)	Meat Loaf	Virgin	15	(1)	
3	10	True Love	Elton John & Kiki Dee	Rocket	7	(56)	
4	-	For Whom The Bell Tolls	Bee Gees	Polydor	9		
5	2	Please Forgive Me	Bryan Adams	A&M	11	(7)	
6	3	Don't Be A Stranger	Dina Carroll	A&M	11		
7	-	It's Alright	East 17	London	10		
8	-	Babe	Take That	RCA	5		
9	-	Stay (Faraway, So Close!) /I've Got You Under My Skin	U2	Island	3		
10	-	Don't Look Any Further	M People	Deconstruction	6		
11	-	Twist And Shout	Chaka Demus & Pliers/ Jack Radics/Taxi Gang	Mango	9		L
12	12	Again	Janet Jackson	Virgin	8	(1)	
13	-	The Perfect Year	Dina Carroll	A&M	7		
14	19	Long Train Runnin'	Doobie Brothers	Warner Bros.	4		F L
15	-	Bat Out Of Hell	Meat Loaf	Epic	5		
16	-	Controversy	Prince	Paisley Park	2		
17	-	The Power Of Love	Frankie Goes To Hollywood	ZTT	4		
18	-	Y.M.C.A. '93 Remix	Village People	Bell	2		L
19	7	Hero	Mariah Carey	Columbia	10	(1)	
20	-	I Wouldn't Normally Do This Kind Of Thing	Pet Shop Boys	Parlophone	3		

◆ British teen idols Take That became the first act to have three successive singles enter at No. 1. They also had three of the country's Top 4 videos.
◆ Chaka Demus & Pliers, the first reggae act to have three successive Top 5 entries, took the song 'Twist And Shout' into the Top 10 for the fourth time.
◆ The year ended with the death of one of rock's true originals, Frank Zappa.

1994

This Mnth	Prev Mnth	Title	Artist	Label	Wks	(US 20 Pos)	
1	11	Twist And Shout	Chaka Demus & Pliers Feat. Jack Radics & Taxi Gang	Mango	9		
2	-	Things Can Only Get Better	D:ream	/Magnet	11		
3	-	Come Baby Come	K7	Tommy Boy	10	(18)	F
4	7	It's Alright	East 17	London	10		
5	1	Mr. Blobby	Mr. Blobby	Destiny Music	7		F L
6	-	All For Love	Bryan Adams/Rod Stewart/Sting	A&M	9	(1)	
7	8	Babe	Take That	RCA	5		
8	4	For Whom The Bell Tolls	Bee Gees	Polydor	9		
9	13	The Perfect Year	Dina Carroll	A&M	7		
10	-	Anything	Culture Beat	Epic	5		
11	-	Cornflake Girl	Tori Amos	East West	4		
12	-	I Miss You	Haddaway	Logic	8		
13	2	I'll Do Anything For Love (But I Won't Do That)	Meat Loaf	Virgin	15	(1)	
14	-	Save Our Love	Eternal	EMI	4		
15	15	Bat Out Of Hell	Meat Loaf	Epic	5		
16	-	Breathe Again	Toni Braxton	Laface	9	(3)	F
17	-	In Your Room	Depeche Mode	Mute	2		
18	-	Here I Stand	Bitty McLean	Brilliant	3		
19	-	A Whole New World (Aladdin's Theme)	Peabo Bryson & Regina Belle	Columbia	5	(1)	L
20	-	Return To Innocence	Enigma	Virgin	11	(4)	L

This Mnth	Prev Mnth	Title	Artist	Label	Wks	(US 20 Pos)	
1	2	Things Can Only Get Better	D:ream	/Magnet	11		
2	16	Breathe Again	Toni Braxton	Laface	9	(3)	F
3	20	Return To Innocence	Enigma	Virgin	11	(4)	L
4	6	All For Love	Bryan Adams/Rod Stewart/Sting	A&M	9	(1)	
5	-	The Power Of Love	Celine Dion	550 Music	6	(1)	
6	-	Without You	Mariah Carey	Columbia	9	(3)	
7	3	Come Baby Come	K7	Tommy Bo	10	(18)	F
8	-	A Deeper Love	Aretha Franklin	Arista	3	(63)	
9	-	Stay Together	Suede	Nude	3		
10	-	Come In Out Of The Rain	Wendy Moten	EMI USA	4		F L
11	11	Cornflake Girl	Tori Amos	East West	4		
12	-	Move On Baby	Cappella	Internal	4		
13	-	I Like To Move It	Reel 2 Real/The Mad Stuntman	Positiva	15	(89)	F
14	-	Let The Beat Control Your Body	2 Unlimited	PWL Continental	5		
15	10	Anything	Culture Beat	Epic	5		
16	-	The Sign	Ace Of Base	Arista	10	(1)	
17	-	Give It Away	Red Hot Chili Peppers	Warner	2	(73)	F
18	-	Sweet Lullaby	Deep Forest	Columbia	3	(78)	F
19	12	I Miss You	Haddaway	Logic/Arista	8		
20	1	Twist And Shout	Chaka Demus & Pliers Feat. Jack Radics & Taxi Gang	Mango	9		

◆ Newcomers Chaka Demus & Pliers became the fourth act to take 'Twist And Shout' into the Top 10 and their recording was also the 700th different single to head the UK chart.

◆ The classic ballad 'Without You' returned to the top, this time by Mariah Carey. Her transatlantic No. 1 was the first single by a female artist to enter the UK lists in pole position.

◆ Among the Brit Award winners were Sting, Dina Caroll, the Stereo MCs, M People and Take That.

March 1994

This Mnth	Prev Mnth	Title	Artist	Label	Wks	(US 20 Pos)	
1	6	Without You	Mariah Carey	Columbia	9	(3)	
2	16	The Sign	Ace Of Base	Arista	10	(1)	
3	-	Doop	Doop	Citybeat	7		F L
4	3	Return To Innocence	Enigma	Virgin	11	(4	L
5	2	Breathe Again	Toni Braxton	Laface	9	(3)	F
6	-	Streets Of Philadelphia	Bruce Springsteen	Columbia	8	(9)	L
7	-	Renaissance	M People	Deconstruction	3		
8	13	I Like To Move It	Reel 2 Real/The Mad Stuntman	Positiva	15	(89)	F
9	-	Girls And Boys	Blur	Food	4	(59)	
10	14	Let The Beat Control Your Body	2 Unlimited	PWL Continental	5		
11	1	Things Can Only Get Better	D:ream	Magnet	11		
12	-	U R The Best Thing	D:ream	Magnet	5		
13	-	Don't Go Breaking My Heart	Elton John & RuPaul	Rocket	3		
14	-	Rocks/Funky Jam	Primal Scream	Creation	2		
15	12	Move On Baby	Cappella	Internal	4		
16	-	Whatta Man	Salt-N-Pepa Featuring En Vogue	Next Plateau	6	(3)	
17	-	Pretty Good Year	Tori Amos	East West	1		
18	-	Shine On	Degrees Of Motion	ffrr	5		F L
19	-	The More You Ignore Me, The Closer I Get	Morrissey	Parlophone	1	(46)	L
20	4	All For Love	Bryan Adams/Rod Stewart/Sting	A&M	9	(1)	

April 1994

This Mnth	Prev Mnth	Title	Artist	Label	Wks	(US 20 Pos)	
1	6	Streets Of Philadelphia	Bruce Springsteen	Columbia	8	(9)	L
2	-	The Most Beautiful Girl In The World	TAFKAP	NPG	9	(3)	
3	-	Everything Changes	Take That	RCA	5		
4	3	Doop	Doop	Citybeat	7		F L
5	8	I Like To Move It	Reel 2 Real/The Mad Stuntman	Positiva	15	(89)	F
6	2	The Sign	Ace Of Base	Arista	10	(1)	
7	-	The Real Thing	Tony Di Bart	Cleveland City	8		F L
8	12	U R The Best Thing	D:ream	Magnet	5		
9	-	Mmm Mmm Mmm Mmm	Crash Test Dummies	Arista	6	(4)	F L
10	16	Whatta Man	Salt-N-Pepa Featuring En Vogue	Next Plateau	6	(3)	
11	-	Dedicated To The One I Love	Bitty McLean	Brilliant	6		L
12	-	I'll Remember	Madonna	Maverick	4	(2)	
13	-	Rock My Heart	Haddaway	Logic	5		
14	1	Without You/Never Forget You	Mariah Carey	Columbia	9	(3)	
15	-	Sweets For My Sweet	CJ Lewis	Black Market	8		F
16	18	Shine On	Degrees Of Motion	ffrr	5		F L
17	-	Dry County	Bon Jovi	Vertigo	2		
18	-	I'll Stand By You	Pretenders	WEA	4	(16)	L
19	-	Light My Fire	Clubhouse Featuring Carl	PWL International	5		L
20	-	Hung Up	Paul Weller	Go! Discs	1		

◆ A record number of European artists reached the chart this quarter and for the first time since the late 1950s, 7" vinyl singles accounted for less than 10% of the market.

◆ 'Everything Changes' gave Take That a record fourth entry at No. 1; the single had logged up 300,000 advance orders. They were the first act since The Beatles to take four successive singles to the top. Also, group member Gary Barlow was named Songwriter of the Year at the Ivor Novello Awards.

1994

This Mnth	Prev Mnth	Title	Artist	Label	Wks	(US 20 Pos)	
1	-	Come On You Reds	Manchester United Squad	Polygram TV	10		
2	-	Inside	Stiltskin	White Water	8		F L
3	7	The Real Thing	Tony Di Bart	Cleveland City	8		F L
4	15	Sweets For My Sweet	CJ Lewis	Black Market	8		F
5	2	The Most Beautiful Girl In The World	TAFKAP	NPG	9	(3)	
6	9	Mmm Mmm Mmm Mmm	Crash Test Dummies	Arista	6	(4)	F L
7	-	Around The World	East 17	London	7		
8	-	Love Is All Around	Wet Wet Wet	Precious	21	(45)	G
9	-	Just A Step From Heaven	Eternal	EMI	6		
10	19	Light My Fire	Clubhouse Featuring Carl	PWL International	5		L
11	-	Always	Erasure	Mute	5	(20)	L
12	-	Get-A-Way	Maxx	Pulse 8	7		F
13	-	The Real Thing	2 Unlimited	PWL	4		
14	-	More To This World	Bad Boys Inc	A&M	4		
15	11	Dedicated To The One I Love	Bitty McLean	Brilliant	6		L
16	5	I Like To Move It	Reel 2 Real/The Mad Stuntman	Positiva	15	(89)	F
17	-	No Good (Start The Dance)	Prodigy	XL	8		
18	18	I'll Stand By You	Pretenders	WEA	4	(16)	L
19	-	Carry Me Home	Gloworm	Go! Discs	6		L
20	-	Under The Bridge	Red Hot Chili Peppers	Warner	3	(2)	

This Mnth	Prev Mnth	Title	Artist	Label	Wks	(US 20 Pos)	
1	8	Love Is All Around	Wet Wet Wet	Precious	21	(45)	G
2	-	Baby I Love Your Way	Big Mountain	RCA	10	(6)	F L
3	1	Come On You Reds	Manchester United Football Squad	Polygram TV	10		
4	17	No Good (Start The Dance)	Prodigy	XL	8		
5	12	Get-A-Way	Maxx	Pulse 8	7		F
6	7	Around The World	East 17	London	7		
7	-	You Don't Love Me (No, No, No)	Dawn Penn	Big Beat	7	(58)	F L
8	-	Swamp Thing	Grid	Deconstruction	12		F
9	-	Don't Turn Around	Ace Of Base	Arista	7	(4)	
10	-	Absolutely Fabulous	Absolutely Fabulous	Spaghetti	3		F L
11	2	Inside	Stiltskin	White Water	8		F L
12	-	Anytime You Need A Friend	Mariah Carey	Columbia	3	(12)	
13	-	I Swear	All-4-One	Blitzz	14	(1)	F L
14	19	Carry Me Home	Gloworm	Go! Discs	6		L
15	4	Sweets For My Sweet	CJ Lewis	Black Market	8		F
16	-	Since I Don't Have You	Guns N' Roses	Geffen	2	(69)	
17	-	Everybody's Talkin'	Beautiful South	Go! Discs	4		
18	13	The Real Thing	2 Unlimited	PWL	4		
19	-	No More Tears (Enough Is Enough)	Kym Mazelle & Jocelyn Brown	Bell	3		L
20	14	More To This World	Bad Boys Inc	A&M	4		

◆ Prince changed his name to a symbol, and released his first single away from Warner Brothers. The record, 'The Most Beautiful Girl In The World', gave him his first British No. 1.

◆ Danish-born Whigfield became the first artist to make their UK chart debut at No. 1. 'Saturday Night', one of Europe's biggest summertime hits, sold over half a million in just three weeks.

July 1994

This Mnth	Prev Mnth	Title	Artist	Label	Wks	(US 20 Pos)	
1	1	Love Is All Around	Wet Wet Wet	Precious	21	(45)	G
2	13	I Swear	All-4-One	Blitzz	14	(1)	F L
3	8	Swamp Thing	Grid	Deconstruction	12		F
4	-	(Meet) The Flintstones	BC-52s	MCA	9	(33)	L
5	2	Baby I Love Your Way	Big Mountain	RCA	10	(6)	F L
6	-	Love Ain't Here Anymore	Take That	RCA	4		
7	-	Shine	Aswad	Bubblin'	9		L
8	-	Crazy For You	Let Loose	Mercury	13		F
9	7	You Don't Love Me (No, No, No)	Dawn Penn	Big Beat	7	(58)	F L
10	-	Go On Move	Reel 2 Real/Mad Stuntman	Positiva	4		
11	9	Don't Turn Around	Ace Of Base	Arista	7	(4)	
12	-	Everybody Gonfi Gon	Two Cowboys	ffrreedom	5		F L
13	-	Regulate	Warren G & Nate Dogg	Death Row	10	(2)	F
14	-	Word Up	Gun	A&M	4		F
15	4	No Good (Start The Dance)	Prodigy	XL	8		
16	-	Run To The Sun	Erasure	Mute	2		
17	-	Searching	China Black	Wild Card	10		F
18	-	U & Me	Cappella	Internal	3		
19	-	Everything Is Alright (Uptight)	CJ Lewis	Black Market	4		
20	-	Shakermaker	Oasis	Creation	2		F

August 1994

This Mnth	Prev Mnth	Title	Artist	Label	Wks	(US 20 Pos)	
1	1	Love Is All Around	Wet Wet Wet	Precious	21	(45)	G
2	8	Crazy For You	Let Loose	Mercury	13		F
3	2	I Swear	All-4-One	Blitzz	14	(1)	F L
4	17	Searching	China Black	Wild Card	10		F
5	-	Compliments On Your Kiss	Red Dragon With Brian/Tony Gold	Mango	9		F L
6	4	(Meet) The Flintstones	BC-52s	MCA	9	(33)	L
7	13	Regulate	Warren G & Nate Dogg	Death Row	10	(2)	F
8	-	7 Seconds	Youssou N'dour/Neneh Cherry	Columbia	9	(98)	F L
9	-	What's Up	DJ Miko	Systematic	6		F L
10	-	No More (I Can't Stand It)	Maxx	Pulse 8	4		L
11	-	Let's Get Ready To Rumble	PJ And Duncan	XSrhythm/	7		F
12	7	Shine	Aswad	Bubblin'	9		L
13	-	Trouble	Shampoo	Food	7		F L
14	3	Swamp Thing	Grid	Deconstruction/RCA	12		F
15	-	Eighteen Strings	Tinman	ffrr	4		F L
16	-	Live Forever	Oasis	Creation	3		
17	19	Everything Is Alright (Uptight)	CJ Lewis	Black Market	4		
18	-	Black Hole Sun	Soundgarden	A&M	2		L
19	-	Midnight At The Oasis	Brand New Heavies	Acid Jazz	3		
20	-	So Good	Eternal	EMI	3		

◆ Sweden's latest hit making machine, Ace Of Base, reached the Top 5 in 30 countries with their album The Sign (aka Happy Nation). Their current transatlantic hit ,'Don't Turn Around' was one of a record seven reggae-styled tracks in the UK Top 30.

◆ In Britain Wet Wet Wet held the top rung for a staggering 15 weeks with a revival of The Troggs' 'Love Is All Around', whilst in the USA 'I'll Make Love To You' by Boyz II Men hogged the No. 1 position for an unprecedented 14 weeks.

September 1994

This Mnth	Prev Mnth	Title	Artist	Label	Wks	(US 20 Pos)	
1	1	Love Is All Around	Wet Wet Wet	Precious	21	(45)	G
2	8	7 Seconds	Youssou N'dour/Neneh Cherry	Columbia	9	(98)	F L
3	5	Compliments On Your Kiss	Red Dragon With Brian & Tony Gold	Mango	9		F L
4	-	Confide In Me	Kylie Minogue	Deconstruction	4		
5	-	I'll Make Love To You	Boyz II Men	Motown	7	(1)	
6	-	The Rhythm Of The Night	Corona	WEA	8	(11)	F
7	-	Saturday Night	Whigfield	Systematic	12		F G
8	2	Crazy For You	Let Loose	Mercury	13		F
9	-	Endless Love	Luther Vandross/Mariah Carey	Columbia	5	(2)	
10	4	Searching	China Black	Wild Card	10		F
11	7	Regulate	Warren G & Nate Dogg	Death Row	10	(2)	F
12	3	I Swear	All-4-One	Blitzz	14	(1)	F L
13	-	Incredible	M-Beat feat General Levy	Renk	5		F
14	-	Always	Bon Jovi	Mercury	12	(4)	
15	9	What's Up	DJ Miko	Systematic	6		F L
16	-	What's The Frequency, Kenneth?	REM	Warner Bros.	3	(21)	
17	-	Parklife	Blur	Food	3		
18	-	Hey Now (Girls Just Want To Have Fun)	Cyndi Lauper	Epic	9	(87)	L
19	-	Right Beside You	Sophie B. Hawkins	Columbia	6	(56)	L
20	15	Eighteen Strings	Tinman	ffrr	4		F L

October 1994

This Mnth	Prev Mnth	Title	Artist	Label	Wks	(US 20 Pos)	
1	7	Saturday Night	Whigfield	Systematic	12		F G
2	14	Always	Bon Jovi	Mercury	12	(4)	
3	-	Baby Come Back	Pato Banton	Virgin	15		F
4	18	Hey Now (Girls Just Want To Have Fun)	Cyndi Lauper	Epic	9	(87)	L
5	6	The Rhythm Of The Night	Corona	WEA	8	(11)	F
6	-	Sure	Take That	RCA	4		
7	-	Sweetness	Michelle Gayle	RCA	10		
8	-	Stay	Lisa Loeb & Nine Stories	RCA	9	(1)	F L
9	9	Endless Love	Luther Vandross & Mariah Carey	Columbia	5	(2)	
10	-	Secret	Madonna	Maverick	5	(3)	
11	-	Steam	East 17	London	4		
12	-	Welcome To Tomorrow	Snap Featuring Summer	Arista	7		
13	-	She's Got That Vibe	R. Kelly	Jive	6	(59)	
14	-	Cigarettes & Alcohol	Oasis	Creation	2		
15	-	Circle Of Life	Elton John	Rocket	6	(18)	
16	5	I'll Make Love To You	Boyz II Men	Motown	7	(1)	
17	1	Love Is All Around	Wet Wet Wet	Precious	21	(45)	G
18	13	Incredible	M-Beat Featuring General Levy	Renk	5		F
19	-	When We Dance	Sting	A&M	3	(38)	
20	-	Seventeen	Let Loose	Mercury	3		

◆ Record piracy rocketed to new heights, sales were up 17% in the UK and 20% in the USA. Interestingly, there had been only nine US No. 1 singles in 1994, fewer than any year since 1955.

◆ In a year when the remaining members of Led Zeppelin reportedly refused $100 million to reform, tours by fellow UK veterans The Rolling Stones and Pink Floyd both surpassed $100 million in ticket sales alone.

November 1994

This Mnth	Prev Mnth	Title	Artist	Label	Wks	(US 20 Pos)	
1	3	Baby Come Back	Pato Banton	Virgin	15		F
2	2	Always	Bon Jovi	Mercury	12	(4)	
3	-	Another Night	(MC Sar &) the Real McCoy	Arista	10	(3)	F
4	13	She's Got That Vibe	R. Kelly	Jive	6	(59)	
5	-	Oh Baby I	Eternal	EMI	7		
6	1	Saturday Night	Whigfield	Systematic	12		F G
7	-	All I Wanna Do	Sheryl Crow	A&M	6	(2)	F
8	-	Let Me Be Your Fantasy	Baby D	Systematic	9		F
9	7	Sweetness	Michelle Gayle	RCA	10		
10	12	Welcome To Tomorrow	Snap Featuring Summer	Arista	7		
11	-	We Have All The Time In The World	Louis Armstrong	EMI	7		L
12	-	Sight For Sore Eyes	M People	Deconstruction	5		
13	-	Some Girls	Ultimate Kaos	Wild Card	5		F
14	4	Hey Now (Girls Just Want To Have Fun)	Cyndi Lauper	Epic	9	(87	L
15	-	True Faith - 94	New Order	Centredate Co.	3		
16	-	Crocodile Shoes	Jimmy Nail	East West	8		
17	-	If I Only Knew	Tom Jones	ZTT	3		L
18	8	Stay	Lisa Loeb & Nine Stories	RCA	9	(1)	F L
19	-	Spin The Black Circle	Pearl Jam	Epic	1	(18)	L
20	-	This D.J.	Warren G	Violator	2	(9)	F

December 1994

This	Prev	Title	Artist	Label	Wks	(US)	
1	-	Stay Another Day	East 17	London	9		
2	-	All I Want For Christmas Is You	Mariah Carey	Columbia	5		
3	8	Let Me Be Your Fantasy	Baby D	Systematic	9		F
4	11	We Have All The Time In The World	Louis Armstrong	EMI	7		L
5	16	Crocodile Shoes	Jimmy Nail	East West	8		
6	-	Love Me For A Reason	Boyzone	Polydor	9		F
7	-	Think Twice	Celine Dion	Epic	20	(95)	G
8	-	Power Rangers	Mighty Morph'n Power Rangers	RCA	5		F L
9	3	Another Night	(MC Sar &) the Real McCoy	Arista	10	(3)	F
10	-	Love Spreads	Stone Roses	Geffen	2		
11	1	Baby Come Back	Pato Banton	Virgin	15		F
12	-	Cotton Eye Joe	Rednex	Internal Affairs	12	(25)	F
13	-	Please Come Home For Christmas	Bon Jovi	Jambco	4		
14	-	Whatever	Oasis	Creation	6		
15	-	Hold Me, Thrill Me, Kiss Me	Gloria Estefan	Epic	6		
16	-	Another Day	Whigfield	Systematic	6		
17	-	Them Girls Them Girls	Zig And Zag	RCA	5		F L
18	7	All I Wanna Do	Sheryl Crow	A&M	6	(2)	F
19	-	Eternal Love	PJ And Duncan	XSrhythm	6		
20	12	Sight For Sore Eyes	M People	Deconstruction	5		

◆ As the ground breaking ceremony took place for the National Black Music Hall Of Fame in New Orleans, a survey pointed out that black American artists were seven times more likely to get a British hit than white ones.

◆ 1994 was a year of unrest for major superstars with George Michael, Prince and Metallica taking legal action against their record companies.

1995

This Mnth	Prev Mnth	Title	Artist	Label	Wks	(US 20 Pos)	
1	12	Cotton Eye Joe	Rednex	Internal Affairs	12	(25)	F
2	7	Think Twice	Celine Dion	Epic	20	(95)	G
3	6	Love Me For A Reason	Boyzone	Polydor	9		F
4	1	Stay Another Day	East 17	London	9		
5	-	Here Comes The Hotstepper	Ini Kamoze	Columbia	11	(1)	F L
6	-	Set You Free	N-Trance	All Around The World	10		F
7	-	Tell Me When	Human League	East West	6	(31)	
8	14	Whatever	Oasis	Creation	6		
9	-	Total Eclipse Of The Heart	Nicki French	Bags of Fun	8	(2)	F L
10	17	Them Girls Them Girls	Zig And Zag	RCA	5		F L
11	16	Another Day	Whigfield	Systematic	6		
12	-	Bump N' Grind	R. Kelly	Jive	6	(1)	
13	-	Basket Case	Green Day	Reprise	3		
14	-	Sympathy For The Devil	Guns N' Roses	Geffen	2	(55)	
15	5	Crocodile Shoes	Jimmy Nail	East West	8		
16	2	All I Want For Christmas Is You	Mariah Carey	Columbia	5		
17	-	Riverdance	Bill Whelan	Son	9		F L
18	-	She's A River	Simple Minds	Virgin	2	(52)	
19	-	Glory Box	Portishead	Go Beat	3		F
20	8	Power Rangers	Mighty Morph'n Power Rangers	RCA	5		F L

This Mnth	Prev Mnth	Title	Artist	Label	Wks	(US 20 Pos)	
1	2	Think Twice	Celine Dion	Epic	20	(95)	G
2	6	Set You Free	N-Trance	All Around The World	10		F
3	1	Cotton Eye Joe	Rednex	Internal Affairs	12	(25)	F
4	-	I've Got A Little Something For You	MN8	Columbia	8		F
5	5	Here Comes The Hotstepper	Ini Kamoze	Columbia	11	(1)	F L
6	9	Total Eclipse Of The Heart	Nicki French	Bags of Fun	8	(2)	F L
7	-	No More 'I Love You's	Annie Lennox	RCA	5	(23)	
8	-	Run Away	Real McCoy	Arista	7	(3)	
9	-	Reach Up (Papa's Got A Brand New Pig Bag)	Perfecto Allstarz	Perfecto	7		F L
10	-	Don't Give Me Your Life	Alex Party	Systematic	9		F L
11	-	Bedtime Story	Madonna	Maverick	2	(42)	
12	17	Riverdance	Bill Whelan	Son	9		F L
13	-	Open Your Heart	M People	Deconstruction	3		
14	13	Basket Case	Green Day	Reprise	3		
15	-	Call It Love	Deuce	London	5		F
16	-	Independent Love Song	Scarlet	WEA	7		F L
17	-	Someday I'll Be Saturday Night	Bon Jovi	Jambco	3		
18	7	Tell Me When	Human League	East West	6	(31)	
19	12	Bump N' Grind	R. Kelly	Jive	6	(1)	
20	-	One Night Stand	Let Loose	Mercury	3		

◆ A survey of 1994 showed that for the first time there were more European than American artists among the UK's Top 100 singles acts. British acts were having their worst spell on the US charts since the start of the Beat Boom, 32 years earlier.

◆ Celine Dion's minor US hit 'Think Twice' was one of the year's biggest sellers in Britain. Canadian Dion held the top single and album positions for five consecutive weeks, a feat last performed by The Beatles.

March 1995

This Mnth	Prev Mnth	Title	Artist	Label	Wks	(US 20 Pos)	
1	1	Think Twice	Celine Dion	Epic	20	(95)	G
2	10	Don't Give Me Your Life	Alex Party	Systematic	9		F L
3	-	Push The Feeling On	Nightcrawlers	ffrr	7		F
4	4	I've Got A Little Something For You	MN8	Columbia	8		F
5	-	Love Can Build A Bridge	Cher/Chrissie Hynde/ Neneh Cherry/Eric Clapton	London	5		L
6	-	The Bomb! (These Sounds Fall Into My Mind)	Bucketheads	Positiva	9	(49)	F L
7	7	No More 'I Love You's	Annie Lennox	RCA	5	(23)	
8	-	Don't Stop (Wiggle Wiggle)	Outhere Brothers	Eternal	11		F
9	-	Turn On, Tune In, Cop Out	Freak Power	4th & Broadway	5		F L
10	-	Axel F/Keep Pushin'	Clock	Media	5		F
11	9	Reach Up (Papa's Got A Brand New Pig Bag)	Perfecto Allstarz	Perfecto	7		F L
12	2	Set You Free	N-Trance	All Around The World	10		F
13	-	Julia Says	Wet Wet Wet	Precious	5		
14	-	Wake Up Boo!	Boo Radleys	Creation	3		F L
15	17	Someday I'll Be Saturday Night	Bon Jovi	Jambco	3		
16	-	Whoops Now/What'll I Do	Janet Jackson	Virgin	4		
17	5	Here Comes The Hotstepper	Ini Kamoze	Columbia	11	(1)	F L
18	11	Bedtime Story	Madonna	Maverick	2	(42)	
19	-	Over My Shoulder	Mike + The Mechanics	Virgin	3		L
20	3	Cotton Eye Joe	Rednex	Internal Affairs	12	(25)	F

April 1995

This Mnth	Prev Mnth	Title	Artist	Label	Wks	(US 20 Pos)	
1	8	Don't Stop (Wiggle Wiggle)	Outhere Brothers	Eternal	11		F
2	-	Back For Good	Take That	Arista	8	(7)	
3	-	Two Can Play The Game	Bobby Brown	MCA	8		
4	-	U Sure Do	Strike	Fresh	5		F L
5	13	Julia Says	Wet Wet Wet	Precious	5		
6	-	Baby Baby	Corona	Eternal	5	(57)	
7	5	Love Can Build A Bridge	Cher/Chrissie Hynde/ Neneh Cherry/Eric Clapton	London	5		L
8	-	Not Over Yet	Grace	Perfecto	4		F L
9	-	Have You Ever Really Loved A Woman?	Bryan Adams	A&M	4	(1)	
10	1	Think Twice	Celine Dion	Epic	20	(95)	G
11	-	If You Love Me	Brownstone	MJJ	6	(8)	F
12	-	Chains	Tina Arena	Columbia	8	(38)	F L
13	-	Key To My Life	Boyzone	Polydor	4		
14	6	The Bomb! (These Sounds Fall Into My Mind)	Bucketheads	Positiva	9	(49)	F L
15	2	Don't Give Me Your Life	Alex Party	Systematic	9		F L
16	-	Baby It's You	Beatles	Apple	2	(67)	L
17	-	If You Only Let Me In	MN8	Columbia	3		
18	9	Turn On, Tune In, Cop Out	Freak Power	4th & Broadway	5		F L
19	-	Best In Me	Let Loose	Mercury	2		L
20	-	Let It Rain	East 17	London	3		

◆ At times re-mixes of singles that flopped when first released hogged half of the UK Top 10. TV actors Robson Green & Jerome Flynn became the first UK act to make their chart debut at No. 1. Their version of the oft-recorded 'Unchained Melody' sold a million in three weeks!

1995

This Mnth	Prev Mnth	Title	Artist	Label	Wks	(US 20 Pos)	
1	-	Guaglione	Perez 'Prez' Prado	RCA	8		L
2	-	Some Might Say	Oasis	Creation	4		
3	-	Dreamer	Livin' Joy	Undiscovered	5	(72)	L
4	2	Back For Good	Take That	Arista	8	(7)	
5	-	Scatman (Ski-Ba-Bop-Ba-Dop-Bop)	Scatman John	RCA	8	(60)	F
6	-	Unchained Melody/ White Cliffs ...	Robson Green/Jerome Flynn	RCA	11		F G
7	13	Key To My Life	Boyzone	Polydor	4		
8	12	Chains	Tina Arena	Columbia	8	(38)	F L
9	3	Two Can Play The Game	Bobby Brown	MCA	8		
10	1	Don't Stop (Wiggle Wiggle)	Outhere Brothers	Eternal	11		F
11	-	We're Gonna Do It Again	Manchester United FC	PolyGram TV	3		L
12	-	Love City Groove	Love City Groove	Planet3	6		F L
13	-	That Look In Your Eye	Ali Campbell	Kuff	6		F L
14	-	Your Loving Arms	Billie Ray Martin	Magnet	6		F L
15	-	Only One Road	Celine Dion	Epic	3	(93)	
16	17	If You Only Let Me In	MN8	Columbia	3		
17	-	Surrender Your Love	Nightcrawlers/John Reid	Final Vinyl	4		
18	-	The Changingman	Paul Weller	Go! Discs	1		
19	9	Have You Ever Really Loved A Woman?	Bryan Adams	A&M	4	(1)	
20	-	This Is How We Do It	Montell Jordan	Def Jam	5	(1)	F

This Mnth	Prev Mnth	Title	Artist	Label	Wks	(US 20 Pos)	
1	6	Unchained Melody/ White Cliffs ...	Robson Green/Jerome Flynn	RCA	11		F G
2	-	Common People	Pulp	Island	7		
3-	-	(Everybody's Got To Learn Sometime) I Need Your....	Baby D	Systematic	6		
4	1	Guaglione	Perez 'Prez' Prado	RCA	8		L
5	-	Scream	Michael & Janet Jackson	Epic	5	(5)	
6	5	Scatman (Ski-Ba-Bop-Ba-Dop-Bop)	Scatman John	RCA	8	(60)	F
7	-	Hold Me, Thrill Me, Kiss Me, Kill Me	U2	Island	10	(16	
8	13	That Look In Your Eye	Ali Campbell	Kuff	6		F L
9	-	This Ain't A Love Song	Bon Jovi	Mercury	3	(14)	
10	-	Think Of You	Whigfield	Systematic	6		
11	-	Boom Boom Boom	Outhere Brothers	Eternal	11	(65)	
12	-	Don't Want To Forgive Me Now	Wet Wet Wet	Precious	3		
13	14	Your Loving Arms	Billie Ray Martin	Magnet	6		F L
14	17	Surrender Your Love	Nightcrawlers/John Reid	Final Vinyl	4		
15	-	Yes	McAlmont & Butler	Hut	3		F
16	-	Right In The Night (Fall In Love With Music)	Jam & Spoon Feat Plavka	Epic	5		F L
17	-	A Girl Like You	Edwyn Collins	Setanta	9	(32)	F L
18	-	Reverend Black Grape	Black Grape	Radioactive	1		F
19	-	Search For The Hero	M People	Deconstruction	3		
20	3	Dreamer	Livin' Joy	Undiscovered	5	(72)	L

◆ Take That's 'Back For Good' sold half a million in two weeks and their LP Nobody Else went double platinum in three days.

◆ Soon after Blur won a record four Brit Awards, arch rivals Oasis clocked up their first chart No. 1, 'Some Might Say' and five of their old singles re-charted.

July 1995

This Mnth	Prev Mnth	Title	Artist	Label	Wks	(US 20 Pos)	
1	11	Boom Boom Boom	Outhere Brothers	Eternal	11	(65)	
2	1	Unchained Melody/ White Cliffs Of Dover	Robson Green/Jerome Flynn	RCA	11		F G
3	-	Shy Guy	Diana King	Work	9	(13)	F
4	7	Hold Me, Thrill Me, Kiss Me, Kill Me	U2	Island	10	(16)	
5	17	A Girl Like You	Edwyn Collins	Setanta	9	(32)	F L
6	-	Alright/Time	Supergrass	Parlophone	7		
7	-	Whoomph! (There It Is)	Clock	Media	5		
8	-	In The Summertime	Shaggy Featuring Rayvon	Virgin	7	(3)	
9	-	I'm A Believer	EMF/Reeves And Mortimer	Parlophone	3		L
10	-	Kiss From A Rose	Seal	ZTT	9	(1)	
11	10	Think Of You	Whigfield	Systematic	6		
12	3	(Everybody's Got To Learn Sometime) I Need Your...	Baby D	Systematic	6		
13	-	This Is A Call	Foo Fighters	Roswell	1		F
14	-	Shoot Me With Your Love	D:ream	Magnet	2		
15	-	Humpin' Around	Bobby Brown	MCA	2		
16	-	3 Is Family	Dana Dawson	EMI	4		F L
17	-	Try Me Out	Corona	Eternal	8		
18	-	Happy	MN8	Columbia	3		L
19	5	Scream	Michael Jackson/Janet Jackson	Epic	5	(5)	
20	-	Stillness In Time	Jamiroquai	Sony	2		

August 1995

This Mnth	Prev Mnth	Title	Artist	Label	Wks	(US 20 Pos)	
1	-	Never Forget	Take That	RCA	6		
2	10	Kiss From A Rose	Seal	ZTT	9	(1)	
3	3	Shy Guy	Diana King	Work	9	(13)	F
4	1	Boom Boom Boom	Outhere Brothers	Eternal	11	(65)	
5	-	Waterfalls	TLC	Laface	10	(1)	
6	17	Try Me Out	Corona	Eterna	8		L
7	-	I Luv U Baby	Original	Ore	5		F L
8	-	So Good	Boyzone	Polydor	3		
9	6	Alright/Time	Supergrass	Parlophone	7		
10	-	Country House	Blur	Food	6		
11	-	Roll With It	Oasis	Creation	4		
12	-	Son Of A Gun	JX	Ffrreedom	3		L
13	-	I'm Only Sleeping/ Off On Holiday	Suggs	WEA	3		F
14	4	Hold Me, Thrill Me, Kiss Me, Kill Me	U2	Island	10	(16)	
15	-	Everybody	Clock	Media	3		
16	-	In The Name Of The Father	Black Grape	Radioactive	2		
17	8	In The Summertime	Shaggy Featuring Rayvon	Virgin	7	(3)	
18	-	Human Nature	Madonna	Maveric	1		
19	-	Don't You Want Me	Felix	Deconstruction	2		
20	5	A Girl Like You	Edwyn Collins	Setanta	9	(32)	F L

◆ For the first time in years, a battle for the top of the charts made the national press, when Oasis and Blur released new singles simultaneously. Blur's 'Country House' came in at No. 1 and 'Roll With It' by Oasis entered in runner-up position.

◆ Records were spending less time on the UK Top 20 than ever before. It was now quite normal for singles to peak in their first chart week and to spend less than three weeks on the Top 20.

1995

This Mnth	Prev Mnth	Title	Artist	Label	Wks	(US 20 Pos)	
1	-	You Are Not Alone	Michael Jackson	Epic	10	(1)	
2	-	I'll Be There For You	Rembrandts	East West	8	(17)	F L
3	10	Country House	Blur	Food	6		
4	-	The Sunshine After The Rain	Berri	Ffrreedom	6		F
5	-	Stayin' Alive	N-Trance Featuring Ricardo Da Force	All Around The World	6		
6	11	Roll With It	Oasis	Creation	4		
7	-	Boombastic	Shaggy	Virgin	8	(3)	
8	7	I Luv U Baby	Original	Ore	5		F L
9	-	Who The F**k Is Alice?	Smokie/Roy Chubby Brown	Now	10		L
10	5	Waterfalls	TLC	Laface	10	(1)	
11	-	Fantasy	Mariah Carey	Columbia	7	(1)	
12	-	Fairground	Simply Red	East West	9		
13	-	Can I Touch You...There?	Michael Bolton	Columbia	4	(27)	L
14	-	Hideaway	De'lacy	Slip'n'slide	4		F L
15	-	Runaway	Janet Jackson	Epic	3	(3)	
16	-	Tu M'Aimes Encore (To Love Me Again)	Celine Dion	Epic	3		
17	-	La La La Hey Hey	Outhere Brothers	Eternal	3		
18	-	Scatman's World	Scatman John	RCA	4		L
19	1	Never Forget	Take That	RCA	6		
20	-	I Feel Love	Donna Summer	Manifesto	2		L

This Mnth	Prev Mnth	Title	Artist	Label	Wks	(US 20 Pos)	
1	12	Fairground	Simply Red	East West	9		
2	7	Boombastic	Shaggy	Virgin	8	(3)	
3	9	Who The F**k Is Alice?	Smokie/Roy Chubby Brown	Now	10		L
4	-	Mis-Shapes/Sorted For Es & Wizz	Pulp	Island	4		
5	1	You Are Not Alone	Michael Jackson	Epic	10	(1)	
6	-	When Love & Hate Collide	Def Leppard	Bludgeon Riffola	6		L
7	11	Fantasy	Mariah Carey	Columbia	7	(1)	
8	-	Gangsta's Paradise	Coolio Featuring L.V.	Tommy Boy	17	(1)	G
9	-	I'd Lie For You (And That's The Truth)	Meat Loaf	MCA	5	(13)	L
10	-	Power Of A Woman	Eternal	EMI	4		
11	-	Light Of My Life	Louise	EMI	4		F
12	-	Somewhere Somehow	Wet Wet Wet	Precious	4		
13	5	Stayin' Alive	N-Trance Featuring Ricardo Da Force	All Around The World	6		
14	-	Higher State Of Consciousness	Josh Wink	Manifesto	3		F L
15	2	I'll Be There For You	Rembrandts	East West	8	(17)	F L
16	-	Something For The Pain	Bon Jovi	Mercury	3		
17	-	Missing	Everything But The Girl	Blanco Y Negro	16	(2)	
18	-	Man On The Edge	Iron Maiden	EMI	1		L
19	-	Renegade Master	Wildchild	Hi-Life	2		F L
20	-	Walking In Memphis	Cher	WEA	2		

◆ The Beatles' 'Free As A Bird' just failed to give them their 18th UK No. 1, which would have topped Elvis Presley's total. Their Anthology I double album sold an unprecedented 500,000 on its first day in America, and the first *Beatles Anthology* TV show attracted 47 million US viewers, double the amount of its nearest competitor.

November 1995

This Mnth	Prev Mnth	Title	Artist	Label	Wks	(US 20 Pos)	
1	8	Gangsta's Paradise	Coolio Featuring L.V.	Tommy Boy	17	(1)	G
2	-	I Believe/Up On The Roof	Robson Green & Jerome Flynn	RCA	10		G
3	17	Missing	Everything But The Girl	Blanco Y Negro	16	(2)	
4	-	Wonderwall	Oasis	Creation	13	(8)	
5	-	Heaven For Everyone	Queen	Parlophone	4		
6	-	Thunder	East 17	London	8		
7	9	I'd Lie For You (And That's The Truth)	Meat Loaf	MCA	5	(13)	L
8	-	You'll See	Madonna	Maverick	8	(8)	
9	-	Fairground	Simply Red	East West	9		
10	6	When Love & Hate Collide	Def Leppard	Bludgeon Riffola	6		L
11	-	The Universal	Blur	Food/Parlophone	3		
12	-	Anywhere Is	Enya	WEA	7		L
13	-	I Believe	Happy Clappers	Shindig/PWL	2		F L
14	3	Who The F**k Is Alice?	Smokie/Roy Chubby Brown	Now	10		L
15	-	Father And Son	Boyzone	Polydor	11		
16	10	Power Of A Woman	Eternal	EMI	4		
17	-	It's Oh So Quiet	Bjork	One Little Indian	9		
18	2	Boombastic	Shaggy	Virgin	8	(3)	
19	-	Goldeneye	Tina Turner	Parlophone	2		L
20	-	He's On The Phone	Saint Etienne	Heavenly	2		L

December 1995

This Mnth	Prev Mnth	Title	Artist	Label	Wks	(US 20 Pos)	
1	15	Father And Son	Boyzone	Polydor	11		
2	-	Earth Song	Michael Jackson	Epic	11		G
3	2	I Believe/Up On The Roof	Robson Green/Jerome Flynn	RCA	10		G
4	1	Gangsta's Paradise	Coolio Featuring L.V.	Tommy Boy	17	(1)	G
5	3	Missing	Everything But The Girl	Blanco Y Negro	16	(2)	
6	17	It's Oh So Quiet	Bjork	One Little Indian	9		
7	4	Wonderwall	Oasis	Creation	13	(8)	
8	-	Free As A Bird	Beatles	Apple	4	(6)	
9	-	One Sweet Day	Mariah Carey & Boyz II Men	Columbia	6	(1)	
10	12	Anywhere Is	Enya	WEA	7		L
11	-	Wonderwall	Mike Flowers Pops	London	3		F L
12	-	Disco 2000	Pulp	Island	6		
13	-	Miss Sarajevo	Passengers	Island	3		F L
14	-	A Winter's Tale	Queen	Parlophone	2		L
15	-	The Gift Of Christmas	Childliners	London	4		F L
16	-	I Am Blessed	Eternal	EMI	7		
17	-	The Best Things In Life Are Free	Luther Vandross/Janet Jackson	A&M	3		
18	8	You'll See	Madonna	Maverick/Sire	8	(8)	
19	-	Gold	TAFKAP	Warner	5		
20	-	Lie To Me	Bon Jovi	Mercury	2		

◆ In Christmas week, a record-shattering 10.6 million albums were sold in the UK. The biggest seller was Robson & Jerome's eponymous debut LP which sold a record-breaking 2 million copies in just seven weeks. The duo also clocked up their second No. 1 single, 'I Believe', which had amassed 600,000 advance orders.

1996

This Mnth	Prev Mnth	Title	Artist	Label	Wks	(US 20 Pos)	
1	2	Earth Song	Michael Jackson	Epic	11		G
2	1	Father And Son	Boyzone	Polydor	11		
3	5	Missing	Everything But The Girl	Blanco Y Negro	16	(2)	
4	7	Wonderwall	Oasis	Creation	13	(8)	
5	-	Jesus To A Child	George Michael	Virgin	4	(7)	
6	-	So Pure	Baby D	Systematic	4		L
7	-	Spaceman	Babylon Zoo	EMI	7		G L
8	6	It's Oh So Quiet	Bjork	One Little Indian	9		
9	11	Wonderwall	Mike Flowers Pops	London	3		F L
10	4	Gangsta's Paradise	Coolio Featuring L.V.	Tommy Boy	17	(1)	F
11	16	I Am Blessed	Eternal	EMI	7		
12	-	Whole Lotta Love	Goldbug	Acid Jazz	3		F L
13	-	Creep '96	TLC	Laface	3		L
14	-	Anything	3T	MJJ	9	(15)	F
15	-	One By One	Cher	WEA	5		L
16	-	If You Wanna Party	Molella Featuring The Outhere Brothers	Eternal	6		F L
17	-	Sandstorm	Cast	Polydor	2		
18	3	I Believe/Up On The Roof	Robson Green/ Jerome Flynn	RCA	10		G
19	-	Too Hot	Coolio	Tommy Boy	2		
20	-	Why You Treat Me So Bad	Shaggy Featuring Grand Puba	Virgin	2		

This Mnth	Prev Mnth	Title	Artist	Label	Wks	(US 20 Pos)	
1	7	Spaceman	Babylon Zoo	EMI	7		G L
2	14	Anything	3T	MJJ	9		F
3	-	Slight Return	Bluetones	Superior Quality	4		
4	-	Lifted	Lighthouse Family	Wild Card	6		F
5	-	I Got 5 On It	Luniz	Noo Trybe	7	(8)	F L
6	6	I Just Want To Make Love To You	Etta James	/MCA	4		F L
7	-	One Of Us	Joan Osborne	Blue Gorilla	4	(4)	F L
8	5	Jesus To A Child	George Michael	Virgin	4	(7)	
9	-	I Wanna Be A Hippy	Technohead	Mokum	9		F L
10	-	Children	Robert Miles	Deconstruction	13	(54)	F
11	-	Do U Still?	East 17	London	3		
12	-	Open Arms	Mariah Carey	Columbia	2		
13	-	Not A Dry Eye In The House	Meat Loaf	Virgin	3		
14	15	One By One	Cher	WEA	5		L
15	-	Street Spirit (Fade Out)	Radiohead	Parlophone	1		
16	12	Whole Lotta Love	Goldbug	Acid Jazz	3		F L
17	-	Stereotypes	Blur	Food	2		
18	-	No Fronts - The Remixes	Dog Eat Dog	Roadrunner	2		F
19	-	Hyperballad	Bjork	One Little Indian	1		L
20	-	Change Your Mind	Upside Down	World	3		F L

◆ The Brit Awards attracted massive media coverage when Jarvis Cocker of Pulp semi-sabotaged Michael Jackson's performance of 'Earth Song'.

◆ The Beatles, whose Anthology I passed the 10 million mark world-wide, ended this last quarter with Anthology 2 at the top.

◆ Take That, Britain's top act of the 1990s, disbanded. Their final single, 'How Deep Is Your Love' giving them eight No.1s from their last nine releases.

March 1996

This Mnth	Prev Mnth	Title	Artist	Label	Wks	(US 20 Pos)	
1	10	Children	Robert Miles	Deconstruction	13	(54)	F
2	-	Don't Look Back In Anger	Oasis	Creation	8		
3	-	How Deep Is Your Love	Take That	RCA	7		L
4	-	Coming Home Now	Boyzone	Polydor	4		
5	-	Give Me A Little More Time	Gabrielle	Go!discs	10		
6	9	I Wanna Be A Hippy	Technohead	Mokum	9		F L
7	2	Anything	3T	MJJ	9		F
8	-	Return Of The Mack	Mark Morrison	WEA	*10		
9	-	I Got 5 On It	Luniz	Noo Trybe	7	(8)	F L
10	-	Firestarter	Prodigy	XL	6		
11	-	Real Love	Beatles	Apple	2	(11)	L
12	-	Stupid Girl	Garbage	Mushroom	2		
13	-	The X Files	Mark Snow	Warner	6		F L
14	-	Passion	Gat Decor	Way Of Life	3		F L
15	-	Spaceman	Babylon Zoo	EMI	7		G L
16	-	Going Out	Supergrass	Parlophone	3		L
17	-	Falling Into You	Celine Dion	Epic	5		
18	-	Perseverance	Terrorvision	Total Vegas	1		F L
19	-	These Days	Bon Jovi	Mercury	2		
20	4	Lifted	Lighthouse Family	Wild Card	6		F

April 1996

This Mnth	Prev Mnth	Title	Artist	Label	Wks	(US 20 Pos)	
1	8	Return Of The Mack	Mark Morrison	WEA	14	(2)	
2	10	Firestarter	Prodigy	XL	6	(30)	
3	-	Ooh Aah...Just A Little Bit	Gina G	Eternal/WEA	11	(12)	F
4	13	The X Files	Mark Snow	Warner	6		F L
5	1	Children	Robert Miles	Deconstruction	14	(21)	F
6	5	Give Me A Little More Time	Gabrielle	Go!Discs	10		
7	-	They Don't Care About Us	Michael Jackson	Epic	5	(30)	
8	-	A Design For Life	Manic Street Preachers	Epic	5		
9	-	California Love	2 Pac Feat Dr Dre	Death Row/Island	3	(1)	F
10	-	Cecilia	Suggs	WEA	8		L
11	-	X-Files	DJ Dado	ZYX	3		F L
12	-	Walking Wounded	Everything But The Girl	Virgin	2		
13	-	Goldfinger	Ash	Infectious	2		
14	-	Peaches	Presidents Of The United States	Columbia	3	(29)	
15	3	How Deep Is Your Love	Take That	RCA	7		L
16	-	You've Got It Bad	Ocean Colour Scene	MCA	2		
17	-	Keep On Jumpin'	Lisa Marie Experience	3 Beat/ffrr	4		F L
18	-	Bulls On Parade	Rage Against The Machine	Epic	1		L
19	2	Don't Look Back In Anger	Oasis	Creation	8	(55)	
20	-	Something Changed	Pulp	Island	1		

◆ Prodigy's tenth Top 20 single, 'Firestarter', took them to new heights. It not only gave the group their first UK No. 1, but it also helped propel their album, The Fat Of The Land, to the top of the charts in many other parts of the world including the USA.

◆ In its 10th month on the chart the album Jagged Little Pill by Canadian Alanis Morissette passed the million sales mark and finally reached No. 1. It headed the UK chart for 10 weeks, a female record which was previously held by Madonna, who owned Morissette's US label!

1996

This Mnth	Prev Mnth	Title	Artist	Label	Wks	(US 20 Pos)	
1	-	Fastlove	George Michael	Virgin	7	(8)	
2	3	Ooh Aah...Just A Little Bit	Gina G	Eternal	11	(12)	F
3	1	Return Of The Mack	Mark Morrison	WEA	14	(2)	
4	10	Cecilia	Suggs	WEA	8		L
5	-	Move Move Move (The Red Tribe)	Manchester United FA Cup Squad	Music Collection	5		L
6	8	A Design For Life	Manic Street Preachers	Epic	5		
7	-	There's Nothing I Won't Do	JX	Ffrreedom	8		
8	-	Charmless Man	Blur	Food/Parlophone	3		
9	-	Pass & Move (It's The Liverpool Groove)	Liverpool FC & The Boot Room Boys	Telstar	2		L
10	-	Nobody Knows	Tony Rich Project	Lafac	10	(2)	F L
11	7	They Don't Care About Us	Michael Jackson	Epic	5	(30)	
12	-	Tonight, Tonight	Smashing Pumpkins	Virgin	2	(36)	
13	-	Cut Some Rug/Castle Rock	Bluetones	Superior Quality	1		
14	-	Before	Pet Shop Boys	Parlophone	1		
15	-	Woo-Hah!! Got You All In Check	Busta Rhymes	Elektra	2	(8)	F
16	17	Keep On Jumpin'	Lisa Marie Experience	/ffrr	4		F L
17	-	Klubbhopping	Klubbheads	AM:PM	3		F L
18	-	24/7	3T	MJJ	3		
19	-	Blue Moon/Only You	John Alford	Love This	2		L
20	-	Sale Of The Century	Sleeper	Indolent	2		

This Mnth	Prev Mnth	Title	Artist	Label	Wks	(US 20 Pos)	
1	-	Three Lions (Official Song Of The England Team)	Baddiel & Skinner & Lightning Seeds	Epic	10		F L
2	-	Mysterious Girl	Peter Andre Feat Bubbler Ranx	Mushroom	13		
3	-	Killing Me Softly	Fugees	Columbia	12		F G
4	-	Because You Loved Me	Celine Dion	Epic	10	(1)	
5	10	Nobody Knows	Tony Rich Project	Laface/Arista	10	(2)	F L
6	2	Ooh Aah...Just A Little Bit	Gina G	Eternal/WEA	11	(12)	F
7	-	Don't Stop Movin'	Livin' Joy	Undiscovered/MCA	9	(67)	
8	-	The Day We Caught The Train	Ocean Colour Scene	MCA	5		
9	-	Always Be My Baby	Mariah Carey	Columbia	5	(1)	
10	7	There's Nothing I Won't Do	JX	Ffrreedom	8		
11	-	Blurred	Pianoman	Ffrreedom	4		F L
12	-	Naked	Louise	Ist Avenue/EMI	3		
13	-	Until It Sleeps	Metallica	Vertigo	2	(10)	
14	1	Fastlove	George Michael	Virgin	7	(8)	
15	-	The Only Thing That Looks Good On Me Is You	Bryan Adams	A&M	2	(52)	
16	-	Fable	Robert Miles	Deconstruction	2		
17	-	Theme From 'Mission: Impossible'	Adam Clayton & Larry Mullen	Mother	7	(7)	F L
18	-	Make It With You	Let Loose	Mercury	2		L
19	-	England's Irie	Black Grape Featuring Joe Strummer & Keith Allen	Radioactive	2		L
20	3	Return Of The Mack	Mark Morrison	WEA	14	(2)	

◆ As Phil Collins departed Genesis, Australasian act Crowded House (whose Very Best Of album topped the chart soon after) announced they were disbanding and The Sex Pistols re-united after 18 years for the Filthy Lucre Tour - the group members netting £750,000 each. The most popular football song of all time, 'Three Lions' by Baddiel & Skinner and The Lightning Seeds, topped the chart and was heard throughout the Euro 96 competition.

July 1996

This Mnth	Prev Mnth	Title	Artist	Label	Wks	(US 20 Pos)	
1	3	Killing Me Softly	Fugees	Columbia	12		F G
2	1	Three Lions (Official Song Of The England Team)	Baddiel & Skinner & Lightning Seeds	Epic	10		F L
3	2	Mysterious Girl	Peter Andre Feat Bubbler Ranx	Mushroom	13		
4	-	Born Slippy	Underworld	Junior Boy's Own	10		F L
5	4	Because You Loved Me	Celine Dion	Epic	10	(1)	
6	-	Wannabe	Spice Girls	Virgin	13	(1)	F
7	-	Forever Love	Gary Barlow	RCA	4		F
8	7	Don't Stop Movin'	Livin' Joy	Undiscovered	9	(67)	
9	-	Tattva	Kula Shaker	Columbia	3		F
10	-	You're Makin' Me High	Toni Braxton	Laface	4	(1)	
11	-	In Too Deep	Belinda Carlisle	Chrysalis	2		
12	-	Jazz It Up	Reel 2 Real	Positiva	3		L
13	-	Oh Yeah	Ash	Infectious	2		
14	-	Crazy	Mark Morrison	WEA	3		
15	-	Macarena (Bayside Boys Mix)	Los Del Rio	RCA	11	(1)	F L
16	-	Keep On Jumpin'	Todd Terry Featuring Martha Wash & Jocelyn Brown	Manifesto	3		F
17	-	Higher State Of Consciousness '96	Wink	Manifesto	5		F L
18	-	Where Love Lies	Alison Limerick	Arista	2		L
19	9	Always Be My Baby	Mariah Carey	Columbia	5	(1)	
20	-	Bad Actress	Terrorvision	Total Vegas	1		

August 1996

This Mnth	Prev Mnth	Title	Artist	Label	Wks	(US 20 Pos)	
1	6	Wannabe	Spice Girls	Virgin	13	(1)	F
2	15	Macarena (Bayside Boys Mix)	Los Del Rio	RCA	11	(1)	F L
3	1	Killing Me Softly	Fugees	Columbia	12		F G
4	-	Why	3T Featuring Michael Jackson	MJJ	3		
5	-	Good Enough	Dodgy	A&M	5		
6	-	Freedom	Robbie Williams	RCA	3		F
7	3	Mysterious Girl	Peter Andre Feat Bubbler Ranx	Mushroom	13		
8	-	How Bizarre	OMC	Polydor	10		F L
9	4	Born Slippy	Underworld	Junior Boy's Own	10		F L
10	-	We've Got It Goin' On	Backstreet Boys	Jive	4	(69)	
11	-	Someday	Eternal	EMI	3		
12	-	Trash	Suede	Nude	2		
13	-	Spinning The Wheel	George Michael	Virgin	4		
14	-	Tha Crossroads	Bone Thugs N Harmony	Epic	5	(1)	F
15	-	Virtual Insanity	Jamiroquai	Sony S^2	7		
16	-	E-Bow The Letter	REM	Warner Bros.	2	(49)	
17	17	Higher State Of Consciousness '96	Wink	Manifesto	5		F L
18	-	Everything Must Go	Manic Street Preachers	Epic	2		
19	-	Undivided Love	Louise	EMI	3		
20	-	Peacock Suite	Paul Weller	Go! Discs	1		

◆ Newcomers the Spice Girls notched up the first of a record shattering six successive UK No. 1 singles with 'Wannabe'. The track, which was the first ever by an all-British girl group to reach the top, went on to top the charts in more than 30 countries and became the biggest selling debut record by a British act.
◆ Veteran duo Los Del Rio scored the biggest ever hit from Spain with 'Macarena', which spent a record breaking 60 weeks on the US Top 100.

1996

This Mnth	Prev Mnth	Title	Artist	Label	Wks	(US 20 Pos)	
1	1	Wannabe	Spice Girls	Virgin	13	(1)	F G
2	-	Ready Or Not	Fugees	Columbia	7		
3	-	Flava	Peter Andre	Mushroom	5		
4	-	I've Got A Little Puppy	Smurfs	EMI TV	5		
5	15	Virtual Insanity	Jamiroquai	Sony S^2	7		
6	-	Hey Dude	Kula Shaker	Columbia	3		
7	-	Breakfast At Tiffany's	Deep Blue Something	Interscope	8	(5)	F L
8	-	One To Another	Charlatans	Beggars Banquet	2		
9	-	I'm Alive	Stretch & Vern Present Maddog	ffrr	4		F L
10	8	How Bizarre	OMC	Polydor	10		F L
11	2	Macarena	Los Del Rio	RCA	11	(1)	F L
12	-	Escaping	Dina Carroll	A&M	4		L
13	13	Spinning The Wheel	George Michael	Virgin	4		
14	-	Seven Days And One Week	BBE	Positiva	5		F
15	-	The Circle	Ocean Colour Scene	MCA	2		
16	-	I Love You Always Forever	Donna Lewis	Atlantic	9	(2)	F L
17	-	Marblehead Johnson	Bluetones	Superior Quality	2		
18	-	Me And You Versus The World	Space	Gut	3		
19	-	Always Breaking My Heart	Belinda Carlisle	Chrysalis	2		
20	-	Oh What A Night	Clock	MCA	7		

This Mnth	Prev Mnth	Title	Artist	Label	Wks	(US 20 Pos)	
1	7	Breakfast At Tiffany's	Deep Blue Something	Interscope	8	(5)	F L
2	-	It's All Coming Back To Me Now	Celine Dion	Epic	7	(2)	
3	-	Setting Sun	Chemical Brothers	Virgin	3		
4	16	I Love You Always Forever	Donna Lewis	Atlantic	9	(2)	F L
5	14	Seven Days And One Week	BBE	Positiva	5		F
6	-	You're Gorgeous	Baby Bird	Echo	8		F
7	-	Words	Boyzone	Polydor	6		
8	2	Ready Or Not	Fugees	Columbia	7		
9	-	Rotterdam	Beautiful South	Go! Discs	4		
10	12	Escaping	Dina Carroll	A&M	4		L
11	-	Say You'll Be There	Spice Girls	Virgin	11	(3)	
12	-	Insomnia	Faithless	Cheeky	6		F
13	-	Loungin'	LL Cool J	Def Jam	4	(3)	
14	-	Flying	Cast	Polydor	2		
15	-	Trippin'	Mark Morrison	WEA	2		
16	3	Flava	Peter Andre	Mushroom	5		
17	-	No Diggity	Blackstreet Featuring Dr Dre	Interscope	3	(1)	F
18	-	Beautiful Ones	Suede	Nude	2		
19	-	Dance Into The Light	Phil Collins	Face Value	2	(45)	L
20	-	Kevin Carter	Manic Street Preachers	Epic	1		

◆ As America's Backstreet Boys and 3T joined the boy band elite, Gary Barlow and Robbie Williams reached the Top 3 with their first solo singles since leaving the 1990s top boy band, Take That.
◆ The Fugees and Deep Blue Something helped keep the flag flying for American groups. The former achieved two No. 1s in three months, with their million selling revival of Roberta Flack's 1973 hit 'Killing Me Softly' and 'Ready Or Not', which was based a 1968 track by The Delfonics. Deep Blue Something were the first US rock band to top the UK chart with a self-penned debut hit since Buddy Holly & The Crickets in 1957.

This Mnth	Prev Mnth	Title	Artist	Label	Wks	(US 20 Pos)	
1	11	Say You'll Be There	Spice Girls	Virgin	11	(3)	
2	-	If You Ever	East 17 Featuring Gabrielle	London	10		
3	-	What Becomes Of The Broken Hearted	Robson Green & Jerome Flynn	RCA	6		L
4	-	Un-Break My Heart	Toni Braxton	Laface	14	(1)	
5	-	Breathe	Prodigy	XL	10		
6	-	What's Love Got To Do t With I	Warren G Featuring Adina Howard	Interscope	6		
7	7	Words	Boyzone	Polydor	6		
8	12	Insomnia (remix)	Faithless	Cheeky	6		F
9	-	Hillbilly Rock Hillbilly Roll	Woolpackers	RCA	9		F L
10	6	You're Gorgeous	Baby Bird	Echo	8		F
11	-	One & One	Robert Miles Featuring Maria Nayler	Deconstruction	10	(54)	
12	-	Stranger In Moscow	Michael Jackson	Epic	3	(91)	
13	-	No Woman No Cry	Fugees	Columbia	3		
14	-	Angel	Simply Red	East West	2		
15	-	Child	Mark Owen	RCA	3		F
16	-	I Belong To You	Gina G	Eternal/WEA	3		
17	-	Place Your Hands	Reef	Sony	3		
18	2	It's All Coming Back To Me Now	Celine Dion	Epic	7	(2)	
19	-	Govinda	Kula Shaker	Columbia	3		
20	-	I'll Never Break Your Heart	Backstreet Boys	Jive	2		

This Mnth	Prev Mnth	Title	Artist	Label	Wks	(US 20 Pos)	
1	4	Un-Break My Heart	Toni Braxton	Laface	14	(1)	
2	5	Breathe	Prodigy	XL	10		
3	11	One & One	Robert Miles Featuring Maria Nayler	Deconstruction	10	(54)	
4	-	A Different Beat	Boyzone	Polydor	5		
5	-	Knockin' On Heaven's Door/ Throw These Guns Away	Dunblane	BMG	4		F L
6	-	I Feel You	Peter Andre	Mushroom	3		
7	-	I Need You	3T	Epic	6		
8	-	2 Becomes 1	Spice Girls	Virgin	9	(4)	
9	-	Forever	Damage	Big Life	5		
10	-	Horny	Mark Morrison	WEA	5		
11	-	Don't Cry For Me Argentina	Madonna	Warner Bros.	6	(8)	
12	-	All By Myself	Celine Dion	Epic	4	(4)	
13	-	Don't Marry Her	Beautiful South	Go! Discs	5		L
14	-	Cosmic Girl	Jamiroquai	Sony S^2	6		
15	6	What's Love Got To Do With It	Warren G Featuring Adina Howard	Interscope	6		
16	9	Hillbilly Rock Hillbilly Roll	Woolpackers	RCA	9		F L
17	-	Your Christmas Wish	Smurfs	EMI TV	3		L
18	2	If You Ever	East 17 Featuring Gabrielle	London	10		
19	-	Australia	Manic Street Preachers	Epic	1		L
20	13	No Woman No Cry	Fugees	Columbia	3		

◆ The debut album by the Spice Girls, Spice, went platinum in the UK after just five days . It became the biggest selling and fastest selling debut album ever by a British act. It also topped the chart in over a dozen other countries and sold close to 20 million copies worldwide. The quintet also won the battle for the Christmas No. 1 with 2 Become 1, which amassed over 700,000 advance orders. It was the fastest selling single since Band Aid.

1997

This Mnth	Prev Mnth	Title	Artist	Label	Wks	(US 20 Pos)	
1	8	2 Become 1	Spice Girls	Virgin	9	(4)	
2	-	Professional Widow (It's Got To Be Big)	Tori Amos	East West	5		L
3	1	Un-Break My Heart	Toni Braxton	Laface/Arista	14	(1)	
4	11	Don't Cry For Me Argentina	Madonna	Warner Bros.	6	(8)	
5	-	Quit Playing Games (With My Heart)	Backstreet Boys	Jive	6	(2)	
6	3	One & One	Robert Miles Featuring Maria Nayler	Deconstruction	10	(54)	
7	-	Say What You Want	Texas	Mercury	6		
8	-	Don't Let Go (Love)	En Vogue	East West America	10	(2)	
9	-	Your Woman	White Town	Chrysalis	5	(23)	F L
10	-	Satan	Orbital	Internal	2		
11	5	Knockin' On Heaven's Door-Throw These Guns Away	Dunblane	BMG	4		F L
12	-	Hey Child	East 17	London	2		L
13	-	People Hold On (The Bootleg Mixes)	Lisa Stansfield Vs The Dirty Rotten Scoundrels	Arista	2		
14	2	Breathe	Prodigy	XL	10		
15	-	Where Do You Go	No Mercy	Arista	12	(5)	F
16	10	Horny	Mark Morrison	WEA	5		
17	4	A Different Beat	Boyzone	Polydor	5		
18	-	Saturday Night	Suede	Nude	1		
19	-	I Can Make You Feel Good	Kavana	Nemesis	3		F
20	-	Come Back Brighter	Reef	Sony	2		

This Mnth	Prev Mnth	Title	Artist	Label	Wks	(US 20 Pos)	
1	15	Where Do You Go	No Mercy	Arista	12	(5)	F
2	9	Your Woman	White Town	Chrysalis	5	(23)	F L
3	-	Ain't Nobody	LL Cool J	Geffen	4	(46)	
4	8	Don't Let Go (Love)	En Vogue	East West America	10	(2)	
5	-	Discotheque	U2	Island	3	(10)	
6	-	Beetlebum	Blur	Food	2		
7	7	Say What You Want	Texas	Mercury	6		
8	-	Don't Speak	No Doubt	Interscope	11		F
9	-	Older/I Can't Make You Love Me	George Michael	Virgin	2		
10	-	Nancy Boy	Placebo	Elevator Music	3		F
11	-	Clementine	Mark Owen	RCA	3		L
12	-	Remember Me	Blue Boy	Pharm	8		F L
13	-	I Shot The Sheriff	Warren G	Def Jam	3	(20)	
14	-	Toxygene	Orb	Island	2		
15	-	The Day We Find Love	911	Ginga	2		
16	-	Barrel Of A Gun	Depeche Mode	Mute	1		
17	-	Do You Know	Michelle Gayle	RCA	2		
18	-	Walk On By	Gabrielle	Go. Beat	2		L
19	-	Ain't Talkin' 'Bout Dub	Apollo Four Forty	Stealth Sonic	3		F L
20	-	Da Funk/Musique	Daft Punk	Virgin	2	(61)	F

◆ Madonna took the song 'Don't Cry For Me Argentina' into the UK Top 5 for the third time, and all the way to the top of the European chart. It was, perhaps surprisingly, the first recording of an Andrew Lloyd Webber song to reach the US Top 10. The track was taken from the soundtrack album to her film Evita, which gave the recent mum her fifth UK No. 1.

◆ Among the acts returning to the Top 20 singles chart after a notable absence were British bands Texas, Depeche Mode and the Bee Gees.

1997

March 1997

This Mnth	Prev Mnth	Title	Artist	Label	Wks	(US 20 Pos)	
1	8	Don't Speak	No Doubt	Interscope	11		F
2	-	Encore Une Fois	Sash!	Multiply	10		F
3	-	Mama/Who Do You Think You Are	Spice Girls	Virgin	7		
4	1	Where Do You Go	No Mercy	Arista	12	(5)	F
5	-	Alone	Bee Gees	Polydor	5	(28)	
6	-	Hush	Kula Shaker	Columbia	3		L
7	-	Rumble In The Jungle	Fugees	Mercury	4		L
8	-	You Got The Love	Source Featuring Candi Staton	React	3		L
9	-	Don't You Love Me	Eternal	EMI	3		
10	-	Isn't It A Wonder	Boyzone	Polydor	3		
11	-	If I Never See You Again	Wet Wet Wet	Precious Org.	3		
12	-	I Believe I Can Fly	R. Kelly	Jive	11	(2)	
13	4	Don't Let Go (Love)	En Vogue	East West America	10	(2)	
14	-	Fresh	Gina G	Eternal	3		
15	-	Anywhere For You	Backstreet Boys	Jive	2		
16	12	Remember Me	Blue Boy	Pharm	8		F L
17	-	Flash	BBE	Positiva	2		L
18	-	Natural	Peter Andre	Mushroom	2		
19	-	Swallowed	Bush	Interscope	2		F L
20	-	Love Guaranteed	Damage	Big Life	2		

April 1997

This Mnth	Prev Mnth	Title	Artist	Label	Wks	(US 20 Pos)	
1	12	I Believe I Can Fly	R. Kelly	Jive	11	(2)	
2	1	Don't Speak	No Doubt	Interscope	11		F
3	-	Belissima	DJ Quicksilver	Positiva	12		F
4	3	Mama/Who Do You Think You Are	Spice Girls	Virgin	7		
5	-	Block Rockin' Beats	Chemical Brothers	Virgin	3		
6	-	Richard III	Supergrass	Parlophone	2		
7	-	Song 2	Blur	Food	2		
8	-	The Saint	Orbital	ffrr	2		L
9	-	Underwater Love	Smoke City	Jive	3		F L
10	-	Old Before I Die	Robbie Williams	RCA	3		
11	-	North Country Boy	Charlatans	Beggars Banquet	2		
12	-	Ready Or Not	Course	The Brothers	4		F
13	-	Staring At The Sun	U2	Island	2	(26)	
14	-	It's No Good	Depeche Mode	Mute	2	(38)	L
15	2	Encore Une Fois	Sash!	Multiply	10		F
16	-	You Might Need Somebody	Shola Ama	WEA	8		F
17	-	Around The World	Daft Punk	Virgin	2	(61)	L
18	-	Don't Leave Me	Blackstreet	Interscope	5		
19	-	Free Me	Cast	Polydor	2		
20	-	Hit 'Em High (The Monstars' Anthem)	B Real/Busta Rhymes/ Coolio/LL Cool J/M. Man	Atlantic	2		F L

◆ It was announced that producer Frank Farian had sold over 80 million records around the globe. The German, who had previously given the world Boney M and Milli Vanilli, was now producing the Cuban-American pop trio, No Mercy.

◆ Jyoti Mishra (aka White Town) was the first British-based solo artist to enter the chart at No. 1 with a debut hit. The Indian born Mishra, who recorded 'Your Woman' in his bedroom, was unkindly tagged "The nerd from nowhere" by the media.

1997

This Mnth	Prev Mnth	Title	Artist	Label	Wks	(US 20 Pos)	
1	-	Lovefool	Cardigans	Stockholm	7		F L
2	1	I Believe I Can Fly	R. Kelly	Jive	11	(2)	
3	16	You Might Need Somebody	Shola Ama	WEA	8		F
4	-	You Are Not Alone	Olive	RCA	6	(56)	F
5	3	Belissima	DJ Quicksilver	Positiva	12		F
6	-	Love Won't Wait	Gary Barlow	RCA	3		
7	-	Wonderful Tonight	Damage	Big Life	4		L
8	-	Time To Say Goodbye (Con Te Partiro)	Sarah Brightman & Andrea Bocelli	Coalition	8		L
9	-	Blood On The Dance Floor	Michael Jackson	Epic	2	(42)	
10	-	Love Shine A Light	Katrina & The Waves	Eternal	4		L
11	-	Bodyshakin'	911	Virgin	4		
12	-	Star People '97	George Michael	Virgin	2		
13	-	I Wanna Be The Only One	Eternal Featuring Bebe Winans	EMI	10		
14	-	Love Is The Law	Seahorses	Geffen	2		F
15	-	Please Don't Go	No Mercy	Arista	3	(21)	
16	-	I'll Be There For You	Rembrandts	East West	5	(17)	L
17	-	Closer Than Close	Rosie Gaines	Big Bang	7		F L
18	-	I'm A Man Not A Boy	North & South	RCA	3		F
19	-	Alright	Jamiroquai	Sony S^2	2	(78)	
20	18	Don't Leave Me	Blackstreet	Interscope	5		

This Mnth	Prev Mnth	Title	Artist	Label	Wks	(US 20 Pos)	
1	-	Mmmbop	Hanson	Mercury	8	(1)	F
2	13	I Wanna Be The Only One	Eternal Featuring Bebe Winans	EMI	10		
3	8	Time To Say Goodbye (Con Te Partiro)	Sarah Brightman & AndreaBocelli	Coalition	8		L
4	17	Closer Than Close	Rosie Gaines	Big Bang	7		F L
5	-	Free	Ultra Naté	AM:PM	12	(75)	F
6	-	Paranoid Android	Radiohead	Parlophone	2		
7	-	I'll Be Missing You	Puff Daddy & Faith Evans	Puff Daddy	15	(1)	G
8	-	Bitter Sweet Symphony	Verve	Hut	7	(12)	F
9	-	Midnight In Chelsea	Jon Bon Jovi	Mercury	2		
10	-	Coco Jamboo	Mr. President	WEA	6	(21)	F L
11	16	I'll Be There For You	Rembrandts	East West	5	(17)	L
12	-	Hundred Mile High City	Ocean Colour Scene	MCA	3		
13	4	You Are Not Alone	Olive	RCA	6	(56)	F
14	-	On Your Own	Blur	Food	1		
15	-	Love Rollercoaster	Red Hot Chili Peppers	Geffen	3		L
16	-	How High	Charlatans	Beggars Banquet	1		
17	-	Hard To Say I'm Sorry	Az Yet	Laface	2	(8)	F L
18	1	Lovefool	Cardigans	Stockholm	7		F L
19	-	Nothing Lasts Forever	Echo & The Bunnymen	London	3		L
20	-	I'll Be	Foxy Brown Featuring Jay Z	Def Jam	1	(7)	

◆ More records entered the UK Top 10 in their first week than ever before (on one week alone there were seven new entries!), and the average single only spent two weeks in the Top 20, another record. For 11 consecutive weeks a new single entered at No. 1.

◆ Among the quarter's No. 1 albums was **OK Computer** by the critically acclaimed Radiohead (it included the hit single 'Paranoid Android'), which sold over 135,000 in its first week, and the US chart topper, **Wu-Tang Forever**, by the Wu-Tang Clan.

This Mnth	Prev Mnth	Title	Artist	Label	Wks	(US 20 Pos)	
1	7	I'll Be Missing You	Puff Daddy & Faith Evans	Puff Daddy	15	(1)	G
2	-	Ecuador	Sash! Featuring Rodriguez	Multiply	7		
3	5	Free	Ultra Naté	AM:PM	12	(75)	F
4	-	D'You Know What I Mean?	Oasis	Creation	6		
5	8	Bitter Sweet Symphony	Verve	Virgin	7	(12)	F
6	1	Mmmbop	Hanson	Mercury	8	(1)	F
7	-	Freed From Desire	Gala	Big Life	10		F
8	-	C U When U Get There	Coolio Featuring 40 Thevz	Tommy Boy	7	(12)	
9	-	Just A Girl	No Doubt	Interscope	3	(23)	
10	-	The Journey	911	Virgin	2		
11	-	Something Goin' On	Todd Terry	Manifesto	5		
12	-	History/Ghosts	Michael Jackson	Epic	3		L
13	2	I Wanna Be The Only One	Eternal Featuring Bebe Winans	EMI	10		
14	-	Piece Of My Heart	Shaggy Featuring Marsha	Virgin	3	(72)	L
15	-	Ain't Nobody	Course	The Brothers	2		L
16	-	Blinded By The Sun	Seahorses	Geffen	2		
17	-	Gotham City	R. Kelly	Jive	3	(9)	L
18	10	Coco Jamboo	Mr. President	WEA	6	(21)	F L
19	-	A Change Would Do You Good	Sheryl Crow	A&M	1		
20	-	Lazy Days	Robbie Williams	Chrysalis	1		

This Mnth	Prev Mnth	Title	Artist	Label	Wks	(US 20 Pos)	
1	1	I'll Be Missing You	Puff Daddy & Faith Evans	Puff Daddy	15	(1)	G
2	7	Freed From Desire	Gala	Big Life	10		F
3	-	Everybody (Backstreet's Back)	Backstreet Boys	Jive	7	(8)	
4	-	Men In Black	Will Smith	Columbia	11		F L
5	-	Picture Of You	Boyzone	Polydor	5		
6	-	Bitch	Meredith Brooks	Capitol	6	(2)	FL
7	-	Mo Money Mo Problems	Notorious B.I.G. Featuring Puff Daddy & Mase	Puff Daddy	5	(1)	L
8	-	Tubthumping	Chumbawamba	EMI	14	(6)	F L
9	8	C U When U Get There	Coolio Featuring 40 Thevz	Tommy Boy	7	(12)	
10	-	All About Us	Peter Andre	Mushroom	3		
11	-	All I Wanna Do	Dannii Minogue	Eternal	4		
12	4	D'You Know What I Mean?	Oasis	Creation	6		
13	-	Yesterday	Wet Wet Wet	Precious Org.	3		L
14	-	Everything	Mary J. Blige	MCA	3	(24)	
15	-	You're The One I Love	Shola Ama	WEA	3		
16	3	Free	Ultra Naté	AM:PM	12	(75)	F
17	-	Black Eyed Boy	Texas	Mercury	3		
18	-	California Dreamin	Mamas & The Papas	MCA	3		L
19	-	Never Gonna Let You Go	Tina Moore	Delirious	9		F
20	-	Filmstar	Suede	Nude	1		L

◆ For the first time since 1981 the UK won the Eurovision Song Contest, and for the first time the singer was American born. 'Love Shine A Light' by British-based Katrina (Leskanich) & The Waves collected the most votes ever and outsold all the other winners from the 1990s.

◆ 'Mmmbop', the debut single from young long-haired American family trio Hanson topped the charts in the UK, US and many other territories including Australia (where they were the first act to enter at No. 1 with their debut single!). In the UK it sold more than 500,000 copies in just four weeks.

1997

This Mnth	Prev Mnth	Title	Artist	Label	Wks	(US 20 Pos)	
1	4	Men In Black	Will Smith	Columbia	11		F L
2	8	Tubthumping	Chumbawamba	EMI	14	(6)	F L
3	-	The Drugs Don't Work	Verve	Hut	7		
4	-	Candle In The Wind 1997/ Something About The...	Elton John	Rocket	17	(1)	P L
5	-	I Know Where It's At	All Saints	London	4	(36)	F L
6	1	I'll Be Missing You	Puff Daddy & Faith Evans	Puff Daddy	15	(1)	G
7	-	Honey	Mariah Carey	Columbia	4	(1)	L
8	-	You Have Been Loved/The Strangest Thing '97	George Michael	Virgin	3		L
9	-	Where's The Love	Hanson	Mercury	4		
10	-	Sunchyme	Dario G	Eternal	8		F L
11	19	Never Gonna Let You Go	Tina Moore	Delirious	9		F
12	-	(Un, Dos, Tres) Maria	Ricky Martin	Virgin	3		F L
13	-	Travellers Tune	Ocean Colour Scene	MCA	2		
14	-	Free	DJ Quicksilver	Positiva	2		L
15	-	Fix	Blackstreet	Interscope	2	(58)	
16	-	Live The Dream	Cast	Polydor	1		
17	2	Freed From Desire	Gala	Big Life	10		F
18	-	Samba De Janeiro	Bellini	Virgin	3		F L
19	-	Karma Police	Radiohead	Parlophone	1		
20	-	All Mine	Portishead	Go Beat	1		L

This Mnth	Prev Mnth	Title	Artist	Label	Wks	(US 20 Pos)	
1	4	Candle In The Wind 1997/ Something About The...	Elton John	Rocket	17	(1)	P L
2	10	Sunchyme	Dario G	Eternal	8		F L
3	-	As Long As You Love Me	Backstreet Boys	Jive	9		L
4	2	Tubthumping	Chumbawamba	EMI	14	(6)	F L
5	-	Stand By Me	Oasis	Creation	3		
6	-	Angel Of Mine	Eternal	EMI	6		L
7	-	Stay	Sash! Featuring La Trec	Multiply	6		
8	-	Got 'Til It's Gone	Janet Featuring Q-Tip And Joni Mitchell	Virgin	4		L
9	-	Arms Around The World	Louise	EMI	3		
10	-	Spice Up Your Life	Spice Girls	Virgin	6	(18)	
11	-	Barbie Girl	Aqua	Universal	13	(7)	F G L
12	-	Raincloud	Lighthouse Family	Wild Card	3		L
13	1	Men In Black	Will Smith	Columbia	11		F L
14	-	On Her Majesty's Secret Service	Propellerheads/David Arnold	East West	2		F
15	-	Just For You	M People	M People	3		L
16	-	Please	U2	Island	1		
17	-	You've Got A Friend	Brand New Heavies	London	4		L
18	11	Never Gonna Let You Go	Tina Moore	Delirious	9		F
19	3	The Drugs Don't Work	Verve	Hut	7		
20	-	U Sexy Thing	Clock	Media	5		

◆ Sean 'Puff Daddy' Coombs produced five of America's 10 No. 1 hits in 1997 and co-wrote and performed on three of them. He was the producer and artist on the most successful rap single ever, 'I'll Be Missing You', which sold over seven million worldwide.

◆ European dance acts continued to clock up major UK hit singles. Among the current chart makers were: German group Mr. President, fellow German Sash!, Italian act Gala, the Course from Holland, Turkish-born DJ Quicksilver and the multi-national group Bellini.

November 1997

This Mnth	Prev Mnth	Title	Artist	Label	Wks	(US 20 Pos)	
1	11	Barbie Girl	Aqua	Universal	13	(7)	F G
2	-	Torn	Natalie Imbruglia	RCA	13		F
3	1	Candle In The Wind 1997/ Something About The...	Elton John	Rocket	17	(1)	P L
4	10	Spice Up Your Life	Spice Girls	Virgin	6	(18)	
5	-	Tell Him	Barbra Streisand & Celine Dion	Epic	8		L
6	7	Stay	Sash! Featuring La Trec	Multiply	6		
7	3	As Long As You Love Me	Backstreet Boys	Jive	9		L
8	-	Never Ever	All Saints	London	17		G L
9	-	Perfect Day	Various	Chrysalis	11		FGL
10	-	Do Ya Think I'm Sexy?	N-Trance Featuring Rod Stewart	All Around The World	4		L
11	2	Sunchyme	Dario G	Eternal	8		F L
12	-	Wind Beneath My Wings	Steven Houghton	RCA	7		F L
13	-	Choose Life	PF Project Featuring Ewan McGregor	Positiva	4		F L
14	-	Party People...Friday Night	911	Ginga	2		L
15	-	I Will Come To You	Hanson	Mercury	2	(9)	L
16	-	You Sexy Thing	Hot Chocolate	EMI	3		L
17	-	Ain't That Just The Way	Lutricia McNeal	Wildstar	7	(63)	F L
18	-	Lonely	Peter Andre	Mushroom	1		
19	-	Open Road	Gary Barlow	RCA	2		L
20	-	James Bond Theme	Moby	Mute	2		L

December 1997

This Mnth	Prev Mnth	Title	Artist	Label	Wks	(US 20 Pos)	
1	9	Perfect Day	Various	Chrysalis	11		FGL
2	1	Barbie Girl	Aqua	Universal	13	(7)	F G
3	-	Teletubbies Say Eh-Oh!	Teletubbies	BBC Worldwide	6		FGL
4	-	Baby Can I Hold You/Shooting Star	Boyzone	Polydor	8		L
5	8	Never Ever	All Saints	London	17		L G
6	12	Wind Beneath My Wings	Steven Houghton	RCA	7		F L
7	2	Torn	Natalie Imbruglia	RCA	13		F
8	-	Together Again	Janet Jackson	Virgin	13	(1)	
9	-	Angels	Robbie Williams	Chrysalis	14		
10	-	Too Much	Spice Girls	Virgin	5	(9)	
11	5	Tell Him	Barbra Streisand & Celine Dion	Epic	8		L
12	3	Candle In The Wind 1997/ Something About The...	Elton John	Rocket	17	(1)	P L
13	17	Ain't That Just The Way	Lutricia McNeal	Wildstar	7	(63)	F L
14	-	Lucky Man	Verve	Hut	1		L
15	-	Slam Dunk (Da Funk)	5	RCA	5		F L
16	-	Sing Up For The Champions	Reds United	Music Collection	5		F L
17	-	Feel So Good	Mase	Puff Daddy	3	(5)	L
18	-	The Reason	Celine Dion	Epic	3		
19	-	Let A Boy Cry	Gala	Big Life	1		L
20	-	If God Will Send His Angels	U2	Island	1		L

◆ No single in history has sold as many copies as Elton John's tribute to Diana, Princess Of Wales, 'Candle In The Wind 1997'. Within three months of its release, it topped the chart in every corner of the world, and over 33 million copies were shipped out. It smashed sales records all over the globe; in the UK, 4.9 million copies were sold and in the US (where it was No. 1 longer than any previous UK recording) it was credited with a record shattering 8 million sales. By mid-December the record had earned £20 million.

1998

This Mnth	Prev Mnth	Title	Artist	Label	Wks	(US 20 Pos)	
1	5	Never Ever	All Saints	London	17		G L
2	1	Perfect Day	Various	Chrysalis	11		FGL
3	8	Together Again	Janet Jackson	Virgin	13	(1)	
4	10	Too Much	Spice Girls	Virgin	5	(9)	
5	9	Angels	Robbie Williams	Chrysalis	14		
6	-	High	Lighthouse Family	Polydor	8		L
7	-	Bamboogie	Bamboo	VC	5		FL
8	-	Renegade Master 98	Wildchild	Hi-Life	5		L
9	-	All Around The World	Oasis	Creation	3		L
10	3	Teletubbies Say Eh-Oh!	Teletubbies	BBC Worldwide	6		FGL
11	-	You Make Me Wanna	Usher	Laface	5	(2)	FL
12	7	Torn	Natalie Imbruglia	RCA	13		F
13	-	Avenging Angels	Space	Gut	3		
14	-	Mulder And Scully	Catatonia	Blanco Y Negro	4		FL
15	-	No Surprises	Radiohead	Parlophone	1		L
16	-	My Star	Ian Brown	Polydor	2		F L
17	2	Barbie Girl	Aqua	Universal	13	(7)	F G
18	4	Baby Can I Hold You/ Shooting Star	Boyzone	Polydor	8		L
19	12	Candle In The Wind 1997/ Something About The...	Elton John	Rocket	17	(1)	P L
20	-	Amnesia	Chumbawamba	EMI	2		L

This Mnth	Prev Mnth	Title	Artist	Label	Wks	(US 20 Pos)	
1	-	Doctor Jones	Aqua	Universal	7		L
2	1	Never Ever	All Saints	London	17		G L
3	-	Gettin' Jiggy Wit It	Will Smith	Columbia	6	(1)	L
4	5	Angels	Robbie Williams	Chrysalis	14		
5	11	You Make Me Wanna	Usher	Laface	5	(2)	F L
6	-	My Heart Will Go On	Celine Dion	Epic	14	(1)	G L
7	-	All I Have To Give	Backstreet Boys	Jive	3		L
8	-	Cleopatra's Theme	Cleopatra	WEA	4		F L
9	6	High	Lighthouse Family	Polydor	8		L
10	-	Brimful Of Asha	Cornershop	Wiiija	8		F L
11	-	Let Me Show You	Camisra	VC	3		F L
12	-	Truly Madly Deeply	Savage Garden	Columbia	*14	(1)	L
13	3	Together Again	Janet Jackson	Virgin	13	(1)	
14	-	When I Need You	Will Mellor	Unity	2		F L
15	14	Mulder And Scully	Catatonia	Blanco Y Negro	4		F L
16	-	Be Alone No More	Another Level	Northwestside	3		F L
17	-	Crazy Little Party Girl	Aaron Carter	Ultra Pop	2		L
18	7	Bamboogie	Bamboo	VC	5		F L
19	-	You're Still The One	Shania Twain	Mercury	4	(2)	F L
20	-	Solomon Bites The Worm	Bluetones	Superior Quality	1		L

◆ 1998 Brit winners included Finley Quaye, Shola Ama, the Verve (three awards including Best Album for Urban Hymns), the Prodigy, U2, the Stereophonics and Chumbawamba, whose Danbert Nobacon (AKA Nigel Hunter) threw a bucket of iced water over deputy Prime Minister, John Prescott.

◆ Celine Dion became the first woman to sell over a million copies of two separate singles in the UK. The latest, 'My Heart Will Go On', topped the charts in most territories. It was featured on her No. 1 album, **Let's Talk About Love**, (her second in a row to sell over 20 million copies globally) and on the record breaking **Titanic** soundtrack.

March 1998

This Mnth	Prev Mnth	Title	Artist	Label	Wks	(US 20 Pos)	
1	6	My Heart Will Go On	Celine Dion	Epic	14	(1)	G L
2	-	Frozen	Madonna	Maverick	7	(2)	L
3	10	Brimful Of Asha	Cornershop	Wiiija	8		F L
4	-	It's Like That	Run-DMC Vs Jason Nevins	Sm:)e Communications	10		G L
5	12	Truly Madly Deeply	Savage Garden	Columbia	*14	(1)	L
6	-	Stop	Spice Girls	Virgin	6		L
7	-	Big Mistake	Natalie Imbruglia	RCA	3		L
8	-	The Ballad Of Tom Jones	Space With Cerys Of Catatonia	Gut	3		L
9	-	When The Lights Go Out	5	RCA	4		L
10	-	How Do I Live	Leann Rimes	Curb	*13	(2)	F L
11	-	Say What You Want/Insane	Texas Featuring Wu Tang Clan	Mercury	2		L
12	1	Doctor Jones	Aqua	Universal	7		L
13	-	Let Me Entertain You	Robbie Williams	Chrysalis	5		L
14	-	Everlasting Love	Cast From Casualty	Warner.esp	2		F L
15	-	No, No, No	Destiny's Child	Columbia	3	(3)	F L
16	-	Here's Where The Story Ends	Tin Tin Out Featuring Shelley Nelson	VC	5		L
17	-	Show Me Love	Robyn	RCA	2	(7)	F L
18	16	Be Alone No More	Another Level	Northwestside	3		F L
19	-	Angel St	M People	M People	2		L
20	-	Uh La La La	Alexia	Dance Pool	3		F L

April 1998

This Mnth	Prev Mnth	Title	Artist	Label	Wks	(US 20 Pos)	
1	4	It's Like That	Run-DMC Vs Jason Nevins	Sm:)e Communications	10		G L
2	1	My Heart Will Go On	Celine Dion	Epic	14	(1)	G L
3	-	La Primavera	Sash!	Multiply	5		L
4	5	Truly Madly Deeply	Savage Garden	Columbia	*14	(1)	L
5	-	Turn It Up/Fire It Up	Busta Rhymes	Elektra	5		L
6	-	Kiss The Rain	Billie Myers	Universal	5	(15)	F L
7	13	Let Me Entertain You	Robbie Williams	Chrysalis	5		L
8	10	How Do I Live	Leann Rimes	Curb	*14	(2)	L
9	-	All I Want Is You	911	Virgin	3		L
10	-	I Get Lonely	Janet Jackson	Virgin	4		L
11	6	Stop	Spice Girls	Virgin	6		L
12	-	Feel It	Tamperer Featuring Maya	Pepper	*6		F L
13	-	Found A Cure	Ultra Nate	AM:PM	3		L
14	-	Give A Little Love	Daniel O'Donnell	Ritz	2		L
15	16	Here's Where The Story Ends	Tin Tin Out Featuring Shelley Nelson	VC	5		L
16	-	All My Life	K-Ci & Jojo	MCA	4	(1)	F L
17	15	No, No, No	Destiny's Child	Columbia	3	(3)	F L
18	-	Kung-Fu	187 Lockdown	East West	1		L
19	-	Say You Do	Ultra	East West	2		F L
20	-	All That Matters	Louise	EMI	2		L

◆ First the good news: Elton John received a knighthood from the Queen and Petula Clark was awarded a CBE. Then the bad: recent deaths included former hitmakers Michael Hutchence (INXS), John Denver, Austria's biggest star Falco, pianist Floyd Cramer, the 1950s top songwriter Bob Merrill and R&R legend Carl Perkins. Also Carl Wilson (Beach Boys), drummer Cozy Powell, Sonny Bono (Sonny & Cher), Linda McCartney, reggae rude boy Judge Dread and "The First Lady of Country Music", Tammy Wynette.

Listings by TITLE

Title	Artist
Abacab	Genesis
Abba-Esque (EP)	Erasure
ABC	Jackson Five
Abracadabra	Steve Miller Band
Abraham Martin & John	Marvin Gaye
Absolute Beginners	David Bowie
Absolute Beginners	Jam
Absolutely Fabulous	Absolutely Fabulous
Achy Breaky Heart	Billy Ray Cyrus
Activ 8 (Come With Me)	Altern 8
Addams Groove	Hammer
Addicted To Love	Robert Palmer
Adoration Waltz	David Whitfield
Africa	Toto
African Waltz	Johnny Dankworth
After All	Frank And Walters
After The Love Has Gone	Earth, Wind & Fire
Agadoo	Black Lace
Again	Janet Jackson
Again And Again	Status Quo
Against All Odds (Take A Look At Me Now)	Phil Collins
Ain't Gonna Bump No More (With No Big Fat Woman)	Joe Tex
Ain't Gonna Kiss Ya (E.P.)	Searchers
Ain't Got No - I Got Life	Nina Simone
Ain't It Fun	Guns N' Roses
Ain't Misbehavin'	Tommy Bruce & The Bruisers
Ain't No Doubt	Jimmy Nail
Ain't No Love (Ain't No Use)	Sub Sub Featuring Melanie Williams
Ain't No Mountain High Enough	Diana Ross
Ain't No Pleasing You	Chas & Dave
Ain't No Stoppin'	Enigma
Ain't No Stoppin' Us Now	McFadden & Whitehead
Ain't No Sunshine	Michael Jackson
Ain't Nobody	Course
Ain't Nobody	LL Cool J
Ain't Nobody	Rufus & Chaka Khan
Ain't Nothin' But A Houseparty	Showstoppers
Ain't Nothing Goin' On But The Rent	Gwen Guthrie
Ain't Talkin' 'Bout Dub	Apollo Four Forty
Ain't That A Shame	Pat Boone
Ain't That Funny	Jimmy Justice
Ain't That Just The Way	Lutricia McNeal
Ain't 2 Proud 2 Beg	TLC
The Air That I Breathe	Hollies
Airport	Motors
Albatross	Fleetwood Mac
Alfie	Cilla Black
Alice I Want You Just For Me	Full Force
Alive And Kicking	Simple Minds
All About Us	Peter Andre
All Alone Am I	Brenda Lee
All Along The Watchtower	Jimi Hendrix Experience
All Around My Hat	Steeleye Span
All Around The World	Oasis
All Around The World	Lisa Stansfield
All Because Of You	Geordie
All By Myself	Celine Dion
All Cried Out	Alison Moyet

Title	Artist
All Day And All Of The Night	Kinks
All Day And All Of The Night	Stranglers
All For Love	Bryan Adams/Rod Stewart/Sting
All For Love	Color Me Badd
All I Ask Of You	Cliff Richard
All I Ever Need Is You	Sonny & Cher
All I Have To Do Is Dream	Everly Brothers
All I Have To Do Is Dream	Bobbie Gentry & Glen Campbell
All I Have To Give	Backstreet Boys
All I Really Want To Do	Byrds
All I Really Want To Do	Cher
All I See Is You	Dusty Springfield
All I Wanna Do	Sheryl Crow
All I Wanna Do	Dannii Minogue
All I Wanna Do Is Make Love To You	Heart
All I Want For Christmas Is A Beatle	Dora Bryan
All I Want For Christmas Is You	Mariah Carey
All I Want Is You	911
All I Want Is You	Roxy Music
All I Want Is You	U2
All Kinds Of Everything	Dana
All Mine	Portishead
All My Life	K-Ci & Jojo
All My Love	Cliff Richard
All Night Long	Rainbow
All Night Long (All Night)	Lionel Richie
(All Of A Sudden) My Heart Sings	Paul Anka
All Of Me Loves All Of You	Bay City Rollers
All Of My Heart	ABC
All Of My Life	Diana Ross
All Or Nothing	Small Faces
All Out Of Love	Air Supply
All Right Now	Free
All She Wants Is	Duran Duran
All Shook Up	Elvis Presley
All Star Hit Parade	Various Artists
All Stood Still	Ultravox
All That Matters	Louise
All That She Wants	Ace Of Base
All The Love In The World	Dionne Warwick
All The Man That I Need	Whitney Houston
All The Things She Said	Simple Minds
All The Way	Frank Sinatra
All The Way From Memphis	Mott The Hoople
All The Young Dudes	Mott The Hoople
All Together Now	Farm
All You Need Is Love	Beatles
Ally's Tartan Army	Andy Cameron
Almaz	Randy Crawford
Almost There	Andy Williams
Almost Unreal	Roxette
Alone	Bee Gees
Alone	Petula Clark
Alone	Heart
Alone Again (Naturally)	Gilbert O'Sullivan
Alone Without You	King
Alphabet Street	Prince
Alright	Jamiroquai
Alright	Supergrass

Title	Artist
Alright Alright Alright	Mungo Jerry
Also Sprach Zarathustra (2001)	Deodata
Alternate Title	Monkees
Always	Atlantic Starr
Always	Bon Jovi
Always	Erasure
Always And Forever	Heatwave
Always Be My Baby	Mariah Carey
Always Breaking My Heart	Belinda Carlisle
Always Look On The Bright Side	Monty Python
Always On My Mind	Pet Shop Boys
Always On My Mind	Elvis Presley
Always There	Incognito Featuring Jocelyn Brown
Always There	Marti Webb
Always Yours	Gary Glitter
Am I That Easy To Forget	Engelbert Humperdinck
Amanda	Stuart Gillies
Amateur Hour	Sparks
Amazing Grace	Judy Collins
Amazing Grace	Royal Scots Dragoon Guards
America: What Time Is Love?	KLF
American Pie	Don McLean
An American Trilogy	Elvis Presley
Americanos	Holly Johnson
Amigo	Black Slate
Amityville (The House On The Hill)	Lovebug Starski
Amnesia	Chumbawamba
Among My Souvenirs	Connie Francis
Amoureuse	Kiki Dee
Anasthasia	T99
And I Love You So	Perry Como
And The Bands Played On	Saxon
And The Beat Goes On	Whispers
And The Heavens Cried	Anthony Newley
Anfield Rap (Red Machine In Full Effect)	Liverpool F.C.
Angel	Madonna
Angel	Simply Red
Angel	Rod Stewart
Angel Eyes	Abba
Angel Eyes	Roxy Music
Angel Eyes (Home And Away)	Wet Wet Wet
Angel Face	Glitter Band
Angel Fingers	Wizzard
Angel Of Harlem	U2
Angel Of Mine	Eternal
Angel St	M People
Angela Jones	Michael Cox
Angelo	Brotherhood Of Man
Angels	Robbie Williams
Angie	Rolling Stones
Angie Baby	Helen Reddy
Animal	Def Leppard
Animal Nitrate	Suede
Annie I'm Not Your Daddy	Kid Creole & The Coconuts
Annie's Song	John Denver
Annie's Song	James Galway
The Anniversary Waltz - Part 1	Status Quo
Another Brick In The Wall (Pt. 2)	Pink Floyd
Another Day	Paul McCartney

Title	Artist	Title	Artist	Title	Artist
Another Day	Whigfield	Autobahn	Kraftwerk	Ballad Of Bonnie & Clyde	Georgie Fame
Another Day In Paradise	Phil Collins	Automatic	Pointer Sisters	The Ballad Of Davy Crockett	
Another One Bites The Dust	Queen	Automatic Lover	Dee D. Jackson		Tennessee Ernie Ford
Another Rock And Roll Christmas		Automatically Sunshine	Supremes	The Ballad Of Davy Crockett	Bill Hayes
	Gary Glitter	Autumn Almanac	Kinks	Ballad Of John And Yoko	Beatles
Another Step (Closer To You)		Avenging Angels	Space	Ballad Of Paladin	Duane Eddy
	Kim Wilde & Junior	Axel F	Clock	The Ballad Of Tom Jones	Space With
Another Tear Falls	Walker Brothers	Axel F	Harold Faltermeyer		Cerys Of Catatonia
Another Time Another Place	Engelbert	Ay Ay Ay Ay Moosey	Modern Romance	Ballroom Blitz	Sweet
	Humperdinck	Babe	Styx	Bamboogie	Bamboo
Answer Me	Frankie Laine	Babe	Take That	Banana Boat Song	Shirley Bassey
Answer Me	David Whitfield	Babooshka	Kate Bush	Banana Boat Song	Harry Belafonte
Ant Rap	Adam & The Ants	Baby Baby	Corona	Banana Republic	Boomtown Rats
Anthem	N-Joi	Baby Baby	Amy Grant	Banana Rock	Wombles
Antmusic	Adam & The Ants	Baby Baby	Frankie Lymon	Banana Splits (Tra La La Song)	
Any Dream Will Do	Jason Donovan		& The Teenagers		Dickies
Any Time, Any Place	Janet Jackson	Baby Can I Hold You	Boyzone	Band Of Gold	Don Cherry
Any Way That You Want Me	Troggs	Baby Come Back	Pato Banton	Band Of Gold	Freda Payne
Anyone Can Fall In Love	Anita Dobson	Baby Come Back	Equals	Band On The Run	Paul McCartney
Anyone Who Had A Heart	Cilla Black	Baby, Come To Me	Patti Austin	Get It On	T. Rex
Anything	3T	(duet with James Ingram)		Bang Bang	B.A. Robertson
Anything	Culture Beat	Baby Don't Change Your Mind	Gladys	Bang Bang (My Baby Shot Me Down)	
Anything For You	Gloria Estefan		Knight & The Pips		Cher
	& The Miami Sound Machine	Baby Don't Go	Sonny & Cher	(Bang Zoom) Let's Go Go	Real Roxanne
Anytime You Need A Friend		Baby Face	Little Richard		With Hitman Howie
	Mariah Carey	Baby I Don't Care	Buddy Holly	Bangin' Man	Slade
Anyway Anyhow Anywhere	Who	Baby I Don't Care	Transvision Vamp	Bangla Desh	George Harrison
Anywhere For You	Backstreet Boys	Baby I Know	Rubettes	Bank Robber	Clash
Anywhere Is	Enya	Baby I Love You	Dave Edmunds	Banks Of The Ohio	Olivia Newton-John
Apache	Shadows	Baby I Love You	Ronettes	Banner Man	Blue Mink
Ape Man	Kinks	Baby I Love You, OK	Kenny	Barbados	Typically Tropical
Apple Blossom Time	Rosemary June	Baby I Love Your Way	Big Mountain	Barbara Ann	Beach Boys
Applejack	Jet Harris & Tony Meehan	Baby I'm A Want You	Bread	Barbie Girl	Aqua
April Love	Pat Boone	Baby It's You	Beatles	Barcelona	Monserrat Caballe
April Skies	Jesus And Mary Chain	Baby Jane	Rod Stewart	Barcelona	Freddie Mercury
Are 'Friends' Electric	Tubeway Army	Baby Jump	Mungo Jerry		& Monserrat Caballe
Are You Gonna Go My Way		Baby Love	Dannii Minogue	Barrel Of A Gun	Depeche Mode
	Lenny Kravitz	Baby Love	Supremes	Basket Case	Green Day
Are You Lonesome Tonight ?		Baby Lover	Petula Clark	Batdance	Prince
	Elvis Presley	Baby Make It Soon	Marmalade	Battle Of New Orleans	Lonnie Donegan
Are You Mine?	Bros	Baby, Now That I Found You		Be Aggressive	Faith No More
Are You Ready To Rock	Wizzard		Foundations	Be Alone No More	Another Level
Are You Sure	Allisons	Baby Please Don't Go	Them	Be Mine	Lance Fortune
Argentine Melody (Cancion De		Baby Sittin' Boogie	Buzz Clifford	Be My Baby	Vanessa Paradis
Argentina)	San Jose	Baby Stop Crying	Bob Dylan	Be My Baby	Ronettes
Aria	Acker Bilk	Babylon's Burning	Ruts	Be My Girl	Jim Dale
Arms Around The World	Louise	Bachelor Boy	Cliff Richard	Be My Guest	Fats Domino
Arms Of Mary	Sutherland Brothers	Back And Forth	Cameo	Be Quick Or Be Dead	Iron Maiden
	And Quiver	Back For Good	Take That	Beach Baby	First Class
Army Game	TV Cast	Back Home	England World Cup Squad	Beach Boy Gold	Gidea Park
Around The World	Bing Crosby	Back Off Boogaloo	Ringo Starr	Beat Dis	Bomb The Bass
Around The World	Daft Punk	Back Street Luv	Curved Air	Beat It	Michael Jackson
Around The World	East 17	Back To Life (However Do You Want		Beat Surrender	Jam
Around The World	Gracie Fields	Me)	Soul II Soul (featuring Caron	Beat The Clock	Sparks
Around The World	Ronnie Hilton		Wheeler)	Beatles Movie Medley	Beatles
Art For Art's Sake	10cc	Back To The Sixties	Tight Fit	Beatnik Fly	Johnny & The Hurricanes
Arthur Daley ('E's Alright)	Firm	Back Together Again	Roberta Flack &	Beautiful Noise	Neil Diamond
Arthur's Theme (Best That You Can Do)			Donny Hathaway	Beautiful Ones	Suede
	Christopher Cross	Backstage	Gene Pitney	Beauty & The Beast	Celine Dion
As I Love You	Shirley Bassey	Bad	Michael Jackson		& Peabo Bryson
As Long As He Needs Me		Bad Actress	Terrorvision	Because I Love You (The Postman	
	Shirley Bassey	Bad Bad Boy	Nazareth	Song)	Stevie B
As Long As You Love Me	Backstreet	Bad Boy	Marty Wilde	Because Of Love	Janet Jackson
	Boys	Bad Boys	Wham!	Because The Night	Patti Smith Group
As Tears Go By	Marianne Faithfull	Bad Girl	Madonna	Because They're Young	Duane Eddy
As Usual	Brenda Lee	Bad Moon Rising	Creedence	Because You Loved Me	Celine Dion
As You Like It	Adam Faith		Clearwater Revival	Bed Sitter	Soft Cell
Ashes To Ashes	David Bowie	Bad Old Days	Coco	Beds Are Burning	Midnight Oil
At The Club	Drifters	Bad To Me	Billy J. Kramer	Bedtime Story	Madonna
At The Hop	Danny & The Juniors		& The Dakotas	Beetlebum	Blur
Atlantis	Shadows	Baggy Trousers	Madness	Before	Pet Shop Boys
Atmosphere	Russ Abbot	Baker Street	Gerry Rafferty	Beg Steal Or Borrow	New Seekers
Atomic	Blondie	Baker Street	Undercover	Begin The Beguine (Volver A Empezar)	
Attention To Me	Nolans	Ball Of Confusion	Temptations		Julio Iglesias
Australia	Manic Street Preachers	Ball Park Incident	Wizzard		

Title	Artist
Behind A Painted Smile	Isley Brothers
Behind The Groove	Teena Marie
Bein' Boiled	Human League
Being With You	Smokey Robinson
Belfast	Boney M
Belfast Child	Simple Minds
Believe	Elton John
Believe In Me	Utah Saints
Belissima	DJ Quicksilver
Bell Bottom Blues	Alma Cogan
Ben	Michael Jackson
Ben	Marti Webb
Bend It	Dave Dee, Dozy, Beaky, Mick & Tich
Bend Me Shape Me	Amen Corner
Bernadette	Four Tops
The Best	Tina Turner
The Best Disco In Town	Ritchie Family
Best In Me	Let Loose
The Best Of Me	Cliff Richard
Best Of My Love	Emotions
Best Of You	Kenny Thomas
The Best Thing That Ever Happened	Gladys Knight & The Pips
The Best Things In Life Are Free	Luther Vandross & Janet Jackson
Best Years Of Our Lives	Modern Romance
Bette Davis Eyes	Kim Carnes
Better Do It Salsa	Gibson Brothers
Better Love Next Time	Dr. Hook
Better The Devil You Know	Kylie Minogue
Betty, Betty, Betty	Lonnie Donegan
Beyond The Reef	Elvis Presley
Beyond The Sea (La Mer)	Bobby Darin
Beyond The Stars	David Whitfield
Bicycle Race	Queen
Big Apple	Kajagoogoo
Big Area	Then Jericho
Big Bad John	Jimmy Dean
Big Eight	Judge Dread
Big Fun	Gap Band
Big Fun	Inner City
Big Girls Don't Cry	Four Seasons
Big Hunk O' Love	Elvis Presley
Big In Japan	Alphaville
Big Log	Robert Plant
Big Love	Fleetwood Mac
Big Man	Four Preps
Big Mistake	Natalie Imbruglia
Big Seven	Judge Dread
Big Ship	Cliff Richard
Big Six	Judge Dread
Big Ten	Judge Dread
Big Time	Peter Gabriel
Big Yellow Taxi	Joni Mitchell
Billie Jean	Michael Jackson
Billy, Don't Be A Hero	Paper Lace
Bimbo	Ruby Wright
Bionic Santa	Chris Hill
Bird Dog	Everly Brothers
Bird Of Paradise	Snowy White
Birdhouse In Your Soul	They Might Be Giants
The Birdie Song (Birdie Dance)	Tweets
Bitch	Meredith Brooks
Bits And Pieces	Dave Clark Five
Bitter Sweet Symphony	Verve
The Bitterest Pill (I Ever Had To Swallow)	Jam
Black And White	Greyhound
Black Betty	Ram Jam
Black Eyed Boy	Texas
The Black Eyed Boys	Paper Lace

Title	Artist
Black Hills Of Dakota	Doris Day
Black Hole Sun	Soundgarden
Black Is Black	Los Bravos
Black Is Black	La Belle Epoque
Black Night	Deep Purple
Black Or White	Michael Jackson
Black Pearl	Horace Faith
Black Skin Blue Eyed Boys	Equals
Black Superman (Muhammad Ali)	Johnny Wakelin & The Kinshasa Band
Black Velvet	Alannah Myles
Black Velvet Band	Dubliners
Blackberry Way	Move
Blame It On The Boogie	Big Fun
Blame It On The Boogie	Jacksons
Blame It On The Pony Express	Johnny Johnson & The Bandwagon
Blanket On The Ground	Billie Jo Spears
Blaze Of Glory	Jon Bon Jovi
Bless You	Tony Orlando
Blind Vision	Blancmange
Blinded By The Light	Manfred Mann's Earth Band
Blinded By The Sun	Seahorses
Block Rockin' Beats	Chemical Brothers
Blockbuster	Sweet
Blood On The Dance Floor	Michael Jackson
Bloodnok's Rock 'n' Roll Call	Goons
A Blossom Fell	Nat 'King' Cole
A Blossom Fell	Ronnie Hilton
A Blossom Fell	Dickie Valentine
Blow The House Down	Living In A Box
Blow Your Mind	Jamiroquai
Blowin' In The Wind	Peter, Paul & Mary
Blowing Wild	Frankie Laine
Blue Angel	Roy Orbison
Blue Bayou	Roy Orbison
Blue Christmas	Elvis Presley
Blue Eyes	Elton John
Blue Eyes	Don Partridge
Blue Guitar	Justin Hayward & John Lodge
Blue Is The Colour	Chelsea F.C.
Blue Jean	David Bowie
Blue Monday	New Order
Blue Moon	John Alford
Blue Moon	Marcels
Blue Moon	Elvis Presley
Blue Room	Orb
Blue Savannah	Erasure
Blue Star	Cyril Stapleton
Blue Suede Shoes	Carl Perkins
Blue Suede Shoes	Elvis Presley
Blue Velvet	Bobby Vinton
Blueberry Hill	Fats Domino
Bluebottle Blues	Goons
Blurred	Pianoman
Bo Diddley	Buddy Holly
The Boat That I Row	Lulu
Bobby's Girl	Susan Maughan
Body And Soul	Mai Tai
Body Rock	Maria Vidal
Body Talk	Imagination
Bodyshakin'	911
Bohemian Rhapsody	Queen
The Bomb! (These Sounds Fall Into My Mind)	Bucketheads
Boney M Megamix	Boney M
Bonnie Came Back	Duane Eddy
Bony Moronie	Larry Williams
Boogie Nights	Heatwave
Boogie On Reggae Woman	Stevie Wonder

Title	Artist
Boogie Oogie Oogie	Taste Of Honey
Boogie Wonderland	Earth, Wind & Fire With The Emotions
The Book	David Whitfield
Book Of Days	Enya
Book Of Love	Mudlarks
Boom Bang-A-Bang	Lulu
Boom Boom Boom	Outhere Brothers
Boom! Shake That Room	Jazzy Jeff & Fresh Prince
Boombastic	Shaggy
Boops (Here To Go)	Sly And Robbie
Borderline	Madonna
Born Free	Vic Reeves/The Roman Numerals
Born In The U.S.A.	Bruce Springsteen
Born Slippy	Underworld
Born To Be Alive	Patrick Hernandez
Born To Be With You	Chordettes
Born To Be With You	Dave Edmunds
Born Too Late	Poni-Tails
Born With A Smile On My Face	Stephanie De Sykes
Boss Drum	Shamen
Both Sides Of The Story	Phil Collins
The Bouncer	Kicks Like A Mule
The Boxer	Simon & Garfunkel
Boxer Beat	Joboxers
Boy From New York City	Darts
A Boy From Nowhere	Tom Jones
A Boy Named Sue	Johnny Cash
Boys	Kim Wilde
The Boys Are Back In Town	Thin Lizzy
Boys Cry	Eden Kane
Boys Keep Swingin'	David Bowie
The Boys Of Summer	Don Henley
Boys (Summertime Love)	Sabrina
Brand New Key	Melanie
Brandy	Scott English
Brass In Pocket	Pretenders
Break Away	Beach Boys
Break Dance Party	Break Machine
Break My Stride	Matthew Wilder
Break The Rules	Status Quo
Breakaway	Tracey Ullman
Breakfast At Tiffany's	Deep Blue Something
Breakfast In America	Supertramp
Breakfast In Bed	UB40
Breakin' Down The Walls Of Heartache	Johnny Johnson & The Bandwagon
Breakin' In A Brand New Broken Heart	Connie Francis
Breakin'...There's No Stopping Us	Ollie & Jerry
Breaking The Law	Judas Priest
Breaking Up Is Hard To Do	Partridge Family
Breaking Up Is Hard To Do	Neil Sedaka
Breakout	Swing Out Sister
Breakthru'	Queen
Breath Of Life	Erasure
Breathe	Prodigy
Breathe Again	Toni Braxton
Breathless	Jerry Lee Lewis
The Breeze And I	Caterina Valente
Bridge Over Troubled Water	Simon & Garfunkel
Bridge To Your Heart	Wax
Bridget The Midget (The Queen Of The Blues)	Ray Stevens
Bright Eyes	Art Garfunkel
Brimful Of Asha	Cornershop
Bring A Little Water Sylvie	Lonnie Donegan

274

Title	Artist
Bring It On Home To Me	Animals
Bring It On Home To Me	Rod Stewart
Bring Me Edelweiss	Edelweiss
Bring Your Daughter To The Slaughter	Iron Maiden
Bringing On Back The Good Times	Love Affair
British Hustle	Hi Tension
The BRITS 1990	Various Artists
Broken Down Angel	Nazareth
Broken Wings	Mr. Mister
Broken Hearted Melody	Sarah Vaughan
Brontosaurus	Move
Brother Louie	Hot Chocolate
Brother Louie	Modern Talking
Brown Eyed Handsome Man	Buddy Holly
Brown Girl In The Ring	Boney M
Brown Sugar	Rolling Stones
Buddy	De La Soul
Buffalo Gals	Malcolm McLaren & The World's Famous Supreme
Buffalo Soldier	Bob Marley & The Wailers
Buffalo Stance	Neneh Cherry
Build Me Up Buttercup	Foundations
Build Your Love	Johnnie Ray
Bulls On Parade	Rage Against The Machine
The Bump	Kenny
Bump N' Grind	R. Kelly
Buona Sera	Acker Bilk
Burlesque	Family
Burn It Up	Beatmasters With P.P. Arnold
Burning Bridges (On And Off And On Again)	Status Quo
Burning Heart	Survivor
Burning Love	Elvis Presley
Bus Stop	Hollies
But I Do	Clarence 'Frogman' Henry
Butterfingers	Tommy Steele
Butterfly	Danyel Gerrard
Butterfly	Charlie Gracie
Butterfly	Andy Williams
By The Light Of The Silvery Moon	Little Richard
Bye Bye Baby	Bay City Rollers
Bye Bye Love	Everly Brothers
C Moon	Paul McCartney
C U When U Get There	Coolio Featuring 40 Thevz
Ca Plane Pour Moi	Plastic Bertrand
Cacharpaya (Andes Pumpsa Daesi)	Incantation
Calendar Girl	Neil Sedaka
California Dreamin	Mamas & The Papas
California Dreamin'	River City People
California Love	2 Pac Feat Dr Dre
California Man	Move
Call It Love	Deuce
Call Me	Blondie
Call Me	Go West
Call Me	Spagna
(Call Me) Number One	Tremeloes
Call Rosie On The Phone	Guy Mitchell
Call Up The Groups	Barron Knights
Calling All The Heroes	It Bites
Calling Occupants Of Interplanetary Craft	Carpenters
Calling Your Name	Marilyn
Cambodia	Kim Wilde
Camouflage	Stan Ridgway
Can Can	Bad Manners

Title	Artist
Can Can You Party	Jive Bunny & The Mastermixers
Can I Play With Madness	Iron Maiden
Can I Take You Home Little Girl	Drifters
Can I Touch You...There?	Michael Bolton
Can The Can	Suzi Quatro
Can You Do It	Geordie
(Can You) Feel The Passion	Blue Pearl
Can You Feel It	Jacksons
Can You Feel The Force	Real Thing
Can You Feel The Love Tonight	Elton John
Can You Forgive Her?	Pet Shop Boys
Can't Be Without You Tonight	Judy Boucher
Can't Buy Me Love	Beatles
Can't Get Along Without You	Frankie Vaughan
Can't Get By Without You	Real Thing
Can't Get Enough Of Your Love	Taylor Dayne
Can't Get Enough Of Your Love, Babe	Barry White
Can't Get Used To Losing You	Beat
Can't Get Used To Losing You	Andy Williams
Can't Give You Anything (But My Love)	Stylistics
(I Can't Help) Falling In Love	UB40
Can't Help Falling In Love	Elvis Presley
Can't Help Falling In Love	Stylistics
Can't Help Falling In Love	Andy Williams
Can't Keep It In	Cat Stevens
Can't Shake The Feeling	Big Fun
Can't Stand Losing You	Police
Can't Stay Away From You	Gloria Estefan & The Miami Sound Machine
Can't Stop The Music	Village People
Can't Take My Eyes Off You	Boystown Gang
Can't Take My Eyes Off You	Pet Shop Boys
Can't Take My Eyes Off You	Andy Williams
Can't Wait Another Minute	Five Star
Can't You See That She's Mine	Dave Clark Five
Candida	Dawn
Candle In The Wind	Elton John
Candle In The Wind (Live)	Elton John
Candle In The Wind 1997	Elton John
Candy Girl	New Edition
Candy Man	Brian Poole & The Tremeloes
Cantina Band	Meco
Capstick Comes Home	Tony Capstick
Captain Beaky	Keith Michel
The Captain Of Her Heart	Double
Captain Of Your Ship	Reperata & The Delrons
Car 67	Driver 67
Car Wash	Rose Royce
Cara Mia	David Whitfield
Caravan Of Love	Housemartins
Cardiac Arrest	Madness
Careless Hands	Des O'Connor
Careless Whisper	Wham! Featuring George Michael
Caribbean Disco	Lobo
Caribbean Queen (No More Love On The Run)	Billy Ocean
The Carnival Is Over	Seekers
Carolina Moon	Connie Francis

Title	Artist
Caroline	Status Quo
Caroline (Live At The N.E.C.)	Status Quo
Carrie	Cliff Richard
Carrie-Anne	Hollies
Carry Me Home	Gloworm
Carry The Blame	River City People
Cars	Gary Numan
Casanova	Coffee
Casanova	Levert
Cast Your Fate To The Wind	Sounds Orchestral
Castle Rock	Bluetones
Cat Among The Pigeons	Bros
The Cat Crept In	Mud
Cat's In The Cradle	Ugly Kid Joe
Catch A Falling Star	Perry Como
Catch The Wind	Donovan
Catch Us If You Can	Dave Clark Five
Cathy's Clown	Everly Brothers
Causing A Commotion	Madonna
Cecilia	Suggs
Celebration	Kool & The Gang
Centrefold	J. Geils Band
A Certain Smile	Johnny Mathis
C'est La Vie	Robbie Nevil
Chain Gang	Sam Cooke
Chain Gang	Jimmy Young
Chain Reaction	Diana Ross
Chains	Tina Arena
Chains Of Love	Erasure
Chance	Big Country
Change	Lisa Stansfield
Change	Tears For Fears
A Change Would Do You Good	Sheryl Crow
Change Your Mind	Upside Down
Changing Partners	Bing Crosby
Changing Partners	Kay Starr
The Changingman	Paul Weller
Chanson D'amour	Manhattan Transfer
Chant No. 1 (I Don't Need This Pressure On)	Spandau Ballet
Chantilly Lace	Big Bopper
Chapel Of The Roses	Malcolm Vaughan
Chariots Of Fire - Titles	Vangelis
Charleston	Winifred Atwell
Charlie Brown	Coasters
Charly	Prodigy
Charmaine	Bachelors
Charmless Man	Blur
Check Out The Groove	Bobby Thurston
Check This Out	L.A. Mix
Chequered Love	Kim Wilde
Cherish	David Cassidy
Cherish	Kool & The Gang
Cherish	Madonna
Cherry Oh Baby	UB40
Cherry Pink And Apple Blossom White	Eddie Calvert
Cherry Pink And Apple Blossom White	Perez Prado
Chi Mai Theme	Ennio Morricone
The Chicken Song	Spitting Image
Chika Boom	Guy Mitchell
Child	Mark Owen
A Child's Prayer	Hot Chocolate
Children	Robert Miles
Children Of The Revolution	T. Rex
China Doll	Slim Whitman
China Girl	David Bowie
China In Your Hand	T'Pau
China Tea	Russ Conway
Chiquitita	Abba

Title	Artist
Chirpy Chirpy Cheep Cheep	Middle Of The Road
Chocolate Box	Bros
Choose Life	PF Project Featuring Ewan McGregor
Chorus	Erasure
The Chosen Few	Dooleys
Christian	China Crisis
Christmas Alphabet	Dickie Valentine
Christmas Island	Dickie Valentine
Christmas Through Your Eyes	Gloria Estefan
Church Of The Poison Mind	Culture Club
Cigarettes & Alcohol	Oasis
Cinderella Rockafella	Esther & Abi Ofarim
Cindy Incidentally	Faces
Cindy, Oh Cindy	Eddie Fisher
Cindy Oh Cindy	Tony Brent
Circle In The Sand	Belinda Carlisle
Circle Of Life	Elton John
The Circle	Ocean Colour Scene
Circles	New Seekers
The Circus	Erasure
Clair	Gilbert O'Sullivan
The Clairvoyant	Iron Maiden
The Clapping Song	Belle Stars
The Clapping Song	Shirley Ellis
Classic	Adrian Gurvitz
Classical Gas	Mason Williams
Claudette	Everly Brothers
Clementine	Bobby Darin
Clementine	Mark Owen
Cleopatra's Theme	Cleopatra
Climb Ev'ry Mountain	Shirley Bassey
Close The Door	Stargazers
Close To Me	Cure
Close (To The Edit)	Art Of Noise
Close To You	Maxi Priest
Closer Than Close	Rosie Gaines
Closest Thing To Heaven	Kane Gang
Cloud Lucky Seven	Guy Mitchell
Cloud Nine	Temptations
Clouds Across The Moon	Rah Band
Club Country	Associates
Club Tropicana	Wham!
C'mon And Get My Love	D. Mob Introducing Cathy Dennis
C'mon Everybody	Eddie Cochran
C'mon Everybody	Sex Pistols
Co-Co	Sweet
Coco Jamboo	Mr. President
Cold Turkey	Plastic Ono Band
Colours	Donovan
The Comancheros	Lonnie Donegan
Combine Harvester (Brand New Key)	Wurzels
Come And Get It	Badfinger
Come And Stay With Me	Marianne Faithfull
Come As You Are	Nirvana
Come Baby Come	K7
Come Back And Finish What You Started	Gladys Knight & The Pips
Come Back And Shake Me	Clodagh Rodgers
Come Back And Stay	Paul Young
Come Back Brighter	Reef
Come Back My Love	Darts
Come In Out Of The Rain	Wendy Moten
Come Into My Life	Joyce Sims
Come Live With Me	Heaven 17
Come On Eileen	Dexy's Midnight Runners

Title	Artist
Come On Let's Go	Tommy Steele
Come On Over To My Place	Drifters
Come On You Reds	Manchester United Football Squad
Come Outside	Mike Sarne And Wendy Richard
Come Prima	Marino Marini
(Come 'Round Here) I'm The One You Need	Smokey Robinson & The Miracles
Come Softly To Me	Fleetwoods
Come Softly To Me	Frankie Vaughan & The Kaye Sisters
Come To Me	Ruby Winters
Come Together	Beatles
Come Tomorrow	Manfred Mann
Come Undone	Duran Duran
Come What May	Vicky Leandros
Coming Home Baby	Mel Torme
Coming Home Now	Boyzone
Coming Round Again	Carly Simon
Coming Up	Paul McCartney
Common People	Pulp
Communication	Spandau Ballet
Complex	Gary Numan
Compliments On Your Kiss	Red Dragon With Brian & Tony Gold
Computer Love	Kraftwerk
Concrete And Clay	Unit 4 Plus 2
Confessin'	Frank Ifield
Confide In Me	Kylie Minogue
Confusion	Electric Light Orchestra
Confusion	New Order
Congratulations	Cliff Richard
Constantly	Cliff Richard
Contact	Edwin Starr
Controversy	Prince
Conversations	Cilla Black
Convoy	C.W. McCall
Convoy GB	Laurie Lingo & The Dipsticks
Cool For Cats	Squeeze
Cool Water	Frankie Laine
Cornflake Girl	Tori Amos
Cosmic Girl	Jamiroquai
Cotton Eye Joe	Rednex
Cottonfields	Beach Boys
Could Have Told You So	Halo James
Could It Be Forever	David Cassidy
Could It Be I'm Falling In Love	David Grant & Jaki Graham
Could It Be Magic	Take That
Could You Be Loved	Bob Marley & The Wailers
Could've Been	Tiffany
Couldn't Get It Right	Climax Blues Band
Count Your Blessings	Bing Crosby
Counting Teardrops	Emile Ford & The Checkmates
Country House	Blur
Cousin Norman	Marmalade
Cover Girl	New Kids On The Block
Coward Of The County	Kenny Rogers
Coz I Luv You	Slade
Crackers International E.P.	Erasure
Cracklin' Rosie	Neil Diamond
Cradle Of Love	Johnny Preston
Crash	Primitives
Crazy	Mark Morrison
Crazy	Mud
Crazy	Seal
Crazy Crazy Nights	Kiss
Crazy For You	Let Loose
Crazy For You	Madonna
Crazy Horses	Osmonds

Title	Artist
Crazy Little Party Girl	Aaron Carter
Crazy Little Thing Called Love	Queen
Crazy Otto Rag	Stargazers
Creep	Radiohead
The Creep	Ken Mackintosh
Creep '96	TLC
Creeque Alley	Mamas & The Papas
Criticize	Alexander O'Neal
Crockett's Theme	Jan Hammer
Crocodile Rock	Elton John
Crocodile Shoes	Jimmy Nail
Cross My Broken Heart	Sinitta
Cross Over The Bridge	Patti Page
The Crown	Gary Byrd & Gb Experience
Cruel Summer	Bananarama
Cruel To Be Kind	Nick Lowe
Cruising	Sinitta
The Crunch	Rah Band
Crush On You	Jets
Cry For Help	Rick Astley
Cry Just A Little Bit	Shakin' Stevens
Cry Like A Baby	Box Tops
Cry Wolf	A-Ha
Cryin' In The Rain	Everly Brothers
Crying	Don McLean
The Crying Game	Dave Berry
Crying In The Chapel	Lee Lawrence
Crying In The Chapel	Elvis Presley
Crying Laughing Loving Lying	Labi Siffre
Crying Over You	Ken Boothe
Cuba	Gibson Brothers
Cubik	808 State
Cuddly Toy	Roachford
Cuff Of My Shirt	Guy Mitchell
Cult Of Snap	Snap
Cum On Feel The Noize	Slade
Cumberland Gap	Lonnie Donegan
Cumberland Gap	Vipers Skiffle Group
Cupid	Sam Cooke
Cupid	Johnny Nash
Cupid-I've Loved You For A Long Time (Medley)	Spinners
Curly	Move
Cut Some Rug	Bluetones
The Cutter	Echo & The Bunnymen
D'You Know What I Mean?	Oasis
D-A-A-A-N-C-E-	Lambrettas
D-Days	Hazel O'Connor
Da Da Da	Trio
Da Doo Ron Ron	Crystals
Da Funk	Daft Punk
Da Ya Think I'm Sexy	Rod Stewart
Daddy Cool	Boney M
Daddy Cool	Darts
Daddy's Home	Cliff Richard
Damned Don't Cry	Visage
Damned On 45	Captain Sensible
Dance Away	Roxy Music
Dance Dance Dance (Yowsah Yowsah Yowsah)	Chic
Dance Into The Light	Phil Collins
Dance Little Lady Dance	Tina Charles
Dance On	Kathy Kirby
Dance On	Shadows
Dance To The Music	Sly & The Family Stone
Dance With The Guitar Man	Duane Eddy
Dance With The Devil	Cozy Powell
Dance Yourself Dizzy	Liquid Gold
Dancin' In The Moonlight (It's Caught Me In The Spotlight)	Thin Lizzy
Dancin' Party	Showaddywaddy
Dancing Girls	Nik Kershaw
Dancing In The City	Marshall Hain

Title	Artist
Dancing In The Dark	Bruce Springsteen
Dancing In The Street	David Bowie
Dancing In The Street	Mick Jagger & David Bowie
Dancing In The Street	Martha & The Vandellas
(Dancing) On A Saturday Night	Barry Blue
Dancing On The Ceiling	Lionel Richie
Dancing On The Floor (Hooked On Love)	Third World
Dancing Queen	Abba
Dancing Tight	Galaxy Featuring Phil Fearon
Dancing With Tears In My Eyes	Ultravox
Dancing With The Captain	Paul Nicholas
Dandelion	Rolling Stones
Danger Games	Pinkees
Dangerous	Roxette
Daniel	Elton John
Dark Is The Night	Shakatak
Darlin'	Beach Boys
Darlin'	Frankie Miller
Dat	Pluto Shervington
Daughter Of Darkness	Tom Jones
Davy's On The Road Again	Manfred Mann's Earth Band
Day After Day	Badfinger
The Day I Met Marie	Cliff Richard
The Day The Rains Came	Jane Morgan
Day Trip To Bangor (Didn't We Have A Lovely Time)	Fiddler's Dram
Day Tripper	Beatles
The Day We Caught The Train	Ocean Colour Scene
The Day We Find Love	911
A Day Without Love	Love Affair
Daydream	Lovin' Spoonful
Daydream Believer	Monkees
Daydreamer	David Cassidy
Days	Kinks
Days	Kirsty MacColl
The Days Of Pearly Spencer	Marc Almond
De Do Do Do, De Da Da Da	Police
Dead End Street	Kinks
Dead Giveaway	Shalamar
Dead Or Alive	Lonnie Donegan
Dead Ringer For Love	Meat Loaf
Deadwood Stage	Doris Day
The Dean And I	10cc
Dear Jessie	Madonna
Dear John	Status Quo
Dear Prudence	Siouxsie & The Banshees
Death Of A Clown	Dave Davies
Debora	Tyrannosaurus Rex
December '63 (Oh What A Night)	Four Seasons
Deck Of Cards	Max Bygraves
Deck Of Cards	Wink Martindale
Dedicated Follower Of Fashion	Kinks
Dedicated To The One I Love	Mamas & The Papas
Dedicated To The One I Love	Bitty McLean
Deep	East 17
Deep, Deep Trouble	Simpsons
Deep Down Inside	Donna Summer
Deep Heat '89	Latino Rave
Deeper And Deeper	Madonna
A Deeper Love	Aretha Franklin
Deeply Dippy	Right Said Fred
Delaware	Perry Como

Title	Artist
Delilah	Sensational Alex Harvey Band
Delilah	Tom Jones
Delta Lady	Joe Cocker
Denis	Blondie
Desafinado	Stan Getz & Charlie Byrd
Desiderata	Les Crane
A Design For Life	Manic Street Preachers
Desire	U2
Destiny	Johnnie Ray
Detroit City	Tom Jones
Deutscher Girls	Adam & The Ants
Devil Gate Drive	Suzi Quatro
Devil Woman	Cliff Richard
Devil Woman	Marty Robbins
Devil's Answer	Atomic Rooster
Diamonds	Jet Harris & Tony Meehan
Diana	Paul Anka
Diane	Bachelors
The Diary Of Horace Wimp	Electric Light Orchestra
Did You Ever	Nancy Sinatra & Lee Hazlewood
Didn't I Blow Your Mind	New Kids On The Block
A Different Beat	Boyzone
A Different Corner	George Michael
Different Strokes	Isotonik
Diggin' On You	TLC
Digging Your Scene	Blow Monkeys
Dime And A Dollar	Guy Mitchell
Dippety Day	Father Abraham & The Smurfs
Dirty Cash	Adventures Of Stevie V
Dirty Diana	Michael Jackson
Disappointed	Electronic
D.I.S.C.O.	Ottawan
Disco 2000	Pulp
Disco Connection	Isaac Hayes
Disco Duck	Rick Dees & His Cast Of Idiots
Disco Inferno	Tina Turner
Disco Queen	Hot Chocolate
Disco Stomp	Hamilton Bohannon
Discoteque	U2
Distant Drums	Jim Reeves
Divine Emotions	Narada
D.I.V.O.R.C.E.	Billy Connolly
D.I.V.O.R.C.E.	Tammy Wynette
Dixie-Narco (EP)	Primal Scream
Dixieland	Winifred Atwell
Dizzy	Vic Reeves & The Wonder Stuff
Dizzy	Tommy Roe
DJs Take Control	SL2
Do Anything You Wanna Do	Rods
Do Anything You Want To	Thin Lizzy
Do I Do	Stevie Wonder
Do It Again	Beach Boys
Do It Again	Raffaella Carra
Do Nothing	Specials
Do That To Me One More Time	Captain & Tennille
Do The Bartman	Simpsons
Do The Conga	Black Lace
(Do) The Hucklebuck	Coast To Coast
Do The Right Thing	Redhead Kingpin & The FBI
(Do The) Spanish Hustle	Fatback Band
Do They Know It's Christmas	Band Aid
Do They Know It's Christmas?	Band Aid 11
Do U Still?	East 17
Do Wah Diddy Diddy	Manfred Mann
Do What You Do	Jermaine Jackson
Do What You Gotta Do	Four Tops
Do What You Gotta Do	Nina Simone

Title	Artist
Do What You Wanna Do	T-Connection
Do Ya Do Ya (Wanna Please Me)	Samantha Fox
Do Ya Think I'm Sexy?	N-Trance Featuring Rod Stewart
Do You Believe In Love	Huey Lewis & The News
Do You Feel My Love	Eddy Grant
Do You Know	Michelle Gayle
Do You Know The Way To San Jose	Dionne Warwick
Do You Love Me	Brian Poole & The Tremeloes
Do You Mind	Anthony Newley
Do You Really Want To Hurt Me	Culture Club
Do You See The Light (Looking For)	Snap
Do You Wanna Dance	Barry Blue
Do You Wanna Dance	Cliff Richard
Do You Wanna Touch Me (Oh Yeah)	Gary Glitter
Do You Want Me	Salt-N-Pepa
Do You Want To Know A Secret	Billy J. Kramer & The Dakotas
Dr. Beat	Miami Sound Machine
Doctor Doctor	Thompson Twins
Doctor Jones	Aqua
Dr. Kildare Theme	Johnny Spence
Dr. Love	Tina Charles
Doctor My Eyes	Jackson Five
Doctor's Orders	Sunny
Doctorin' The House	Coldcut Featuring Yazz & The Plastic Population
Doctorin' The Tardis	Timelords
Does Your Chewing Gum Lose Its Flavour	Lonnie Donegan
Does Your Mother Know	Abba
Dog Eat Dog	Adam & The Ants
Doin' The Doo	Betty Boo
Doing Alright With The Boys	Gary Glitter
Dolce Vita	Ryan Paris
Dolly My Love	Moments
Dominique	Singing Nun (Soeur Sourire)
Domino Dancing	Pet Shop Boys
Don Quixote	Nik Kershaw
Don't	Elvis Presley
Don't Answer Me	Cilla Black
Don't Be Cruel	Bobby Brown
Don't Believe A Word	Thin Lizzy
Don't Blame It On That Girl	Matt Bianco
Don't Blame Me	Frank Ifield
Don't Break My Heart	UB40
Don't Bring Lulu	Dorothy Provine
Don't Bring Me Down	Animals
Don't Bring Me Down	Electric Light Orchestra
Don't Bring Me Down	Pretty Things
Don't Bring Me Your Heartaches	Paul & Barry Ryan
Don't Cry	Guns N' Roses
Don't Cry Daddy	Elvis Presley
Don't Cry For Me Argentina	Julie Covington
Don't Cry For Me Argentina	Madonna
Don't Cry For Me Argentina	Shadows
Don't Cry Out Loud	Elkie Brooks
Don't Do It Baby	Mac & Katie Kissoon
Don't Drive My Car	Status Quo
Don't Ever Change	Crickets
Don't Forbid Me	Pat Boone
Don't Forget To Remember	Bee Gees
Don't Get Me Wrong	Pretenders
Don't Give Me Your Life	Alex Party

Title	Artist
Don't Give Up	Peter Gabriel & Kate Bush
Don't Give Up On Us	David Soul
Don't Go	Yazoo
Don't Go Breaking My Heart	Elton John & Rupaul
Don't Go Breaking My Heart	Elton John & Kiki Dee
Don't It Make My Brown Eyes Blue	Crystal Gayle
Don't Knock The Rock	Bill Haley & His Comets
Don't Know Much	Linda Ronstadt (featuring Aaron Neville)
Don't Laugh At Me	Norman Wisdom
Don't Leave Me	Blackstreet
Don't Leave Me This Way	Communards
Don't Leave Me This Way	Thelma Houston
Don't Leave Me This Way	Harold Melvin & The Blue Notes
Don't Let Go (Love)	En Vogue
Don't Let It Die	Hurricane Smith
Don't Let Me Be Misunderstood	Animals
Don't Let The Sun Catch You Crying	Gerry & The Pacemakers
Don't Let The Sun Go Down On Me	George Michael/Elton John
Don't Look Any Further	M People
Don't Look Back In Anger	Oasis
Don't Look Down-The Sequel	Go West
Don't Make Me Wait	Bomb The Bass
Don't Make My Baby Blue	Shadows
Don't Make Waves	Nolans
Don't Marry Her	Beautiful South
Don't Miss The Partyline	Bizz Nizz
Don't Play That Song	Aretha Franklin
Don't Play Your Rock 'n' Roll To Me	Smokey
Don't Push It, Don't Force It	Leon Haywood
Don't Sleep In The Subway	Petula Clark
Don't Speak	No Doubt
Don't Stand So Close To Me	Police
Don't Stay Away Too Long	Peters & Lee
Don't Stop (Wiggle Wiggle)	Outhere Brothers
Don't Stop It Now	Hot Chocolate
Don't Stop Me Now	Queen
Don't Stop Movin'	Livin' Joy
Don't Stop The Carnival	Alan Price Set
Don't Stop The Music	Yarbrough & Peoples
Don't Stop Till You Get Enough	Michael Jackson
Don't Take Away The Music	Tavares
Don't Talk Just Kiss	Right Said Fred/Jocelyn Brown
Don't Talk To Him	Cliff Richard
Don't Talk To Me About Love	Altered Images
Don't Tell Me	Blancmange
Don't That Beat All	Adam Faith
Don't Throw Your Love Away	Searchers
Don't Treat Me Like A Child	Helen Shapiro
Don't Turn Around	Ace Of Base
Don't Turn Around	Aswad
Don't Turn Around	Merseybeats
Don't Walk Away	Jade
Don't Wanna Lose You	Gloria Estefan
Don't Want To Forgive Me Now	Wet Wet Wet
Don't Waste My Time	Paul Hardcastle

Title	Artist
Don't Worry	Kim Appleby
Don't Worry Be Happy	Bobby McFerrin
Don't You (Forget About Me)	Simple Minds
Don't You Know It	Adam Faith
Don't You Love Me	Eternal
Don't You Rock Me Daddy-O	Lonnie Donegan
Don't You Rock Me Daddy-O	Vipers Skiffle Group
Don't You Think It's Time	Mike Berry
Don't You Want Me	Felix
Don't You Want Me	Human League
Donald Where's Your Troosers	Andy Stewart
Donna	10cc
Donna	Marty Wilde
Doobedood'ndoobe	
Doobedood'ndoobe	Diana Ross
Doop	Doop
Double Barrel	Dave & Ansil Collins
Double Dutch	Malcolm McLaren
Down Down	Status Quo
Down On The Beach Tonight	Drifters
Down On The Street	Shakatak
Down The Dustpipe	Status Quo
Down To Earth	Curiosity Killed The Cat
Down Under	Men At Work
Down Yonder	Johnny & The Hurricanes
Downtown	Petula Clark
Downtown Train	Rod Stewart
Dr Kiss Kiss	5000 Volts
Dragging Me Down	Inspiral Carpets
Dragnet	Ray Anthony
Dragnet	Ted Heath
Drama!	Erasure
Dreadlock Holiday	10cc
Dream A Lie	UB40
Dream A Little Dream Of Me	Mama Cass
Dream Baby	Roy Orbison
Dream Lover	Bobby Darin
A Dream's A Dream	Soul II Soul
Dreamboat	Alma Cogan
Dreamer	Supertramp
Dreamin'	Johnny Burnette
Dreaming	Blondie
Dreaming	Cliff Richard
Dreamlover	Mariah Carey
Dreams	Gabrielle
Dreams Can Tell A Lie	Nat 'King' Cole
Dress You Up	Madonna
Drinking Song	Mario Lanza
Drive	Cars
Drive-In Saturday	David Bowie
Driven By You	Brian May
Driving My Car	Madness
Drop The Boy	Bros
Drowning In Berlin	Mobiles
The Drugs Don't Work	Verve
Drummer Man	Tonight
Dry County	Bon Jovi
Dub Be Good To Me	Beats International
Duke Of Earl	Darts
Durham Town (The Leavin')	Roger Whittaker
Dyna-Mite	Mud
E=mc2	Big Audio Dynamite
E-Bow The Letter	REM
Each Time You Break My Heart	Nick Kamen
Early In The Morning	Vanity Fare
Earth Angel	Crew-Cuts
The Earth Dies Screaming	UB40
Earth Song	Michael Jackson
Easier Said Than Done	Shakatak

Title	Artist
Easy	Commodores
Easy Going Me	Adam Faith
Easy Lover	Philip Bailey & Phil Collins
Ebb Tide	Frank Chacksfield
Ebeneezer Goode	Shamen
Ebony And Ivory	Paul McCartney & Stevie Wonder
Echo Beach	Martha & The Muffins
Ecuador	Sash! Featuring Rodriguez
Edelweiss	Vince Hill
The Edge Of Heaven	Wham!
Egyptian Reggae	Jonathan Richman & The Modern Lovers
18 And Life	Skid Row
Eighteen Strings	Tinman
Eighteen With A Bullet	Pete Wingfield
Eighth Day	Hazel O'Connor
Einstein A Go-Go	Landscape
El Bimbo	Bimbo Jet
El Lute	Boney M
Eleanor Rigby	Beatles
Elected	Alice Cooper
Election Day	Arcadia
Electric Avenue	Eddy Grant
Electric Youth	Debbie Gibson
Elenore	Turtles
Elephant Stone	Stone Roses
Eloise	Damned
Eloise	Barry Ryan
Elusive Butterfly	Val Doonican
Elusive Butterfly	Bob Lind
Embarrassment	Madness
Emma	Hot Chocolate
Emotions	Samantha Sang
Emotional Rescue	Rolling Stones
Encore Une Fois	Sash!
End Of The Road	Boyz II Men
Endless Love	Diana Ross & Lionel Richie
Endless Love	Luther Vandross & Mariah Carey
Endless Sleep	Marty Wilde
England We'll Fly The Flag	England World Cup Squad
England's Irie	Black Grape Featuring Joe Strummer & Keith Allen
English Country Garden	Jimmie Rodgers
Enjoy The Silence	Depeche Mode
Enola Gay	Orchestral Manoeuvres In The Dark
Enter Sandman	Metallica
Ernie (The Fastest Milk Man In The West)	Benny Hill
Erotica	Madonna
Escaping	Dina Carroll
Especially For You	Kylie Minogue & Jason Donovan
Et Les Oiseaux Chantaient (And The Birds Were Singing)	Sweet People
Eternal Flame	Bangles
Eternal Love	PJ And Duncan
The Eton Rifles	Jam
European Female	Stranglers
Ev'ry Time We Say Goodbye	Simply Red
Ev'rybody's Twistin'	Frank Sinatra
Ev'rywhere	David Whitfield
Evapor 8	Altern 8
Eve Of Destruction	Barry McGuire
Eve Of The War (Ben Liebrand Remix)	Jeff Wayne
Even Better Than The Real Thing	U2
Even The Bad Times Are Good	Tremeloes
Ever Fallen In Love	Fine Young Cannibals

Title	Artist
Evergreen (Love Theme From 'A Star Is Born')	Barbra Streisand
An Everlasting Love	Andy Gibb
Everlasting Love	Cast From Casualty
Everlasting Love	Love Affair
Evermore	Ruby Murray
Every Beat Of My Heart	Rod Stewart
Every Breath You Take	Police
Every Day Hurts	Sad Cafe
Every Day (I Love You More)	Jason Donovan
Every Day Of My Life	Malcolm Vaughan
Every Little Step	Bobby Brown
Every Little Thing She Does Is Magic	Police
Every Loser Wins	Nick Berry
Every 1's A Winner	Hot Chocolate
Every Rose Has Its Thorn	Poison
Everybody	Clock
Everybody	Tommy Roe
Everybody (Backstreet's Back)	Backstreet Boys
Everybody Dance	Chic
Everybody Get Together	Dave Clark Five
Everybody Gonfi Gon	Two Cowboys
Everybody Hurts	R.E.M.
Everybody In The Place (EP)	Prodigy
Everybody Knows	Dave Clark Five
Everybody Loves Somebody	Dean Martin
Everybody Needs Somebody To Love	Blues Brothers
Everybody Salsa	Modern Romance
Everybody Wants To Rule The World	Tears For Fears
Everybody Wants To Run The World	Tears For Fears
(Everybody's Got To Learn Sometime) I Need Your Loving	Baby D
Everybody's Free (To Feel Good)	Rozalla
Everybody's Gonna Be Happy	Kinks
Everybody's Got To Learn Sometime	Korgis
Everybody's Laughing	Phil Fearon & Galaxy
Everybody's Somebody's Fool	Connie Francis
Everybody's Talkin'	Beautiful South
Everyday	Slade
Everyday Is Like Sunday	Morrissey
Everyone's Gone To The Moon	Jonathan King
Everything	Mary J. Blige
Everything About You	Ugly Kid Joe
Everything Changes	Take That
Everything Counts	Depeche Mode
(Everything I Do) I Do It For You	Bryan Adams
Everything I Am	Plastic Penny
Everything I Own	Ken Boothe
Everything I Own	Boy George
Everything Is Alright (Uptight)	CJ Lewis
Everything Is Beautiful	Ray Stevens
Everything Must Change	Paul Young
Everything Must Go	Manic Street Preachers
Everything She Wants	Wham!
Everything's Alright	Mojos
Everything's Tuesday	Chairmen Of The Board
Everytime You Go Away	Paul Young
Everywhere	Fleetwood Mac

Title	Artist
Evil Hearted You	Yardbirds
The Evil That Men Do	Iron Maiden
Evil Woman	Electric Light Orchestra
Excerpt From A Teenage Opera	Keith West
Excitable	Amazulu
Exhale (Shoop Shoop)	Whitney Houston
Exodus	Ferrante & Teicher
Experiments With Mice	Johnny Dankworth
Express	Dina Carroll
Express Yourself	Madonna
Extended Play E.P.	Bryan Ferry
Exterminate!	Snap Featuring Niki Haris
Eye Level	Simon Park Orchestra
Eye Of The Tiger	Survivor
Fable	Robert Miles
Fabulous	Charlie Gracie
Faces	2 Unlimited
Fade To Grey	Visage
Fading Like A Flower (Every Time You Leave)	Roxette
Fairground	Simply Red
Fairytale	Dana
Fairytale Of New York	Pogues
Faith	George Michael
Fall In Love With You	Cliff Richard
Falling	Julee Cruise
Falling	Roy Orbison
Falling Apart At The Seams	Marmalade
Falling Into You	Celine Dion
Fame	Irene Cara
Fancy Pants	Kenny
Fanfare For The Common Man	Emerson, Lake & Palmer
Fantastic Day	Haircut 100
Fantasy	Black Box
Fantasy	Mariah Carey
Fantasy	Earth, Wind & Fire
Fantasy Island	Tight Fit
Far Far Away	Slade
Farewell	Rod Stewart
Farewell Is A Lonely Sound	Jimmy Ruffin
Farewell My Summer Love	Michael Jackson
Fascinating Rhythm	Bass-O-Matic
Fashion	David Bowie
Fast Car	Tracy Chapman
Fastlove	George Michael
Fat Bottomed Girls	Queen
Father And Son	Boyzone
Father Christmas Do Not Touch Me	Goodies
Fattie Bum-Bum	Carl Malcolm
Favourite Shirts (Boy Meets Girl)	Haircut 100
F.B.I.	Shadows
Fear Of The Dark (Live)	Iron Maiden
Feel It	Tamperer Featuring Maya
Feel Like Making Love	Pauline Henry
Feel So Good	Mase
Feel So High	Des'ree
Feel So Real	Steve Arrington
Feel The Need In Me	Detroit Emeralds
Feel The Need In Me	Detroit Emeralds
Feelings	Morris Albert
(Feels Like) Heaven	Fiction Factory
Feels Like Heaven	Urban Cookie Collective
Feels Like I'm In Love	Kelly Marie
Fernando	Abba
Ferry 'cross The Mersey	Marsden/McCartney/Johnson/Christians
Ferry Across The Mersey	Gerry & The Pacemakers
Fever	Peggy Lee

Title	Artist
Fever	Madonna
Fields Of Fire (400 Miles)	Big Country
Figaro	Brotherhood Of Man
Filmstar	Suede
The Final Countdown	Europe
Finally	Ce Ce Peniston
Finchley Central	New Vaudeville Band
Find My Love	Fairground Attraction
Find The Time	Five Star
Fine Time	New Order
Fine Time	Yazz
Finger Of Suspicion	Dickie Valentine
Fings Ain't What They Used T'be	Max Bygraves
Fire	Crazy World Of Arthur
Fire	Prodigy
Fire Brigade	Move
Fire It Up	Busta Rhymes
Fireball	Deep Purple
Firestarter	Prodigy
First Cut Is The Deepest	Rod Stewart
First Of May	Bee Gees
The First Time	Robin Beck
The First Time	Adam Faith
5-4-3-2-1	Manfred Mann
Five Live (EP)	George Michael & Queen
5-7-0-5	City Boy
Fix	Blackstreet
Flash	Bbe
Flash	Queen
Flashdance....What A Feeling	Irene Cara
Flava	Peter Andre
F.L.M.	Mel & Kim
Float On	Floaters
The Floral Dance	Brighouse And Rastrick
Flowers In The Rain	Move
Floy Joy	Supremes
The Fly	U2
Flying	Cast
Fog On The Tyne (Revisited)	Gazza And Lindisfarne
The Folk Singer	Tommy Roe
Follow That Dream (E.P.)	Elvis Presley
Follow You Follow Me	Genesis
Food For Thought	UB40
A Fool Am I	Cilla Black
A Fool Such As I	Elvis Presley
Fool To Cry	Rolling Stones
Fool's Gold	Stone Roses
Foolish Beat	Debbie Gibson
Fools Rush In	Rick Nelson
Foot Tapper	Shadows
Footloose	Kenny Loggins
Footsee	Wigan's Chosen Few
Footsteps	Steve Lawrence
For All We Know	Shirley Bassey
For America	Red Box
For Once In My Life	Stevie Wonder
For The Good Times	Perry Como
For Whom The Bell Tolls	Bee Gees
For You	Rick Nelson
For Your Babies	Simply Red
For Your Eyes Only	Sheena Easton
For Your Love	Yardbirds
Forever	Damage
Forever	Roy Wood
Forever & Ever	Slik
Forever Autumn	Justin Hayward
A Forever Kind Of Love	Bobby Vee
(Forever) Live And Die	Orchestral Manoeuvres In The Dark
Forever Love	Gary Barlow
Forget About You	Motors
Forget Him	Bobby Rydell

279

Title	Artist
Forget Me Not	Eden Kane
Forget Me Not	Martha & The Vandellas
Forget Me Nots	Patrice Rushen
Forgive Me, Girl	Spinners
Fort Worth Jail	Lonnie Donegan
48 Crash	Suzi Quatro
40 Miles Of Bad Road	Duane Eddy
Found A Cure	Ultra Nate
Four Bacharach & David Songs (EP)	Deacon Blue
Four From Toyah E.P.	Toyah
Four Letter Word	Kim Wilde
Four More From Toyah E.P.	Toyah
Fox On The Run	Manfred Mann
Fox On The Run	Sweet
Frankie	Sister Sledge
Free	Dj Quicksilver
Free	Ultra Nate
Free	Deniece Williams
Free As A Bird	Beatles
Free E.P.	Free
Free Me	Cast
Free Your Mind	En Vogue
Freebird	Will To Power
Freed From Desire	Gala
Freedom	Wham!
Freedom	Robbie Williams
Freedom Come Freedom Go	Fortunes
Freek'n You	Jodeci
Freight Train	Chas McDevitt Skiffle Group
French Kiss	Lil Louis
French Kissin' In The USA	Debbie Harry
Fresh	Gina G
Fresh	Kool & The Gang
Friday, I'm In Love	Cure
Friday Night (Live Version)	Kids From 'Fame'
Friday On My Mind	Easybeats
Friend Or Foe	Adam Ant
Friendly Persuasion	Pat Boone
Friends	Arrival
Friends	Shalamar
Friends	Amii Stewart
Friends And Neighbours	Max Bygraves & The Tanner Sisters
Friends And Neighbours	Billy Cotton & His Band
Friggin' In The Riggin'	Sex Pistols
Frightened City	Shadows
From A Distance	Cliff Richard
From A Jack To A King	Ned Miller
From A Window	Billy J. Kramer & The Dakotas
From Here To Eternity	Frank Sinatra
From Me To You	Beatles
From New York To L.A.	Patsy Gallant
From The Underworld	Herd
Frozen	Madonna
Frozen Orange Juice	Peter Sarstedt
Full Metal Jacket (I Wanna Be Your Drill Instructor)	Abigail Mead & Nigel Goulding
Funeral Pyre	Jam
Funkin' For Jamaica (N.Y.)	Tom Browne
Funky Gibbon	Goodies
Funky Jam	Primal Scream
Funky Moped	Jasper Carrott
Funky Town	Pseudo Echo
Funky Weekend	Stylistics
Funkytown	Lipps Inc.
Funny Familiar Forgotten Feeling	Tom Jones
Funny Funny	Sweet
Funny How Love Can Be	Ivy League

Title	Artist
Future Love (EP)	Seal
Gal With The Yaller Shoes	Michael Holliday
Galveston	Glen Campbell
Gambler	Madonna
Gamblin' Man	Lonnie Donegan
Game Of Love	Wayne Fontana & The Mindbenders
Games People Play	Joe South
Games Without Frontiers	Peter Gabriel
Gangsta's Paradise	Coolio Featuring L.V.
Gangsters	Specials
Garden Of Eden	Gary Miller
Garden Of Eden	Frankie Vaughan
Gasoline Alley Bred	Hollies
Gaye	Clifford T. Ward
Gee Baby	Peter Shelley
Gee Whiz It's You	Cliff Richard
Geno	Dexy's Midnight Runners
Gentle On My Mind	Dean Martin
Georgy Girl	Seekers
Geronimo	Shadows
Get A Life	Soul II Soul
Get Away	Georgie Fame
Get Back	Beatles
Get Back	Rod Stewart
Get Dancing	Disco Tex & The Sex-O-Lettes
Get Down	Gene Chandler
Get Down	Gilbert O'Sullivan
Get Down And Get With It	Slade
Get Down On It	Kool & The Gang
Get Here	Oleta Adams
Get It	Darts
Get Lost	Eden Kane
Get Off Of My Cloud	Rolling Stones
Get Outta My Dreams Get Into My Car	Billy Ocean
Get Ready	Temptations
Get Ready For This	2 Unlimited
Get The Message	Electronic
Get Up And Boogie (That's Right)	Silver Convention
Get Up (Before The Night Is Over)	Technotronic
Get-A-Way	Maxx
Gett Off	Prince
Gettin' Jiggy Wit It	Will Smith
Ghetto Child	Detroit Spinners
Ghetto Heaven	Family Stand
Ghost Town	Specials
Ghostbusters	Ray Parker Jr.
Ghosts	Michael Jackson
Ghosts	Japan
Giddy-Up-A-Ding-Dong	Freddie Bell & The Bellboys
The Gift Of Christmas	Childliners
Gigi	Billy Eckstine
Gilly Gilly Ossenfeffer Katzenellen Bogen By The Sea	Max Bygraves
Gimme All Your Lovin'	ZZ Top
Gimme Dat Ding	Pipkins
Gimme Gimme Gimme (A Man After Midnight)	Abba
Gimme Gimme Good Lovin'	Crazy Elephant
Gimme Hope Jo'anna	Eddy Grant
Gimme Little Sign	Brenton Wood
Gimme Some	Brendon
Gimme Some Loving	Spencer Davis Group
Gin House Blues	Amen Corner
Ginny Come Lately	Brian Hyland
Girl	St. Louis Union

Title	Artist
The Girl Can't Help It	Darts
The Girl Can't Help It	Little Richard
Girl Crazy	Hot Chocolate
Girl Don't Come	Sandie Shaw
Girl I'm Gonna Miss You	Milli Vanilli
The Girl Is Mine	Michael Jackson
The Girl Is Mine	Paul McCartney & Michael Jackson
A Girl Like You	Edwyn Collins
A Girl Like You	Cliff Richard
Girl Of My Best Friend	Elvis Presley
Girl Of My Dreams	Tony Brent
Girl You Know It's True	Milli Vanilli
Girlfriend	Pebbles
Girlie Girlie	Sophia George
Girls	Moments And Whatnauts
Girls And Boys	Blur
Girls Girls Girls	Sailor
Girls Just Want To Have Fun	Cyndi Lauper
Girls On Film	Duran Duran
Girls Talk	Dave Edmunds
Give A Little Love	Aswad
Give A Little Love	Bay City Rollers
Give A Little Love	Daniel O'donnell
Give In To Me	Michael Jackson
Give It Away	Red Hot Chili Peppers
Give It To Me	Troggs
Give It Up	Goodmen
Give It Up	KC & The Sunshine Band
Give Me A Little More Time	Gabrielle
Give Me Back My Heart	Dollar
Give Me Just A Little More Time	Chairmen Of The Board
Give Me Just A Little More Time	Kylie Minogue
Give Me Love (Give Me Peace On Earth)	George Harrison
Give Me The Night	George Benson
Give Me Your Heart Tonight	Shakin' Stevens
Give Me Your Word	Tennessee Ernie Ford
Give Peace A Chance	Plastic Ono Band
Givin' Up Givin' In	Three Degrees
Giving It All Away	Roger Daltrey
G.L.A.D.	Kim Appleby
Glad All Over	Dave Clark Five
Glad It's All Over	Captain Sensible
Glass Of Champagne	Sailor
Globetrotter	Tornados
Gloria	Laura Branigan
Glory Box	Portishead
Glory Of Love	Peter Cetera
Glow	Spandau Ballet
Go	Moby
Go Away	Gloria Estefan
Go Away Little Girl	Mark Wynter
Go (Before You Break My Heart)	Gigliola Cinquetti
Go Buddy Go	Stranglers
Go Now!	Moody Blues
Go On By	Alma Cogan
Go On Move	Reel 2 Real
Go West	Pet Shop Boys
Go Wild In The Country	Bow Wow Wow
God Gave Rock & Roll To You II	Kiss
God Only Knows	Beach Boys
God Save The Queen	Sex Pistols
Goin' Back	Dusty Springfield
Going Back To My Roots	FPI Project
Going Back To My Roots	Odyssey
Going Down The Road	Roy Wood
Going Home	Osmonds
Going In With My Eyes Open	David Soul

Title	Artist
I'm Leaving It (All) Up To You	Donny & Marie Osmond
I'm Living In Shame	Diana Ross & The Supremes
I'm Looking Out The Window	Cliff Richard
I'm Mandy Fly Me	10cc
I'm Not A Juvenile Delinquent	Frankie Lymon & The Teenagers
I'm Not In Love	10cc
I'm Not Scared	Eighth Wonder
I'm On Fire	5000 Volts
I'm On Fire	Bruce Springsteen
I'm Only Sleeping	Suggs
I'm So Excited	Pointer Sisters
I'm Sorry	Brenda Lee
I'm Sorry I Made You Cry	Connie Francis
I'm Still Standing	Elton John
I'm Still Waiting	Diana Ross
I'm Stone In Love With You	Johnny Mathis
I'm Stone In Love With You	Stylistics
I'm Telling You Now	Freddie & The Dreamers
I'm The Leader Of The Gang (I Am)	Gary Glitter
I'm The Lonely One	Cliff Richard
I'm The One	Gerry & The Pacemakers
I'm The Urban Spaceman	Bonzo Dog Doo-Dah Band
I'm Too Sexy	Right Said Fred
I'm Walking Backwards For Christmas	Goons
I'm Your Baby Tonight	Whitney Houston
I'm Your Man	Wham!
I've Been A Bad Bad Boy	Paul Jones
I've Been Losing You	A-Ha
I've Been Thinking About You	Londonbeat
I've Got A Little Puppy	Smurfs
I've Got A Little Something For You	MN8
I've Got News For You	Feargal Sharkey
I've Got You Under My Skin	Four Seasons
I've Got You Under My Skin	U2
I've Gotta Get A Message To You	Bee Gees
(I've Had) The Time Of My Life	Bill Medley & Jennifer Warnes
I've Lost You	Elvis Presley
I've Never Been To Me	Charlene
I've Told Every Little Star	Linda Scott
I've Waited So Long	Anthony Newley
The Ice Cream Man	Tornados
Ice Ice Baby	Vanilla Ice
Ice In The Sun	Status Quo
Idle Gossip	Perry Como
Idle On Parade (EP)	Anthony Newley
If	Telly Savalas
If Anyone Finds This I Love You	Ruby Murray
If Every Day Was Like Christmas	Elvis Presley
If God Will Send His Angels	U2
If I Can Dream	Elvis Presley
If I Can't Have You	Yvonne Elliman
If I Can't Have You	Kim Wilde
If I Could Turn Back Time	Cher
If I Didn't Care	David Cassidy
If I Give My Heart To You	Doris Day
If I Give My Heart To You	Joan Regan
If I Had A Hammer	Trini Lopez

Title	Artist
If I Had Words	Scott Fitzgerald & Yvonne Keeley
If I Never See You Again	Wet Wet Wet
If I Only Had Time	John Rowles
If I Only Knew	Tom Jones
If I Said You Had A Beautiful Body	Bellamy Brothers
If I Was	Midge Ure
If I Were A Carpenter	Bobby Darin
If I Were A Carpenter	Four Tops
If I Were A Rich Man	Topol
If It Happens Again	UB40
If Not For You	Olivia Newton-John
If Not You	Dr. Hook
If Only I Could	Sydney Youngblood
(If Paradise Is) Half As Nice	Amen Corner
If She Should Come To You	Anthony Newley
If The Kids Are United	Sham 69
If The Whole World Stopped Loving	Val Doonican
If We Hold On Together	Diana Ross
If You Believe	Johnnie Ray
If You Can't Give Me Love	Suzi Quatro
If You Can't Stand The Heat	Bucks Fizz
If You Don't Know Me By Now	Harold Melvin & The Blue Notes
If You Don't Know Me By Now	Simply Red
If You Ever	East 17 Featuring Gabrielle
If You Go Away	Terry Jacks
If You Go Away	New Kids On The Block
If You Gotta Go, Go Now	Manfred Mann
If You Gotta Make A Fool Of Somebody	Freddie & The Dreamers
If You Leave Me Now	Chicago
If You Let Me Stay	Terence Trent D'Arby
If You Love Me	Brownstone
If You Only Let Me In	MN8
If You Think You Know How To Love Me	Smokey
If You Wanna Party	Molella Featuring The Outhere Brothers
If You Were Here With Me Now	Kylie Minogue/Keith Washington
If You're Lookin' For A Way Out	Odyssey
Iko Iko	Natasha
Il Silenzio	Nini Rosso
Imagine	John Lennon
In A Broken Dream	Python Lee Jackson
In All The Right Places	Lisa Stansfield
In And Out Of Love	Diana Ross & The Supremes
The In Betweenies	Goodies
The In Crowd	Bryan Ferry
In Dreams	Roy Orbison
In Dulce Jubilo	Mike Oldfield
In For A Penny	Slade
In My Defence	Freddie Mercury
In My Own Time	Family
In Old Lisbon	Frank Chacksfield
In Private	Dusty Springfield
In Summer	Billy Fury
In The Air Tonight	Phil Collins
In The Army Now	Status Quo
In The Bad Bad Old Days	Foundations
In The Bush	Musique
In The Closet	Michael Jackson
In The Country	Cliff Richard
In The Ghetto	Elvis Presley
In The Middle Of Nowhere	Dusty Springfield

Title	Artist
In The Midnight Hour	Wilson Pickett
In The Mood	Ernie Fields
In The Mood	Glenn Miller
In The Name Of The Father	Black Grape
In The Navy	Village People
In The Summertime	Mungo Jerry
In The Summertime	Shaggy Featuring Rayvon
In The Year 2525 (Exordium & Terminus)	Zager & Evans
In These Arms	Bon Jovi
In Thoughts Of You	Billy Fury
In Too Deep	Belinda Carlisle
In Yer Face	808 State
In Your Eyes	George Benson
In Your Room	Depeche Mode
In Zaire	Johnny Wakelin
Incommunicado	Marillion
Incredible	M-Beat Featuring General Levy
Independence	Lulu
Independent Love Song	Scarlet
Indian Love Call	Slim Whitman
Indian Reservation	Don Fardon
Indiana Wants Me	R. Dean Taylor
Infinite Dreams	Iron Maiden
Infinity	Guru Josh
Informer	Snow
An Innocent Man	Billy Joel
Innuendo	Queen
Insane	Texas Featuring Wu Tang Clan
Insanity	Oceanic
Inside	Stiltskin
Inside-Looking Out	Animals
Inside Out	Odyssey
Insomnia (remix)	Faithless
Instant Karma	John Lennon, Yoko Ono & The Plastic Ono Band
Instant Replay	Dan Hartman
Instant Replay	Yell!
Instinction	Spandau Ballet
International Bright Young Thing	Jesus Jones
International Jet Set	Specials
International Rescue	Fuzzbox
Into The Groove	Madonna
Into The Valley	Skids
Intuition	Linx
Invisible Sun	Police
Invisible Touch (Live)	Genesis
I.O.U.	Freeez
Ire Feelings (Skanga)	Rupie Edwards
The Irish Rover	Pogues & The Dubliners
Iron Lion Zion	Bob Marley & The Wailers
Is It A Dream	Classix Nouveaux
Is It Love You're After	Rose Royce
Is There Anybody Out There?	Bassheads
Is There Something I Should Know	Duran Duran
Is This Love	Bob Marley & The Wailers
Is This Love	Alison Moyet
Is This Love	Whitesnake
Island In The Sun	Harry Belafonte
Island Of Dreams	Springfields
Island Of Lost Souls	Blondie
Islands In The Stream	Kenny Rogers & Dolly Parton
Isn't It A Wonder	Boyzone
Isn't Life Strange	Moody Blues
Isn't She Lovely	David Parton
Israelites	Desmond Dekker & The Aces
It Ain't Over 'Til It's Over	Lenny Kravitz

Title	Artist
Let's Have A Ding Dong	Winifred Atwell
Let's Have A Party	Winifred Atwell
Let's Have A Quiet Night In	David Soul
Let's Have Another Party	Winifred Atwell
Let's Hear It For The Boy	Deniece Williams
Let's Jump The Broomstick	Brenda Lee
Let's Party	Jive Bunny & The Mastermixers
Let's Pretend	Lulu
Let's Put It All Together	Stylistics
Let's Spend The Night Together	Rolling Stones
Let's Stay Together	Al Green
Let's Stay Together	Tina Turner
Let's Stick Together	Bryan Ferry
Let's Talk About Love	Helen Shapiro
Let's Talk About Sex	Salt-N-Pepa
Let's Think About Living	Bob Luman
Let's Try Again	New Kids On The Block
Let's Turkey Trot	Little Eva
Let's Twist Again	Chubby Checker
Let's Wait Awhile	Janet Jackson
Let's Work Together	Canned Heat
The Letter	Box Tops
Letter From America	Proclaimers
A Letter To You	Shakin' Stevens
LFO	LFO
Licence To Kill	Gladys Knight
Lido Shuffle	Boz Scaggs
Lie To Me	Bon Jovi
Lies	Status Quo
Life	Haddaway
Life Is A Long Song	Jethro Tull
Life Is A Minestone	10cc
Life Is Too Short Girl	Sheer Elegance
Life On Mars	David Bowie
Lifeline	Spandau Ballet
Lifted	Lighthouse Family
Light My Fire	Clubhouse Featuring Carl
Light My Fire	Doors
Light My Fire	Jose Feliciano
(Light Of Experience) Doina De Jale	Georghe Zamfir
Light Of My Life	Louise
Lightnin' Strikes	Lou Christie
Lights Of Cincinati	Scott Walker
Massachusetts	Bee Gees
Like A Baby	Len Barry
Like A Prayer	Madonna
Like A Rolling Stone	Bob Dylan
Like A Virgin	Madonna
Like Clockwork	Boomtown Rats
Like I Do	Maureen Evans
Like I've Never Been Gone	Billy Fury
Like Sister And Brother	Drifters
Like To Get To Know You Well	Howard Jones
Lil' Devil	Cult
Lily The Pink	Scaffold
Lily Was Here	David A. Stewart Introd. Candy Dulfer
The Lion Sleeps Tonight	Tight Fit
The Lion Sleeps Tonight	Tokens
Lip Up Fatty	Bad Manners
Lipstick On Your Collar	Connie Francis
Liquidator	Harry J. & The All Stars
Listen To Me	Hollies
Listen To What The Man Said	Paul McCartney
Listen To Your Heart	Roxette
Listen To Your Heart	Sonia
Little Arrows	Leapy Lee
Little Bird	Annie Lennox

Title	Artist
A Little Bit Me, A Little Bit You	Monkees
A Little Bit More	Dr. Hook
A Little Bit Of Soap	Showaddywaddy
Little Bit Of Love	Free
A Little Bitty Tear	Burl Ives
A Little Boogie Woogie (In The Back Of My Mind)	Shakin' Stevens
Little Brown Jug	Glenn Miller
Little Children	Billy J. Kramer & The Dakotas
Little Darlin'	Diamonds
Little Devil	Neil Sedaka
Little Does She Know	Kursaal Flyers
Little Donkey	Beverley Sisters
Little Donkey	Nina & Frederick
Little Drummer Boy	David Bowie
Little Drummer Boy	Royal Scots Dragoon Guards
Little Drummer Boy	Harry Simeone Chorale
The Little Drummer Boy	Beverley Sisters
Little Fluffy Clouds	Orb
Little Lies	Fleetwood Mac
A Little Love, A Little Kiss	Karl Denver
A Little Love And Understanding	Gilbert Becaud
A Little Loving	Fourmost
Little Man	Sonny & Cher
Little Miss Lonely	Helen Shapiro
A Little More Love	Olivia Newton-John
A Little Peace	Nicole
Little Red Corvette	Prince & The Revolution
Little Red Rooster	Rolling Stones
A Little Respect	Erasure
The Little Shoemaker	Petula Clark
The Little Shoemaker	Frank Weir
Little Things	Dave Berry
Little Things Mean A Lot	Alma Cogan
Little Things Mean A Lot	Kitty Kallen
Little Things Mean A Lot	Jimmy Young
A Little Time	Beautiful South
Little Town Flirt	Del Shannon
Little White Bull	Tommy Steele
Little Willie	Sweet
Live And Let Die	Guns N' Roses
Live And Let Die	Paul McCartney
Live Forever	Oasis
Live In Trouble	Barron Knights
Live Is Life	Opus
Live It Up	Mental As Anything
Live The Dream	Cast
Live To Tell	Madonna
Live Together	Lisa Stansfield
Live Your Life Be Free	Belinda Carlisle
Lively	Lonnie Donegan
Liverpool Lou	Scaffold
Livin' On A Prayer	Bon Jovi
Livin' Thing	Electric Light Orchestra
Living After Midnight	Judas Priest
Living By Numbers	New Muzik
The Living Daylights	A-Ha
Living Doll	Cliff Richard
Living Doll	Cliff Richard & The Young Ones
Living In A Box	Living In A Box
Living In America	James Brown
Living In Harmony	Cliff Richard
Living In The Past	Jethro Tull
Living Next Door To Alice	Smokie
Living On My Own	Freddie Mercury
Living On The Ceiling	Blancmange
Living On The Front Line	Eddy Grant

Title	Artist
Living On Video	Trans-X
The Living Years	Mike + The Mechanics
L-L-Lucy	Mud
Loadsamoney (Doin' Up The House)	Harry Enfield
Loco In Acapulco	Four Tops
The Loco-Motion	Little Eva
The Loco-Motion	Kylie Minogue
Locomotion	Orchestral Manoeuvres In The Dark
The Logical Song	Supertramp
Lola	Kinks
Lollipop	Chordettes
Lollipop	Mudlarks
London Calling	Clash
London Nights	London Boys
The Lone Ranger	Quantum Jump
Lonely	Peter Andre
Lonely	Acker Bilk
Lonely Boy	Paul Anka
Lonely Boy	Andrew Gold
Lonely Pup (In A Christmas Shop)	Adam Faith
Lonely This Christmas	Mud
Lonesome	Adam Faith
Long Haired Lover From Liverpool	Little Jimmy Osmond
Long Hot Summer	Style Council
Long Legged Woman Dressed In Black	Mungo Jerry
Long Live Love	Olivia Newton-John
Long Live Love	Sandie Shaw
Long Tall Glasses	Leo Sayer
Long Tall Sally	Little Richard
Long Train Runnin'	Doobie Brothers
The Look	Roxette
Look Around	Vince Hill
Look Away	Big Country
Look For A Star	Garry Mills
Look Homeward Angel	Johnnie Ray
The Look Of Love	Madonna
The Look Of Love (Part 1)	ABC
Look Through Any Window	Hollies
Look Wot You Dun	Slade
Lookin' Through The Eyes Of Love	Partridge Family
Lookin' Through The Windows	Jackson Five
Looking After Number One	Boomtown Rats
Looking For A New Love	Jody Watley
Looking Through Patient Eyes	P.M. Dawn
Looking Through The Eyes Of Love	Gene Pitney
Looking Up	Michelle Gayle
Loop De Loop	Frankie Vaughan
Loop Di Love	Shag
Loser	Beck
Losing My Mind	Liza Minnelli
Losing You	Brenda Lee
Losing You	Dusty Springfield
Lost In France	Bonnie Tyler
Lost John	Lonnie Donegan
Louise	Human League
Loungin'	LL Cool J
Love Action (I Believe In Love)	Human League
Love Ain't Here Anymore	Take That
Love And Affection	Joan Armatrading
Love & Kisses	Dannii Minogue
Love And Marriage	Frank Sinatra
Love & Pride	King
Love And Understanding	Cher
Love Bites	Def Leppard

Title	Artist
Nobody Knows	Tony Rich Project
Nobody Needs Your Love	Gene Pitney
Nobody Told Me	John Lennon
Nobody's Child	Karen Young
Nobody's Darlin' But Mine	Frank Ifield
Nobody's Diary	Yazoo
Nobody's Fool	Haircut 100
Non Ho L'eta Per Amarti	Gigliola Cinquetti
North Country Boy	Charlatans
Northern Lights	Renaissance
Not A Dry Eye In The House	Meat Loaf
Not Fade Away	Rolling Stones
Not Over Yet	Grace
Nothin' My Love Can't Fix	Joey Lawrence
(Nothin' Serious) Just Buggin'	Whistle
Nothing Can Divide Us	Jason Donovan
Nothing Comes Easy	Sandie Shaw
Nothing Compares 2 U	Sinead O'Connor
Nothing Else Matters	Metallica
Nothing Ever Happens	Del Amitri
Nothing Lasts Forever	Echo & The Bunnymen
Nothing Rhymed	Gilbert O'Sullivan
Nothing's Gonna Change My Love For You	Glenn Medeiros
Nothing's Gonna Stop Me Now	Samantha Fox
Nothing's Gonna Stop Us Now	Starship
Notorious	Duran Duran
November Rain	Guns N' Roses
November Spawned A Monster	Morrissey
Now And Forever	Richard Marx
Now I'm Here	Queen
Now Is The Time	Jimmy James & The Vagabonds
Now That We've Found Love	Heavy D. & The Boyz
Now That We've Found Love	Third World
Now Those Days Are Gone	Bucks Fizz
Nuff Vibes (EP)	Apache Indian
Numero Uno	Starlight
Nut Rocker	B. Bumble & The Stingers
Nutbush City Limits	Ike & Tina Turner
O Superman	Laurie Anderson
Ob-La-Di Ob-La-Da	Marmalade
Obsession	Animotion
Ode To Billie Joe	Bobbie Gentry
Off On Holiday	Suggs
Off The Wall	Michael Jackson
Oh Babe What Would You Say?	Hurricane Smith
Oh Baby I...	Eternal
Oh Boy	Brotherhood Of Man
Oh Boy	Mud
Oh, Boy!	Crickets
Oh Carol	Smokie
Oh! Carol	Neil Sedaka
Oh Carolina	Shaggy
Oh Diane	Fleetwood Mac
Oh Happy Day	Edwin Hawkins Singers
Oh Julie	Shakin' Stevens
Oh L'amour	Dollar
Oh Lonesome Me	Craig Douglas
Oh Lori	Alessi
Oh Mein Papa	Eddie Calvert
Oh! My Pa-Pa	Eddie Fisher
Oh No Not My Baby	Manfred Mann
Oh No Not My Baby	Rod Stewart
Oh Pretty Woman	Roy Orbison
Oh Well	Fleetwood Mac

Title	Artist
Oh What A Circus	David Essex
Oh What A Night	Clock
Oh What A Shame	Roy Wood
Oh Yeah	Ash
Oh Yeah (On The Radio)	Roxy Music
Oh Yes! You're Beautiful	Gary Glitter
Oh You Pretty Thing	Peter Noone
O.K.	Rock Follies
O.K. Fred	Erroll Dunkley
Okay!	Dave Dee, Dozy, Beaky, Mick & Tich
Ol' Macdonald	Frank Sinatra
Ol' Rag Blues	Status Quo
Old Before I Die	Robbie Williams
Older	George Michael
Oldest Swinger In Town	Fred Wedlock
Ole Ola (Muhler Brasileira)	Rod Stewart
Oliver's Army	Elvis Costello
Olympic	808 State
On A Carousel	Hollies
On A Ragga Tip	SL2
On A Slow Boat To China	Emile Ford & The Checkmates
On Bended Knee	Boyz Ii Men
On Her Majesty's Secret Service	Propellerheads/David Arnold
On Horseback	Mike Oldfield
On My Own	Patti Labelle & Michael McDonald
On My Radio	Selecter
On My Word	Cliff Richard
On Our Own	Bobby Brown
On The Beach	Cliff Richard
On The Inside (Theme 'Prisoner-Cell Block H')	Lynne Hamilton
On The Rebound	Floyd Cramer
On The Road Again	Canned Heat
On The Street Where You Live	Vic Damone
On The Street Where You Live	David Whitfield
On The Wings Of Love	Jeffrey Osborne
On With The Motley	Harry Secombe
On Your Own	Blur
Once Bitten Twice Shy	Vesta Williams
Once In A Lifetime	Talking Heads
Once Upon A Dream	Billy Fury
Once Upon A Long Ago	Paul McCartney
One	U2
The One	Elton John
One & One	Robert Miles Featuring Maria Nayler
One And One Is One	Medicine Head
The One And Only	Chesney Hawkes
One Broken Heart For Sale	Elvis Presley
One By One	Cher
One Day At A Time	Lena Martell
One Day I'll Fly Away	Randy Crawford
One Day In Your Life	Michael Jackson
100% Pure Love	Crystal Waters
One In Ten	UB40
One Inch Rock	Tyrannosaurus Rex
One Love	Bob Marley & The Wailers
One Love	Prodigy
One Love	Stone Roses
One Man Band	Leo Sayer
One Moment In Time	Whitney Houston
One More Dance	Esther & Abi Ofarim
One More Night	Phil Collins
One More Sunrise (Morgen)	Dickie Valentine
One Nation Under A Groove (Pt. 1)	Funkadelic
One Night	Elvis Presley
One Night In Bangkok	Murray Head

Title	Artist
One Night In Heaven	M People
One Night Stand	Let Loose
10538 Overture	Electric Light Orchestra
One Of Us	Abba
One Of Us	Joan Osborne
One Shining Moment	Diana Ross
One Step Beyond	Madness
One Step Further	Bardo
One Sweet Day	Mariah Carey & Boyz II Men
137 Disco Heaven	Amii Stewart
One To Another	Charlatans
1-2-3	Len Barry
1-2-3	Gloria Estefan & The Miami Sound Machine
One Two Three O'Leary	Des O'Connor
One Vision	Queen
One Way Love	Cliff Bennett & The Rebel Rousers
One Way Ticket	Eruption
Onion Song	Marvin Gaye & Tammi Terrell
Only Crying	Keith Marshall
Only Fools (Never Fall In Love)	Sonia
Only In My Dreams	Debbie Gibson
The Only Living Boy In New Cross	Carter-USM
Only Love	Nana Mouskouri
The Only One I Know	Charlatans
Only One Road	Celine Dion
Only One Woman	Marbles
The Only Rhyme That Bites	MC Tunes Versus 808 State
Only Sixteen	Craig Douglas
Only The Lonely	Roy Orbison
The Only Thing That Looks Good On Me Is You	Bryan Adams
The Only Way Is Up	Yazz & The Plastic Population
The Only Way Out	Cliff Richard
Only When You Leave	Spandau Ballet
Only Women Bleed	Julie Covington
Only Yesterday	Carpenters
Only You	John Alford
Only You	Flying Pickets
Only You	Platters
Only You	Praise
Only You	Yazoo
Only You	Hilltoppers
Only You Can	Fox
Ooh Aah...Just A Little Bit	Gina G
Ooh La La La (Let's Go Dancing)	Kool & The Gang
Ooh To Be Ah	Kajagoogoo
Ooh! What A Life	Gibson Brothers
Ooh-Wakka-Doo-Wakka-Day	Gilbert O'Sullivan
Oops Up	Snap
Oops Upside Your Head	Gap Band
Open Arms	Mariah Carey
Open Road	Gary Barlow
Open Your Heart	Human League
Open Your Heart	M People
Open Your Heart	Madonna
Open Your Mind	Usura
Opportunities (Let's Make Lots Of Money)	Pet Shop Boys
Opposites Attract	Paula Abdul (duet With The Wild Pair)
Ordinary Day	Curiosity Killed The Cat
Ordinary World	Duran Duran
Orinoco Flow	Enya
Orville's Song	Keith Harris & Orville
Ossie's Dream (Spurs Are On Their Way To Wembley)	Tottenham Hotspur F.A.Cup Final Squad

Title	Artist	Title	Artist	Title	Artist
Rockin' Around The Christmas Tree	Brenda Lee	Runaway Train	Soul Asylum	Save Your Love	Renee And Renato
Rockin' Around The Christmas Tree	Kim Wilde & Mel Smith	The Runner	Three Degrees	Saved By The Bell	Robin Gibb
A Rockin' Good Way	Shaky & Bonnie	Running Bear	Johnny Preston	Saving All My Love For You	Whitney Houston
Rockin' Over The Beat	Technotronic Featuring Ya Kid K	Running In The Family	Level 42	Saviour's Day	Cliff Richard
Rockin' Robin	Michael Jackson	Running Scared	Roy Orbison	Say A Little Prayer	Bomb The Bass
Rockin' Roll Baby	Stylistics	Running Up That Hill	Kate Bush	Say, Has Anybody Seen My Sweet	
Rockin' Through The Rye	Bill Haley & His Comets	Running With The Night	Lionel Richie	Gypsy Rose	Dawn Featuring Tony Orlando
Rocking Goose	Johnny & The Hurricanes	Rupert	Jackie Lee	Say Hello Wave Goodbye	Soft Cell
Rockit	Herbie Hancock	Rush Hour	Jane Wiedlin	Say I Won't Be There	Springfields
Rocks	Primal Scream	Rush Rush	Paula Abdul	Say I'm Your No. 1	Princess
Rodrigo's Guitar Concerto De Aranjuez	Manuel & His Music Of The Mountains	Russians	Sting	Say It Again	Jermaine Stewart
Rok Da House	Beatmasters Featuring The Cookie Crew	S-S-S-Single Bed	Fox	Say Say Say	Paul McCartney & Michael Jackson
Roll Away The Stone	Mott The Hoople	Sabre Dance	Love Sculpture	Say What You Want	Texas
Roll Over Beethoven	Electric Light Orchestra	Sacrifice	Elton John	Say What You Want	Texas Featuring Wu Tang Clan
Roll Over Lay Down	Status Quo	Sad Songs (Say So Much)	Elton John	Say Wonderful Things	Ronnie Carroll
Roll With It	Oasis	Sad Sweet Dreamer	Sweet Sensation	Say You Do	Ultra
Rollin' Stone	David Essex	Saddle Up	David Christie	Say You Don't Mind	Colin Blunstone
Rolling Home	Status Quo	Sadness Part 1	Enigma	Say You, Say Me	Lionel Richie
Romeo	Petula Clark	The Safety Dance	Men Without Hats	Say You'll Be There	Spice Girls
Romeo	Mr. Big	Sail On	Commodores	Scarlett O'Hara	Jet Harris & Tony Meehan
Romeo And Juliet	Dire Straits	Sailing	Rod Stewart	Scatman (Ski-Ba-Bop-Ba-Dop-Bop)	Scatman John
Room In Your Heart	Living In A Box	Sailing On The Seven Seas	OMD		
Rose Garden	Lynn Anderson	Sailor	Petula Clark	Scatman's World	Scatman John
Rose Garden	New World	Sailor	Anne Shelton	School Love	Barry Blue
A Rose Has To Die	Dooleys	St. Elmo's Fire (Man In Motion)	John Parr	School's Out	Alice Cooper
Rose Marie	Slim Whitman	The Saint	Orbital	Scotch On The Rocks	Band Of The Black Watch
Roses Are Red	Ronnie Carroll	St. Therese Of The Roses	Malcolm Vaughan	Scream	Michael Jackson & Janet Jackson
Roses Are Red	Mac Band Featuring The McCampbell Brothers	St. Valentine's Day Massacre E.P.	Headgirl	Sea Of Love	Marty Wilde
Roses Are Red (My Love)	Bobby Vinton	The Saints Rock 'n Roll	Bill Haley & His Comets	Sealed With A Kiss	Jason Donovan
Roses Of Picardy	Vince Hill	Sal's Got A Sugar Lip	Lonnie Donegan	Sealed With A Kiss	Brian Hyland
Rosetta	Fame And Price Together	Sale Of The Century	Sleeper	Search For The Hero	M People
Rosie	Don Partridge	Sally	Gerry Monroe	Searchin'	Hazell Dean
Rotterdam	Beautiful South	Sally Don't You Grieve	Lonnie Donegan	Searchin'	Hollies
Roulette	Russ Conway	Saltwater	Julian Lennon	Searching	Change
Round And Round	Jaki Graham	Sam	Olivia Newton-John	Searching	China Black
The Roussos Phenomenon E.P.	Demis Roussos	Samantha	Kenny Ball	Seaside Shuffle	Terry Dactyl & The Dinosaurs
Roxanne	Police	Samba De Janeiro	Bellini	Seasons In The Sun	Terry Jacks
Royal Event	Russ Conway	The Same Old Scene	Roxy Music	Secret	Madonna
Rubber Ball	Bobby Vee	San Bernadino	Christie	Secret Love	Bee Gees
Rubber Ball	Marty Wilde	San Franciscan Nights	Eric Burdon & The Animals	Secret Love	Doris Day
Rubber Bullets	10cc	San Francisco (Be Sure To Wear Flowers In Your Hair)	Scott McKenzie	Secret Love	Kathy Kirby
Rubberband Girl	Kate Bush	Sanctify Yourself	Simple Minds	Secret Lovers	Atlantic Starr
Ruby, Don't Take Your Love To Town	Kenny Rogers & The First Edition	Sandstorm	Cast	The Secrets That You Keep	Mud
Ruby Tuesday	Melanie	Sandy	John Travolta	See Emily Play	Pink Floyd
Ruby Tuesday	Rolling Stones	Santa Bring My Baby Back To Me	Elvis Presley	See My Baby Jive	Wizzard
Ruby Tuesday	Rod Stewart	Santa Claus Is Comin' To Town	Bruce Springsteen	See My Friend	Kinks
Rude Boys Outa Jail	Specials	Santo Natale	David Whitfield	See The Day	Dee C. Lee
Ruff In The Jungle	Prodigy	Sat In Your Lap	Kate Bush	See Those Eyes	Altered Images
Rumble In The Jungle	Fugees	Satan	Orbital	See You	Depeche Mode
Run Away	Real McCoy	Saturday Love	Cherrelle & Alexander O'Neal	See You Later Alligator	Bill Haley & His Comets
Run, Baby Run (Back Into My Arms)	Newbeats	Saturday Night	Suede	Self Control	Laura Branigan
Run For Home	Lindisfarne	Saturday Night	Whigfield	Semi-Detached Suburban Mr.James	Manfred Mann
Run Run Run	Jo Jo Gunne	Saturday Night At The Movies	Drifters	Send In The Clowns	Judy Collins
Run Runaway	Slade	Saturday Night's Alright For Fighting	Elton John	Senses Working Overtime	XTC
Run To Him	Bobby Vee	The Savage	Shadows	Sentinel	Mike Oldfield
Run To Me	Bee Gees	Save A Prayer	Duran Duran	Senza Una Donna (Without A Woman)	Zucchero/Paul Young
Run To The Hills	Iron Maiden	Save Me	Dave Dee, Dozy, Beaky, Mick & Tich	Separate Lives	Phil Collins & Marilyn Martin
Run To The Sun	Erasure	Save Our Love	Eternal	September	Earth, Wind & Fire
Run To You	Bryan Adams	Save The Best For Last	Vanessa Williams	Serenade	Slim Whitman
Run To You	Rage	Save The Last Dance For Me	Drifters	Serious	Donna Allen
Runaround Sue	Dion	Save Your Kisses For Me	Brotherhood Of Man	Sesame's Treet	Smart E's
Runaway	Janet Jackson			Set Adrift On Memory Bliss	P.M. Dawn
Runaway	Del Shannon			Set Me Free	Jaki Graham
Runaway Boys	Stray Cats				

295

Title	Artist
Set Me Free	Kinks
Set You Free	N-Trance
Setting Sun	Chemical Brothers
Seven Days And One Week	BBE
Seven Drunken Nights	Dubliners
747 (Strangers In The Night)	Saxon
Seven Little Girls Sitting In The Back Seat	Avons
Seven Rooms Of Gloom	Four Tops
Seven Seas Of Rhye	Queen
7 Seconds	Youssou N'dour
Seven Tears	Goombay Dance Band
7 Ways To Love	Cola Boy
7 Teen	Regents
Seventeen	Let Loose
Sexcrime (Nineteen Eighty Four)	Eurythmics
(Sexual) Healing	Marvin Gaye
Sexy Eyes	Dr. Hook
Sexy MF	Prince
Sh-Boom	Crew-Cuts
Sh-Boom	Stan Freberg
Sha La La	Manfred Mann
Sha La La La Lee	Small Faces
Shaddup You Face	Joe Dolce
Shadow Waltz	Mantovani
Shake It Down	Mud
Shake, Rattle And Roll	Bill Haley & His Comets
Shake You Down	Gregory Abbott
Shake Your Body (Down To The Ground)	Jacksons
Shake Your Head	Was (Not Was)
Shake Your Love	Debbie Gibson
Shakermaker	Oasis
Shakin' All Over	Johnny Kidd & The Pirates
The Shakin' Stevens E.P.	Shakin' Stevens
Shame, Shame, Shame	Shirley And Company
Shang-A-Lang	Bay City Rollers
Shapes Of Things	Yardbirds
Shattered Dreams	Johnny Hates Jazz
Shazam	Duane Eddy
She	Charles Aznavour
She Ain't Worth It	Glenn Medeiros Featuring Bobby Brown
She Don't Let Nobody	Chaka Demus & Pliers
She Drives Me Crazy	Fine Young Cannibals
She Loves You	Beatles
She Makes My Day	Robert Palmer
She Means Nothing To Me	Phil Everly & Cliff Richard
She Wants To Dance With Me	Rick Astley
She Wears My Ring	Solomon King
She'd Rather Be With Me	Turtles
She's A Lady	Tom Jones
She's A River	Simple Minds
She's Got Claws	Gary Numan
She's Got That Vibe	R. Kelly
She's In Love With You	Suzi Quatro
She's Leaving Home	Billy Bragg
She's Not There	Santana
She's Not There	Zombies
She's Not You	Elvis Presley
She's On It	Beastie Boys
She's Out Of My Life	Michael Jackson
She's So Modern	Boomtown Rats
Sheffield Grinder	Tony Capstick
Sheila	Tommy Roe
Sherry	Adrian Baker
Sherry	Four Seasons

Title	Artist
Shindig	Shadows
Shine	Aswad
Shine A Little Love	Electric Light Orchestra
Shine On	Degrees Of Motion
Shiny Happy People	R.E.M.
Ship Of Fools	Erasure
Shiralee	Tommy Steele
Shirley	Shakin' Stevens
Shocked	Kylie Minogue
The Shoop Shoop Song (It's In His Kiss)	Cher
Shoot Me With Your Love	D:ream
Shooting Star	Boyzone
Shoplifters Of The World Unite	Smiths
Short Short Man	20 Fingers
Shortsharpshock (EP)	Therapy?
Shotgun Wedding	Roy 'C'
Shout	Louchie Lou & Michie One
Shout	Lulu
Shout	Tears For Fears
Shout To The Top	Style Council
The Show	Doug E. Fresh & The Get Fresh Crew
Show Me Heaven	Maria McKee
Show Me Love	Robin S.
Show Me Love	Robyn
Show Me The Way	Peter Frampton
Show Me You're A Woman	Mud
The Show Must Go On	Leo Sayer
Show You The Way To Go	Jacksons
Showdown	Electric Light Orchestra
Showing Out	Mel & Kim
The Shuffle	Van McCoy
Shut Up	Madness
Shy Boy	Bananarama
Shy Guys	Diana King
Sick Man Blues	Goodies
Side Saddle	Russ Conway
Side Show	Barry Biggs
Sight For Sore Eyes	M People
The Sign	Ace Of Base
Sign O' The Times	Prince
Sign Of The Times	Belle Stars
Sign Your Name	Terence Trent D'Arby
Signed, Sealed, Delivered I'm Yours	Stevie Wonder
Silence Is Golden	Tremeloes
Silent Night	Bros
Silhouettes	Herman's Hermits
Silhouettes	Cliff Richard
Silly Games	Janet Kay
Silly Love Songs	Paul McCartney
Silly Thing	Sex Pistols
Silver Dream Machine (Pt. 1)	David Essex
Silver Lady	David Soul
Silver Machine	Hawkwind
Silver Star	Four Seasons
Simon Says	1910 Fruitgum Co.
Simon Smith & His Amazing Dancing Bear	Alan Price Set
Simon Templar	Splodgenessabounds
Simple Game	Four Tops
Since I Don't Have You	Guns N' Roses
Since Yesterday	Strawberry Switchblade
Since You've Been Gone	Rainbow
Sincerely	McGuire Sisters
Sing A Song Of Freedom	Cliff Richard
Sing Baby Sing	Stylistics
Sing It With Joe	Joe 'Mr. Piano' Henderson
Sing Little Birdie	Pearl Carr & Teddy Johnson
Sing Me	Brothers

Title	Artist
Sing Our Own Song	UB40
Sing Up For The Champions	Reds United
Singin' In The Rain (Pt. 1)	Sheila B. Devotion
The Singing Dogs (Medley)	Singing Dogs
Singing The Blues	Guy Mitchell
Singing The Blues	Tommy Steele
Single Life	Cameo
Sippin' Soda	Guy Mitchell
Sir Duke	Stevie Wonder
Sister	Bros
Sister Jane	New World
Sister Of Mercy	Thompson Twins
Sisters Are Doin' It For Themselves	Eurythmics & Aretha Franklin
Sit Down	James
Sittin' In The Park	Georgie Fame
(Sittin' On) The Dock Of The Bay	Otis Redding
The Six Teens	Sweet
16 Bars	Stylistics
Sixteen Reasons	Connie Stevens
Sixteen Tons	Tennessee Ernie Ford
Sixteen Tons	Frankie Laine
The Size Of A Cow	Wonder Stuff
Ska Train	Beatmasters
Skiing In The Snow	Wigan's Ovation
Skin Deep	Duke Ellington
Skin Deep	Ted Heath
Skweeze Me Pleeze Me	Slade
Sky High	Jigsaw
The Skye Boat Song	Roger Whittaker & Des O'Connor
Slam Dunk (Da Funk)	5
Slam Jam	WWF Superstars
Slave To Love	Bryan Ferry
Slave To The Rhythm	Grace Jones
Slave To The Vibe	Aftershock
Sledgehammer	Peter Gabriel
Sleeping Satellite	Tasmin Archer
Sleepy Joe	Herman's Hermits
Sleepy Shores	Johnny Pearson Orchestra
Slight Return	Bluetones
The Slightest Touch	Five Star
Slip Your Disc To This	Heatwave
Sloop John B	Beach Boys
Slow Down	John Miles
Slow Hand	Pointer Sisters
Slow It Down	East 17
Smalltown Boy	Bronski Beat
Smarty Pants	First Choice
Smells Like Teen Spirit	Nirvana
Smile	Nat 'King' Cole
Smoke Gets In Your Eyes	Platters
Smooth Criminal	Michael Jackson
The Smurf Song	Father Abraham & The Smurfs
Snap Mega Mix	Snap
Snooker Loopy	Matchroom Mob With Chas & Dave
Snoopy Vs The Red Baron	Royal Guardsmen
Snoopy Vs. The Red Baron	Hotshots
Snot Rap	Kenny Everett
Snow Coach	Russ Conway
So Cold The Night	Communards
So Do I	Kenny Ball
So Emotional	Whitney Houston
So Good	Boyzone
So Good	Eternal
So Good To Be Back Home Again	Tourists
So Hard	Pet Shop Boys

Title	Artist
So Lonely	Police
So Long Baby	Del Shannon
So Macho	Sinitta
So Pure	Baby D
So Sad (To Watch Good Love Go Bad)	
	Everly Brothers
So You Win Again	Hot Chocolate
Softly As I Leave You	Matt Monro
Softly Softly	Ruby Murray
Softly Whispering I Love You	
	Congregation
Soldier Blue	Buffy Sainte Marie
Soley Soley	Middle Of The Road
Solid	Ashford & Simpson
Solid Bond In Your Heart	Style Council
Solid Gold Easy Action	T. Rex
Solitaire	Andy Williams
Solomon Bites The Worm	Bluetones
Solsbury Hill	Peter Gabriel
Some Day	Frankie Laine
Some Girls	Racey
Some Girls	Ultimate Kaos
Some Guys Have All The Luck	
	Maxi Priest
Some Kind Of A Summer	David Cassidy
Some Kind-A Earthquake	Duane Eddy
Some Might Say	Oasis
Some Of Your Lovin'	Dusty Springfield
Some People	Cliff Richard
Somebody Else's Guy	Jocelyn Brown
(Somebody) Help Me Out	Beggar & Co
Somebody Help Me	Spencer Davis
	Group
Somebody To Love	Queen
Somebody's Watching Me	Rockwell
Someday	Eternal
Someday	Ricky Nelson
Someday	Jodie Sands
Someday I'll Be Saturday Night	Bon Jovi
Someday (I'm Coming Back)	Lisa
	Stansfield
Someday One Day	Seekers
Someday We'll Be Together	Diana Ross
	& The Supremes
Someday We're Gonna Love Again	
	Searchers
Someone	Johnny Mathis
Someone Else's Baby	Adam Faith
Someone Else's Roses	Joan Regan
Someone On Your Mind	Jimmy Young
Someone Someone	Brian Poole
	& The Tremeloes
Someone's Looking At You	Boomtown
	Rats
Somethin' Stupid	Nancy & Frank
	Sinatra
Something	Shirley Bassey
Something	Beatles
Something 'Bout You Baby	Status Quo
Something About The Way You Look	
Tonight	Elton John
Something About You	Level 42
Something Better Change	Stranglers
Something Changed	Pulp
Something Else	Sex Pistols
Something For The Pain	Bon Jovi
Something Goin' On	Todd Terry
Something Good	Utah Saints
Something Got Me Started	Simply Red
Something Happened On The Way To	
Heaven	Phil Collins
Something Here In My Heart (Keeps	
A-Tellin' Me No)	Paper Dolls
(Something Inside) So Strong	Labi
	Siffre

Title	Artist
Something In The Air	Thunderclap
	Newman
Something Old, Something New	
	Fantastics
Something Tells Me (Something Is	
Gonna Happen Tonight)	Cilla Black
Something's Burning	Kenny Rogers &
	The First Edition
Something's Gotta Give	Sammy Davis Jr.
Something's Gotten Hold Of My Heart	
	Marc Almond Featuring Gene Pitney
Something's Gotten Hold Of My Heart	
	Gene Pitney
Something's Happening	
	Herman's Hermits
Sometimes	Erasure
Sometimes When We Touch	Dan Hill
Somewhere	P.J. Proby
Somewhere In My Heart	Aztec Camera
Somewhere Out There	Linda Ronstadt
Somewhere Somehow	Wet Wet Wet
Son Of Hickory Holler's Tramp	
	O.C. Smith
Son Of My Father	Chicory Tip
Son-Of-A Preacher Man	Dusty Springfield
Song 2	Blur
Song For Guy	Elton John
Song For Love	Extreme
Song For Whoever	Beautiful South
Song Of The Dreamer	Johnnie Ray
Songs For Swinging Lovers (L.P.)	
	Frank Sinatra
Sorrow	David Bowie
Sorrow	Merseys
Sorry I'm A Lady	Baccara
Sorry Seems To Be The Hardest Word	
	Elton John
Sorry Suzanne	Hollies
Sorted For Es & Wizz	Pulp
S.O.S.	Abba
Sound	James
Sound And Vision	David Bowie
The Sound Of Silence	Bachelors
Sound Of The Suburbs	Members
Southern Freeez	Freeez
Souvenir	Orchestral Manoeuvres
	In The Dark
Sowing The Seeds Of Love	Tears For
	Fears
The Space Jungle	Adamski
Space Oddity	David Bowie
Spaceman	Babylon Zoo
Spanish Eyes	Al Martino
Spanish Flea	Herb Alpert
The Sparrow	Ramblers
Speak Like A Child	Style Council
Speak To Me Pretty	Brenda Lee
Special Brew	Bad Manners
The Special Years	Val Doonican
Speedy Gonzales	Pat Boone
Spend The Night	Coolnotes
Spice Up Your Life	Spice Girls
Spiders & Snakes	Jim Stafford
Spies Like Us	Paul McCartney
Spin The Black Circle	Pearl Jam
Spinning The Wheel	George Michael
Spirit In The Sky	Doctor & The Medics
Spirit In The Sky	Norman Greenbaum
Spirits In The Material World	Police
Splish Splash	Charlie Drake
Spot The Pigeon E.P.	Genesis
Squeeze Box	Who
Staccato's Theme	Elmer Bernstein
Stagger Lee	Lloyd Price
Stairway Of Love	Michael Holliday

Title	Artist
Stairway To Heaven	Far Corporation
Stairway To Heaven	Rolf Harris
Stairway To Heaven	Neil Sedaka
Stand And Deliver	Adam & The Ants
Stand By Me	Oasis
Stand By Your Man	Tammy Wynette
Stand Up For Your Love Rights	Yazz
Standing In The Road	Blackfoot Sue
Standing In The Shadows Of Love	
	Four Tops
Standing On The Corner	King Brothers
Star	Kiki Dee
Star	Erasure
Star On A TV Show	Stylistics
Star People '97	George Michael
Star Trekkin'	Firm
Stardust	David Essex
Stardust	Billy Ward & His Dominoes
Staring At The Sun	U2
Starmaker	Kids From 'Fame'
Starman	David Bowie
Starry Eyed	Michael Holliday
Stars	Simply Red
Stars On 45	Stars On 45
Stars On 45 (Vol 2)	Starsound
Stars Shine In Your Eyes	Ronnie Hilton
Start	Jam
Start Me Up	Rolling Stones
Start Movin'	Sal Mineo
Starting Together	Su Pollard
Stay	Jackson Browne
Stay	Eternal
Stay	Hollies
Stay	Lisa Loeb & Nine Stories
Stay	Sash! Featuring La Trec
Stay	Shakespears Sister
Stay	Maurice Williams & The Zodiacs
Stay Another Day	East 17
Stay Awhile	Dusty Springfield
Stay (Faraway, So Close!)	U2
Stay On These Roads	A-Ha
Stay Out Of My Life	Five Star
Stay Together	Suede
Stay With Me	Blue Mink
Stay With Me	Faces
Stayin' Alive	Bee Gees
Stayin' Alive	N-Trance Featuring
	Ricardo Da Force
Steam	East 17
Steam	Peter Gabriel
Step Back In Time	Kylie Minogue
Step By Step	New Kids On The Block
Step By Step	Joe Simon
Step Inside Love	Cilla Black
Step It Up	Stereo MCs
Step Off (Pt. 1)	Grandmaster Melle Mell
	& The Furious Fiv
Step On	Happy Mondays
Steppin' Out	Joe Jackson
Stereotype	Specials
Stereotypes	Blur
Stewball	Lonnie Donegan
Stick It Out	Right Said Fred
Still	Commodores
Still	Karl Denver
Still I'm Sad	Yardbirds
Still Water (Love)	Four Tops
Stillness In Time	Jamiroquai
Stir It Up	Johnny Nash
Stomp!	Brothers Johnson
Stoned Love	Supremes
The Stonk	Hale & Pace
Stool Pigeon	Kid Creole & The Coconuts
Stop	Sam Brown
Stop	Spice Girls

Title	Artist
Teacher	Jethro Tull
A Tear Fell	Teresa Brewer
Teardrops	Shakin' Stevens
Teardrops	Womack & Womack
Tears	Ken Dodd
The Tears I Cried	Glitter Band
Tears In Heaven	Eric Clapton
Tears Of A Clown	Beat
The Tears Of A Clown	Smokey Robinson & The Miracles
Tears On My Pillow	Kylie Minogue
Tears On My Pillow	Johnny Nash
Tease Me	Chaka Demus & Pliers
Teddy Bear	Elvis Presley
Teddy Bear	Red Sovine
Teen Beat	Sandy Nelson
Teenage Dream	Marc Bolan & T. Rex
Teenage Lament '74	Alice Cooper
Teenage Rampage	Sweet
A Teenager In Love	Craig Douglas
A Teenager In Love	Marty Wilde
Telegram Sam	T. Rex
Telephone Line	Electric Light Orchestra
Telephone Man	Meri Wilson
Teletubbies Say Eh-Oh!	Teletubbies
Tell Her About It	Billy Joel
Tell Him	Billie Davis
Tell Him	Hello
Tell Him	Barbra Streisand & Celine Dion
Tell It To My Heart	Taylor Dayne
Tell Laura I Love Her	Ricky Valance
Tell Me What He Said	Helen Shapiro
Tell Me When	Applejacks
Tell Me When	Human League
Tell Me Why	Elvis Presley
Telstar	Tornados
Temma Harbour	Mary Hopkin
Temple Of Love (1992)	Sisters Of Mercy
Temptation	Everly Brothers
Temptation	Heaven 17
The Tender Trap	Frank Sinatra
Tenderly	Nat 'King' Cole
Tennessee Wig Walk	Bonnie Lou
Tequila	Champs
Terry	Twinkle
Tetris	Doctor Spin
Tha Crossroads	Bone Thugs N Harmony
Thank U Very Much	Scaffold
Thanks For The Memory (Wham Bam Thank You Mam)	Slade
That Girl Belongs To Yesterday	Gene Pitney
That Look In Your Eye	Ali Campbell
That Ole Devil Called Love	Alison Moyet
That Same Old Feeling	Pickettywitch
That Sounds Good To Me	Jive Bunny & The Mastermixers
That'll Be The Day	Crickets
That's All!	Genesis
That's Amore	Dean Martin
That's How A Love Song Was Born	Ray Burns
That's Living (Alright)	Joe Fagin
That's My Home	Acker Bilk
That's The Way	Honeycombs
That's The Way (I Like It)	KC & The Sunshine Band
That's The Way God Planned It	Billy Preston
That's The Way It Is	Mel & Kim
That's The Way Love Goes	Janet Jackson
That's The Way Love Is	Ten City
That's What Friends Are For	Deniece Williams

Title	Artist
That's What I Like	Jive Bunny & The Mastermixers
That's What Love Will Do	Joe Brown & The Bruvvers
Them Girls Them Girls	Zig And Zag
Theme For A Dream	Cliff Richard
Theme For Young Lovers	Shadows
Theme From 'Mission:Impossible'	Adam Clayton & Larry Mullen
Theme From 'A Summer Place'	Percy Faith
Theme From Dixie	Duane Eddy
Theme From Dr. Kildare (Three Stars Will Shine Tonight)	Richard Chamberlain
Theme From Harry's Game	Clannad
Theme From M.A.S.H.	Manic Street Preachers
Theme From M*A*S*H* (Suicide Is Painless)	Mash
Theme From Mahogany (Do You Know Where You're Going To)	Diana Ross
Theme From New York New York	Frank Sinatra
Theme From 'Shaft'	Isaac Hayes
Theme From S'Express	S'Express
Theme From 'The Legion's Last Patrol'	Ken Thorne & His Orchestra
Theme From 'The Threepenny Opera'	Billy Vaughn
Theme From The Deer Hunter (Cavatina)	Shadows
Theme From The Threepenny Opera	Louis Armstrong
Then He Kissed Me	Crystals
Then I Kissed Her	Beach Boys
There Are More Questions Than Answers	Johnny Nash
There But For Fortune	Joan Baez
There Goes My Everything	Engelbert Humperdinck
There Goes My Everything	Elvis Presley
There Goes My First Love	Drifters
There Is A Mountain	Donovan
There It Is	Shalamar
There Must Be A Reason	Frankie Laine
There Must Be A Way	Frankie Vaughan
There Must Be An Angel (Playing With My Heart)	Eurythmics
There There My Dear	Dexy's Midnight Runners
There Won't Be Many Coming Home	Roy Orbison
There's A Ghost In My House	R. Dean Taylor
There's A Gold Mine In The Sky	Pat Boone
There's A Heartache Following Me	Jim Reeves
There's A Kind Of Hush	Herman's Hermits
There's A Whole Lot Of Loving	Guys & Dolls
(There's) Always Something There To Remind Me	Sandie Shaw
There's No One Quite Like Grandma	St. Winifred's School
There's No Other Way	Blur
There's Nothing I Won't Do	JX
These Boots Are Made For Walkin'	Nancy Sinatra
These Days	Bon Jovi
These Dreams	Heart
They Don't Care About Us	Michael Jackson
They Don't Know	Tracey Ullman

Title	Artist
(They Long To Be) Close To You	Carpenters
They'll Be Sad Songs (To Make You Cry)	Billy Ocean
They're Coming To Take Me Away Ha-Haaa!	Napoleon XIV
Thieves In The Temple	Prince
The Thin Wall	Ultravox
A Thing Called Love	Johnny Cash
Things	Bobby Darin
Things Can Only Get Better	D:ream
Things Can Only Get Better	Howard Jones
Things That Make You Go Hmmmm....	C&C Music Factory Feat. Freedom Williams
Things We Do For Love	10cc
Think It Over	Crickets
Think Of You	Whigfield
Think Twice	Celine Dion
Thinking About Your Love	Kenny Thomas
Thinking Of You	Colour Field
Thinking Of You	Maureen
Thinking Of You	Sister Sledge
This Ain't A Love Song	Bon Jovi
This Beat Is Technotronic	Technotronic Featuring MC Eric
This Corrosion	Sisters Of Mercy
This D.J.	Warren G
This Flight Tonight	Nazareth
This Golden Ring	Fortunes
This Guy's In Love With You	Herb Alpert
This Is A Call	Foo Fighters
This Is How We Do It	Montell Jordan
This Is It	Adam Faith
This Is It	Dannii Minogue
This Is It	Melba Moore
This Is My Song	Petula Clark
This Is My Song	Harry Secombe
This Is Not A Love Song	Pil
This Is Tomorrow	Bryan Ferry
This Little Bird	Marianne Faithfull
This Old Heart Of Mine	Isley Brothers
This Old Heart Of Mine	Rod Stewart
This Old House	Billie Anthony
This Ole House	Rosemary Clooney
This Ole House	Shakin' Stevens
This One's For The Children	New Kids On The Block
This Time I Know It's For Real	Donna Summer
This Time (We'll Get It Right)	England World Cup Squad
This Town Ain't Big Enough For The Both Of Us	Sparks
This Used To Be My Playground	Madonna
This Wheel's On Fire	Julie Driscoll, Brian Auger & The Trinity
Thorn In My Side	Eurythmics
Those Were The Days	Mary Hopkin
Thought I'd Died And Gone To Heaven	Bryan Adams
3 A.M. Eternal	KLF
The Three Bells	Browns
Three Coins In The Fountain	Tony Brent
Three Coins In The Fountain	Four Aces
Three Coins In The Fountain	Frank Sinatra
3 Is Family	Dana Dawson
Three Lions (The Official Song Of The England Football Team)	Baddiel & Skinner & Lightning Seeds
Three Little Pigs	Green Jelly

Title	Artist
Three Steps To Heaven	Eddie Cochran
Three Steps To Heaven	Showaddywaddy
Three Times A Lady	Commodores
3 X 3 E.P.	Genesis
Thriller	Michael Jackson
Through The Barricades	Spandau Ballet
Throw Down A Line	Cliff Richard
Throw These Guns Away	Dunblane
Thunder	East 17
Thunder In Mountains	Toyah
Thunderbirds Are Go	Fab Featuring MC Parker
Ticket To Ride	Beatles
The Tide Is High	Blondie
Tie A Yellow Ribbon Round The Old Oak Tree	Dawn
Tie Me Kangaroo Down Sport	Rolf Harris
Tiger Feet	Mud
('Til) I Kissed You	Everly Brothers
Till	Tom Jones
Till The End Of The Day	Kinks
Time	Craig Douglas
Time	Supergrass
Time After Time	Cyndi Lauper
Time (Clock Of The Heart)	Culture Club
Time Drags By	Cliff Richard
The Time Has Come	Adam Faith
Time Is Tight	Booker T. & The M.G.'s
Time To Make You Mine	Lisa Stansfield
Time To Say Goodbye (Con Te Partiro)	Sarah Brightman & Andrea Bocelli
The Time Warp (SAW Remix)	Damian
Times They Are A-Changin'	Bob Dylan
Tin Soldier	Small Faces
Tired Of Being Alone	Al Green
Tired Of Waiting For You	Kinks
To Be Loved	Malcolm Vaughan
To Be Or Not To Be	B.A. Robertson
To Be With You	Mr. Big
To Be With You Again	Level 42
To Cut A Long Story Short	Spandau Ballet
To Know Him, Is To Love Him	Teddy Bears
To Know You Is To Love You	Peter & Gordon
To Love Somebody	Nina Simone
To Love Somebody	Jimmy Somerville
To Whom It Concerns	Chris Andrews
Tobacco Road	Nashville Teens
Toccata	Sky
Today	Talk Talk
Together	Connie Francis
Together	P.J. Proby
Together Again	Janet Jackson
Together Forever	Rick Astley
Together In Electric Dreams	Giorgio Moroder & Phil Oakey
Together We Are Beautiful	Fern Kinney
Tokoloshe Man	John Kongos
Tokyo Melody	Helmut Zacharias Orchestra
Tom Dooley	Lonnie Donegan
Tom Dooley	Kingston Trio
Tom Hark	Elias & His Zigzag Jive Flutes
Tom Hark	Piranhas
Tom-Tom Turnaround	New World
Tom Traubert's Blues (Waltzing Matilda)	Rod Stewart
Tom's Diner	DNA Featuring Suzanne Vega
Tomboy	Perry Como
Tomorrow	Johnny Brandon
Tomorrow	Sandie Shaw

Title	Artist
Tomorrow Night	Atomic Rooster
Tomorrow's (Just Another Day)	Madness
Tonight	Kool & The Gang
Tonight	Move
Tonight	New Kids On The Block
Tonight	Rubettes
Tonight I Celebrate My Love	Peabo Bryson & Roberta Flack
Tonight I Celebrate My Love	Roberta Flack
Tonight I'm Yours (Don't Hurt Me)	Rod Stewart
Tonight's The Night (Gonna Be Alright)	Rod Stewart
Tonight, Tonight	Smashing Pumpkins
Too Blind To See It	Kym Sims
Too Busy Thinking About My Baby	Marvin Gaye
Too Funky	George Michael
Too Good To Be Forgotten	Amazulu
Too Good To Be Forgotten	Chi-Lites
Too Hot	Coolio
Too Hot To Handle	Heatwave
Too Late For Goodbyes	Julian Lennon
Too Many Broken Hearts	Jason Donovan
Too Much	Bros
Too Much	Elvis Presley
Too Much	Spice Girls
Too Much Heaven	Bee Gees
Too Much Love Will Kill You	Brian May
Too Much, Too Little, Too Late	Johnny Mathis & Deniece Williams
Too Much Too Young (E.P.)(Special Aka Live!)	Specials
Too Nice To Talk To	Beat
Too Shy	Kajagoogoo
Too Soon To Know	Roy Orbison
Too Young	Donny Osmond
Too Young To Die	Jamiroquai
Too Young To Go Steady	Nat 'King' Cole
Top Of The World	Carpenters
Torch	Soft Cell
Torn	Natalie Imbruglia
Torn Between Two Lovers	Mary MacGregor
Tossing And Turning	Ivy League
Total Eclipse Of The Heart	Nicki French
Total Eclipse Of The Heart	Bonnie Tyler
The Total Mix	Black Box
Touch Me	49ers
Touch Me (All Night Long)	Cathy Dennis
Touch Me (I Want Your Body)	Samantha Fox
Touch Me In The Morning	Diana Ross
Touch Me Touch Me	Dave Dee, Dozy, Beaky, Mick & Tich
A Touch Too Much	Arrows
Touchy!	A-Ha
Tougher Than The Rest	Bruce Springsteen
Tower Of Strength	Mission
Tower Of Strength	Frankie Vaughan
Town Called Malice	Jam
Toxygene	Orb
Toy Balloons	Russ Conway
Toy Boy	Sinitta
Toy Soldiers	Martika
The Tracks Of My Tears	Smokey Robinson & The Miracles
Tracy	Cuff Links
Tragedy	Bee Gees
The Trail Of The Lonesome Pine	Laurel & Hardy
Train Of Thought	A-Ha

Title	Artist
Trains And Boats And Planes	Burt Bacharach
Trains And Boats And Planes	Billy J. Kramer & The Dakotas
Tramp	Salt 'n' Pepa
Trapped	Colonel Abrams
Trash	Suede
Travelin' Band	Creedence Clearwater Revival
Travelin' Man	Ricky Nelson
Travellers Tune	Ocean Colour Scene
Travellin' Light	Cliff Richard
Tribal Dance	2 Unlimited
Tribute (Right On)	Pasadenas
Tricky Disco	Tricky Disco
A Trip To Trumpton	Urban Base
Trippin'	Mark Morrison
The Trooper	Iron Maiden
Trouble	Shampoo
Truck On (Tyke)	T. Rex
Trudie	Joe 'Mr. Piano' Henderson
True	Spandau Ballet
True Blue	Madonna
True Colors	Cyndi Lauper
True Faith	New Order
True Faith - 94	New Order
True Love	Bing Crosby
True Love	Elton John & Kiki Dee
True Love Ways	Peter & Gordon
True Love Ways	Cliff Richard
Truly	Lionel Richie
Truly Madly Deeply	Savage Garden
Try Me Out	Corona
Try To Remember	Gladys Knight & The Pips
Tu M'Aimes Encore (To Love Me Again)	Celine Dion
Tubthumping	Chumbawamba
Tulane	Steve Gibbons Band
Tulips From Amsterdam	Max Bygraves
Tumbling Dice	Rolling Stones
The Tunnel Of Love	Fun Boy Three
Turn It On Again	Genesis
Turn It Up	Busta Rhymes
Turn It Up	Conway Brothers
Turn On, Tune In, Cop Out	Freak Power
Turn The Music Up	Players Association
Turn Up The Bass	Tyree Featuring Kool Rock Steady
Turning Japanese	Vapors
Turtle Power	Partners In Kryme
Tusk	Fleetwood Mac
Tweedle Dee	Little Jimmy Osmond
Tweedle Dee Tweedle Dum	Middle Of The Road
The Twelfth Of Never	Donny Osmond
The Twelfth Of Never	Cliff Richard
20th Century Boy	T. Rex
25 Or 6 To 4	Chicago
24/7	3T
Twenty Four Hours From Tulsa	Gene Pitney
Twenty Tiny Fingers	Stargazers
Twilight Time	Platters
Twilight Zone	2 Unlimited
Twist & Shout	Deacon Blue
Twist And Shout	Chaka Demus & Pliers/Jack Radics/Taxi Gang
Twist And Shout	Brian Poole & The Tremeloes
Twist And Shout	Salt 'n' Pepa
Twist And Shout (E.P.)	Beatles
The Twist (Yo, Twist)	Fat Boys
Twistin' The Night Away	Sam Cooke
2 Become 1	Spice Girls

Title	Artist
Who's In The House	Beatmasters Featuring Merlin
Who's Leaving Who	Hazell Dean
Who's Sorry Now	Connie Francis
Who's That Girl	Eurythmics
Who's That Girl	Madonna
Who's Zoomin' Who	Aretha Franklin
Whodunit	Tavares
Whole Lotta Shakin' Goin' On	Jerry Lee Lewis
Whole Lotta Love	Goldbug
Whole Lotta Woman	Marvin Rainwater
A Whole New World (Aladdin's Theme)	Peabo Bryson & Regina Belle
The Whole Of The Moon	Waterboys
Whoomph! (There It Is)	Clock
Whoops Now	Janet Jackson
Why	3T Featuring Michael Jackson
Why?	Bronski Beat
Why	Annie Lennox
Why	Anthony Newley
Why	Donny Osmond
Why	Carly Simon
Why Can't I Wake Up With You?	Take That
Why Can't This Be Love	Van Halen
Why Can't We Live Together	Timmy Thomas
Why Do Fools Fall In Love	Frankie Lymon & The Teenagers
Why Do Fools Fall In Love	Diana Ross
Why Oh Why Oh Why	Gilbert O'Sullivan
Why You Treat Me So Bad	Shaggy Featuring Grand Puba
Wichita Lineman	Glen Campbell
Wicked Game	Chris Isaak
Wide Boy	Nik Kershaw
Wide Eyed And Legless	Andy Fairweather-Low
Wig Wam Bam	Sweet
Wiggle It	2 In A Room
The Wild Boys	Duran Duran
Wild In The Country	Elvis Presley
The Wild One	Suzi Quatro
Wild One	Bobby Rydell
Wild Side Of Life	Status Quo
Wild Thing	Troggs
Wild West Hero	Electric Light Orchestra
Wild Wind	John Leyton
Wild World	Jimmy Cliff
Wild World	Maxi Priest
Wilfred The Weasel	Keith Michel
Will I What	Mike Sarne
Will You	Hazel O'Connor
Will You Be There	Michael Jackson
Will You Love Me Tomorrow	Shirelles
Willie Can	Alma Cogan
Wimoweh	Karl Denver
Winchester Cathedral	New Vaudeville Band
Wind Beneath My Wings	Steven Houghton
Wind Beneath My Wings	Bette Midler
The Wind Cries Mary	Jimi Hendrix Experience
Wind It Up (Rewound)	Prodigy
Wind Me Up (Let Me Go)	Cliff Richard
Wind Of Change	Scorpions
Windmills Of Your Mind	Noel Harrison
Wings Of A Dove	Madness
The Winner Takes It All	Abba
Winter In July	Bomb The Bass
Winter World Of Love	Engelbert Humperdinck
A Winter's Tale	David Essex

Title	Artist
A Winter's Tale	Queen
Wipe Out	Surfaris
Wipeout	Fat Boys & Beach Boys
Wired For Sound	Cliff Richard
Wisdom Of A Fool	Norman Wisdom
Wishful Thinking	China Crisis
Wishin' And Hopin'	Merseybeats
Wishing	Buddy Holly
Wishing I Was Lucky	Wet Wet Wet
Wishing (If I Had A Photograph Of You)	Flock Of Seagulls
Wishing On A Star	Fresh 4
Wishing On A Star	Rose Royce
Wishing Well	Terence Trent D'Arby
Wishing Well	Free
Wishing You Were Somehow Here Again	Michael Crawford/Sarah Brightman
The Witch	Rattles
Witch Doctor	Don Lang
Witch Doctor	David Seville
Witch Queen Of New Orleans	Redbone
The Witch's Promise	Jethro Tull
Witchcraft	Frank Sinatra
With A Girl Like You	Troggs
With A Little Help From My Friends	Joe Cocker
With A Little Help From My Friends	Wet Wet Wet
With A Little Luck	Paul McCartney
With All My Heart	Petula Clark
With Or Without You	U2
With The Beatles L.P.	Beatles
With These Hands	Tom Jones
With You I'm Born Again	Billy Preston & Syreeta
Without Love	Tom Jones
Without You	Mariah Carey
Without You	Nilsson
Woman	John Lennon
A Woman In Love	Frankie Laine
Woman In Love	Barbra Streisand
Woman (Uh-Huh)	Jose Ferrer
Wombling Merry Christmas	Wombles
The Wombling Song	Wombles
Women In Love	Three Degrees
Won't Get Fooled Again	Who
Won't Somebody Dance With Me	Lynsey De Paul
Won't Talk About It	Beats International
The Wonder Of You	Elvis Presley
Wonderful Christmastime	Paul McCartney
Wonderful Dream	Ann-Marie David
Wonderful Land	Shadows
Wonderful Life	Black
Wonderful Secret Of Love	Robert Earl
A Wonderful Time Up There	Pat Boone
Wonderful Tonight	Damage
Wonderful World	Sam Cooke
Wonderful World	Herman's Hermits
Wonderful World Beautiful People	Jimmy Cliff
Wonderful World Of The Young	Danny Williams
Wonderland	Big Country
Wonderous Stories	Yes
Wonderwall	Mike Flowers Pops
Wonderwall	Oasis
Woo-Hah!! Got You All In Check	Busta Rhymes
Wood Beez (Pray Like Aretha Franklin)	Scritti Politti
Wooden Heart	Elvis Presley
Woodstock	Matthews Southern Comfort

Title	Artist
Wooly Bully	Sam The Sham & The Pharaohs
The Word Girl (Feat. Ranking Ann)	Scritti Politti
Word Up	Cameo
Word Up	Gun
Words	Bee Gees
Words	Boyzone
Words	F.R. David
Wordy Rappinghood	Tom Tom Club
Work Rest & Play E.P.	Madness
Work That Body	Diana Ross
Workaholic	2 Unlimited
Working In The Coal Mine	Lee Dorsey
Working Man	Rita McNeil
World	Bee Gees
World In Motion	Englandneworder
World In Union	Kiri Te Kanawa
A World Of Our Own	Seekers
A World Without Love	Peter & Gordon
Would I Lie To You?	Charles & Eddie
Wouldn't Change A Thing	Kylie Minogue
Wouldn't It Be Good	Nik Kershaw
Wow	Kate Bush
Wrapped Around Your Finger	Police
Wrestlemania	WWF Superstars
Wuthering Heights	Kate Bush
The X Files	Mark Snow
X-Files	DJ Dado
Xanadu	Olivia Newton-John/Electric Light Orchestra
Y Viva Espana	Sylvia
Ya Ya Twist	Petula Clark
Yah Mo B There	James Ingram & Michael McDonald
Yakety Yak	Coasters
Years May Come, Years May Go	Herman's Hermits
Yeh Yeh	Georgie Fame
Yellow River	Christie
Yellow Rose Of Texas	Ronnie Hilton
Yellow Rose Of Texas	Gary Miller
Yellow Rose Of Texas	Mitch Miller
Yellow Submarine	Beatles
Yes	McAlmont & Butler
Yes I Will	Hollies
Yes My Darling Daughter	Eydie Gorme
Yes Sir I Can Boogie	Baccara
Yes Tonight Josephine	Johnnie Ray
Yester-Me, Yester-You, Yesterday	Stevie Wonder
Yesterday	Beatles
Yesterday	Matt Monro
Yesterday	Wet Wet Wet
Yesterday Has Gone	Cupid's Inspiration
Yesterday Man	Chris Andrews
Yesterday Once More	Carpenters
Yesterdays	Guns N' Roses
Ying Tong Song	Goons
Y.M.C.A.	Village People
You	Ten Sharp
You Ain't Seen Nothin' Yet	Bachman-Turner Overdrive
You Always Hurt The One You Love	Connie Francis
You Always Hurt The One You Love	Clarence 'Frogman' Henry
You And Me Tonight	Aurra
You Are Everything	Diana Ross
You Are My Destiny	Paul Anka
You Are My Love	Liverpool Express
You Are Not Alone	Michael Jackson
You Are Not Alone	Olive
You Are The One	A-Ha